D1477757

Expert Oracle and Java Security

Programming Secure Oracle Database Applications with Java

THE IET LIBRARY
2 SAVOY PLACE, LONDON WC2R 0BL

92590

MAR 2012

+44 (0)20 7344 5461 L... ...@theiet.org
SHELF 681.3:002.7 COF
LOC.

92590

David Coffin

Apress®

Expert Oracle and Java Security: Programming Secure Oracle Database Applications with Java

Copyright © 2011 by David Coffin

All rights reserved. No part of this work may be reproduced or transmitted in any form or by any means, electronic or mechanical, including photocopying, recording, or by any information storage or retrieval system, without the prior written permission of the copyright owner and the publisher.

ISBN-13 (pbk): 978-1-4302-3831-7

ISBN-13 (electronic): 978-1-4302-3832-4

Trademarked names, logos, and images may appear in this book. Rather than use a trademark symbol with every occurrence of a trademarked name, logo, or image we use the names, logos, and images only in an editorial fashion and to the benefit of the trademark owner, with no intention of infringement of the trademark.

The use in this publication of trade names, trademarks, service marks, and similar terms, even if they are not identified as such, is not to be taken as an expression of opinion as to whether or not they are subject to proprietary rights.

President and Publisher: Paul Manning
Lead Editor: Jonathan Gennick
Technical Reviewer: Josh Juneau
Editorial Board: Steve Anglin, Mark Beckner, Ewan Buckingham, Gary Cornell, Jonathan Gennick, Jonathan Hassell, Michelle Lowman, Matthew Moodie, Jeff Olson, Jeffrey Pepper, Frank Pohlmann, Douglas Pundick, Ben Renow-Clarke, Dominic Shakeshaft, Matt Wade, Tom Welsh
Coordinating Editor: Adam Heath
Copy Editor: Tracy Brown
Compositor: Bytheway Publishing Services
Indexer: BIM Indexing & Publishing Services
Artist: SPI Global
Cover Designer: Anna Ishchenko

Distributed to the book trade worldwide by Springer Science+Business Media, LLC., 233 Spring Street, 6th Floor, New York, NY 10013. Phone 1-800-SPRINGER, fax (201) 348-4505, e-mail orders-ny@springer-sbm.com, or visit www.springeronline.com.

For information on translations, please e-mail rights@apress.com, or visit www.apress.com.

Apress and friends of ED books may be purchased in bulk for academic, corporate, or promotional use. eBook versions and licenses are also available for most titles. For more information, reference our Special Bulk Sales–eBook Licensing web page at www.apress.com/bulk-sales.

The information in this book is distributed on an "as is" basis, without warranty. Although every precaution has been taken in the preparation of this work, neither the author(s) nor Apress shall have any liability to any person or entity with respect to any loss or damage caused or alleged to be caused directly or indirectly by the information contained in this work.

The source code for this book is available to readers at www.apress.com. You will need to answer questions pertaining to this book in order to successfully download the code.

In memory of my dad, Colonel Monty D. Coffin,
the best teacher I ever had
--David Coffin

Contents at a Glance

Contents

About the Author

■ **David Coffin** has over 30 years' experience in multi-platform network integration and systems programming. He has worked for large government contractors throughout his career. As a perpetual student, he has earned one Master's degree and has started a couple others. As a family man, he has raised eight children. David is a tri-athlete and distance swimmer who competes in the middle of the pack. He is also a classical guitar player, but he's not quitting his day job.

About the Technical Reviewer

 **Josh Juneau** has been developing software since the mid-1990s. Database application programming has been the focus of his career since the beginning. He is an Oracle database administrator and has adopted the PL/SQL language for performing administrative tasks and developing applications for Oracle database. As his skills evolved, he began to incorporate Java into his PL/SQL applications, and later began to develop stand-alone applications in Java. During his tenure as a developer, he has combined his knowledge of PL/SQL and Java to develop robust Oracle database applications that harness the great features offered by both technologies. He has extended his knowledge of the JVM by learning and developing applications with other JVM languages, such as Jython and Groovy. Since 2006, Josh has been the editor and publisher for the *Jython Monthly* newsletter. In late 2008, he began a podcast dedicated to the Jython programming language. Josh was the lead author for *The Definitive Guide to Jython*, and *Oracle PL/SQL Recipes*, both published by Apress. He is the lead for the Django-Jython project (http://code.google.com/p/django-jython/). He loves to spend time with his four wonderful kids and excellent wife. To hear more from Josh, follow his blog at http://jj-blogger.blogspot.com. You can also follow him on Twitter via @javajuneau.

Acknowledgments

Writing this book was as much about expressing who I am as it is about the work I do. It was on New Year's Eve, 2009 that I decided I would write 100 pages of my own creation during 2010. I started writing an autobiography, but that turned out to be too complex. I have read Benjamin Franklin's autobiography, and maybe one day I will be that concise.

I decided to write about something that I think about day in and day out: computer security. Thankfully, I have one family member who gets this stuff—my son Matthew. Thank you, Matthew, for taking an interest and giving me encouragement. Also, thanks again for getting me through my refresher course on differential equations, 30 years after finishing college. You tutor me and I mentor you, all right big guy?

I wouldn't have gotten very far without the encouragement of my wife, Linda. I guess she sees the ideas bouncing around in my head, because she has always encouraged me to write. She claims I'll be like Emily Dickinson and have my writings published only after I die. Linda, I hope this assuages your concerns about sorting through my notebooks when I'm gone. Thanks for loving me through this process!

Kids, thanks for putting up with your dad's time on the computer. I love you!

I have had many technical mentors on the job. Many folks were willing to share their ideas and understanding with me, and also let me run with my own thoughts. Among my best mentors were my peers in the Intranet Development Group. I'm glad I have this opportunity to tell you guys how much you expanded my horizons during our time as a development team. I'm very glad we spent time in the Skunk Works together. A special thanks to our Fearless Leader—your ideas for application authentication came together into Chapter 10 of this book.

I also want to thank God. He has given me natural abilities in computer administration and security, and he has been my source of peace and joy for as long as I've known Him, and even before.

Introduction

Every day I read e-mails and articles dealing with computer security attacks and breaches, and the repercussions that follow. I have been getting onboard with computer security for decades, and there is no end in sight for this effort. Each and every professional in information technology has a commitment to keep with regard to computer security. We have, most of us, signed computing codes of conduct, and further we have aligned ourselves with those who protect the computing resources of our respective companies.

Of course, computer security professionals are on the front lines, and they draw the ranks of system and network engineers and administrators along into the fray. Hopefully these soldiers are joined by the software system administrators—database administrators and web services administrators. How often is that the limit of personnel dedicated to securing corporate resources on a daily basis?

Application programmers need to join this battle. Programmers cannot depend blindly on the work of those front-line combatants to protect their work and their careers. In the ranks of IT professionals, there are no civilians—we are all in the fight.

I speak like this is a war. Do I think we are dealing with so-called cyber warfare? No, not really. People are not dying. But the battle has become economic, and has threatened the wealth and economic security of each of us. This is more like theft, and we are more like guards and policemen.

You are a guard for the computer resources and data of your company, and you need to fulfill that responsibility. It is my intention to provide you tools and knowledge that you can put to immediate use. But even more than that, I want to get you thinking about how you can write bulletproof applications of your own. Your requirements will differ from those presented in this book, so you will be coming up with defenses of your own. It's my hope that, after working through this book and honing your skills, your arsenal will be greatly strengthened.

In Part 1, Chapters 2 through 4, we will build a foundation for secure programming in Java and Oracle, and their common ground, Java Stored Procedures (JSP). This is not an encyclopedic coverage of these expansive domains. Rather, I focus on the specific topics that touch on that special discipline of "secure" programming.

In Part II, Chapters 5 through 7, we explore a couple varieties of encryption, using only a couple sets of protocols. Once again, this is not encyclopedic. But after reading these chapters, you will be prepared to encrypt data in your applications, and over the network in a client-server application. You will find that, with Java running in the Oracle database as well as on the client computer, our tightly coupled client-server application can transmit sensitive data with bulletproof, session-specific encryption.

In Part III, Chapters 8 through 10, we will expand our toolset to include single sign-on, two-factor authentication and application verification. These are practices that will keep intruders from getting access to our applications, and will keep unauthorized applications and users from getting access to our Oracle credentials and data. Single sign-on has the added benefit of reducing the number of times a user needs to type his user ID and password. Two-factor authentication, on the other hand, requires that the user have a specific mobile phone or registered device to receive a code that authorizes her access to the application. Application verification helps assure that an application is authorized access, and allows us to assign applications to users.

In Part VI, Chapters 11 and 12, we enhance the security we have been building and then build an administrative interface to get it running and keep it running. The security enhancements we will add include application-specific encryption on disk and use of a hardened Oracle database instance for application verification. In the administrative interface, we will discuss how the security data is maintained, and we will also look at some good practices for GUI application development in Java.

At several points in the book, we will prepare a template that we can provide to other application programmers so that they can implement the same security structures. The simplest and most complete template for implementing this security in a GUI application is presented in Chapter 12—the Login class. When you get to the end of that chapter, you will be the expert. You can do your part for computer security, and you can assist your associates in doing theirs. Thank you!

CHAPTER 1

Introduction

This book is a walk through Oracle and Java technology. I will weave the story of Oracle Database and Java security on the loom of these pages. The particular thread we will weave is code. This is a story for programmers.

This story will take you through several large tasks to help you start securing your Oracle applications. We will not be building any specific application, but will focus on the security aspects in building an application. In order to make this learning effort feel like a practical application, we will apply our efforts to the HR sample schema that is available with the Oracle Database 11g installation.

I hope to maintain a conversational tone, because I want to teach the concepts of secure programming. We are going to have "the talk" about secure programming. When you have read this book, you will be well equipped for the most difficult application programmer assignment of our day: defending our applications and computers.

Requirements

In order to work through the examples in this book, you will need an installation of Oracle Database 11g, Enterprise Edition, Release 11.2 or later. You will also need to have the Java Development Kit, 1.5 or later, installed on your workstation. That is it.

I will refer to some other products as we go along, but the intent of this book is to cover topics and approaches that will be useful to Oracle and Java programmers, rather than committing to any additional products. However, you should note that much of what we will do here can be acquired through commercial products from Oracle corporation and elsewhere.

Notably, two of the features we will be building in this book—data encryption over the network and data encryption on disk—are available in a product from Oracle called Oracle Advanced Security. That product is relatively easy to configure and use, although it is expensive. But adding encryption onto a badly secured database or application will just hide the things you, as a programmer, should be addressing. So even if you use Oracle Advanced Security, you would still do well to learn about programming secure Oracle Database applications with Java.

For Windows and UNIX/Linux Users

It is not a requirement that you be a Windows user to accomplish the tasks in this book. All of the code is in PL/SQL and Java, and will run cross-platform. However, I've had to be a bit focused in the development of this material. All of the descriptions of filesystem directories, command prompt, environment settings, services, scripts, and processes are written using Microsoft Windows as the model.

To avoid the appearance of a strong Windows bias, let me remind you that we are talking about Java and Oracle here. I've been using UNIX for longer than Windows has been around. I didn't start using

Windows until Windows 3.1, when the trumpet winsock tcp/ip stack became available. I started out in UNIX with SunOS 4.1 as a system administrator, along with Netware servers. Then for a few years I was a business UNIX system administrator. I ran dozens of machines and over a half-dozen flavors of UNIX. These I managed centrally with a lot of willpower and a thorough the application of scripting and Perl over NFS with scheduled *cron* updates, and by knowing the unique attributes of BSD, System 5, and AIX flavors. I combined that with standardization—for example, the Korn shell (or mksh) and lprNG.

So why not write this book for UNIX/Linux users? In the first place, you guys likely already know how to do what I'm saying in Windows-speak on your Linux systems. Secondly, I can talk about Windows and only rarely have to mention the differences between Windows 7 and Windows XP. There is no way I could talk about UNIX and Linux with that much clarity. UNIX is not an operating system; it is a foundation for many operating systems. That is also true of OSX.

Additionally, there is not just one command prompt, but many shells in UNIX. There is not just one UNIX batch/command language, but innumerable scripting options.

Background

So, why write or study code that can be purchased off the shelf? As a programmer, I believe in the importance of knowing how programs on my computers and servers work, even if I didn't write the programs. I think all programmers by nature enjoy seeing new functions in code; it is educational and empowering. My goal with this book is reader understanding, perhaps with a measure of career development built in.

And if it is your goal to achieve application security using the basic Oracle Database and Java services, without going out to spend your tens of thousands of dollars, this book will give you a foundation for doing just that. You can write secure Oracle applications with Java!

I will keep things clear and concise, so I don't clutter the message. This book is also intended as a primer (I like that word, no matter which way you pronounce it) for both Oracle Database and Java security. I am not going to assume too much foreknowledge, but if some terms are unfamiliar, I suggest a quick Internet search for clarification. Also, I am deeply indebted to the Oracle Documentation Library, and to Sun's (Oracle's) Java Documentation, and I recommend you keep links to those resources close for frequent reference. They can be found at:

http://www.oracle.com/technetwork/indexes/documentation/index.html
http://download.oracle.com/javase/6/docs/

How to Use This Book

You will need to refer to the source code. You can read this book from cover to cover and understand everything and become the expert you are meant to be. But you have other responsibilities and distractions. So you will need to leave and come back and get re-oriented from time to time. This book will proceed with the assumption that you are reading from cover to cover and have complete retention, but I've never really met anyone who does.

I much prefer assuming you are mortal, like me. You'll be asking yourself the questions, "Now, where was I, and what are we doing?" Also, even if you are willing to take it on faith that we are proceeding in a logical order and are actually making forward progress, reading on even though you might be a bit disoriented, you will still have the question, "What does this have to do with anything?"

These questions can be answered pretty easily with a quick reference to the code. You will want to be able to search the code for the keywords that you are reading about, find the code in question, and find references to it. You'll want to see the code in context, and you'll want to see how the code starts and runs. Now, I've incorporated large and small chunks of code throughout this text, and I don't talk about code without showing it to you, but you will want to see it in context.

I organized the text and code to easily walk hand in hand together. For the most part, you will only need to have one source code file open at a time as you read through the text. In Chapter 2, which is coming right up, you will complete Oracle Database security tasks as several different users—for each user, there is a corresponding source code file. The chapter is organized around those files. In fact, it would be best if you also open a SQL client and execute each portion of the code as it is discussed.

Organization of This Book

There are four main sections in this book. In Part I (Chapters 2–4), you will learn the technical ins and outs of secure programming in Oracle Database, secure programming in Java, and Java Stored Procedures (Java running in the Oracle Database engine). From novice Oracle PL/SQL programmers and novice Java programmers to experienced Oracle application programmers using Java, these chapters will fill in the missing concepts that you need to master for security' sake.

In Part II (Chapters 5–7), we build on the Java and Oracle Database secure programming foundation. We develop a strong layer of encryption—specifically, encryption in transit. You will build this for yourself using Java Cryptography Extension (JCE), rather than a purchased package or SSL service. Because encryption plays such a key (pun intended) role in secure programming today, you need to have a solid grasp of these data encryption concepts, and you also need something more: you need to know when to apply encryption and how to evaluate your encryption strategy to determine if you have successfully protected your data. We will cover all of that.

In Part III (Chapters 8–10), we get into some fun topics that will permit you to provide the solutions your company is seeking: single sign-on, two-factor authentication, and something you may not have realized you need: application identification and authorization. In application authorization, we will be providing a secure data store for our application passwords—one that not only avoids embedded passwords, but also provides enhanced security along with ease of management and central distribution.

In the last section, Part IV (Chapters 11–12), we will harden the security with additional data encryption in the Oracle Database store, with a further hardened Oracle Database and with some additional programming efforts, such as obfuscation. We also establish a simple user interface for administering the tables and data we've built to accomplish security, and do that securely.

Java Objects and Oracle Database Structures

In this book, I will be using certain terms non-interchangeably that are used interchangeably elsewhere. Often schemas, tables, indexes, and other items in Oracle Database are referred to as both *objects* and *structures*. Because *object* is a technical term in Java and not just another word for *thing*, I will reserve the word for our discussion of Java objects. In Oracle Database, I'm calling things by their primary type name and collectively or generically as *structures*, so tables will be called both *tables* and *structures*. I will also have a need to refer to collections of Oracle tables and views and indexes and things, which I will call collectively *structures*. We will define all these terms later, so don't be alarmed if they are new to you.

Chapter Review

It is my sincere hope that you will enjoy working through this book. I believe the best way to learn and use this material is to take your time with each chapter, executing the code as you come to it. You will be building a secure Oracle application environment with Java. Definitely test all the places I've provided you with test cases, scenarios, and test code. If you find other situations, test those too, and please send me your comments and results when I need to address an issue—my aim is to serve you.

CHAPTER 2

Oracle Database Security

As you might imagine, the subject of this chapter could fill a whole book, or even several, if I tried to cover the entire scope of Oracle security. Instead, I will cover the essentials, and also some particular aspects of Oracle security to which a programmer can relate. An example of essential Oracle security is using roles and granting privileges to those roles. An example of a programmer's extension of Oracle security is secure application roles.

The basic goals of this chapter are as follows:

- Create two users: a security administrator user and an application security user. These users will be granted privileges and delegated responsibilities for achieving application security.

- Use Oracle roles to control access and enhance application security, and learn about secure application roles identified by Oracle stored procedures.

- Distinguish between sensitive and non-sensitive data in the EMPLOYEES table.

Prepare to delve into many aspects of database administration and design. This chapter will get you started with Oracle security, and we will build on the concepts covered here throughout the remainder of the book. Some aspects, such as proxy connections, will only be really clear when presented in context. I want to be sure you really understand what is covered in the book, rather than just be exposed to it.

Finding a Test Oracle Database

We are going to hit the ground running. I hope you already have access to the SYS account on your database. If not, I hope you are good friends with the database administrator (DBA) for the server, and that you are recognized as a database security administrator. If so, you can ask your DBA friend to do the small portion of this work that must be done by SYS or a DBA.

If you'd like to learn the concepts in this chapter, but you don't want to use a managed server—and if you have sufficient computer power in your personal workstation—then you can download and install the Oracle Database 11g Enterprise Edition server and do the tasks that I describe in this chapter locally. I highly recommend that approach in any case, because you should definitely demonstrate and test the security measures that I describe in this chapter for your own peace of mind, before you place any of them in production.

Working from an Existing Oracle Database

If you are working from an existing database installation, you may have some issues to address. If you have a default Oracle Database 11.2 installation, then you need only consider the steps you have taken since installation to see if you have undone any built-in/default security. At minimum, you need to assure password complexity and secrecy. However, if you have a database that has been around for a while and has been upgraded from previous releases of Oracle, then you may have to spend some time and effort correcting the security issues.

I recommend you adopt a resource that Arup Nanda of the Oracle Technology Network has produced, called Project Lockdown. Project Lockdown is a series of checklists, tasks, and projects that will effectively enable and enforce Oracle database security. You can find this resource on the Oracle Technology Network web site at www.oracle.com/technetwork/articles/project-lockdown-133916.pdf.

Project Lockdown may take as much as several months to accomplish, depending on how lax your current security stance is. However, the first couple phases, which are the most critical, may be accomplished in a week.

Oracle Users and Schemas

Once Oracle Database 11g is up and running, you will want to consider users and user security, even before you think about the data, because users create data. Even application databases that don't belong to any particular person are associated with a user in an Oracle database. Each user on a local database has an associated schema, which is basically an organized storage allocation for Oracle structures (or objects) such as tables and indexes that belong to the user. See Table 2-1 for a list of users we will discuss.

Table 2-1. Oracle Users We Will Use or Create

Username	Description
SYS	Default Oracle system administrator.
HR	Human resources user/schema; installs with sample Oracle structures.
secadm	Our security administrator; we will create this account and give it privileges to implement all the security measures we need.
appsec	Our application security user; we will create this user and load code and other structures into her schema that we can use for app security.
appusr	Our first application user account; this account will only have the privileges needed to use the client application.
osuser	This is a pseudonym for any operating system username on your system; e.g., the username you use to log into Windows.
appver	User for application verification, covered in Chapter 10.

osadmin   This is another pseudonym for any operating system username on your system, in particular one who will be responsible for managing Oracle connection strings for applications.

SQL*Plus, SQL Developer, JDeveloper, or TOAD

I am going to assume that, if you are reading this, you are already doing some work as an Oracle developer. I'm going to further assume that you have some tool for submitting commands on an Oracle database, such as the prompt in SQL*Plus or the editor in TOAD, SQL Developer, or JDeveloper. SQL*Plus comes with Oracle, so if you don't have one of the other tools, you still have SQL*Plus. That is all you need to do the tasks outlined in this book.

■ **Note** Some of these tools are more sensitive than others to multi-line commands. They may require a slash character (/) on the line following a multi-line command.

Many of the SQL script files included in the source code for this book will need specific values edited, to be unique to your computer and corporate or home environment. Those values are listed at the top of the SQL files. After editing as appropriate, most of the SQL files can be executed as scripts; just be sure you are connected as the appropriate Oracle user.

Organization of the Next Few Sections

I want to make the process of working through this material as easy as possible for you. Toward that end, I have separated into sections the tasks and concerns of each of three users: SYS (the database administrator), the security administrator that we will be creating here, and the HR (human resource) schema owner.

For the most part, SYS as the database administrator could do all these tasks, but it is my intent to demonstrate security with delegation. We will have each of these users accomplish the tasks that are specific to their delegated responsibility. The commands to be executed by each of these users are consolidated into a single script file per user, and it is possible for us to focus on tasks and concerns of each of those users in turn, one at a time.

Each of these users must address a number of diverse topics, all related to security. These concerns are addressed in the order in which they are needed as we work toward the goals of this text. We will continue to build on all the topics I introduce here throughout this book.

You should have access to the code as we progress through this material. If you are reading this away from your computer, I hope to have provided enough of the code right in the text for you to completely understand the discussion. However, it is also my intention that you implement this code, and that this text will guide your understanding of what is occurring at each juncture.

When you work through the code, you will find that the best way to execute the commands in the various script files is to copy the file contents to a SQL command editor like TOAD or JDeveloper, and to execute one command at a time. That is preferred over executing the entire code as a script, because you will see each command as it gets executed. Remember, the goal is to understand secure programming, not just to implement security software.

Working as the SYS User

SYS has a schema (by the same name) and has lots of structures belonging to his account. You can connect (log in) to a database as SYS, but a unique requirement of that user is that you have to specify that you are using the SYSDBA privilege. (Note that in the text I will be using all uppercase for reserved words in Oracle commands and for default Oracle users, schemas, and structures.)

```
CONNECT sys AS sysdba;
```

At that point, you will have to enter the password associated with the SYS user.

■ **Note** You can find a script of the following commands in the file named *Chapter2/Sys.sql*.

System Privileges

SYSDBA is a unique system privilege; let's call it a "super" system privilege. It provides practically unlimited administrative ability. It can be granted to any user, but is best left granted only to SYS. As SYS you can check who has SYSDBA:

```
SELECT * FROM sys.v$pwfile_users;
```

With this query, you request to SELECT (see) all the columns of data (*) from the V$PWFILE_USERS view. The sys. prefix on that view name indicates the schema (user) that owns the view. You will see a couple of other super system privileges listed in this query: SYSOPER and SYSASM. These should also only be granted to SYS.

Besides the super system privileges, there are several dozen other system privileges that can be granted to provide such administrative abilities as creating other users and granting them privileges. We will be granting privileges as we explore Oracle security.

In addition to system privileges, there are schema object privileges. These allow, for example, another user to read your data. We will grant these privileges also. They have a much more tailored impact on Oracle application security.

Roles

Roles are collections of granted privileges that are much more granular and diverse and limited than the super system privileges. Instead of granting SYSDBA, the preferred method for giving users access to the various privileges is to grant the privileges to a role, then grant the role to the user. If you do this, you can always substitute a different user in a job, or replicate the privileges required for a job to another user by simply granting the existing role to the new user. (Privileges can be granted directly to users, but we will mostly avoid that.)

For example, I can create a role named appaccess and grant the ability to read the application tables to that role. Then I can grant that role to a user. When I have another user who needs access to the same application, I can permit that by granting the appaccess role to the new user as well. And when I delete the first user, the permissions required for other users to access the application do not disappear in the process.

I need to grant access to the application data as described previously, because the data tables will be in a schema belonging to the application, and each user will have her own schema. Users cannot read data in other schemas unless that access is specifically granted to them or to a special user named PUBLIC. Anything granted to PUBLIC is granted to all users. See Table 2-2 for a list of Oracle roles we will discuss.

Table 2-2. *Oracle Roles We Will Use or Create*

Role Name	Description
DBA	This predefined role comes with Oracle upon installation and provides system administrative privileges for the database; we will not grant this role to any user.
CONNECT	This predefined role allows users to connect to Oracle; we are encouraged not to use predefined roles, so we won't.
create_session_role	Our role to allow users to connect to Oracle.
secadm_role	Our security administrator role; we will grant the privileges required to perform security administration to this role, and we will grant this role to the SECADM user.
hrview_role	Our secure application role for granting access to data in the human resources (HR) sample schema.
appsec_role	A non-default role used by APPSEC when configuring application security.
appver_role	Secure application role for running application verification, which I cover in Chapter 10.

The DBA Role

The DBA role is named for the job it enables: database administrator. It is similar to the SYSDBA super system privilege. Traditionally, the DBA role was granted to those users who needed to manage the database. The DBA role is almost as powerful as the SYSDBA privilege, but it can be modified to have some of its privileges removed.

In recent releases of Oracle, database administrators have been discouraged from using the DBA role. Rather, they are encouraged to create their own roles and to grant just those administrative privileges that are required. Therefore, we will not grant DBA role to any user.

We will be creating a security administrator role, secadm_role. We will use this role for most of our administrative actions. It will have a variety of privileges, but only those required for the scope of this book. This approach adheres to the concept of "least privilege," which means providing only the privileges required for the task at hand.

Oracle Database Vault is a product that allows you to use DBA and other privileged roles while restricting their access. This is geared toward Department of Defense and national security users, where a database administrator does not necessarily have access to the data.

The Create-Session Role

We will also create a simple role, create_session_role, which will only have one privilege: CREATE SESSION. The CREATE SESSION privilege is required for a user to connect to an Oracle database. Traditionally, this has been accomplished through a predefined role (it exists when you install Oracle) named CONNECT. In current releases of Oracle database, CONNECT only has the one privilege. But in this case, as with the DBA role, Oracle recommends that administrators create their own roles and not rely on the predefined roles (like CONNECT). Do this as SYS:

```
CREATE ROLE create_session_role NOT IDENTIFIED;
GRANT CREATE SESSION TO create_session_role;
```

We will be granting this role to all users in the database. It would take the exact amount of effort to grant the CREATE SESSION privilege to each user as it takes to grant create_session_role. However, there is a benefit to roles as a centralization of privileges. For example, if we wanted to quickly give another privilege to all users, we could grant it to the create_session_role; although, I don't recommend that. More likely there might be a time when you need to keep the database running, but want to keep all users from connecting to it. That can be done by a single command, revoking CREATE_SESSION from create_session_role.

NOT IDENTIFIED

I hope the CREATE ROLE syntax is fairly obvious. The only odd feature is the NOT IDENTIFIED keyword. That merely indicates that when a user is acquiring this role, we do not have any password or encoded process to verify his access to it. A role of this type has to be granted to a user (or to another role) by an administrative command. Generally, roles that are designated as NOT IDENTIFIED are also default roles, which a user acquires automatically when he connects to the Oracle database. This is the most usual configuration of a role.

Using Roles

Most roles get created as default roles. When a user connects to an Oracle database, he acquires all his default roles, and all the privileges associated with those roles. Any regular NOT IDENTIFIED role can be set to be default or non-default.

▪ **Note** In Oracle Database 11g, default roles that are identified by a password are no longer acquired when a user first connects—the user must enter the password. More on that later.

At any time, the Oracle user can acquire a role that has been granted by executing a SET ROLE command. This is true for both default and non-default roles.

When we SET ROLE to a new role, it becomes the only role in use, even if other roles were in use before. Fortunately, the session has already been created (we are already connected when the new role is set), so we can stand to lose the create_session_role (which will happen). I can imagine a scenario wherein we would require every role to be granted CREATE SESSION privilege so that when you SET ROLE, you still have CREATE SESSION in the new role.

There is a way to add to existing roles, keeping those that exist. By issuing the command:

```
SET ROLE ALL;
```

This command cannot be used to set a role that is IDENTIFIED by a password or a procedure. However, after you acquire a password-protected role or secure application role (we will discuss those in a minute), you can SET ROLE ALL and restore your default roles as well.

I should mention that roles can be granted to roles, which we will do. Setting your role replaces whatever you had before, but will include not only the role you set, but all the roles granted to that role, and so on, recursively. There is a constraint to these cascading grants so that no endless loops can be formed.

Password-Protected Roles

Let me preface this discussion with a note regarding Oracle 11g: starting with this version of Oracle, in order to set password-protected roles from an active connection, you have to supply the password, even if it's a default role. This may catch you off guard. Previously, if a role was protected by a password but it was a default role, the user got that role by default when she connected.

I agree with this change to Oracle; and for the same reasons, we will not have any password-protected roles in this book. The only reason to have a password-protected role is in a case where the role is granted to a user, but you don't want the user to use the role. You protect the role by setting a password, and don't let the user know. But, we have to ask, "Why did we grant him the role in the first place?"

A better approach is to only grant the role to the users who need it. Perhaps this is a bit muddied by the possibility for many people to connect as a specific Oracle user, where some of those people need access to the role and some don't. In that case, I recommend you either make the people who need the role enter the role password, or, better yet, revisit your users and roles and sort them out.

One possibility is to have a secure application role, validated by a procedure. That role can be granted based on user id or some group membership. Then no role password is needed. You just need to maintain a list of acceptable users or a group membership list.

I have observed a corporate policy of securing every application role with a password. The idea is that people sitting at a general SQL client, like SQL*Plus, will not have access to the role, because they don't know the password. But from the application where we want them to have the role, a procedure is called to set the role by looking up the role password in a database table. It may be that this configuration provides a small impediment to casual Oracle users getting the application roles; however, the bare facts to observe here are that the person who has been granted the role will have access to the role either by that same procedure that the application calls, or by the same code that's in that procedure. From SQL*Plus, the user may simply call the procedure, get the password, and set the role.

Perhaps the role could be protected from bald access by assuring that only a certain client application is being used; again, this is a job for a secure application role. But the real problem here is that a role has been granted to an Oracle user, and the administrator does not want the user to access the role. Password-protected roles provide only the illusion of enhanced security, unless you make specific users memorize and manually enter the password to set the role. That is the thinking behind the new policy in Oracle 11g.

Security Administrator User

Let's go ahead and start defining our security administrator. The security administrator is going to be a separate non-person user; that is, an account and password that can be delegated to various people who rotate into and out of the job responsibility. The security administrator will be doing tasks that would typically be done by a DBA or even by SYS, but we are going to limit the privileges we give to the security administrator to just those aspects related to application security.

First, as SYS we will create the user secadm and grant him the create_session_role, in one step. Substitute a real password for "password" in this command:

```
GRANT create_session_role TO secadm IDENTIFIED BY password;
```

■ **Caution** Be sure to give a very complex password to this user; it will be powerful enough to be dangerous in the wrong hands. This warning goes for the SYS and SYSTEM accounts as well.

Security Administrator Role

Next, we will create the security administrator role, secadm_role. It will be the role that is granted all the privileges needed to do security administration. We can then grant this role to any user, but we will limit it to just one user, secadm.

At the outset, I want to set some requirements regarding how and when this role can be used, so I will not use the NOT IDENTIFIED keywords that we saw with create_session_role. Rather, I will have it be identified (verified) by a procedure. You can see the name of the verification procedure, sys.p_check_secadm_access in this command:

```
CREATE ROLE secadm_role IDENTIFIED USING sys.p_check_secadm_access;
```

A role that is identified by a procedure is called a secure application role.

Security Administration Role Verification

As I mentioned, all the privileges that the security administrator needs will be granted to secadm_role, so we are going out of our way to protect it. The keywords IDENTIFIED USING sys.p_check_secadm_access indicate that when a user attempts to acquire secadm_role, he will have to get it from the procedure named p_check_secadm_access, which exists in the SYS schema.

A stored procedure (procedure) is a named block of Procedural Language/Structured Query Language (PL/SQL) code that is stored and run (executed) on the Oracle database. Generally, a procedure takes parameters and does work. It can also return information through its parameters. In Oracle there are also stored functions (functions), which are very similar to procedures except that they usually take values; do research or calculations; and then return a single value as the result. We will be using both procedures and functions.

The specific procedure used for verifying secadm_role, p_check_secadm_access does not take any parameters (arguments or values passed to the procedure for evaluation), and does not return any results. Most procedures do take parameters, but they don't have to.

In the Listing 2-1, we are creating the procedure to be used for acquiring the security administrator role. Note that the simple goal I have for this procedure is to require that the security administrator be running on the same computer as the Oracle database server (the IP address 127.0.0.1 is also known as the localhost or the loopback address). This requirement may not be appropriate for your system; if not, you can still create the procedure, but comment out the three lines that start with IF, THEN, and END IF by placing two dashes (minus signs) in front of it. You can execute this command as SYS, and the procedure will be created.

Listing 2-1. p_check_secadm_access *Procedure for Secure App Role*

```
CREATE OR REPLACE PROCEDURE sys.p_check_secadm_access
AUTHID CURRENT_USER
AS
BEGIN
    -- This is a comment
    IF( SYS_CONTEXT( 'USERENV', 'IP_ADDRESS' ) = '127.0.0.1' )
    THEN
        EXECUTE IMMEDIATE 'SET ROLE secadm_role';
    END IF;
END;
/
```

We will want to come back and visit (replace) this procedure later, adding whatever additional security constraints we deem appropriate. For now, our Security Administrator must be connected directly to the Oracle Database (running SQL*Plus on the server.)

As a programmer, you will already understand the IF/THEN/END IF syntax and realize there are other PL/SQL grammar requirements like the BEGIN/END and the semicolons.

Look at the code between the BEGIN flag and the last END flag. Between there it says, in English, "if the user's environment has an *Internet Protocol* (IP) address of the local host, then immediately set his role to secadm_role." We are using the SYS_CONTEXT *context* to get the IP address from the *user environment*, and we are determining if the address is equal to 127.0.0.1 (localhost). If that test is true, then we immediately set the role for the current *session* to secadm_role.

INVOKER'S RIGHTS VERSUS DEFINER'S RIGHTS

In the procedure we defined above, we say AUTHID CURRENT_USER so that this procedure is executed as the current user, not as SYS (the one who defined the procedure.) So when executed, this procedure will use what is called "Invoker's Rights" (CURRENT_USER) as opposed to "Definer's Rights" (the default or owner, which in this case is SYS). If we didn't do this, the environment and identity would appear to be SYS when we execute the procedure, but we want to be able to determine the acceptability of (authorize) the specific, current user. Another reason we need to execute with invoker's rights is that otherwise we are not allowed to set a role from a procedure—we can only set the role for the *authenticated* (current) user.

Security Administrator Role Acquisition

We are not nearly done defining our Security Administrator yet. We need to permit the Security Administrator to execute the procedure we created. We do that by issuing the following command:

```
GRANT EXECUTE ON sys.p_check_secadm_access TO secadm;
```

Notice that we don't need to grant secadm_role to secadm; rather, if the user meets all the requirements of the procedure (p_check_secadm_access), then that IDENTIFIED USING procedure will set his role to secadm_role. There is an analogous restriction here: either you grant a role or you grant the ability to execute a procedure, which will set the role. In both cases you are limiting access to the role by requiring a specific grant. However, by using the procedure to set the role, you can place further restrictions on access.

Notice that in this case, we are granting a privilege (to execute the procedure) to a user directly, instead of, as we recommended previously, granting permissions to a role and granting the role to a user. Every rule has exceptions! The reason for this specific exception is that we are protecting a role with a procedure. We do not need to further protect the procedure with a role.

The Security Administrator, secadm user can acquire secadm_role by executing the procedure as shown below. In fact, every time secadm connects to Oracle Database, he will need to call that procedure to get the secadm_role role.

```
EXEC sys.p_check_secadm_access;
```

System Privileges Granted to the Security Administrator Role

The bulk of privileges that we want our Security Administrator to have will be granted by SYS:

```
GRANT
    CREATE USER
    ,ALTER USER
    ,CREATE ROLE
    ,GRANT ANY OBJECT PRIVILEGE
    ,GRANT ANY PRIVILEGE
    ,GRANT ANY ROLE
    ,CREATE ANY PROCEDURE
    ,CREATE ANY TRIGGER
    ,CREATE ANY CONTEXT
    ,CREATE PROFILE
    ,AUDIT SYSTEM
    ,AUDIT ANY
TO secadm_role;
```

Most of these system privileges that we are granting to secadm_role permit us to do some of what we have been doing already as SYS. We will allow our security administrator to create and modify users and to create roles and grant them to users. secadm will grant privileges for roles to work with Oracle objects (structures) in other schemas. He will grant certain system privileges to roles. He will also create procedures and triggers, which are like procedures, but execute when certain events occur (we'll discuss this more in a bit.) We will also create an application context when we get to Chapter 10. And the security administrator will create profiles, which we will see when we get to Chapter 8. For now, we rely on the default profile.

We will also be setting up some auditing as security administrator. We will audit a variety of system events, and we are going to audit access to tables and other structures in the HR schema—hence the AUDIT ANY privilege. Any time you see ANY in an object privilege grant, you can read that as "in any schema." Generally, a user already has those privileges in his own schema.

These are not all the system and schema object privileges that our security administrator will need to do his job, but they will get us started. We will come back as SYS and give the security administrator a bit more privileges later.

The Audit Trail

Finally, as SYS, we are going to set up some initial auditing on the auditing trail itself. This will deter a rogue database administrator from doing something wrong and then erasing their tracks by deleting their audit records:

```
AUDIT SELECT, UPDATE, DELETE
    ON sys.aud$
    BY ACCESS;
```

When we designate BY ACCESS for auditing, we are saying that we want detailed information. The other (possibly default) option is BY SESSION. This gives less detail, but still audits each occurrence, rather than only providing a single audit record per session, as in earlier releases of Oracle.

The Data Dictionary

We want our security administrator to be able to view all data in the Data Dictionary, which is a collection of views in the SYS schema that list structures and system data in Oracle. (A *view* is a defined way to look at a table of data.) For example, we may want to list details about all the database users:

```
SELECT * FROM sys.dba_users;
```

There are many columns in the DBA_USERS view that are not available in the PUBLIC data dictionary views: ALL_USERS (fewer details) and USER_USERS (a bit more detail, but only for the current user).

Much of the data dictionary has been granted to PUBLIC by default, and can be selected by every user. For the most part, this is needed. But we will deal with this a bit more stringently in Chapter 11, *Enhancing Our Security*. However, selecting some parts of the Data Dictionary requires the SELECT_CATALOG_ROLE. Grant that role to the secadm_role:

```
GRANT select_catalog_role TO secadm_role;
```

Note that this is a role granted to a role. From now on, when we set the role to secadm_role, we will also have the SELECT_CATALOG_ROLE.

Working as the Security Administrator

Now that our security administrator has been defined with the privileges he needs to do his job, we are going to put him to work. Go ahead and connect:

```
CONNECT secadm;
```

▪ **Note** You can find a script of the following commands in the file named *Chapter2/SecAdm.sql*.

As you will recall from our creation of the security administrator role, secadm_role, we required that it be validated by a procedure. We have only permitted one account, secadm to execute the procedure. Execute it now to acquire secadm_role:

```
EXEC sys.p_check_secadm_access;
```

Note that when secadm connects to Oracle, he does not automatically acquire secadm_role. Because it is a secure application (verified) role, and not directly granted to secadm, it cannot be a default role. Every time the secadm user connects, he will have to execute the procedure to gain his Security Administrator role and privileges.

This is in contrast to roles that are granted directly to a user, which are default roles initially. That status of default role can be unset.

Acquire secadm_role from a SQL*Plus Local Connection

There are always gotcha's, and here's one that will probably get you a few times if you use SQL*Plus as your primary client: when you are sitting at a command prompt on the Oracle database, you can connect locally to the default instance. Do that by executing SQL*Plus without any arguments, like this:

```
sqlplus
```

You can connect then as secadm user by entering the username and the password. If you then attempt to execute the procedure, sys.p_check_secadm_access that sets secadm_role, it will not succeed. Why does it not succeed? Our address should be that of localhost, which should be okay. Well, when connecting locally, SQL*Plus doesn't use the network at all—it just talks directly to the database. You can see the lack of IP address information by executing this command:

```
SELECT SYS_CONTEXT( 'USERENV', 'IP_ADDRESS' ) FROM DUAL;
```

This has some implications for security. When connected locally like this, the commands you enter do not traverse the network adapter and have no possibility of leaking out on the network to snooping devices.

So how, you might ask, are we supposed to connect as secadm and run sys.p_check_secadm_access from SQL*Plus on the Oracle Database? There is a way, and it only requires that you act like you're not connecting locally by adding the arguments for user and instance name (orcl in this example) on the command line. Actually orcl in this context is a TNS alias with the same name as the instance. We will discuss TNS aliases in Chapter 11.

```
sqlplus secadm@orcl
```

At that point, you have an IP address in the session context, and you can successfully set role through the procedure:

```
SELECT SYS_CONTEXT( 'USERENV', 'IP_ADDRESS' ) FROM DUAL;
EXEC sys.p_check_secadm_access;
```

Toggle Between Roles

You can see the effects of running SET ROLE by observing your current session roles as you toggle back and forth between create_session_role and secadm_role. As secadm user, do this and observe the list of roles when you do each SELECT query:

```
SELECT * FROM sys.session_roles;
SET ROLE create_session_role;
SELECT * FROM sys.session_roles;
EXECUTE sys.p_check_secadm_access;
SELECT * FROM sys.session_roles;
```

You will see three roles when you execute the procedure and then select from SESSION_ROLES. The procedure itself sets your role to secadm_role. To that role, we granted SELECT_CATALOG_ROLE. And the

SELECT _CATALOG_ROLE has been granted HS_ADMIN_SELECT_ROLE. All of those will be listed as current roles of the session. If you have additional packages or different versions installed on your Oracle Database, you may see additional roles related to those packages.

Create an Application Security User

We will need a couple more users to develop and demonstrate our security. The first user is our Application Security user, appsec. She will own all the structures that make our application security work.

Please take note of the differentiation I am making between Oracle security, which we've delegated to security administrator, and application security. The security administrator has been granted a number of system privileges so that he can create users and do other tasks in Oracle. The application security user, on the other hand, will own a number of procedures and structures that are used for application security processes. The application security user will not connect as part of any particular application; rather, she will grant access to her logic and data to application users.

```
GRANT create_session_role TO appsec IDENTIFIED BY password;
```

■ **Caution** Be sure to give a very complex password to this user; she does not have significant privileges in the database, but she owns some logic and data that we do not want to expose to corruption.

Application Security Role

Our application security user needs to create procedures, functions, Java stored procedures, tables, and views. When creating those items, appsec requires the CREATE PROCEDURE, CREATE TABLE, and CREATE VIEW system privileges. We will grant those privileges to a role named appsec_role, and grant that role to the appsec user:

```
CREATE ROLE appsec_role NOT IDENTIFIED;
GRANT CREATE PROCEDURE TO appsec_role;
GRANT CREATE TABLE TO appsec_role;
GRANT CREATE VIEW TO appsec_role;
GRANT appsec_role TO appsec;
```

Non-Default Role

Our application Security user only requires these privileges (for example, CREATE PROCEDURE) on occasion. Our preference would be for her to set her role to appsec_role as needed, but currently it is a default role. In order to change the behavior for roles created as NOT IDENTIFIED from being default roles to be non-default, we need to issue the ALTER USER command. In the following command, we ask Oracle to make all the roles granted to appsec user to be DEFAULT except this one we want to exclude:

```
ALTER USER appsec DEFAULT ROLE ALL EXCEPT appsec_role;
```

Hereafter, when appsec connects in order to create new structures, she will have to issue one of the SET ROLE commands. (Do not execute these commands as secadm user—at this point, they are for explanation only.)

```
SET ROLE appsec_role;
SET ROLE ALL;
```

The second command listed above will set the current session for appsec to enable ALL the roles that have been granted to her, both default and non-default.

Create an Application User

As an example user for connecting to Oracle to run an application, we will create an application user, appusr. For our purposes, appusr is not tied to a single person, but is what Oracle refers to as a "one big application user" model user. In this model, numerous people will use an application, and the application will connect all of them to Oracle as our one big application user. They do not need individual person accounts and passwords for this access.

```
GRANT create_session_role TO appusr IDENTIFIED BY password;
```

■ **Caution** Be sure to give a very complex password to this user—they can potentially select data and do updates to application data. We only want that activity to take place from within the application. I hope you are getting used to this warning about passwords and can even anticipate it.

INDIVIDUAL PERSON ACCOUNTS

We will have an opportunity to create Oracle user accounts that are specific to individual people; however, the administrative requirement for maintaining those users (and granting, validating, and revoking the required privileges) is a huge responsibility. I think there are better, less tedious and more secure ways to recognize and authorize individual people in the database, and we will look at that in Chapter 8.

Create the HR View Role

We are going to begin securing access to the data in the Human Resources (HR) Sample Schema. We will create a role named hrview_role. Through that role we will grant access to the data needed by a variety of applications that we plan to build. At the outset, we only want folks who are on our internal network to access this data, and only during our normal office hours of 7 AM to 7 PM.

To accomplish these constraints, we will create the role and require that it be verified by a procedure. Oracle calls this a secure application role because that is its function – it is a role that gives access to application data, but it is secured by some encoded constraints. This is the same thing we did to secure secadm_role.

```
CREATE ROLE hrview_role IDENTIFIED USING appsec.p_check_hrview_access;
```

Verify HR View Role by a Procedure

Just as we did previously for the secadm_role, we will create a procedure to protect access to the hrview_role. At the end of the procedure, if the CURRENT_USER meets the requirements encoded in this procedure, we will SET ROLE to the hrview_role.

Create the procedure by executing the code in Listing 2-2 as secadm. Here, we are creating a procedure in another schema. Notice the schema name, appsec. prepended on the procedure name. To do this requires secadm to have the CREATE ANY PROCEDURE system privilege.

Listing 2-2. p_check_hrview_access Procedure for Secure App Role

```
CREATE OR REPLACE PROCEDURE appsec.p_check_hrview_access
AUTHID CURRENT_USER
AS
BEGIN
    IF( ( SYS_CONTEXT( 'USERENV', 'IP_ADDRESS' ) LIKE '192.168.%' OR
        SYS_CONTEXT( 'USERENV', 'IP_ADDRESS' ) = '127.0.0.1' )
    AND
        TO_CHAR( SYSDATE, 'HH24' ) BETWEEN 7 AND 18
    )
    THEN
        EXECUTE IMMEDIATE 'SET ROLE hrview_role';
    END IF;
END;
/
```

Notice that, here again, we have the statement AUTHID CURRENT_USER. We are going to execute with invoker's rights (IR) instead of the default definer's rights (DR). In this procedure we have encoded two tests in the IF statement. And for those sessions that pass both tests, we set the role to hrview_role.

Test for Subnet

The first test in p_check_hrview_access, shown in Listing 2-2, gets the IP Address of the client from the user environment and tests that it begins with the string "192.168." The LIKE syntax indicates that the address should consist of the specified characters followed by zero or more characters (the "%" symbol is a wildcard). The test assures that the client exists on our internal corporate subnet. ("192.168" is a non-routed subnet, and can be used behind firewalls or on test subnets. It is typically the subnet used for a home network that attaches to the Internet through a DSL or cable modem.) Your corporate subnet is most likely different from this subnet, so modify the code for the procedure before you create it. At the command prompt, you can find the IP address and other networking information of your Windows workstation by issuing a command:

```
C:\>ipconfig /all
```

Probably the first two octets (sets of three or fewer digits separated by dots, or sets of eight bits in binary) of your workstation's IP address are representative of your corporate subnet. Contact your networking support personnel to determine exactly what to use.

This procedure also allows you to connect to Oracle from the Oracle database server itself. If the IP address is 127.0.0.1, the localhost address (that is, the Oracle database server itself), then the procedure also succeeds.

Test for Normal Business Hours

The second test in p_check_hrview_access, shown in Listing 2-2, contains the statement TO_CHAR (SYSDATE, 'HH24') BETWEEN 7 AND 18. Let's take a minute to break this down. SYSDATE is the name for the current time and date on the Oracle database. You can SELECT (request) SYSDATE from the server, and you can set date values to be equal to SYSDATE when you update data in Oracle. In this case, we are requesting SYSDATE and using the TO_CHAR function to format just the hour (HH24) portion the date into a character string using the 24-hour format. In this format, when it is 7AM, the TO_CHAR function will return 7; and when it is 7PM, 19. So we check that the hour is BETWEEN 7 and 18 (at 6:59PM, this test will still be true; but at 7PM, false.) We have determined that our normal business hours are between 7AM and 7PM, so these tests are valid.

■ **Caution** There is no code here to disconnect the user from Oracle when 7PM arrives. This code only prevents further connections from being established after 7PM.

Permit Application User to Acquire HR View Role

Every user that needs to get access to the HR data will have to execute the p_check_hrview_access procedure to have the hrview_role set. It is only the hrview_role that has access to the data, and the only way to set that role is by executing the procedure. We will grant the EXECUTE privilege for this procedure to our application user, appusr. As secadm, execute this:

```
GRANT EXECUTE ON appsec.p_check_hrview_access TO appusr;
```

We will have to grant EXECUTE on this procedure to all users who need access to the data. Alternatively, we could grant the EXECUTE privilege to PUBLIC, but we would only want to do that if every user of the database required access to the HR data. Do not grant privileges to PUBLIC without considering the implications.

Audit Changes to Security Administrator Procedures

We will close out this part of the chapter by establishing some additional auditing. Because we are working as SECADM, the default structures for which we define auditing are in the SECADM schema. We will audit any change to procedures in our schema, because they are security related. We need to assure that any changes have been vetted.

```
AUDIT ALTER ANY PROCEDURE BY ACCESS;
```

This is actually one of the privileges that is audited by default when the secconf.sql script is run as part of the database creation.

Audit Failed Attempts to Access HR Data

Our first audit on access to the HR data is really an audit on attempted execution of the p_check_hrview_access procedure, which sets the hrview_role. We don't want to know when this procedure succeeds, but we would like to know when invalid access is attempted, so we use the keywords WHENEVER NOT SUCCESSFUL.

```
AUDIT EXECUTE ON appsec.p_check_hrview_access
    BY ACCESS
    WHENEVER NOT SUCCESSFUL;
```

Working as the HR Schema User

For several aspects of the endeavors put forth in this book, we are going to use the HR sample schema that can be installed with Oracle 11g. If you haven't got that schema installed, you will have had difficulties in the preceding step that configured auditing on HR schema structures. Please browse to the Oracle web site for instructions on how to install the sample schemas after the fact.

Now, at the installation of Oracle, you also had the opportunity to configure a password for the HR user. If the sample schemas exist but the HR user is not configured (or simply to reconfigure the user), you can issue the ALTER USER command (as SYS or secadm):

```
ALTER USER hr ACCOUNT UNLOCK IDENTIFIED BY password;
```

■ **Caution** Be sure to give a very complex password to this user; HR owns the data that we are going to attempt to protect.

Connect to Oracle as the HR user:

```
CONNECT hr;
```

HR has no system privileges outside his own schema, but has been granted the privileges required to connect to the database and create a number of structures in his own schema: tables, views, indexes, and the like.

■ **Note** You can find a script of the following commands in the file named *Chapter2/HR.sql*.

Sensitive Data in the HR Sample Schema

In the HR sample schema, which can be installed with Oracle 11g, there is a table named EMPLOYEES. That table has a couple columns that we should call "sensitive": SALARY and COMMISSION_PCT. We are going to make it our goal to grant access to that table without compromising the sensitive data.

View the contents of the EMPLOYEES table with this command, as HR:

```
SELECT * FROM hr.employees;
```

Let's pretend that it is our company's goal to publish an online personnel directory (phone book), and that this table is the primary source data. We could export just the non-sensitive portions of the data for use in the phone book, but it would be much better to grant secure access directly to the primary data in this table, rather than replicating the data (assuming our database server will support the additional load).

Public View of Employees

The most basic method for granting limited access to a data table is to create a view. A view is like a filter that we put on the data table that can show only certain data, reorganize the data, format the data and provide data from multiple tables or other views. We will create a view named v_employees_public that only includes the non-sensitive columns of data:

```
CREATE OR REPLACE VIEW hr.v_employees_public
AS SELECT
    employee_id,
    first_name,
    last_name,
    email,
    phone_number,
    hire_date,
    job_id,
    manager_id,
    department_id
FROM hr.employees;
```

Test the new view to assure it returns just the data we've requested. We should notice that the SALARY and COMMISSION_PCT columns are missing:

```
SELECT * FROM hr.v_employees_public;
```

Because we have omitted the sensitive columns (SALARY and COMMISSION_PCT) from this view, we can grant access to this view to the entire company without exposing sensitive data. We could grant it to PUBLIC; however, we still feel a bit protective of our data, and we want to be sure access is controlled, so we grant access to the view to our secure application role, hrview_role rather than to PUBLIC. HR user has the privilege to grant access to structures in his own schema:

```
GRANT SELECT ON hr.v_employees_public TO hrview_role;
```

With this grant we are permitting hrview_role to SELECT data from the view. Other common privileges one might grant to a view are INSERT, UPDATE and DELETE. We are not granting any of those privileges at this time. The hrview_role can see but not modify the non-sensitive data through the v_employees_public view.

Sensitive View of EMPLOYEES

Now that we have our non-sensitive view configured, it should be obvious how to create a sensitive view of all columns of the EMPLOYEES table. As HR, we create a view:

```
CREATE OR REPLACE VIEW hr.v_employees_sensitive
    AS SELECT *
    FROM hr.employees;
```

The asterisk (*) represents all columns, and this view selects all the data from all the columns. Test that this view returns all the data from the EMPLOYEES table:

```
SELECT * FROM hr.v_employees_sensitive;
```

This view might be useful at some point in the application—for instance, when we want to let certain financial analysts count how many people earn a certain salary in preparation for annual raises. We might also want to use this view for a financial application that we want to grant UPDATE access for giving out those raises. It would also be useful to have this view to allow Human Resources to INSERT and DELETE folks from the database as they are hired and terminated.

However, given the sensitivity of the data (how much money you and I or our managers earn), we are not going to grant access to this view at all. Later, we are going to provide access to this data through much more heavily guarded and encrypted channels.

Our first audit statement on HR data was given previously in the section "Audit Failed Attempts to Access HR Data." Our second audit statement for HR data follows. With it, we intend to audit any direct access to the sensitive view of the EMPLOYEES table. Later, we will look at auditing the selection of just those fields that we consider to be sensitive, no matter what view or table they are selected from.

```
AUDIT SELECT ON hr.v_employees_sensitive BY ACCESS;
```

Test Application User Access

To test our security, we need to try things that we believe should not work (because of our security measures) as well as the things that we permitted to succeed. To do this, you will need to connect to Oracle as appusr user:

```
CONNECT appusr;
```

■ **Note** You can find a script of the following commands in the file named *Chapter2/AppUsr.sql*.

The next three commands, we believe, will fail because the appusr user has not been directly granted access to anything in the HR schema. He only has his default roles, which also do not have access. We should see an error message that those tables or views don't exist.

```
SELECT * FROM hr.employees;
SELECT * FROM hr.v_employees_sensitive;
SELECT * FROM hr.v_employees_public;
```

Now we will execute the procedure that will check our validity, and then set role to hrview_role. This should succeed if we are on our corporate subnet (or on the Oracle Database server, itself) and it is between 7AM and 7PM:

```
EXEC appsec.p_check_hrview_access;
```

Then we will test our access to the EMPLOYEES structures in the HR schema. We do not expect the first two commands to work; again we should see an error message that those structures don't exist. The hrview_role does not give access to the sensitive data:

```
SELECT * FROM hr.employees;
SELECT * FROM hr.v_employees_sensitive;
```

On this last command, we should see the data from the EMPLOYEES table; however, we note that there are two columns missing from the data: SALARY and COMMISSION_PCT.

```
SELECT * FROM hr.v_employees_public;
```

Audit Trail Logs for the Sensitive View

Let's find the audit log entries for this access. HR user does not have access to read the audit logs (if he tries, he will be audited), but if you will connect as secadm and execute the following commands, you will see the audit logs that were generated by HR querying v_employees_public:

```
EXEC sys.p_check_secadm_access;

SELECT OBJECT_NAME, STATEMENT_TYPE, RETURNCODE FROM DBA_COMMON_AUDIT_TRAIL
      WHERE DB_USER='HR'
      ORDER BY EXTENDED_TIMESTAMP DESC;
```

While we are still here as secadm, we should try to access the sensitive view and see the audit log entries for this failed attempt (secadm cannot read the sensitive view). You will also see logs of the audit trail SELECT statements executed by secadm.

```
SELECT OBJECT_NAME, STATEMENT_TYPE, RETURNCODE FROM DBA_COMMON_AUDIT_TRAIL
      WHERE DB_USER='SECADM'
      ORDER BY EXTENDED_TIMESTAMP DESC;
```

A RETURNCODE of 0 is a success, while a non-zero RETURNCODE indicates a failure.

Regarding Synonyms

Synonyms are like extra names for structures in Oracle, primarily for tables and views. The most persuasive argument for synonyms is the use of public synonyms. If we create a public synonym for a view, then anyone selecting from that view need not prefix the schema name on the view name. HR user can do the following to create a public synonym. (Do not do this—this example is for discussion only.)

```
CREATE PUBLIC SYNONYM v_employees_public FOR hr.v_employees_public;
```

This does not change the security or accessibility of the view or data. However, it permits the role hrview_role to select the data without the hr. schema name prefix, as in:

```
SELECT * FROM v_employees_public;
```

It is also possible to give a name to the synonym that is different from the name of the structure it represents, like the following:

```
CREATE PUBLIC SYNONYM employees FOR hr.v_employees_public;
```

Perhaps this can simplify the name—and if we expected our users to type all their queries at the command prompt, this might be helpful. (Do not do this—this example is for discussion only.) You can imagine there might also be some confusion for the successor database administrator coming along behind the DBA who set this up. An employee might complain that they cannot select from EMPLOYEES, and the successor administrator might reply that no one can, not knowing that the employee was talking about the synonym, not the table or view. Also, if ever the view hr.v_employees_public is dropped (deleted), the synonym will be broken.

An individual user might create a private synonym for her own use (use by only that specific user/schema). She might do this so she can call HR.EMPLOYEES by her favorite term, "PEERS." However, when she tries to share any database queries or code with her associates, they will be frustrated by her private synonyms. Queries using her private synonyms won't work for others.

I have also observed attempts to incorporate synonyms into a security strategy, hiding the original table with a public or private synonym by the same name. It would be foolish to trust in such a ruse.

Probably the best reason for synonyms is to make it slightly easier for programmers to write code, by not having to remember to prefix the table and view names with those pesky schema names. However, I have observed application failures when a table or view is migrated from a development environment (Oracle *instance*) to production, but the public synonym is left behind. I know this should never happen, but it does. Then the data is there in production, but the application fails, because it is missing the synonym or merely missing the schema name in the code. That can be very difficult to troubleshoot.

I recommend that you rarely if ever use synonyms, and that you just make the developers address the tables and views where they reside, with the schema name prefix. I don't really expect everyone to follow my advice, but please at least consider it.

One further argument for synonyms is to be a reference to a structure on another database instance. In this case, the synonym can also include a database link. I can't really argue against that use of synonyms, because it is certainly easier to specify and update if the database link name changes. I do caution that you need to protect data wherever it appears, even across database links. There should also be restrictions on the visibility and use of production data in non-production environments; and even more so, vice-versa.

Chapter Review

Now you have a security administrator user who is not a DBA, but who can handle most of the Oracle security tasks required. Also, you have an application security user who will be handling the transactions we require for Oracle application security.

You have locked down our Oracle database and added some basic auditing, and learned about the data dictionary views. We discussed roles: predefined roles, default roles, non-default roles, and secure application roles. In our first foray into application security, we built a couple of secure application roles and the procedures that protect them.

In the application data schema, HR, we distinguished between sensitive and non-sensitive data and created a public view of only the non-sensitive data. We also created a view of both the sensitive and non-sensitive data, but we haven't permitted anyone to see that yet. Then we viewed the audit trail logs for entries related to our sensitive view of EMPLOYEES.

Secure Java Development Concepts

This chapter goes beyond what would traditionally be covered in a chapter on Java security, and it does not cover strictly Java security topics in depth. Rather, it addresses fundamental Java development concepts. We should make sure that we are on a solid foundation in Java development. You can develop very secure code in Java, but if you do not realize what you are doing, your code can be unwittingly insecure.

This chapter will also help Java Integrated Development Environment (IDE) programmers better understand the development process outside of the tools (such as JDeveloper, NetBeans, or Eclipse). IDEs do a pretty good job, but do not blindly trust one to understand and enforce secure development practices for you. If you have a strong background in Java, this chapter may be unnecessary—in that case, just skim it to see if there are any areas you need to review.

Java Development Kit

The Java Standard Edition (SE) Java Development Kit (JDK) is available both stand-alone and bundled with Sun's (Oracle's) IDE, NetBeans. You can download either one from Oracle's web site at `java.sun.com` (www.oracle.com/technetwork/java). You will need JDK 1.5 or later, and you will find that earlier versions, such as 1.5, may only be available on the Previous Releases web page.

We need JDK 1.5 or later because that is the version of the JDK that has been included in the Oracle database: the Oracle Java Virtual Machine. We will discuss virtual machines shortly. We want to have at least that same revision level of Java on our workstation as on the Oracle database.

You can also download the Java Runtime Environment (JRE.) Because you are downloading the JDK, you do not need to also download the JRE. A JRE is that portion of the JDK required to run Java applications, but it does not have the tools required to compile Java.

If you have a Java IDE installed, then you also have the JDK included with your IDE. If that is version 1.5 or later, you can simply use the JDK that came with your IDE.

Oracle Java Database Connectivity

Download a copy of the Oracle Java Database Connectivity (JDBC) code library from Oracle's web site at *www.oracle.com/technetwork/indexes/downloads*. Scroll down to [Drivers]. The file you download can be for the latest release of Oracle database (11g) and must be suitable for JDK 1.5 or later. Note, however, that you should not use JDBC drivers that are later than the JDK you are using (e.g., do not use *ojdbc6.jar* with JDK 1.5). So you will download *ojdbc5.jar*, or *ojdbc6.jar* if you are using JDK 1.6 or later.

JAR File Directory Separator

A Java Archive (JAR) file (like the `ojdbc6.jar` file that we downloaded previously) is a compressed directory tree with compiled Java files and other files for use as a set. You can, and later we will, create a JAR file with the JAR utility in the JDK. You can look at the contents of a JAR file with any ZIP utility.

In a JAR file, you would find a directory tree. For example, inside the `ojdbc6.jar` file you would see these directories (and many others):

```
/oracle
/oracle/sql
```

In the `/oracle/sql` directory, you would see files like `ARRAY.class`. The `ARRAY.class` file is a compiled Java file.

Do not be disturbed by my use of the / (slash) for a directory separator character. This is the standard separator character for UNIX, and it is the default for Java. Java will understand slash, but the standard Microsoft backslash must be escaped (explained) to Java, in most situations. The backslash serves another purpose in Java as the escape character itself, so an escaped backslash looks like this \\. The following two filenames are equivalent in Java on a Windows box, but I will always use the first style.

```
"C:/Program Files/Internet Explorer/SIGNUP/install.ins"
"C:\\Program Files\\Internet Explorer\\SIGNUP\\install.ins"
```

Java Packages

We don't have the Java code of the Oracle JDBC drivers, but we can deduce that the code of the `ARRAY` class (mentioned previously) was in a file named `ARRAY.java`. And in that file was a package statement:

```
package oracle.sql;
```

Notice how the package name correlates with the directory tree, using a dot (.) separator character for the package, instead of a slash for the directory. At Oracle, the corporate developers keep the file `ARRAY.java` in a directory named `sql,` which is in a directory named `oracle`. They compile the class in a matching directory tree. And they create the JAR file by collecting all the compiled content, starting with the `oracle` directory.

You need to keep this fundamental concept in mind: packages equal directory paths. Packages also provide security and affect how we reference Java code and how we compile and run it, as we shall see.

Development at Command Prompt

I have coached many developers, new and experienced, who have primarily accomplished their Java development efforts or education with an IDE. When I ask them to do any troubleshooting or test their application from the command prompt, often they don't know where to begin. I believe you need to be prepared to execute (run) Java from the command prompt, and we will be doing some of that here.

Environment

When you get to the command prompt and you want to compile or run your code, you will need a couple of operating system environment settings: your `PATH` to find the JDK executables, and your `CLASSPATH` to find your code and the Oracle JDBC code. From wherever the recent JDK executables exist, they are able to find their own libraries of code (Java can find Java libraries, although it hasn't always been that way), so you don't have to specify them in the `CLASSPATH`.

Let's imagine that you have installed the JDK in this directory:

```
C:\Program Files\java\jdk1.6
```

Imagine you also placed the Oracle JDBC file at this location:

```
C:\Program Files\java\ojdbc6.jar
```

You do not need to set the environment variables, but the difference in Java command line syntax is significant. Following are two examples of running the Java Oracle application MyApp from the command prompt. In the first command, we have set and rely on our environment settings. The second would be required if we do not have our environment set.

```
java MyApp
C:/Program Files/java/jdk1.6/bin/java -cp ".;C:\Program Files\java\ojdbc6.jar" MyApp
```

You can readily see how much easier it is to run from the command line if your environment is properly configured. If you're running Windows XP or later, then right click on **My Computer** on the desktop and choose Properties, or right-click on Computer in your Start menu and choose Properties. Select the Advanced tab or button and click on Environment Variables. At the top, create two (new) user variables (or modify existing) with the settings listed in Table 3-1.

Table 3-1. Environment Variables

Variable Name	Variable Value
PATH	C:\Program Files\java\jdk1.6\bin;
CLASSPATH	.;C:\Program Files\java\ojdbc6.jar;%CLASSPATH%

The PATH user environment variable will be automatically appended to the System PATH, and will tell Windows how to find the Java compiler (javac.exe) and Java runtime (java.exe) executables.

Beware that even after setting your path, there might be other java.exe executables earlier in the PATH. Assure that the versions of javac.exe and java.exe are both 1.5 or later. Open the command prompt from your Start menu and check the results of these commands:

```
javac -version
java -version
```

In the CLASSPATH user environment variable, we are saying several things. First of all the dot (.) tells Java to find classes in the current directory. Trust me, you do not want to be caught asking Java, "Why can't you find the file—it's right here?" The second thing we point to is the Oracle code in the ojdbc6.jar file—we want Java to automatically find that code. And the third thing we are saying is that we want whatever system environment CLASSPATH already exists (%CLASSPATH%) appended to our CLASSPATH.

Just to elaborate a bit, the CLASSPATH is a list of places that we want Java to look for compiled classes. These places are really just starting points, and can include directories (like our "dot" current directory) and archive files (JAR files or ZIP files). When we compile or run our own code and need to use existing code, we can find it along the CLASSPATH. Java opens archive files and looks at the included directories and files to see if what we need is there. If I refer to oracle.sql.ARRAY in my code, Java will eventually open the ojdbc6.jar file from the CLASSPATH and find the oracle directory. It will then continue to find the sql directory, and from there, the ARRAY.class file.

Beginning Java Syntax

Let's put a couple Java code files on display here so that we can talk about some specific programming concerns with concrete references. For discussion only, we will have two .java files exist in a directory named mypkg, and mypkg is in a directory named **javadev**. The directory structure and filenames look like this:

```
javadev/
        mypkg/
                MyApp.java
                MyRef.java
```

■ **Note** You will find the files in the javadev/mypkg directory.

Consider the following code listings for our two Java files, shown in Listings 3-1 and 3-2. Note that these files don't do anything, but they are valid Java code.

Listing 3-1. MyApp.java

```
package mypkg;
import oracle.sql.ARRAY;
public class MyApp {
    ARRAY myArray;
    MyRef myRef;
}
```

Listing 3-2. MyRef.java

```
package mypkg;
public class MyRef {
}
```

We will cover several aspects of the syntax of Java code here, but we will be introducing the bulk of the syntax a bit later. Notice that both of the Java code files begin with the declaration of their package. Looking at MyRef.java, we see the simple declaration of the class with the modifier public. The code for a class is enclosed in a pair of curly brackets ({}). Each .java file must have only one top-level class declaration, and the top-level class must be named identical to the file (in this case, MyRef).

■ **Note** Often these top-level classes are declared public, but they don't have to be. They cannot be private or protected, but they can be default, or package accessible with no modifier.

Another observation at this point is in the MyApp.java file. First, we have an import statement, import oracle.sql.ARRAY. A statement like this is required every time you use a class from a different package. If we were using lots of classes from the `oracle.sql package`, we could import them all with the shorthand statement `import oracle.sql.*`. Because `MyRef` is in the same package as `MyApp`, we do not need to import `MyRef`, even though we do refer to it in `MyApp`.

Also notice that, inside the class definition (between the curly brackets) of `MyApp`, we have declared two member classes: one instance (copy) of `ARRAY` that we will refer to as `myArray`, and one instance of `MyRef`, which we will refer to as `myRef`. Notice that Java is case sensitive: compare `myRef` with `MyRef`.

I will be using the terms *member* and *instance* frequently. Briefly, in object-oriented parlance, an object that is created in computer memory is an instance of whatever kind of class it is; we call the creation of objects instantiation. The object that is created by another object and referenced therein is called a member of the object that created it.

Byte Code Compilation and the Java Virtual Machine

I have already used the word compile, and you will see it a lot in this book. In Java, you will write human-readable code and place your code in files with a .java extension on the filename. In order to run the code, it first needs to be compiled. The compile step creates a file that humans cannot read with a .class extension. This .class file cannot be executed by the computer operating system; it is in byte-code format. Class files are run by the Java Runtime Environment (JRE) executable, java.exe.

The Java runtime creates a Java Virtual Machine (JVM) in computer memory that can interpret and run the byte code. The value of having a JVM read and run the byte code is that, in most cases, the byte code can be written once, run anywhere–a fundamental goal of the Java language. You write it and compile it wherever it is convenient for you, the developer, and then place it on any computer with a compatible JVM to be run: in a workstation, server, browser, cell phone, or web server. The JVM handles all the specifics of talking to the operating system and to the hardware.

We will see the power of this concept in our code, which we will write, compile, and run on our workstation. We will then load it onto an Oracle database (actually, we will store it in the database), and have the Oracle JVM run it also in Oracle.

Using the Java Compiler

The JDK has a number of command-line utilities in the bin subdirectory. One of these is the primary Java compiler, javac.exe. Another is the primary Java executable for running applications, java.exe.

To compile Java code, you execute javac.exe, passing the name of the Java code file as a parameter, like this (assuming your command prompt is in the directory `javadev/mypkg`):

```
javac MyApp.java
```

You must include the .java extension on the code file name. This command will find the file `MyApp.java` in the current directory and, if successful, it will place a compiled Java file named `MyApp.class` in the current directory. This is true whether or not `MyApp` is in a package. If `MyApp.java` refers to other compiled classes that are not in the current directory, then they must be found along the `CLASSPATH` (for example, the compiler can find `oracle.sql.ARRAY` when `ojdbc6.jar` is listed in the `CLASSPATH`).

If there are other Java code files referred to by `MyApp` that can be found along the `CLASSPATH`, and the code has not been compiled or has been updated since the last compilation, then `javac.exe` will compile those classes also. The referenced code will be compiled and the compiled class file will be placed in the same directory with the referenced Java code file. For example, `MyRef.class` will be placed in the same directory as `MyRef.java`.

Additionally, you can compile multiple Java classes or all in a specific directory by specifying a wildcard, like this:

```
javac *.java
javac mypkg/*.java
```

Finding Referenced Code/Classes

There is a "gotcha" with compiling Java that you need to understand and anticipate, or at least quickly recognize. When your code refers to other Java code that is not on your CLASSPATH, the Java compiler will not find the code, even if the referenced code is in the current directory. Let's imagine your code is in package (directory) named mypkg and that your MyApp.java refers to MyRef.java in the same package. If your CLASSPATH does not refer to the parent directory of the mypkg subdirectory, then *javac.exe* will not find the MyRef.java file. Having dot (.) in your CLASSPATH will not fix this gotcha, because the mypkg directory is not in the current directory, rather we are in mypkg. Remember, CLASSPATH (even dot) is merely a list of starting places for packages. Looking in the current directory, we cannot find the package (subdirectory) named mypkg nor the code or class file named mypkg/MyRef.class.

One way to correct that gotcha is to change directories to the parent of mypkg. Once there, you can compile your code, and the dot (.) in your CLASSPATH will find the referenced code in the mypkg directory. In this case, however, you need to tell javac.exe that your MyApp.java code is in a subdirectory (both the forward and back slashes are acceptable as directory separator characters in this context), like this:

```
javac mypkg/MyApp.java
```

That is a valid approach, but probably the best way to address this issue is to have a development directory (like javadev) and to place all your package directories underneath that directory. Then add your development directory to your CLASSPATH.

```
set CLASSPATH = C:\javadev;%CLASSPATH%
```

Often, especially if you manage your development using an IDE, you will not be able to put your packages in a single development directory. Each project will store files in a separate directory.

Perhaps now you are thinking, "Man, I'm just going to let the IDE handle all this for me!" I don't want to disparage IDEs, but being satisfied to take that approach is like voluntarily going to jail because work is hard. Don't quit working hard! Often you don't need an IDE to write, compile, and run your code, so take those opportunities to work at the command prompt. Once you set your environment variables, it is just a matter of knowing about packages and CLASSPATH and recognizing problems.

Running Compiled Code

Once your code is compiled, running (executing) it can be easy:

```
java mypkg.MyApp
```

Please observe that to run a Java class, you need to specify the package it is in. There is no shortcut around this.

The same requirements for finding all classes needed for your application along the CLASSPATH apply for execution as they do for compiling. In order to run your Java code as just shown, java.exe needs to be able to find the mypkg package in one of the starting points listed in CLASSPATH. In our example, if you are in the javadev directory and you have the "dot" in your CLASSPATH, then java.exe can find mypkg, and can run your code in mypkg/MyApp.class. This must be true for all classes that your code refers to, like oracle.sql.ARRAY. For that reference, java.exe needs to find ojdbc6.jar listed in CLASSPATH.

There is an alternative to having CLASSPATH defined in your Operating System environment. You can pass CLASSPATH to java.exe, or javac.exe for that matter, using the -cp parameter.

```
java -cp ".;C:\Program Files\java\ojdbc6.jar" mypkg.MyApp
```

In this example, we alert **java.exe** that the CLASSPATH parameter (**-cp**) is provided. The quotation marks are required, because there is a space in the directory name Program Files. Note that forward slashes would also work in this context.

Java Code and Syntax Concepts

I'm going to give a brief example of Java code. It is 20 lines long and not too complex, but it will introduce you to many Java syntax concepts. You do not need to memorize the details of these concepts—they will present themselves in every program you write in Java.

Throughout the following discussion, we are going to consider some aspects of the code in Listing 3-3. Keep a bookmark at this page for reference as you read the next few sections.

Listing 3-3. MyApp2.java

```
package pkg2;
import oracle.sql.ARRAY;
import mypkg.MyRef;
public class MyApp2 {
    private ARRAY myArray = null;
    static MyRef myRef;
    public static void main( String[] args ) {
        MyApp2 m = new MyApp2();
        MyRef useRef = new MyRef();
        m.setRef( useRef );
        ARRAY mA = m.getArray();
        myRef = new MyRef();
    }
    public ARRAY getArray() {
        return myArray;
    }
    void setRef( MyRef useRef ) {
        myRef = useRef;
    }
}
```

■ **Note** Find this code in the file named *javadev/pkg2/MyApp2.java*

Continuing our previous discussions about Java syntax, we see that this new code, *MyApp2.java*, is in a new package (directory), *pkg2*. For that reason, we have to import (refer to) the *MyRef* code in our original package. Recall that both of those packages need to be found from some starting point in your CLASSPATH in order to compile and run this code.

Methods

In the code for `MyApp2` (`MyApp2.java`) you will see three blocks of code named `main()`, `getArray()`, and `setRef()`. Find them by looking for open and close curly brackets within the curly brackets that define the body of the class `MyApp2`. These three blocks of code are called methods (programmers may think of them like subroutines or functions).

Each standard method requires two things: a set of parentheses where parameters (input values or objects) may be passed to the method, and a declaration of the return type (being handed back to whatever code called the method). When I mention methods in this text, I will append the open and close parentheses. Later, I will discuss in more detail the `public` and `private` modifiers. For now, know that they are not return types.

Look at the middle method first. `getArray()` has an empty set of parentheses that indicates it doesn't take any input parameters. Before the name of the method, it has the word `ARRAY`, which shows that it returns an object of type `ARRAY`.

Notice that both the `main()` and `setRef()` methods have a return type of `void`, which is a way to say that those methods do not return anything.

The `main()` method takes a single parameter named `args`, and the type of that parameter is an array of `Strings`. *String* is the term for a series of characters, like the word "tremendous," or the sentence, "This is good!" An array of any type is indicated by open and close square brackets ([ ]). Any single element in the array can be referenced by placing an integer in the square brackets to indicate its place, its index. For example, `args[0]` is the first element of the array of `Strings` passed to the `main()` method. When defining an array, you can put the square brackets on either the type or the name; the following are identical:

```
String[] sAr;
String sAr[];
```

There is another kind of method that is different from the standard methods—it is called a constructor. Constructors are called when an instance of a class is created in computer memory. Constructors do not have a return type, and the name of the constructor method is the same as the name of the class. For example, a constructor for `MyApp2` might look like this:

```
public MyApp2() {
}
```

Notice that there is no return type indicated. If you do not define a constructor in your code, your class will use the default constructor, which would look very much like this example constructor. Also compare this default constructor with the `MyApp2` class definition; they are very different things, but bear some resemblance: `public MyApp2() {` compared with `public class MyApp2 {`.

Values

In our example code for `MyApp2`, shown in Listing 3-3, we have statements where we set a member variable equal to a value. For example, we said the following:

```
ARRAY mA = m.getArray();
```

In describing this statement, I am as likely to say, "set `mA` equal to `m.getArray()`" as I am to say, "get `m.getArray()` into `mA`." But what I should be saying, and what you need to understand, is that the member variable `mA` is a pointer to an object of type `ARRAY`. What I am doing in this statement is setting the value of the pointer to the address in memory of the object that is returned by `m.getArray()`. Even this is not precise. It is more precise to say that `m.getArray()` is returning a pointer to the location of an `ARRAY`, and I am setting the pointer `mA` to that same location.

This matters, because you need to remember that you are never replicating an object when you pass it around and set member variables equal to it, you are merely setting more pointers to the same location. The only time an object is created is when you instantiate it by a call to new or some method that generates a new object and returns it. We will also look at the clone method, which can be used to return the address of a new copy of an object instead of returning the address of the original object.

The following examples might help. In the first, we just point another member at the existing object; and in the second, a new object is created and we point the new member variable at it. When we set the name member in the first example, we set the value in the originally existing object; and any other code that points at the original object will see the changed name. In the second example, the change, so far, is only seen locally.

```
ExampleObject newMember = existingObject;
newMember.name = "New Name";

ExampleObject newMember = new ExampleObject();
newMember.name = "Another Name";
```

Something different happens with primitive values. They are not Java objects and their value, rather than their address, is passed in all references.

Members

Objects have both methods and members. Members in object-oriented programming are variables. By variable, I mean a pointer. This variable might point to a primitive—like an int (integer)—or a Java object (like a Date class). In Java, Strings are objects, not primitives. Plain old arrays are also objects (with no methods).

Often, both methods and variables are referred to as "members" of a class, but I prefer to say "methods and member variables. In this discussion, methods are not called *members*. And also, member variables are correctly referred to as *fields*. I can't help throwing that in once in a while. If I used the terms *fields* and *methods* I wouldn't need to say *members*; but I like the word *members* and am in the habit of saying it, so I will say *members* and *methods*.

In our sample code, MyApp2 has several members. The first two we see are named myArray and myRef. Those are both class member variables, because they exist in the class, outside of any methods, which you can see from the code (repeated in the following). Methods know about the class member variables as you can see in the getArray() method, which returns the class member myArray. You can also see that the setRef() method sets the value of the myRef class member to be equal to the parameter that is passed to the method, useRef.

```
private ARRAY myArray = null;
static MyRef myRef;
public ARRAY getArray() {
    return myArray;
}
void setRef( MyRef useRef ) {
    myRef = useRef;
}
```

If you look for a minute at the main() method (repeated in the following), you will see that there are three members declared: m, useRef and mA. These are method members, because they exist solely in the method. Note that they can be handed around to be used elsewhere. For instance, the main() method hands useRef to the method m.setRef(), which then sets the myRef class member (remember, we are handing and setting memory pointers or references). The main() method is unique, and I will discuss it more when I cover the static modifier, a little later.

```java
public static void main( String[] args ) {
    MyApp2 m = new MyApp2();
    MyRef useRef = new MyRef();
    m.setRef( useRef );
    ARRAY mA = m.getArray();
    myRef = new MyRef();
}
```

Objects

The words *object*, *class*, and *instance* are practically interchangeable. You have classes (theoretically) before you create any instances. An instance only exists when you instantiate a new one in memory. You have objects that you can move around and store even if you don't know what type they are. Objects can be placed on disk or sent across the network, even when they don't exist as instances in memory.

So, you create an instance in memory of a class type, which is an object that can be moved out of memory (stored on disk), at which point it is not an instance, but can still exist as an object.

Classes and Null

I have already used the term *instance* in our discussion. In Listing 3-3, there are three instances of classes being created. To pick out the instances, look for the word *new*. Whenever you see the statement new, an object is being instantiated.

Sometimes you will call other classes in order to get an instance of some type; however, even though you don't use the word new in your code, that word was used somewhere down the line to get the instance. In the example code for MyApp2, we see the main() method setting the member mA equal to an ARRAY that is returned from the method getArray(). You may notice that the getArray() method in MyApp2 does not use the new statement, and when we define myArray at the class level (top), we do not say new. Instead, we used the word null in the definition. When the method getArray() returns myArray, it is returning a null instead of an instance of ARRAY. And when the main() method set mA equal to what's returned from getArray(), it is setting mA equal to null. This is not very productive, but it is valid Java code.

To explain null, we will consider what the following statements mean:

```java
MyRef useRef = new MyRef();
new MyRef();
ARRAY myArray;
ARRAY myArray = null;
```

The first line instantiates a new instance of MyRef class and assigns a member reference (name) to it. The name we will use is useRef.

We can instantiate a new instance without assigning it to a name as in the second line. This is often done in graphical user interface (GUI) apps when they get started. The initial Frame is instantiated and displays itself on screen—no name is required.

We can also create a new name for a certain type of class and not assign it to any instance, as in the third line. The fourth line is identical in effect to the third line except that in the fourth line we are specifically telling Java that we are assigning the member name myArray to a non-existent instance, hence null. In effect, myArray points at *no* memory location.

We say that member variable names point to instances. At any time, we can point a member variable name at another instance. In hardware, this actually works out to pointing the member at an address in memory. When we point the member at `null`, we are saying that it doesn't point to any address in memory.

Garbage Collection

A Java application in computer memory can be pictured as a basket full of Java objects, all referencing one another, calling each other's methods and returning data, and getting and setting one-another's members. In Java, we do not have to manually keep track of what objects are in use and release the memory of unused objects, the Java runtime does that through a process called garbage collection. When an object is no longer referenced by any other object in the basket, it falls out of the basket. It doesn't disappear until the periodic garbage collection process walks through memory and sweeps the fallen objects away.

Primitives

In addition to objects (described previously), we have Java primitives. Some of the primitive types are `int` (integer), `byte`, and `char` (character). Member variables can be of types from both the Java classes (objects) and the primitives (values).

Primitives do not have any methods and do not have any members. You can have arrays of primitives, just like arrays of Java objects.

There are also Java classes that encapsulate the primitives, letting us hold primitives in an object instance and retrieve primitives from an instance. For example, `Integer`, is a class that can encapsulate an `int`. From `Integer`, we can get the `int` value of a `String` by calling `Integer.parseInt( String s )`.

Some Java constructs can only handle objects, not primitives; for example, a `Vector` (a dynamic array object), so we will need to encapsulate our primitive values if we intend to store them in a `Vector`.

Strings

A `String` is an immutable Java object, meaning you can't change it; however, you can replace it with (point your member variable at) a `new String`. `String` has methods that look like you are changing the object, but that is not the case. For example, you might call the `String.toUpperCase()` method:

```
myString.toUpperCase();
```

This invocation of `toUpperCase()` does not change the value of `myString` at all, but it has a return type of `String`, and what gets returned is the value of `myString` in uppercase. The only way to set `myString` to uppercase is to set it equal to the return value. In effect, you are setting `myString` to point at a new uppercase `String` that is created by the `toUpperCase()` method:

```
myString = myString.toUpperCase();
```

A very common error when handling `Strings` is to try to compare them like you can do with the primitive types, using equal signs for instance:

```
if( stringOne == stringTwo )
```

This is frighteningly valid code, but does not accomplish the test you intend. It is as bad as accidentally using one equals sign in a test like this:

```
if( int1 = int2 )
```

I imagine this intended to compare `int1` with `int2`, but it ended up setting the value of `int1` equal to the value of `int2`. Bad, very bad—too bad.

Because `String` is an object, you need to treat it like an object and call its methods for comparisons. We call `String.equals()` method to compare `Strings`.

```
if( stringOne.equals( stringTwo ) )
```

This requirement for using methods of objects to do comparisons applies to all object types. However, it is most common to run into coding errors in this regard when dealing with `Strings`: they probably appear to programmers to be more like the primitives.

Static Modifier and the main() Method

You have seen the modifier `static` already. It was in our code example in the definition of the `main()` method, and in the definition of the `myRef` member. Both members and methods can be static. To describe what static means, let me step back for a second.

Imagine you executed `java.exe` and are running some Java code. Picture the JVM holding a bunch of objects (instances). If our code created 100 instances of the `MyApp` class, each one would have certain aspects of our `MyApp.java` code; however, some aspects would only exist one time in the JVM. Those things that only exist one time per JVM are labeled `static`. Items that are `static` exist outside any instance of `MyApp` and are shared by all. An interesting phenomenon that results from existence outside an instance of a class is that those aspects of the class that are `static` are available even when you haven't created an instance.

For example, the first line in my code could be this:

```
if( MyApp2.myRef == null ) {
```

In that line, I do not have an instance of `MyApp2` that I'm referring to by name; rather, I am referring to the class itself and testing the value of the static class member variable, `myRef`.

Now, this is precisely what we need to start running some Java code. By default, if I execute `java.exe` and give it a class name to run, it will run the `main()` method. If I provide any arguments on the command line when I execute `java.exe`, these arguments will be passed to the `main()` method as parameters: an array of `Strings`. For instance, if I give this command:

```
java MyApp2 this is a test
```

Then there are four arguments passed to the `main()` method of `MyApp2`: this, is, a, and test.

Here is the definition of `main()` from our code:

```
public static void main( String[] args ) {
```

After I describe the modifier `public` in the next section, you will know the meaning of that entire definition. This specific syntax for the `main()` method is identical for any class that you want to run from the command prompt (except that you can call the array of `Strings`, the arguments, anything you want, not just `args`).

We need to have a static method to start running Java code, because at that point we have not instantiated any classes. Look again at the `main()` method in Listing 3-3 (repeated in the following). We do something there that is quit typical. In the `main()` method, we instantiate an instance of the class itself—we create a `new` `MyApp2` instance, named `m`. To use the non-static methods of `MyApp2`, we need to call them within our instance of `MyApp2`, so we call `m.setRef()` and `m.getArray()`. The `m.` prefix indicates that we are calling the methods of our instance of `MyApp2` named `m`.

```
public static void main( String[] args ) {
```

```
    MyApp2 m = new MyApp2();

    MyRef useRef = new MyRef();
    m.setRef( useRef );
    ARRAY mA = m.getArray();
    myRef = new MyRef();
}
```

Notice one last thing in the main() method definition. It sets the value of the static myRef member to an instance of MyRef. From a static method, only static members of the class can be referenced. If we tried to set the value of myArray from within main(), we would get an error at compile time, because until we create an instance of MyApp2, there is no myArray member—it is not static.

Public and Private Modifiers

public and private modifiers can exist on both methods and member variables. These help delineate the items in a class that the user of a class has direct access to, from those items that the user of a class cannot see (directly). These are scope modifiers. That is the important thing about public and private: it is important because it has some implications for security that we will discuss later.

In Listing 3-3, the myArray member is private, so someone using this class cannot get or modify myArray directly. However, we have provided the method getArray() which is public and can return myArray to anyone.

```
    private ARRAY myArray = null;
    static MyRef myRef;
    public ARRAY getArray() {
        return myArray;
    }
    void setRef( MyRef useRef ) {
        myRef = useRef;
    }
```

By default, methods and members, like the myRef member and the setRef() method, which are not declared as private or public, are generally only accessible to other classes that come from the same package. One additional scope modifier is protected. Protected scope is like the default, except it allows you to permit subclasses of your class that are defined outside your package to see your members and methods.

One design pattern (approach) declares all the class member variables are private, then sets about establishing getters and setters (public methods that provide a way for other objects to get or set the private members) to read from and write to the members. This is a feature of JavaBeans, and often of Enterprise Java Beans, and lends to their usefulness as components in an IDE. They can be distributed and incorporated into an IDE or application server without prior knowledge or definition by virtue of their getters and setters—by reflection (or XML definition), the IDE can list the public getter and setter methods of a bean and provide access to the private members.

We have provided a getter method in our example code for the myArray member: getArray(). We have also provided a setter method for the myRef member: setRef(); although, our method names don't conform to JavaBeans standards, because we are not writing JavaBeans, and we needn't implement all that boilerplate code.

Exceptions

Good and secure code must have a plan in place for handling errors. Java has included a framework on which we can build error (exception) handling. You have several choices when dealing with exceptions, and Java helps you accomplish any of the following that you choose:

- Do nothing with the exception, but *throw* it to the code that called the code with the exception. Throwing exceptions generates a stack trace, which lists the place (line number and code) where the exception occurred and the place that called this block of code (method) and the place that called that method, and so on. You can print the stack trace and see where you were and what happened. Often, the exception itself will tell you why the exception happened; no further troubleshooting required.

- Catch the exception and deal with it locally, and then either continue running or break out of the code, or even throw the exception after catching it.

- Catch the exception and throw a different exception.

Exception Handling Syntax

Let's explore some of the syntax and functionality of exception handling. Listing 3-4, ExceptionDemoA.java, shows two blocks inside the main() method: try and catch, each surrounded by curly brackets. They go together, so I have concatenated the catch block to the close curly bracket of the try block. In the second block, the catch, we catch the general Exception.

■ **Note** You can find this Java file and the next file in the folder named *Chapter3*.

Listing 3-4. ExceptionDemoA.java

```java
import java.io.FileInputStream;
public class ExceptionDemoA {
    public static void main( String[] args ) {
        try {
            ExceptionDemoA m = new ExceptionDemoA();
            String mS = m.doWork();
            System.out.println( mS );
        } catch( Exception x ) {
            System.out.println( x.toString() );
        }
        System.exit(0);
    }
    String doWork() throws Exception {
        FileInputStream tempFileIS = new FileInputStream( "C:/Windows/win.ini" );
        tempFileIS.open();
        //…
        if( tempFileIS != null ) tempFileIS.close();
```

```
        return "success";
    }
}
```

Notice that the `doWork()` method is declared with `throws Exception`. The `Exception` class is the mother of all exceptions and represents any of them. Some of her children exceptions are `IOException` when dealing with files or the network, `SQLException` when dealing with databases and `NullPointerException` when your Java code tries to call a method of a nonexistent object. We can have a separate `catch` block for each kind of exception that we are anticipating. A method can throw multiple types of exceptions that may occur.

Catching the general `Exception` would be appropriate whenever we are calling an external block of code (in this case, our call to the `m.doWork()` method) that may throw any number of exceptions. It would also be appropriate if, no matter what exception we catch, we handle it identically, as in this case.

Print the Exception Message to System Output Stream

Whatever the exception is that we catch, we will print the identity in the catch block using this command:

```
System.out.println( x.toString() );
```

Every object in Java has a `toString()` method, including exception objects and the objects that you will create. The `toString()` method is inherited from the `Object` object – more on that later. The `toString()` method returns a `String` type, which can be used to provide the identity or some details about the object—in the case of exceptions, it provides the exception name.

`System.out.println()` sends text to the command prompt window, ending with a line ending character. Line ending characters differ from one kind of computer to another, for instance, from Windows to UNIX. Lines end with a carriage return character or line feed character or both.

These terms come from the days of typewriters where the paper rolled around a platen in a carriage and the carriage moved from right to left as you typed. At the end of each line, the typist would swing a lever that rolled the platen to feed a line, and push the lever to the left, which would return the carriage to the start.

Appending a line ending character to a string means the next character will appear underneath the first character on the current line, i.e., on the next line.

STACKED CALLS

Note that we call `x.toString()` in the `catch` block and pass the returned `String` immediately as a parameter to `System.out.println()`. We don't create a `String` member variable to hold the value before printing it. For lack of a better name, I'm going to call this a *stacked call*. See if you can find two very similar examples of such a call in the code in the next section, Listing 3-5, `ExceptionDemoB.java`. We will begin to use stacked calls frequently in Chapter 6.

Clean Up as part of Exception Handling

There is a problem with the code of `ExceptionDemoA.java` in Listing 3-4. (The code is repeated in the following). There are things that get done in the `doWork()` method that need to get undone there as well.

Primarily, we open a `FileInputStream` (probably to read the contents of a file). From there, anything could happen—specifically, an exception could occur.

```
String doWork() throws Exception {
    FileInputStream tempFileIS = new FileInputStream( "C:/Windows/win.ini" );
    tempFileIS.open();
    //…
    if( tempFileIS != null ) tempFileIS.close();
    return "success";
}
```

If an exception were thrown before we close the `FileInputStream`, then the `doWork()` method would throw the exception to whoever called it (see the `throws` modifier on the line that defines `doWork()`). The line that closes the `FileInputStream` (`close()` method) would never be reached, and in some instances the file would remain open. This could have dire consequences for applications running on the computer. In many cases, a file that is currently open in one application cannot be read by another, so a file that is not closed after an exception might not get backed up, and it might lock up other computer operations.

Clean Up in a finally Block

With exception handling, there is a third block called `finally` that can be used, as in Listing 3-5. With each `try` block, there must also be a `catch` block, a `finally` block or both. We will rarely have a `try` without a `catch` block (see the sidebar called "`try`/`finally` Tack-on Debugging and Synchronization" later in this chapter). The idea is that whether you complete the `try` block successfully or generate and catch an exception before finishing the `try`, you can do things to clean up in the `finally`. The `finally` block runs, even if your `catch` block throws an exception. Look at the syntax of the `doWork()` method in Listing 3-5.

Listing 3-5. ExceptionDemoB.java

```
import java.io.FileInputStream;
public class ExceptionDemoB {
    public static void main( String[] args ) {
        ExceptionDemoB m = new ExceptionDemoB();
        System.out.println( m.doWork() );
        System.exit(0);
    }
    String doWork() {
        String returnString = "attempt";
        FileInputStream tempFileIS = null;

        try {

            tempFileIS = new FileInputStream( "C:/Windows/win.ini" );
            tempFileIS.open();
            //…
            returnString = "success";

        } catch( Exception x ) {

            System.out.println( x.toString() );
```

```
    } finally {
        try {
            if( tempFileIS != null ) tempFileIS.close();
        } catch( Exception y ){}

    }

    return returnString;
    }
}
```

In doWork() we have a try block around the open() of the FileInputStream. If anything should happen to cause an exception to be thrown, we will catch it in the next block. Then whether we have caught an exception or not, we will enter the finally block and execute the FileInputStream.close() method.

You might have a couple questions. The first might be, "Why can't we close the FileInputStream in both the try and in the catch blocks?" The answer is you *can* do that. However, repeating code is bad practice, and you may have a problem with the close() in the catch block that will cause another exception to be handled, thus compounding the troubleshooting effort.

A second question you may have is. "Why don't we just put the FileInputStream.close() outside both the try and the catch, and skip the finally block?" That is a bad idea because sometimes you will both catch an exception and throw it or another exception, like this:

```
} catch( IOException x ) {
    throw new AppException( x.toString() );
}
FileInputStream.close();
```

If this were your code, and you caught an IOException, you would never reach the FileInputStream.close() line. The throw statement inside your catch, since it is not caught here, would exit the current method, throwing an AppException to whatever code called this method.

Looking back up at our example, you will see this set of blocks within the finally block:

```
    } finally {

        try {

            if( tempFileIS != null ) tempFileIS.close();
        } catch( Exception y ){}
    }
```

Closing the FileInputStream can throw an IOException, and we need to deal with it (catch it or throw it). I choose to catch it and do nothing, at this point. I use this as my standard syntax for a finally block. Generally, we are just doing cleanup, and whatever work I might have been doing should have been completed, or would have thrown an exception, which I've already handled.

If I can't clean this up (e.g., close the FileInputStream), then it is true I may need to fix something, but if I've gotten this far, then I've already used the resource, in which case I should be able to close it. If I failed to use it, then I've already handled a related exception, and another exception here would be superfluous. So I usually do nothing inside the catch block that I have inside my finally block.

TRY/FINALLY TACK-ON DEBUGGING AND SYNCHRONIZATION

There is one case where I have found the need for a set of `try` and `finally` blocks, without a `catch` block. If you have written a method and you need to temporarily add debugging to it without over-cluttering your existing code, you can use a `try` and `finally` block pair to your advantage. Look at the following skeleton of a method named `methodName()`:

```
returnType methodName() throws Exception {
    try {
        while() {
            if() {
            }
        }
        for() {
        }
    catch( Exception x ) {
    } finally {
    }
}
```

To do temporary spot debugging on this method, we could declare a file output before the `try` block, then write debug messages to it throughout the method. For completeness, security and good practice, we would then `flush()` the file and `close()` it in the existing `finally` block. The only problem with that is that we have cluttered up our code, and making those changes and then cleaning it up later (removing the debugging) gives an abundance of opportunity to introduce more errors. In brief, that approach would yield code that appears more like permanent debugging code, like this:

```
returnType methodName() throws Exception {
    PrintStream debugOut = null;

    try {
        debugOut = new PrintStream ( new FileOutputStream( "debug.txt" ) );

        while() {
            debugOut.println( "message 1" );
            if() {
            }
        }
        for() {
        }
    catch( Exception x ) {
    } finally {
        if( debugOut != null ) {
            debugOut.flush();

            debugOut.close();

        }
    }
}
```

We can reduce the potential for introducing errors with a simpler try/finally block pair. If we are seeing problems that we know are happening in the while block in our example method, then we can surround just that block with our troubleshooting. (Be aware that you cannot break existing blocks by putting a new code block around just the open or close of an existing block.) Our solution might look like the following (the code in bold has been added):

```
returnType methodName() throws Exception {
    try {

        // temp code
        PrintStream debugOut = null;

        try {
        debugOut = new PrintStream ( new FileOutputStream( "debug.txt" ) );

        // to here

        while() {
            debugOut.println( "message 1" );
            if() {
                debugOut.println( "message 2" );
            }
            debugOut.println( "message 3" );
        }

        // temp code
        debugOut.println( "message 4" );
        } finally {
            if( debugOut != null ) {
                debugOut.flush();

                debugOut.close();

            }
        }
        // to here

        for() {
        }
    catch( Exception x ) {
    } finally {
    }
}
```

We have successfully added spot debugging, right where needed, and we have used good coding practice by closing our file output in a finally block. Note that if our method is not already catching or throwing an IOException, we will need a new catch block before our new finally block, and we will need a set of try/catch blocks within our added finally block, around the flush() and close(). Cleaning this up (removing the debugging) only requires removing the opening and closing sections of code (our new try and finally declarations and the surrounding code we added) and removing each of the debugOut.println() statements.

When tacking code on like this, it is good to remember the context and the synchronization demands. If this were a method that is being called by a multithreaded server application, then we would need to assure that only one user at a time will be opening, writing and closing the file. One way to accomplish that would be to declare the method to be *synchronized* (add the `synchronized` keyword to the method signature, before the return type declaration). Another way that doesn't involve changing the existing method signature is to *synchronize* on an object. It can be any type of object, but it should be a static class member so that everyone is synchronizing on the same thing.

Often you will attempt to synchronize the smallest section of code that you can, and in that case you might synchronize each `debugOut.println()` statement. But in that case you might also need to declare your `debugOut PrintStream` as a static class member. However to add synchronization to our spot debugging, we will synchronize a larger section and allow each request of the `methodName()` method to have exclusive access to the debug.txt file from open to close. It will look like this:

```
static String synchOnThis = "";
returnType methodName() throws Exception {

    try {

        PrintStream debugOut = null;

        synchronized( synchOnThis ) {

        try {
        debugOut = new PrintStream ( new FileOutputStream( "debug.txt" ) );

        while() {
            debugOut.println( "message 1" );
            if() {
                debugOut.println( "message 2" );
            }
            debugOut.println( "message 3" );
        }

        debugOut.println( "message 4" );
        } finally {
            if( debugOut != null ) {
                debugOut.flush();

                debugOut.close();

            }
        } }

        for() {
        }
    catch( Exception x ) {
    } finally {
    }
}
```

Notice that we open a `synchronized` block before our added `try` block, and we close the `synchronized` block (with an extra close curly bracket) after our added `finally` block. Everything within that `synchronized` block will be executed exclusively by one call to the `methodName()` method (by one user) at a time.

We are synchronizing on a blank `String` named `synchOnThis`. It is a `static` class member. Let me point out how we might capitalize on this synchronization arrangement. Let's say we have an additional method in this same class that we need to debug. We can add identical `try`/`finally` blocks and debugging in that second method, again synchronizing on the `synchOnThis` member. Not only will each call to those methods get exclusive access to write to our file, but also a call to either method will have exclusive access—e.g., someone in our first method cannot have access to the file while someone in the second method has `synchronized` on it. If you want to debug a method in a different class to this same file, you can synchronize on the same static member, `synchOnThis` in this class.

There is one assumption in synchronization that you must understand: synchronization is only effective within a single JVM. If you have, for example, two web servers on the same computer, each one will likely be running its own JVM. Those two JVMs cannot coordinate synchronized access to a file (for example). So if one of the JVMs is writing to the file, the other JVM may try to write to the file at the same time. That will likely fail.

Exception Handling Approaches

There are a variety of philosophies and practices regarding exception handling. I have not seen any proposals that I have entirely agreed with. However, I do have practices that I like, and I do try to be consistent. Allow me to propose a few ideas that help define my approach.

Don't Code Multiple Exceptions When One Will Do

I find that it is a very rare circumstance that will provoke me to do one thing for one specific exception thrown in a `try` block, and a different thing for another kind of exception in the same block. So I usually only have one `catch` block per `try` block. One "exception" to this rule is when I am throwing generic app exceptions (more on this is a bit).

Additionally, I will frequently have `try` and `catch` blocks inside other `try` and `finally` blocks. You have already seen me do that in the `finally` block listed previously.

Catch and Handle an Exception Where It Occurs

Deal with the exception immediately. If you're not sure what to do in the current method, it will be even harder to do something from a more remote method. An "exception" to this is when your design is intended to throw exceptions in order to create a complete stack trace.

I'm thankful that the classes provided by Sun and Oracle corporations are designed to throw their exceptions to my code. They are certainly not in a position to handle them like I as the application programmer can. But it's true for you like it's true for me, what my graduate professor once said: "You're the doctor now." It's your job to deal with the exception.

It almost goes without saying that there are many times when the best way to deal with an exception is to ignore it. One way I frequently ignore exceptions is by returning a blank `String`. Let's say, for example, you are passing a phone number that you selected from Oracle database to a Java method that formats phone numbers with parentheses and dashes (e.g., (800)555-1212). However, the current record has a `null` phone number. You wouldn't want to throw an exception for that trivial concern. You can do one of 2 things (or both):

1. Test if the incoming phone number is `null` and immediately return a blank `String`.

2. Format whatever, and if it throws an exception, return a blank `String`—but don't throw an exception from your phone number format method.

Why wouldn't you just take approach number (1)? Well there might be other problems with formatting a phone number besides a `null` value. What if the phone number is too short or contains alphabetic characters? Therefore, to prevent throwing an exception for this simple formatting problem, we would prefer approach number (2). Note that this example is for data coming from a database, if you were dealing with user input, you would probably want to notify the user of format problems so they could fix them.

Give Feedback from Your Catch Block

Some exceptions need to be documented and communicated, especially in those cases where a system administrator needs to take immediate action to correct an error, or when the application programmer needs to fix a processing problem. In those cases, sufficient situational details (like the stack trace and the data being processed) need to be transmitted. There are three common ways to transmit the data:

*   Log it in an error log file or database.

*   Send an e-mail or other message to an on-call support address.

*   Print a message to the console or application window.

In client/server applications, the application user is rarely the person who needs to get the error details, so sending that data to the console or application window will not help solve the problem, but you do need to inform the user that there is a problem, with a sensible message like, "An error has occurred. We have informed the administrator. Please try again later. Thank you."

If an error is not likely to be urgent, you might rely on logging the details and hope the administrator reviews the logs at some time; otherwise, you may need to send a message directly to the administrator by e-mail or some other messaging system.

Govern the Amount of Exception Reporting in Any Major Outage

When catching exceptions and logging or sending e-mails or other messages, beware of the potential to make the problem worse by excessively reporting the problem. When everyone in your organization runs into the same problem at the same time, you don't want your administrator's e-mail to fill up immediately with 1,000 or 10,000 of the exact same error messages. You need to govern the flow.

My approach (not detailed here) is to send the first 10 identical messages, then every tenth in the first hundred, then every hundredth. In this way, the administrator gets less than 30 messages, even if 1,000s are generated.

Consider Throwing A Generic Exception

For web applications, I have used the approach of throwing generic exceptions. No matter how deep you are in an application's methods, when you catch an exception, you deal with it, and then throw a generic application exception. The exception you throw is nothing special – it is an ordinary exception that extends Exception perhaps, but has no other members.

Why would you create such a façade as a generic exception? We need something simple and unique to our application that we can use like a flag. The generic exception is a flag that lets us know that we have already dealt with the exception and are just notifying the chain of command. In all application methods, no matter how deep, you also catch this generic application exception. Let's call this façade exception GenAppException. Your standard try/catch syntax would look like this:

```
try {
        …
} catch( GenAppException g ) {
        throw g;
} catch( Exception x ) {
        // Deal with x
        throw new GenAppException();
} finally{
        …
}
```

The thing to note here is that no matter what exception we catch here, if we can't just ignore it, we end up throwing a GenAppException. We either throw the GenAppException we caught from some deeper level, or we throw a new one.

You know two things when you catch one of these generic application exceptions:

- There was an exception that we need to take note of.

- It was handled earlier in the code, so all we need to do is pass it along (throw it).

And here is the clincher: when you get to the top level, ready to present something from the web application to the user's browser, you catch any exception and present a sensible error page to the user. They don't want to read your stack trace or exception details, and displaying that data might be a security concern. All that information should have been logged or e-mailed to the system administrator or application programmer when you initially dealt with the original exception.

Close Local Resources in a finally Block

We have already discussed this in our example code. Let me conclude by saying that every time you open a database Connection, Statement, or ResultSet, you need to embed the open() and all use of that resource in a try block, and close the resource in the associated finally block. This rule applies not only to Oracle Connections, but also to Files, Buffers, Streams, and so on.

Java Virtual Machine Sandbox

We have already explored the JVM and seen that it is the interface between the compiled Java byte code and the particular machine hardware and operating system where it is running. This gives Java byte code the ability to "run anywhere"—anywhere there is a JVM, that is.

In addition to lending portability, the JVM can enhance security by establishing a runtime security sandbox. The sandbox is a set of rules that apply to all Java code running in the JVM. In most cases where a security policy is in effect, these rules prevent the Java code from reading from or writing to the hard drive, and from opening network connections. When the JVM is running in a browser (like Internet Explorer or FireFox), the Java code (usually a Java applet) is not allowed to communicate with any other machine on the network except the machine from which it was loaded (the web server that provided the web page that included the applet tag).

At the command prompt and in many Java web servers, there is no sandbox in the JVM. In that case, your Java code can open and write files and read from other machines on the network.

In the Oracle JVM, the sandbox is quite rigid, preventing the Java code from reading from/writing to the hard drive; and from communicating on the network at all; however, it provides open access to the Oracle database, limited by the Oracle privileges granted to the Oracle user who is executing the Java code, and his roles.

With every sandbox, additional privileges can be granted in a number of ways. With applets, the code needs to be signed with a certificate in order to be granted extra privileges. When it runs in a browser, the browser presents the certificate to the computer user, who has to accept the certificate and privileges before the privileges become functional. Once the certificate is accepted, the applet is permitted to perform the privileged actions.

On the Oracle database, privileges are granted by administrative commands and are stored in the database. Privilege grants can be broad or very granular. We will be using extended privileges for Java code running in Oracle database in order to communicate to other machines over the Internet. You will see some very granular grants for those privileges when we get to Chapter 9.

Chapter Review

Although this has been only a brief introduction to the Java language, it has provided you with enough of the fundamentals to get you started. You cannot build security on sand; rather, you need a foundation. There are many options and styles in Java programming, and we want to intentionally choose our coding practices to assure, enhance and maintain security.

We learned about packages and their relationship to directory paths. We also learned about the `CLASSPATH` environment variable.

There were a boatload of terms and concepts introduced in this chapter, including class, instance, object, method, member, and constructor. Also the modifiers `static`, `public`, and `private` were covered. And we discussed the `main()` method.

Finally, we covered exception handling and the `try/catch/finally` syntax.

We will be using all these Java syntax elements throughout the rest of this book. If they are new to you now, don't worry. They will be like second nature to you before long.

CHAPTER 4

Java Stored Procedures

When I first discovered Java stored procedures, I made a formal presentation of my findings to the IT department of the company where I worked, giving several examples, including using Java in an Oracle database to send e-mail, to read web pages, and to calculate Unix crypt values for the authentication of application users. That was in 2001, and as we shall see as we go through this text, I am still presenting the same ideas. However, it is only now that these ideas can be realized, on account of the upgrade to the Oracle JVM that happened with Oracle database 11g. With Oracle database 11g, Oracle has upgraded the Oracle JVM to run with Java version 1.5, which includes a significant upgrade to the Java cryptography extension (JCE) package included with the JVM.

So, what does Java encryption have to do with Oracle? Well, the standard Oracle database does not provide encryption of data for transmission to client applications out of the box. You can buy add-ons, such as Oracle Advanced Security, to provide it, but with the Oracle JVM running in the database, we can use Java to do data encryption on the Oracle database. The only way to get to that Java functionality in Oracle database is through Java stored procedures. Having the power of programs written in Java running in the Oracle database will give us encryption and much more.

There was no impediment to running enhanced encryption in previous versions of the Oracle JVM, and I have been doing so ever since my initial presentation in 2001. The only problem was one of effort and standardization, and the vetting (acceptance) of the algorithms. Before enhancements to JCE in Java 1.5, we had to acquire algorithms or write them ourselves and manually install them in Oracle database. However, for encryption, we are now able to call on the standard functions and algorithms included in JCE.

In this chapter, we will learn how to connect from SQL queries on the Oracle database to the Oracle JVM in order to let Java do our processing and return data to us. We will also cover the basics of connecting to Oracle database from Java and running database queries. In fact, we will connect from Oracle through Java, using Java to read Oracle.

Java Stored Procedure Example

Nothing speaks to a programmer more clearly than code. Let the example that I'm going to present serve as a guide to begin understanding how Java stored procedures work. You will see an Oracle header to the Java code shown in Listing 4-1 in bold font. And you will also observe the definition of an Oracle function, following the Java code, which encapsulates the Java code. You cannot call Java code directly from an Oracle query, but you can call the Oracle function or procedure which will then call and run the Java.

Place a bookmark here so you can refer back Listing 4-1 in the discussion that follows. We will load this code into the Oracle database shortly.

Listing 4-1. MyApp4 and f_get_oracle_time

```
SET ROLE appsec_role;

CREATE OR REPLACE AND RESOLVE JAVA SOURCE NAMED myapp4 AS
package pkg4;
import java.sql.*;
import oracle.jdbc.driver.OracleDriver;
public class MyApp4 {
    public static String getOracleTime() {
        String timeString = null;
        Statement stmt = null;
        try {
            //Class.forName( "oracle.jdbc.driver.OracleDriver" );
            //new oracle.jdbc.OracleDriver();
            //Connection conn = new OracleDriver().defaultConnection();
            Connection conn = DriverManager.getConnection("jdbc:default:connection");
            stmt = conn.createStatement();
            ResultSet rs = stmt.executeQuery( "select sysdate from dual" );
            if( rs.next() ) {
                timeString = rs.getString(1);
            }
        } catch( Exception x ) {
            timeString = x.toString();
        } finally {
            try {
                if( stmt != null ) stmt.close();
            } catch( Exception y ) {}
        }
        return timeString;
    }
}
/

CREATE OR REPLACE FUNCTION f_get_oracle_time
    RETURN VARCHAR2
    AS LANGUAGE JAVA
    NAME 'pkg4.MyApp4.getOracleTime() return java.lang.String';
/
```

▪ **Note** The code in Listing 4-1 can be found in the file named *Chapter4/AppSec.sql.*

I want to point out one thing about this example code before we go any further. I know I said that packages, like pkg4 in our example class MyApp4, are coordinated with directories, but there is no *pkg4* directory. I also said that there is always one public class defined in each *.java* file with the class having the same name as the file. However in our example, there is no *MyApp4.java* file, and the file we have is not even named "MyApp4" dot anything.

The reason for this discrepancy is that we are only defining this class on the Oracle database. As it is right now, we can't compile or run it on the client. And when we load it into the Oracle database, the things I said about packages and classes suddenly becomes true again. The Oracle database creates a virtual package directory that it can search like a CLASSPATH to find the class. Also, it compiles the code just like a regular **.java* file and creates the class files, that is virtual files, stored in the database.

Acquiring the Privilege to Load a Java Stored Procedure

Application security user, `appsec`, needs the `CREATE PROCEDURE` privilege to load Java into the database. She gets that privilege through the `appsec_role`. Recall that we set the `appsec_role` to be a non-default role for `appsec` user. For that reason, when `appsec` connects to Oracle database, she does not have that role at the outset. Rather, she has to enable it by setting `appsec_role` for her current session. The method shown (`SET ROLE appsec_role`) is sufficient, and as you recall, the new role becomes the only role that `appsec` has in her current session. An alternative approach is to request that all roles granted to `appsec` (both default and non-default) be enabled in the current session with this command:

```
SET ROLE ALL;
```

Loading Java in the Oracle Database

There are a couple ways to get Java code into the Oracle database. One way is to use the *loadjava.exe* utility. That utility is available in both the Oracle database and in some versions of the Oracle client software. It is in the same bin directory as *sqlplus.exe* and other Oracle applications. Using *loadjava*, we can submit a java file (or *sqlj* file, with SQL embedded in Java code), a class file, or even a jar file to the Oracle database. The server handles whatever we submit in an appropriate manner. Here is an example `loadjava` command that we might have used to load a Java file named *MyApp4.java* (refer to Listing 4-1).

```
loadjava -force -resolve -user appsec/password@orcl pkg4/MyApp4.java
```

That command would attach to Oracle database as `appsec` user, then read the *MyApp4.java* file from the *pkg4* directory and submit it to Oracle database. The new code would overwrite anything that existed previously by the same name, and the Oracle database would compile the code and place a virtual *MyApp4.class* file in a virtual *pkg4* directory.

Another approach we can use to load Java code into Oracle database is what we've used in our example, Listing 4-1. We have the Java code for the MyApp4 class listed after this Oracle statement:

```
CREATE OR REPLACE AND RESOLVE JAVA SOURCE NAMED myapp4 AS
```

We can run this `CREATE` statement while connected to Oracle database, and it will accomplish the same things that we would have accomplished through the `loadjava` command.

Handling Exceptions in a Java Stored Procedure

As you can see in the `getOracleTime()` method in the `MyApp4` class in Listing 4-1, we start out with a `try/catch/finally` block. Whenever you are dealing with databases, you must be prepared to catch or throw a `SQLException`. There are many cases when a `SQLException` would be thrown; for example, if you misspell a table name or a column name or if you don't have permission to read the data or if the Oracle database has a problem responding. `IOExceptions` can also be generated when doing input/output (IO). Communicating with Oracle database is I/O as is reading and writing files, and as is reading from network resources, like web servers.

Based on the discussions on exception handling in Chapter 3, we select to catch all exceptions and deal with them locally, setting the string that we are about to return to be equal to the value returned from `Exception.toString()`. When we get to the end of the `try` / `catch` / `finally` blocks, the last line returns `timeString`, which may be the Oracle database data and time if successful, else it will be the `Exception.toString()` message. (Please note that the `toString()` method in `Exception` is not static. You will need an instance of `Exception`, like `x`, to call `x.toString()`. I'm just saying `Exception.toString()` for discussion clarity.)

Here is an example `Exception.toString()` message:

```
java.sql.SQLException: Invalid Oracle URL specified.
```

In the `finally` block, we close the `Statement` object, `stmt`. Again, we are dealing with Oracle database, so we must be prepared for and catch any `SQLExceptions`. However, we needn't do anything with exceptions in this case. Notice that we test to see if `stmt` is `null` before we try to close it. That test will keep us from generating a `NullPointerException` in case we never instantiated the `Statement` object. (`NullPointerException` is generated when we attempt to use methods or members of a class that has not been instantiated.) Maybe you already surmised correctly that we don't need to do the test on whether `stmt` is `null`. Since we are in a `try`/`catch` block and doing nothing with exceptions, we could just attempt to close the `stmt` and it will either succeed or we will catch the `NullPointerException`. That is true, but I don't like generating exceptions needlessly, so we test if `stmt` is `null`.

Another notable item at this point in our exploration of Java is the declaration of `timeString` and `stmt`. First, notice that we declare (mention) them before the `try` block. We need to do that so that we can return `timeString` outside the `try` block, and so that we can close the `stmt` in the `finally` block, which is outside the `try` block. Member variables are contextual, and only reside within the scope of their declaration. That is to say, a member variable only exists within the block (curly braces) where it is declared. For example, the `ResultSet` member does not exist outside of the `try` block.

The second thing to notice about the declaration of `timeString` and `stmt` is that they are both declared initially to be `null`. As I mentioned earlier, they would point to no object (`null`) even if we didn't declare them as `null`. This is true of all Java objects, not just Strings and Statements. However, the compiler looks ahead and sees that we are going to return `timeString`, and it doesn't like to return unknowns. If you tried to compile a method with these two lines:

```
String myString;
Return myString;
```

The compiler will report an error and refuse to compile your code, saying that `myString` may not have been *initialized* (set to point at an object or at a value). But if you change the declaration of `myString` to be:

```
String myString = null;
```

then the compiler will accept that (at least) *you* take responsibility for the `null` value, and it will compile your code.

You might ask why the compiler doesn't see that `timeString` is initialized later on (we say `timeString` = `rs.getString(1)`) when we are reading through the `ResultSet`? *Javac* is a pretty smart compiler. It sees the initialization there but notices that the initialization occurs *conditionally*—meaning, it happens after the `if` statement.

So, why is `stmt` declared to be `null`? It's for a very similar reason. If you declared `stmt` like this, without initializing it even to `null`; then, when the compiler looks ahead and sees that you are going to test `stmt` in an `if` block, it reports an error that `stmt` might not have been initialized.

```
Statement stmt;
...
```

```
if( stmt == null ) …
```

In this case, the complaint is that we are trying to use something in our logic that may not have been initialized. Java wants to make informed decisions and sees this as a potential for confusion, even at compile time.

Calling Oracle Database from Java

Within the Java method named `getOracleTime()`, in Listing 4-1, are calls to four classes that are used for interfacing with Oracle database: `OracleDriver`, `Connection`, `Statement`, and `ResultSet`. The following sections describe each of those four classes and what they do.

OracleDriver

The first call is to load the `OracleDriver` in the Java database connectivity (JDBC) drivers registry (list). (You can use multiple drivers; e.g. Oracle database, SQL Server, and MySQL. Each would need to be registered.) I show several options for registering the `OracleDriver`. They are all commented for reasons I'll explain in a second.

```
//Class.forName( "oracle.jdbc.driver.OracleDriver" );
//new oracle.jdbc.OracleDriver();
//Connection conn = new OracleDriver().defaultConnection();
```

The first option uses a call to instantiate an `OracleDriver` class, sight unseen, by using the `Class.forName()` call. The `Class.forName()` method is a way to instantiate an object by simply stating its fully qualified name. By instantiating the `OracleDriver` this way, it is automatically loaded into the drivers registry. This is the standard practice for loading the `OracleDriver`, and you will see it frequently.

The second option is to instantiate a `new OracleDriver()`, which automatically gets loaded in the drivers registry. Lastly, we have an option to create a new instance of `OracleDriver` (again automatically loaded in the drivers registry) and in the same line of code, use the `OracleDriver` to get a `Connection` object.

Now, let me tell you why all of these invocations are commented. There are two reasons. The first has to do with the fact that we are running this code as a Java stored procedure on the Oracle database. As part of the Oracle session, the Oracle JVM automatically loads and registers the `OracleDriver`.

The second reason, but one that is less dependable, is that from Java version 1.6 on, the `OracleDriver` is loaded automatically, as needed (with *ojdbc6.jar* in the `CLASSPATH` and a hint from the connection string, e.g. "*jdbc:oracle:thin*"). This is less dependable, because you as the developer have the option of compiling and running this code with whatever version of Java you have available. You are only required to have JDK 1.5 or later to follow this book, so we will continue to load the `OracleDriver` in any code that will run on your client workstation.

Connection and Statement

Next in Listing 4-1, we establish a connection to Oracle database (repeated in the following). We define the connection based on the default, "*jdbc:default:connection.*" We will place this Java code into the Oracle database, so we do not need to specify an Oracle server or Oracle listener port number, nor do we need to identify an Oracle user or password. By default, the Java stored in the database runs as the user associated with the schema where the Java is loaded. Because we are creating this Java structure using the `appsec` user, it will run with the default roles and privileges of `appsec`.

```
Connection conn = DriverManager.getConnection("jdbc:default:connection");
stmt = conn.createStatement();
```

We use our instance of `Connection` to create a `Statement` by calling `conn.createStatement()`. Note that these are the standard Java classes used in Java to talk to any vendor's SQL database, including SQL Server and DB2. Yet, because we requested (or received by default) the `OracleDriver` to give us the `Connection`, we have a `Connection` that is specific to Oracle database.

Each database vendor must implement these standard interfaces (Connection and Statement) to enable our Java code to talk with their databases using vendor-specific drivers. The Oracle-specific drivers and classes are what we get by including *ojdbc6.jar* in our `CLASSPATH`. There are several additional types of `Statements` and `Connections` that we will use—the variations being specific to Oracle database.

ResultSet

Once you have your `Statement` object, you can execute Oracle commands, like the one that we execute in the example, Listing 4-1 and repeated in the following. When we execute a query by calling `stmt.executeQuery()`, we expect to get data back. Data from a query is returned in a `ResultSet` object (`rs` in our example). By calling the `next()` method of the `ResultSet`, we bring the values from the next (first) row into the `ResultSet` object so we can request each value (each column in the row specified in the query) with a "getter" method, like the call to `rs.getString()` in our example code.

```
ResultSet rs = stmt.executeQuery( "select sysdate from dual" );
if( rs.next() ) {
        timeString = rs.getString(1);
}
```

An interesting thing about the `ResultSet` "getter" methods is that, for some types that are returned, a translation can be done automatically. For example, in our code, we are requesting a `Date` type (value), because in our query we `SELECT`ed (asked for) the value of `SYSDATE` which is the time and date of the Oracle database. Yet in our call to the `ResultSet` we asked to `getString()`, so the `ResultSet` does a translation from `Date` type to `String` type.

Picture the data being returned in the `ResultSet` as a spreadsheet with rows of data entries, and for each row there are multiple columns of associated values. When you call `ResultSet.next()`, you are getting the equivalent of the next row into the current `ResultSet` values space. Once there, you can get the value from each column using the column number. In our example, we get the value from the first column with the statement:

```
rs.getString(1);
```

Uniquely, the index for a `ResultSet` is 1-based; that is, the first column value is at index 1. This is different from everything else in Java (that I can think of). Java arrays and `Collections` are typically 0-based, and the first element is at index 0. Also, character places in a `String` start with 0.

We will almost always want to see if there is any data being returned in the `ResultSet` before we try to use it. For that reason, we put a `ResultSet.getString()` call in the `if` condition statement that tests whether there is a next row. Alternatively, we could just say:

```
rs.next();
rs.getString(1);
```

However, if we did this and there were no "next," then the `ResultSet` values space would be `null`, and when we call `rs.getString(1)`, we'd generate an `Exception`.

Also, we will almost always be expecting one or more rows to be returned in a `ResultSet`, and calling `if( rs.next() )` would only ever test whether a single row is returned. When we expect to be getting several rows, we will use a `while` block to process the `ResultSet`, for example:

```
while( rs.next() ) {
...
}
```

Method Syntax in Java Stored Procedures

I described the function of the modifier `static` in the `main()` method in Chapter 3. In Java stored procedures, we will see that Oracle database only calls `static` methods from Java stored procedures. This is for a similar reason to what we saw for the `main()` method: Oracle is calling these methods without instantiating an object of that class beforehand. We do not create an instance of `MyApp4` (listing 4-1) before we call the `getOracleTime()` method. However, just as the `main()` method can instantiate itself or any other object, these static methods (like `getOracleTime()`) called as Java stored procedures can instantiate themselves or other objects as needed (not everything used in a static method is static).

Calling Java from Oracle Database

The second part of our example code for a Java stored procedure (function) in Listing 4-1 is an Oracle statement to create a function, `f_get_oracle_time`. The syntax (repeated in the following) should be familiar—most of the Oracle keywords are identical to what we saw in Chapter 2 when we created procedures. With Java stored procedures (and functions), we modify the procedure definition with an indication that the code performing the processing is in a different language—in our case, Java. We indicate what Java code is going to be called by providing the full Java method specification:

```
CREATE OR REPLACE FUNCTION f_get_oracle_time

    RETURN VARCHAR2

    AS LANGUAGE JAVA
    NAME 'pkg4.MyApp4.getOracleTime() return java.lang.String';
/
```

Notice that our specification of the Java method includes the package name (`pkg4`), the class name (`MyApp4`) and the method name `getOracleTime()`. In this example, we also see that the return type being sent back from Java is specified as `java.lang.String`. If you look at the definition of the return type from the Oracle function, it says:

```
RETURN VARCHAR2
```

The Oracle `VARCHAR2` type corresponds to the Java `String` type. In case you hadn't already guessed, *java.lang* is the package where Sun (Oracle) keeps the `String` class. Specifying a fully qualified package as part of the parameter and return value types is required in Java stored procedure definitions.

We do need to coordinate the consistency of Java return types with the return types available in Oracle database. Oracle includes Java classes that encapsulate their return types in the *oracle.sql* package, and for many Oracle types, there are corresponding generic Java classes in the *java.sql* package. We will see some of these as we proceed. For more information on the Oracle database types and associated Java types, refer to the Oracle Documentation and to Appendix A of the document called *Oracle® Database JDBC Developer's Guide*.

Although this technology is called Java stored procedures, you'll see that for the most part we will be calling Java methods from Oracle functions. Java methods can only return one value. While that value can be a complex array of objects or an object with many members, it is still a single return value—a model that is analogous to Oracle functions. Oracle defines a stored procedure as code that performs a process, and a stored function as code that returns a value. Of course, an Oracle procedure can return multiple values through OUT parameters, and it would be handy if we could map that to a Java stored procedure that returns multiple values, but we cannot easily do that. And of course, an Oracle function can perform a process before returning a value. Oracle functions can also return multiple values through OUT parameters, but that is discouraged.

VARCHAR OR VARCHAR2

When creating database tables and writing PL/SQL, it is customary to define string columns and variables as type VARCHAR2. For historical reasons, there is no VARCHAR1. Oracle database does currently recognize VARCHAR as a synonym (a subtype in PL/SQL) for VARCHAR2, but Oracle warns against the use of VARCHAR in their official documentation. You can read that warning at the following link:

http://download.oracle.com/docs/cd/E11882_01/server.112/e17118/sql_elements001.htm#sthre f117

There is no reason to go against Oracle's advice, and I recommend VARCHAR2 when creating tables and writing PL/SQL. There is an exception to using VARCHAR2 as the string type, and that exception occurs when writing Java code to interface with the database. Later on when we define the parameters that we intend to pass from Java to Oracle in an Insert or Update statement, we will call them OracleTypes.VARCHAR. There is no OracleTypes.VARCHAR2 defined. OracleTypes is a class provided by Oracle, so VARCHAR2 as a type is conspicuous in its absence.

The important thing to remember here, is that one uses VARCHAR2 when creating a database column, or when defining a PL/SQL variable, and one uses OracleTypes.VARCHAR when defining a Java variable or parameter to be compatible with VARCHAR2 values from Oracle database.

Installing and Testing the Example Code

Run the code from Listing 4-1. You can run it using any of *SQL*Plus, SQL Developer, JDeveloper, TOAD* or any other database code editor that enables execution of code. The first portion is one line to set your role to appsec_role. The second portion of Listing 4-1 creates the Java Source named MyApp4. And the third portion creates the f_get_oracle_time function.

After running the code, you can test the Java stored procedure by calling the Oracle function f_get_oracle_time. The function will return the current date and time from the Oracle database.

```
SELECT f_get_oracle_time FROM DUAL;
```

A note here about the FROM DUAL clause. In order to select data, the SELECT query must have a source. The source will typically be an Oracle table or view. In this case, however, we are selecting the return value from a function. By saying FROM DUAL we are fulfilling the requirement for a source in the SELECT query syntax, but essentially saying "from the database." DUAL is actually a dummy table with one column named DUMMY and one row with DUMMY = 'X'. You can see this from the following query:

```
SELECT * FROM DUAL;
```

If you have by now surmised that we could have selected SYSDATE from any table or view, you would be correct! However, we would get a result for each and every row in the view or table we specified. Try this query and you will see results like those shown:

```
SELECT USERNAME, SYSDATE FROM SYS.ALL_USERS ORDER BY USERNAME;
```

```
ANONYMOUS            09-JUN-11
APEX_030200          09-JUN-11
APEX_PUBLIC_USER     09-JUN-11
APPQOSSYS            09-JUN-11
APPSEC               09-JUN-11
APPUSR               09-JUN-11
APPVER               09-JUN-11
```

A row for each user is returned, but the only values we return are username and SYSDATE for each row. This is a feature of the SELECT statement that we can use to our advantage. For example, if we select all the managers from a list of personnel, we might insert the words "Pointy-Haired" between the first and last names, like this:

```
SELECT FIRST_NAME || ' Pointy-Haired ' || LAST_NAME
    FROM HR.EMPLOYEES
    WHERE EMPLOYEE_ID IN (
        SELECT DISTINCT MANAGER_ID FROM EMPLOYEES
);
```

The double pipes "||" is a way to *concatenate* strings in Oracle database. We have a sub-query in the parentheses that selects all the *distinct* (unique) EMPLOYEE_IDs that are listed in the MANAGER_ID column of EMPLOYEES. For all employees that have one of those MANAGER_IDs as their EMPLOYEE_ID, we concatenate their FIRST_NAME, the words "Pointy-Haired" and their LAST_NAME, just for fun mind you.

We can select whatever we want for each row that is returned from a query. We can SELECT SYSDATE for each row, or we can SELECT "First Pointy-Haired Boss" for each row.

Review The Roster of Participants

The following is a quick rundown of the participants in our test of the example code:

1. Your client (Oracle command line) calling.

2. The function on the Oracle database that encapsulates.

3. The Java source named MyApp4 (Listing 4-1) that queries.

4. The Oracle database to select SYSDATE.

When we created the MyApp4 Java source, the Oracle database compiled the code and created the package *pkg4* and the class MyApp4. Our Oracle function calls the static method getOracleTime() in the MyApp4 class. In the getOracleTime() method, we open a connection to the Oracle database and request the system time, SYSDATE which we then return as a String. Our function receives the time string and returns it to our client as a VARCHAR2, and the client displays the date and time string.

You can see how these participants relate to one another in Figure 4-1.

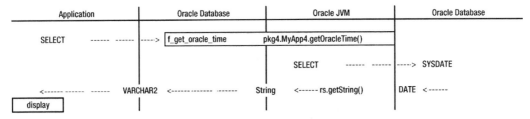

Figure 4-1. *Flow of a Java stored procedure*

There are two things that stand out in Figure 4-1 that I want to emphasize. First is that the Java stored procedure, function `f_get_oracle_time`, and the associated Java method, `getOracleTime()` are so closely related that I show them in a single box. You might say they are "joined at the hip." All that the function `f_get_oracle_time` does is pass its parameters to the Java method and return the value that is returned from the method.

The second thing I'd like to emphasize is that as the return value is passed along its return path, it is consecutively seen as a `DATE` type, then a `String` type, then a `VARCHAR2` type.

Cleaning Up

What we have just seen is merely an example of how Java stored procedures operate. You wouldn't normally invoke a Java stored procedure just to get the time from a `SELECT` statement. It would be much simpler to just invoke the built-in `SYSDATE` function. For example:

```
SELECT SYSDATE FROM DUAL;
```

The real usefulness of Java stored procedures is to do something hard or impossible to do in PL/SQL.

So let's remove this example from the database with these commands:

```
DROP FUNCTION f_get_oracle_time;
DROP JAVA SOURCE myapp4;
```

The Oracle Java Virtual Machine

When Oracle corporation first included a JVM in its database, it called it Aurora. You will still find some references to Aurora in the directories and files included with Oracle Database 11g.

The Oracle JVM in Oracle Database 11g is heavily customized, and cannot be upgraded or replaced with a standard JVM downloaded from Sun (Oracle corporation). The Oracle JVM has a comprehensive security structure and sandbox that is tied in with the Oracle database. That sandbox is part of what makes the Oracle JVM impossible to replace with a standard JVM. Sandbox security settings can be queried from the database and set with Oracle commands (we will see that in Chapter 9 when we discuss two-factor authentication).

Oracle JVM Based on Java SE 1.5

Probably because of the amount of tailoring that Oracle corporation needed to do to build the Oracle JVM, it is a release behind the current standard JVM. The Oracle JVM is based on Java Standard Edition (SE) version 1.5, while 1.6 is currently supported. 1.7 was released in July 2011. Talking about versions can really make a text like this look dated, and this paragraph may fall behind quickly; but in a few years when you have Java 1.7 or 1.8 on your workstation and you are using Oracle Database 12, you may still be using an Oracle JVM based on Java 1.5 – the Oracle JVM gets that far behind.

In any case, Java 1.5 is what we needed in Oracle database to support our use of JCE. So we won't criticize or lament.

A Separate JVM for Each Oracle Session

When you connect to Oracle database and use Java, you start a separate JVM for use only by your session. You cannot share any Java objects or data with other running JVMs (Oracle sessions), unless you store them in the database for others to query or hand the objects around through network port services (e-mail, ftp, web, etc.)

When you disconnect from Oracle database, your Oracle session closes and the JVM is terminated. If you immediately make a new connection to Oracle, you get a brand new JVM and nothing in your previous JVM is retained or carried over to the new JVM.

This has repercussions for us. Primarily, since we are going to be generating cryptographic keys (you might have already guessed that), we want to use them for a time to send encrypted data back and forth before we close the connection to Oracle database and the keys are discarded. We could save the keys in the database, or in what Oracle calls a wallet, which is basically a secure file on the hard drive of the server and/or the client. But if they are stored anywhere, then we don't know who might get access to them. No, what we will do is generate the keys on the fly and use them for a time, keeping our connection open during the key exchange and multiple queries, and only close the connection when we are done.

Oracle JVM Sandbox

We briefly discussed the Oracle JVM sandbox at the end of the last chapter. To recap that discussion, this particular sandbox prevents the Java code in Oracle database from reading from/writing to the hard drive; and from communicating on the network at all; however, it provides open access to the Oracle database, limited by the Oracle privileges granted to the Oracle user who is executing the Java code, and his roles. For example, if the HR user owns and is executing the Java stored procedure, it will have access to all of the HR schema data.

Extended security privileges can be granted to Java code in Oracle database to perform functions normally denied by the sandbox. These privileges are granted by administrative commands and are stored in the database. Privilege grants can be broad or very granular. We will be using extended privileges for Java code running in Oracle database in order to communicate to other machines over the internet. You will see some very granular grants for those privileges when we get to Chapter 9.

Auto-Commit Disabled in the Oracle JVM

In SQL databases, COMMIT means to incorporate changes into the existing database. Until COMMIT is executed, data updates are held in a cache. The session that made the updates can see the changes, but everyone else sees the data as it existed before the updates. When the session executes COMMIT, everyone can see the changes that were made. This is a powerful concept for transactions that have multiple steps. In a single session, each step can be performed, and each successive step can base its actions on updates already made in the session. When all the steps are completed, the session can issue a COMMIT, and all the updates will be made to the existing database. However, if there is a problem in any later step, all the completed steps can be *rolled back* (reversed) and not written to the existing database. You can see how this might be handy if a bank is transferring money from you to me—they will take it from your account and put it in my account. But if they have problems giving me your money, you want them to also reverse the step where they took it from you.

Generally, in Oracle database, a `COMMIT` must be issued as needed, which is sometime after every data update (`INSERT`, `UPDATE` or `DELETE`). Oracle *procedures* that update data should not issue a `COMMIT` – they assume that they are just part of a transaction and that whatever code called them will issue a `COMMIT` when all the parts are successful. Tom Kyte, author of *Expert Oracle Database Architecture: Oracle Database 9i, 10g, and 11g Programming Techniques and Solutions* (Apress, 2010) explains on his blog (`asktom.oracle.com`) that procedures do *atomic* units of work, and all transactions must be controlled (and `COMMIT` executed) by the invoker (the one who called the procedure).

Auto-commit is a mode of operation that you can employ where every update is immediately committed to the database. You can turn this feature on by executing:

```
SET AUTOCOMIT ON;
```

You might think that this would defeat the ability to do multiple-step transactional updates, and you would be right. However, this is the default mode for JDBC. So from a Java client, when you update the database, that update is immediately committed, and you cannot roll it back. One benefit is that you don't have to execute another Oracle statement using JDBC to `COMMIT` the update.

Actually you can turn off the auto-commit mode in JDBC by calling the `setAutoCommit()` method of your `Connection`, like this:

```
conn.setAutoCommit(false);
```

Then when appropriate, you can commit or rollback your transaction manually with one of these commands:

```
conn.commit();
conn.rollback();
```

Auto-commit is one area where pure Java is not "run anywhere." For Java code running in the Oracle database (Java stored procedures), the default mode is for auto-commit to be turned off. This adheres to the proposition that procedures are atomic and that transactions are committed by the invoker, but it is the opposite of what you'd expect from JDBC.

This is something to keep in mind as we develop Java stored procedures. If we update data, we need to issue a `COMMIT`.

Chapter Review

This has been a rather brief chapter in which we've been able to focus on running Java in the Oracle database, or Java stored procedures. We saw a couple techniques of loading Java into Oracle.

It may be off that subject, but we also discussed in some detail the reverse process of calling Oracle database from Java using the `Connection` and `Statement` classes. We also diverged into a discussion of `FROM DUAL` and the `SELECT` query.

As we must do as we proceed, we stepped back to talk about general programming issues. In this chapter, we covered some additional aspects of exception handling, and we covered declaring and initializing members.

Most important, we discussed the Oracle JVM and its transient nature and association with a specific Oracle session. Also, we talked about the Oracle JVM sandbox.

Public Key Encryption

I'm sure you've heard of public key encryption (PKE). You probably use it every day—if not in your code or on your servers, then on the Internet. When you use secure socket layers (SSL) in your browser or when you see the lock or key symbol and see `https:\\` (with the s) as the protocol in the address bar, you are using PKE and other encryption. SSL is used to send private data such as your credit card number in encrypted form to online merchants.

The basic concept of PKE is that two entities share a set of two keys (one public and one private) and use them to encrypt data for and decrypt data from each other. The keys are tied to one another so that anything encrypted with one of the pair (e.g., the private key) can only be decrypted with the other (e.g., the public key). This encryption/decryption works in both directions.

The most important aspect of PKE is that one of the keys is private. The private key is never disclosed to anyone; however, the public key can be given to any and all requestors. How does this help privacy?

The one requesting the public key can be sure that if that key successfully decrypts data, then it came from the entity with the private key. Only the private key can encrypt data that can be decrypted with the public key.

The converse is also true: only the public key can encrypt data that can be decrypted by the private key, so the one using the public key can be sure that only the entity with the private key can decrypt data that they encrypted.

Because the public key is, well, public, anyone can decrypt data sent from the originator. Also anyone can encrypt data and send it to the originator for decryption. This is not a flaw, but it is an aspect of PKE that we need to be aware of and account for.

Generate Keys on the Client

We will have the client computer generate a set of keys. That computer will send artifacts (components) of the public key to the Oracle database so that Oracle can build a copy of the public key. Then the Oracle database can encrypt data using the public key that only the originating client can decrypt.

This approach may sound like a complete solution, but there are a couple concerns that we will not address until we get to the next chapter's discussion on secret password encryption. First, anyone can read the public key artifacts as they traverse the network (that is, anyone with software to read all packets going across the network, like a sniffer.) That means that we have to assume that everyone has the public key and that everyone sees and can decrypt data (if any) that the client encrypts with the private key and sends to the server.

The second concern is that PKE, at least the version we are using, does not lend itself to encrypting large amounts data. It is a block cipher with a limited block size. For example, if the block size for our PKE keys is limited to 128 bytes, we would have to break the data into portions of that size and encrypt each portion individually. On the other side of this transaction, the recipient would have to decrypt each portion and reassemble the original data.

To handle larger amounts of data, there are a couple of methods: cipher block chaining (CBC) and stream encryption. With CBC, large data is broken up into appropriate block sizes for encryption and then decrypted and reassembled automatically for the user. (Whew, that takes a lot of burden off our shoulders.) With stream encryption, each bit, byte, or block of bytes would be encrypted/decrypted as it passed through the stream. A stream is simply a channel for data en route. You put bytes of data into a stream, and take bytes of data out in the same order: first in first out (fifo). A stream can exist when reading/writing data to storage, or across the network, or simply from one place (structure) in memory to another.

RSA Public Key Cryptography

We will be using RSA public key cryptography for our PKE encryption algorithm. RSA stands for the last names of the creators of the algorithm: Rivest, Shamir, and Adleman.

Because RSA uses a different key for encryption (e.g., private) from what is required for decryption (e.g., public), it is called an asymmetric algorithm. All PKE is asymmetric encryption. With a long key length, RSA is a very trustworthy encryption algorithm.

Java Code to Generate and Use RSA Keys

All our code for accomplishing Oracle database and Java security will reside in a single Java class (there are some small exceptions; we will have some separate Java classes for testing our processes). As we walk through the remaining chapters of this book, we are going to develop security code in phases, adding layers and concepts as we progress. Our single Java class will grow over time.

Our class will be called `OracleJavaSecure`, and we will define it in a package called `orajavsec`. Because we do not have a single version of this file, we are going to have multiple directories (one per chapter) where different versions of this Java code reside. This will make compiling and running a bit more difficult, but I will provide instructions as needed to reference these files.

■ **Note** You can find the following code in the file *Chapter5/orajavsec/OracleJavaSecure.java*. I recommend that you open that file and refer to it as we proceed through this chapter.

Creating a Set of Keys

Listing 5-1 shows the code that is used for creating a set of PKE keys. This code, along with other Java code in this chapter, comes from the `OracleJavaSecure` class.

Listing 5-1. Create PKE Keys, makeLocRSAKeys()

```
private static SecureRandom random;
private static int keyLengthRSA = 1024;
private static Key locRSAPrivKey;
private static RSAPublicKey locRSAPubKey;
private static void makeLocRSAKeys() throws Exception {
    random = new SecureRandom();
    KeyPairGenerator generator = KeyPairGenerator.getInstance( "RSA" );
```

```
    generator.initialize( keyLengthRSA, random );
    KeyPair pair = generator.generateKeyPair();
    locRSAPrivKey = pair.getPrivate();
    locRSAPubKey = ( RSAPublicKey )pair.getPublic();
}
```

We use the JCE class named `KeyPairGenerator` to generate our private and public keys. First, we instantiate a `KeyPairGenerator` named `generator`. We specify that `generator` will create keys conforming to the RSA algorithm. (Notice we call the static method `KeyPairGenerator.getInstance()` and ask it to get an instance of itself.) We initialize `generator` with both the key length (1024 bits) and with an instance of the `SecureRandom` class named `random`. `SecureRandom` is a trustworthy random number generator. We will use `random` to even greater purposes in the next chapter.

Note Someday, a 1024 bit RSA key may be insufficient, but at this time, it is still considered relatively unbreakable.

`KeyPairGenerator` generates a single object: a `KeyPair` that we call `pair`. We get our separate public and private keys (`locRSAPubKey` and `locRSAPrivKey`) by calling methods in `KeyPair`. Notice also that we cast the public key that we get from `KeyPair` as an `RSAPublicKey` type in this statement:

`locRSAPubKey = ( RSAPublicKey )pair.getPublic();`

Casting can add functionality to an object as long as the object you cast to implements (is a superset of) the object in hand. In this case `RSAPublicKey` is a superset of the `PublicKey` class. When `RSAPublicKey` was defined, the definition looked like this:

`public class RSAPublicKey implements PublicKey …`

We cast the `PublicKey` to an `RSAPublicKey` so that we can use some methods that only exist for the `RSAPublicKey` class. We will see those in the next section.

When we run Listing 5-1, we end up with the keys. The `locRSAPrivKey` is our private key. We will not share our private key with anyone. We will do our encryption and decryption using the private key—so an entity with our public key can then decrypt data from us and encrypt data to us. The `locRSAPubKey` is the public key of our key pair. We intend to give that key to all requestors.

Hand the Public Key Across the Network

We intend to give `locRSAPubKey` to all requestors (actually we just hand it directly to the Oracle database); however, we don't know (for arguments' sake) which platform they will be running on, so we can't just give them our Java cryptographic extensions (JCE) version of the key. Instead, we will give them two artifacts, which together can be used to build our public key on whatever system.

We can only build another key of the same type with our two artifacts. Our artifacts are `locRSAPubMod` and `locRSAPubExp`. These are the RSA public key modulus and exponent, two numbers that we can use to calculate the public key. Listing 5-2 shows how we generate those artifacts.

Listing 5-2. Generating Public Key Artifacts

```
    private static BigInteger locRSAPubMod = null;
```

```
private static BigInteger locRSAPubExp;
…
locRSAPubMod = locRSAPubKey.getModulus();
locRSAPubExp = locRSAPubKey.getPublicExponent();
```

The methods getModulus() and getPublicExponent() are available in the RSAPublicKey class, but not in the PublicKey class. We cast the PublicKey as an RSAPublicKey in order to use these methods (see previous section). In essence, we ask the RSA public key to give us the value of its modulus and exponent.

These numeric values are too large to handle without wrapping them in Java objects. We get them as BigInteger objects. They can be very large numbers (especially the modulus) that don't fit well into standard primitive types like integers or longs, and for that reason, we often handle and transmit these numbers as if they were Strings.

You might have noticed that we declared locRSAPubMod to be null. You will recall our reasons for this from the section called "Declaring and Initializing Members" in Chapter 4. In this case, we plan to test whether locRSAPubMod is null to see if we need to generate the keys or if they already exist.

Serialize Objects

We are not limited to transmitting only simple type values to and from Oracle database. In Oracle, we can define new types that hold arrays or data structures, and we can transmit objects in RAW format (an ordered sequence of bytes). If we want to transmit very large objects, we can transmit and store them as binary large objects (BLOBs) in Oracle.

There is one requirement for transmitting a Java object across the network, and for storing a Java object, for that matter; that is, the Java object must implement the Serializable interface. Normally, an interface is a set of members and methods that must be implemented (set in code) by any class that implements the interface. (We will create our own interface in Chapter 10.) However, with the Serializable interface, there are no members or methods to be implemented; rather, implementing the interface just indicates that you intend to package an instance of your class for transmission or storage. You can send an object that is Serializable across an ObjectStream or write it to a File with an ObjectWriter class.

Some objects cannot be serialized (cannot implement Serializable). If something about the state of an object exists by association rather than as a value, then the object cannot be serialized. For example, if our object has an Oracle Connection member, then the connection cannot be serialized (you can't save a connection for use later), and our object cannot be serialized.

Building the Public Key from Artifacts

On the other side of the encryption/decryption process, we want to get the necessary artifacts (components) of the public key, and we want to rebuild the key. We are going to look at how we transmit the components from the client to the server in just a minute, but for this discussion and for testing, we can simply get them locally and build the key (we will use the same code on the server side). Listing 5-3 shows the code to build the public key from components of the key.

Listing 5-3. Building Public Key from Artifacts, `makeExtRSAPubKey()`

```
private static RSAPublicKey extRSAPubKey = null;
private static void makeExtRSAPubKey( BigInteger extRSAPubModulus,
    BigInteger extRSAPubExponent ) throws Exception
{
    RSAPublicKeySpec keySpec =
        new RSAPublicKeySpec( extRSAPubModulus, extRSAPubExponent );
    KeyFactory kFactory = KeyFactory.getInstance( "RSA" );
    extRSAPubKey = ( RSAPublicKey )kFactory.generatePublic( keySpec );
}
```

We hand both the RSA Modulus and the RSA Exponent to this method, `makeExtRSAPubKey()`. Then we instantiate a new instance of the `RSAPublicKeySpec` named `keySpec`, which is a specification object for a key. We also get an instance of a `KeyFactory` named `kFactory`, based on the RSA algorithm. We pass the `keySpec` to the `kFactory` to generate the public RSA key. This key is equivalent to the public key that was originally generated, so we can use it to decode data that is encoded with the original private key.

What does all this mean? How will we use this so-called equivalent key? We generate the key pair on the client. Then we pass the public key modulus and exponent to Oracle database. We assemble an identical public key on the Oracle database. At that point, our plan is to encrypt data with the public key on Oracle and transmit the encrypted data to the client. The client alone will be able to decrypt the data using the private key.

Generating the RSA Cipher

A cryptographic key is really nothing more than a mathematical construct; it does not inherently have the functionality we need to put it to use. Instead, we need to have a `Cipher` class that can use the key to do our work. We generate the `Cipher`, `cipherRSA` with the code shown in Listing 5-4.

Listing 5-4. Generate RSA Cipher, `makeCryptUtilities()`

```
private static Cipher cipherRSA;
private static void makeCryptUtilities() throws Exception {
    cipherRSA = Cipher.getInstance( "RSA" );
}
```

Our `makeCryptUtilities()` method will be called from the client when we call `makeLocRSAKeys()`, and from the Oracle database when we call `makeExtRSAPubKey()`.

The `Cipher` class can generate a cipher of various types. We are specifically creating a new instance of `Cipher` that uses the RSA algorithm.

Note that we don't say new `Cipher()`, but we call the static `Cipher.getInstance()` method to get a specific instance of itself. If you review the code we've seen so far in this chapter, you will see that quite frequently we are not instantiating an object in our code with the new statement; rather, we are getting new instances from some provider method, some factory or some other provider. It is important to understand that somewhere in that process, some method or other got a new instance to deliver to us.

Using the RSA Cipher

We will use `cipherRSA` to do encryption and decryption. To use it, we will have to provide it with the key and tell it what mode to use (encryption or decryption), then we will ask it to perform that task on some data. The `cipherRSA` method calls in Listing 5-5 will be used for that process.

Listing 5-5. Initialize the Cipher to Do Encryption

```
cipherRSA.init( Cipher.ENCRYPT_MODE, extRSAPubKey, random );
byte[] encodedBytes = cipherRSA.doFinal( clearBytes );
```

The first method called here is used for initializing the `Cipher` to a specific mode: encrypt or decrypt. In this case, we have asked it to be ready to encrypt data (`Cipher.ENCRYPT_MODE`). To decrypt, we would initialize the `Cipher` to `Cipher.DECRYPT_MODE`.

The second method of `cipherRSA` that we call is `doFinal()`. This method does the encryption or decryption that we initialized on the data we provide in the parameter (e.g., encrypt `clearBytes`). Note that the `doFinal()` method of `Cipher` takes a byte array as its parameter and returns a byte array. For that reason, we will be converting `Strings` and other objects to and from byte arrays as we perform encryption. Note also that a byte is simply eight bits and a bit is just one memory position being turned Off or On (value of 0 or 1). A byte array is simply a series of bytes assembled in and handled as a single list. If some of these concepts are unfamiliar, you can explore computer architecture at `www.wikipedia.org`.

JAVA CONSTANTS

Notice how we specify `ENCRYPT_MODE` in the `Cipher` initialization call in Listing 5-5. This is a member variable (notice it is not a method call—no parentheses or parameters.) Notice also that it must be static; we do not refer to a specific instance of `Cipher` to get `ENCRYPT_MODE`, but to the static class definition. Lastly, notice that the member name is in all uppercase. The uppercasing of this member variable and underscore characters between words indicates, by Java naming conventions, that this is a constant. In `Cipher`, it would have been declared like this:

```
public static final int ENCRYPT_MODE = <some int>;
```

The modifier `final` helps identify this member as a constant, but `final` may not mean what you might think at first. It does not mean that the value cannot change, but that the address pointed to in memory cannot be changed to a new address. For primitive and simple types, like the `int ENCRYPT_MODE`, this amounts to the same thing. That includes `Strings`, because they are immutable (refer to Chapter 3).

However, if you had a constant `Date` member, defined like the following

```
public static final Date BERLIN_WALL_FELL = new Date( 89, 10, 9 );
```

you could not prevent someone from coming along later and setting:

```
BERLIN_WALL_FELL.setYear( 80 );
```

Even though this `Date` is declared `static final`. Wouldn't it be nice to improve history!

This method for defining a Date with three integers representing year, month, and day is *deprecated*, which means it is still available but no longer approved for use in code. Potentially, deprecated features will be removed in future versions of the JDK. I use it here only for illustration purposes. Perhaps the reason that this Date constructor is deprecated is the inconsistency in specifying the integers. This constructor adds 1900 to the year specification and adds 1 to the month. The month specification is 0-based (0-11), but the day is 1-based (1-31).

Note that the BERLIN_WALL_FELL Date member still points at the same instance of Date (we did not instantiate a new Date), but we changed the value. In fact, that member variable meets all the requirements for a Java constant, but it turned out to be changeable (rather than constant)! So, my advice is to choose some other, simpler, primitive or immutable type to be a constant, like this String:

```
public static final String BERLIN_WALL_FELL = "November 9, 1989";
```

If you must use a mutable class instance as a constant, then I suggest you make it private and have a getter method that is public. Do not provide a setter method. In addition, recall that when you provide an object through a getter method, you are passing the reference to the original object, not sending a copy of the original object to the caller. If you just return your private member, and it is mutable, then the caller can change it. To avoid this problem, create a new instance of your constant class type by cloning the object, and return the clone (actually return a reference to the clone).

Here is how that all might look:

```
private static final Date BERLIN_WALL_FELL = new Date( 89, 10, 9 );
public static final Date getBERLIN_WALL_FELL() {

     return (Date)BERLIN_WALL_FELL.clone();

}
```

Because our constant is private, no one can modify it, unless we expose it. We allow people to get its value through the getter method, getBERLIN_WALL_FELL(). However, we don't return a reference to our constant, but rather we return a reference to a clone of our constant. We can do that because Date implements the Cloneable interface. Note that the clone() method returns an Object, which we have to cast as a Date to return.

The one who calls this getter could always change his personal reference to this Date or the value of the Date; but even so, each one who calls the original getBERLIN_WALL_FELL() method will get a Date with the correct value.

While we're on the subject of the final modifier, we should observe that the getBERLIN_WALL_FELL() method is declared final in the last section. This has a couple of effects. The first idea that we need to be prepared to adhere to is that anything we call final should never change. The primary reason is that *any* code that refers to something we've called final *will* need to be recompiled if we ever modify our code. We should consider these final methods to be constant methods. (Perhaps we should agree to indicate this fact by giving our methods all upper case names with underscore characters between words. There is no convention for that, yet.) The exceptions to this idea of recompiling all referencing code are difficult to identify, so this idea is like a rule you should follow.

final methods, like final members, can be automatically compiled inline, which means the code or value is included in the referrer byte code when compiled. This has some performance benefit, but that is usually outweighed by the requirement to recompile if the final code ever changes.

The second effect of declaring our methods to be final is that they cannot be overridden by some other class that implements our class. This is our primary reason for declaring methods in OracleJavaSecure.java to be final. We are protecting our logic from being modified or spoofed. We must abide the rule that our final methods may never change, or that the final methods are all private so that we are the only one that refers to them. Continue with this thought in the following section.

Getting RSA Public Key Artifacts

You may have noticed in Listings 5-1 through 5-4 that all our keys and components thereof are declared not only **static**, but also **private**. We do not give direct access to any of those. If you were very astute, you might have also noticed that our methods so far were declared **private**: that is makeLocRSAKeys(), makeCryptUtilities() and makeExtRSAPubKey() are all **private**. We never expect our client applications, nor our Java-stored procedures in Oracle to call these methods directly. We will define some **public** methods that will call these **private** methods as needed.

The first two **public** methods that we will meet now are for getting the public RSA key artifacts. We will ask client applications to call these methods shown in Listing 5-6.

Listing 5-6. Methods to Get Public Key Artifacts, getLocRSAPubMod() and getLocRSAPubExp()

```
private static BigInteger locRSAPubMod = null;
private static BigInteger locRSAPubExp;
public static final String getLocRSAPubMod() {
    String rtrnString = "getLocRSAPubMod() failed";
    try {
        if ( null == locRSAPubMod ) makeLocRSAKeys();
        rtrnString = locRSAPubMod.toString();
    } catch ( Exception x ) {
        x.printStackTrace();
    }
    return rtrnString;
}
public static final String getLocRSAPubExp() {
    String rtrnString = "getLocRSAPubExp() failed";
    try {
        if ( null == locRSAPubMod ) makeLocRSAKeys();
        rtrnString = locRSAPubExp.toString();
    } catch ( Exception x ) {}
    return rtrnString;
}
```

I'd like to point out several things in these **public** methods. First of all, notice that we test whether locRSAPubMod is null. Recall that when we first declared locRSAPubMod (at top of this code) we set it to null. (If we had declared it with this statement **private static BigInteger locRSAPubMod**, it would have also been null, but because we put it into an if test, we would get a "might not have been initialized" error when we try to compile.) If in the if test, locRSAPubMod is no longer null, then we must have already created the RSA key pair. However, if it is still null, then we call the **private** method makeLocRSAKeys().

Also, note the test syntax, if(null == locRSAPubMod) which is identical to if(locRSAPubMod == null). There is a benefit in using the first syntax. A common error, using one equals sign instead of two, will not be caught by the compiler in the second syntax. But in the first syntax, this would be flagged as an error if(null = locRSAPubMod).

Each of these members, locRSAPubMod and locRSAPubExp are BigInteger classes – a type that doesn't exist in Oracle. I mentioned earlier that we often handle and transmit these large numbers as Strings, and that is the case here. We call the BigInteger.toString() method. When we get to the Oracle JVM, we will recreate BigIntegers based on these Strings.

We are returning a String, rtrnString and if there is a problem (an Exception or other problem getting locRSAPubMod or locRSAPubExp), then we can return an error message in our regular return value. You can see that we define the error message at the top of each method as rtrnString, in one case "getLocRSAPubMod() failed". Then if we are successful, we overwrite rtrnString with the requested key artifact. But in the case that there's a problem, we send back that original message. In a client/server application, we need to send meaningful error messages when there's a problem.

Because we are running on the client at this point, we can easily include a statement to dump the stack trace from the exception, as we do in the catch block of the first method, above. That is generally the first method called in our class, so it is a good place to catch an Exception, if there are going to be any. Note that in the code I'm providing, the troubleshooting and debugging has been accomplished and much of the error reporting has been removed.

Using Static Methods and Private Constructor

Recall that we have a new Oracle JVM for each Oracle session that needs Java. As long as we maintain that session, our JVM is retained. Also recall that Java stored procedures can only call static methods, because no instance is available to call from the stored procedure. We could always instantiate the OracleJavaSecure class and then use non-static methods of our instance; however, it will be much simpler, if we can get away with it, and we can, to make everything static that we do and touch inside our class. You can see that approach in the code examples we've seen so far.

Note that any members declared inside a method are not and cannot be declared as static. The static modifier can only be applied to items outside our methods, at the class level (i.e., class members).On the flip side, any class members referred to within a static method *must* be static. That is because in a static method, you can only refer to members in the class that also exist with or without an instance of the class (i.e., static members).

One way to assure that our class is ever and always static is to guarantee that it is never instantiated. We can guarantee that by making the default and only constructor for the class to be private. We have accomplished that with the code in Listing 5-7.

Listing 5-7. Private Constructor

```
private OracleJavaSecure() {
}
```

Instantiating a Connection Member from a Static Initializer

In our code, we will need to have an Oracle Connection member. When we run on the client, we will pass a Connection to a setter method to store the Connection for use in our class, but when running in the Oracle Database, we don't have a good method to use to instantiate the Connection. We could instantiate the Connection in every public static method where it might be used, but a better approach is to have a *static initializer*. That approach looks like what we have in Listing 5-8.

Listing 5-8. Static Initializer for Connection

```
private static Connection conn;
static {
    try {
        conn = new OracleDriver().defaultConnection();
    } catch ( Exception x ) {}
}
```

The `static` modifier in front of an independent block of code is a static initializer—this is not a method. Notice that we have to prepare to catch any exceptions that might be generated by instantiating the `Connection`. We do not have to do anything with the possible exceptions (if there is an `Exception`, then our problems are more systemic than our code), but we have to establish the `try` /`catch` blocks to make the code valid for compiling.

As a `static` block, it executes one time and exists in the class, outside of and without an instance of the class.

Using One Code for Both Client and Server

For me, one of the most enjoyable aspects of coding in Java and Java stored procedures is the ability to write code that operates on both sides of the client/server communication. This is especially helpful when it comes to testing our code—we can, in many cases, test it all on our workstation prior to deploying it to the Oracle database.

Some aspects of our code will only be executed on the client; for example the method to generate the RSA key pair. Likewise, some portions of our code will normally only be executed on the Oracle database, for example rebuilding our RSA public key from the artifacts. However for testing, we can execute the methods destined for Oracle on our workstation.

■ **Note** Please refer to Appendix A for a list of all the methods of `OracleJavaSecure` and the indication of their primary usage(client or Oracle Database or both).

In other instances, we will have to provide specific logic to permit our code to run in both environments. One case in point is the `Connection` member. In the last section, I mentioned the static initializer that will instantiate a `Connection` for use on the Oracle database. That code also runs on the client, but has no effect—there is no local, default Oracle database for the code to connect to. So we provide an additional method called `setConnection()` that will take a `Connection` from some client application code and set the `static Connection` member to that `Connection`, as shown in Listing 5-9.

Listing 5-9. Setter Method for Client Connection, `setConnection()`

```
public static final void setConnection( Connection c ) {
    conn = c;
}
```

We will have some additional examples of specific logic to run on either the client or the server, which I will point out as we go along.

In my member naming scheme, I could have chosen about any names with the same effect, but I chose to name the keys and artifacts that I generate locally with a loc prefix, like locRSAPrivkey. Artifacts passed to me and keys generated from those artifacts I prefix with an ext prefix (for "external"), like extRSAPubKey. This will help us keep things straight, especially as we execute both the client and the server side code on our workstation.

Testing on the Client

Our code in OracleJavaSecure is intended to be run as a client-server application to encrypt data on one end (e.g., server) and decrypt it at the other (e.g., client). However, it is nice to be able to test our code without introducing some of the complexities of client-server communication. So we will test all of our code so far on the client only. On the client we will generate the keys, encrypt data with the private key, build an equivalent public key from the public key artifacts, and decrypt data with the equivalent public key.

Writing the main() Method

In my experience, the best place to put test code is right in the class whose functions you are testing. Obviously you have to run your code in order to test it, and if you can run it from the command prompt, then you needn't build or depend on another class to do your testing. Whenever we are talking about executing from the command prompt, we are talking about using the main() method. The client-only testing portion of the OracleJavaSecure.main() method is shown in Listing 5-10.

Listing 5-10. Method for Testing on the Client Only, OracleJavaSecure.main(), Part A

```
public static void main( String[] args ) {
    try {
        // As a client application
        String clientPubModulus = getLocRSAPubMod();
        String clientPubExponent = getLocRSAPubExp();
        // Send modulus and exponent to Oracle Database, then
        // As if I were the Oracle Database
        makeExtRSAPubKey( clientPubModulus, clientPubExponent );
        cipherRSA.init( Cipher.ENCRYPT_MODE, extRSAPubKey, random );
        Date clientDate = new Date();
        String sampleData = clientDate.toString();
        byte[] clearBytes = sampleData.getBytes();
        byte[] cryptBytes = cipherRSA.doFinal( clearBytes );
        // Send the cryptBytes back to the client application, then
        // As a client application
        cipherRSA.init( Cipher.DECRYPT_MODE, locRSAPrivKey );
        byte[] newClearBytes = cipherRSA.doFinal( cryptBytes );
        String newSampleData = new String( newClearBytes );
        System.out.println( "Client date: " + newSampleData );
    } catch ( Exception x ) {
        x.printStackTrace();
    }
    System.exit( 0 );
}
```

In the `main()` method, we have two method `String` members, `clientPubModulus` and `clientPubExponent`. We set those members by calling our two public methods, `getLocRSAPubMod()` and `getLocRSAPubExp()`. We are acting as the client application, calling those methods. We continue to act as the client application, but only imagine sending those values to the Oracle Database (at this point, we are just going to use those values locally.)

Now, pretending that we are the Oracle Database, we use those values we just "received," and we call the `makeExtRSAPubKey()` method in order to generate a replica of the public key. (Although, on the server that method is `private` and will not be called directly.) Then the server uses (we use) that public key to encrypt some clear sample data. The sample data, `sampleData` we are using is the date and time that we get by instantiating a new `Date` class.

We initialize `cipherRSA` using `extRSAPubKey`, the public key copy that we built, and we set it to `ENCRYPT_MODE`. Then we call the `doFinal()` method, encrypting the `clearBytes` **into** `cryptBytes`. Note again that the `cipherRSA.doFinal()` method takes a byte array as its parameter and returns a byte array, so we convert the `sampleData String` to a byte array using `String.getBytes()`, in order to submit the `clearBytes` to `cipherRSA.doFinal()`. We end up with `cryptBytes`, a byte array of encrypted data.

Then back at the client, we "receive" the `cryptBytes` encrypted byte array. (The process of calling the Oracle Database to return encrypted data is a bit more complex than this first test, and we will see the details in the second half of this chapter.) Acting as the client, then, we initialize our own `cipherRSA` using the `locRSAPrivKey` private key, to `DECRYPT_MODE`. Then we call the `doFinal()` method. This should return the original clear byte array, from which we create a new `String` instance named `newSampleData`, and which we print. If all has gone well, what we will see is the `newSampleData`, the client date and time as the output.

Notice at the end of Listing 5-10 that there is a call to `System.exit(0)`. That call actually terminates the running JVM. It is important to include that call at the end of most `main()` methods, because if your application is running other threads of code, the JVM may not terminate when you get to the end of `main()`, even though you are done with it. Be aware that you do not normally call `System.exit(0)` in `main()` for GUI applications where your `main()` method displays the GUI interface and then ends. The `main()` ends, but the GUI exists until some control in the GUI (like an **Exit** button) issues a similar `System.exit(0)` call. By the way, the `0` (zero) means exit with an OK status code. Any other number is considered an error code which can be sensed by the operating system, as needed.

Also take note of the `catch` block and our call to `Exception.printStackTrace()`. With that call, any exception caught in the `main()` method will print out a list of each consecutive method call and the line number from which each consecutive call is made. The line number in `main()` where the exception occurred will be at the bottom of the list and the method it called and line number where the exception occurred will be listed above that, and so on. At the top of the list will be the specific exception that occurred and the method and line number where it happened. That list is called a stack trace.

Running the Code

If you have set your `PATH` and `CLASSPATH` as described in Chapter 3, then your job is easier. First run a command prompt (**Start Menu ↗ Programs ↗ Accessories ↗ Command Prompt**). Then change directories to *Chapter5*. Compile the code with this command:

```
javac orajavsec/OracleJavaSecure.java
```

Then run the code from that same directory with this command:

```
java orajavsec.OracleJavaSecure
```

If you have not set your `PATH` and `CLASSPATH`, then you need to locate your compiler (*javac.exe*). And you need to go to the same directory as mentioned previously. For example, if *javac.exe* is in

C:\java\jdk1.6\bin and *ojdb6.jar* is in *C:\java*, you would execute the following commands (from a command prompt in the *Chapter5* directory):

```
C:\java\jdk1.6\bin\javac.exe -cp .;C:\java\ojdbc6.jar orajavsec/OracleJavaSecure.java
C:\java\jdk1.6\bin\java.exe -cp .;C:\java\ojdbc6.jar orajavsec.OracleJavaSecure
```

As a result, you will see the client date displayed:

```
Client date: Sat Dec 04 11:29:39 EST 2010
```

This date `string` was generated, encrypted with the public key and decrypted with the private key all on the client.

Key Exchange

So far, we have created our RSA private and public keys and demonstrated building a copy of the public key with two components: the exponent and the modulus. We have also demonstrated encrypting a `Date` string with our copy of the public key and decrypting it with the private key. These are all the aspects of our RSA key pair that we are going to utilize; however, we will be building the copy of the private key on the Oracle database, doing our encryption there and decrypting the data with the private key on the client. To do that, we are going to need some Oracle structures.

We will define a function and a procedure in our Application Security, `appsec` schema. To do this, connect to Oracle as the `appsec` user and set your role to the privileged `appsec_role`:

```
CONNECT appsec;
SET ROLE appsec_role;
```

▥ **Note** You can find a script of the following commands in the file named *Chapter5/AppSec.sql*.

Creating a Function to Encrypt Data with Public Key

The Oracle script in Listing 5-11 defines a function that calls the `OracleJavaSecure.getRSACryptData()` method. This will encrypt data using the copy of the RSA public key that we will build on the Oracle Database. Execute the command in Listing 5-11 while connected to Oracle Database as the Application Security user, `appsec`.

Listing 5-11. Oracle Function to RSA Encrypt Data

```
CREATE OR REPLACE FUNCTION f_get_rsa_crypt(
    ext_rsa_mod VARCHAR2, ext_rsa_exp VARCHAR2, cleartext VARCHAR2 )
    RETURN RAW
    AS LANGUAGE JAVA
    NAME 'orajavsec.OracleJavaSecure.getRSACryptData( java.lang.String, java.lang.String,
java.lang.String ) return oracle.sql.RAW';
/
```

There are three `VARCHAR2` (`String`) parameters that we are going to pass to the function: the public key modulus, the public key exponent, and the clear-text string that we want to encrypt.

Note that the NAME keyword must point to a single line of text. Here we have word wrap, but the definition of the Java method must all appear on a single line. Additionally, both the input and output parameters must be fully qualified—they must have the entire path prepended to the Class name. That includes classes that are naturally part of the Java language like java.lang.String.

Recall that Oracle functions can take parameters, do work and return a single value. In this case, we are going to encrypt a string and return it as a RAW data type. RAW is an immutable byte array that can be transferred between Oracle Database and Java without any interpretation or translation (casting). RAW data retains *fidelity* between Oracle and Java, server and client. The limit of a RAW data element is either 32767 bytes in PL/SQL code (our case) or 2000 bytes when stored in the database.

Creating a Procedure to get SYSDATE in Encrypted Form

We will add a procedure that does not call Java, so it is not a Java stored procedure, but it calls our Java stored function, f_get_rsa_crypt. Execute the command in Listing 5-12 as the appsec user.

Listing 5-12. Oracle Procedure to Encrypt Date and Time String, p_get_rsa_crypt_sysdate

```
CREATE OR REPLACE PROCEDURE p_get_rsa_crypt_sysdate(
    ext_rsa_mod    IN VARCHAR2,
    ext_rsa_exp    IN VARCHAR2,
    crypt_sysdate OUT RAW,
    m_err_no      OUT NUMBER,
    m_err_txt     OUT VARCHAR2 )
IS BEGIN
    m_err_no := 0;
    crypt_sysdate := f_get_rsa_crypt( ext_rsa_mod, ext_rsa_exp,
        TO_CHAR( CURRENT_TIMESTAMP, 'DY MON DD HH24:MI:SS TZD YYYY' ) );
EXCEPTION
    WHEN OTHERS THEN
        m_err_no := SQLCODE;
        m_err_txt := SQLERRM;
END p_get_rsa_crypt_sysdate;
/
```

This is fairly simple procedure. It gets the CURRENT_TIMESTAMP from the Oracle Database, converts it to a string using the TO_CHAR SQL function, uses f_get_rsa_crypt (that we defined previously) to encrypt it, and then returns it to the caller.

So why have I complicated it with what appears to be error handling? Well now is as good a time as any to introduce a template for procedures of this type. We don't want to burden the Oracle database with the task of dealing with most of the errors our procedures may generate, and we also want to be able to deal with the errors back at our application. We need Oracle database to tell us what the error is, and we need to be able to deal with it in a logical fashion.

For this reason, we have declared several of our parameters as OUT parameters. The first OUT parameter is a RAW that contains our encrypted timestamp string. The second OUT parameter is the error number that is generated by Oracle Database – every Oracle error type has a distinct error number that is indexed in the Oracle documentation. And the third OUT parameter is the error message.

In our template, when an exception occurs, we don't throw it back to the calling application; rather, we allow the procedure to complete in an orderly way and return the error number (SQLCODE) and message (SQLERRM) to the caller in the OUT parameters. Back in the calling code, before we handle any other of the returned data, we will check to see if the error number is anything besides 0, and if it is, we report it to the user or handle it in the application. If there is an error, it is usually not beneficial to continue processing the data. There will be examples of this template in action later in our code.

A WORD ABOUT TIME ZONES

You'll notice that Listing 5-12 gets the current time of the Oracle Database with this call:

```
TO_CHAR( CURRENT_TIMESTAMP, 'DY MON DD HH24:MI:SS TZD YYYY' )
```

The goal is to match the time format with what Java on the local client gives us, just for presentation's sake. The time right now (for me), from Java is:

```
Sat Dec 04 11:29:39 EST 2010
```

Notice the format string includes the element "TZD" which presents the time zone. My time zone is EST (eastern standard time). We use CURRENT_TIMESTAMP instead of SYSDATE in order to get the time zone. Oracle timestamp data must be directed to retain time zone if you want that. Generally, Oracle database assumes the time zone of the client for data generated during a session; however, often the time zone provided by the session is some number of hours offset from Greenwich mean time (GMT). Living in the southeast United States with daylight saving time means that our time zone is usually minus 5 hours from GMT.

Note that to get completely identical results, you would have to uppercase the date String returned by Java. When we compare the results to what is returned by Oracle database, we'll see that Oracle gives names of the days of the week and names of the months in all uppercase. Looking ahead, we will see these date and time representations:

```
Client date: Sat Dec 04 14:59:49 EST 2010
Server date: SAT DEC 04 14:59:50 EST 2010
```

You'll be interested to know (or just consider) that many cities, states, countries and continents share this offset (minus 5 GMT). Therefore, knowing the offset doesn't guarantee that Oracle database can report the time zone in TZD format; although, the offset can be reported.

With some Oracle clients, like TOAD, the client does not inform the server what time zone name to use. The server knows the offset, but not the name. Observe the output from these commands to observe the phenomenon.

```
SELECT TO_CHAR( CURRENT_TIMESTAMP, 'DY MON DD HH24:MI:SS TZD YYYY' ) FROM DUAL;
SELECT * FROM sys.gv_$timezone_names
    WHERE tzname LIKE 'America%' --AND tzabbrev = 'EST'
;
ALTER SESSION SET TIME_ZONE = 'America/New_York';

SELECT TO_CHAR( CURRENT_TIMESTAMP, 'DY MON DD HH24:MI:SS TZD YYYY' ) FROM DUAL;
```

After altering our session to specify our time zone name, Oracle database can correctly report EST or whatever is your current time zone. Here's what I see as the results:

```
SAT DEC 04 11:57:49  2010
```

```
SAT DEC 04 11:58:31 EST 2010
```

On the other hand, the Java client automatically informs Oracle database of its time zone name, so we do not need to manually set it. There is more complexity to time zones that I am not covering here, especially as it relates to daylight saving time.

Loading OracleJavaSecure Java into Oracle Database

Now that we have our Oracle function and procedure defined, we are ready to put our Java logic (code) into the Oracle Database. There are a couple ways to do this. The first would be to use the *loadjava* utility that comes with the Oracle client and server software. We have made that a bit difficult for ourselves since the role that is needed to accomplish that command as the application security, appsec user is not a default role. Instead of using *loadjava*, let's just connect to Oracle Database (or remain connected) as appsec.

The next line is at the top of our Java code in the *OracleJavaSecure.java* file. Uncomment it and copy the entire code into your Oracle client.

```
CREATE OR REPLACE AND RESOLVE JAVA SOURCE NAMED appsec."orajavsec/OracleJavaSecure" AS
...
```

For security, scroll down to the class body and *assure you do not have a valid password* in the connection string. If you do, remove the password from the connection string before executing this command in Oracle Database. You do not want to store any passwords in the code on Oracle – they are not needed there, and having them there makes them available to hackers.

```
private static String appsecConnString =
    "jdbc:oracle:thin:AppSec/password@localhost:1521:Orcl";
```

Execute the script in your Oracle client (e.g., SQL*Plus) to load the Java code into the Oracle Database, which compiles it.

Encrypting Data with Public Key

We saw in our definition of the Oracle function f_get_rsa_crypt, previously, that we intended to call a method named getRSACryptData(). We have just loaded that Java method into Oracle Database in the last section. The code for getRSACryptData() is shown in Listing 5-13. We will have the Oracle Database encrypt data with the public key – later we will decrypt it at the client with the private key.

Listing 5-13. Encrypt Data with Public Key, getRSACryptData()

```
public static final RAW getRSACryptData( String extRSAPubMod,
    String extRSAPubExp, String clearText )
{
    RAW rtrnRaw =
        new RAW( "getRSACryptData() failed".getBytes() );
    try {
        if ( ( null == extRSAPubKey ) ||
            ( !saveExtRSAPubMod.equals( extRSAPubMod ) ) )
            makeExtRSAPubKey( extRSAPubMod, extRSAPubExp );
        cipherRSA.init( Cipher.ENCRYPT_MODE, extRSAPubKey, random );
        rtrnRaw = new RAW( cipherRSA.doFinal( clearText.getBytes() ) );
    } catch ( Exception x ) {}
```

```
        return rtrnRaw;
    }
```

During development, I had occasions to catch exceptions in `getRSACryptData()` and similar methods, but in the debugged code, I'm depending on another mechanism to report errors. You can see that the `catch` block has a close brace } immediately after the open brace {. That is a way of ignoring the exception. This method will successfully return a valid `RAW` value whether an exception is thrown or not. If there is a problem completing the encryption (the last line within the `try` block), then our original "error" message is returned in the `RAW`. That original message informs the client that the method failed. We translate the message into a `RAW` by getting the bytes of the `String` from `getBytes()` and sending them to the `RAW` constructor. If there is no problem when executing the code, then our member `rtrnRaw` is set to the encrypted value, and that is returned; else the error message is returned in `RAW` form.

The first test we do in `getRSACryptData()` is to see whether we have already built a copy of the RSA public key. We pass this method the public artifacts each time we call it, but only want to go through building the key one time. So, we test if `extRSAPubKey` is `null`. We also test to see if the value of the modulus artifact has changed (that should never be the case). If either of these is true, we build our copy of the RSA public key by calling `makeExtRSAPubKey()`.

We initialize the `cipherRSA` to do encryption, `Cipher.ENCRYPT_MODE`. Then we encrypt our clear text by calling the `doFinal()` method.

After this chapter, we will not be calling `getRSACryptData()` directly from our client code, so we will be changing this from a `public` to a `private` method. Eventually, the only thing we will be encrypting with our RSA public key is a secret passphrase. We will be exploring that in the next chapter.

Use Stacked Calls

Let me point out the syntax in one line of code from Listing 5-13:

```
rtrnRaw = new RAW( cipherRSA.doFinal( clearText.getBytes() ) );
```

We call the `getBytes()` method of the `clearText` `String`, then instead of pointing a byte array member at it, we pass the bytes directly to the `cipherRSA.doFinal()` method to encrypt (it takes a byte array and returns a byte array). Then instead of pointing a local byte array member at the encrypted bytes, we pass the array to a new `RAW` instance constructor.

I call this syntax stacked calls, and I like it. I prefer densely packed code over spacious code. It's just my opinion that it reads and prints easier. The key to reading stacked calls is to look at the innermost pair of parentheses first, and read from the inside out. This is more difficult to read from left to right than from right to left.

Decrypting Data with Private Key

The next method that we need for the demonstrations in this chapter is a method to decrypt the data on the client with our RSA private key. Listing 5-14 defines that method.

Listing 5-14. Decrypingt Data with Private Key, getRSADecryptData()

```
public static final String getRSADecryptData( RAW cryptData ) {
    String rtrnString = "getRSADecryptData failed";
    try {
        cipherRSA.init( Cipher.DECRYPT_MODE, locRSAPrivKey );
        rtrnString = new String( cipherRSA.doFinal( cryptData.getBytes() ) );
    } catch ( Exception x ) {
```

```
        x.printStackTrace();
    }
    return rtrnString;
}
```

This method takes a `RAW` parameter named `cryptData`. The code gets the byte array from `cryptData` and passes it to the `cipherRSA.doFinal()` method to decrypt. We instantiate a new `String` from the decrypted byte array, and return that `String` to the caller.

You will recognize the similarities in error handling between this and the `getRSACryptData()` method described above. One additional measure we are taking here is to print out the stack trace of any `Exception` that's thrown.

This method is not needed in future chapters, because we will not be encrypting just any old data with our RSA public key; rather, with the RSA keys we will only be encrypting / decrypting specific artifacts of our secret password key that we create in the next chapter. So we will repackage this decryption call specifically for that purpose.

Testing on Client and Server

Earlier in this chapter, you compiled *OracleJavaSecure.java* on your workstation. Let's make a couple changes to the code now. First of all, if you saved the version that we installed on the Oracle Database, then you may have uncommented the first line. If so, comment it again:

```
//CREATE OR REPLACE AND RESOLVE JAVA SOURCE NAMED appsec."orajavsec/OracleJavaSecure" AS
```

Down a little ways from the top of the file, in the body of the class code, set the `boolean` named `testingOnServer` to `true`. That change will cause the second half of the `main()` method to execute.

```
private static boolean testingOnServer = true;
private static String appsecConnString =
    "jdbc:oracle:thin:AppSec/password@localhost:1521:Orcl";
```

Additionally, we want to connect from this client code to the Oracle Database, so edit the next line down with the correct host, port, instance and password needed to connect as `appsec` user. Be sure to save your changes.

Inside the `main()` method, after the code we discussed previously, we have another section for testing client/server public key encryption. We check the `testingOnServer` boolean that we set previously, and if `true` we continue our testing. The first thing we want to do is establish our Oracle `Connection`, `conn` based on the `appsecConnString` we edited above. See Listing 5-15.

Listing 5-15. Testing PKE on Client and Server

```
if( testingOnServer ) {
    // Since not on the Server, must load Oracle-specific Driver
    Class.forName( "oracle.jdbc.driver.OracleDriver" );
    // This will set the static member "conn" to a new Connection
    conn = DriverManager.getConnection( appsecConnString );
```

Using IN and OUT Parameters in an OracleCallableStatement

Also in the `main()` method, you will see our code to prepare an `OracleCallableStatement`. We are using a `Statement` class of that type so that we can read the `OUT` parameters. Notice as we prepare the call, in Listing 5-16, that we list the procedure name and have a list of question marks for the parameters we are going to pass. We also register parameters 3, 4, and 5 as OUT parameters that we will be able to read later. If we fail to register the parameters that way, we may be surprised when we go to read them later—they won't be available.

Listing 5-16. An OracleCallableStatement for Client/Server Encryption

```
OracleCallableStatement stmt =
    ( OracleCallableStatement )conn.prepareCall(
    "CALL p_get_rsa_crypt_sysdate(?,?,?,?,?)" );
stmt.registerOutParameter( 3, OracleTypes.RAW );
stmt.registerOutParameter( 4, OracleTypes.NUMBER );
stmt.registerOutParameter( 5, OracleTypes.VARCHAR );
stmt.setString( 1, clientPubModulus );
stmt.setString( 2, clientPubExponent );
stmt.setNull(  3, OracleTypes.RAW );
stmt.setInt(   4, 0 );
stmt.setNull(  5, OracleTypes.VARCHAR );
stmt.executeUpdate();
```

After preparing the Statement, we set the input parameters. The only parameters we have to pass to the procedure are our RSA public key modulus and exponent. We call stmt.setString() for each of those parameters.

Notice, however, that we set the remainder of the parameters to null using the stmt.setNull() method, or to 0 in the case of the int. There are two things to mention about setting these to null: first, it may not be necessary because we don't read or test the values of those parameters in the Oracle procedure, but we do it to satisfy our desire to *address all potential concerns.* Consider it to be just one more part of the secure programming approach—cover all your bases. Second, these are the same parameters that we are expecting to read from—OUT parameters. We want to assure that unless the Oracle procedure puts a value in those parameters, there will be nothing there to read.

Oracle procedures can define their parameters as one of three types: IN (the default), OUT, and INOUT. On occasion you will want to use a single INOUT parameter to both submit data to an Oracle procedure and to read the results coming back. I find it can be more concise to use INOUT parameters, but it can also be a bit confusing in the procedure code—deciding what value is currently being handled. So, for a more security conscientious approach, we will avoid INOUT parameters.

Both when we register OUT parameters and when we set those parameters to null, we have to declare the data type of the parameter. We refer to the types in the OracleTypes class, as in OracleTypes.RAW and OracleTypes.NUMBER. We find OracleTypes in the *oracle.jdbc* package (from *ojdbc6.jar*) and import it from there. Earlier we mentioned this one inconsistency in the use of VARCHAR instead of VARCHAR2. It is in the OracleTypes class, as you can see in Listing 5-16.

The last line of this section of code executes the Statement. That is, it calls the Oracle stored procedure, passing the IN parameters, and retrieving the OUT parameters.

Handle Errors Reported by Oracle Database

We will build our Oracle procedures to send the error number and error message back in two of the OUT parameters. This will be our standard approach for handling errors in processing—it places the responsibility for dealing with errors into the hands of the application developer. This code from the main() method, Listing 5-17, follows the execution of the Statement. First we read the errNo parameter. If it is not equal to zero, some problem has occurred, and we print out the error message; otherwise, we will continue.

Listing 5-17. Handling Errors from a Stored Procedure

```
int errNo = stmt.getInt( 4 );
if( errNo != 0 ) {
    String errMsg = stmt.getString( 5 );
    System.out.println( "Oracle error " + errNo + ", " + errMsg );
    System.out.println( (stmt.getRAW( 3 )).toString() );
}
```

Notice how we also print out the data that is returning to us in the RAW parameter, number 3. Normally that would hold the encrypted data (SYSDATE) from the p_get_rsa_crypt_sysdate procedure; but when there's an error, it will hold the name of the Java method, running in the Oracle JVM, where the error occurred. This information is difficult to gather unless you go to these efforts, or log the errors in the Oracle JVM and read through the logs. We will do both.

Decrypting at the Client

Normally, when there is no error, we read our non-error-related OUT parameter, number 3, the RAW element that is our encrypted data. Here we read it and assign the value to the cryptData RAW. Then we call the getRSADecryptData() method to decrypt it. And finally, we print out the data, which is the server timestamp. These actions are shown in Listing 5-18.

Listing 5-18. Decrypting the Data from the Stored Procedure

```
else {
    RAW cryptData = stmt.getRAW( 3 );
    newSampleData = getRSADecryptData( cryptData );
    System.out.println( "Server date: " + newSampleData );
}
```

Running Our Code Again

If you have any troubles completing this, refer to the previous section in this chapter, "Running Our Code." You will have to have loaded the Java code on the Oracle Database as described in the section "Load OracleJavaSecure Java into Oracle Database."

You will change directories to *Chapter5* and compile the code with the following command. As a reminder, you will need to have *ojdbc.jar* in your CLASSPATH.

```
javac orajavsec/OracleJavaSecure.java
```

Then run the code from that same directory with this command:

```
java orajavsec.OracleJavaSecure
```

Observing the Results

With the edits you made in the second half of this chapter to *OracleJavaSecure.java*, the main() method will continue to run the client/server tests. The first line shown below is printed from the encryption/decryption methods running on the client only; and the second line comes from the client/server encryption/decryption process:

```
Client date: Sat Dec 04 14:59:49 EST 2010
```

```
Server date: SAT DEC 04 14:59:50 EST 2010
```

Both of these sets of test used our rebuilt copy of the RSA public key to encrypt the date `String`, and used the RSA private key to decrypt the date `String`. In the second set of tests, the public key was rebuilt on the Oracle Database and the date `String` was encrypted there. Then the encrypted `RAW` data was returned to the client, where it was decrypted and printed. Ta da! You have accomplished client-server encrypted data transmission! This process is depicted in Figure 5-1.

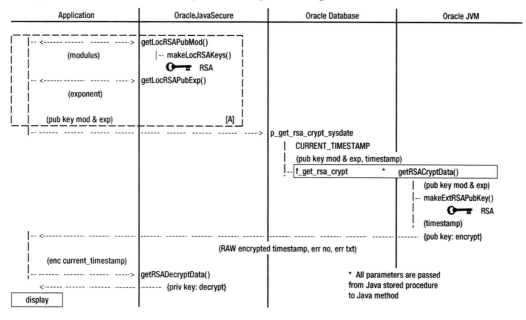

Figure 5-1. *Client/server public key encryption*

There is a section of Figure 5-1 that is outlined and labeled as **[A]**. That section is a depiction of the generation of the RSA key pair. Within that outline is an image of a key which represents the RSA key pair as it exists on the client.

The client application makes one call to the Oracle Database, to the procedure named `p_get_rsa_crypt_sysdate`. In that call, the RSA public key modulus and exponent are sent to the database. On the database, a java stored procedure, `f_get_rsa_crypt` is called, which in turn calls Java in the Oracle JVM, to a method named `getRSACryptData()`. That is the starting point for building an equivalent RSA public key, depicted by the key image on the right side of Figure 5-1.

The Oracle JVM uses the equivalent public key to encrypt the `CURRENT_TIMESTAMP` value from the Oracle database, and then returns that encrypted value to the client application. From there, the client will decrypt the value using the RSA private key. The private key only exists in this client, so only this client can decrypt the data being returned by the Oracle database.

Removing the Demonstration Oracle Structures

We are not going to need the Oracle function or procedure that we built in this chapter. They were just for our use in demonstrating our client/server RSA public key encryption. We will be building some more-enduring functions and procedures in the next chapter. But because we are done here, let's clean up after ourselves and remove these structures with the following commands as `appsec` user:

```
DROP PROCEDURE p_get_rsa_crypt_sysdate;
DROP FUNCTION f_get_rsa_crypt;
```

Chapter Review

Perhaps this was a lot of ground to cover in a few short pages, but there wasn't a lot of code required. I think you'll agree that if this is all that's required to do Public Key Encryption, we should all be doing it!

Here is a list of PKE-related steps we took:

- Created the public and private key set.

- Got the modulus and exponent of the public key.

- Re-created the public key from the modulus and exponent.

- Generated an appropriate `Cipher.`

- Initialized the `Cipher` to do encryption or decryption using either the public or private key.

- Called the `Cipher.doFinal()` method to do both encryption and decryption.

In addition to the PKE aspects, we learned about the `Serializable` interface and about how we can serialize objects to pass them around and store them.

We also established a standard form for calling Oracle procedures from an `OracleCallableStatement` that will allow us to exchange data and provide good error reporting back to the client, in a controlled fashion to be handled by the application programmer.

We discussed `final` methods, Java constants, `static` methods, `private` constructors, and `static` initializers, with an aside on time zones.

All of this took place within our introductions to the `OracleJavaSecure` class that we will be building and extending during the course of this book.

CHAPTER 6

Secret Password Encryption

What I am calling secret password encryption (password encryption) is also known as shared secret passphrase encryption and password-based encryption (PBE). Basically, the idea is that a single passphrase (or password—I will be using those words interchangeably) is known by two parties, and they each encrypt messages or data to pass to each other using that password. The same password is used by the recipient to decrypt the messages and data. No one else can decrypt the data because the password is a secret, shared only by the two parties.

Password encryption is beneficial to us for several reasons, chief of which is that it can be used for encryption of larger blocks of data. We will be using the U.S. data encryption standard (DES) with cipher block chaining (CBC) to automatically break any size data into appropriate blocks for encryption; then upon decryption, assemble the results back into the original data.

Another benefit of password encryption is that there is no public key—that is, no one else knows the key we are using to encrypt the data, assuming we have adequately protected the password. An alternative approach is to have public key encryption from both client and the server, each encrypting the data with the other's public key, only to be read by the recipient. And for added assurance, have each encrypt their messages first with their own private key, then with the other's public key. Think that through and you'll see that not only can only the recipient decrypt the message, but also only the expected sender could send it. (Add a trusted Certificate Authority (CA) like VeriSign and you have identity assurance as well—everyone is who they say they are.) However, we are going to get most of those benefits with only our secret password encryption.

We are going to create a passphrase on the Oracle server and pass it back to the client in secret. We will make it secret by encrypting the passphrase with the client's RSA public key. To do this, the client will have already passed the public key artifacts (modulus and exponent) to the Oracle server. Only the client can decrypt the secret passphrase using the private key.

One last benefit of using password encryption in addition to RSA public key encryption is that any assailant will have to attack both protocols to intercept our data.

Approach

As you read through this chapter, you will want to open the referenced files to follow along in the full code listing. First we are going to discuss the Java code that we implement for secret password encryption, because it is in Java that we will be building the encryption key and doing the encryption. However, we will not compile and run the Java code until the end of the chapter. Then we will run it in two phases: the first will be doing both encryption and decryption in Java on the client computer; the second phase will accomplish secret password encryption key exchange between the client computer and Oracle database and will demonstrate client/server encryption/decryption.

Before we get to the testing phases at the end of the chapter, we will also discuss the Oracle SQL code required for this process. Feel free to execute the SQL code to create the structures we need on

Oracle database as we discuss it, or you can execute all the SQL code at the end before we do the phase two tests.

Java Code for Secret Password Encryption

We are returning to add code to and edit the `OracleJavaSecure` class that we introduced in the last chapter. This class will form the core of all our security processes on both the client and the Oracle database. You will benefit by opening *OracleJavaSecure.java* and referring to the full code listing as we progress through this section. We will replace the `OracleJavaSecure` class in the Oracle database and compile and run the updated code on our client computer when we get to the end of the chapter and do some testing.

Sharing the Artifacts of a Secret Password Key

There are several artifacts of DES password-based encryption that must be shared between the client and server in order to have an identical encryption key and `Cipher` at each end. First, there is a passphrase, which is known only to the two parties involved in the encrypted dialog.

There are two other artifacts that must be shared, but are often treated as constants in a specific context. Those are the salt and the iteration count. Fixing those two parameters as constants is a major weakness. Vendors will often obfuscate (make hidden) their code in order to hide those values. Any hacker who can steal the salt and iteration count has a leg up on decrypting your data.

Our plan is to generate all three artifacts to be different for each session. We will use the `SecureRandom` instance to generate a random iteration count and a random salt. We will also generate a maximum-length passphrase from random acceptable characters.

Generating the Password and Artifacts

While we're on the subject, let's go ahead and see how we generate these artifacts. We do it in the `makeSessionSecretDESPassPhrase()` method, the code for which is shown in Listing 6-1.

Listing 6-1. Generating DES Password Artifacts makeSessionSecretDESPassPhrase()

```
private static SecureRandom random = new SecureRandom();

private static final int SALT_LENGTH = 8;
private static int maxPassPhraseBytes;
private static char[] sessionSecretDESPassPhraseChars = null;
private static byte[] salt;
private static int iterationCount;
private static void makeSessionSecretDESPassPhrase() {
    // Pass Phrase, Buffer size is limited by RSACipher class (on Oracle JVM)
    // Max size of data to encrypt is equal to the key bytes minus padding
    // (key.bitlength/8)-PAD_PKCS1_LENGTH (11 Bytes)
    maxPassPhraseBytes = ( keyLengthRSA/8 ) - 11;
    sessionSecretDESPassPhraseChars = new char[maxPassPhraseBytes];
    for( int i = 0; i < maxPassPhraseBytes; i++ ) {
        // I want printable ASCII characters for PassPhrase
        sessionSecretDESPassPhraseChars[i] =
                ( char )( random.nextInt( 126 - 32 ) + 32 );
```

```
    }
    // Appreciate the power of random
    iterationCount = random.nextInt( 10 ) + 15;
    salt = new byte[SALT_LENGTH];
    for( int i = 0; i < SALT_LENGTH; i++ ) {
        salt[i] = ( byte )random.nextInt( 256 );
    }
}
```

■ **Note** You can find this code in the file *Chapter6/orajavsec/OracleJavaSecure.java*.

Calculating the Size of the Password

The first thing you'll notice in Listing 6-1 is a definition of the maximum size of the passphrase. It is calculated based on the size of the RSA key.

```
maxPassPhraseBytes = ( keyLengthRSA/8 ) - 11;
```

The reason we base our password length on the size of the RSA key is that we are going to encrypt our passphrase with the public key, and RSA can only encrypt a byte array smaller than its own key, minus the padding.

We could have made maxPassPhraseBytes a constant, but we might have been tempted to try something larger (okay, I tried it) had we not known the derivation. Also, we may at some point increase the RSA key size, which will automatically translate into a larger passphrase length.

Respecting the Power of Random

In our method, shown in Listing 6-1, we instantiate a byte array the size of maxPassPhraseBytes and populate it with random characters in the **for** loop. Notice the parameters for the random character. We want our passphrase to be made up of printable characters in the ASCII range of 32 to 126.

We will set the iteration count to be a random number between 15 and 25.

And we will populate the salt byte array with random bytes between 0 and 256. Our salt byte array size is fixed at eight bytes. We declare SALT_LENGTH as a constant (static final).

All of these artifacts of our password-based encryption will be generated for each Oracle session and passed back to the client. They will be encrypted using the RSA public key prior to transmission. The client will decrypt them using the private key. Then with those artifacts in hand, the client will create an identical secret password key to use in sending and receiving encrypted data.

Initializing Static Class Members

We are going to move the initialization of two static class members from their previous location in a method out into the class body. See Listing 6-2. Instead of two separate calls to the makeCryptUtilities() method (one on the client and a different one on the server), we unify the process of creating these components. We will instantiate the **SecureRandom** at the point of definition, and we will instantiate the **cipherRSA** in a static initializer block (catching Exceptions, as required).

Listing 6-2. Static Class Members

```java
private static SecureRandom random = new SecureRandom();
private static Cipher cipherRSA;
static {
    try {
        cipherRSA = Cipher.getInstance( "RSA" );
    } catch( Exception x ) {}
}

private static Cipher cipherDES;
private static SecretKey sessionSecretDESKey = null;
private static AlgorithmParameterSpec paramSpec;

private static String sessionSecretDESAlgorithm = "PBEWithSHA1AndDESede";
```

In addition to the artifacts of the DES password-based encryption key described in the previous section, we will declare the key itself and the DES `Cipher` we will be using. We will also build and use an `AlgorithmParameterSpec` member for the DES key.

Evaluating the Java 1.5 Password-Based Encryption Bug

We get to select what algorithm we intend to use for our secret password encryption. U.S. (DES) is good, but Triple DES (3DES or DESede) is stronger, and AES even more so; and SHA1 is a better cryptographic hash than MD5. So we would like to use the password-based encryption algorithm fully indicated by `PBEWithSHA1AndDESede`, and we specify it as shown in Listing 6-2.

But wait, there is a problem. In the Java Runtime Edition version 1.5, there is a bug. It is reported at this link: `http://bugs.sun.com/bugdatabase/view_bug.do?bug_id=6332761`.

The Oracle JVM is based on JRE 1.5, so it manifests that bug. When we generate our secret key specifying our preferred algorithm, the key generator will return a weaker key of type `PBEWithMD5AndDES` instead.

Coding an Automatic Upgrade: Negotiated Algorithm

It is the job of programmers to debug issues like the bug described in the previous section when we run across them, and to build bridges over the obstacles. We will have a method that shows us the algorithm in actual use; that will display the bug. Additionally, we will not assume that what we specify is what we get—we will return the actual algorithm to the client and build the copy of the secret password key using the actual algorithm.

The benefits of this approach are that we will negotiate a common algorithm and continue to specify a stronger encryption algorithm. Continuing to specify the stronger algorithm will predispose our code to use the stronger algorithm whenever it becomes available in the Oracle JVM.

So we will specify `PBEWithSHA1AndDESede`, but at this time we will be using `PBEWithMD5AndDES`. When Oracle next upgrades the Oracle JVM, we are prepared to use the stronger algorithm. Both of these algorithms use CBC as their mode, so they will work equally well for what we are doing.

Generating the Password Key

Now that we have all the artifacts of our secret password key, let's build the key. In Listing 6-3, we have a method to create the key, `makeSessionSecretDESKey()`. The first step in this method checks to see if the key has already been generated (is the passphrase char array null), and if it has not been generated, we call the method we described previously, `makeSessionSecretDESPassPhrase()` to build the artifacts.

Listing 6-3. Generating the Password Key, `makeSessionSecretDESKey()`

```
private static void makeSessionSecretDESKey() throws Exception {
    // DES Pass Phrase is generated on server and passed to client
    if( null == sessionSecretDESPassPhraseChars )
        makeSessionSecretDESPassPhrase();
    paramSpec = new PBEParameterSpec( salt, iterationCount );
    KeySpec keySpec = new PBEKeySpec( sessionSecretDESPassPhraseChars, salt,
            iterationCount );
    // Try with recommended algorithm
    sessionSecretDESKey = SecretKeyFactory.getInstance(
        sessionSecretDESAlgorithm ).generateSecret( keySpec );
    // See what algorithm used
    sessionSecretDESAlgorithm = sessionSecretDESKey.getAlgorithm();
    cipherDES = Cipher.getInstance( sessionSecretDESKey.getAlgorithm() );
}
```

Using our secret passphrase key artifacts, we first instantiate `paramSpec`, which is a `static` class member. We use that `paramSpec` member in multiple methods, so we create it as a static class member. It will be available in future Java stored procedure calls to static methods, from the same Oracle session.

We also instantiate a `KeySpec` class, which is local to the method and is only used here. The `keySpec` member is used by the `SecretKeyFactory` to generate a key of the algorithm type described in the `sessionSecretDESAlgorithm` member. This algorithm type is subject to the bug, so we will actually get a key of the algorithm type supported by the Oracle JVM version. After that, we get the actual algorithm by calling `sessionSecretDESKey.getAlgorithm()`. We also get an instance of our DES `Cipher` based on that algorithm.

Remember that we have passed our RSA public key from the client to Oracle. Now, on Oracle database we are building our secret password key, artifacts of which we will encrypt with the client public key and pass back to the client. We will also pass back the actual algorithm to the client, so we establish a common algorithm on the client.

Encrypting with the Public RSA Key

We have seen this code before, in the last chapter. We encrypt clear data (on Oracle) using our server-built copy of the RSA public key. However, previously this was a public method that we were calling directly to demonstrate RSA public key encryption. Now we are using it as a utility method to encrypt artifacts of our secret password key to send to the client, so we've made it private. Look at the code in Listing 6-4.

Listing 6-4. Encrypting with the RSA Public Key, `getRSACryptData()`

```
private static final RAW getRSACryptData( String extRSAPubMod,
    String extRSAPubExp, String clearText ) throws Exception
{
    byte[] clearBytes = clearText.getBytes();
    return getRSACryptData( extRSAPubMod, extRSAPubExp, clearBytes );
}
```

```
private static final RAW getRSACryptData( String extRSAPubMod,
    String extRSAPubExp, byte[] clearBytes ) throws Exception
{
    if( ( null == extRSAPubKey ) ||
        ( !saveExtRSAPubMod.equals( extRSAPubMod ) ) )
        makeExtRSAPubKey( extRSAPubMod, extRSAPubExp );
    cipherRSA.init( Cipher.ENCRYPT_MODE, extRSAPubKey, random );
    return new RAW( cipherRSA.doFinal( clearBytes ) );
}
```

Notice also that we have two methods now by the same name: getRSACryptData(). They are different, however, by taking different arguments: one takes its clear text in String form; the other, in byte array form. These methods are said to have different signatures. We call this method overloading when we have multiple methods with the same name but different signatures.

The first method takes the clear text String and creates a byte array. Then to keep from repeating any code, the first method simply calls the second method and returns what the second method returns: the RAW encrypted text. We will be calling each of these methods multiple times to encrypt all the artifacts of our secret password key.

Returning Secret Password Key Artifacts to the Client

You will see so much similarity between the following four methods, that we will only describe each aspect once. These four methods return the passphrase, algorithm, salt, and iteration count, which when combined can be used to generate the DES secret password key.

These methods will be called from Java stored procedures, so they are public and static. Notice that these methods take the RSA public key artifacts as parameters, which they will use to encrypt the secret password key artifacts. The methods return the key artifacts as RAW data types, so we maintain fidelity of the data between Oracle database and the client. Let's look at the first of the bunch in Listing 6-5. It returns the passphrase.

Listing 6-5. Encrypt the Passphrase, getCryptSessionSecretDESPassPhrase()

```
public static final RAW getCryptSessionSecretDESPassPhrase(
    String extRSAPubMod, String extRSAPubExp )
{
    RAW rtrnRAW =
        new RAW( "getCryptSessionSecretDESPassPhrase() failed".getBytes() );
    try {
        if( null == sessionSecretDESKey ) makeSessionSecretDESKey();
        byte[] sessionSecretDESPassPhraseBytes =
            charArrayToByteArray( sessionSecretDESPassPhraseChars );
        rtrnRAW = getRSACryptData( extRSAPubMod, extRSAPubExp,
            sessionSecretDESPassPhraseBytes );
    } catch( Exception x ) {

        java.io.CharArrayWriter errorText =
            new java.io.CharArrayWriter( 32767 );
        x.printStackTrace( new java.io.PrintWriter( errorText ) );
        rtrnRAW = new RAW( errorText.toString().getBytes() );

    }
    return rtrnRAW;
```

}

We've discussed a lot of the Exception handling already. This method is generally called first of the current foursome, and includes a bit more error reporting. Because we are returning a RAW, we can return up to 32,767 bytes of data. In the catch block, we instantiate a CharArrayWriter of size 32,767 characters in an array in memory. Then by stacked calls, we instantiate a PrintWriter, which points at the CharArrayWriter. Then we print the Exception *s*tack trace to that PrintWriter. As a result, we get the stack trace in a char array writer, errorText. We call errorText.toString().getBytes() to get a byte array of the stack trace, and then we instantiate a RAW from that, which we can pass back to the client.

At the client, if we have trouble deciphering the passphrase that we are seeking from the RAW that has been returned, we can read the RAW as a String and see the Exception stack trace. This is a handy troubleshooting practice in a client/server environment when you'd like to see the error that the server sees, not just the error at the client.

Listing 6-6 shows the second of this bunch of methods. This one returns the name of the actual algorithm that's in use on the Oracle database. In the try block, you'll see a feature common to all these methods. We test to see if the sessionSecretDESKey is null, and if it is, we call makeSessionSecretDESKey() (described earlier) to create the secret password key.

Listing 6-6. Encrypt the Algorithm Name, getCryptSessionSecretDESAlgorithm ()

```
public static final RAW getCryptSessionSecretDESAlgorithm(
    String extRSAPubMod, String extRSAPubExp )
{
    RAW rtrnRAW =
        new RAW( "getCryptSessionSecretDESAlgorithm() failed".getBytes() );
    try {
        if( null == sessionSecretDESKey ) makeSessionSecretDESKey();
        rtrnRAW = getRSACryptData( extRSAPubMod, extRSAPubExp,
            sessionSecretDESAlgorithm );
    } catch( Exception x ) {}
    return rtrnRAW;
}
```

The last common call in the try block is a call to the getRSACryptData() method described previously) to encrypt the secret password key artifact; in this case, the algorithm name. That generates a RAW data type containing the encrypted artifact, which will be returned to the client.

Please take note of what is returned if an exception is called. We still return rtrnRAW, but its value is the bytes of the string "getCryptSessionSecretDESAlgorithm() failed". Having this reported back to the client can be helpful for troubleshooting. Also, note how we get the bytes of that String—we treat the value between quotation marks as if it were already *a* String object, calling the getBytes() method. Is that allowed? Yes!

The last two methods in this group, shown in Listings 6-7 and 6-8, return the salt and iteration count as encrypted RAW data types.

Listing 6-7. Encrypt the Salt, getCryptSessionSecretDESSalt ()

```
public static final RAW getCryptSessionSecretDESSalt( String extRSAPubMod,
    String extRSAPubExp )
{
    RAW rtrnRAW = new RAW( "getCryptSessionSecretDESSalt() failed".getBytes() );
    try {
        if( null == sessionSecretDESKey ) makeSessionSecretDESKey();
```

```
        rtrnRAW = getRSACryptData( extRSAPubMod, extRSAPubExp, salt );
    } catch( Exception x ) {}
    return rtrnRAW;
}
```

Listing 6-8. Encrypt the Itteration Count, getCryptSessionSecretDESIterationCount ()

```
public static final RAW getCryptSessionSecretDESIterationCount(
    String extRSAPubMod, String extRSAPubExp )
{
    RAW rtrnRAW =
        new RAW( "getCryptSessionSecretDESIterationCount() failed".getBytes() );
    try {
        if( null == sessionSecretDESKey ) makeSessionSecretDESKey();

        byte[] sessionSecretDESIterationCountBytes =
            { ( byte )iterationCount };

        rtrnRAW = getRSACryptData( extRSAPubMod, extRSAPubExp,
            sessionSecretDESIterationCountBytes );
    } catch( Exception x ) {}
    return rtrnRAW;
}
```

This last method for returning the encrypted iteration count creates a byte array of one **byte**. The only **byte** in the array is the iteration count **int**, cast as a **byte**. In that way, we can call the same method to encrypt the iteration count as a byte array. We will have to reverse that process when we decrypt it at the client.

Encrypting Data with Our Secret Password

We will call the same method on both the client and Oracle database to encrypt data using the secret password key. The syntax, in Listing 6-9, should be familiar by now. This method takes a **String** of clear text data and returns a **RAW** of encrypted data. Notice that initializing the **Cipher** using the **sessionSecretDESKey** is very similar to how we do it with the RSA keys, except that we also provide the **paramSpec**.

Listing 6-9. Encrypt Data with Secret Password, getCryptData()

```
public static final RAW getCryptData( String clearData ) {
    if( null == clearData ) return null;
    RAW rtrnRAW = new RAW( "getCryptData() failed".getBytes() );
    try {
        if( null == sessionSecretDESKey ) makeSessionSecretDESKey();
        cipherDES.init( Cipher.ENCRYPT_MODE, sessionSecretDESKey, paramSpec );
        rtrnRAW = new RAW( cipherDES.doFinal( clearData.getBytes() ) );
    } catch( Exception x ) {}
    return rtrnRAW;
}
```

Like the methods we described earlier for encrypting and returning our secret password key artifacts, this method tests whether the **sessionSecretDESKey** has been instantiated, and attempts to create it if not. This is good practice on the Oracle database, but is presumptuous on the client (where we do not want to originate the secret password key.) It is mandatory that developers understand that the client MUST get the secret password key from the Oracle database first, and only then may use it to encrypt data for insert or update to Oracle. No harm will come if developers fail to follow that guideline, but their code will not work.

Oracle Structures for Secret Password Encryption

In the last chapter, we created an Oracle function and a procedure to demonstrate use of our RSA public key encryption in a client/server environment. Now we will create an Oracle package with multiple functions and procedures, including Java stored procedures, to handle our secret password encryption.

The package will be placed in the Application Security, appsec schema. As the appsec user, first set your role to the non-default role, appsec_role with this command:

```
SET ROLE appsec_role;
```

■ **Note** You can find a script of the following commands in the file named *Chapter6/AppSec.sql*.

As you read through this section, you can follow along in the referenced code file, and see in context the code that's discussed in this text. Also, you can execute the code to create the Oracle structures as you read about them. We will use these structures when we run tests at the end of the chapter.

Package to Get Secret Password Artifacts and Encrypted Data

A package in Oracle database is a set of functions and procedures that can be configured as a group. Permissions to access the functions and procedures in a package are granted by granting executable permission on the package. We will learn one additional benefit of Oracle packages when we get to Chapter 7: we can define new data types and use them in Oracle packages.

An Oracle package has two parts, the specification and the body. The specification provides the signature for each procedure or function, but the actual code is only included in the body. This two-part identity for packages allows PL/SQL programmers to share the functionality (the specification) without sharing the code (the body). You might do this for separation of duty, security through obfuscation, or simply to protect your intellectual property. C programmers will recognize this approach as being analogous to having a header file for each code file.

Application Security Package Specification

An Oracle package specification merely defines the functions and procedures, listing the expected parameters and the return type for functions. Listing 6-10 shows the app_sec_pkg package specification. Execute this as appsec user.

Listing 6-10. Package Specification for Secret Password Encryption

```
CREATE OR REPLACE PACKAGE appsec.app_sec_pkg IS

    -- For Chapter 6 testing only - move to app in later versions of this package
```

```
     PROCEDURE p_get_shared_passphrase(
          ext_modulus              VARCHAR2,
          ext_exponent             VARCHAR2,
          secret_pass_salt      OUT RAW,
          secret_pass_count     OUT RAW,
          secret_pass_algorithm OUT RAW,
          secret_pass           OUT RAW,
          m_err_no              OUT NUMBER,
          m_err_txt             OUT VARCHAR2 );

     -- For Chapter 6 testing only - remove in later versions of this package
     PROCEDURE p_get_des_crypt_test_data(
          ext_modulus              VARCHAR2,
          ext_exponent             VARCHAR2,
          secret_pass_salt      OUT RAW,
          secret_pass_count     OUT RAW,
          secret_pass_algorithm OUT RAW,
          secret_pass           OUT RAW,
          m_err_no              OUT NUMBER,
          m_err_txt             OUT VARCHAR2,
          test_data                VARCHAR2,
          crypt_data            OUT RAW );

     FUNCTION f_get_crypt_secret_pass( ext_modulus VARCHAR2,
          ext_exponent VARCHAR2 ) RETURN RAW;

     FUNCTION f_get_crypt_secret_algorithm( ext_modulus VARCHAR2,
          ext_exponent VARCHAR2 ) RETURN RAW;

     FUNCTION f_get_crypt_secret_salt( ext_modulus VARCHAR2,
          ext_exponent VARCHAR2 ) RETURN RAW;

     FUNCTION f_get_crypt_secret_count( ext_modulus VARCHAR2,
          ext_exponent VARCHAR2 ) RETURN RAW;

     FUNCTION f_get_crypt_data( clear_text VARCHAR2 ) RETURN RAW;

     FUNCTION f_get_decrypt_data( crypt_data RAW ) RETURN VARCHAR2;

     -- For Chapter 6 testing only - remove in later versions of this package
     FUNCTION f_show_algorithm RETURN VARCHAR2;

END app_sec_pkg;
/
```

See the list of functions in the second half of the package specification. We have one function to return the encrypted RAW data for each of the secret password key artifacts: f_get_crypt_secret_pass, f_get_crypt_secret_ algorithm, f_get_crypt_secret_ salt, and f_get_crypt_secret_ count. We also have functions to encrypt clear text and return an encrypted RAW, f_get_crypt_data, and to decrypt a RAW and return clear text, f_get_decrypt_data (we have not seen the Java side of that process yet).

Above our functions, we specify two procedures: p_get_shared_passphrase and p_get_des_crypt_test_data. Each of these procedures takes the client RSA public key modulus and exponent as input parameters, and returns the secret password key artifacts as OUT parameters. We are handling errors as we described in the previous chapter with OUT parameters for the error number and error text. Additionally, the p_get_des_crypt_test_data procedure takes a clear text input parameter and returns an encrypted RAW as an additional OUT parameter.

Both of these procedures are for testing in this chapter only and will be moved or removed from the package in future chapters. The last function, f_show_algorithm, is also for testing only in this chapter and will be removed later.

Application Security Package Body: Functions

The function and procedure definitions in our package specification must be duplicated exactly in our package body. The body contains not just the definitions, but also the code of the procedures and functions. You can execute this package body at this time; the package will be created in the Oracle database.

Here is one example function from the body listing for our consideration, in Listing 6-11. We pass our RSA public key modulus and exponent to the function f_get_crypt_secret_pass. It passes them along to the Java method named getCryptSessionSecretDESPassPhrase() (discussed above). That Java method returns a RAW, the secret password key passphrase, encrypted with the RSA public key. And the function returns the RAW value that the Java method returned to it.

Listing 6-11. Function to Return the Secret Passphrase

```
FUNCTION f_get_crypt_secret_pass( ext_modulus VARCHAR2,
                ext_exponent VARCHAR2 )

RETURN RAW

AS LANGUAGE JAVA
NAME 'orajavsec.OracleJavaSecure.getCryptSessionSecretDESPassPhrase( java.lang.String,
java.lang.String ) return oracle.sql.RAW';
```

This same approach is taken to get each artifact of the secret password key, and to get encrypted and decrypted data. We also have a function that takes no input parameters and returns the algorithm string as an OUT parameter. That function, f_show_algorithm, is just for testing in this chapter.

Application Security Package Body: Procedures

The procedures in the package body are the locus of our primary efforts. These procedures are shown in Listings 6-12 and 6-13. Note that both of these procedures are for testing only in this chapter and will be removed and replaced in future chapters. The first procedure we will look at is p_get_shared_passphrase, which returns the artifacts of a secret password key to the client. If the key does not yet exist, it will be created when we call f_get_crypt_secret_salt. Remember that our encryption keys are specific to an Oracle session, so we need to keep the session open in order to use the secret password key for encryption.

Listing 6-12. Procedure to get the Shared Password Key, p_get_shared_passphrase

```
PROCEDURE p_get_shared_passphrase(
    ext_modulus             VARCHAR2,
    ext_exponent            VARCHAR2,
    secret_pass_salt        OUT RAW,
```

```
            secret_pass_count      OUT RAW,
            secret_pass_algorithm OUT RAW,
            secret_pass            OUT RAW,
            m_err_no               OUT NUMBER,
            m_err_txt              OUT VARCHAR2 )
    IS BEGIN
        m_err_no := 0;
        secret_pass_salt := f_get_crypt_secret_salt( ext_modulus, ext_exponent );
        secret_pass_count := f_get_crypt_secret_count( ext_modulus, ext_exponent );
        secret_pass := f_get_crypt_secret_pass( ext_modulus, ext_exponent );
        secret_pass_algorithm :=
            f_get_crypt_secret_algorithm( ext_modulus, ext_exponent );
    EXCEPTION
        WHEN OTHERS THEN
            m_err_no := SQLCODE;
            m_err_txt := SQLERRM;
    END p_get_shared_passphrase;
```

Observe the list of IN and OUT parameters in the Oracle procedure, p_get_shared_passphrase, in Listing 6-12. We provide the RSA public key modulus and exponent, then get out the artifacts of the secret password key, and the error number and text. Each of the artifacts is acquired by a call to one of the Oracle functions, like this:

```
secret_pass := f_get_crypt_secret_pass( ext_modulus, ext_exponent );
```

Each of the functions, like f_get_crypt_secret_pass, that are called from p_get_shared_passphrase are Java stored procedures. We saw the code for one of those functions in Listing 6-11. All the substantial work of the Java stored procedures is done in our Java code, OracleJavaSecure on the Oracle database

A second procedure that we will look at here is p_get_des_crypt_test_data. It is very similar to p_get_shared_passphrase except that p_get_des_crypt_test_data has two additional parameters, one IN and one OUT, as shown in Listing 6-13. These parameters will be used to submit clear text to Oracle database and to return that text in encrypted form—encrypted with the secret password key.

Listing 6-13. Procedure to get Encrypted Data, p_get_des_crypt_test_data

```
    PROCEDURE p_get_des_crypt_test_data(
        ext_modulus            VARCHAR2,
        ext_exponent           VARCHAR2,
        secret_pass_salt       OUT RAW,
        secret_pass_count      OUT RAW,
        secret_pass_algorithm OUT RAW,
        secret_pass            OUT RAW,
        m_err_no               OUT NUMBER,
        m_err_txt              OUT VARCHAR2,
        test_data              VARCHAR2,
        crypt_data             OUT RAW )
    IS BEGIN
        m_err_no := 0;
        secret_pass_salt := f_get_crypt_secret_salt( ext_modulus, ext_exponent );
        secret_pass_count := f_get_crypt_secret_count( ext_modulus, ext_exponent );
        secret_pass := f_get_crypt_secret_pass( ext_modulus, ext_exponent );
        secret_pass_algorithm :=
```

```
            f_get_crypt_secret_algorithm( ext_modulus, ext_exponent );
    crypt_data := f_get_crypt_data( test_data );
EXCEPTION
    WHEN OTHERS THEN
        m_err_no := SQLCODE;
        m_err_txt := SQLERRM;
END p_get_des_crypt_test_data;
```

We send clear text `test_data` from the client to Oracle, and this procedure returns `crypt_data` after encryption by a call to the `f_get_crypt_data` function. That function is also a Java stored procedure.

Java Methods for Secret Password Decryption

Once we've called the `appsec` procedures to get the DES secret password key artifacts and encrypted data back to the client, we need to

1) decrypt the artifacts with the RSA private key

2) generate the DES secret password key

3) decrypt the data with the secret password key

As a rule, I try to limit the number of steps that I require of developers to accomplish work. Why make a developer call three methods when they can call a single method that accomplishes the other calls for them? The application developer's goal is to decrypt data, so we provide a method for them to do just that.

■ **Note** You can find this code in the file *Chapter6/orajavsec/OracleJavaSecure.java*.

Decrypting Data Using the Secret Password Key

After the client application has called the `p_get_des_crypt_test_data` procedure, we have them call the method `getDecryptData()` shown in Listing 6-14.

Listing 6-14. Build Secret Password and Decrypt Data, `getDecryptData()`

```
public static final String getDecryptData( RAW cryptData,
    RAW cryptSecretDESPassPhrase, RAW cryptSecretDESAlgorithm,
    RAW cryptSecretDESSalt, RAW cryptSecretDESIterationCount )
{
    String rtrnString = "getDecryptData() A failed";
    try {
        if( ( null == sessionSecretDESKey ) || testAsClientAndServer ) {
            decryptSessionSecretDESPassPhrase( cryptSecretDESPassPhrase,
                cryptSecretDESAlgorithm, cryptSecretDESSalt,
                cryptSecretDESIterationCount );
            makeSessionSecretDESKey();
        }
```

```
        rtrnString = getDecryptData( cryptData );
    } catch( Exception x ) {
        x.printStackTrace();
    }
    return rtrnString;
}
```

The first thing we do in the try block is to test whether the sessionSecretDESKey has already been instantiated. If not, then we call two methods: decryptSessionSecretDESPassPhrase() (discussed in the next section) and makeSessionSecretDESKey(). We discussed makeSessionSecretDESKey() earlier in this chapter—it is the same method we called to build to the secret password key initially on the Oracle database. We are calling it again on the client to build an identical key.

When we test whether we already have the sessionSecretDESKey, we also test the boolean testAsClientAndServer. The testAsClientAndServer boolean is always false, unless we are testing the OracleJavaSecure class from its main() method. In the main(), when we set this boolean to true, we can replace a locally generated DES secret password key with one coming from Oracle database at different stages of testing. We will examine the code of the main() method a bit later in this chapter.

The getDecryptData() method is overloaded with a version that assumes the secret password key has been built and does the decryption. It takes a RAW and returns the clear text as a String. The first getDecryptData() method (shown previously) calls this second getDecryptData() method, see Listing 6-15.

Listing 6-15. Decrypt Data with Existing Secret Password, getDecryptData()

```
public static final String getDecryptData( RAW cryptData ) {
    if( null == cryptData ) return null;
    String rtrnString = "getDecryptData() B failed";
    try {
        cipherDES.init( Cipher.DECRYPT_MODE, sessionSecretDESKey, paramSpec );
        rtrnString = new String( cipherDES.doFinal( cryptData.getBytes() ) );
    } catch( Exception x ) {
        //x.printStackTrace();
        //rtrnString = x.toString();
    }
    return rtrnString;
}
```

This same, second getDecryptData() method is also called to decrypt data on the Oracle database for encrypted data inserts and updates coming from the client. There on the Oracle database, we presumably know that we already have our DES secret password key.

Decrypting the DES Passphrase using RSA Private Key

The decryptSessionSecretDESPassPhrase() method uses the client's RSA private key to decrypt all the artifacts of the server DES secret password key. The code is presented in Listing 6-16.

Listing 6-16. Decrypt Secret Password Key Artifacts, decryptSessionSecretDESPassPhrase()

```
private static void decryptSessionSecretDESPassPhrase(
    RAW cryptSecretDESPassPhrase, RAW cryptSecretDESAlgorithm,
    RAW cryptSecretDESSalt, RAW cryptSecretDESIterationCount )
    throws Exception
```

```
    {
        cipherRSA.init( Cipher.DECRYPT_MODE, locRSAPrivKey );
        byte[] cryptBytes;
        cryptBytes = cryptSecretDESPassPhrase.getBytes();
        sessionSecretDESPassPhraseChars =
            byteArrayToCharArray( cipherRSA.doFinal( cryptBytes ) );
        cryptBytes = cryptSecretDESAlgorithm.getBytes();
        sessionSecretDESAlgorithm = new String( cipherRSA.doFinal( cryptBytes ) );
        cryptBytes = cryptSecretDESSalt.getBytes();
        salt = cipherRSA.doFinal( cryptBytes );
        cryptBytes = cryptSecretDESIterationCount.getBytes();
        iterationCount = cipherRSA.doFinal( cryptBytes )[0];
        //System.out.println( "\n" + new String( sessionSecretDESPassPhraseChars ) );
        //System.out.println( sessionSecretDESAlgorithm );
        //System.out.println( new String( salt ) );
        //System.out.println( iterationCount );
    }
```

For each artifact, we convert the encrypted RAW into a byte array and pass it to the cipherRSA member to be decrypted. We use the byte array coming back from the Cipher to populate our static class members with an appropriate data type. Keep the value as a byte array for salt, char array for sessionSecretDESPassPhraseChars by calling the byteArrayToCharArray() method, String for sessionSecretDESAlgorithm by instantiating a new String(), and a single byte, automatically cast as an int for iterationCount.

If you are interested in observing these session-specific, random artifacts and the negotiated algorithm as they arrive at the client, you can uncomment the System.out.println() calls at the end of the method. However, you should only do this temporarily: the System.out.println() calls have been removed from the code in the next chapter.

Ancillary Methods for Array Conversion

In two places in the preceding code, we called some ancillary array conversion methods that we have defined in the OracleJavaSecure code, shown in Listing 6-17. One takes a byte array and converts it to a char array. The other does the opposite. We call byteArrayToCharArray() from decryptSessionSecretDESPassPhrase() (see Listing 6-16) when we get sessionSecretDESPassPhraseChars, and we call charArrayToByteArray() from getCryptSessionSecretDESPassPhrase() (see Listing 6-5) when we are encrypting sessionSecretDESPassPhraseChars.

Listing 6-17. Array Conversion Methods, byteArrayToCharArray() and charArrayToByteArray()

```
    static char[] byteArrayToCharArray( byte[] bytes ) {
        char[] rtrnArray = new char[bytes.length];
        for ( int i = 0; i < bytes.length; i++ ) {
            rtrnArray[i] = ( char )bytes[i];
        }
        return rtrnArray;
    }

    static byte[] charArrayToByteArray( char[] chars ) {
        byte[] rtrnArray = new byte[chars.length];
```

```
        for ( int i = 0; i < chars.length; i++ ) {
            rtrnArray[i] = ( byte )chars[i];
        }
        return rtrnArray;
    }
```

We can normally convert these array types back and forth just by casting, as in the following example. However, we need to be aware of the implications of narrowing and widening conversions. We must restrict the char values in our array to standard ASCII characters, not 16-bit Unicode characters, in order to not lose information in the conversions.

```
byte[] bAr = new byte[10];
char[] cAr = (char[])bAr;
bAr = (byte[])cAr;
```

That kind of array casting is not supported from within the JDeveloper IDE (and possibly elsewhere), so we will instead rely on our ancillary methods. JDeveloper is nice because it is free, and it is highly tailored for working with Oracle databases; it handles Oracle views better than any other IDE. You can find JDeveloper on the Oracle corporate web site at www.oracle.com.

You may wonder why we maintain the passphrase as a char array. That is the format we need when we build the PBEKeySpec.

Method Used to Show Actual Algorithm

Listing 6-18 presents the showAlgorithm() method. This is actually duplicative functionality. Take a look at the code for the decryptSessionSecretDESPassPhrase() method (shown previously) and you will see that we get sessionSecretDESAlgorithm from Oracle database to a String on the client that we could simply print out.

The only additional assurance in selecting this directly from the Oracle database (via the function f_show_algorithm) is that there is no mix up during transfer. We have already built the function in app_sec_pkg that will call this method to return the algorithm name. We can also call this method from the client (before calling the server) and compare the algorithms used.

Listing 6-18. Display the Secret Password Algorithm Name in Use, showAlgorithm()

```
    public static final String showAlgorithm() {
        String rtrnString = "showAlgorithm failed";
        try {
            rtrnString = sessionSecretDESKey.getAlgorithm();
        } catch( Exception x ) {
            rtrnString = x.toString();
        } finally {
            return rtrnString;
        }
    }
```

This is a temporary method for testing only in the chapter, and we will remove it, and the Oracle function that calls it, from the code in future chapters.

Testing DES Encryption on the Client Only

Once again, we are going to do our client-side-only testing by calling our methods from the `main()` method of `OracleJavaSecure`. The code for the first part of `main()` is shown in Listing 6-19. Start out by getting our client public key modulus and exponent, which in the process generates the RSA Public/private key pair, if not existing.

Listing 6-19. Code for Client-Only Testing, from `main()`

```
String clientPubModulus = getLocRSAPubMod();
String clientPubExponent = getLocRSAPubExp();

// Emulates server actions
RAW mCryptSessionSecretDESPassPhrase =
    getCryptSessionSecretDESPassPhrase( clientPubModulus,
    clientPubExponent );
RAW mCryptSessionSecretDESSalt =
    getCryptSessionSecretDESSalt( clientPubModulus,
    clientPubExponent );
RAW mCryptSessionSecretDESAlgorithm =
    getCryptSessionSecretDESAlgorithm( clientPubModulus,
    clientPubExponent );
RAW mCryptSessionSecretDESIterationCount =
    getCryptSessionSecretDESIterationCount( clientPubModulus,
    clientPubExponent );
RAW cryptData = getCryptData( "Monday" );

testAsClientAndServer = true;

// As client
System.out.println( getDecryptData( cryptData,
    mCryptSessionSecretDESPassPhrase, mCryptSessionSecretDESAlgorithm,
    mCryptSessionSecretDESSalt, mCryptSessionSecretDESIterationCount ) );
System.out.println( showAlgorithm() );
```

Next, we emulate the server, having received the modulus and exponent, getting the DES secret password key artifacts from `getCryptSessionSecretDESPassPhrase()` and other methods. In the process, a copy of the public key is built from the artifacts, the DES secret password key is generated and each of the secret password key artifacts is encrypted using the RSA public key.

We also emulate the server, encrypting some data with the secret password key:

```
RAW cryptData = getCryptData( "Monday" );
```

Our next step in testing assumes we are back on the client, and having received all the encrypted secret password key artifacts, we generate a copy of the secret password key from those artifacts. To do that, we set `testAsClientAndServer` to be `true` in order to overwrite the secret password key that we just created while emulating the server (even though the key will be identical):

```
testAsClientAndServer = true;
```

Now again as the client, we call `getDecryptData()` with all the DES secret password key artifacts, and the encrypted data. This will create a new DES secret key based on the artifacts, then decrypt the data

101

using that key. We will print out the decrypted data, which should be the same as what we encrypted earlier. Also, we will print out the DES algorithm name that we used for secret password encryption.

Running the Code

We assume you followed the procedure to run the code in the previous chapter. This chapter will use an identical procedure. In a command prompt, change directories to *Chapter6*. Compile the code with this command:

```
javac orajavsec/OracleJavaSecure.java
```

If you have any problems, refer to Chapter 3 for directions on compiling at the command prompt and setting your environment CLASSPATH to include *ojdbc6.jar*. Then run the code from that same directory with this command:

```
java orajavsec.OracleJavaSecure.OracleJavaSecure
```

Observing the Results

The following two lines will be printed as a result of the commands issued in the preceding section:

```
Monday
PBEWithSHA1AndDESede
```

We encrypted the string "Monday" using the DES secret password key when we emulated the server, and we passed the encrypted data back to the client, along with the secret password key artifacts, encrypted with the client RSA public key. Back at the client, we built a duplicate DES key using the artifacts, and decrypted the encrypted data. We printed out the decrypted data and saw "Monday" at the command prompt. Then we printed the negotiated algorithm. If you are using JDK 1.6 or later on your workstation, you will see PBEWithSHA1AndDESede; however, if you are using JDK 1.5, you will see PBEWithMD5AndDES.

Coding to Test Client/Server Secret Password Encryption

The next line is at the top of our Java code in *OracleJavaSecure.java*. Uncomment it and copy the entire code into your Oracle client.

```
CREATE OR REPLACE AND RESOLVE JAVA SOURCE NAMED appsec."orajavsec/OracleJavaSecure" AS
```

For security, scroll down to the class body and assure you do not have a valid password in the connection string. If you do, remove the password from the connection string before executing this command in Oracle.

```
private static String appsecConnString =
    "jdbc:oracle:thin:AppSec/password@localhost:1521:Orcl";
```

Execute the script in your Oracle client (e.g., SQL*Plus) to load the Java code into the Oracle database. This command, as we have seen, loads the Java code into the Oracle database and compiles it.

Setting the Code to Test Server as well as Client

To compile and execute OracleJavaSecure on your client, that first line that we uncommented to run on the Oracle database, needs to be commented:

```
//CREATE OR REPLACE AND RESOLVE JAVA SOURCE NAMED appsec."orajavsec/OracleJavaSecure" AS
```

Scroll down to the class body and set the password in the connection string. Also correct any of the other addresses and names for your connection string.

```
private static String appsecConnString =
    "jdbc:oracle:thin:AppSec/password@localhost:1521:Orcl";
```

Also set the testingOnServer boolean to true:

```
private static boolean testingOnServer = true;
```

Save the file.

You may have already executed the app_sec_pkg package specification and body on Oracle, from earlier in this chapter. If you haven't done so, do that now. This will create the Oracle structures we need to do secret password encryption.

Consider the Server Portion of the main() Method

This time when we run through the main() method of OracleJavaSecure, we will pass the testingOnServer test, so we will execute the remainder of main(), as shown in Listing 6-20. We declare a couple member variables to hold the error number and error message coming back from Oracle, errNo and errMsg.

Because we are running from the client (not on Oracle database), we need to load the Oracle-specific driver (assuming we might not be using JDK 1.6 or later). And we will set up the Oracle connection for use: note that we will be connecting as appsec user.

We will be using an Oracle-specific OracleCallableStatement, which allows us to retrieve OUT parameters back from Oracle, and to transfer Oracle-specific data types.

Listing 6-20. Code for Client/Server Testing, from main()

```
if( testingOnServer ) {
    int errNo;
    String errMsg;
    // Since not on the Server, must load Oracle-specific Driver
    Class.forName( "oracle.jdbc.driver.OracleDriver" );
    // This will set the static member "conn" to a new Connection
    conn = DriverManager.getConnection( appsecConnString );
    OracleCallableStatement stmt;
```

Getting the DES Secret Password from Oracle

Our first procedure call, in Listing 6-21, is to p_get_shared_passphrase. This will simply test the exchange of RSA and DES keys between our client and Oracle. We hand the procedure our RSA public key modulus and exponent, and in return get the DES secret password key artifacts, encrypted by the Oracle database using the public key. Notice that we register the OUT parameters and either set or setNull all our parameters.

Listing 6-21. Get Shared Passphrase, from main()

```
stmt = ( OracleCallableStatement )conn.prepareCall(
    "CALL app_sec_pkg.p_get_shared_passphrase(?,?,?,?,?,?,?,?)" );
```

```
stmt.registerOutParameter( 3, OracleTypes.RAW );
stmt.registerOutParameter( 4, OracleTypes.RAW );
stmt.registerOutParameter( 5, OracleTypes.RAW );
stmt.registerOutParameter( 6, OracleTypes.RAW );
stmt.registerOutParameter( 7, OracleTypes.NUMBER );
stmt.registerOutParameter( 8, OracleTypes.VARCHAR );
stmt.setString( 1, clientPubModulus );
stmt.setString( 2, clientPubExponent );
stmt.setNull(   3, OracleTypes.RAW );
stmt.setNull(   4, OracleTypes.RAW );
stmt.setNull(   5, OracleTypes.RAW );
stmt.setNull(   6, OracleTypes.RAW );
stmt.setInt(    7, 0 );
stmt.setNull(   8, OracleTypes.VARCHAR );
stmt.executeUpdate();

errNo = stmt.getInt( 7 );
if( errNo != 0 ) {
    errMsg = stmt.getString( 8 );
    System.out.println( "Oracle error " + errNo +
        ", " + errMsg );
    System.out.println( (stmt.getRAW( 3 )).toString() );
} else {
    mCryptSessionSecretDESSalt = stmt.getRAW( 3 );
    mCryptSessionSecretDESIterationCount = stmt.getRAW( 4 );
    mCryptSessionSecretDESAlgorithm = stmt.getRAW( 5 );
    mCryptSessionSecretDESPassPhrase = stmt.getRAW( 6 );
}
if( null != stmt ) stmt.close();
```

After executing the statement, we get the error number, errNo coming back from Oracle database and assure it's 0. If not, we report the error.

If there was no error, then we, as the client application, set a method member equal to each of the encrypted artifacts, like the mCryptSessionSecretDESSalt. Now we have everything we need to build an exact copy of the secret password key that was generated on the Oracle database. At this point, we have fully exchanged keys; however, we have not yet built a copy of the DES secret password key on the client. Later in this code, we will decrypt each artifact using our private key, then build the secret password key and use it to exchange encrypted data with Oracle.

Because we are done with this statement, we close it. It is a matter of consistency and diligence that before we close the statement we assure that it is not null. In reality, if stmt were null, we would have thrown an exception in the earlier code with the first registerOutParameter() call.

Seeing the Negotiated Algorithm for Password-Based Encryption

We call the function, f_show_algorithm in order to display the algorithm name that the Oracle database selected (see Listing 6-22). Because the Oracle 11g JVM is based on the standard JVM version 1.5, we will see that Oracle database manifests the aforementioned bug in this regard and selects PBEWithMD5AndDES as the protocol, instead of what we requested, PBEWithSHA1AndDESede. This will serve as the common algorithm negotiated with the client.

Listing 6-22. Show Algorithm, from main()

```
stmt = ( OracleCallableStatement )conn.prepareCall(
    "{? = call app_sec_pkg.f_show_algorithm}" );
stmt.registerOutParameter( 1, OracleTypes.VARCHAR );
stmt.executeUpdate();
System.out.println( stmt.getString(1) );
if( null != stmt ) stmt.close();
```

Of note here is the syntax for calling an Oracle function, rather than a procedure. The function always returns a value. The leading "? =" represents the return value, and our statement parameter (1) is that value. Each question mark in a prepared callable statement is a parameter, whether it comes before or after the procedure or function name. The parameters are always numbered from left to right with 1 (one) being the first.

The format used in this function call, with the open and close curly brackets, is referred to as SQL92 syntax. That is a reference to the international standard for SQL that was adopted in 1992. Another form of syntax that can be used for calling stored procedures and functions is the PL/SQL Block syntax (with begin and end statements). I have found that with much older versions (e.g., jdbc14.jar) of the Oracle drivers (although not as old as SQL92) the PL/SQL Block syntax will work when the SQL92 syntax will not. Here is the same prepareCall() method call from Listing 6-22 in PL/SQL Block syntax:

```
stmt = ( OracleCallableStatement )conn.prepareCall(
    "begin ? = call app_sec_pkg.f_show_algorithm; end;" );
```

Calling Oracle Database to get Encrypted Data

Next we want to demonstrate getting encrypted data back from Oracle database and decrypting it on the client with a local copy of the DES secret password key. In Listing 6-23, you can see we call the procedure, p_get_des_crypt_test_data. Again, we pass our public key artifacts and retrieve the encrypted secret password key artifacts. Because this process is something we will see repeated throughout the remainder of this book, I will just call this "key exchange". We just returned from another procedure that retrieved the secret password key artifacts, so we don't bother to set our method members again—those lines are commented. Note that all these calls are occurring in the same Oracle session, so existing keys are used—there is no additional key generation.

Listing 6-23. Get DES Crypt Test Data, from main()

```
stmt = ( OracleCallableStatement )conn.prepareCall(
    "CALL app_sec_pkg.p_get_des_crypt_test_data(?,?,?,?,?,?,?,?,?,?)" );
stmt.registerOutParameter( 3, OracleTypes.RAW );
stmt.registerOutParameter( 4, OracleTypes.RAW );
stmt.registerOutParameter( 5, OracleTypes.RAW );
stmt.registerOutParameter( 6, OracleTypes.RAW );
stmt.registerOutParameter( 7, OracleTypes.NUMBER );
stmt.registerOutParameter( 8, OracleTypes.VARCHAR );
stmt.registerOutParameter( 10, OracleTypes.RAW );
stmt.setString( 1, clientPubModulus );
stmt.setString( 2, clientPubExponent );
stmt.setString( 9, "Tuesday" );
stmt.setNull(   3, OracleTypes.RAW );
stmt.setNull(   4, OracleTypes.RAW );
stmt.setNull(   5, OracleTypes.RAW );
stmt.setNull(   6, OracleTypes.RAW );
```

```
    stmt.setInt(    7, 0 );
    stmt.setNull(   8, OracleTypes.VARCHAR );
    stmt.setNull(  10, OracleTypes.RAW );
    stmt.executeUpdate();
    errNo = stmt.getInt( 7 );
    if( errNo != 0 ) {
        errMsg = stmt.getString( 8 );
        System.out.println( "Oracle error " + errNo +
            ", " + errMsg );
        System.out.println( (stmt.getRAW( 10 )).toString() );
    } else {
        //mCryptSessionSecretDESSalt = stmt.getRAW( 3 );
        //mCryptSessionSecretDESIterationCount = stmt.getRAW( 4 );
        //mCryptSessionSecretDESAlgorithm = stmt.getRAW( 5 );
        //mCryptSessionSecretDESPassPhrase = stmt.getRAW( 6 );
        cryptData = stmt.getRAW( 10 );

        System.out.println( getDecryptData( cryptData,

            mCryptSessionSecretDESPassPhrase,
            mCryptSessionSecretDESAlgorithm, mCryptSessionSecretDESSalt,
            mCryptSessionSecretDESIterationCount ) );
    }
    if( null != stmt ) stmt.close();
```

Along with key exchange, we send the string "Tuesday" to the p_get_des_crypt_test_data procedure to be encrypted on Oracle database using the secret password key. So, after executing the Statement, we retrieve the encrypted data, and then decrypt the data by calling getDecryptData() locally on the client and print out the decrypted String. Notice that the getDecryptData() method takes all the encrypted secret password key artifacts.

If the secret password key has not yet been built, then getDecryptData() calls makeSessionSecretDESKey(). When we call getDecryptData() we pass sufficient parameters, the artifacts of the secret password key, to build the key; but if it has already been built, we do not repeat that effort. We may call getDecryptData() multiple times for multiple pieces of encrypted data, but the effort to build the secret password key will only be undertaken once.

Testing Oracle Database Encrypt and Local Decrypt Data

The next test in Listing 6-24 is even more concise, if unrealistic. We will call the temporary function, f_get_crypt_data to get encrypted data representing a clear text String, "Wednesday". We will get the encrypted data RAW back from the statement and call the getDecryptData() method locally to decrypt it, printing the result.

Listing 6-24. Get Crypt Data, from main()

```
    stmt = ( OracleCallableStatement )conn.prepareCall(
        "{? = call app_sec_pkg.f_get_crypt_data(?) }" );
    stmt.registerOutParameter( 1, OracleTypes.RAW );
    stmt.setString( 2, "Wednesday" );
    stmt.executeUpdate();
    cryptData = stmt.getRAW( 1 );
```

```
System.out.println( getDecryptData( cryptData,
    mCryptSessionSecretDESPassPhrase,
    mCryptSessionSecretDESAlgorithm, mCryptSessionSecretDESSalt,
    mCryptSessionSecretDESIterationCount ) );
if( null != stmt ) stmt.close();
```

Normally we wouldn't call Oracle database to encrypt clear text data from the client, and then decrypt it at the client to obtain the clear text. Nevertheless, that is precisely what we did here.

Sending Encrypted Data to Oracle

In our last test in Listing 6-25, we will encrypt clear text data, "Thursday" on the client. We encrypt it with the copy of the DES secret password key, based on the artifacts we got from Oracle. Then we submit the encrypted data to Oracle database by calling the **f_get_decrypt_data** function. Oracle database will decrypt the data using the original secret password key, and then our client will read the clear text **String** that is returned as parameter 1. We print that result and close the **Statement**.

Listing 6-25. Get Decrypt Data, from main( )

```
cryptData = getCryptData( "Thursday" );
stmt = ( OracleCallableStatement )conn.prepareCall(
    "{? = call app_sec_pkg.f_get_decrypt_data(?) }" );
stmt.registerOutParameter( 1, OracleTypes.VARCHAR );
stmt.setRAW( 2, cryptData );
stmt.executeUpdate();
System.out.println( stmt.getString( 1 ) );
if( null != stmt ) stmt.close();
```

This is another unlikely scenario where we are calling an Oracle function to decrypt data for use on the client. Don't worry about exposing unneeded functionality to the client; we will be sorting this out as we continue. In fact, we already have! Our client applications will not be connecting as **appsec** user, and only **appsec** will be able to execute procedures and functions in the **app_sec_pkg** package.

Testing Our Secure Client/Server Data Transmission

In a Command Prompt, Change directories to *Chapter6*. Compile the code with this command:

```
javac orajavsec/OracleJavaSecure.java
```

Again, if you have any problems, refer to Chapter 3 for directions on compiling at the command prompt and setting your environment **CLASSPATH** to include *ojdbc6.jar*. Then run the code from that same directory with this command:

```
java orajavsec.OracleJavaSecure
```

The following six lines will be printed as a result:

```
Monday
PBEWithSHA1AndDESede
PBEWithMD5AndDES
Tuesday
Wednesday
```

Thursday

The first two lines show the same client-only tests that we performed earlier in this chapter. After that, because `testingOnServer` is `true`, the `main()` method continues to get the DES secret password key from Oracle. Then we call `f_show_algorithm` and display the negotiated algorithm at the command prompt, which will likely be `PBEWithMD5AndDES`.

After that, we send the string "Tuesday" to Oracle database for encryption by `p_get_des_crypt_test_data` procedure. We read the encrypted data, decrypt it with a copy of the secret password key, and display it, "Tuesday".

We also call the function `f_get_crypt_data` directly, handing it the clear text string "Wednesday". We read the encrypted data returned by the function, decrypt it again with the copy of the secret password key and display it, "Wednesday". By this time, it is obvious that the session of our Oracle connection is retaining and reusing the same RSA and DES keys for multiple queries.

Finally, we encrypt the string, "Thursday" on the client and submit it to the Oracle function `f_get_decrypt_data`. Oracle database decrypts the data with the original secret password key. We read the returned clear text string and print it, "Thursday."

Chapter Review

We find ourselves at the end of another chapter. Looking back, let's see what ground we've covered.

- We learned about DES secret password encryption. In particular, we learned about the various artifacts that make up the secret password key: passphrase, salt, iteration count, and the algorithm. We also devised a way to observe and report and work around a bug in JCE, even coding to accommodate an eventual JVM upgrade that will not have the bug.

- We found out how to generate the secret password key on Oracle, do key exchange, then build an identical key on the client. With identical keys (a shared password), we can exchange encrypted data. We also saw how to use the RSA public key to encrypt the DES key so that we can exchange it between Oracle database and the client, but still keep it secret.

- We made extensive use of the `SecureRandom` class in order to generate a random passphrase, salt, and iteration count for each session.

- We explored Oracle packages, something we will depend on for organization and security.

Figures 6-1 and 6-2 illustrate the secret password encryption processes we have covered in this chapter. These processes will be used throughout the remainder of this book. In Figure 6-1, at the top, you will see that we refer to block [A] of Figure 5-1—that is where we saw the standard process of generating an RSA public/private key pair on the client. We pass the public key exponent and modulus to Oracle database when we call `p_get_shared_pass_phrase`. You can see in Figure 6-1, on the far right, that an equivalent public key is built on Oracle database, represented by the key image labeled RSA. Another key image on the far right, labeled DES depicts the shared password key that we create on the Oracle database.

Each of the artifacts of the shared password key is encrypted on the Oracle database with the public key and returned to the client. Each encrypted artifact is placed in one of the OUT parameters of the `p_get_shared_pass_phrase` procedure. We have outlined this whole process and labeled it as block [B] in Figure 6-1. This is our standard process for exchanging the shared password key, and we will refer to it in future Figures.

At the bottom of Figure 6-1, we illustrate how the client calls methods to decrypt the secret password key artifacts and to build an equivalent secret password key. The key image at the bottom represents the secret password key on the client.

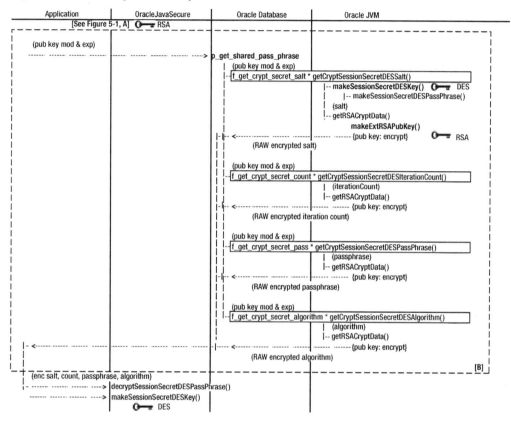

Figure 6-1. Key exchange

In Figure 6-2 you can see an illustration of the example processes for exchanging encrypted data between the client and Oracle database. In the top one third of Figure 6-2, you see the process of doing key exchange and encrypting data on the Oracle database. That encrypted data is returned to the client in the OUT parameters of the p_get_des_crypt_test_data procedure. Here we refer to block [B] of Figure 6-1, where we saw the secret password key being built on Oracle database and returned to the client. In Figure 6-2, in addition to building the secret password key, we use that key to encrypt data that is returned to the client in encrypted form.

In the middle section of Figure 6-2, by a call to the getDecryptData() method (version A of two methods with that name), we see an illustration of how the client decrypts data coming from Oracle database. We outline this section of Figure 6-2 and label it as block [C]—it illustrates a standard process for decrypting data. You can see that an equivalent secret password key, labeled DES, is built on the client (as needed) during the decryption process.

The last section of Figure 6-2, at the bottom shows the mirror image of this process. In that illustration, the client uses the equivalent secret password key that has already been built to encrypt data. The encrypted data is then sent to the Oracle database by a call to the **f_get_decrypt_data** function. The Oracle database then decrypts the data using the original secret password key. In our example code, that decrypted, clear-text data is returned to the client for display.

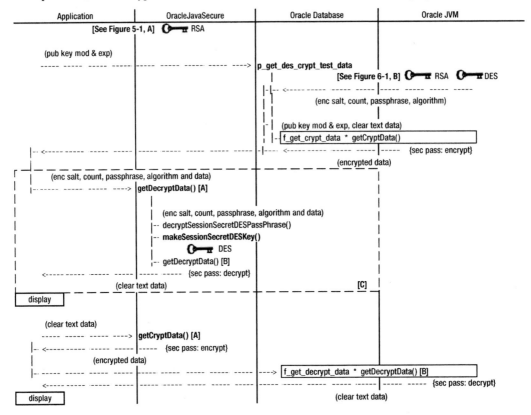

Figure 6-2. *Encrypted data exchange example*

CHAPTER 7

Data Encryption in Transit

In Chapter 6, we laid the foundation for data encryption between Oracle database and a Java client. We proved that we can exchange keys securely and then send encrypted data back and forth, successfully decrypting the data at the recipient, and at the Oracle database.

In this chapter, we will complete the foundation for encryption, which we will continue to build in the application security, appsec Oracle schema. Then we will take on the role of an application developer, using the appsec structures to secure access to our data. Specifically, we will secure access to data in the HR example schema.

Consider the last chapter and observe that we have been both building and testing our application security structures and code as the appsec user. It is not the intent to have every application run as appsec. Rather, we will allow each application that needs our security to execute our security functions, and we will be demonstrating that in this chapter.

Also, we need to provide developers access to our Java structures to include with their desktop applications. We will discuss that at the end of this chapter.

Security Administrator Activities

Our security administrator, secadm, needs to provide a few more permissions. Some of the permissions are system privileges, and some are grants to packages in the appsec and HR schemas.

Note You can find a script of the following commands in the file named *Chapter7/SecAdm.sql*.

Connect to Oracle database as SECADM user, and acquire the secure application role, secadm_role.

```
EXECUTE sys.p_check_secadm_access;
```

We are going to be creating a table in the appsec schema for logging errors. We are also going to create a trigger associated with that table. Our trigger is like a procedure that runs when certain events occur—in our case, our trigger will run when a record is inserted into our table.

We want to have a central table for application errors, because the error messages will be returned to, potentially, dozens or hundreds of applications. How will we, as the application security administrator, get reports from all these sources? If our application developers are conscientious, they will let us know what problems they are seeing, but we are not going to count on that happening. We will watch for errors from our remote listening post—the error table.

Granting More System Privileges to the Application Security User

In order to succeed at setting up the error logging table, we need to allow appsec to store data in a tablespace. The default tablespace is "USERS," and that will suffice for us. We need to specify how much space appsec may use, a *quota*. We'll start out permitting two megabytes of space. Execute the following as appsec:

```
ALTER USER appsec DEFAULT TABLESPACE USERS QUOTA 2M ON USERS;
```

Additionally, for appsec to be able to create a trigger, we need to grant the CREATE TRIGGER system privilege. We will grant it to her non-default role (she'll only need it occasionally):

```
GRANT CREATE TRIGGER TO appsec_role;
```

Permitting Users to Execute Packages in Other Schemas

We want HR to execute the appsec security structures. We'd like to create a role to which we might grant execute on a package, and then grant that role to whomever needs it. However, let's examine why this approach does not always work. Consider the following statements, which you should not execute:

```
--CREATE ROLE appsec_user_role NOT IDENTIFIED;
--GRANT EXECUTE ON appsec.app_sec_pkg TO appsec_user_role;
--GRANT appsec_user_role TO hr;
```

Specifically, the approach illustrated here does not work when procedures, functions, and packages call procedures, functions, and packages in other schemas. To get a bit ahead of ourselves, we will be creating procedures in the HR schema that we want to have execute the app_sec_pkg package (you know, we want HR to call functions to encrypt data).

The problem is that the HR procedures, functions, and packages cannot gain privileges from a role. This is a restriction (based on the dependency model) designed to keep the HR procedures from getting invalidated every time we logout or set role. We remedy the restriction by granting execute on the app_sec_pkg package directly to HR user. For example, execute the following code:

```
GRANT EXECUTE ON appsec.app_sec_pkg TO hr;
```

By way of stark contrast, our application user, appusr, and other application users will be calling the procedures, functions, and packages in the HR schema directly, as needed. We do not imagine appusr calling our procedures from their own procedures. So we can grant access to our (yet to be configured) HR Security Package, hr_sec_pkg, to a role that appusr has, the hrview_role. The following is the GRANT statement, which we will execute later after creating the hr.hr_sec_pkg package:

```
--GRANT EXECUTE ON hr.hr_sec_pkg TO hrview_role;
```

Later we will execute a script named HR.sql. This script creates the hr.hr_sec_pkg package, and also executes the preceding GRANT statement.

Application Security User Activities

We are going to create an error log table, and an insert trigger, and we will also be adding procedures to do logging to app_sec_pkg package.

■ **Note** You can find a script of the following commands in the file named *Chapter7/AppSec.sql*.

Connect to Oracle database as `appsec` user, and set your role to the non-default role, `appsec_role`:

```
SET ROLE appsec_role;
```

Creating a Table for Error Logging

Next, create a table for error logging. Probably, you want to pull out your DBA skills or get a DBA to help you define this table, setting its performance parameters and estimating initial storage and growth plans, none of which is defined here. Execute the code in Listing 7-1 to create the table using the defaults.

Listing 7-1. Create the Application Security Error Log Table, `t_appsec_errors`

```
CREATE TABLE appsec.t_appsec_errors (
    err_no      NUMBER,
    err_txt     VARCHAR2(2000),
    msg_txt     VARCHAR2(4000) DEFAULT NULL,
    update_ts   DATE DEFAULT SYSDATE
);
```

We are going to capture the Oracle error number, `err_no`, and text, `err_txt`, and provide ourselves with another field, `msg_txt`, for helpful information (e.g., method name or stack trace). We will also capture the time of the error, `update_ts`, which helps in two ways: first, we want to know when things happened, or what is happening; second, we want to throw away log records when they are too old to be helpful.

Note that the last two column definitions in the listing specify default values using the keyword `DEFAULT`. To insert a record, you only need to insert the first two fields. The third will default to `NULL`, and the fourth will default to the current date and time on the Oracle database, `SYSDATE`. In fact, we do not want to insert a date in `UPDATE_TS`. We want to accept the default. Because `appsec` is the only one who will be entering data in this table (this is an error log for application security use, not for general use), we do not need to enforce the default `UPDATE_TS`.

In order to accomplish our sorting and selection of records by date, we are going to set up an index on the `UPDATE_TS` column. Execute the code in Listing 7-2 to create the index.

Listing 7-2. Index for the Application Security Error Log Table, `t_appsec_errors`

```
CREATE INDEX i_appsec_errors00 ON appsec.t_appsec_errors (
    update_ts
);
```

Indexes, once created, are maintained automatically as you insert or update rows. Also, they are automatically used when you select records from the table. Which index is used is a logical choice made by Oracle database that can be overridden by a hint, if desired. One thing to be aware of is that a select query that does not mention the leading column of an index will not benefit directly from the index. For example, if we selected all rows from the `t_appsec_errors` table where the `msg_txt` column contains the string "Exception," we would not directly use the index we just created. If we created an index on columns (`update_ts, msg_txt`), that index would not benefit our query directly either. To get the direct benefits of an index when we select from `msg_txt`, we would want to create an index mentioning `msg_txt` as the first column, for example (`msg_txt, update_ts`).

The Oracle database optimizer may actually use any index to improve the performance of a query by doing a *skip scan*. A skip scan can improve performance in simple queries, potentially reducing the reliance on full-table scans (those cause very bad performance). You can also use a skip scan hint to explicitly name an index for use. It may take some trial and error and a bit of engineering to get the best performance from a skip scan hint. Here is an example, taken from the Oracle documentation. The comment section (/* */) with the plus symbol and hint name serve as a hint to the optimizer.

```
SELECT /*+ INDEX_SS(e emp_name_ix) */ last_name
    FROM employees e
    WHERE first_name = 'Steven';
```

Notice that the skip scan hint, `INDEX_SS` directs the optimizer to use the index `emp_name_ix` for our query. Even though we're selecting records where the `first_name` column is 'Steven,' we ask to benefit from the index on `last_name, first_name`. For a better understanding of skip search optimization, I recommend doing an Internet search for examples.

You might want to sort or select from `t_appsec_errors` table based on different columns, but unless there is a frequent query that requires this column to be ordered, you will not need an index. Because this table is really only intended for troubleshooting after an error, we don't expect to have other indexes—we will always select the most recent records (based on `update_ts`).

We will create a view of the table that we are prepared to grant select on; however, we don't have anyone in mind at present who may need to view it. Perhaps down the road we will have a savvy app developer who wants to help debug his application's use of the **appsec** packages. We may arrange for her to select from our view. Execute the following:

```
CREATE OR REPLACE VIEW appsec.v_appsec_errors AS SELECT * FROM appsec.t_appsec_errors;
```

Creating a Table for Managing Our Error Log Table

Remember, we only gave our application security, **appsec**, user two megabytes of space in the USERS tablespace. It would be inconsiderate, if not negligent, to create a table, especially a log table, without any provision for regular cleaning and maintenance.

Now to let you in on a secret: we are building a robot. Not a mechanical contraption to fetch our coffee, but a software sentinel to help us manage the error log table, especially when we are not looking. We are going to do automatically remove old records from our table with a trigger that runs whenever we insert a record into our table.

The tricky thing is, there is some effort involved in managing our table, so we want to minimize how frequently the management tasks occur. In fact, we only want to manage our error log table once a day. We also won't mind knowing when the table was last managed. The best way to accomplish both those goals is to create another table to store the date whenever our error log table is managed. Execute the code in Listing 7-3 to create the error log maintenance table.

Listing 7-3. Creating the Application Security Error Log Table and Index, t_appsec_errors_maint

```
CREATE TABLE appsec.t_appsec_errors_maint (
    update_ts DATE DEFAULT SYSDATE
);
CREATE UNIQUE INDEX i_appsec_errors_maint00 ON appsec.t_appsec_errors_maint (
        update_ts );
```

Once again, selecting by date is important for performance, so we will create an index on the UPDATE_TS column, the only column.

This time, we made it a UNIQUE index, meaning that we will only have one entry with a specific timestamp. On our error log table, the index was not UNIQUE, because we may have multiple errors and entries in the table at the exact same time.

The t_appsec_errors_maint table is for internal use only, so we won't create a view and don't anticipate ever granting privileges on the table.

Creating an Error Log Management Procedure

Our table management task is instigated by a trigger, but before we can define the trigger, we need to define our procedure that accomplishes the management task. Our management procedure will be named p_appsec_errors_janitor, and it has no parameters.

We want it to run independently; therefore, we define it with the modifier PRAGMA AUTONOMOUS_TRANSACTION. This allows the procedure to do inserts and deletes and commit the changes, even if the program that called this transaction does not commit. Without this modifier, if we issue a commit here, we are asking Oracle database to commit every update, insert, or delete we've made in the current session. When we're dealing with an error, we specifically want to avoid committing anything except the insert of an error message in our log and cleanup of old entries. Execute the script in Listing 7-4 to create the procedure.

Listing 7-4. Procedure to Manage to Error Log Table, p_appsec_errors_janitor

```
CREATE OR REPLACE PROCEDURE appsec.p_appsec_errors_janitor
AS
    PRAGMA AUTONOMOUS_TRANSACTION;
    m_err_no NUMBER;
    m_err_txt VARCHAR2(2000);
BEGIN
    INSERT INTO t_appsec_errors_maint ( update_ts ) VALUES ( SYSDATE );
    COMMIT;
    -- Remove error log entries over 45 days old
    DELETE FROM t_appsec_errors WHERE update_ts < ( SYSDATE - 45 );
    COMMIT;
    INSERT INTO t_appsec_errors
        ( err_no, err_txt, msg_txt ) VALUES
        ( 0, 'No Error', 'Success managing log file by Janitor' );
    COMMIT;
EXCEPTION
    WHEN OTHERS
    THEN
        m_err_no := SQLCODE;
        m_err_txt := SQLERRM;
        INSERT INTO t_appsec_errors
            ( err_no, err_txt, msg_txt ) VALUES
            ( m_err_no, m_err_txt, 'Error managing log file by Janitor' );
        COMMIT;
END;
/
```

Our first step (after the BEGIN header) is to insert the current date in our management table. That will prevent others from also trying to manage the error log table. We commit it, which is only allowed here because we are an autonomous transaction.

The second step is to delete records in the error log that are over 45 days old. Notice that we do some date arithmetic involving SYSDATE, in this case SYSDATE - 45, which is equivalent to 45 days ago. We will use similar date arithmetic in our trigger. We also commit this deletion.

The last thing under the BEGIN header is to insert a "Success" message in the error log, and commit it. Why not? That seems like a good place.

As in our other procedures we've seen so far, we are going to catch errors. In this case, we will insert the error into our error log table (once again, why not? It'll be nice to have all our troubleshooting messages in one place.) And commit it.

Creating a Trigger to Maintain the Error Log Table

The maintenance procedure we defined above will work every time you call it, and however you call it. You could hire someone to manually run that procedure once a day. Oracle database has a scheduler (the DBMS_SCHEDULER PL/SQL package or the older DBMS_JOB PL/SQL package) that you could alternatively use to run it once a day.

Instead, we are going to make the table self-governing by adding a trigger. A trigger has a lot of similarities to a procedure, so it is consistent with the syntax we've been discussing. Execute the code in Listing 7-5 to create and enable a trigger on the t_appsec_errors table that will run after each row (log entry) is inserted in the table.

Listing 7-5. Insert Trigger on Error Log Table, t_appsec_errors_iar

```
CREATE OR REPLACE TRIGGER appsec.t_appsec_errors_iar
    AFTER INSERT ON t_appsec_errors FOR EACH ROW
DECLARE
    m_log_maint_dt DATE;
BEGIN
    SELECT MAX( update_ts ) INTO m_log_maint_dt FROM t_appsec_errors_maint;
    -- Whenever T_APPSEC_ERRORS_MAINT is empty, M_LOG_MAINT_DT is null
    IF( ( m_log_maint_dt IS NULL ) OR
        ( m_log_maint_dt < ( SYSDATE - 1 ) ) )
    THEN
        p_appsec_errors_janitor;
    END IF;
END;
/
ALTER TRIGGER appsec.t_appsec_errors_iar ENABLE;
```

This trigger runs after each insert, AFTER INSERT; however, we only want our procedure to run once a day. To accomplish this, we get the MAX(update_ts) of the last time our procedure was run from the t_appsec_errors_maint table, and store that date in m_log_maint_dt. (Note this example of SELECT INTO syntax—selecting a value into a variable.) Then we check to see if m_log_maint_dt is NULL (whenever t_appsec_errors_maint table is empty) or m_log_maint_dt is earlier than 24 hours ago (< SYSDATE - 1). If it is, then we run our procedure, p_appsec_errors_janitor.

Testing the Trigger

While you are connected to Oracle database as `appsec` user, you can test the trigger. First execute the following lines to insert an error log entry and commit it:

```
INSERT INTO appsec.v_appsec_errors (err_no, err_txt ) VALUES (1, 'DAVE' );
COMMIT;
```

Note that our autonomous procedure can only deal with data that exists independently. Our inserts and updates do not exist in the database independently until we `COMMIT` the data.

Note also that we are depending on the default values for `msg_txt` and `update_ts`—those columns are not part of our insert statement.

Query each of our tables, the error logs and the maintenance record, and observe that our previous insert succeeded and that the Janitor procedure ran. Here's an example:

```
SELECT * FROM appsec.v_appsec_errors ORDER BY update_ts;
SELECT * FROM appsec.t_appsec_errors_maint ORDER BY update_ts;
```

Now insert an error log entry that pretends to be 60 days old (note the arithmetic with `SYSDATE`):

```
INSERT INTO appsec.v_appsec_errors (err_no, err_txt, msg_txt, update_ts)
    VALUES (2, 'DAVE', 'NONE', SYSDATE - 60 );
COMMIT;
```

Again query each of our tables to assure that our insert worked and that our janitor procedure did not run again (because it has already run on this day):

```
SELECT * FROM appsec.v_appsec_errors ORDER BY update_ts;
SELECT * FROM appsec.t_appsec_errors_maint ORDER BY update_ts;
```

Now change the data of our last janitor maintenance run date to yesterday (actually, 24 hours ago), and assure that the change was effective (if you have more than one entry in this table, this `UPDATE` won't work. The index on `UPDATE_TS` in this table is a `UNIQUE` index):

```
UPDATE appsec.t_appsec_errors_maint SET update_ts = SYSDATE-1;
COMMIT;
SELECT * FROM appsec.t_appsec_errors_maint ORDER BY update_ts;
```

And submit another record from today (default, `SYSDATE`):

```
INSERT INTO appsec.v_appsec_errors (err_no, err_txt ) VALUES (3, 'DAVE' );
COMMIT;
```

For the last time in these tests, query each of our tables to assure that our insert worked and that our janitor procedure ran a second time, and that the mock-old record (the one with `err_no = 2`) was deleted:

```
SELECT * FROM appsec.v_appsec_errors ORDER BY update_ts;
SELECT * FROM appsec.t_appsec_errors_maint ORDER BY update_ts;
```

Updating the Application Security Package

In Chapter 6, we had two procedures (`p_get_shared_passphrase` and `p_get_des_crypt_test_data`) and one function (`f_show_algorithm`) that we described as being "temporary". They were used for testing only in Chapter 6, and we will remove them from `app_sec_pkg` in this chapter. The remainder of the functions in **app_sec_pkg** will remain and have not been changed. Look at the file, *Chapter7/AppSec.sql* to see the full listing. We have one new procedure that we introduce in this chapter: **p_log_error**.

Creating an Error Logging Procedure

The **p_log_error** procedure takes a **NUMBER** and one or two **VARCHAR2** (text) parameters. The **err_txt** field is limited to 2,000 characters, but a **VARCHAR2** column may have up to 4000 characters; so we truncate the **m_err_txt** parameter to 2,000 characters, if needed, to fit our **err_txt** column.

Note that this procedure (the package), and the table being updated are in the **appsec** schema, but the one calling this procedure may be an application in another schema (like **HR**). We have already granted execute on **app_sec_pkg** package to the **HR** user, and we need to grant execute to any other application user who needs our Application Security processes.

If you will, think back to when we defined the **t_appsec_errors** table. Recall that we set the **msg_txt** and **update_ts** columns to be nullable, and to have default values (**NULL** and **SYSDATE**). That allowed us to do data inserts by just providing data elements for the first two columns. We could insert data without even mentioning the last two columns. In fact, we said that we don't want to insert a value for **update_ts**; but rather, allow the Oracle database to assign the current default value of **SYSDATE**.

Well, now we are creating a procedure (shown in Listing 7-6) for various applications to call in order to insert error records into our table, and the procedure accounts for those default values. First of all, the procedure doesn't accept a value for **update_ts**; rather, the default **SYSDATE** will be used. Second, the value for **msg_txt** has a default value of **NULL** so that application users can call this procedure with or without a value for **msg_txt**.

Listing 7-6. Procedure to Insert Log Entries, p_log_error

```
PROCEDURE p_log_error( m_err_no NUMBER, m_err_txt VARCHAR2,
    m_msg_txt VARCHAR2 DEFAULT NULL )
IS
    l_err_txt VARCHAR2(2000);
BEGIN
    l_err_txt := RTRIM( SUBSTR( m_err_txt, 1, 2000 ) );
    INSERT INTO v_appsec_errors ( err_no, err_txt, msg_txt )
        VALUES ( m_err_no, l_err_txt, m_msg_txt );
    COMMIT;
END p_log_error;
```

We use the **substring** function, **SUBSTR**, to get only the first 2,000 characters of the error text. Then we use the right trim function, **RTRIM** to remove any spaces at the right end of the remaining text. If **m_err_txt** is NULL, SUBSTR returns a NULL, and RTRIM returns a NULL.

At the end of the **p_log_error** procedure, we simply insert the error data into our error log table and **COMMIT**.

Executing Package Specification and Body

Execute the two blocks in the file named *Chapter7/AppSec.sql* to replace the **app_sec_pkg** package specification and body. You can see that both those blocks begin with the command **CREATE OR REPLACE**. Because we already have a package named **app_sec_pkg**, this command will replace it. The absolute best thing about this command is that we can execute it on a running Oracle database, and the applications that use the package will not fail. That is, if the package specification does not need to change. Consider another option: if we had to **DROP** and then separately **CREATE** these structures, we would have to wait until the Oracle database was off-line, or at least until the dependent applications were not running; otherwise, applications would fail during the interim between the DROP and the CREATE.

Methods for Using and Testing Encryption in Transit

Our working model will not be tested from the main() method of OracleJavaSecure; rather, we are going to demonstrate how we come in as a separate application and use the structures of our Application Security package, app_sec_pkg. We are going to add two more methods to the OracleJavaSecure class: one just for testing, resetKeys(); and another to prepare the client to encrypt data for updates / inserts to Oracle database, makeDESKey().

We want the ability to do data updates from our client application with a minimum of effort. The least effort requires these steps:

1. Generate RSA keys on client and pass public key to Oracle.

2. Generate DES secret password key on Oracle database,
   encrypt the artifacts with RSA public key, and pass back to the client.

3. Build a copy of the DES key on the client.

4. Encrypt data with DES key and send to Oracle database for decrypt and
   update.

We have already demonstrated an Oracle procedure, p_get_shared_passphrase, which allowed us to combine steps 1 and 2 into a single step. However, step 4 requires a second Oracle statement. Therefore, we are going to have to make at least two calls to Oracle database to do the first update. Within the same Oracle session, we can do additional updates, each in a single call. We only need to do the combined steps 1, 2 and 3 once (key exchange); and then after the keys have been established, we can do as many updates and inserts as we'd like using existing keys.

Method to Build the Secret Password Key

In Chapter 6, we used the p_get_shared_passphrase Oracle procedure to get all the DES secret password key artifacts to the client; however, we didn't build the secret password key until we received encrypted data from Oracle database that we wanted to decrypt on the client.

In this chapter, we are going to need the DES secret key even without data to decrypt. We are going to do data encryption on the client and send it to Oracle database as an independent task. So, we need a Java method that independently builds the secret password key. Listing 7-7 shows the code for that method.

Listing 7-7. Method to Call to Build Secret Password Key, makeDESKey( )

```
public static final void makeDESKey(
    RAW cryptSecretDESPassPhrase, RAW cryptSecretDESAlgorithm,
    RAW cryptSecretDESSalt, RAW cryptSecretDESIterationCount )
{
    try {
        decryptSessionSecretDESPassPhrase( cryptSecretDESPassPhrase,
            cryptSecretDESAlgorithm, cryptSecretDESSalt,
            cryptSecretDESIterationCount );
        makeSessionSecretDESKey();
    } catch( Exception x ) {
        x.printStackTrace();
    }
}
```

Within the **try** block is most of the body of our previous **getDecryptData()** method, sans the call to actually decrypt data. This provides us an opportunity to do some refactoring, improving the design of our code. Because our new method does most of what we did in **getDecryptData()**, let's rewrite **getDecryptData()** to call the new method, as in Listing 7-8.

Listing 7-8. Decrypt Data with the Secret Password Key, getDecryptData( )

```
public static final String getDecryptData( RAW cryptData,
    RAW cryptSecretDESPassPhrase, RAW cryptSecretDESAlgorithm,
    RAW cryptSecretDESSalt, RAW cryptSecretDESIterationCount )
{
    String rtrnString = "getDecryptData() A failed";
    try {
        if( ( null == sessionSecretDESKey ) || testAsClientAndServer ) {
            makeDESKey( cryptSecretDESPassPhrase, cryptSecretDESAlgorithm,
                cryptSecretDESSalt, cryptSecretDESIterationCount );
        }
        rtrnString = getDecryptData( cryptData );
    } catch( Exception x ) {
        x.printStackTrace();
    }
    return rtrnString;
}
```

The bold text, our call to **makeDESKey()**, is where we previously had the code that we have moved into the body of **makeDESKey()**.

Temporary Method to Reset All Keys

The second method we are adding to **OracleJavaSecure** is **resetKeys()**. The **resetKeys()** method is only for testing in this chapter (however, we will resurrect it in Chapter 10). Later we will describe several test scenarios, one of which will emulate starting a new connection/session on the client (by running this method) and trying to use existing keys on Oracle database. This scenario will fail, but we will do the test just to demonstrate that scenario.

In `resetKeys()`, Listing 7-9, we set back to `null` those static members that we set to `null` initially. Recall that they were `null` in order to facilitate testing those variables for `null` and/or for testing comparison to other members. We needed to set them to `null` initially in order to compile past the "may not have been initialized" error message.

We also reset the value of `sessionSecretDESAlgorithm` to its pre-negotiated value.

Listing 7-9. Reset all Keys, `resetKeys()`

```
public static final void resetKeys() {
    locRSAPubMod = null;
    saveExtRSAPubMod = null;
    extRSAPubKey = null;
    sessionSecretDESPassPhraseChars = null;
    sessionSecretDESKey = null;
    sessionSecretDESAlgorithm = "PBEWithSHA1AndDESede";
}
```

Loading Updated OracleJavaSecure Class into Oracle

Connect or remain connected to Oracle database as application security, `appsec`, user with the non-default role, `appsec_role` and copy/paste the code from the file *Chapter7\orajavsec\OracleJavaSecure.java* into your Oracle client. Uncomment the first line then run the script to replace our Java class in Oracle database.

```
CREATE OR REPLACE AND RESOLVE JAVA SOURCE NAMED appsec."orajavsec/OracleJavaSecure" AS
```

Security Structures for the HR User

Our working model of application encryption will consist of reading data from the `HR` schema, with sensitive columns being encrypted as they are transmitted across the network. Part of the responsibility falls to the *application* developers who must assure that sensitive data is only available to the client in encrypted form. Our application security schema, `appsec`, can provide the tools, but our application developers, like `HR`, will need to implement them.

Let's explore what `HR` does to encrypt his data first. Then we'll look at what the Application Security manager can provide to all application developers as a template for implementing this.

Exploring Privileges That Enable HR Tasks

`HR`, as provided by Oracle, is a sample schema and already has a variety of system privileges. `HR` has the default role, `RESOURCE`, and via that role, has this list of privileges:

```
CREATE SEQUENCE,
CREATE TRIGGER,
CREATE CLUSTER,
CREATE PROCEDURE,
CREATE TYPE,
CREATE OPERATOR,
CREATE TABLE,
CREATE INDEXTYPE
```

All application schemas that intend to implement our application security will need the CREATE PROCEDURE system privilege.

Recall that to have access to the application security structures, we also need to grant each application schema the object privilege to execute the **app_sec_pkg** package, like we did (already as secadm) for HR:

```
GRANT EXECUTE ON appsec.app_sec_pkg TO hr;
```

Creating the HR Security Package

HR will have a package of his own procedures and functions that provide access to HR tables, but return any sensitive columns in encrypted form only. Let's examine the package and then create it at the end.

■ **Note** You can find a script of the following commands in the file named *Chapter7/HR.sql*.

```
CREATE OR REPLACE PACKAGE hr.hr_sec_pkg IS
    TYPE RESULTSET_TYPE IS REF CURSOR;
```

Within the Specification of our package, we will define a TYPE. We will name it RESULTSET_TYPE, and it will represent a CURSOR, also known as a ResultSet in Java. When we call procedures to get our encrypted HR data, we are going to hand back from Oracle database, a number of OUT parameters. Many of the OUT parameters will be artifacts of our secret password key, as we have seen, and one might also be a RESULTSET_TYPE, which will hold *multiple rows of encrypted data.*

Selecting Sensitive Data Columns from EMPLOYEES

The code in Listing 7-10 is the body of an Oracle procedure named **p_select_employees_sensitive**. You should be very familiar with this format. The list of parameters and the code used to set the secret password key artifacts look like what we've seen before. We do have an OUT parameter named resultset_out that will hold a RESULTSET_TYPE (rows of data):

Listing 7-10. Procedure to Select Sensitive Data from Employees Table, p_select_employees_sensitive

```
PROCEDURE p_select_employees_sensitive(
    ext_modulus              VARCHAR2,
    ext_exponent             VARCHAR2,
    secret_pass_salt      OUT RAW,
    secret_pass_count     OUT RAW,
    secret_pass_algorithm OUT RAW,
    secret_pass           OUT RAW,
    resultset_out         OUT RESULTSET_TYPE,
    m_err_no              OUT NUMBER,
    m_err_txt             OUT VARCHAR2 )
IS BEGIN
    m_err_no := 0;
    secret_pass_salt :=
        appsec.app_sec_pkg.f_get_crypt_secret_salt( ext_modulus, ext_exponent );
```

```
        secret_pass_count :=
            appsec.app_sec_pkg.f_get_crypt_secret_count( ext_modulus, ext_exponent );
        secret_pass :=
            appsec.app_sec_pkg.f_get_crypt_secret_pass( ext_modulus, ext_exponent );
        secret_pass_algorithm :=
            appsec.app_sec_pkg.f_get_crypt_secret_algorithm(ext_modulus, ext_exponent);

        OPEN resultset_out FOR SELECT

            employee_id,
            first_name,
            last_name,
            email,
            phone_number,
            hire_date,
            job_id,
            appsec.app_sec_pkg.f_get_crypt_data( TO_CHAR( salary ) ),
            appsec.app_sec_pkg.f_get_crypt_data( TO_CHAR( commission_pct ) ),
            manager_id,
            department_id
        FROM employees;
EXCEPTION
    WHEN OTHERS THEN
        m_err_no := SQLCODE;
        m_err_txt := SQLERRM;
        appsec.app_sec_pkg.p_log_error( m_err_no, m_err_txt,
            'HR p_select_employees_sensitive' );
END p_select_employees_sensitive;
```

Filling the RESULTSET_TYPE

In the middle of the p_select_employees_sensitive procedure, we open the RESULTSET_TYPE to gather a CURSOR from a query. Note that we don't actually transmit all the data when we return to the client; rather, we provide the client with a handle for the CURSOR so that the client can gather and process rows of data, one at a time.

The query we are using selects all the columns from the EMPLOYEES table. Notice in Listing 7-10 that we encrypt the SALARY and COMMISSION_PCT with these calls:

```
appsec.app_sec_pkg.f_get_crypt_data( TO_CHAR( salary ) ),
appsec.app_sec_pkg.f_get_crypt_data( TO_CHAR( commission_pct ) ),
```

Our encryption methods require that we pass the data in for encryption using a String. Both SALARY and COMMISSION_PCT are number columns, so we first convert them to VARCHAR2 and then pass them to our Application Security Java Stored Procedure (function), appsec.app_sec_pkg.f_get_crypt_data.

That function returns a RAW type that holds the encrypted data. The client will decrypt the data back to a clear-text String. And we will convert the data back to its original type (Date, number, etc.), as needed at the client.

You're probably asking, "But can't we encrypt non-String data?" The answer is yes. Actually, we can encrypt anything that can be represented as a byte array, which is really anything, after some conversion. However, if you can see the data on a screen or print it out, then you can also represent the data as a String, and it's often clearer when we convert to / from Strings and often the case that we eventually want a String anyway.

▪ **Note** At the end of this chapter, you will have a solid foundation to extend the encryption we have built here. You'll be able to extend what you've learned in order to encrypt objects or BLOBS, or other types of data.

Logging the Error Message

At the end of our procedure, we catch any Oracle exceptions and log the error. We call our new `p_log_error` procedure. We will log the error in the `appsec` schema so our application security manager can catch errors in the `appsec` structures, and can assist in debugging problems in individual applications using those structures. We will not strand the application developer but will provide assistance in the debugging effort.

Selecting All Data as a Single Sensitive String

HR has implemented another method that encrypts all the selected data, not as individual columns, but as one long, concatenated VARCHAR2 per row. The only difference between this procedure, `p_select_employees_secret` shown in Listing 7-11, and the last one we looked at is the definition of the RESULTSET_OUT.

Listing 7-11. Portion of Procedure to Encrypt All Data as Single String, p_select_employees_secret

```
OPEN resultset_out FOR SELECT

    appsec.app_sec_pkg.f_get_crypt_data(
        TO_CHAR( employee_id ) ||', '||
        first_name ||', '||
        last_name ||', '||
        email ||', '||
        phone_number ||', '||
        TO_CHAR( hire_date ) ||', '||
        job_id ||', '||
        TO_CHAR( salary ) ||', '||
        TO_CHAR( commission_pct ) ||', '||
        TO_CHAR( manager_id ) ||', '||
        TO_CHAR( department_id )
    )
FROM employees;
```

The double-pipe characters "||" are the symbol used in Oracle database to concatenate text. Notice that we call the TO_CHAR function for columns that are not already of type VARCHAR2. After we've concatenated all of these columns together, we pass the resulting VARCHAR2 to the f_get_crypt_data function for encryption and we return a single RAW per row in RESULTSET_OUT.

Note that at the client we may have to parse the data, once we decrypt it, to get the individual columns. We have used a comma as a separator between columns, but parsing on commas presumes that no commas exist in our data. Each application will have to plan their use of our Application Security structures, and the best approach to provide their data in a form appropriate for use by their client. This concatenated format would probably be better for a client that doesn't need individual elements of a record.

Selecting Sensitive Data for an Employee ID

We will explore one more example of procedures to select encrypted data from HR. This Oracle procedure, `p_select_employee_by_id_sens`, is almost identical to the previous two procedures, except that it also takes a parameter representing a single `EMPLOYEE_ID`. That is shown in Listing 7-12.

Listing 7-12. Portion of Procedure to Select Sensitive Data by ID, p_select_employee_by_id_sens

```
m_employee_id      employees.employee_id%TYPE
...
OPEN resultset_out FOR SELECT
    employee_id,
    ...
FROM employees
WHERE employee_id = m_employee_id;
```

The query for the `resultset_out` parameter selects data where the `EMPLOYEE_ID` equals that input parameter.

This procedure should only return one row of data.

Revising Procedure to Get Shared Passphrase

We saw the `p_get_shared_passphrase` procedure in Chapter 6. We are embellishing it a bit in this chapter with error logging. Error logging can assist application security in supporting the application developer.

The biggest change is that we are pulling `p_get_shared_passphrase` from the `app_sec_pkg` package into our individual application package, `hr_sec_pkg`. We have it in `hr_sec_pkg` now so that our client application, which may be running with `hr_view` role, can execute the procedure. We allow HR to execute the `app_sec_pkg` structures, but we don't allow `hr_view` to do so. So, `hr_view` executes HR structures and HR structures execute `appsec` structures.

We call `p_get_shared_passphrase` and follow up with a call to our new `OracleJavaSecure.makeDESKey()` method to complete a key exchange and build the shared secret password key. We must do this before attempting data updates.

Updating Sensitive Data Columns in EMPLOYEES

We are at the point now where we can implement encrypted updates to our data. We will define a procedure `p_update_employees_sensitive` shown in Listing 7-13, in the package `hr_sec_pkg` to take data for all the columns of the `EMPLOYEES` table. For the sensitive columns, we will be submitting `RAW` types that encapsulate the encrypted data. The only `IN` parameters are the table column data, and the only `OUT` parameters are the error number and text. Notice what is missing here—there are no parameters representing our encryption keys. We have to assume that key exchanges have already taken place. If we have not already exchanged keys in the current Oracle session, then the user application is trying to submit unencrypted data in the fields that require encryption, or they are encrypting the data with keys from a different session; and the Oracle database will not be able to decrypt the data.

We are defining our parameter types using an anchored datatype form that refers to the definition of the original data. We anchor this datatype declaration to a previous definition. For example, in this declaration:

```
m_employee_id          employees.employee_id%TYPE,
```

We are saying that the `m_employee_id` parameter is of the same type as the `EMPLOYEE_ID` column in the `EMPLOYEES` table. We will use this form of "type specification by reference" whenever appropriate to further establish the relation between the data we are receiving and the table it is destined for. This practice is helpful for at least two reasons. The first is that our procedure will only accept data that is appropriate for the field into which it will be inserted or updated. This is a further protection against a SQL injection attack (see a detailed discussion in the next section). The second reason anchoring datatypes is good is that we can change the definition of that column in the table without having to also change this procedure.

Listing 7-13. Update Sensitive Data in the Employees Table, p_update_employees_sensitive

```
PROCEDURE p_update_employees_sensitive(
    m_employee_id       employees.employee_id%TYPE,
    m_first_name        employees.first_name%TYPE,
    m_last_name         employees.last_name%TYPE,
    m_email             employees.email%TYPE,
    m_phone_number      employees.phone_number%TYPE,
    m_hire_date         employees.hire_date%TYPE,
    m_job_id            employees.job_id%TYPE,
    crypt_salary        RAW,
    crypt_commission_pct RAW,
    m_manager_id        employees.manager_id%TYPE,
    m_department_id     employees.department_id%TYPE,
    m_err_no        OUT NUMBER,
    m_err_txt       OUT VARCHAR2 )
IS
    test_emp_ct     NUMBER(6);
    v_salary        VARCHAR2(15); -- Plenty of space, eventually a NUMBER
    v_commission_pct VARCHAR2(15);
BEGIN
    m_err_no := 0;
    v_salary := appsec.app_sec_pkg.f_get_decrypt_data( crypt_salary );
    v_commission_pct :=
        appsec.app_sec_pkg.f_get_decrypt_data( crypt_commission_pct );
    SELECT COUNT(*) INTO test_emp_ct FROM employees WHERE
        employee_id = m_employee_id;
    IF test_emp_ct = 0
    THEN
        INSERT INTO employees
            (employees_seq.NEXTVAL, first_name, last_name, email, phone_number,
            hire_date, job_id, salary, commission_pct, manager_id, department_id)
        VALUES
            (m_employee_id, m_first_name, m_last_name, m_email, m_phone_number,
            m_hire_date, m_job_id, v_salary, v_commission_pct, m_manager_id,
            m_department_id);
    ELSE
        -- Comment update of certain values during testing - date constraint
        UPDATE employees
        SET first_name = m_first_name, last_name = m_last_name, email = m_email,
            phone_number = m_phone_number,
            -- Job History Constraint -- hire_date = m_hire_date, job_id = m_job_id,
```

```
                salary = v_salary, commission_pct = v_commission_pct,
                manager_id = m_manager_id
                -- Job History Constraint -- , department_id = m_department_id
            WHERE employee_id = m_employee_id;
        END IF;
    EXCEPTION
        WHEN OTHERS THEN
            m_err_no := SQLCODE;
            m_err_txt := SQLERRM;
            appsec.app_sec_pkg.p_log_error( m_err_no, m_err_txt,
                'HR p_update_employees_sensitive' );
    END p_update_employees_sensitive;

END hr_sec_pkg;
/
```

Procedure Variables and Data Decryption

We cannot modify the IN parameters like we did with OUT parameters in previous example procedures, but we want to capture the output of our decryption, so we establish a couple procedure variables: v_salary and v_commission_pct. We also define a numeric procedure variable named test_emp_ct:

```
test_emp_ct       NUMBER(6);
v_salary          VARCHAR2(15); -- Plenty of space, eventually a NUMBER
v_commission_pct  VARCHAR2(15);
```

Our procedure body, under the BEGIN header, includes two calls to the f_get_decrypt_data Oracle function which will return a VARCHAR2 data type representing the SALARY and the COMMISSION_PCT. Note again that use of this procedure assumes that you have already done key exchange:

```
m_err_no := 0;
v_salary := appsec.app_sec_pkg.f_get_decrypt_data( crypt_salary );
v_commission_pct :=
    appsec.app_sec_pkg.f_get_decrypt_data( crypt_commission_pct );
```

Inserting or Updating

I have found that a multifunction procedure is often the best choice for managing data inserts and updates. At most, we grant SELECT privilege to a view of the data and EXECUTE privilege to the management procedure. We regularly pass a transaction code (usually A, U, or D) that indicates whether we are going to be inserting (adding), updating, or deleting a record. For a simple, bi-functional procedure (insert or update), we do not need a transaction code, but can examine the data and 1) update an existing record or 2) insert a new record if no existing record matches the key columns.

In our management procedure body, we will populate test_emp_ct by using SELECT INTO syntax with a count of the number of employees whose EMPLOYEE_ID matches the m_employee_id that is being passed in for update. There should never be more than one, so we expect a value of 0 or 1 from the count.

```
SELECT COUNT(*) INTO test_emp_ct FROM employees WHERE
    employee_id = m_employee_id;
```

We then test to see if test_emp_ct is 0 – if so, we do an INSERT; if not, an UPDATE:

```
IF test_emp_ct = 0
THEN
    INSERT INTO employees
        ...
ELSE
    UPDATE employees
    SET first_name = m_first_name, last_name = m_last_name, email = m_email,
        phone_number = m_phone_number, hire_date = m_hire_date,
        -- Job History Constraint -- job_id = m_job_id,
        salary = v_salary, commission_pct = v_commission_pct,
        manager_id = m_manager_id
        -- Job History Constraint -- , department_id = m_department_id
    WHERE employee_id = m_employee_id;
END IF IF;
```

Integrity Constraint on Employees Table

You will see in the previous code that we skip updating two of the columns: JOB_ID and DEPARTMENT_ID. The reason is that there is an existing trigger on the EMPLOYEES table that inserts a record in JOB_HISTORY when either of those 2 columns in an EMPLOYEES' record is updated. The trigger code is shown in Listing 7-14.

Listing 7-14. An Existing Integrity Constraint on Employees Table, HR.update_job_history

```
CREATE OR REPLACE TRIGGER HR.update_job_history
  AFTER UPDATE OF job_id, department_id ON HR.EMPLOYEES FOR EACH ROW
BEGIN
  add_job_history(:old.employee_id, :old.hire_date, sysdate,
                  :old.job_id, :old.department_id);
END;
```

You can see the trigger in Listing 7-14 calls a procedure, add_job_history. All that procedure does is INSERT a record into the JOB_HISTORY table. However, the JOB_HISTORY table includes a UNIQUE index on (EMPLOYEE_ID, **START_DATE**).

To summarize the problem: if you try to update an EMPLOYEES' JOB_ID, or DEPARTMENT_ID more than once a day, it fails because the trigger cannot insert another record in the JOB_HISTORY table for that same user on the same day. This is a business rule that the developers of the HR sample schema are enforcing through a UNIQUE index—employees can't change jobs more than once a day.

UPDATE TRIGGER SYNTAX

I'd like to point out one aspect of the trigger syntax. Do you see the :old. prefix in Listing 7-14? That prefix indicates that we are using the value that already exists in the table. Because this is an AFTER UPDATE trigger, the value that exists in the table is the same value we submitted in the update. This runs after the data has been updated.

Often triggers can be used to test, filter, and manipulate data being submitted to a table before it is stored. For example, if I am updating the last name of an employee, I might say:

```
update employees set last_name = 'coffin' where employee_id = 700;
```

This may be a problem if we require all our `last_name` entries to be in upper case! We can catch and correct this problem with a `BEFORE UPDATE OR INSERT` trigger. In the middle of our trigger, we might say:

```
:new.last_name := upper(:new.last_name);
```

This will capitalize the new value we are submitting for last_name. If we want to complain that the user is trying to update the last name with the same last name that already exists, we can compare the capitalized new value with the old value, like this:

```
IF :new.last_name = :old.last_name
THEN
    Raise_Application_Error(-20000, 'Same last name as before!');
```

A `BEFORE UPDATE` trigger has access to both the existing value in the database (`:old`) and the new value being submitted (`:new`). That ability is often utilized in triggers.

Avoiding SQL Injection

If a computer user saves the html source of a web page that submits data and is able to modify the web page to send data that is not normally allowed, that would be an example of cross-sight scripting (the user's own web page being one site, submitting data to the web server being another site.) For example, you might have a web page that submits a ZIP code for an address and only allows numeric data. I might maliciously modify the web page so my copy submits a web link (URL) in the ZIP code field. The only real prevention for cross-site scripting is to assume it will always happen and take steps on the server to catch and handle it.

Perhaps your web page submits data to Oracle database, and a malicious user modifies a copy of your web page to submit Oracle SQL or PL/SQL commands in the zip code field. That hacker might put this code in the field, "`11111;delete from employees;--`". If you are building a dynamic query that simply embeds the submitted data in a query, then instead of executing:

```
UPDATE EMPLOYEES SET ZIP=11111 WHERE EMPLOYEE_ID=300;
```

You might execute this set of commands:

```
UPDATE EMPLOYEES SET ZIP=11111;delete from employees;-- WHERE EMPLOYEE_ID=300;
```

That works out to three lines: an update for all employees, deleting all records from employees, and a comment. That is an example of SQL injection.

A typical SQL injection attack modifies a select statement by tacking on an extra where test that is true for all data. For example, if I accept user input of a last name to search employees and the user types "King' or 'a'='a'", my dynamic SQL might look like this:

```
SELECT * FROM EMPLOYEES WHERE LAST_NAME='King' or 'a'='a';
```

If this were a test for password matching a value stored in Oracle database, then the SQL injection might look like this:

```
SELECT count(*) FROM EMPLOYEES WHERE LAST_NAME='King' and
    PASSWORD='whatever' or 'a'='a';
```

The select statement will return a number greater than 0 and the user might get access even though he doesn't know the password.

At the Oracle database, you can prevent SQL injection from happening by several methods. One traditional way is to filter the incoming data and/or escape the data (make it a sequence of individual characters rather than text.) However, a better way is to always use parameterized input. We do that with our stored procedures that take parameters. We are not building dynamic queries but are pumping parameters into PL/SQL that has already been staged in Oracle database. The database *binds* the variables to our query/update framework.

We can also prevent SQL injection from the client with prepared statements in Java like the following. The value of `userInputEmpID` is bound to the query parameter at the question mark (?).

```
String query = "SELECT * FROM EMPLOYEES WHERE EMPLOYEE_ID = ? ";
PreparedStatement pstmt = connection.prepareStatement( query );
pstmt.setString( 1, userInputEmpID );
```

Having a `PreparedStatement` accept our parameter and populate the query with it, keeps malicious code from being tacked onto the query. Once again, the `PreparedStatement` is staged in Oracle database and our parameters are set there, Oracle database binds them to the update/query.

If you need to place code for an Oracle database query in your application (java or other), use a `PreparedStatement`, as seen previously, rather than concatenating user input into a query string.

Demonstrating Failure to SQL Inject in Stored Procedure

I have included two more procedures in the `hr_sec_pkg` that will demonstrate attempts at SQL injection in stored procedures. I don't hail from Missouri, but I am from the "Show-Me State" of mind: trust, but verify. Let's try SQL injection when doing a select query on `LAST_NAME`. In the procedure partially shown in Listing 7-15, `p_select_employee_by_ln_sens`, we will pass in a tenth parameter, the `LAST_NAME` and modify our select in the procedure to use it:

Listing 7-15. Select Employees Data by Last Name and Attempt SQL Injection

```
PROCEDURE p_select_employee_by_ln_sens(
    ...
    m_last_name      employees.last_name%TYPE )
IS BEGIN
    ...
    OPEN resultset_out FOR SELECT
       ...
    FROM employees
    WHERE last_name = m_last_name;
```

Let's also see if we can sneak some SQL injection in by embodying it in a `RAW` (like we do with our encrypted data updates) and by casting the `RAW` to a `VARCHAR2` in the `WHERE` clause. We do that in a test procedure named `p_select_employee_by_raw_sens` in Listing 7-16.

Listing 7-16. Select Employees Data by RAW Value and Attempt SQL Injection

```
PROCEDURE p_select_employee_by_raw_sens(
    ...
    m_last_name      RAW )
IS BEGIN
    ...
    OPEN resultset_out FOR SELECT
       ...
```

```
    FROM employees
    WHERE last_name = UTL_RAW.CAST_TO_VARCHAR2( m_last_name );
```

You will be happy to note that when we test this, these attempts at subterfuge are not successful. In both these cases, as is intended, Oracle database says, "give me something to plug into the test `WHERE LAST_NAME = ?;`".

We will be giving Oracle database this string: "King' or 'a'='a", which one might imagine being wrapped in single quotes to become:

```
WHERE LAST_NAME = 'King' or 'a'='a';
```

However, Oracle database sees our string as a *single data element* and checks to see if anyone's `LAST_NAME` is (in escaped form): "King\' or \'a\'=\'a" or "{King' or 'a'='a}".

Executing the HR Package Specification and Body

Now that we have described the procedures in the `hr_sec_pkg` package, we will go ahead and execute the `CREATE` statements for the package specification and the package body. Execute the two blocks in the file named *Chapter7/HR.sql* to create the `hr_sec_pkg` package specification and body. After you have created `hr_sec_pkg`, you will need to grant execute on the package to the `hrview_role` role

```
GRANT EXECUTE ON hr.hr_sec_pkg TO hrview_role;
```

Inserting an EMPLOYEES Record: Update a Sequence

We need a fixed `EMPLOYEE_ID`, number 300 for a record in the `EMPLOYEES` table in order for our example code to work. When the sample `EMPLOYEES` table is initially installed, there are about 100 records, with `EMPLOYEE_IDs` from 100 to about 200. Generally, inserts into the `EMPLOYEES` table use the next value of the *sequence*, `EMPLOYEES_SEQ` like this (do not execute this yet—this is for reference only):

```
INSERT INTO employees
    (employee_id, first_name, last_name, email, phone_number, hire_date,
    job_id, salary, commission_pct, manager_id, department_id)
VALUES
    (employees_seq.NEXTVAL, 'David', 'Coffin', 'DAVID.COFFIN',
    '800.555.1212', SYSDATE, 'SA_REP', 5000, 0.20, 147, 80);
```

Every time that `SEQUENCE.NEXTVAL` is called, the value is incremented. To see the current (next) value of `EMPLOYEES_SEQ`, execute this command:

```
SELECT last_number FROM user_sequences WHERE sequence_name='EMPLOYEES_SEQ';
```

■ **Note** You can find a script of the commands in this section in the file named *Chapter7/HR.sql*.

There is no sanctioned way to manually set the `LAST_NUMBER` for a sequence. However, we can adjust the increment value to get the desired effect. First, assure that the current `LAST_NUMBER` returned in the command above is less than 300 (our example `EMPLOYEE_ID`.) If it's not, you may have to substitute a number larger than the `LAST_NUMBER` in our example code or update the data at `EMPLOYEE_ID` 300.

To get set up to insert our example EMPLOYEES record at EMPLOYEE_ID = 300, we need to get the LAST_NUMBER of EMPLOYEES_SEQ to be equal to 300 We are going to do that with an anonymous (unnamed) PL/SQL block. This doesn't get saved to a named stored procedure but gets executed once to accomplish our plan.

■ **Note** We use LAST_NUMBER from the user_sequences view instead of the current value, CURRVAL of the sequence. We do this because we may not have a CURRVAL in this session. CURRVAL only exists after we have executed NEXTVAL on the sequence in this session. Then we can get the current value of the sequence.

See Listing 7-17. We have a NUMBER, offset into which we select the value (300 – LAST_NUMBER) from our sequence. If our LAST_NUMBER is currently 207 for example, the value of offset will be 300 – 207 or 93. We concatenate a command string, alter_command to ALTER the sequence to set the INCREMENT BY value to that offset. We pass that ALTER command to EXECUTE IMMEDIATE. Then the next time we call EMPLOYEES_SEQ.NEXTVAL, we will get the value of 207 + 93 = 300. To finish this plan, we set the INCREMENT BY value for the sequence back to 1.

Execute all of the commands in Listing 7-17 at this time. You will create our test user as employee_id = 300. Feel free to insert your own personal data in the INSERT command at the end.

Listing 7-17. Anonymous PL/SQL Block to Reset Sequence

```
DECLARE
    offset NUMBER;
    alter_command VARCHAR2(100);
    new_last_number NUMBER;
BEGIN
    SELECT (300 - last_number) INTO offset FROM user_sequences
        WHERE sequence_name='EMPLOYEES_SEQ';

    alter_command := 'ALTER SEQUENCE employees_seq INCREMENT BY ' ||
        TO_CHAR(offset) || ' MINVALUE 0';
    EXECUTE IMMEDIATE alter_command;

    SELECT employees_seq.NEXTVAL INTO new_last_number FROM DUAL;
    DBMS_OUTPUT.PUT_LINE( new_last_number );

    EXECUTE IMMEDIATE 'ALTER SEQUENCE employees_seq INCREMENT BY 1';
END;
/

SELECT last_number FROM user_sequences WHERE sequence_name='EMPLOYEES_SEQ';

INSERT INTO employees
    (employee_id, first_name, last_name, email, phone_number, hire_date,
    job_id, salary, commission_pct, manager_id, department_id)
VALUES
    (employees_seq.NEXTVAL, 'David', 'Coffin', 'DAVID.COFFIN',
```

```
'800.555.1212', SYSDATE, 'SA_REP', 5000, 0.20, 147, 80);
```

```
COMMIT;
```

A brute-force way to increment a sequence without inserting records is to SELECT SEQUENCE.NEXTVAL a sufficient number of times. You can also set the INCREMENT BY value to a negative number to reduce the value of LAST_NUMBER in a sequence.

We can see the new LAST_NUMBER setting in EMPLOYEES_SEQ by selecting it again. Assure that it is 300, and then insert our example record for EMPLOYEE_ID = 300. Finally COMMIT the updates. See our new entry by selecting:

```
SELECT * FROM employees WHERE employee_id=300;
```

I should mention that there is an existing INSERT/UPDATE/DELETE trigger on the EMPLOYEES table named SECURE_DML. This trigger limits changing the EMPLOYEES data to weekdays from 8 AM to 6 PM. It is similar to the restrictions we enforced in Chapter 2. However, by default this trigger is disabled.

Demonstrations and Tests of Encrypted Data Exchange

We are going to execute a separate Java class, TestOracleJavaSecure to emulate a client application of the HR schema. Our client application will call the stored procedures that we defined within the hr_sec_pkg, doing several queries and a few updates.

We will only explore several small and large snippets of the application code. You should have the TestOracleJavaSecure.java file open to refer to while we go through this section.

■ **Note** You can find this code in the file *Chapter7/TestOracleJavaSecure.java*.

Some Preliminary Steps

Before we get into the big individual demonstrations and tests, we want to get our bearings. The next few subsections set us up for the demonstrations and tests that follow.

The main() Method and Method Members

The entire code of the TestOracleJavaSecure class resides within the main() method. So, we simply run the code from top to bottom when we call Java with this class from the command line.

The first thing we do in the main() method is establish an Oracle connection, shown in Listing 7-18. Edit the connection string to use the password you assigned to the Application User, appusr, and with your specific server name and port.

Listing 7-18. Beginning of Code to Test Encryption in Transit, TestOracleJavaSecure Class

```
public class TestOracleJavaSecure {
    public static void main( String[] args ) {
        Connection conn = null;
        try {
```

```
private static String appusrConnString =
    "jdbc:oracle:thin:AppUsr/password@localhost:1521:Orcl";
Class.forName( "oracle.jdbc.driver.OracleDriver" );
conn = DriverManager.getConnection( appusrConnString );
```

Getting Ready for Encryption

We do not need the Connection in OracleJavaSecure because we won't be calling Oracle database directly from that class. The only function of OracleJavaSecure on the client (in this chapter) is to build keys and encrypt/decrypt data. See Listing 7-19.

Listing 7-19. Get Ready for Encryption

```
//OracleJavaSecure.setConnection( conn );
String locModulus = OracleJavaSecure.getLocRSAPubMod();
String locExponent = OracleJavaSecure.getLocRSAPubExp();
```

We get our RSA key pair, and get the public key exponent and modulus to pass to Oracle database.

Setting Non-Default Role

The appusr user has the privilege to execute the appsec.p_check_hrview_access procedure (refer back to Chapter 2), which will set the Secure Application Role, hrview_role. We execute the procedure as shown in Listing 7-20.

Listing 7-20. Set Non-Default Role

```
stmt = ( OracleCallableStatement )conn.prepareCall(
    "CALL appsec.p_check_hrview_access()" );
// Comment next line to see Exception when non-default role not set
stmt.executeUpdate();
```

We need to execute the statement in order to acquire the role. If you want to assure yourself that access without the role will fail, comment the line to executeUpdate() and run TestOracleJavaSecure. Be sure to uncomment that line after you run that test, so you can run our primary tests.

Reusing a Callable Statement

Inasmuch as an OracleCallableStatement is an interface that implements Statement, we can use it like a regular Statement. A regular Statement can be used over and over again to execute queries and updates. In my experience, though, if you have OUT parameters from a procedure called from your OracleCallableStatement, then you should not reuse it—just get a new OracleCallableStatement.

That first call to set our role in Listing 7-20, leaves us with an OracleCallableStatement that we can reuse for getting a count of the rows in our non-sensitive view of EMPLOYEES. We will count the rows two ways, both shown in Listing 7-21: once by iterating through the ResultSet of all the rows, incrementing our count, cnt as we go; and once by selecting the count(*) of all rows. Selecting count(*) is a much more efficient way:

Listing 7-21. Get a Count of Rows in the Public View of Employees

```
rset = stmt.executeQuery(
    "SELECT * FROM hr.v_employees_public" );
int cnt = 0;
while( rset.next() ) cnt++;
System.out.println( "Count data in V_EMPLOYEES_PUBLIC: " + cnt );

rset = stmt.executeQuery(
    "SELECT COUNT(*) FROM hr.v_employees_public" );
if( rset.next() ) cnt = rset.getInt(1);
System.out.println( "Count data in V_EMPLOYEES_PUBLIC: " + cnt );

if( null != stmt ) stmt.close();
```

Selecting Encrypted Data from EMPLOYEES

Here is our textbook process for selecting encrypted data from Oracle database, Listing 7-22. It resembles the test procedures we used in the last chapter. We pass the public key modulus and exponent to Oracle database and receive back the encrypted artifacts of our DES secret password key. In addition, we have an OUT parameter that is of type OracleTypes.CURSOR. We will draw on the OracleTypes.CURSOR (ResultSet in Java) to read our data.

Listing 7-22. Java Code to Select Sensitive Data from Employees, from p_select_employees_sensitive

```
stmt = ( OracleCallableStatement )conn.prepareCall(
    "CALL hr.hr_sec_pkg.p_select_employees_sensitive(?,?,?,?,?,?,?,?,?)" );
stmt.registerOutParameter( 3, OracleTypes.RAW );
stmt.registerOutParameter( 4, OracleTypes.RAW );
stmt.registerOutParameter( 5, OracleTypes.RAW );
stmt.registerOutParameter( 6, OracleTypes.RAW );
stmt.registerOutParameter( 7, OracleTypes.CURSOR );
stmt.registerOutParameter( 8, OracleTypes.NUMBER );
stmt.registerOutParameter( 9, OracleTypes.VARCHAR );
stmt.setString( 1, locModulus );
stmt.setString( 2, locExponent );
stmt.setNull(    3, OracleTypes.RAW );
stmt.setNull(    4, OracleTypes.RAW );
stmt.setNull(    5, OracleTypes.RAW );
stmt.setNull(    6, OracleTypes.RAW );
// This must go without saying - unsupported type for setNull
//stmt.setNull( 7, OracleTypes.CURSOR );
stmt.setInt(     8, 0 );
stmt.setNull(    9, OracleTypes.VARCHAR );
stmt.executeUpdate();

errNo = stmt.getInt( 8 );
if( errNo != 0 ) {
    errMsg = stmt.getString( 9 );
    System.out.println( "Oracle error 1) " + errNo +
```

```java
            ", " + errMsg );
        } else {
            System.out.println( "Oracle success 1)" );
            sessionSecretDESSalt = stmt.getRAW( 3 );
            sessionSecretDESIterationCount = stmt.getRAW( 4 );
            sessionSecretDESAlgorithm = stmt.getRAW( 5 );
            sessionSecretDESPassPhrase = stmt.getRAW( 6 );
            rs = ( OracleResultSet )stmt.getCursor( 7 );
            //while( rs.next() ) {
            // Only show first row
            if( rs.next() ) {
                System.out.print( rs.getString( 1 ) );
                System.out.print( ", " );
                System.out.print( rs.getString( 2 ) );
                System.out.print( ", " );
                System.out.print( rs.getString( 3 ) );
                System.out.print( ", " );
                System.out.print( rs.getString( 4 ) );
                System.out.print( ", " );
                System.out.print( rs.getString( 5 ) );
                System.out.print( ", " );
                System.out.print( rs.getString( 6 ) );
                System.out.print( ", " );
                System.out.print( rs.getString( 7 ) );
                System.out.print( ", " );
                System.out.print( OracleJavaSecure.getDecryptData(
                    rs.getRAW( 8 ), sessionSecretDESPassPhrase,
                    sessionSecretDESAlgorithm, sessionSecretDESSalt,
                    sessionSecretDESIterationCount ) );
                if ( null != rs.getRAW( 8 ) )
                    System.out.print( " (" + rs.getRAW( 8 ).stringValue() +
                            ")" );
                System.out.print( ", " );
                // Most initial commissions in database are null
                System.out.print( OracleJavaSecure.getDecryptData(
                    rs.getRAW( 9 ), sessionSecretDESPassPhrase,
                    sessionSecretDESAlgorithm, sessionSecretDESSalt,
                    sessionSecretDESIterationCount ) );
                if ( null != rs.getRAW( 9 ) )
                    System.out.print( " (" + rs.getRAW( 9 ).stringValue() +
                            ")" );
                System.out.print( ", " );
                System.out.print( rs.getString( 10 ) );
                System.out.print( ", " );
                System.out.print( rs.getString( 11 ) );
                System.out.print( "\n" );
            }
        }
        if( null != rs ) rs.close();
        if( null != stmt ) stmt.close();
```

Our error handling is identical to what we did in the last chapter: we hand back the error number and message through two of the `OUT` parameters. If there is no error, we continue by getting the secret password key artifacts into local method members, and we also get the `CURSOR` into a `ResultSet` so we can walk through the data. Since there are about 100 entries in the `EMPLOYEES` table, we will only show the first one (by reading the `ResultSet.next()` in an `if` block rather than in a `while` block).

Most of the columns are clear text, so we just print them out. But the `SALARY` and `COMMISSION_PCT` values are handed to us by Oracle database as `RAW` encrypted data. (Note that the encrypted `SALARY` is in the 8th position in the `ResultSet`, and the `ResultSet` is in the seventh position in the `Statement`. Those element numberings are independent.) We will send those `RAW` values to the `getDecryptData()` method, along with the secret password key artifacts. If we haven't yet built our local copy of the secret password key, we will build it there; in any case, we will decrypt the data and return it as a `String`. We will also print that out.

For our demonstration purposes only, we are also going to print out the actual `RAW` (if not `null`), within parentheses, "()". If we want to track that across multiple runs through this code, we will see that it is different each time—owing to using different secret password keys in different Oracle sessions.

At the end of each call to our stored procedures for data encryption, we will close the `OracleCallableStatement`. We may also close the `ResultSet`, even though it is unnecessary—it is inherently closed when we close the `Statement`, because it was acquired through the `Statement`. However, it is good practice to explicitly close each `ResultSet`, especially because it is common practice to reuse a `Statement`—you may open multiple `ResultSets` during the life of a single `Statement`, and to assure that you are freeing up Oracle resources, you should close each `ResultSet` when you are done with it.

Selecting All Columns in Encrypted String

Our second example procedure for selecting encrypted data from Oracle database, `p_select_employees_secret` does not select and encrypt individual columns, but rather selects all the columns and concatenates them into a single, comma-delimited `VARCHAR2` to be encrypted. In this case, none of the data is sent in clear-text form. At the client, if individual columns of the data are needed, you will need to parse the decrypted string to acquire individual data elements.

Also in this example, we are using a comma as a delimiter between fields. This assumes that there are no commas in the data—not often a valid assumption. You can use a different delimiter that is less likely to occur in the data, like a caret (^)or tilde (~). This is an example only, and you would need to evaluate your specific requirements for the data before building a procedure like this for your application.

We call the procedure, decrypt the data and print the results as in partial Listing 7-23.

Listing 7-23. Encrypt All Data Selected from Employees, from p_select_employees_secret

```
stmt = ( OracleCallableStatement )conn.prepareCall(
    "CALL hr.hr_sec_pkg.p_select_employees_secret(?,?,?,?,?,?,?,?,?)" );
    ...
    if( rs.next() ) {
        System.out.print( OracleJavaSecure.getDecryptData( rs.getRAW( 1 ),
            sessionSecretDESPassPhrase,
            sessionSecretDESAlgorithm, sessionSecretDESSalt,
            sessionSecretDESIterationCount ) );
        if( null != rs.getRAW( 1 ) )
            System.out.print( " (" + rs.getRAW( 1 ).stringValue() +
                ")" );
```

```
            System.out.print( "\n" );
```

Again, we print the String value of the encrypted RAW in parentheses beside the data. In this case there is a single RAW that represents the entire row of concatenated data.

Sending Encrypted Data to Oracle Database for Insert/Update

I wouldn't say that this next example procedure bears no resemblance to our previous examples, but you will notice there are none of the trappings of key exchange in either direction. This is an update, and in order to encrypt the data at the client, we would already have had to exchange keys. Listing 7-24 shows the code to call our encrypted data update procedure, p_update_employees_sensitive.

Listing 7-24. Update Sensitive Data in Employees, call p_update_employees_sensitive

```
stmt = ( OracleCallableStatement )conn.prepareCall(
    "CALL hr.hr_sec_pkg.p_update_employees_sensitive(?,?,?,?,?,?,?,?,?,?,?,?,?)" );
stmt.registerOutParameter( 12, OracleTypes.NUMBER );
stmt.registerOutParameter( 13, OracleTypes.VARCHAR );
stmt.setInt(    1, 300 );
stmt.setString( 2, "David" );
stmt.setString( 3, "Coffin" );
stmt.setString( 4, "DAVID.COFFIN" );
stmt.setString( 5, "800.555.1212" );
stmt.setDate(   6, new Date( ( new java.util.Date() ).getTime() ) );
stmt.setString( 7, "SA_REP" );
// Note - may not have locModulus, locExponent,  at this time!
stmt.setRAW(    8, OracleJavaSecure.getCryptData( "9000.25" ) );
stmt.setRAW(    9, OracleJavaSecure.getCryptData( "0.15" ) );
stmt.setInt(   10, 147 );
stmt.setInt(   11, 80 );
stmt.setInt(   12, 0 );
stmt.setNull(  13, OracleTypes.VARCHAR );
stmt.executeUpdate();

errNo = stmt.getInt( 12 );
if( errNo != 0 ) {
    errMsg = stmt.getString( 13 );
    System.out.println( "Oracle error 3) " + errNo + ", " + errMsg );
}
else System.out.println( "Oracle success 3)" );
if( null != stmt ) stmt.close();
```

For our encrypted data, we first call the getCryptData() method. Then we set a RAW parameter in our Oracle procedure. When we execute this statement, both the clear-text and encrypted data values get sent to Oracle database for Insert or Update, as determined by the procedure.

A TALE OF TWO DATE CLASSES

As in our previous examples, here in Listing 7-24 we are setting our parameters, except that this time, we are setting data instead of key artifacts. In our sixth parameter, we are instantiating a java.util.Date class. The constructor with no arguments creates a `Date` with the current date and time. Frequently with Oracle database, we will be using instances of `java.sql.Date` (notice the package *java.sql* instead of *java.util*), which does not have such a constructor; however, we can construct a `java.sql.Date` with the long (milliseconds) coming from the `java.util.Date.getTime()` method. We could also use the same statement used by `java.util.Date()` constructor to instantiate a `java.sql.Date` object, like this:

```
java.sql.Date( System.currentTimeMillis() );
```

I have one observation about the syntax we use in our code. The parentheses around our instantiation of a (`new java.util.Date()`) allow us immediate access to it as an object, to its `getTime()` method, like this:

```
stmt.setDate( 6, new Date( ( new java.util.Date() ).getTime()));
```

Okay, so why doesn't `java.sql.Date` have a `Date()` constructor, didn't it inherit one by extending `java.util.Date`? Oh, excellent question! The short answer is that constructors are not considered members of a class, so they are not inherited by the subclass. You can, however, get access to the parent constructors by a call to the `super()` method as the first line in any subclass constructor. There can be multiple `super()` methods with differing signatures, one for each constructor in the parent class.

We will be coming back to the subject of *java.sql* and *java.util* `Dates` again in Chapter 9. We need a standard practice for exchanging dates, and I will propose one there.

Selecting a Single Row from EMPLOYEES

Perhaps we don't want to select the entire table, but only records that meet a certain criteria. We can provide criteria to be made part of the `WHERE` clause in our query. In this procedure, `p_select_employee_by_id_sens`, Listing 7-25, we are providing a tenth parameter, the `EMPLOYEE_ID`.

Listing 7-25. *Select by ID, Sensitive Data from Employees, from* `p_select_employee_by_id_sens`

```
stmt = ( OracleCallableStatement )conn.prepareCall(
    "CALL hr.hr_sec_pkg.p_select_employee_by_id_sens(?,?,?,?,?,?,?,?,?,?)" );
...
stmt.setInt(  10, 300 ); // Employee ID 300
stmt.executeUpdate();
```

The remainder of the procedure call is identical to our previous query examples, except that we only expect one or zero records to be returned (the `EMPLOYEE_ID` is a `UNIQUE` key for this table.) So we can handle the `ResultSet` in an `if( rs.next() )` block instead of `while( rs.next() )`.

Selecting EMPLOYEES Data by Last Name: Try SQL Injection

We can also query all records meeting some other criteria that is perhaps not `UNIQUE`. One example that we will show queries `EMPLOYEES` by `LAST_NAME` using the `p_select_employee_by_ln_sens` procedure, in partial Listing 7-26. There are two entries with the `LAST_NAME` "King". So this would return two rows.

Listing 7-26. *Select by Last Name, Sensitive Data from Employees, from* `p_select_employee_by_ln_sens`

```
stmt = ( OracleCallableStatement )conn.prepareCall(
```

```
    "CALL hr.hr_sec_pkg.p_select_employee_by_ln_sens(?,?,?,?,?,?,?,?,?,?)" );
...
stmt.setString(  10, "King" ); // Employees Janette and Steven King
...
while( rs.next() ) {
```

Iterate through the ResultSet using a while block to see all returned rows.

We can attempt a SQL injection here by replacing our previous parameter 10 setting with the following:

```
stmt.setString(  10, "King' or 'a'='a" );
```

What we will see is that *no data is returned*, because no EMPLOYEES have the LAST_NAME {King' or 'a'='a}.

Selecting EMPLOYEES Data by RAW: Try SQL Injection

Perhaps, one might think, we can break through and accomplish SQL injection if we hand our data back as a RAW and only convert it to a VARCHAR2 at the point of making our selection (refer to the Oracle procedure, p_select_employee_by_raw_sens which we described earlier and in Listing 7-16.) This procedure call, partial Listing 7-27, attempts that strategy.

Listing 7-27. Select by RAW Value, Sensitive Data from Employees, from p_select_employee_by_raw_sens

```
stmt = ( OracleCallableStatement )conn.prepareCall(
    "CALL hr.hr_sec_pkg.p_select_employee_by_raw_sens(?,?,?,?,?,?,?,?,?,?)" );
...
stmt.setRAW(  10, new RAW("King' or 'a'='a".getBytes()) );
```

You will see that once again, our attempt at SQL injection in a stored procedure fails. It seems that passing parameters, as opposed to embedding user-provided text in dynamic SQL, is quite resistant to SQL injection.

Also note how we are treating the value between quotation marks as if it were already a String object, calling the getBytes() method. We saw that first in Chapter 6.

Testing Encryption Failure with New Client Keys

Perhaps you need to see this for yourself, or perhaps not. In any case, you can test calling procedures with keys on the client that don't match what's on Oracle database: it will fail. Take note that in the Java code thus far in the TestOracleJavaSecure.main() method, we have exchanged keys, and those would continue to work. We will take a split-second to remove or disable the keys on the client. We do that with a call to the resetKeys() method (see Listing 7-28).

Listing 7-28. Test Encryption with Mixed Keys

```
OracleJavaSecure.resetKeys(); // Method for Chapter 7 testing only
locModulus = OracleJavaSecure.getLocRSAPubMod();
locExponent = OracleJavaSecure.getLocRSAPubExp();
```

We also establish new keys on the client by calling the getLocRSAPubMod() method, and we get the public modulus and exponent. If we make no effort to pass these public key artifacts to Oracle database and retrieve new secret password key artifacts in return, then an update (which doesn't exchange keys) will fail. This is what we will test.

Note that it is unlikely that we will accidentally reset our keys, and calling the `getLocRSAPubMod()` method or other methods of `OracleJavaSecure` multiple times will not create new keys if they already exist, but rather will return the existing keys. The keys are `static`, so they will not disappear on their own as long as the Java Virtual Machine continues to run. So, this test is really just for fun: answering a "what if" question.

Testing Failure with New Oracle Connection

Another test that we can demonstrate is the scenario wherein we close the `Connection` to Oracle database and establish a new one. The server-side keys will disappear—both the client public key and the secret password key. We can reset the `Connection` and prepare to call our encryption procedures by setting our Secure Application Role to `HRVIEW_ROLE` as in Listing 7-29.

Listing 7-29. Reset Connection and Re-Set Secure Application Role

```
if ( null != conn ) conn.close();
conn = DriverManager.getConnection( appusrConnString );
OracleJavaSecure.setConnection( conn );
stmt = ( OracleCallableStatement )conn.prepareCall(
    "CALL appsec.p_check_hrview_access()" );
stmt.executeUpdate();
```

Again, in the case of doing an encrypted Oracle update, we will see a failure because Oracle database has neither the public key nor the secret password key. This code is initially commented.

Some Closing Remarks

I've covered all the big demonstrations and tests in the preceding sections. Now, it's your turn to modify the tests and try some of your own. Feel free to comment and uncomment those sections of test code that we just described. When you recompile and run those sections of `TestOracleJavaSecure` you will see a message on an attempted data update that indicates we have "Failed where expected—OK."

If You Need To Close/Open Your Connection

Resetting your Oracle connection poses another potential problem when we do a select of encrypted data, for certainly we will pass our public key to Oracle database, and the database will build the secret password key and hand it back. However, we still retain an old copy of the secret password key on the client and will run into problems decrypting the data. We can remedy that after getting and decrypting the secret password key artifacts on the client with an immediate call to the `OracleJavaSecure.makeDESKey()` method, before we try to decrypt the data.

I think the best rule of thumb, and an examination on your code review checklist, is to retain the Oracle connection for the duration of your queries and updates. If there are long pauses and you need to close the Oracle connection, when you open a new connection, pass your public key artifacts to Oracle database via the `p_get_shared_passphrase` procedure (described in the following) and build a replacement secret password key on the client by calling the `makeDESKey()` method.

Running Basic Key Exchange Without Data Encryption

For those times when all we want to do is submit encrypted data updates to Oracle database, or we want to be prepared to update before doing any selects, we need to assure that we have exchanged keys beforehand. We can do that by calling the p_get_shared_passphrase procedure (in our current design, this procedure must be included in every individual application package, like hr_sec_pkg). Listing 7-30 presents the fundamentals of basic key exchange from a Java client.

Listing 7-30. Basic Key Exchange

```
stmt = ( OracleCallableStatement )conn.prepareCall(
    "CALL hr.hr_sec_pkg.p_get_shared_passphrase(?,?,?,?,?,?,?,?)" );
...
OracleJavaSecure.makeDESKey( sessionSecretDESPassPhrase,
    sessionSecretDESAlgorithm, sessionSecretDESSalt,
    sessionSecretDESIterationCount );
```

We will get and decrypt each artifact of our secret password key, and pass that to the makeDESKey() method. At that point, we have completed our key exchange and ready to exchange encrypted data and do decryption on both the client and Oracle database.

After we call the p_get_shared_passphrase procedure and call OracleJavaSecure.makeDESKey(), the TestOracleJavaSecure class will again try to do an encrypted data update, and will succeed.

Executing the Demonstrations and Tests

We are going to run our demonstrations and tests now. To do that, we will again edit our code, as needed, and then compile and run it. In a command prompt, change directories to *Chapter7*. Edit *TestOracleJavaSecure.java* if not already, placing the correct password for appusr and correct host and port number in the Oracle connection string, near the top.

```
private static String appusrConnString =
    "jdbc:oracle:thin:appusr/password@localhost:1521:Orcl";
```

Compile the code with these commands, or just the second which will automatically compile the first (be sure the first line of *OracleJavaSecure.java* is commented, the line to CREATE the Java structures in Oracle database).

```
javac orajavsec/OracleJavaSecure.java
javac TestOracleJavaSecure.java
```

Then run the code from that same directory with this command:

```
java TestOracleJavaSecure
```

Observing the Results

When you execute TestOracleJavaSecure (as distributed), all of the tests listed previously will run straight through from top to bottom. The results will look like this:

```
Count data in V_EMPLOYEES_PUBLIC: 108
Count data in V_EMPLOYEES_PUBLIC: 108
Oracle success 1)
```

```
198, Donald, OConnell, DOCONNEL, 650.507.9833, 2007-06-21 00:00:00, SH_CLERK, 2600
(E27811A8C7C9D9F3), null, 124, 50
Oracle success 2)
198, Donald, OConnell, DOCONNEL, 650.507.9833, 21-JUN-07, SH_CLERK, 2600, , 124, 50
(F7EA4E97B2F39E036AF6E880B2E5CA3EB78332BF8CE82B7585A4CBC7B340FEBDE4862830927
D118D27A1DDE3304478D9A463EBA9BC78E3188217884D5F5EA92F54A6EA2FB62598D1419F003295D
F1C076E48BC6D07058E3B)
Oracle success 3)
Oracle success 4)
300, David, Coffin, DAVID.COFFIN, 800.555.1212, 2010-08-30 00:00:00, SA_REP, 9000.25, .15,
147, 80
Oracle success 5) No data on failed SQL Injection
Oracle success 6) No data on failed SQL Injection
Failed where expected - OK. Need key exchange.
Oracle success 8)
Oracle success 9)
```

Demonstrating Scenarios

Here is a list in relatively plain English of the scenarios we have demonstrated. There is a lot of code to accomplish all these different scenarios. The code for each scenario is very similar to some of the other scenarios, with modifications for the specific demonstration.

- We queried the EMPLOYEES table and got the SALARY and COMMISSION_PCT columns back in encrypted form. For both of these, we print out the decrypted String, and in parentheses, the stringValue() of the encrypted RAW (unless null). We only show the first row of the ResultSet.

- We queried the table and got all the columns back in one concatenated String, in encrypted form. We print the decrypted data, and in parentheses, the stringValue() of the encrypted RAW. Again, we only show the first row.

- We do an insert or update to the EMPLOYEES table, inserting EMPLOYEE_ID = 300. If it already exists, we do an update. At that point, the salary is 9000.25 (now I'm dreaming).

- We select a single row from EMPLOYEES, requesting data WHERE EMPLOYEE_ID = 300.

- We attempt to query EMPLOYEES through our procedures with a sample SQL injection string. This fails, and no data is returned.

- We attempt again to query EMPLOYEES through our procedures with a sample SQL injection string, this time transmitted as a RAW and only converted when we do the SELECT. This also fails, and no data is returned.

- We can alternately compile TestOracleJavaSecure to test resetting the client keys or resetting the Oracle connection. After that, our attempt to send encrypted data to Oracle database for insert/update fails, as expected.

- We successfully call the p_get_shared_passphrase procedure and run the makeDESKey() method to complete key exchange.

- Again, we send encrypted data to Oracle database for insert/update, and we succeed. Now the salary is 9700.75 (now my wife is dreaming).

Querying Employees to See Updates

You can see the status of the record we inserted / updated by connecting to Oracle database as the HR user and executing the following command:

```
SELECT * FROM employees WHERE employee_id=300;
```

Packaging Template to Implement Encryption

I know that folks find the cost of security, like the cost of quality, to be unpalatable; but the potential cost of insecurity is inordinately higher. Our security structures are only valuable if put to use. We will add some value in the next few chapters, but as it stands now, getting folks to use our security structures may be like pulling teeth. This is not one of those "if you build it, they will come" moments.

We are going to lower the threshold of entrance into these security structures by providing application developers with templates that they can use to quickly implement the back end Oracle structures for their application, and the front end Java calls to those structures.

Template for Oracle Application Security Structures

The first file that we will give to developers provides the code for an Oracle security package that they will need to implement in their application schema. In the file, there are generic names for the application schema, the package, procedures, tables/views and columns. Developers should search and replace those names with the actual names they will use.

■ **Note** You can this file at *Chapter7/AppPkgTemplate.sql*.

Your security administrator, secadm, will need to grant execute on the appsec.app_sec_pkg to the developers' application schema user so the application can use the app_sec_pkg procedures and functions.

In order to create the application package, the developer will need the CREATE PROCEDURE system privilege. Also, in order for the application user(s) to use the application package, all application users will need the EXECUTE object privilege on the package granted to them.

We have four template procedures in the package:

```
p_get_shared_passphrase
p_select_APPTABLE_sensitive
p_select_APPTABLE_by_COLUMN1_sens
p_update_APPTABLE_sensitive
```

There is nothing new being introduced to you here—you have seen all these structures used in the HR schema.

Template for Java Calls to Application Security

We will also provide our application developers with a template Java file. Each developer will search and replace the generic names for schema, table, procedure etc. to whatever names are appropriate in their application.

▨ **Note** You can find the Java code for the `AppAccessSecure` template class in the file *Chapter7/ AppJavaTemplate.java*.

This file bears strong resemblance to our test code for the structures in the `HR` schema, *TestOracleJavaSecure.java*. It consists of a `main()` method that establishes an Oracle connection and calls the application structures that the developer will define in the application schema.

Perhaps this will be the most intimidating code for your application developers because of the bulk required to do key exchange. You are the expert now, so you will do well to give your application developers some assistance. In fact, it will save you some headaches down the road if you can assist the developers in implementing this correctly, and avoiding any security weaknesses, like we did with the `HR.EMPLOYEES` table.

Java Archive for Use by Applications

In addition to providing your developers with the two template files, you need to give them the *orajavsec/OracleJavaSecure.class* file. I recommend that you do not give developers the *OracleJavaSecure.java* code file, just to assure yourself that no modified version of the class is in use in your organization.

Probably the best form to use to distribute the class file is in the form of a Java archive (JAR) file. To create an appropriate jar file for distribution, you can run the JAR Tool that comes with the JDK. If your `PATH` and `CLASSPATH` are still set as described in Chapter 2, you can get a command prompt window and change directory to the *Chapter7* directory. From there, execute this command:

```
jar cvf orajavsec.jar orajavsec/OracleJavaSecure.class
```

This will create a file named *orajavsec.jar* in the current directory. Distribute this file and instruct your application developers to place this file name in their `CLASSPATH` both during development and when their application code is run.

Don't Stop Now

With templates in hand, we are at a point where we can bring Oracle application developers into the encrypted data over the network fold, and you would do well to take one of your applications and configure it to use these structures and approaches, to blaze the way. But this is only a half-way house for security respite. We are going to introduce some powerful concepts in the following chapters that will entice your application developers to hang with the program. Stepping into secure application development and operation is like getting your life back. Security is a sense of well-being. It requires work, but with the work, you determine your own secure computing destiny.

Chapter Review

We took our key exchange and data encryption concepts that we learned in Chapter 6 and applied them to a specific Oracle application, the HR schema. Is this one of those great moments in science? Perhaps not, but it is a milestone, and a springboard for us into bigger and better things in regard to our application security. We have successfully encrypted our sensitive application data as it traversed the network.

We built structures for error logging, specifically to track errors and events involving our application security processes, no matter what client application is currently using them. Additionally, we built a trigger to automatically manage the logs, discarding records over 45 days old.

There was a lot of code, both PL/SQL and Java, presented in this chapter. The goal of this code is fairly straightforward—to use our existing data encryption processes when retrieving sensitive data and records from the HR schema, and when updating sensitive data and records.

Along the way, I introduced the following concepts:

- Using indexes for performance

- Triggers, autonomous transactions, and COMMIT

- Use and manipulation of sequences

- Default procedure parameters

- Use of the CURSOR TYPE

- Use of type specification by reference, anchored declaration of a datatype

- Use of java.util.Date and java.sql.Date

We spent significant time evaluating and testing our protections against SQL injection attacks.

Finally, we presented templates that can be delivered to application programmers so that they can implement these security constructs in their applications.

Please study Figures 7-1 and 7-2 for a visual overview of secure application data query and update processes. Figure 7-1 illustrates the process of querying Oracle database for sensitive data and retrieving it in encrypted form. At the top, you see a reference to Figure 5-1 [A] which is where we saw the RSA private/public key pair created on the client. Then in Figure 7-1, we see the client calls p_check_hrview_access to set the role for access to the sensitive HR data.

At that point, we have the execute privilege to call the hr_sec_pkg package. We call p_select_employees_sensitive to get both public and sensitive data from the EMPLOYEES table. The first order of business is to accomplish key exchange. You can see to the right of Figure 7-1 that we create an equivalent RSA public key on the Oracle database, and we create the secret password (DES) key which we will return to the client. We saw the details of that process in Figure 6-1 [B].

The next order of business of the procedure on Oracle database is to query the EMPLOYEES table and encrypt both the SALARY and COMMISSION_PCT fields. Finally the procedure returns the data, both clear text fields and encrypted forms of the sensitive fields in a ResultSet to the client.

Back at the client (the left side of Figure 7-1), we build an equivalent secret password key based on the artifacts that the Oracle database returned. See the key image at the bottom of the illustration. Then we display the data from the ResultSet, using the secret password key to decrypt the sensitive data components.

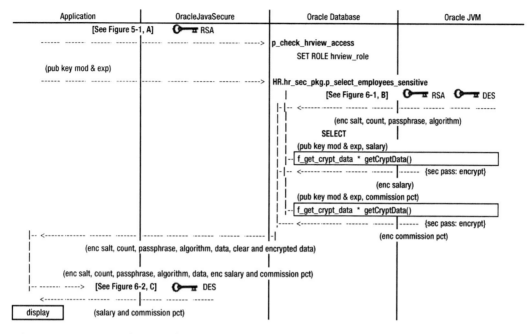

Figure 7-1. *Secure application data query*

Figure 7-2 illustrates the process for updating sensitive data. For that process we encrypt the sensitive data on the client, using the secret password key. We do that by calling the **getCryptData()** method. Then we submit both clear text fields and encrypted sensitive fields to Oracle database by calling the **p_update_employees_sensitive** procedure.

The key exchange must have already taken place, so that the Oracle database can use the equivalent (original) secret password key to decrypt the data. Then the procedure executes an **INSERT** or **UPDATE** command to store the data.

Application	OracleJavaSecure	Oracle Database	Oracle JVM

[Have already accomplished key exchange]

(new salary and commission pct)
------ ------ ------ -----> getCryptData() [A]
|-- <-------- ------ ------ |------ {sec pass: encrypt}
(enc salary and commission pct)

(encrypted and clear text data)
|-- ------- ------ ------ ------ ------ -----> HR.hr_sec_pkg.p_update_employees_sensitive
(enc salary and commission pct)
|-- f_get_decrypt_data * getDecryptData()
|-- <------ ------ ------ ------ |------ {sec pass: decrypt}
(clear text data)
|-- **INSERT or UPDATE**

Figure 7-2. *Secure application data update*

CHAPTER 8

Single Sign-On

Single sign-on (SSO) is a relatively simple concept. Did you log in when you turned on your computer, before you were able to start working? If so, then we ought to be able to find out who you logged in as and assume that your identity is the same when you use our applications.

Part of the mystery here revolves around assurance and trust. Can I trust that initial log in to be secure enough so that only the actual user can authenticate as himself? Can I be sure that no one else has that username and password, and that no one can pretend to be that user (spoof the user)? This assurance comes not only from the power of the encryption and the strength of the password storage protection, but also from the computer security code of conduct: frequency of password change, password composition and strength rules, screen-lock rules, rules against password sharing and posting, education about malware and viruses, and social engineering. This assurance also comes from network access control (NAC). Do we assure that each client computer has the latest updates and anti-virus software? Do we assure that client computers are correctly configured with security options, like our password-protected screen lock? Do we protect mobile computers with hard disk encryption, firewall software, and virtual private network (VPN) when they communicate with our company over public networks? And do we use NAC to do all this *before* we allow those computers to connect to our corporate network?

If I am sure of all these things, and anything else that is required to combat a computer security threat, then I can trust the original log in to be good enough for any further identity requirements. There is a large foundation that we require before we can continue building our application security with SSO.

Another Layer of Authentication?

We could always add another authentication in our application—a chance for the user to reenter the username and password (possibly a different password), but beyond frustrating the user, have we improved on security? (In the next chapter, we will try to improve on security with 2-Factor Authentication.)

I'm not saying that extra authentications are a bad thing. Sometimes you do not have the trust and assurances I listed previously, so SSO is not valid. The problems come when you have ten or tens of passwords. At that point, two things happen: your authentication support systems get heavily taxed because of lost or forgotten passwords and innumerable password resets, and your organization's (and personal) security decreases. Can it be true that security decreases with increased quantity of passwords? Yes, because now you have placed users in the position where they have too many passwords, changing too often to remember—they must be written down.

Perhaps your users are savvy enough to keep a list of all the places they have passwords, and when they change them one place, they change them all places. I'm not sure you can count on that, even in a computing organization with less than 10 people. And there are always exceptions—passwords that change more frequently and passwords that have different composition rules.

Additionally, are your users able to distinguish the list of secure, corporate sites where the single work password can be synchronized from all other insecure or non-work-related sites that should not have access to their work password? Work passwords that grant access to sensitive information should never be used on external systems—who knows what security those external systems maintain?

In the end, we need to strive for SSO. First, we need to establish the foundation of trust and assurance with NAC. Then we should push for adoption of SSO everywhere we can achieve it. Our Java and Oracle applications are one of those places.

Who Is Logged-In on the Client?

If you are on a Microsoft Windows client or a UNIX client, the operating system (OS) retains knowledge of the identity you claimed when you authenticated or logged in. That identity is published in your environment settings for easy access from scripts, but the environment can be changed by those scripts so that, judging from your environment settings alone, you can spoof a different user.

To see this spoofing, bring up a command prompt window (on Windows) and type SET to see your settings. Perhaps you have a setting called USERNAME near the end. Observe what it is. In the same window, type:

```
set USERNAME=coffin
```

Now type SET again and observe what the value of USERNAME is. Note that this doesn't change your identity in the operating system, but it could change your identity for any script that uses the current environment as its source.

Because the environment is so malleable and transient, it is not a trustworthy source of identity. Do not read a user's identity from the environment—if you are doing that, change your ways!

Find a Better Source of OS User Identity

Windows is willing to tell our applications who the logged-in user is. Specifically, the Active Directory authenticated user ID is available to all who know how to read it. The JRE for Windows has a class that can acquire the user ID. That class is named NTSystem, and it is in the *com.sun.security.auth.module* package—it is automatically available to the Java applications on Windows.

There is an alphabet soup of acronyms that will help us define what NTSystem does. NTSystem calls functions in a dynamic load library (DLL) named *jaas_nt.dll*—part of the Java authentication and authorization system (JAAS) package. That DLL is included in the JRE (and JDK) for Windows. NTSystem makes native code calls using Java Native Interface (JNI) to the DLL. I suspect that NTSystem was named for the precursor to Active Directory, NT Directory Service. For Microsoft, the Windows NT (marketed in 1993 as New Technology) server operating system was a source of many names, including NT Domains.

Use NTSystem or UnixSystem to Get Identity

When you use NTSystem, you are not relying on the environment or other intermediary, but are going directly to the OS to get the user identity. Listing 8-1 shows the code for that functionality.

Listing 8-1. Use NTSystem to Get Windows User Identity

```
import com.sun.security.auth.module.NTSystem;

NTSystem mNTS = new NTSystem();
String name = mNTS.getName();
```

Now, wasn't that easy?

If you have UNIX clients, you can use a similar JAAS component through the UnixSystem class, as in Listing 8-2.

Listing 8-2. Use UnixSystem to Get UNIX User Identity

```
import com.sun.security.auth.module.UnixSystem;

UnixSystem mUX = new UnixSystem();
String name = mUX.getUsername();
```

These classes are not both available on either client, and you can only compile the code shown above on the system where the class exists. So you should only include one or the other calls to NTSystem or UnixSystem in your application code. You can include each of these and comment one to compile the other for distribution to those clients where appropriate.

There are other ways to use Java to read the current user identity from Windows Active Directory, for example as a lightweight directory access protocol (LDAP) service; however, security and configuration will be very specific to your corporate environment. I will not cover that approach here.

Do Cross-Platform-Specific Coding with Reflection

That approach of "pick your client platform" is not very satisfying, nor does it meet the Java goal of "run anywhere." But we have to deal with the fact that NTSystem and UnixSystem classes are not only platform-specific, but also not available cross-platform. There is an approach that can solve this problem: *reflection*. With reflection, we can forget those pesky either/or import statements and commenting the platform-inappropriate code.

With reflection we can write code that is compiled with possibilities rather than specifics. It is possible we will be running on a Windows platform, and in that case we want to use NTSystem. But it is also possible we are running on a UNIX platform, in which case we want UnixSystem to run.

With reflection, we will load a platform-appropriate class, sight-unseen (like going on a blind date), and then we will use the resources of that class. Reflection uses runtime type introspection to find and use properties of a specific class.

Listing 8-3 shows the code to get the user identity from the Windows OS using reflection. The code for UNIX is similar but uses the UnixSystem class rather than the NTSystem class.

▓ **Note** You will find the code in Listing 8-3 in the file *Chapter8/PlatformReflectTest.java*.

Listing 8-3. Use Reflection to Get OS User Identity

```
//import com.sun.security.auth.module.NTSystem;
import java.lang.reflect.Method;

//NTSystem mNTS = new NTSystem();
Class mNTS = Class.forName( "com.sun.security.auth.module.NTSystem" );

//String name = mNTS.getName();
Method classMethod = mNTS.getMethod( "getName" );
String name = ( String )classMethod.invoke( mNTS.newInstance() );
```

Notice first in this code that we no longer import the Windows specific class, NTSystem. We would not be able to compile code with that import statement on a UNIX platform. Instead, we are importing the reflection class, Method. Method can represent any specific method in a class.

Next, notice that we do not instantiate an NTSystem class, as we had done before. Now we get an NTSystem class by using the Class.forName() method and giving the fully qualified name of NTSystem. Where have we seen this before? Oh that's right; we used this syntax when we load the OracleDriver. Using this syntax, the compiler has no trouble—it sees the fully qualified name as a String, so even if NTSystem doesn't exist on a UNIX box, you can compile this code there.

Next, we know we need to access a method named getName(), so we pass the name of the method to Class.getMethod(), which returns a Method class, classMethod representing the getName() method.

We do not yet have an instance of NTSystem, but we have a handle, mNTS, to what might amount to a static class. Our next step requires that we call the getName() method on an instance of NTSystem. To call the method, we call classMethod.invoke(), but we need a real instance (object) of NTSystem, so we instantiate the object by calling Class.newInstance().

At this point, our instance of NTSystem returns the OS user name from the getName() method. However, because we are calling this through the Method class, we will get an Object type returned, which we need to cast as a String.

We will do more with reflection when we get to Chapter 10. There we use reflection to restore classes and objects from storage in the Oracle database and from transmission over the network. In the end, we will read their members and call their methods.

Assure More Stringent OS Identity

What would we like to know before we accept the NTSystem report of the user ID? We'd like to know first that we are on a Windows client. One possible pursuit of spoofing our code would be to run on a UNIX client with an imposter class named *com.sun.security.auth.module.NTSystem* found in the client CLASSPATH. There would be problems trying to accomplish that, but we will avoid the issue by simply assuring we are on a Windows machine. See Listing 8-4.

Knowing we are on a Windows client also informs us about which JAAS source to use: NTSystem instead of UnixSystem.

Listing 8-4. Get OS User Identity, getOSUserID()

```
private static String expectedDomain = "ORGDOMAIN";

//System.getProperties().list(System.out);
if( ( System.getProperty("os.arch").equals("x86") ||
    System.getProperty("os.arch").endsWith("64")) &&
```

```
    System.getProperty("os.name").startsWith("Windows") )
{
    // Using reflection
    Class mNTS = Class.forName( "com.sun.security.auth.module.NTSystem" );

    Method classMethod = mNTS.getMethod( "getDomain" );
    String domain = ( String )classMethod.invoke( mNTS.newInstance() );
    domain = domain.toUpperCase();

    classMethod = mNTS.getMethod( "getName" );
    String name = ( String )classMethod.invoke( mNTS.newInstance() );
    name = name.toUpperCase();

    System.out.println( "Domain: " + domain + ", Name: " + name );
    if ( ( name != null ) && ( !name.equals( "" ) ) &&
        ( domain != null ) &&
        domain.equalsIgnoreCase( expectedDomain ) )
    {
        rtrnString = name;
    } else {
        System.out.println( "Expecting domain = " + expectedDomain );
        System.out.println( "User " + name + " must exist in Oracle"  );
    }
}
```

The `if` statement tests two properties of `System` to assure our OS architecture (`os.arch` system property) and OS name (`os.name` system property) are consistent with a Windows client.

To see all the properties of `System`, you can uncomment the top line of code. Calling the `list()` method of a `Properties` object will "print" the properties to an output stream—`System.out`, in our case.

The Expected Domain

In our identity code in Listing 8-4, we also get the Windows domain name from the `NTSystem.getDomain()` method. This must match the `expectedDomain` that we have hard coded.

Assume that our application code needs to get to resources on our organizational network, like Oracle databases; we should have a high threshold that client machines must cross before being allowed access to our corporate network. We do this with a NAC system. Part of NAC supervision is assuring that our clients are connected to our corporate domain services (Active Directory). The user would have to be logged into our domain to get network access.

If our network is not protected by NAC that assures our domain, then another avenue of attempted spoofing might be available. A hacker might set up her own domain with an imposter user identity (she may be posing as one of us), and have our code get the spoofed ID from her domain by `NTSystem`.

We avoid that potential issue, even if we have NAC, by requiring that the client computer be attached to our corporate domain. That is, `NTSystem` must return our expected domain name, or we don't accept the claim of user identity.

▨ **Note** On a stand-alone system, the domain name may equal the system name alone.

USING UNIXSYSTEM

If you are going to use UnixSystem for your clients, then you will want to assure that your clients and the Oracle database are using the same naming services. This information is not provided by the UnixSystem class.

There is something you could use. UnixSystem provides the user identifier, uid, which is a numeric value representing the user. The uid is not necessarily unique, but in a single naming system, a specific user will have a specific uid.

To use the uid, your clients could transmit what they see for uid to Oracle database, and the database could assure that it sees the same uid for that user in its naming service. The level of assurance provided by this check is quite low, so I'm not advising it.

On the contrary, I recommend you use NAC to assure that all your UNIX and Linux clients are using the required naming service before they can get access to the network and the Oracle Database. I like NAC! That sounds like a campaign slogan, but that was before my time.

Case Sensitivity

You will notice in our code that we uppercase both the user name and domain. We also test the domain using the equalsIgnoreCase() method. That case-insensitive test of domain is just in case someone implements this code and neglects to type the expectedDomain in all caps. No matter how the domain name is cased coming from NTSystem, if the spelling is the same, it is the same domain.

In Java, we can do case-insensitive tests, but in Oracle database, we are always case sensitive. In the Windows/NT domains (Active Directory), depending on how user IDs are entered, you will find mixed cases. Windows domains are case insensitive: the user COFFIN is the same as Coffin or coffin.

There is a possibility that you or your application developers will use an equals() method instead of an equalsIgnoreCase() method in Java when dealing with the user ID. There is also a possibility (especially if you follow this book) that you will send the user ID to Oracle database and save it there or test it for existence in a database. For these possibilities, we will assure that our data is consistently cased where case-sensitivity is an issue. We will handle user IDs in upper case.

Access Oracle Database as Our Identified User

Oracle JDBC transmits a number of identity characteristics from the client to the server. Among these are the OS user ID, the IP address and in certain cases the *terminal* (client computer) name. We can query these items and use them for validation. Additionally, we can pass identity information to Oracle database, and we can assume a valid alternate identity and use the connected identity as a proxy.

All of these aspects of identity, when appropriately set, allow us to authorize access, and as importantly, to audit access to data. We want to know, monitor, and report who did what.

Examine the Oracle SSO Options for Programmers

Let's examine some of our options at this point. I am going to limit the options for doing single sign-on with Oracle database to the following:

- Have a standard connection to Oracle database as `appusr` and pass the OS user identity for authorization (perhaps) and auditing (certainly).

- Have a proxy session to Oracle database. The Oracle user will be named the same as our OS user, and will proxy through `appusr`. This requires a minimal Oracle user for each OS user, with the same name as the OS user. (This will be the default approach used throughout the chapters following this one. But if you are using another scheme at present, you will be glad to know that we can achieve SSO in that approach as well.)

- Have a connection pool for the app with Oracle users named the same as our OS users, all proxying through `appusr`. We will examine both lightweight (thin) connection pools and heavyweight (Oracle call interface, or OCI) connection pools. We will also implement the newest connection pool technology from Oracle database: universal connection pool (UCP).

Set a Client Identifier

The client identifier is an identity trait we can set for each Oracle connection. It can be used for a number of things, but for our purposes, we will set it equal to the user identity we get from `NTSystem` or `UnixSystem`.

Using an `OracleConnection` class (which extends the standard `Connection` class), we can set the client identifier using the code in Listing 8-5.

Listing 8-5. Set the Client Identifier, doTest1()

```
userName = OracleJavaSecure.getOSUserID();

String metrics[] =
    new String[OracleConnection.END_TO_END_STATE_INDEX_MAX];
metrics[OracleConnection.END_TO_END_CLIENTID_INDEX] = userName;
conn.setEndToEndMetrics( metrics, ( short )0 );
```

The last line is a call to set the end-to-end metrics for the connection. That call takes a `String` array, `metrics`, and an index of type `short` (a smaller integer) equal to 0—we cast the value 0 as a `short`. We set the size of the `String` array equal to the constant member of `OracleConnection` named `END_TO_END_STATE_INDEX_MAX`, and we place the user identity in the array at the constant index `END_TO_END_CLIENTID_INDEX`.

Later, when we want to see what the client identifier is set to, we will examine it on the Oracle database by querying `SYS_CONTEXT('USERENV','CLIENT_IDENTIFIER')`. Oracle database provides the facility for creating and using application contexts in addition to the session context, `SYS_CONTEXT`. Contexts are a convenience feature for storing information in the session as opposed to storing that data in a database table. Often application contexts are mentioned along with the security topic of Fine-Grained Access (FGA) control (See Chapter 12), but contexts by themselves do not provide security—just another storage place for information.

Prepare to Access HR Data

In all cases, we want to access data in the `HR` schema, so we can do a couple things to prepare for that. First, we will call the `appsec.p_check_hrview_access` procedure to acquire our secure application role, `hrview_role`. Then, we can set our current schema to the `HR` schema. This has no effect on access, but allows us to call on views and procedures in the HR schema without prefixing each call with "HR." The code in Listing 8-6 does these things.

Listing 8-6. Prepare to Access HR Data

```
stmt.execute("CALL appsec.p_check_hrview_access()");
stmt.execute("ALTER SESSION SET CURRENT_SCHEMA=hr");
rs = stmt.executeQuery( "SELECT COUNT(*) FROM v_employees_public" );
```

Notice there is no "HR." prefix on the view name, v_employees_public.

Update p_check_hrview_access Procedure, Non-Proxy Sessions

We will be making a couple sweeping changes to the appsec.p_check_hrview_access procedure: one to handle regular connections, and one to handle proxy sessions. Once you decide which approach you will implement, you may comment or remove one or the other blocks of code. In the body of appsec.p_check_hrview_access, we will place this code, Listing 8-7 for non-proxy sessions.

Listing 8-7. Verify Non-Proxy Sessions

```
IF( ( SYS_CONTEXT( 'USERENV', 'IP_ADDRESS' ) LIKE '192.168.%' OR
      SYS_CONTEXT( 'USERENV', 'IP_ADDRESS' ) = '127.0.0.1' )
AND TO_CHAR( SYSDATE, 'HH24' ) BETWEEN 7 AND 18
AND SYS_CONTEXT( 'USERENV', 'SESSION_USER' ) = 'APPUSR'
AND SYS_CONTEXT( 'USERENV', 'CLIENT_IDENTIFIER' ) = just_os_user )
THEN
    --DBMS_SESSION.SET_ROLE('hrview_role');
    EXECUTE IMMEDIATE 'SET ROLE hrview_role';
END IF;
```

■ **Note** You can find this script in the file named *Chapter8/AppSec.sql*.

The first two tests in the if statement, regarding IP_ADDRESS and SYSDATE time constraints, are the same as what we implemented in Chapter 2. The third test assures that the SESSION_USER is 'APPUSR'; that is, that the appusr user is connected to Oracle database. Prior to this point, we have limited the execution privilege for appsec.p_check_hrview_access to appusr, but now with proxy sessions, we need to permit any Oracle user to execute our procedure, and assure that they are connected as appusr after the fact. We grant execute to PUBLIC (everybody) like this:

GRANT EXECUTE ON appsec.p_check_hrview_access TO PUBLIC;

Remember, the goal of all these checks is to eventually set the role to hrview_role, if everything checks out. There are at least the following two ways to set the role:

- Call to DBMS_SESSION.SET_ROLE.

- Immediately execute the SET ROLE command.

Both are valid, but we will continue to use the second form. It is more generic, and we will use the EXECUTE IMMEDIATE syntax in additional situations.

Assure Client Identifier and OS_USER

The fourth test in our procedure, shown Listing 8-7, assures that the OS user identity that we are passing to Oracle database as the client identifier is equal to the OS_USER connection trait that JDBC passes to the database. This is merely a second check for us to assure that the client identifier set by the application, which represents the OS user identity, is the same as the OS user identity sensed by the Oracle Database. We assure that the application has not set client identity to something other than the OS user identity.

We get the OS user that was sensed by Oracle database, just_os_user through the JDBC client using the code in Listing 8-8. Really, it is just another session context environment setting; however, we need to massage the value.

Listing 8-8. Getting the OS User Sensed by Oracle

```
just_os_user      VARCHAR2(40); -- Windows users are 20, allow 20 for domain
backslash_place NUMBER;
BEGIN
    -- Upper case OS_USER and discard prepended domain name, if exists
    just_os_user := UPPER( SYS_CONTEXT( 'USERENV', 'OS_USER' ) );
    -- Back slash is not an escape character in this context
    -- Negative 1 indicates count left from the right end, get last backslash
    backslash_place := INSTR( just_os_user, '\', -1 );
    IF( backslash_place > 0 )
    THEN
        just_os_user := SUBSTR( just_os_user, backslash_place + 1 );
    END IF;
```

Note that we need to upper-case the OS_USER sent by JDBC to Oracle Database using the UPPER function so that we can match by case the uppercase user identity we set in client identifier. In some cases, the domain name is prepended on the OS_USER with a backslash separator like this: *ORGDOMAIN\OSUSER*. We use the INSTR (in string) function to find the place of the backslash, if any. Then we remove the domain name and backslash using the SUBSTR (substring) function. Looking back at Listing 8-7, it is this massaged OS_USER, just_os_user that we compare to the value we set in the client identifier.

Testing that all these user identity traits are identical doesn't really buy us a lot of additional security, but sets another hurdle to trip up would-be hackers. You might be surprised at how often that one extra hurdle is all you needed to prevent a break-in, and how often a simple added hurdle is sold as a commercial security solution.

Audit Activity with Client Identifier Set

The following query will show you audit trail entries for connections where the client identifier is set. You may not have any just yet, but we will see these connections after our tests.

```
SELECT * FROM sys.dba_audit_trail
WHERE client_id IS NOT NULL
ORDER BY TIMESTAMP DESC;
```

■ **Note** You can find this script in the file named *Chapter8/SecAdm.sql*.

Proxy Sessions

The idea behind proxy sessions is that we can connect as our application user but do work as an identified person user. This allows us to securely connect as our application user (no individual person passwords are used, nor indeed are they needed), and to audit the activities of individual persons. These goals do not differ radically from what we accomplish with setting our client identifier to the OS user identity, as in the previous section. The primary differences (in our efforts) are:

- With proxy sessions, we are not doing work as our application user, but as our individual user.
- With proxy sessions, an Oracle user must exist for each individual person who is going to connect.

Create Individual Person Users in Oracle

Why would we want to go to the effort of setting up individual person users in Oracle database when our application account is all we need to do the work? That is a good question, and the answer may give you reasons to choose to take either of the two routes we are describing in this section:

1) Using standard connections and placing the OS user identity in the Oracle client identifier.

2) Using proxy sessions.

Individual (human) users require some administrative activity; however, it can be minimal. Let's create one example user named OSUSER (feel free to substitute your user ID for OSUSER in these commands):

```
CREATE USER osuser IDENTIFIED EXTERNALLY;
GRANT create_session_role TO osuser;
ALTER USER osuser GRANT CONNECT THROUGH appusr;
```

For each individual user, you only need to execute these commands. Each user must have the Create Session system privilege because proxying requires creation of an additional session. You will have one connection (as the application user) and two sessions—one as the application user and one as the proxying user.

You could script user creation from a list of all the users in your organization and quickly create an Oracle user for each person. The ease with which these users can be created is not an argument in their favor, as there is still an effort required. There is also an administrative effort required to remove or disable users when employees are no longer around.

Another argument against individual users in Oracle database is that some access and allocation is provided for each user. Each user will have an associated schema. This schema will not consist of much, but it will exist. And when you scroll through the list of schemas (in an IDE) to get to the one you want, you may be scrolling through dozens, hundreds, or thousands belonging to individual persons.

Proxy from Users IDENTIFIED EXTERNALLY

Perhaps your organization already uses the Oracle Internet directory (OID) and/or enterprise user security, if so it is possible to create individual person users who do not have schemas on each instance of Oracle Database, and can be used in proxy sessions. Those users would be IDENTIFIED GLOBALLY.

Perhaps, you trust another directory service or the operating system to identify your users. In that case, you would still have a unique schema for each user, but the authentication (ID and password) would be retained externally. For instance, you might set an OS_AUTHENT_PREFIX like "OPS$" (typical) for your database, and create an Oracle user named OPS$OSUSER. The OSUSER user would not provide a password when connecting to Oracle database, but would gain access by virtue of being authenticated to the operating system as OSUSER. There are steps required to set this up, including gaining access to your directory or domain server from the Oracle database. This is a form of single sign-on.

However, what we are doing is intentionally different. We are creating individual users in Oracle Database that have no authentication. They have no password, and the IDENTIFIED EXTERNALLY modifier simply tells Oracle Database that the user is not authenticated by the database.

Another way to have done this would be to create the users identified by a random password that not even the administrator retains. If no one knows the password, no one can authenticate with it. The problem with that is that any password that exists needs to be managed and at least periodically changed (to another random password).

Establish a Proxy Session

To establish a proxy session, we do 2 things. First we create a Properties class (basically a hash table with keys and values, e.g., key=PROXY_USER_NAME and value=OSUSER). Then we pass this Properties class to the openProxySession() method of the OracleConnection class, as shown in Listing 8-9. This code is from the doTest2() method of the OraSSOTests class. Also see the main() method.

■ **Note** Find the test code in the file named *Chapter8/OraSSOTests.java.*

Note that we already have an existing connection at this point. We are connected to Oracle database as our application user. The goal here is to have our OS user account proxy through the application user.

Listing 8-9. Open a Proxy Session, doTest2()

```
userName = OracleJavaSecure.getOSUserID();
Properties prop = new Properties();
prop.setProperty( OracleConnection.PROXY_USER_NAME, userName );
conn.openProxySession(OracleConnection.PROXYTYPE_USER_NAME, prop);

String metrics[] =
    new String[OracleConnection.END_TO_END_STATE_INDEX_MAX];
metrics[OracleConnection.END_TO_END_CLIENTID_INDEX] = userName;
conn.setEndToEndMetrics( metrics, ( short )0 );
```

Notice we get the OS user identity into userName from NTSystem or UnixSystem and set it as the PROXY_USER_NAME. When we open the session, we tell it we are basing the proxy on user name, PROXYTYPE_USER_NAME.

We also set the client identifier to the OS user name—that is a good handle for searching audit logs. At this point we have a proxy session, and we can validate it with this query:

```
SELECT USER
, SYS_CONTEXT('USERENV','PROXY_USER')
, SYS_CONTEXT('USERENV','OS_USER')
, SYS_CONTEXT('USERENV','SESSION_USER')
, SYS_CONTEXT('USERENV','OS_USER')
, SYS_CONTEXT('USERENV','IP_ADDRESS')
, SYS_CONTEXT('USERENV','TERMINAL')
, SYS_CONTEXT('USERENV','CLIENT_IDENTIFIER')
FROM DUAL;
```

This will return a series of identity values like this:

```
user                  : OSUSER
userenv proxy_user    : APPUSR
userenv current_user  : OSUSER
userenv session_user  : OSUSER
userenv os_user       : OSUser (occasionally OrgDomain\OSUser)
userenv ip_address    : 127.0.0.1
userenv terminal      : unknown
userenv client_id     : OSUSER
```

In our Oracle proxy session, the USER, CURRENT_USER, and SESSION_USER also are set to OSUSER. Oracle database saw that our OS user from JDBC was OSUser, as shown for the OS_USER session environment value.

Finally, we connected as appusr, which allows proxying through by OSUSER, so we see APPUSR as the PROXY_USER. If you look at the code of OraSSOTests, you'll see that we connect as appusr:

```
private String appusrConnString =
    "jdbc:oracle:thin:appusr/password@localhost:1521:orcl";

conn = (OracleConnection) DriverManager.getConnection( appusrConnString );
```

So we connected as appusr, but after establishing our proxy session, you can see that our user is OSUSER.

We close our proxy connections with a bit different syntax:

```
conn.close( OracleConnection.PROXY_SESSION );
```

In this context (the doTest2() method), the effect is the same as the standard conn.close(), but for cached connections/connection pools this new syntax only closes the current session but keeps the connection available for others.

PROXY USER VERSUS PROXY USER NAME

Unfortunately, Oracle has used the words "proxy user" for both sides of the "connect as user" and "proxy through user" relationship. Proxy user, proxy_user, is the Oracle user that connects to the database as in our session environment, SYS_CONTEXT('USERENV', 'PROXY_USER'). And PROXY_USER_NAME is the name of the user getting access through the proxy user as when we set up our proxy connection, prop.setProperty(OracleConnection.**PROXY_USER_NAME**, userName). Perhaps it would have been better to delineate these players with the names "proxy host user" and "proxy client user," or "proxy connect user" and "proxy session user."Despite the confusion, we will need to keep them straight. One user initially connects to Oracle database with his password (called the proxy user), and another user proxies through (connects through) that user. That second user owns the session that will do all the work and we will see him in our audit logs.

Update p_check_hrview_access Procedure, Proxy Sessions

Our secure application role procedure, `appsec.p_check_hrview_access` must be updated again to verify proxy sessions and grant the `hrview_role`, as appropriate. We have added the code shown in Listing 8-10 to the body of the procedure for that purpose (find this in the file *AppSec.sql*).

Listing 8-10. Verify Proxy Session

```
IF( SYS_CONTEXT( 'USERENV', 'PROXY_USER' ) = 'APPUSR'
AND ( SYS_CONTEXT( 'USERENV', 'IP_ADDRESS' ) LIKE '192.168.%' OR
    SYS_CONTEXT( 'USERENV', 'IP_ADDRESS' ) = '127.0.0.1' )
AND TO_CHAR( SYSDATE, 'HH24' ) BETWEEN 7 AND 18
AND SYS_CONTEXT( 'USERENV', 'SESSION_USER' ) =
    SYS_CONTEXT( 'USERENV', 'CLIENT_IDENTIFIER' )
AND SYS_CONTEXT( 'USERENV', 'CLIENT_IDENTIFIER' ) = just_os_user )
THEN
    EXECUTE IMMEDIATE 'SET ROLE hrview_role';
END IF;
```

The first test within the `if` statement assures us that we are dealing with a proxy session and that the proxy user is `appusr`. If you recall, we initially only allowed `appusr` to execute this procedure, but now we have granted execute to `PUBLIC`. However, we are still permitting access only to `appusr` by assuring that either the `SESSION_USER` is `appusr` (when only setting client identifier) or that the `PROXY_USER` is `appusr` (for proxy sessions).

Next we have the standard tests for IP Address and `SYSDATE` time constraints. Then we have two more tests that basically assure that these three identity traits are identical:

```
SESSION_USER = CLIENT_IDENTIFIER = OS_USER
```

The user proxying this session is the same as the OS user we got from `NTSystem` or `UnixSystem` and is the same as the OS user that is presented by JDBC to Oracle Database. If all that is true, then we set the secure application role, `hrview_role`.

Audit Proxy Sessions

We want to audit activity specific to proxy sessions. We can configure that with these commands:

```
AUDIT UPDATE TABLE, INSERT TABLE BY appusr ON BEHALF OF ANY;
-- This would be nice, but every java class gets audited with this command
--AUDIT EXECUTE PROCEDURE BY appusr ON BEHALF OF ANY;
NOAUDIT EXECUTE PROCEDURE BY appusr ON BEHALF OF ANY;
```

Because `appusr` is the proxy user, we can audit whatever he does on behalf of others. Here we are auditing all update and insert queries. We decided against auditing all calls to execute procedures.

These queries will display audit trail entries generated by proxy sessions. The first query displays all proxy sessions—they have a PROXY_SESSIONID.

```
SELECT * FROM DBA_AUDIT_TRAIL WHERE PROXY_SESSIONID IS NOT NULL;
```

This next query finds the specific proxy connection associated with the session and shows the proxy user for the connection. The results might appear as shown in Table 8-1. Our query actually returns more columns than those shown in the Table.

```
SELECT p.username proxy, u.os_username, u.username, u.userhost, u.terminal,
u.timestamp, u.owner, u.obj_name, u.action_name, u.client_id, u.proxy_sessionid
FROM sys.dba_audit_trail u, sys.dba_audit_trail p
WHERE u.proxy_sessionid = p.sessionid
ORDER BY u.timestamp DESC;
```

Table 8-1. *Example Audit Log Entries for Proxy Session*

PROXY	OS_USERNAME	USERNAME	ACTION_NAME	CLIENT_ID	PROXY_SESSIONID
APPUSR	OSUSER	OSUSER	LOGOFF	OSUSER	68325
APPUSR	OSUSER	OSUSER	LOGON		68325

Using Connection Pools

If you are strictly concerned with desktop client applications, then you can skip this section. Connection pools are generally only needed for multi-threaded, multi-user Server applications. A connection pool is a collection of connections that are available for use by clients or client threads. As needed, a client will acquire a connection from the pool, use it to query or update the Oracle database, and then return it to the pool.

A connection pool usually exists for the duration of the JVM. Consider this scenario: a web application server (for example, Tomcat) starts running and an application requests a connection from a pool. At that point, a pool of connections is established, and one of the connections is provided to the application. That specific application thread (typically tied to a user request—a browser seeking a dynamic web page) will return the connection to the pool when the thread is done with it. Our connection pool exists for use by all the web application threads (users browsing dynamic web pages) until the web application server (Tomcat) is shut down.

We are going to spend sufficient effort here to demonstrate that our single sign-on will work from any of the available connection pooling approaches. If you are using a Java Enterprise Edition (J2EE) container (like a web application server) and you use Enterprise Java Beans (EJBs), then chances are good that you are using connection pooling by way of a "container-managed connection pool."

Proxy Connections from an OCI Connection Pool

An Oracle call interface (OCI) connection pool is a traditional approach to connection pools, and our approach to single sign-on can succeed within it. OCI is a technology that supersedes Java and is not a "pure java" implementation. We would say that using ojdbc, Java is able to call OCI as an external resource.

Configure the Pool

The first step we must take is to establish the connection pool through an `OracleOCIConnectionPool` class. We set the URL (connection string), user, and password (`appusrConnURL`, `appusrConnUser`, `appusrConnPassword`) that all connections in the pool will have, as shown in Listing 8-11. They will all connect as `appusr`.

Be sure to edit the code in *OraSSOTests.java* to correctly identify your host, port, instance and network domain (in `SERVICE_NAME`). Notice that the connection URL is specified as "jdbc:oracle:oci:". That is the designation of a heavyweight, OCI connection type. The connection string is specified in *TNSNames* (transparent network substrate) format, `appusrConnOCIURL`.

Listing 8-11. Configure OCI Connection Pool

```
private String appusrConnOCIURL =
    "jdbc:oracle:oci:@(description=(address=(host=" +
    "127.0.0.1)(protocol=tcp)(port=1521))(connect_data=" +
    "(INSTANCE_NAME=orcl)(SERVICE_NAME=orcl)))";
    // Or
    //"(INSTANCE_NAME=orcl)(SERVICE_NAME=orcl.org.com)))";
private String appusrConnUser = "appusr";
private String appusrConnPassword = "password";

OracleOCIConnectionPool cpool = new OracleOCIConnectionPool();
cpool.setURL(appusrConnOCIURL);
cpool.setUser(appusrConnUser);
cpool.setPassword(appusrConnPassword);

Properties prop = new Properties();
prop.put (OracleOCIConnectionPool.CONNPOOL_MIN_LIMIT, "2");
prop.put (OracleOCIConnectionPool.CONNPOOL_MAX_LIMIT, "10");
prop.put (OracleOCIConnectionPool.CONNPOOL_INCREMENT, "1");
cpool.setPoolConfig(prop);
```

Next, we configure the connection pool by building a `Properties` object with the basic parameters: the minimum pool size (also initial size), maximum pool size, and growth increment. We pass the `Properties` to our connection pool through the `setPoolConfig()` method. Note that these properties apply to the pool itself, not to any specific connection.

Get the Proxy Connection

We add one more parameter to the existing (for convenience) `Properties` object—the `PROXY_USER_NAME`. When we get a connection from the pool, we specifically want a proxy connection. All connections in the pool connect as `appusr`, but each proxy connection coming from the pool can be associated with a different user connecting through `appusr`. We set the `PROXY_USER_NAME` for this connection to `userName`, the OS user identity that we got from `NTSystem` or `UnixSystem`. When we request a proxy connection from the `cpool.getProxyConnection()` method, Listing 8-12, we pass the `Properties` with the `PROXY_USER_NAME` in our request.

Listing 8-12. Get Proxy Connection from OCI Connection Pool

```
prop.setProperty(OracleOCIConnectionPool.PROXY_USER_NAME, userName );
conn = (OracleConnection)cpool.getProxyConnection(
    OracleOCIConnectionPool.PROXYTYPE_USER_NAME, prop);
```

For this connection from an OCI pool, we set the client identifier the same way we did previously for standard connections.

View the Proxy Session

At this point, if you query the `OracleConnection.isProxySession()` method, you will find that this is not a proxy session. Don't let that disturb you. If you query Oracle Database you will find that the `PROXY_USER` is `appusr`, and the `USER`, `CURRENT_USER`, and `SESSION_USER` are all set to our OS user identity. This is, by virtue of acquiring it through the `getProxyConnection()` method, a proxy connection and a proxy session.

It is unnecessary, but if you must have the `isProxySession()` method return `true`, you can generate another session through the `OracleConnection` class—you would have three sessions at that point. Using this code will also nullify your client identifier, which will interfere with the procedure that sets our secure application role. So if you do this, modify the SSO procedures (e.g., `appsec.p_check_hrview_access`) to skip testing the client identifier.

```
//prop = new Properties();
//prop.setProperty(OracleConnection.PROXY_USER_NAME, userName );
//conn.openProxySession(OracleConnection.PROXYTYPE_USER_NAME, prop);
```

Note that this code instantiates a new `Properties` class. The reason for that is that our prior `Properties` had numeric keys based on the `OracleOCIConnectionPool` constants, and this `Properties` instance needs `String` keys based on the `OracleConnection` constants.

See the Proxy Connection

Here are the results from our test queries in the `OraSSOTests.doTest3()` method. These results are from an OCI connection pool proxy connection.

```
Is proxy session: false
user                  : OSUSER
userenv proxy_user    : APPUSR
userenv current_user  : OSUSER
userenv session_user  : OSUSER
userenv os_user       : ORGDOMAIN\OSUSER
userenv ip_address    : 127.0.0.1
userenv terminal      : MYCOMPUTER
userenv client_id     : OSUSER
Read HR view!!T!!!!!!!!!!!!!!!!!!!!
```

Notice the first line. As described in the previous section, the `OracleConnection.isProxySession()` method returns `false`; however, this is a proxy session through a proxy connection. You can see that in the `PROXY_USER` identity trait, contrasted with the other user traits.

One of the nice things about heavy-weight OCI connections is that they can report the terminal name. Notice also that in the OS_USER parameter the OCI connection reports the domain name. It may be that you can implement some additional security checks based on those identity traits.

Close the Proxy Session

Our proxy connection close method, in this context, closes the proxy session and returns the connection to the pool for reuse. Notice in Listing 8-13 that we pass the PROXY_SESSION constant value to the OracleConnection.close() method. This is identical to how we close the proxy connection without connection pooling, except without pooling both the proxy session and the Oracle connection get closed.

Listing 8-13. Close Proxy Connection

```
conn.close( OracleConnection.PROXY_SESSION );
```

Review All the Pool Properties

We can examine all the properties that are used by the connection pool, even those properties that we did not explicitly set. The code in Listing 8-14 gets the complete list of configuration properties and prints each key/value pair.

Listing 8-14. Display all OCI Connection Pool Properties

```
prop = cpool.getPoolConfig();
Enumeration enumer = prop.propertyNames();
String key;
while( enumer.hasMoreElements() ) {
    key = (String)enumer.nextElement();
    System.out.println( key + ", " + prop.getProperty( key ) );
}
```

We see the following list as the result from that code:

```
connpool_active_size, 0
connpool_pool_size, 2
connpool_max_limit, 10
connpool_min_limit, 2
connpool_timeout, 0
connpool_is_poolcreated, true
connpool_increment, 1
connpool_nowait, false
```

Summary of the OCI Connection Pool

The OCI connection pool handles our single sign-on approach very well. We are able to verify the user, pass our secure application role procedure tests and access HR data.

Our OracleConnection class from an OCI connection pool does not recognize the proxy session, but a proxy session exists nonetheless.

OCI connection pool connections recognize the terminal name and can return the Domain name along with the OS user name.

Here is the catch. An OCI connection pool *is very slow to be set up*, the connections are heavyweight and demand more resources. Once set up, and using existing connections in the pool, performance is not an issue. For this reason, an OCI connection pool is suitable for server-based applications with a long runtime duration (e.g., within a web application server).

Proxy Sessions from a Thin Client Connection Pool

While connection pools are generally only needed for Server applications supporting multiple, concurrent users, you might have some call for a multi-threaded, stand-alone or client application that will perhaps need to reuse multiple connections from a pool—be creative! A thin-client connection pool or cache is a great way to accomplish this. Our approach to single sign-on can succeed within it.

Configuring the Pool/Cache

We establish the lightweight (thin) connection pool through an `oracle.jdbc.pool.OracleDataSource` class. Set the URL (connection string), user, and password that all connections in the pool will have. They will all connect as `appusr`.

Edit the connection string (URL), `appusrConnURL`, setting the appropriate host, port, and instance; and set the correct password for `appusr` in `appusrConnPassword`. The URL is specified in TNSNames format. Notice in Listing 8-15 that the URL specifies a thin (light-weight) connection as "jdbc:oracle:thin". Thin connections require fewer resources and are set up faster than OCI connections. Thin connections use only java to communicate by SQL*Net protocol with Oracle Database, as opposed to using OCI as an external, non-java resource to run SQL*Net. We name our connection cache (pool), "APP_CACHE."

Listing 8-15. Configure Thin-Client Connection Pool

```
private String appusrConnThinURL =
    "jdbc:oracle:thin:@(description=(address=(host=" +
    "127.0.0.1)(protocol=tcp)(port=1521))(connect_data=" +
    "(INSTANCE_NAME=orcl)(SERVICE_NAME=orcl.org.com)))";

OracleDataSource cpool = new OracleDataSource();
cpool.setURL(appusrConnThinURL);
cpool.setUser(appusrConnUser);
cpool.setPassword(appusrConnPassword);

// Enable Connection Caching
cpool.setConnectionCachingEnabled(true);
cpool.setConnectionCacheName("APP_CACHE");

Properties prop = new Properties();
prop.setProperty("InitialLimit", "3");
prop.setProperty("MinLimit", "2");
prop.setProperty("MaxLimit", "10");
cpool.setConnectionCacheProperties(prop);
```

We will also set up some initial properties for the connection pool and pass them to the `setConnectionCacheProperties()` method. These are similar to the pool properties we saw earlier for the OCI connection pool, but the key names are quite different.

Use Statement Caching

You will see some confusion when doing research on the web regarding lightweight connection pooling. Much of this confusion stems from the availability of statement caching in the `OracleDataSource` class. It is particularly muddled by the reference to connection pooling as connection caching. For good measure, let's enable statement caching as in Listing 8-16. This has nothing to do with connection pooling.

Listing 8-16. Enable Statement Caching

```
cpool.setImplicitCachingEnabled(true);
```

With statement caching, when you call a prepared statement, the local connection caches it. Should you call the statement again, it executes faster than it would if not cached.

Implicit caching, which we enabled by calling `setImplicitCachingEnabled(true)`, happens automatically. You can also enable *explicit* statement caching which requires you to designate a key string (name) for the statement and to recall it by that name. For more information, do an Internet search on Oracle explicit statement caching.

Get the Proxy Session

We request a thin connection from the pool through the `getConnection()` method, as shown in Listing 8-17. After getting the pooled connection, we request a proxy session. Pass the user identity from `NTSystem` or `UnixSystem` as a property value to the `openProxySession()` method of the `OracleConnection`. Again, for convenience, we just add another value, `PROXY_USER_NAME` to the *existing* Property class.

Listing 8-17. Get Proxy Connection from Thin-Client Connection Pool

```
conn = (OracleConnection)cpool.getConnection();
prop.setProperty(OracleConnection.PROXY_USER_NAME, userName );
conn.openProxySession(OracleConnection.PROXYTYPE_USER_NAME, prop);
```

When we close the proxy session, the connection will return to the pool for reuse:

```
conn.close( OracleConnection.PROXY_SESSION );
```

See the Proxy Session

The results from our queries on the thin client proxy session are as we would expect. We have set both our client identifier and our proxying user, `osuser` through the proxy user, `appusr`. The connection passes the tests for our secure application role and is able to read data from the HR schema.

```
Is proxy session: true
user               : OSUSER
userenv proxy_user : APPUSR
userenv current_user : OSUSER
```

```
userenv session_user : OSUSER
userenv os_user      : OSUSER
userenv ip_address   : 127.0.0.1
userenv terminal     : unknown
userenv client_id    : OSUSER
Read HR view!!!!!!!!!!!!!!!!!!!!!
```

Review All the Pool Properties

We can also retrieve and review all the connection pool properties:

```
prop = cpool.getConnectionCacheProperties();
```

```
MaxStatementsLimit, 0
AbandonedConnectionTimeout, 0
MinLimit, 2
TimeToLiveTimeout, 0
LowerThresholdLimit, 20
InitialLimit, 3
ValidateConnection, false
ConnectionWaitTimeout, 0
PropertyCheckInterval, 900
InactivityTimeout, 0
LocalTransactionCommitOnClose, false
MaxLimit, 10
ClosestConnectionMatch, false
AttributeWeights, NULL
```

COMPILING, DEPRECATED METHODS AND ANNOTATIONS

When you compile OraSSOTests.java you will receive two warnings. Two of the methods we are calling here are deprecated; that is, they are no longer promoted as current programming practices. You can see what methods those are by providing an argument on the command line, like this:

```
javac -Xlint:deprecation OraSSOTests.java
```

```
OraSSOTests.java:265: warning: [deprecation] setConnectionCachingEnabled(boolean
) in oracle.jdbc.pool.OracleDataSource has been deprecated
                  cpool.setConnectionCachingEnabled(true);
                       ^
OraSSOTests.java:274: warning: [deprecation] setConnectionCacheProperties(java.u
til.Properties) in oracle.jdbc.pool.OracleDataSource has been deprecated
            cpool.setConnectionCacheProperties(prop);
                 ^
2 warnings
```

Wouldn't you know it, these are the two methods we are calling to enable and configure our connection pool (cache)!?! Why are they deprecated? Even with those warnings, the code will still compile correctly and will run just fine. It is rare, in my experience, that a deprecated method actually disappears—sometimes they are actually revived. Fear not!

These methods are only recently deprecated, and I suspect the reason is that Oracle has developed a new package to do thin-client connection pooling, universal connection pool (UCP). We will implement UCP later in this chapter.

We can keep these deprecation warnings from bothering us when we compile by placing a @SuppressWarnings *annotation* on the method with our deprecated calls as shown below. Notice that there is no semicolon at the end of the annotation; it applies to the following method, doTest4().

```
@SuppressWarnings("deprecation")
void doTest4() {
```

Annotations are not part of the Java syntax, but they are included in the Java code and the byte code (after compilation) in order to instruct the Java utilities and tools (like *java.exe* and *javac.exe*). The variety of uses of annotations are quite numerous, and you can extend them by defining your own annotation types and by writing Java code for use by the Java tools in responding to annotations.

Many annotations like this are not acceptable to the Oracle JVM, so we will comment them in our code before creating the Java structures in Oracle Database.

Summary of the Thin Client Connection Pool

Thin client connection pooling is quick and convenient. It supports our approach to SSO by proxy and by client identifier.

It is a little disturbing to see the key methods used for connection pooling being labeled as "deprecated." But that is not a roadblock.

Universal Connection Pool

UCP is the newest kid on the block for connection pooling. Because it is so new, it would behoove you to watch for and implement any updates to UCP.

░ **Note** Find the test code for UCP in the file named *Chapter8/OraSSOTests2.java.*

Compile/Run with UCP

As yet, the UCP package has not been incorporated into the Oracle drivers jar (ojdbc6.jar). You will need to download a separate *ucp.jar* file from Oracle at *www.oracle.com/technetwork/indexes/downloads.* Scroll down and find the file in the [**Drivers**] section.

Our test code for UCP is in a separate file, *OraSSOTests2.java*. When you compile and run this code, you will need to include the *ucp.jar* file in your CLASSPATH, as shown in Listing 8-18.

Listing 8-18. Command to Compile and Run with UCP.jar

```
javac -classpath "%CLASSPATH%";ucp.jar OraSSOTests2.java
java -classpath "%CLASSPATH%";ucp.jar OraSSOTests2
```

A better approach, if you are going to use UCP, would be to add it to your CLASSPATH in the OS environment, as described in Chapter 3.

Use a Connection Pool Factory

UCP uses a PoolDataSourceFactory class to instantiate the pool connections. We provide the PoolDataSource with the fully-qualified name of the class to be used for each connection, "oracle.jdbc.pool.OracleDataSource," and we set the URL (connection string) to be used for the connections. See Listing 8-19.

Listing 8-19. Configure UCP Connection Pool

```
private String appusrConnString =
    "jdbc:oracle:thin:appusr/password@localhost:1521:orcl";

PoolDataSource cpool = PoolDataSourceFactory.getPoolDataSource();
cpool.setConnectionFactoryClassName("oracle.jdbc.pool.OracleDataSource");
cpool.setURL( appusrConnString );

cpool.setInitialPoolSize(5);
cpool.setMinPoolSize(2);
cpool.setMaxPoolSize(10);
```

We call methods of the PoolDataSource class, cpool to set some properties of the connection pool.

Note That UCP Is a Thin Client Implementation

Notice that the URL we specify (above) is a lightweight, thin connection. We are also able to specify the URL in the straightforward connection string syntax, as shown in Listing 8-20. If desired, we could specify the URL in TNSNames format and provide the user and password in separate method calls. We can also specify the straightforward connection string syntax, leaving out the user and password, and provide user and password in separate method calls.

Listing 8-20. Alternative UCP Connection Pool Specification

```
cpool.setURL(appusrConnURL);
cpool.setUser(appusrConnUser);
cpool.setPassword(appusrConnPassword);
// Or
cpool.setURL("jdbc:oracle:thin:@localhost:1521:Orcl" );
cpool.setUser(appusrConnUser);
cpool.setPassword(appusrConnPassword);
```

One reason I very much prefer connection string syntax, including user name and password, is that I can provide them all the connection details, including password, from a secure external source as a single string. We will plumb the depths of this topic in Chapter 10 and Chapter 11. Providing connection strings from a secure external source means that we can do the following:

- Avoid embedding passwords in our application code.

- Centralize the storage, maintenance, and distribution of our connection strings (thereby allowing us to change the parameters of a connection string in one place and have the change applied wherever we use the connection).

Get and Use the UCP Connection

This will look very familiar. We get a connection from the pool, get a proxy session and set the client identifier exactly as we did for our non-UCP thin connection pool. The results are identical as well.

Summary of Universal Connection Pool

If you don't mind living a bit on the cutting edge, then UCP is the way to go. It will require you to watch for updates to the UCP package, and eventual inclusion of UCP in the Oracle drivers, *ojdbc6.jar*. You will also need to incorporate *ucp.jar* into your CLASSPATH (refer to Chapter 3). As far as our goal of Oracle SSO is concerned, UCP works without a hitch.

Application Use of Oracle SSO

The presumptive requirement we are making in this chapter is that the user has authenticated on the client. The goal we have in our code is to leverage that existing authentication and make it available to application developers so that they can tap into Oracle SSO without burdening them with the inner workings.

I'm going to implement only one of the five options for Oracle SSO that we've examined. We will select a non-pooled connection with proxy session (refer to the doTest2() method in *OraSSOTests.java*). If you want to implement non-proxy connections or pooled connections, you should be able to do that easily enough based on the *OraSSOTests.java* code.

Our Example Application Oracle SSO

We will examine this from the outside in; that is, from the application developers' point of view first. After we explore what the developer needs to do, we'll discuss what changes we need to make to the `OracleJavaSecure` class in order to support the developers.

Use the Application Oracle Connection

Each application will make connections to different Oracle instances as different application user accounts. That logic has to exist within the application. Our example application gets data from the HR schema as the `appusr` user, so we connect as that user in Listing 8-21.

Listing 8-21. Application Oracle Connection Specification

```
String urlString = "jdbc:oracle:thin:appusr/password@localhost:1521:orcl";
Class.forName( "oracle.jdbc.driver.OracleDriver" );
OracleConnection conn =
    (OracleConnection)DriverManager.getConnection( urlString );
```

■ **Note** You can find this code in the file named *Chapter8/AppOraSSO.java*.

Another approach, and one you would use if you were implementing a connection pool in the `OracleJavaSecure` class rather than in the client application, would *not* instantiate a connection in the application; rather, you would simply pass the application-specific URL, `urlString` to `OracleJavaSecure` in order to configure the connection pool. And you would get back an `OracleConnection` from the pool for use in your application. At least, that's how I would do it.

Get a Proxy Connection for SSO

Preferably, the developers can make a single method call to acquire a proxy connection that will successfully pass the tests in our secure application role procedure. Let's call that method `setConnection()`. The application developer would call it like this:

```
conn = OracleJavaSecure.setConnection( conn );
```

This would overwrite the existing `conn` with the `OracleConnection` returned by that method. In reality, remember that these are just references (pointers) to objects in memory, and there has been no new instance of this object created, so the object pointer has not changed. We passed a reference to the `OracleConnection` from the application to `OracleJavaSecure` (everything resides in a single JVM.) Then `OracleJavaSecure` set the proxy session and the client identifier on that `OracleConnection`. When we go to use it back in the application, those features are now part of our original `OracleConnection`. We can and will just use the syntax shown in Listing 8-22.

Listing 8-22. Add Proxy Features to Existing Connection, setProxyConnection()

```
OracleJavaSecure.setProxyConnection( conn );
```

The results will be the same—the original `OracleConnection`, `conn` now has the proxy features.

If we were passing the URL only, we would call this method, which returns an `OracleConnection` with proxy session and client identifier:

```
OracleConnection conn = OracleJavaSecure.setConnection( urlString );
```

Close the Proxy Connection

We want to allow for the possibility that these connections may come from a connection pool, and we want to be sure to close the proxy session in that case, so we will instruct the developers to call a method to close the connection, like this:

```
OracleJavaSecure.closeConnection();
```

Updates to OracleJavaSecure

The generic `Connection` class does not support proxy connections nor setting the client identifier. We will be using instances of `OracleConnection` from here out. Our static class member, `conn` is now an `OracleConnection`, see Listing 8-23. Also our static initializer for `conn` casts the `Connection` as an `OracleConnection`.

Listing 8-23. OracleJavaSecure Static OracleConnection

```
private static OracleConnection conn;

static {
    try {
        // The following throws an exception when not running within an Oracle Database
        conn = (OracleConnection)(new OracleDriver().defaultConnection());
    } catch( Exception x ) {}
}
```

Update setConnection() Method

We are going to overload the `setConnection()` method (see Listing 8-24), retaining one that takes a `Connection` parameter and adding one that takes an `OracleConnection`. The first will call the second so that both configure a proxy connection with the client identifier set. The OS user identity from `NTSystem` or `UnixSystem` is used for proxying and in the client identifier:

Listing 8-24. Set Internal Connection in OracleJavaSecure and Configure, setConnection()

```
public static final OracleConnection setConnection( Connection c ) {
    return setConnection( (OracleConnection)c );
}
public static final OracleConnection setConnection( OracleConnection c ) {
```

```java
    conn = null;
    // We are going to require that only we will set up initial proxy connections
    if( c == null || c.isProxySession() ) return null;
    else try {
        // Set up a non-pooled proxy connection with Client Identifier
        // To use an alternate solution, refer to code in OraSSOTests.java
        String userName = getOSUserID();
        if ( ( userName != null ) && ( !userName.equals( "" ) ) ) {
            Properties prop = new Properties();
            prop.setProperty( OracleConnection.PROXY_USER_NAME, userName );
            c.openProxySession(OracleConnection.PROXYTYPE_USER_NAME, prop);

            String metrics[] =
                new String[OracleConnection.END_TO_END_STATE_INDEX_MAX];
            metrics[OracleConnection.END_TO_END_CLIENTID_INDEX] = userName;
            c.setEndToEndMetrics( metrics, ( short )0 );

            // If we don't get here, no Connection will be available
            conn = c;
        } else {
            // This is not a valid user
        }
    } catch ( Exception x ) {
        x.printStackTrace();
    }
    return conn;
}
```

This code is exactly what we have been discussing for Oracle SSO. Notice that if the connection that is handed to us is already a proxy connection, we discard it and nullify our Connection. We will not recognize any proxy connections that are configured elsewhere—for security sake, we are jealous and protective of our role in this.

Add an Overloaded setConnection() Method

We are returning the resultant, configured OracleConnection from the setConnection() methods listed in 8-24, and these will support an additional setConnection() method. The additional method (Listing 8-25) takes the URL as a String, instantiates a Connection and calls the core setConnection() method, which configures the connection with a proxy session and client identifier. It then returns the configured OracleConnection. It is made relatively easy with a call to the other setConnection() methods, and returning what they return.

Listing 8-25. Alternate Set Internal Connection, setConnection()

```java
public static final OracleConnection setConnection( String URL ) {
    Connection c = null;
    try {
        Class.forName( "oracle.jdbc.driver.OracleDriver" );
        c = DriverManager.getConnection( URL );
    } catch ( Exception x ) {
        x.printStackTrace();
```

```
        }
        return setConnection( c );
    }
```

■ **Note** If you were going to implement a connection pool inside the OracleJavaSecure class, this is where you would do it. You would want to assure that the URL string had not changed with each subsequent call.

Close the Proxy Connection

Have the developers call a method on OracleJavaSecure to close the configured proxy connection, in order to assure the call is appropriate (Listing 8-26). We must assure that we close the proxy session, which may be an additional session on a single connection.

Listing 8-26. Close the Internal Connection, closeConnection ()

```
public static final void closeConnection() {
    try {
        conn.close( OracleConnection.PROXY_SESSION );
    } catch( Exception x ) {}
}
```

A Code Template to Give Developers

The lines shown in Listing 8-27 are all the Java that application developers will need in order to do Oracle SSO, by using the OracleJavaSecure class.

Listing 8-27. Method Calls for Application Developers

```
OracleConnection conn = OracleJavaSecure.setConnection( connectionString );
// Do Oracle queries here
OracleJavaSecure.closeConnection();
```

Refer to the instructions at the end of Chapter 7 in order to create a jar file containing OracleJavaSecure to give the application developers.

Note that there will also need to be a secure application role, protected by a procedure like the p_check_hrview_access in order to complete the SSO protection of our data.

In the case where we are doing proxy connections, there will need to be an Oracle user for each OS user identity that we want to have accessing our applications. And those Oracle individual person users will need to be granted "proxy through" on our application user.

Chapter Review

In this chapter, we discussed how to identify the Windows or UNIX user using the JAAS classes, NTSystem, and UnixSystem. Because those classes are not provided cross-platform, we delved into using reflection to both instantiate and call methods in those classes.

After establishing the OS identity, we explored the code needed to use that identity when authenticating to Oracle Database. The end goal is that our Oracle application users will be able to use our applications without entering their passwords. In fact, they won't need passwords at all on Oracle database, but we will be able to track each user's actions by one of two methods:

1) We set the connection client identifier equal to the user ID and then assure it exists in the connection before granting access. We can then find that client ID in the audit trail logs.

2) We create an Oracle user for each Windows/UNIX user, although the Oracle user does not need a password or any privileges besides CONNECT. We then proxy those individual users through our application user. We can query the audit logs for the proxy user identity.

We explored several varieties of Oracle connection pools we might establish. There are three connection pool technologies we may use:

1) Lightweight, thin client connection pools

2) Heavyweight, OCI connection pools

3) Universal connection pooling (UCP)

Finally, we built some setConnection() methods in OracleJavaSecure that make it easy for an Oracle application developer to tap into this technology.

Figure 8-1 illustrates the basic SSO process. The client application calls OracleJavaSecure.setConnection() method with an appropriate connection string. That method further calls getOSUserID() which gets the user ID (username) from the operating system using NTSystem or UnixSystem, as appropriate. With that OS user ID, we open a proxy session for our Connection through an Oracle user by the same name.

Using our proxy session, we call the p_check_hrview_access procedure, which assures our SSO credentials are in order, then sets the secure application role, hrview_role. At that point, we have done SSO to Oracle database—notice we didn't enter a password for the specific Oracle user. We can then select sensitive data from the EMPLOYEES table using the privileges granted to hrview_role.

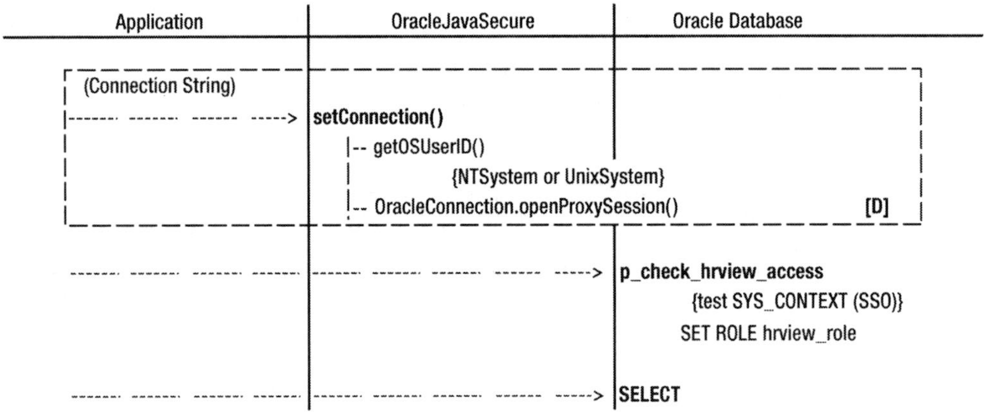

Figure 8-1. *SSO procedure*

CHAPTER 9

Two-Factor Authentication

What would life be like if there were no imposters, no charlatans, and no thieves? Sorry, that rhetorical question does not provide any security. Neither does putting on a set of rose-colored glasses and believing that we are secure just because we've implemented substantial security measures. We will always be susceptible to trickery and carelessness. The weakest link, even with upright associates, is always a person taking shortcuts. Social engineering and lack of attention to our computer security code of conduct (like, don't write down your password, don't share your password, use complex passwords, and change your password periodically) give thieves entrance to our most secure systems.

So, we are looking for further constraints on identity that can assure us that the person sitting at the keyboard is who they claim to be. There are many things that are being done in computer security to attempt to achieve this, such as the following:

- Requiring a second password or PIN code.

- Assuring there is a person at the computer instead of an automated program by having the person enter a non-computer-readable graphic representation of a word, called a CAPTCHA, which stands for completely automated public turing test to tell computers and humans apart (named in part after Alan Turing, the father of computer science and artificial intelligence).

- Requiring the user to answer personal questions, like giving the name of their first pet.

- Having a biometric scanner, like fingerprint, retina, or facial recognition.

- Having a secure ID token that synchronizes a code with the server to provide a one-time password, along with a PIN code.

- Out-of-band communication to a separate account or device, e.g., pass codes sent to your e-mail, pager, or cell phone.

Several of these efforts can be considered two-factor authentication. Combining them, you can even achieve three-factor authentication. For example:

1) What you know (passwords and PIN)

2) Who you are (human and biometric)

3) What you have (a Secure ID token or cell phone)

Perhaps a second password or additional PIN could also be considered two-factor authentication, but not so much. It is still just (1) what you know.

We are going to implement two-factor authentication that uses the single sign-on from Chapter 8, and a code that we will send to a separate account, preferably on a separate device. We will send pass codes to pagers, cell phones, and, as a last resort if neither of the first two is available, to an e-mail account.

Get Oracle Database to Send E-Mail

Our two-factor authentication will primarily contact pagers and cell phones and not send the pass code to a user's e-mail account. However, we are going to have the e-mail option. Also, the easiest way to send messages to commercial cell phones is by using the cell phone providers' short message service (SMS), texting hosts that often accept e-mail messages bound for the cell phones. So we are going to implement e-mail from Oracle database.

Oracle database provides a package called UTL_MAIL that enables us to send e-mail from the database. We will implement that; although, we could also load a Java class to send e-mail, and configure it to execute from a Java stored procedure. Perhaps we would use the JavaMail API or we might open a plain Java Socket and write simple mail transport protocol (SMTP) commands to it (so we don't have to load the JavaMail *mail.jar* file into Oracle database). Later in this chapter we will call a Java-stored procedure to read a web page, and sending e-mail could be done similarly.

Installing UTL_MAIL

The UTL_MAIL package is not installed in Oracle database by default. We will have to install it manually. Actually, we will ask the SYS user to install it for us. The package resides in two files that are located in a server directory resembling this path: *oracle\product\11.2.0\dbhome_1\RDBMS\ADMIN*. The files are called *utlmail.sql* and *prvtmail.plb*.

A *.plb* file is a wrapped PL/SQL file. Wrapped files can be considered obfuscated (not easily read), but not encrypted. The wrapped format lends severe difficulty to reverse engineering, but doesn't prevent it; although, you'd need to be a hacker to obtain the resources to unwrap the file. To create a wrapped procedure, function, package, or type, you pass a *.sql* file containing the CREATE statement for those structures to the wrap utility (comes with the Oracle Database software). This creates a non-reversible *.plb* file. Make sure you save an archive of the original *.sql* file in a secure location in case you ever need to edit it. Wrapped package files are used to hide the PL/SQL code, perhaps to protect intellectual property or to otherwise add security.

As SYS, you or your DBA friend need to open each of these files in order: *utlmail.sql* then *prvtmail.plb*; and execute them within the database. This can be done through TOAD, for example, by loading the files into the SQL Editor and executing them as a script. From SQL*Plus, SYS can run:

```
@C:\app\oracle\product\11.2.0\dbhome_1\RDBMS\ADMIN\utlmail.sql
```

```
@C:\app\oracle\product\11.2.0\dbhome_1\RDBMS\ADMIN\prvtmail.plb
```

■ **Note** You can find these commands listed in the file named *Chapter9/Sys.sql*.

Granting Access to UTL_MAIL

We are only going to allow one Oracle user to access the UTL_MAIL package: the appsec user. We will include code in the app_sec_pkg package to send out 2-factor pass codes using UTL_MAIL. First, let's enable our Security Administrator, secadm user to make entries in the database Access Control Lists (ACLs). Have SYS make the grants shown in Listing 9-1, including grant execute on the UTL_MAIL package to the appsec_role.

Listing 9-1. Grant Access to UTL_MAIL, as SYS user

```
GRANT EXECUTE ON sys.dbms_network_acl_admin TO secadm_role;
GRANT EXECUTE ON sys.utl_mail TO appsec_role;
```

Then as secadm user, execute the commands in Listing 9-2 to establish access control list (ACL) entries that will permit appsec to open port 25 and send e-mail. Be sure to edit the second command in the listing, inserting the name of your corporate SMTP server into the "host" field.

Listing 9-2. ACL Entries to Send E-Mail, as Secadm User

```
BEGIN
  DBMS_NETWORK_ACL_ADMIN.CREATE_ACL (

    acl          => 'smtp_acl_file.xml',
    description  => 'Using SMTP server',
    principal    => 'APPSEC',
    is_grant     => TRUE,
    privilege    => 'connect',
    start_date   => SYSTIMESTAMP,
    end_date     => NULL);

  COMMIT;

END;
/

BEGIN
  DBMS_NETWORK_ACL_ADMIN.ASSIGN_ACL (

    acl          => 'smtp_acl_file.xml',
    host         => 'smtp.org.com',
    lower_port   => 25,
    upper_port   => NULL);
  COMMIT;

END;
/
```

▨ **Note** You can find a script of the commands in Listing 9-2 in the file named *Chapter9/SecAdm.sql*.

You will notice that this syntax is quite different from what we're used to when calling procedures. These are, after all, simply calls to the `CREATE_ACL` and `ASSIGN_ACL` procedures in the `DBMS_NETWORK_ACL_ADMIN` package that is installed by default in the Oracle Database. In Listing 9-2, we are specifying the parameters for these procedures using *named notation,* as opposed to our usual *positional notation.* (I've given named notation here because every example I've seen has used that notation; we probably all just copy the example given in the Oracle documentation).

In named notation, the value being assigned to each parameter is given after the defined parameter name and the assignment operator `=>`, e.g., `acl => 'smtp_acl_file.xml'`. When we call a procedure using positional notation, we list the parameters in the order they were defined in the procedure (hence the name *positional*); but in named notation, the order is not important.

Another difference between positional and named notation is in how optional parameters are handled. You will recall that our error logging table, `t_appsec_errors`, has two optional parameters, `msg_txt` and `update_ts`. They are optional because we configured them with default values. The default value for `update_ts` is SYSDATE. In our `p_log_error` procedure, we never provide a value for `update_ts`. We want the default SYSDATE.

Back to the topic at hand: in positional notation, only optional parameters that are defined after all the required parameters may be ignored. With named notation, we can skip providing optional parameters no matter where they occur in the parameters definition, as long as we supply values for all the required parameters by name.

In the two procedures being called in Listing 9-2, `CREATE_ACL` and `ASSIGN_ACL`, the optional parameters are the last two defined for each procedure, so there is no compelling reason to call these procedures using named notation. In addition, the two calls that I have listed provide a value (or NULL) for each parameter, including the optional ones.

Again as `SYS` user or `DBA`, you can list the ACLs to ensure that your entries were made. Execute these queries:

```
SELECT * FROM sys.dba_network_acls;
SELECT * FROM sys.dba_network_acl_privileges;
```

The results of the first command will resemble this:

```
"HOST"           "LOWER_PORT" "UPPER_PORT" "ACL"                        "ACLID"
"smtp.org.com" "25"         "25"         "/sys/acls/smtp_acl_file.xml" "004B...
```

The results of the second command will resemble this:

```
"ACL"                        "ACLID"  "PRINCIPAL" "PRIVILEGE" "IS_GRANT" ...
"/sys/acls/smtp_acl_file.xml" "004B... "APPSEC"    "connect"   "true"     ...
```

Testing Sending E-Mail

While we are here, we should execute a test to be sure we can send e-mail. We are going to execute the test as our Application Security, `appsec` user. I apologize for bouncing around between these accounts, but we are delegating tasks and checking our work at each step.

■ **Note** You can find a script of the commands to follow in this section in the file named *Chapter9/AppSec.sql*.

We have already configured the Network ACL for **appsec** to be able to open port 25 on your SMTP mail host, but for each session we also need to tell the **UTL_MAIL** package to use that server as our SMTP host. As **appsec**, we add a property to our Oracle session that the **UTL_MAIL** package will read:

```
ALTER SESSION SET SMTP_OUT_SERVER = 'smtp.org.com';
```

Then we send an e-mail message. The arguments we provide are our e-mail address, address of the recipient, title of the message, and text of the message.

```
CALL UTL_MAIL.SEND( 'myname@org.com', 'myname@org.com', '', '',
    'Response','2FactorCode' );
```

Getting Oracle Database to Browse Web Pages

Besides sending two-factor authentication pass codes by e-mail/SMS to cell phones (and possibly e-mail accounts), we are going to send the pass codes to pagers. At our company, we send text messages to corporate pagers from a web page interface. This may or may not be the approach you will need to take to distribute two-factor authentication pass codes to pagers; however, it is relevant to any message distribution, because e-mail and web services are the primary modes of text messaging distribution from a user application.

Delegating Java Policy to Security Administrator

We already saw how we can add an ACL to allow a user to open a port. Now, in order to open a port as a Java stored procedure, we will need to grant Java security permissions. We are, in effect, allowing Java to perform an activity that is normally denied by the Oracle JVM security sandbox.

First, we will have **SYS** or a **DBA** delegate the policy permission to manage specific Java sandbox privileges to our security administrator, the **secadm** user. As **SYS**, do this with the code in Listing 9-3.

Listing 9-3. Grant Policy for Security Administrator to Grant Socket Permissions

```
CALL DBMS_JAVA.GRANT_POLICY_PERMISSION(
    'SECADM_ROLE', 'SYS',
    'java.net.SocketPermission',

    '*');

COMMIT;
```

The DBMS_JAVA.GRANT_POLICY_PERMISSION command specifies **secadm_role** as the recipient of the permission. **SYS** is the schema in which the grant is effective. The kind of permission being granted is a SocketPermission. And **secadm_role** can thereby manage any socket (*).

Assure that the Java policy permission has been granted with the following command. The policies are granted to a grantee number, GRANTEE#. We look up the name of that user in the USER$ table where user number, USER# matches the grantee number.

```
SELECT u.user#, u.name, p.name, p.type_name, p.action
FROM sys.user$ u, sys.java$policy$ p
WHERE p.name LIKE '%java.net.SocketPermission%'

AND p.grantee# = u.user#;
```

The results of this query will resemble the following. `JAVA_ADMIN` has a grant to `SocketPermission` on installation.

```
"USER#"  "NAME"        "NAME_1"                          "TYPE_NAME"
"40"     "JAVA_ADMIN"  "0:java.net.SocketPermission#*"   "oracle.aurora.rdbms...

"93"     "SECADM_ROLE" "0:java.net.SocketPermission#*"   "oracle.aurora.rdbms...
```

We are delegating a limited permission to manage the policy regarding opening sockets (network ports) to the `secadm_role`. There are other policies we might grant, like the policy regarding opening files on the Oracle server file system, but we don't need that here.

Permitting Application Security User to Read Web Pages

Now, as the `secadm` user, let's grant permission for our application security, the `appsec` user, to actually open a port to the web server that sends text messages to our corporate pagers. Change the name and port number of your web server, as required, then execute the code in Listing 9-4 as `secadm` user.

Listing 9-4. Grant Socket Permission to Application Security User

```
CALL DBMS_JAVA.GRANT_PERMISSION(
    'APPSEC',
    'java.net.SocketPermission',

    'www.org.com:80',
    'connect, resolve'
);
```

By this Java permission grant, we are heavily restricting what can actually be done.

- We will only permit connections to a specific server at a specific port, e.g. *www.org.com:80.*

- We will only permit one user to open the connection, `appsec.`

- And we will only allow the "connect" and "resolve" actions, which are sufficient to read a web page (and via the `GET` method, submit data in the URL). We need `resolve` action so that we (in the Oracle database) can do a DNS lookup/name resolution on (for example) `www.org.com`, to find the IP Address. We need the `connect` action so that we can actually establish a connection on a network port. Those are actions that are not permitted by default from the Oracle JVM security sandbox.

This call to `GRANT_PERMISSION` will likely throw an "uncaught Java exception" error. We cannot fix that, and it's nothing to worry about. Perhaps Oracle doesn't expect us to call procedures in the `DBMS_JAVA` package from the SQL command line.

Testing our ability to read web pages from Java on the Oracle database will require that we configure a Java stored procedure and update our Java code. Let's wait and test the fully functional code after we write it.

The Two-Factor Authentication Process

We are going to have Oracle applications attempting to read sensitive data that we are protecting. And we are going to require that these applications do database authentication first; they will need to pass our single sign-on tests, which were described in Chapter 8. Then they will need to request and receive a two-factor pass code that we will send to them from Oracle database. It is that process of requesting and receiving the two-factor pass code that we will be implementing in this chapter.

Once the user receives the two-factor pass code, they will submit that along with their request for data (and do the encryption key exchanges that we finished discussing in Chapter 7). At that point, if the user clicks his heels together and says "There's no place like home", he will be back in Kansas with access to read and update the data, as authorized.

Here's the catch: we can't assume that this two-factor code exchange will be instantaneous; otherwise, we would just require that the two-factor code exchange and the data requests occur in the same session. On the contrary, we will need to cache the two-factor codes in Oracle database for a set time limit to assure that the user and code go together. Certain other facts about the user need to correlate as well, such as the address of the computer from which the requests are being made.

Can you picture what we need to make all this happen? First of all, we need some data about our application users. We need their corporate pager numbers, cell phone numbers, and corporate e-mail addresses. The e-mail address is already stored in the `HR.EMPLOYEES` table. We will build another table in the `HR` schema to hold cell phone and pager numbers.

Along with the cell phone number, we will want to designate a carrier. Each carrier (e.g., AT&T) has a different address to which we will send messages for the cell phone. In the case of AT&T cell phones, we will send SMS messages to `10-digit-phone-number@txt.att.net`. There are SMS aggregators who will deliver SMS messages to phones handled by a number of carriers. If you have paid access to an aggregator, then you can use that as the carrier for all phones.

Security Considerations for Two-Factor Distribution Avenues

Two-factor authentication messages can be delivered to our application users via a variety of devices. We are going to consider delivering the messages by cell phone, pager, and e-mail. With each of those devices we have to consider the security implications. Our preference will be to send the two-factor code to a cell phone or a pager. Only if those fail will we want to send the code to an e-mail address.

Security Issues with Two-Factor Delivery to E-Mail

E-mail in and of itself is a fairly secure application. It is password protected and it is usually well managed. However, the data is usually not protected in transit by encryption, and it is extremely easy to impersonate an e-mail sender and send mail as them. There is no inherent problem with exchanging non-sensitive data using e-mail as long as you are willing to filter out the junk and verify the sender by an alternate means, as needed.

▧ **Note** I love e-mail because it lets us communicate in a non-concurrent, non-collocated, and person-to-person or broadcast fashion. It also can serve as a tactical record of a dialog and as a communication archive.

However, the whole idea with two-factor authentication is that we require a user to have two different and separate identifying traits. Yes, e-mail and our Oracle application are different pieces of code, but they may be running on the same computer, so they may not be separate.

If a hacker breaks into my computer and my e-mail is running, or she also breaks into my e-mail on my computer, and then if I send two-factor codes to e-mail, she can also run the Oracle application as me; even though the Oracle application is supposed to be protected by two-factor authentication.

Security Issues with Two-Factor Delivery to Pagers

I cannot speak regarding all pagers because some may operate differently, more like cell phones; however, the pagers I'm familiar with are quite simple devices, like AM radios. Two-way pagers generally use paging broadcast signals to deliver pages, but responses are returned through cellular telephone signals. Do not assume that page messages are individually delivered to your specific pager. That is not how the system works.

Page messages are delivered to a radio tower and broadcast, sometimes in data blocks of many messages. Each message is prefixed with a code. Your pager and all pagers in your system, listen to everything being broadcast from the radio antenna. The pager is programmed with a code or a list of codes to listen for. If the pager "sees" a code that it recognizes, it displays the associated message on the screen. If your pager is turned off, or the physics of the radio waves are not quite right (for instance, you're in a basement full of pipes), then you miss the broadcast and there's no way for your pager to retrieve the message later.

Now, picture the eaves-dropper sitting in a nearby hotel room with a scanner and a printer. He is listening to the radio frequency that the pager antenna is emitting, and he is printing out messages that are going to target codes, or he is printing out (or saving to a file) all messages. Also picture the hacker with his own radio and antenna, around the corner, sending his own devious page messages to target pager codes.

Now that you know the security issues, I will hasten to say that pagers are a great way to send immediate, simple, non-sensitive messages to people who may be traveling or away from a computer and phone. Paging is also a great way to broadcast messages to a number of people (via a paging group) simultaneously. Just don't send anything you don't want the world to see. And if you have doubts about the authenticity of a message, check with the sender. Also if you are a sender, don't assume the recipient got the page.

Pagers are probably a technology that will quickly disappear now that cell phone texting has become so popular. Pagers have the advantage of being inexpensive to buy and have inexpensive service plans. They are also allowed into some secure facilities where cell phones are not permitted, so pagers may be required in order to contact people in those facilities who are not at a landline phone or computer.

Security Issues with Two-Factor Delivery to Cell Phones

Unlike pagers, cell phones messages are delivered from a specific antenna to a specific cell phone. As you pass from the area covered by one antenna (cell tower) to another, your communication is handed off to the other cell.

Generally, this communication is fairly secure, with what passes as encryption. The key to reading and sending data is contained in the subscriber identity module (SIM) card in your phone. We have all seen television shows and movies depicting how a SIM card can be cloned, and an imposter cell phone can eaves drop on a call to the original phone. I don't think that happens much in real life, but be aware of the possibility.

Once my son broke the keypad on his cell phone and got another one with the same phone number. I suppose that they cloned his SIM card in the new phone. For a while, both phones received all the texting messages that were sent to him, so I can assure you that cloning (cell phones) works.

I like to remind my kids that the text messages they send, even if addressed only to a single other cell phone, are going into a system that can be read by many people that they don't even know: the service provider technical staff and law enforcement who may request access. That's not even mentioning the parents, siblings, friends, and other snoops or thieves who might browse the phone at some time.

We need to remember that any data (including voice, photograph, and video) which is made into a signal should be considered publicly accessible. That includes signals sent by plain old telephone systems (POTS), cell phones, the Internet, and so on. That includes electrical, radio wave, light, and sound transmissions.

Preferred Two-Factor Delivery

Cell phones are the most secure avenue for delivering our two-factor pass codes. However, there is nothing sensitive about the pass codes, so pretty much any delivery route is fine. If a code is read by an eavesdropper, to use the code that person would have to be sitting at the computer that initiated the Oracle application, logged in as the initiating user and within the code cache timeout period (10 minutes). If someone sends a fraudulent code, that is not likely to have an effect other than frustrating the user who is trying to use it for two-factor authentication.

The only preference we have is that if cell phone or pager delivery is available, we do not want to send the code to e-mail. Because e-mail may be running on the same computer as the Oracle application, sending the code to e-mail does not meet our goals for two-factor authentication, which is separate and distinct identity traits. Specifically, the two factors we are counting on are what you know (SSO initial login password), and What you have (a separate cell phone or pager).

Oracle Structures Supporting Two-Factor Authentication

In order to accomplish two-factor authentication, we will create some new tables and incorporate them into our security processes. We will create a table to hold cell phone and pager numbers for users. Additionally, we will create a table to hold the SMS gateway address for each cell phone carrier whose phones we need to support. During our 10-minute cache timeout period, while we wait for the 2-factor codes to be delivered to the user's cell phone, pager or e-mail, we will store the two-factor codes in the Oracle database, in another new table that we will create.

In addition to new tables, we will also create functions to send and to test the two-factor codes. We will also modify the `p_check_hrview_access` procedure to accept and test the two-factor code before setting the secure application role, `hrview_role`.

Creating the SMS Carrier Host Table

Most, if not all, cell phone service providers (carriers) offer access to text their phones through an e-mail server (SMTP.) For example, if you have a personal cell phone that is provided by AT&T, you can send an e-mail message to your phone number at the AT&T SMTP server (e.g., 8005551212@txt.att.net), and they will route your text message to the phone as an SMS message.

Each carrier has its own SMTP to SMS gateway and address; for example, AT&T has txt.att.net. We need a table to store those addresses so that we can send our two-factor authentication codes to cell phones provided by a variety of carriers. We will create a table, `sms_carrier_host`, to hold those addresses. See Listing 9-5. We also create a unique index based on `sms_carrier_cd` that we designate as our primary key. And we create a view (`v_sms_carrier_host`) of the table. Create this table in the HR schema.

■ **Note** You can find the commands in Listing 9-5 in the file named *Chapter9/HR.sql*.

Listing 9-5. Create an SMS Carrier Host Table

```
CREATE TABLE hr.sms_carrier_host
(
    sms_carrier_cd  VARCHAR2(32 BYTE) NOT NULL,
    sms_carrier_url VARCHAR2(256 BYTE)
);

CREATE UNIQUE INDEX sms_carrier_host_cd_pk ON hr.sms_carrier_host
    (sms_carrier_cd);

ALTER TABLE hr.sms_carrier_host ADD (
    CONSTRAINT sms_carrier_host_cd_pk
    PRIMARY KEY
    (sms_carrier_cd)
    USING INDEX sms_carrier_host_cd_pk
);

CREATE OR REPLACE VIEW hr.v_sms_carrier_host AS SELECT * FROM hr.sms_carrier_host;
```

After creating the table, you will want to pre-populate it with the addresses of the major carriers, and any other carriers that are popular with your workforce. Be aware that some of the smaller cell-phone providers piggyback on the major carrier's systems, especially phones from providers that are offered strictly as pre-pay phones.

You can find comprehensive lists of provider's SMS gateways on the Internet. One fairly comprehensive list can be found at http://en.wikipedia.org/wiki/List_of_SMS_gateways. I do not want to promote any specific carrier, but offer these example addresses (URLs) in Listing 9-6 that you may want to insert for your use.

Listing 9-6. Insert Sample SMS Carrier Host Entries

```
INSERT INTO hr.sms_carrier_host
    ( sms_carrier_cd, sms_carrier_url ) VALUES
    ( 'Alltel', 'message.alltel.com' );

INSERT INTO hr.sms_carrier_host
    ( sms_carrier_cd, sms_carrier_url ) VALUES
    ( 'AT_T', 'txt.att.net' );
```

```
INSERT INTO hr.sms_carrier_host

    ( sms_carrier_cd, sms_carrier_url ) VALUES

    ( 'Sprint', 'messaging.sprintpcs.com' );

INSERT INTO hr.sms_carrier_host

    ( sms_carrier_cd, sms_carrier_url ) VALUES

    ( 'Verizon', 'vtext.com' );
```

Creating a Table of Employee Mobile Numbers

We already have a table in the HR schema that includes the e-mail address for personnel: the EMPLOYEES table. However, we also need to store pager numbers and cell-phone numbers for employees, so we will create a table to hold those data values, the emp_mobile_nos table. We need one more data value to tie all this together: when a user log's in, and we identify her through our SSO process, we need a way to associate the HR EMPLOYEES and emp_mobile_nos data with the user. We will add a column named user_id to the emp_mobile_nos table to make that association. See Listing 9-7 for the creation command.

The HR.EMPLOYEES table includes a primary key index on EMPLOYEE_ID, which is an independent numeric value: each employee that is hired is assigned the next numeric value, sequentially. Whatever that value is, we will use to assign mobile numbers to that same employee. We are further associating that numeric EMPLOYEE_ID with an SSO logged-in user, the user_id column.

Listing 9-7. Create a Table for Employee Mobile Phone Numbers

```
-- Adjust length of Pager_No and Phone_No as needed
CREATE TABLE hr.emp_mobile_nos
(
    employee_id     NUMBER (6) NOT NULL,

    user_id         VARCHAR2(20 BYTE) NOT NULL,

    com_pager_no    VARCHAR2(32 BYTE),

    sms_phone_no    VARCHAR2(32 BYTE),

    sms_carrier_cd  VARCHAR2(32 BYTE)
);
```

At this point, I will point out an important fact that you need to consider. As we go forward in our security structures and procedures, we become dependent on the security that we established previously. Our two-factor authentication depends on SSO; we need to identify the user who is requesting two-factor authentication in order to send the two-factor code to the correct devices.

Additionally, we need to know what EMPLOYEE_ID is associated with a user_id. Two-factor authentication can only succeed for employees who have an entry in the emp_mobile_nos *table,* or an alternative. Consider the possibility that we might have added these columns directly to the HR.EMPLOYEES table. It would have been correct to do so as far as data normalization standards dictate; unless it can be proved that not all employees need access to our applications.

It may seem a bit backward to have the computer user_id field in a table of mobile phone numbers instead of in the primary EMPLOYEES table, but we are adding this functionality onto the existing HR structures, and we decided to do it all in one place, the emp_mobile_nos table.

It is a great idea to enforce some integrity constraints on the data by way of unique indexes. We do this with the commands shown in Listing 9-8. We only permit one record in this table per `employee_id`. We also only allow a `user_id` to be associated with one record, and hence with one `employee_id`. Notice in the table definition that neither `employee_id` nor `user_id` are permitted to be null.

Listing 9-8. *Create Indexes for Employee Mobile Phone Numbers Table*

```
CREATE UNIQUE INDEX emp_mob_nos_emp_id_pk ON hr.emp_mobile_nos
    (employee_id);

CREATE UNIQUE INDEX emp_mob_nos_usr_id_ui ON hr.emp_mobile_nos

    (user_id);

ALTER TABLE hr.emp_mobile_nos ADD (

    CONSTRAINT emp_mob_nos_emp_id_pk
    PRIMARY KEY

    (employee_id)
    USING INDEX emp_mob_nos_emp_id_pk,
    CONSTRAINT emp_mob_nos_usr_id_ui
    UNIQUE (user_id)

    USING INDEX emp_mob_nos_usr_id_ui
);

ALTER TABLE hr.emp_mobile_nos ADD (

  CONSTRAINT employee_id_fk

  FOREIGN KEY (employee_id)

  REFERENCES employees (employee_id),
  CONSTRAINT sms_carrier_cd_fk

  FOREIGN KEY (sms_carrier_cd)

  REFERENCES sms_carrier_host (sms_carrier_cd));
```

The unique index on `employee_id` is both our primary key on this table, and is a foreign key. Refer to the commands in Listing 9-8. By the foreign key relationship, we are establishing the constraint that in order to create a record in the `emp_mobile_nos` table for a certain `employee_id`, there must already exist a record in the EMPLOYEES table with that EMPLOYEE_ID.

Similarly, we have a foreign key constraint, `sms_carrier_cd_fk` on the table. (Again, see Listing 9-8) That constraint restricts us to writing (insert or update) `sms_carrier_cds` in the `emp_mobile_nos` table only if they already exist in the `sms_carrier_host` table.

You need to be aware that foreign keys are binding on both tables. Once we insert a record with a specific `employee_id` in the `emp_mobile_nos` table, we cannot delete the record for that EMPLOYEE_ID from the EMPLOYEES table until we've already deleted the associated record from `emp_mobile_nos`. We've encoded the rule that we can't have a record in `emp_mobile_nos` for an `employee_id` unless an associated record exists in EMPLOYEES; if we deleted the associated record from EMPLOYEES, we would no longer meet that requirement. Oracle database will not let us do that.

We always want to have a view of our table that is our primary reference to the table, so we create one with the code in Listing 9-9. If we are granting and using a view, then we can change the table (or tables) it refers to while maintaining the view, and keep from breaking any code.

Listing 9-9. Create a View of Employee Mobile Phone Numbers Table

```
CREATE OR REPLACE VIEW v_emp_mobile_nos AS SELECT * FROM hr.emp_mobile_nos;

INSERT INTO hr.v_emp_mobile_nos

    ( employee_id, user_id, com_pager_no, sms_phone_no, sms_carrier_cd )

    VALUES ( 300, 'OSUSER', '12345', '8005551212', 'Verizon' );


COMMIT;
```

Insert mobile numbers for our example user ID, OSUSR, into the table. Note that `employee_id` 300 is what we forced when we updated the sequence and inserted our example user in Chapter 7. While we're here, let's also insert a record for you. Use an insert statement like that just given, substituting the `user_id` you use to log in (perhaps to Windows) and your pager number, cell phone number, and carrier code (whatever name you will use for all cell phones from the same provider you use). You will also need to insert a record in the `HR.EMPLOYEES` table for you (first name, last name, and e-mail address.) Use the commands in Listing 9-10 as templates.

Listing 9-10. Template Commands to Create Employees and Add Their Mobile Numbers

```
INSERT INTO hr.employees
    (employee_id, first_name, last_name, email, phone_number, hire_date,

    job_id, salary, commission_pct, manager_id, department_id)
VALUES
    (hr.employees_seq.NEXTVAL, 'First', 'Last', 'EMAddress',
    '800.555.1212', SYSDATE, 'SA_REP', 5000, 0.20, 147, 80);


INSERT INTO hr.v_emp_mobile_nos

    ( employee_id, user_id, com_pager_no, sms_phone_no, sms_carrier_cd )

    VALUES ( (
        select employee_id from hr.employees where

        first_name = 'First' and last_name = 'Last'
    ), 'UserID', '12345', '8005551212', 'Verizon' );

COMMIT;
```

Be sure to `COMMIT` the inserts and updates you've made in order to make them visible to other sessions and other users.

Accessing HR Tables from Application Security Procedures

We are going to continue to have our application security user, appsec, run all the security procedures. In order to accomplish our two-factor authentication, she will need to read the EMPLOYEES table from HR, as well as the tables that we just created. We grant her access as shown in Listing 9-11.

Listing 9-11. *Grant Application Security User Access to See Our Views*

```
GRANT SELECT ON hr.v_employees_public TO appsec;
GRANT SELECT ON hr.v_sms_carrier_host TO appsec;

GRANT SELECT ON hr.v_emp_mobile_nos TO appsec;
```

Create the Two-Factor Codes Cache Table

Now that we have defined the tables in HR that hold the addresses and numbers where we are going to send our two-factor authentication codes, we need to consider how we will abide the interim between sending the code and having the user enter it in our application. It may require several minutes for the two-factor authentication code to traverse the Internet and the cell phone system to the user's phone. We do not want to keep our connections open to Oracle database for the whole duration of this out-of-band communication, so we need to think about how to store the two-factor codes for later comparison, and how to assure that the same user to whom we issued and sent the two-factor code is entering it.

With our SSO process and the mapping between login users (user_id) and employee_ids (in the emp_mobile_nos table), we can save a two-factor authentication code for the specific user who logged in. At this point, we will allow one two-factor code per user (although we will modify that in the next Chapter), so we index by employee_id.

We create a table to cache (retain) two-factor authentication codes for a time. This is shown in Listing 9-12. We are creating this in the appsec schema, so connect to Oracle database as appsec, if not already, and execute SET ROLE appsec_role to get the Application Security role in order to accomplish this step.

Listing 9-12. *Create a Table to Cache Two-Factor Authentication Codes*

```
CREATE TABLE appsec.t_two_fact_cd_cache
(
    employee_id   NUMBER(6) NOT NULL,

    two_factor_cd VARCHAR2(24 BYTE),

    ip_address    VARCHAR2(45 BYTE) DEFAULT SYS_CONTEXT( 'USERENV', 'IP_ADDRESS' ),

    distrib_cd    NUMBER(2),
    cache_ts      DATE DEFAULT SYSDATE
);
```

Now this is pure conjecture and creative imagination, but I believe that codes in the following format will be sufficiently complex for security and easy to enter. A series of 12 random numeric characters in groups of 4four separated by dashes, e.g., 1234-5678-9012. Perhaps you disagree and believe another format is better, and that is okay—you have the PL/SQL code and can change it as desired. Just note that this table is being created with a maximum **two_factor_cd** length of 24 characters.

Notice also that we are sizing a column for `ip_address` to be 45 characters. I may have over-specified it a bit, but while an IPv4 address is limited to 15 characters, an IPv6 address can be up to 39. Furthermore, an IPv4 address, mapped to IPv6 can be represented by up to 45 characters.

We also have a field in the `t_two_factor_cd_cache` table for the timestamp, `cache_ts`. It is set to default to SYSDATE, but that only has effect when we insert. When we update, we will "manually" set it to SYSDATE. Why do we need a cache timestamp? Here is some more creative imagination: you will find in the code that we consider a two-factor authentication code to be good for 10 minutes. We will not send another two-factor authentication code to the same user within that time period, and after 10 minutes, the code we sent is no longer valid.

The last column that we need to explore in this table, `distrib_cd`, is a numeric value that indicates how the two-factor code was distributed. Table 9-1 shows the potential values.

Table 9-1. *Two-Factor Code Distribution Values*

Value	Distribution
0	Not Distributed
1	To Pager
2	To Cell Phone
3	To Pager and Cell Phone
4	To E-Mail
5	To Pager and E-Mail
6	To Cell Phone and E-Mail
7	To Pager, Cell Phone and E-Mail

I won't show it here, but on this table the `employee_id` is both a unique index and the primary key. We also create the view, `v_two_fact_cd_cache`. Code for creating the indexes can be found in the file, *Chapter9/AppSec.sql*.

Testing Cache Aging

Let's insert a record and play with the aging algorithm we are going to use.

```
INSERT INTO appsec.v_two_fact_cd_cache
( employee_id ,two_factor_cd )
VALUES
(300,'FAKE');
```

Now, select the record to see that the timestamp is set.

```
SELECT * FROM appsec.v_two_fact_cd_cache;
```

Execute the following command a couple times. It will show the time elapsed since the timestamp was set, and it should count up as you run it.

```
SELECT (SYSDATE-cache_ts)*24*60
FROM appsec.v_two_fact_cd_cache WHERE employee_id=300;
```

That command uses date arithmetic like what we've seen before. We subtract the cache_ts from SYSDATE. Normally what you see when adding and subtracting from SYSDATE is some number of days. Always behind the scene is more precision, which is expressed in fractions of days. In a 10-minute span, there is only a small fraction of a day. We multiply it by 24 to get the fraction of an hour. And we multiply it by 60 to get the number of minutes.

Verifying Current Cached Two-Factor Pass Code

A specific user (determined by SSO) will hand a two-factor authentication code to this procedure. What questions do we need to ask about the code to determine if it is acceptable? First we ask if there is an existing code for the user. Second we ask if the existing code was requested from the same address that the current user is using. And third we ask if the existing code is less than 10 minutes old. We ask all those questions in the SELECT query that we have in the function f_is_cur_cached_cd, shown in Listing 9-13. If a code that meets those requirements exists, it is returned in the cached_two_factor_cd variable.

Listing 9-13. Test User-Entered Two-Factor Code Against Cached Version, f_is_cur_cached_cd

```
CREATE OR REPLACE FUNCTION appsec.f_is_cur_cached_cd( just_os_user VARCHAR2,
    two_factor_cd t_two_fact_cd_cache.two_factor_cd%TYPE )

RETURN VARCHAR2

AS
    cache_timeout_mins NUMBER := 10;
    return_char VARCHAR2(1) := 'N';

    cached_two_factor_cd v_two_fact_cd_cache.two_factor_cd%TYPE;

BEGIN
    SELECT c.two_factor_cd INTO cached_two_factor_cd

    FROM v_two_fact_cd_cache c, hr.v_emp_mobile_nos m

    WHERE m.employee_id = c.employee_id

    AND m.user_id = just_os_user

    AND c.ip_address = SYS_CONTEXT( 'USERENV', 'IP_ADDRESS' )

    AND ( SYSDATE - c.cache_ts )*24*60 < cache_timeout_mins;

    IF cached_two_factor_cd = two_factor_cd
    THEN

        return_char := 'Y';
    END IF;
    RETURN return_char;
END f_is_cur_cached_cd;

/
```

The last thing we do is compare the `cached_two_factor_cd` we found to the `two_factor_cd` that the user handed us. If they are equal, we return a "Y" (equivalent to a `boolean true`, but easier.) Otherwise, we return the default "N".

Notice that this is one of two places where you need to set a different cache duration, if 10 minutes is not correct for your application. The other place is in the `OracleJavaSecure.distribute2Factor()` method.

As with other procedures and functions defined in this chapter, we are not placing them in an Oracle package. Because of the different grants (none or `PUBLIC`) to these structures, we would need different packages with only one or two procedures or functions each. In the next chapter, we will add many similar procedures and functions and we will organize them into packages at that time.

Sending Two-Factor Pass Codes

If we have determined that we need to send two-factor codes to a user, we will call the function `f_send_2_factor` on Oracle database. It is a Java stored procedure that calls Java code on the Oracle Database to do what we cannot (easily) do in PL/SQL.

In this case, we call the `distribute2Factor()` method (see Listing 9-14), which generates the two-factor code, attempts to send it to pagers and cell-phones, and stores the code in the cache table.

Listing 9-14. Send the Two-Factor Code to the User, f_send_2_factor

```
CREATE OR REPLACE FUNCTION appsec.f_send_2_factor( just_os_user VARCHAR2 )
RETURN VARCHAR2

AS LANGUAGE JAVA

NAME 'orajavsec.OracleJavaSecure.distribute2Factor( java.lang.String ) return
java.lang.String';
/
```

Updating the Secure Application Role, HRVIEW_ROLE Procedure

Recall our secure application role, `hrview_role`. Without it we cannot read the data that we've deemed sensitive in the HR schema. We originally created the procedure, `p_check_hrview_access`, in Chapter 2 to provide access to the secure application role. At that time, we just checked IP Address and time of day.

In the last chapter, we updated the procedure to do SSO. If the user connection passed our SSO requirements, we set the role; otherwise, not.

Now in this chapter, we are adding another test – has the user passed a valid two-factor authentication code? See Listing 9-15. In order to accommodate that test, we have to modify the procedure to take an argument: the two-factor code that the user has entered. We also return error codes, as we've done in other procedures. In this case, we will return our distribution code (remember 1 if by pager?) in the `err_txt` field if there is no actual error (no `err_no`).

Listing 9-15. Secure Application Role Procedure Header, p_check_hrview_access

```
CREATE OR REPLACE PROCEDURE appsec.p_check_hrview_access(
    two_factor_cd t_two_fact_cd_cache.two_factor_cd%TYPE,

    m_err_no  OUT NUMBER,
    m_err_txt OUT VARCHAR2 )
```

```
AUTHID CURRENT_USER
AS
    just_os_user     VARCHAR2(40);

    backslash_place NUMBER;
BEGIN
```

I'm leaving out the bulk of the body of this procedure here, but I wanted to point out the section that is specifically used for two-factor authentication, shown in Listing 9-16. If we have passed SSO and other connection tests, then we enter this code. If the user did not pass us a two-factor authentication code, then we call the `f_send_2_factor` function. Otherwise, we test the two-factor code to see if it passes muster by calling the `f_is_cur_cached_cd` function. If the two-factor code is good, we set the secure application role; however, if not we let them know by raising a `NO_DATA_FOUND` exception: they entered the wrong code, or perhaps just an old (older than 10 minutes) code.

Listing 9-16. Secure Application Role Procedure Body, p_check_hrview_access

```
THEN
        IF( two_factor_cd IS NULL OR two_factor_cd = '' )

        THEN
            m_err_txt := f_send_2_factor( just_os_user );

        ELSIF( f_is_cur_cached_cd( just_os_user, two_factor_cd ) = 'Y' )

        THEN
            EXECUTE IMMEDIATE 'SET ROLE hrview_role';

        ELSE
            -- Wrong or Old 2_factor code. Could return message in M_ERR_TXT,
            -- or this will get their attention.
            RAISE NO_DATA_FOUND;

        END IF;
END IF;
```

Notice that when we call `f_send_2_factor`, we set `m_err_txt` to the return value. That is so we can pass the distribution code (summary of what devices the two-factor code is delivered to) coming out of `f_send_2_factor` back to the client.

Update OracleJavaSecurity.java for Two-Factor Authentication

There are several updates and additions we will make to *OracleJavaSecure.java* to support two-factor authentication. The biggest addition will be a new method to distribute the two-factor authentication codes, `distribute2Factor()`. We will discuss that method at length.

We see how to set some static member variables to hold the specific addressing data we intend to use. We also explore the individual methods that send two-factor codes to SMS devices, pagers, and e-mail.

Setting Some Company-Specific Addresses

Several settings in *OracleJavaSecure.java* are specific to your corporate implementation of two-factor authentication: the DNS domain name within your organization, the host name that handles mail routing for your company, and perhaps a web application URL from which text pager messages can be sent. We will add these to your organization's Windows domain name that we set for SSO as items that you need to edit in *OracleJavaSecure.java* before compiling. See Listing 9-17.

■ **Note** Edit the code found in the file named *Chapter9/orajavsec/OracleJavaSecure.java*.

Listing 9-17. Set Company Specific Mail and Paging Addresses

```
private static String expectedDomain = "ORGDOMAIN";
private static String comDomain = "org.com";
private static String smtpHost = "smtp." + comDomain;
private static String baseURL =
    "http://www.org.com/servlet/textpage.PageServlet?ACTION=2&PAGERID=";

private static String msgURL = "&MESSAGE=";
```

Compile Two-Factor Delivery Route Codes: Binary Math

We assemble a single code to represent the compilation of delivery routes selected for transmitting the two-factor authentication code. For each route selected, we add a constant value (static final) to our cumulative distribution code. At the end of processing, the single code represents all routes that were used. Like bits in a byte (eight bits, each with a value double the previous, represent 256 unique values), we use binary math to accumulate our distribution code. The initial constants are listed in Listing 9-18.

Listing 9-18. Delivery Route Constants

```
private static final int USE_PAGER = 1;
private static final int USE_SMS = 2;

private static final int USE_EMAIL = 4;
```

Table 9-1 lists how the sums represent all the different combination of delivery routes. Notice that the maximum value is one less than double the largest value (7 is the max value, which is one less than double 4, the largest constant).

If you haven't already guessed, the next constant would have the value of 8, then 16 and 32. We have only sized the `distrib_cd` column in the `t_two_fact_cd_cache` table to hold 2 digits, so we are limited to those six constant values. The maximum sum of those six constants is 63. The next, seventh constant would be 64, but a max sum including that value would be 127, a three-digit value.

Exploring a Method to Distribute the Two-Factor Codes

When we defined the `f_send_2_factor` Oracle function earlier, we noted that it simply calls the `distribute2Factor()` Java method: it is a pass-through Oracle function, as most Java stored procedures are. The reasoning is a bit esoteric. You see, we are already executing on Oracle database, and in the middle of running the `p_check_hrview_access` procedure when we call `f_send_2_factor`. Why not just call the Java `distribute2Factor()` method from `p_check_hrview_access`? That would be a nice capability, but it is not available. We need to approach the Oracle JVM through a dedicated Java stored procedure that is declared AS LANGUAGE JAVA. We cannot mix PL/SQL with a Java call in the same function or procedure; hence, we call a separate PL/SQL function as a Java stored procedure to get access to the Java method.

When we get to the `distribute2Factor()` method, we already know who the user is from our SSO processing. We pass that user ID to the method so that we can send our two-factor code to the devices owned by the intended recipient. Set up and closure of the method are familiar, as you can see in Listing 9-19. This method returns a String which represents the distribution code (summary of routes the two-factor code was sent).

Listing 9-19. Method to Distribute Two-Factor Codes: Framework, distribute2Factor()

```
public static final String distribute2Factor( String osUser ) throws Exception {
    // Do not resend this two-factor authentication code,
    //   nor a new one using this session
    if ( twoFactorAuthChars != null ) return "0";

    int distribCode = 0;

    Statement stmt = null;
    try {
        ...
    } catch( Exception x ) {
        java.io.CharArrayWriter errorText = new java.io.CharArrayWriter( 4000 );
        x.printStackTrace( new java.io.PrintWriter( errorText ) );
        stmt.executeUpdate( "CALL app_sec_pkg.p_log_error( 0, '" +

            errorText.toString() + "', '')" );
    } finally {
        try {
            if( stmt != null ) stmt.close();
        } catch( Exception y ) {}
    }
    return String.valueOf( distribCode );

}
```

Notice the ellipses (…) in the middle of Listing 9-19. That is where the code resides that we discuss in the subsections that follow.

Creating the Two-Factor Code

Within the `distribute2Factor()` method, we generate two-factor authentication codes that adhere to our prescribed format: 12 numeric characters in three groups of four, separated by dashes (e.g., 1234-5678-9012). I propose that this format is easily read and entered by users. Additionally, and this is significant, very old, numeric-only pagers are only capable of displaying a limited number of characters; often only numeric characters and dashes. The prescribed format conforms to that lowest common denominator.

We build our two-factor code as a character array of 14 characters, as shown in Listing 9-20. We put a random numeric character in each place. Within the ASCII character set, numeric values run from 48 to 58. That span is size 10, and we basically select the next random integer between 0 and 9. We add the first ASCII value for numeric character "0", (48), so in essence we get a random value between 48 and 58 that we cast as a char and set in the twoFactorAuthChars array.

As we march through the for loop, we observe our position. After every four characters, we want to place a dash. We do a modulus 5 (% 5) to test our position. When the next place, modulus 5 equals 0, we need to set the next place to a dash character. The first array position is 0, so we add one, and we want to test our next place, so we add another one. We test (i+2)%5.

When our test is positive, we go ahead and increment it so we can set the next place to a dash and continue; however, we don't want to try to tack another dash character on the end of our array, so we only set a dash if (i < twoFactorLength).

Listing 9-20. Build the Two-Factor Code

```
private static int twoFactorLength = 14;
private static char[] twoFactorAuthChars = null;


twoFactorAuthChars = new char[twoFactorLength];

for ( int i = 0; i < twoFactorLength; i++ ) {
    // Use numeric only to accommodate old pagers
    twoFactorAuthChars[i] = ( char )( random.nextInt( 58 - 48 ) + 48 );

    // Insert dashes (after every 4 characters) for readability
    if( 0 == ( ( i + 2 ) % 5 ) ) {
        i++;
        if ( i < twoFactorLength )
            twoFactorAuthChars[i] = '-';
    }
}
String twoFactorAuth = new String( twoFactorAuthChars );
```

We are only using the String representation of our two-factor authentication code in this method, so we set a method member. Everywhere else, the two-factor authentication code is referred to as a char array. We test the existence of twoFactorAuthChars array when we enter this method (see Listing 9-19), and we retain it as a static class member.

Dealing with Oracle and Java Dates: Standard Practice

Are you familiar with the Jim Croce song, "Time in a Bottle"? One of my favorite lines from that song is, "I've been around enough to know that you're the one I want to go through time with." Some old coding practices are like that. One particular standard practice I maintain is the exchange of dates between Oracle database and Java. I have never gotten into trouble when abiding by this plan, which I'm about to describe.

The only potential problem with what I am going to present to you is that the precision is limited to seconds. If you need milliseconds precision, you will need to modify the approach somewhat. Well, there is also the issue of time zone, which we have discussed; you may have to deal with that if your company is spread across multiple time zones.

The first standard I propose is to always use java.util.Date, and never use java.sql.Date. Besides the confusion due to the fact that they have the same name (but are mutually exclusive), there is the problem that they operate differently. Learn java.util.Date. Always import it and use it exclusively. You can use both Date classes, but great care is required to always address them as either java.util.Date or java.sql.Date, and to refer to them correctly. But more reasonably, you will have to choose one or the other. Choose java.util.Date.

One benefit we might garner from using java.sql.Date (not our preferred approach) would be that we could call ResultSet.getDate() and get a java.sql.Date object directly, without casting. However, the most important single function that is missing from java.sql.Date is the ability to get the current time and date. This topic came up in Chapter 7, in the sidebar "A Tale of Two Date Classes." On the other hand, with java.util.Date, we simply get a new Date(), and the default constructor builds a Date based on the current milliseconds value. A second reason to avoid java.sql.Date is that if you decided to standardize on that Date in an application, you would have to import it from the java.sql package even in some classes that have no interaction with SQL databases. In those cases, I would argue, java.sql.Date is out of place.

The format Strings and a SimpleDateFormat class shown in Listing 9-21 are what we need to do date exchange between Oracle database and Java. This is used in our distribute2Factor() method.

Listing 9-21. Standard Date Exchange Between Oracle Database and Java

```
import java.text.SimpleDateFormat;
import java.util.Date;


    String oraFmtSt = "YYYY-MM-DD HH24:MI:SS"; // use with to_char()
    String javaFmtSt = "yyyy-MM-d H:m:s";
    SimpleDateFormat ora2JavaDtFmt = new SimpleDateFormat( javaFmtSt );
```

The next standard practice I propose is that you always exchange dates as Strings / VARCHAR2s. We will define analogous formats for dates that allow us to exchange them as strings and rebuild representative dates on both Java and Oracle Database. On Oracle database, we use the TO_CHAR and TO_DATE functions; and in Java, we use SimpleDateFormat.parse() and SimpleDateFormat.format() methods. The standard methods for exchanging dates between Oracle database and Java are presented in Table 9-2.

Table 9-2. Methods for Exchanging Dates Between Oracle Database and Java

Perspective for Date Exchange	Method Used for Date Representation
Sending date from Oracle to Java	SELECT TO_CHAR(SYSDATE, 'YYYY-MM-DD HH24:MI:SS') FROM DUAL;
Receiving date string in Oracle from Java	MY_DATE DATE := TO_DATE(CHAR_DATE, 'YYYY-MM-DD HH24:MI:SS');
Receiving date string in Java from Oracle	Date javaDate = ora2JavaDtFmt.parse(rs.getString(1));
Sending date from Java to Oracle	stmt.setString(ora2JavaDtFmt.format(javaDate));

What Routes Are Available for the User?

The next step in the `distribute2Factor()` method is to query the HR data to see what devices the user has: pagers, cell-phones, etc., to which we might send the two-factor authentication code. While we're at it, in one fell swoop, we will get the cached two-factor code, if any, the timestamp when it was cached and the IP Address from which it was requested.

Notice in our query (Listing 9-22) that we are using the Oracle `TO_CHAR` method to get the timestamp and using the format string which we pass from Java.

Listing 9-22. Query for Distribution Routes Available

```
    stmt = conn.createStatement();
    ResultSet rs = stmt.executeQuery(
"SELECT m.employee_id, m.com_pager_no, m.sms_phone_no, s.sms_carrier_url, e.email, " +

"SYS_CONTEXT( 'USERENV', 'IP_ADDRESS' ), " +
"TO_CHAR( c.cache_ts, '" + oraFmtSt + "' ), c.ip_address " +

"FROM hr.v_emp_mobile_nos m, hr.v_employees_public e, hr.v_sms_carrier_host s, " +

"v_two_fact_cd_cache c WHERE m.user_id = '" + osUser + "' " +

"AND e.employee_id =  m.employee_id " +

"AND s.sms_carrier_cd (+)= m.sms_carrier_cd " +

"AND c.employee_id (+)= m.employee_id " );

    if ( rs.next() ) {
        String empID     = rs.getString( 1 );
        String pagerNo   = rs.getString( 2 );
        String smsNo     = rs.getString( 3 );
        String smsURL    = rs.getString( 4 );
        String eMail     = rs.getString( 5 );
        String ipAddress = rs.getString( 6 );
```

There is a bit of fault tolerance built into this query. Do you see the `(+)=` symbols? Those indicate what is called an *outer join*. Notice we are getting the `sms_carrier_url` from the `v_sms_carrier_host` view where the user's `sms_carrier_cd` matches what's in `v_sms_carrier_host`. Now, what if the user doesn't have a cell phone or `sms_carrier_cd`? If we left this query as a straight join (`s.sms_carrier_cd = m.sms_carrier_cd`), we would not get a record for that user. However, by adding the outer join indicator, `(+)` we are asking the query to return a result with the primary data even if this secondary data does not exist. We do another outer join on the two-factor cache data, because the user may not already have a two-factor authentication code in the cache.

I want to reiterate that if the user does not have an entry in the `t_emp_mobile_nos` table, he will not be able to do two-factor authentication. He does not necessarily need to have a cell phone or pager, but the association of SSO user ID (`user_id`) and `employee_id` requires that there be an entry in `t_emp_mobile_nos` for the user. If the user's record in `t_emp_mobile_nos` has no SMS phone number or pager number, then the distribute2Factor() method sends the message to the user's e-mail.

Is the Current Pass Code Still Valid?

In `distribute2Factor()` we want to determine if the user is coming back to request another two-factor authentication code before the 10-minute timeout on an existing two-factor code has expired. The user may or may not have an existing, cached two-factor authentication code: we may get `nulls` back for values from that table. For that reason, we bracket the following code (Listing 9-23) in a try/catch block. Getting `nulls` into our `String` members is no problem, but parsing a `null` into a `Date` and comparing `nulls` with the `String.equals()` method will throw exceptions.

Listing 9-23. *Test Validity of Cached Two-Factor Authentication Code*

```
try{
    String cTimeStamp = rs.getString( 7 );
    String cIPAddr    = rs.getString( 8 );
    // Ten minutes ago Date
    Date tmaDate = new Date( (new Date()).getTime() - 10*60*1000 );

    Date cacheDate = ora2JavaDtFmt.parse( cTimeStamp );
    // If user coming from same IP Address within 10 minutes
    // do not distribute Code (will overwrite code from new IP Addr)
    if( ipAddress.equals( cIPAddr ) && cacheDate.after( tmaDate ) )
        return "0";

} catch( Exception z ) {}
```

The heart of this code is the last line where we test if the user is coming from the same IP Address for which we generated the two-factor code, and if the date is less than 10 minutes old. If that is the case, we do not generate a new two-factor code, and we do not resend the existing code; we simply return.

While here, take a minute to read through the line of code we use to calculate ten minutes ago, `tmaDate`. We get the milliseconds of the current date and subtract 10 minutes of 60 seconds of 1,000 milliseconds.

Distribute the Pass Code to Routes

Next on our agenda in the `distribute2Factor()` method is to send the generated two-factor code to the preferred and/or existing devices. By preference, we will send the two-factor code to the user's pager and cell phone. If neither of those is available, we will send the code to the user's e-mail. See Listing 9-24.

To send the code to a cell phone, the user must have both a phone number and a carrier code. If he does, we call the `distribToSMS()` method. Notice that we add the return value, `int` to our cumulative `distribCode`. Similarly, we send the two-factor code to a pager if the user has pager number. In the following sections, we explore the individual methods to send 2-factor codes to specific devices.

Listing 9-24. *Call Methods to Distribute to SMS, Pager, and/or E-Mail*

```
if( ( smsNo != null ) && ( !smsNo.equals( "" ) ) &&
    ( smsURL != null ) && ( !smsURL.equals( "" ) )
)
    distribCode += distribToSMS( twoFactorAuth, smsNo, smsURL );

if( ( pagerNo != null ) && ( !pagerNo.equals( "" ) ) )
    distribCode += distribToPagerURL( twoFactorAuth, pagerNo );
```

```
// Recommend not send to e-mail unless no other distrib option succeeds
// !Uncomment code in next line!
if( //( distribCode == 0 ) &&

    ( eMail != null ) && ( !eMail.equals( "" ) )
)
        distribCode += distribToEMail( twoFactorAuth, eMail );
```

Currently, we have commented a test that we will want to implement that avoids sending the two-factor code to e-mail if we were successful in sending the code to a pager or cell phone. We've commented the test so that you can also see the e-mail route in action, but you may want to uncomment the test in production. Also, we can only send the code to e-mail if the user has an e-mail address.

Cache the Pass Code in Oracle

Once we have distributed our two-factor authentication code, if we actually found a route to deliver it (distribCode > 0), we want to cache it for comparison to any code the user enters. The following statement from the distribute2Factor() method (Listing 9-25) updates the entry, if it exists. One feature of an update statement is that it returns an integer that indicates how many rows were updated. If we see that less than 1 row was updated, we assume we need to insert a row to cache codes for this particular user. In other words, we attempt an update which also serves as a test to see if we need to insert a row. Once we've got most users entered for most applications, we will almost always want to do an update, so this order, update then insert, is the most efficient.

Listing 9-25. Cache the Two-Factor Authentication Code

```
if( distribCode > 0 || isTesting ) {
    int cnt = stmt.executeUpdate(
"UPDATE v_two_fact_cd_cache SET two_factor_cd = '" + twoFactorAuth +

"', ip_address = '" + ipAddress + "', distrib_cd = " +

String.valueOf( distribCode ) + ", cache_ts=SYSDATE " +

"WHERE employee_id = " + empID );

    if( cnt < 1 )

        stmt.executeUpdate(
"INSERT INTO v_two_fact_cd_cache( employee_id ,two_factor_cd, distrib_cd ) VALUES " +

"( " + empID + ", '" + twoFactorAuth +"', " + String.valueOf( distribCode ) + " )" );

}
```

Distributing the Code to SMS

We saw earlier in this chapter, in our testing, that we need to set a session property for our SMTP server. That is the first statement we execute in Listing 9-26. After that, we call the UTL_MAIL package to send a message to the user's cell phone. The arguments for the send function are sender's e-mail, recipient e-mail, two other distributions we are not concerned with, the message title ("Response"), and the message text (our two-factor authentication code).

We build the recipient e-mail address from the user's cell phone number, smsNo, and the SMS gateway address for his carrier, smsURL.

Listing 9-26. Distribute the Code to SMS, distribToSMS()

```
private static final int distribToSMS( String twoFactorAuth, String smsNo,
    String smsURL )
{
    int distribCode = 0;

    Statement stmt = null;
    try {
        stmt = conn.createStatement();
        stmt.executeUpdate( "ALTER SESSION SET SMTP_OUT_SERVER = '" +
            smtpHost + "'" );
        stmt.executeUpdate( "CALL UTL_MAIL.SEND( 'response@" +

            comDomain + "', '" + smsNo + "@" + smsURL +
            "', '', '', 'Response','" + twoFactorAuth + "' )" );
        distribCode += USE_SMS;

    } catch ( Exception x ) {
    } finally {
        try {
            if( stmt != null ) stmt.close();
        } catch( Exception y ) {}
    }
    return distribCode;

}
```

As an example, this message would look like the following.

```
From: response@org.com
To: 8005551212@txt.att.net
Subject: Response
1234-5678-9012
```

Notice also in this message that we are using the try/catch/finally block to close the statement. We set a method member, distribCode, to 0 at the outset. If we succeed in sending the code to the cell phone, we add the value of the USE_SMS constant to distribCode. And finally we return distribCode.

Distributing the Code to Pager URL

The distribToPagerURL() method has many similarities to distribToSMS(), which we just discussed. The main difference is that we are not using an Oracle package to send e-mail but are using a pure Java URL class to read a web page. See Listing 9-27. In actuality, we are not concerned with what a browser would see when going to this web page. The entry form that a user would see in his browser window is never loaded. It is bypassed because we are submitting the input fields data as part of the URL address. We are using what is called the GET method to pass values to the web server on the URL line. Our URL will resemble this:

```
www.org.com/servlet/textpage.PageServlet?PAGERID=12345&MESSAGE=1234-5678-9012
```

We indicate what pager to send in the PAGERID argument and what the message will be in the MESSAGE argument. After we create a new URL instance with this address, we call its getContent() method to "browse" the web address. At that point, the web server with the paging application has responded to the GET method, and if no exception is thrown, we can continue on with returning the value of the USE_PAGER constant.

Listing 9-27. Distribute the Code to Pager, distribToPagerURL()

```
private static final int distribToPagerURL( String twoFactorAuth,
    String pagerNo )
{
    int distribCode = 0;

    try {
        URL u = new URL( baseURL + pagerNo + msgURL + twoFactorAuth );
        u.getContent();
        distribCode += USE_PAGER;

    } catch ( Exception x ) {}
    return distribCode;

}
```

This method is the most likely to require special editing to be functional in your organization. You will have to research how page messages are sent to your corporate pagers, if at all. Even if you do not have pagers, this code may serve as an example of how you might send the two-factor codes to some other web service.

Distributing the Code to E-Mail

Our distribToEMail() method is not only similar, but also almost identical to the distribToSMS() method, except that the recipient in this case is the user's e-mail address. I'm leaving out the code, but the message resembles this:

```
From: response@org.com
To: OSUSER@org.com
Subject: Response
1234-5678-9012
```

If successful, we return the value of the USE_EMAIL constant.

Testing Two-Factor Authentication

In this section, we again draw on all our resources to demonstrate and test two-factor authentication along with everything else we have discussed so far. We will test our two-factor authentication by using the code we have been examining to generate and transmit two-factor authentication codes. In order to experience this fully, you will need to enter your pager, cell phone, and/or e-mail addresses in the database, as we described. Alternatively, you can query the database to select the generated two-factor codes from the appsec.v_two_fact_cd_cache view.

If you haven't been executing the SQL commands we've been exploring throughout this chapter as we discussed them, you will need to open the *Chapter9* folder and the files *Sys.sql*, *SecAdm.sql*, *AppSec.sql*, and *HR.sql* and execute those commands as the appropriate user. You can execute them in about that order, but when you get about halfway through *AppSec.sql*, you will need to stop and execute *HR.sql* before continuing as appsec.

You will also need to execute *OracleJavaSecure.java* in the Oracle database to create the Java structure there. We will then run the class TestOracleJavaSecure on the client to accomplish all our demonstrations and tests.

Updating OracleJavaSecure Java in Oracle

If you haven't already, edit the code for *OracleJavaSecure.java* to provide our company-specific addresses for two-factor authentication. We saw this previously in Listing 9-17. Edit the code found in the file named *Chapter9/orajavsec/OracleJavaSecure.java*.

```
private static String expectedDomain = "ORGDOMAIN";
private static String comDomain = "org.com";
private static String smtpHost = "smtp." + comDomain;
private static String baseURL =
    "http://www.org.com/servlet/textpage.PageServlet?ACTION=2&PAGERID=";

private static String msgURL = "&MESSAGE=";
```

Load the new *orajavsec/OracleJavaSecure.java* code into Oracle database. You will be loading this into the appsec schema, so you should be connected to Oracle Database as that user and don't forget to set your role to appsec_role. Again, uncomment the top line that begins CREATE OR REPLACE AND RESOLVE JAVA… and execute it in your SQL client (SQL*Plus, SQL Developer, JDeveloper, or TOAD). Remember to set the role first. (This file will also be compiled and executed on the client, so re-comment the first line before saving the file.)

You may also need to modify the environment of your SQL client in order to include an ampersand in your URL string, as in the example baseURL, shown previously. Notice the ampersand between the parameters for "ACTION=2" and "PAGERID=". When some SQL clients see an ampersand like that, they will assume it is a marker for a variable to be substituted on execution, in this case "&PAGERID". Most times that would be a good assumption, but not in this case and never with Java code that we are loading into Oracle database. We can remedy this situation in one of two ways: we can use a different SQL client, or even resort to using the loadjava utility, as described in Chapter 4. However, a simpler and more immediate fix is to tell our SQL client not to do variable substitution with this simple command.

```
SET DEFINE OFF;
```

Editing the Test Code

We are going to execute a separate Java class, TestOracleJavaSecure, to test our two-factor authentication. Edit the code near the top to set the appropriate password and connection string for the appusr user.

■ **Note** You can find the code for the TestOracleJavaSecure class in the file *Chapter9/TestOracleJavaSecure.java*.

Planning to Pass the Two-Factor Code as an Argument to Main

The entire code of the TestOracleJavaSecure class resides within the main() method. So, we simply run the code from top to bottom when we call Java with this class from the command line. This is similar to how we did testing in Chapter 7. Here, however, we will have to call the class two times. The first time, we call it without any arguments. At the end of that call, if all goes as planned, a two-factor authentication code will have been sent to our cell phone, pager, and e-mail.

Once we have received that code on any of our devices, and within 10 minutes, we can execute Java again calling TestOracleJavaSecure, except this time we will include the two-factor code as an argument. The two commands that we execute later will resemble these:

```
java TestOracleJavaSecure
java TestOracleJavaSecure 1234-5678-9012
```

If you don't have any devices or e-mail on which to receive two-factor authorization codes, you can set the isTesting boolean to true in *OracleJavaSecure.java* and reload it in Oracle database. Then recompile and run the commands given above. This will place a two-factor code in the t_two_fact_cd_cache table, even if no distribution devices are found. You may then get the generated two-factor code from this query:

```
SELECT * FROM appsec.v_two_fact_cd_cache;
```

Arguments on the command line are delivered to the main() method as an array of Strings. We can test for the presence of a two-factor code by testing if the String array length is greater than 0. We also assure ourselves that the first element of the array is not null, as shown in Listing 9-28.

Listing 9-28. Pass Two-Factor Code to TestOracleJavaSecure main() Method

```
public static void main( String[] args ) {
    try {
        // Passing 2-factor code in as argument on command line
        String args0 = "";
        if( args.length != 0 && args[0] != null ) args0 = args[0];
        args0 = OracleJavaSecure.checkFormat2Factor( args0 );
```

When the person enters the code he received on his cell phone, we want to make sure we put the least amount of burden on him to understand our formatting rules. If he only types in the numeric characters, leaving off the dashes, we want to accept that. If he appends other characters, like time and date or whatever his phone displays, we should pick out our two-factor code, if readily available. We send whatever he provides at the command prompt to the OracleJavaSecure.checkFormat2Factor() method. If you find other typographical errors are frequent, you might add some more intelligence to that method.

Planning to Acquire the Secure Application Role

Whether or not we have a two-factor code, we call our Oracle procedure, p_check_hrview_access, for the secure application role, hrview_role. If we do not have a two-factor code yet, we pass an empty string to the procedure; otherwise, we pass the code. You are now familiar with reading procedures like this, in Listing 9-29.

Listing 9-29. Set Secure Application Role from TestOracleJavaSecure

```
stmt = ( OracleCallableStatement )conn.prepareCall(
    "CALL appsec.p_check_hrview_access(?,?,?)" );

stmt.registerOutParameter( 2, OracleTypes.NUMBER );
stmt.registerOutParameter( 3, OracleTypes.VARCHAR );
stmt.setString( 1, args0 );
stmt.setInt(    2, 0 );
stmt.setNull(   3, OracleTypes.VARCHAR );
stmt.executeUpdate();
errNo = stmt.getInt( 2 );
errMsg = stmt.getString( 3 );
if( errNo != 0 ) {
    System.out.println( "Oracle error 1) " + errNo + ", " + errMsg );
} else if( args0.equals( "" ) ) {
    System.out.println( "DistribCd = " + errMsg );
    System.out.println( "Call again with 2-Factor code parameter" );
} else {
    if( null != stmt ) stmt.close();
    System.out.println( "Oracle success 1)" );

    OracleResultSet rs = null;
    RAW sessionSecretDESPassPhrase = null;
    RAW sessionSecretDESAlgorithm = null;
    RAW sessionSecretDESSalt = null;
    RAW sessionSecretDESIterationCount = null;

    String locModulus = OracleJavaSecure.getLocRSAPubMod();

    String locExponent = OracleJavaSecure.getLocRSAPubExp();


    stmt = ( OracleCallableStatement )conn.prepareCall(
        "CALL hr.hr_sec_pkg.p_select_employees_sensitive(?,?,?,?,?,?,?,?,?)" );
```

We report any errors coming back from the procedure. One definite potential error is the possibility that the user has entered a wrong or old code, in which case a "DATA NOT FOUND" error will be returned.

If there are no errors and we didn't have a two-factor code when we called, then we presume the two-factor code was distributed, and we display the distribution code that was returned in the errMsg and ask the user to come again with their two-factor code. If they had a two-factor code when they called, and no errors, then we assume the p_check_hrview_access succeeded, and the user's connection has been granted the hrview_role and can proceed to read the data.

Our TestOracleJavaSecure class will execute the p_select_employees_sensitive procedure to demonstrate that access has succeeded. You are, no doubt, all too familiar with that procedure.

Running the Tests and Observing the Results

To recap the requirements: To run the test, you must have created the tables, procedures, and grants that we have described in this chapter. You will have inserted a record for your user ID in the

HR.emp_mobile_nos table. And you will also have edited the company-specific values at the top of *Chapter9/orajavsec/OracleJavaSecure.java*. You should also uncomment the top line of *OracleJavaSecure.java* and execute it in Oracle database to load the Java structures.

After loading OracleJavaSecure into Oracle database, restore the comment on the top line and save the file. From a command prompt in the *Chapter9* directory, compile both *OracleJavaSecure.java* and *TestOracleJavaSecure.java* with these commands.

```
javac orajavsec/OracleJavaSecure.java
javac TestOracleJavaSecure.java
```

Then run the test by executing the first line, java TestOracleJavaSecure, and see the results. Execute the same command again to see that the two-factor code is not sent again (DistribCd = 0). After you receive the two-factor authentication code, execute the last command, passing the two-factor code on the command line.

```
java TestOracleJavaSecure
    DistribCd = 5
    Call again with 2-Factor code parameter
java TestOracleJavaSecure

    DistribCd = 0
java TestOracleJavaSecure 1234-5678-9012

    DistribCd = null
    Oracle success 1)
    Oracle success 2)
    198, Donald, OConnell, DOCONNEL, 650.507.9833, 2007-06-21 00:00:00, SH_CLERK, 26
    00 (AD6E5035FAB394A8), null, 124, 50
```

After 10 minutes have elapsed, the two-factor code will no longer succeed in getting access. Try executing TestOracleJavaSecure again after 10 minutes with the same code and observe the "no data found" error message.

```
java TestOracleJavaSecure 1234-5678-9012
    DistribCd = ORA-01403: no data found
    Oracle error 1) 100, ORA-01403: no data found
```

Chapter Review

We enabled Oracle Database to send E-Mail messages and to browse to web pages. Using those abilities, we developed a process to send 2-factor authentication codes to our application users on their cell phones, pagers and e-mail accounts. Users will have to enter those 2-factor codes in order to get access to our application data.

We built a table to hold mobile phone numbers for users and another to hold web addresses of SMS gateways for each cell phone carrier. We also added a table to hold cached 2-factor codes.

We implemented foreign keys to maintain referential integrity between our tables. And we discussed a coding standard for exchanging dates between Oracle Database and Java.

An overview of the 2-factor code distribution process is provided in Figure 9-1. Notice a reference in this Figure to Figure 8-1, block [D]. It was there that we saw an illustration of the process of getting our SSO proxy connection. Using that connection, we call the p_check_hrview_access procedure two times. The first time, we don't have a two-factor authentication code. Therefore, we do the process depicted in block [E1] in Figure 9-1. In that block, we see an illustration of the process used to distribute the two-factor code to the individual devices associated with the user.

The second time we call **p_check_hrview_access**, we provide the two-factor authentication code as an argument. Because we have returned with that code, we perform the process depicted in block [E2] of Figure 9-1. It is there that we see the tests for validity of the two-factor code, and if all is well, the SET ROLE command to acquire the **hrview_role**.

With that role, our user can continue on to select and update sensitive data in the HR schema using encryption. Those processes are included in Figure 9-1 by a reference to Figures 7-1 and 7-2.

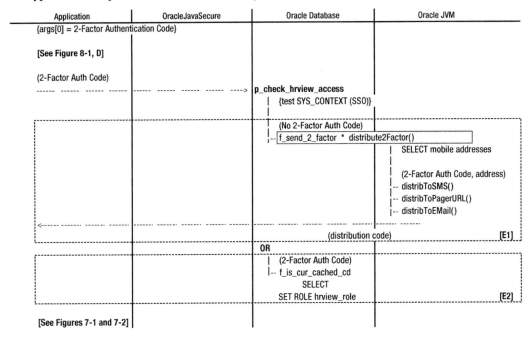

Figure 9-1. *The two-factor authentication code process*

CHAPTER 10

Application Authorization

Every Oracle application connects to one or more Oracle database instance, perhaps as one or more user. We have already seen how we can accomplish this with security and encryption for one application at a time. Our first application attached as the `appusr` account and had access to data in the HR schema via the `hr_view` role.

For that application, and any similar one, the developer will develop a procedure for a secure application role, like our `p_check_hrview_access`. But for all our security, there is one aspect that we haven't addressed: developers are still required to hard-code application user passwords into their code (or find another mechanism.) What if we provide a secure password store for them, one that is not as susceptible to imposter applications as other solutions?

In this chapter, we are going to build a dynamic Oracle procedure for use in validating *all* secure application roles. Individual developers will not have to provide such procedures for their applications. Instead, they will provide a list of three unique items related to their secure application role: the application ID (name), the application user, and the secure application role name. We will store those elements in a table. Then we will provide the dynamic procedure for all secure application roles, and organize our code around it.

Next we will build out some of our other tables to handle multiple applications per user, keeping application-specific security data for users separate from security data for that user for other applications.

We will also have each application send us a representative piece of code—an application-specific class, provided as an object represented by a byte array. (The details of that will become clearer.) By examining that object, we will know what application is requesting services, and in return we will provide that application with a list of the specific connection strings needed by the application. Of course, all of this is done with encryption and security in mind.

We will store the application connection strings in an Oracle table. Some procedures, functions, and Java code are required to accomplish this, and a bit more code will be required to update the data once stored. We will also support multiple versions of an application.

We are storing all the data in Oracle database, and using the security of Oracle database, but recall that we do not have our application Oracle connections until after we have passed the security checks. This is a quandary along the lines of, "which came first, the chicken or the egg?" Or in our case, "which came first, an Oracle connection or our list of Oracle connection strings (passwords)?" The answer is that we need a connection to Oracle database first, so we will use an alternate Oracle application verification, the `appver` user, to provide the necessary initial connection for all applications. The `appver` user will be a hardened user with as many restrictions as we can muster. His sole purpose is to guard and provide application-specific Oracle connection strings.

Because we will want to muster all our security forces before distributing connection strings, we will have `appver` determine the specific application, as described previously. He will also provide the single sign on (SSO) and two-factor Authentication we have discussed in earlier chapters. And he will establish an initial set of encryption keys for use in distributing and decrypting the connection strings.

Note that each new connection established for an application may require a new and distinct set of encryption keys. There are limitations to how many sets of keys we will maintain for concurrent use in the code provided in this book. We will retain the encryption keys for the **appver** connection, in order to continue decrypting the connection strings for this application, and we will allow each application user to use one additional set of encryption keys at a time. Additional Oracle connections without encryption can be used concurrently. However, a diligent programmer can overcome those limitations.

Secure Application Role Procedure for Multiple Applications

Thinking back on our secure application role—**hrview_role** and the procedure that sets the role—what application-specific features did it implement? It tested for a number of things that are not application specific: IP address, time of day, two-factor authentication, and most important, SSO identity. However, a couple things were application-specific: the user who was seeking the role (**appusr**) and the role itself (**hrview_role**).

Our goal at this juncture is to build a single secure application role procedure that will work for any application, enforcing all our connection security requirements, but granting the specific role required to the specific application user. We can build a procedure to handle that, but first we need a registry of those application-specific features. We will create the **t_application_registry** table in the **appsec** schema to hold the data. The code for creating this table is in Listing 10-1.

■ **Note** You can find the script in Listing 10-1 in the file named *Chapter10/AppSec.sql*.

Listing 10-1. Application Registry Table of Salient Features

```
CREATE TABLE appsec.t_application_registry
(
    application_id VARCHAR2(24 BYTE) NOT NULL,
    app_user       VARCHAR2(20 BYTE) NOT NULL,
    app_role       VARCHAR2(20 BYTE) NOT NULL
);
```

We will also create a view of the table for general use. And, though not shown here, we will make the **application_id** and **app_user** columns a unique index and our primary key. We will not depend on that key until we get to Chapter 12. For now, suffice it to say that each application may use multiple secure application roles. We will acquire these roles by proxying through a variety of application users. So a pair of **application_id** and **app_user** is a unique key to acquire an **app_role**.

While we're at it, let's insert a data record with the labels we already know: user **APPUSR** and role **HRVIEW_ROLE**. We give those settings to the **application_id** of **HRVIEW**, as shown here:

```
INSERT INTO appsec.v_application_registry ( application_id, app_user, app_role )
VALUES ( 'HRVIEW', 'APPUSR', 'HRVIEW_ROLE' );
```

We are introducing the **application_id** column here as a handle to acquire the required role. Each application will need a unique **application_id**, which, with a couple more additions, will allow our existing code to provide two-factor authentication, SSO, and secure application roles to multiple applications.

Rebuild Two-Factor Cache Table for Multiple Applications

It is possible that a user will want to use more than one application at a time, and we will want them to operate independently. These applications will have grants to diverse data and will use diverse sets of Oracle instances. They may also be started at the client within the ten-minute, two-factor time to live off one another.

To provide for the independent operation of these applications, we will add the `application_id` column as a part of the primary key for the `t_two_fact_cd_cache` table. See Listing 10-2. In this way, we can create and assign a two-factor authentication code for each application that a user uses. This makes obvious the fact that two-factor authentication for applications is already a step away from single sign on. If your corporate computing environment enforces two-factor authentication for the initial logon (e.g., Windows password and a Secure ID token), then there is no need for two-factor authentication to applications. However, two-factor authentication for basic computer access, whether secure tokens, biometric scanners, or electronic badges, still seems more prevalent in movies than in the corporate setting. If you have a computer with biometric interface (fingerprint or facial recognition) or a secure card slot, it is not two-factor authentication as a substitute for entering a password. Only when you use it in addition to entering a password is it two-factor authentication.

So we will build two-factor authentication, independent for each application. We start by dropping the previous `t_two_fact_cd_cache` table, and creating a new one with an `application_id` column.

Listing 10-2. Redo Two-Factor Code Cache Table

```
DROP TABLE appsec.t_two_fact_cd_cache CASCADE CONSTRAINTS;

CREATE TABLE appsec.t_two_fact_cd_cache
(
    employee_id    NUMBER(6) NOT NULL,
    application_id VARCHAR2(24 BYTE) NOT NULL,
    two_factor_cd  VARCHAR2(24 BYTE),
    ip_address     VARCHAR2(45 BYTE) DEFAULT SYS_CONTEXT( 'USERENV', 'IP_ADDRESS' ),
    distrib_cd     NUMBER(1),
    cache_ts       DATE DEFAULT SYSDATE
);

CREATE UNIQUE INDEX two_fact_cd_emp_id_pk ON appsec.t_two_fact_cd_cache
    (employee_id,application_id);
```

We also recreate a view (code not shown) of this table for general references. There is an example insert and some cache aging test code in the file *Chapter10/AppSec.sql*.

Update Two-Factor Code Functions to Use Application ID

Please refer to the full listing of the code in AppSec.sql file. We modify our existing `f_is_cur_cached_cd` function to take the `application_id` as an argument and to select from `v_two_fact_cd_cache` based on the `application_id`. We also update our existing `f_send_2_factor` function to take the `application_id` as an argument, and to pass it to the `distribute2Factor()` method.

Move Test for SSO to Separate Function

For division of labor among pieces of our code, we are going to separate the SSO process into a separate function, f_is_sso. Into this function, we pass the value for application user. Traditionally, appusr has been our application user, but we will pass whatever user we find registered for the application in the t_application_registry table. Recall that for SSO, the application user has to either be the connected user for our session, or the proxy user. The f_is_sso function will return the validated SSO user ID, or an empty string if invalid. Listing 10-3 shows just the signature of f_is_sso.

Listing 10-3. Function to Test if User Passes SSO Requirements, f_is_sso

```
CREATE OR REPLACE FUNCTION appsec.f_is_sso( m_app_user VARCHAR2 )
RETURN VARCHAR2
AUTHID CURRENT_USER
AS
    return_user      VARCHAR2(40) := '';
...
```

Note Procedures and functions that execute as AUTHID CURRENT_USER are never placed in packages, and they are usually granted EXECUTE to PUBLIC.

Add an Oracle Package for Use Only by Application Security

We will be increasing the number of functions and procedures for use strictly by our application security user, appsec, by almost an order of magnitude, so we are going to employ a package to group and organize them. We'll call this package the appsec_only_pkg package. The package also allows us to secure the code in one location – in this case, we will not grant anyone execute on appsec_only_pkg. We will drop the functions f_is_cur_cached_cd and f_send_2_factor, and move them into our package as in Listing 10-4.

Listing 10-4. Package for Application Security Use Only

```
DROP FUNCTION appsec.f_is_cur_cached_cd;
DROP FUNCTION appsec.f_send_2_factor;

CREATE OR REPLACE PACKAGE appsec.appsec_only_pkg IS

    FUNCTION f_is_cur_cached_cd(
        just_os_user      VARCHAR2,
        m_application_id v_two_fact_cd_cache.application_id%TYPE,
        m_two_factor_cd  v_two_fact_cd_cache.two_factor_cd%TYPE )
    RETURN VARCHAR2;

    FUNCTION f_send_2_factor(
        just_os_user      VARCHAR2,
```

```
    m_application_id v_two_fact_cd_cache.application_id%TYPE )
RETURN VARCHAR2;
```

Add Helper Function to Get APP_ROLE

We are going to need one piece of data from the t_application_registry table, the secure application role name, when we run the procedure that sets those roles. We have already discussed the need to run our secure application role procedure as AUTHID CURRENT_USER. We do this so we can assure the validity of the current user, not the schema owner, appsec. This is called invoker's rights. Also, this is the only way that roles may be set, by the CURRENT_USER.

In order to execute the secure application role procedure, we need to grant execute on the procedure to PUBLIC. However, we do not want to grant data privileges to PUBLIC on the v_application_registry view. If we have a helper function that belongs to the same schema as the v_application_registry and the secure application role procedure, then the helper function can be executed by the procedure and read the data in the table on its behalf. PUBLIC has execute on the procedure, but no grants on the view or the functions; yet the procedure has access to the functions in order to select on the view. The result of this is that we can run a procedure to grant the role, but not expose the data used to evaluate access.

We read the application role name, based on the application_id and app_user from the f_get_app_role function. We will add this function to our appsec_only_pkg package. See Listing 10-5.

Listing 10-5. Helper Function to get Application Role Name

```
FUNCTION f_get_app_role(
    m_application_id v_two_fact_cd_cache.application_id%TYPE,
    m_app_user       v_application_registry.app_user%TYPE )
RETURN VARCHAR2
AS
    m_app_role v_application_registry.app_role%TYPE;
BEGIN
    SELECT app_role INTO m_app_role
    FROM v_application_registry
    WHERE application_id = m_application_id
    AND app_user = m_app_user;
    RETURN m_app_role;
END f_get_app_role;
```

Replace Procedure for hrview_role Access with Dynamic Procedure

We will be replacing the application-specific procedure, p_check_hrview_access, which set the hrview_role with a generic procedure, p_check_role_access, which will set the secure application role for any application. Each application will require an entry (one or more) in the t_application_registry table. With this new procedure, we can easily apply our SSO and two-factor authentication to multiple applications.

Code for the New Procedure

By way of cleaning up, we will drop the old p_check_hrview_access procedure. That will assure us that we are using the new procedure, even for setting hrview_role. Refer to Listing 10-6.

Our new procedure, p_check_role_access looks very similar to our previous secure application role procedure. We enter this procedure with a connection that is already proxying through our application Oracle user, which we get into app_user variable. The new procedure takes the additional application_id argument, which it in turn passes with the app_user identity to our new f_get_app_role helper function in order to read the role name from v_application_registry. Also, instead of having the code for SSO right in this method, we pass the app_user to our new f_is_sso function to get back the validated user.

Listing 10-6. Dynamic Secure Application Role Procedure, p_check_role_access

```
DROP PROCEDURE appsec.p_check_hrview_access;

CREATE OR REPLACE PROCEDURE appsec.p_check_role_access(
    --m_two_factor_cd      v_two_fact_cd_cache.two_factor_cd%TYPE,
    m_application_id      v_two_fact_cd_cache.application_id%TYPE,
    m_err_no         OUT NUMBER,
    m_err_txt        OUT VARCHAR2 )
AUTHID CURRENT_USER
AS
    return_user VARCHAR2(40);
    m_app_user  v_application_registry.app_user%TYPE;
    m_app_role  v_application_registry.app_role%TYPE;
BEGIN
    m_err_no    := 0;

    m_app_user   := SYS_CONTEXT('USERENV','PROXY_USER');

    m_app_role  := appsec_only_pkg.f_get_app_role( m_application_id, m_app_user );
    return_user := f_is_sso( m_app_user );
    IF( return_user IS NOT NULL )
    THEN
-- Code for two-factor Auth moved to appver login process
--      IF( m_two_factor_cd IS NULL OR m_two_factor_cd = '' )
--      THEN
--          m_err_txt := appsec_only_pkg.f_send_2_factor( return_user, m_application_id );
--      ELSIF( appsec_only_pkg.f_is_cur_cached_cd( return_user, m_application_id,
--          m_two_factor_cd ) = 'Y' )
--      THEN
            EXECUTE IMMEDIATE 'SET ROLE ' || m_app_role;
--      ELSE
--          RAISE NO_DATA_FOUND;
--      END IF;
        app_sec_pkg.p_log_error( 0, 'Success getting SSO and setting role, ' ||
            SYS_CONTEXT( 'USERENV', 'OS_USER' ) );
    ELSE
        app_sec_pkg.p_log_error( 0, 'Problem getting SSO, ' ||
            SYS_CONTEXT( 'USERENV', 'OS_USER' ) );
    END IF;
EXCEPTION
    WHEN OTHERS THEN
        m_err_no := SQLCODE;
        m_err_txt := SQLERRM;
```

```
        app_sec_pkg.p_log_error( m_err_no, m_err_txt,
            'APPSEC p_check_role_access' );
END p_check_role_access;
/
```

Notice that the two-factor code is no longer required, and all the logic related to processing two-factor authentication has been commented. We are moving that logic to take place immediately after the application verification, the appver user, connects. The job of appver, after controlling initial application access, is to provide a list of connection strings to the application. It is in this process, a call to a new procedure, P_GET_APP_CONNS that we will do two-factor authentication.

If we pass SSO, then we proceed to set the role to the value we looked up in v_application_registry. If the user's connection/session fails to pass our SSO requirements, then we log the error "Problem getting SSO," and return without setting the role. Something is seriously wrong with that user, and we don't want to deal with him at all.

Put Dynamic Secure Application Role Procedure to Work

As a one-stop-shop for all applications to gain the privileges needed to operate, p_check_role_access needs to be executable by all. We will grant execute on p_check_role_access to PUBLIC. The procedure runs with AUTHID CURRENT_USER, so it doesn't have direct access to data in the appsec schema; however, this procedure, by virtue of its definition in the appsec schema, can execute other functions and procedures in the appsec schema, like the f_get_app_role helper function, which provides the required data. Following is our grant of execute privileges:

```
GRANT EXECUTE ON appsec.p_check_role_access TO PUBLIC;
```

We will add some additional auditing, because we want to see if there is a trend of errors in this procedure. We can combine this audit information with information in the v_appsec_errors log view. For example:

```
AUDIT EXECUTE ON appsec.p_check_role_access
    BY ACCESS WHENEVER NOT SUCCESSFUL;
```

■ **Note** You can find a script with the preceding statements in the file named *Chapter10/SecAdm.sql*.

As you may recall, when we initially created the hrview_role back in Chapter 2, we specified that it would be IDENTIFIED USING appsec.p_check_hrview_access. We are going to have to redirect it to be identified by our new procedure. We will drop the role and recreate it. Also, we need to repeat the grants that we had made to that role as shown in Listing 10-7.

Listing 10-7. Recreate HR View Role Identified by New Procedure

```
DROP ROLE hrview_role;
CREATE ROLE hrview_role IDENTIFIED USING appsec.p_check_role_access;

GRANT EXECUTE ON hr.hr_sec_pkg TO hrview_role;
```

Rewrite and Refactor Method to Distribute Two-Factor Code

We are going to make one more pass at the `distribute2Factor()` method. We need to incorporate the `application_id` in several places. While we are here, we are also going to *refactor* the code with a bit more security and organization.

If you look back at this method in the last chapter, you will see that we have two dynamic queries: one query we build to get data from the `HR.emp_mobile_nos` table and others, and another query we build to update the `v_two_fact_cd_cache` view. For security, we prefer parameterized procedures and functions to dynamic queries. This method and these dynamic queries run in the Oracle database and are unlikely to be susceptible to SQL injection, but we should consider the possibility. What would it take to do SQL injection in those queries?

The first query takes two parameters. It takes the `oraFmtSt` string for formatting dates, which is defined locally—that is tamper-proof. It also takes the `osUser` name, which is passed from `f_send_two_factor`, which is in turn passed from our secure application role procedure and is derived from our SSO process. I can surmise that, in order to accomplish SQL injection in that dynamic query, the user would have to have an extremely bizarre user name in the operating system—not likely.

The second query (update or insert) takes the two-factor code that we generated locally (tamper-proof), the IP Address which is sensed by Oracle database (only suspect in our wildest dreams), and the employee ID, which we got from our `HR` tables and must meet rigid type constraints, `NUMBER(6)`. Once again, this is not a likely candidate for SQL injection.

Our impetus for moving these queries out of our Java code and into stored procedures, then, is not justified as a counter to SQL injection. We will do it in any case, because having the database logic in a stored procedure makes our Java code less dependent on the data organization and more tolerant of database changes. If the DBAs or our application security manager requires that data tables be changed or moved, our procedure can be modified to accommodate the changes without requiring a change to the Java code. We would prefer that database changes only affect native database structures, not Java.

Procedure to get Employee Addresses for Two-Factor Code Delivery

We build a procedure to get the pager, phone, and other numbers that we will use to distribute our two-factor authentication code. At the same time, with a single query, we can get the employee e-mail address and the IP address of the session. We will also get the cached two-factor authentication code for this user on this application, and the timestamp of the cache. Getting all these data elements at once, based on the user ID and the application ID provides sufficient data for all our two-factor code distribution tests and delivery.

Take a look at the list of parameters in Listing 10-8. You'll see that they are mostly `OUT` parameters— we are returning a lot of data. We only pass three parameters to this procedure: the user ID, the date format string we discussed in the last chapter, and the application ID that we introduced in this chapter. We will place `p_get_emp_2fact_nos` in the `appsec_only_pkg` package.

Listing 10-8. Procedure to Get Addresses for Two-Factor Code Distribution

```
PROCEDURE p_get_emp_2fact_nos(
    os_user            hr.v_emp_mobile_nos.user_id%TYPE,
    fmt_string             VARCHAR2,
    m_employee_id      OUT hr.v_emp_mobile_nos.employee_id%TYPE,
    m_com_pager_no     OUT hr.v_emp_mobile_nos.com_pager_no%TYPE,
    m_sms_phone_no     OUT hr.v_emp_mobile_nos.sms_phone_no%TYPE,
```

```
        m_sms_carrier_url OUT hr.v_sms_carrier_host.sms_carrier_url%TYPE,
        m_email           OUT hr.v_employees_public.email%TYPE,
        m_ip_address      OUT v_two_fact_cd_cache.ip_address%TYPE,
        m_cache_ts        OUT VARCHAR2,
        m_cache_addr      OUT v_two_fact_cd_cache.ip_address%TYPE,
        m_application_id      v_two_fact_cd_cache.application_id%TYPE,
        m_err_no          OUT NUMBER,
        m_err_txt         OUT VARCHAR2 )
IS BEGIN
        m_err_no := 0;
        SELECT e.employee_id, m.com_pager_no, m.sms_phone_no, s.sms_carrier_url,
            e.email, SYS_CONTEXT( 'USERENV', 'IP_ADDRESS' ),
            TO_CHAR( c.cache_ts, fmt_string ), c.ip_address
        INTO m_employee_id, m_com_pager_no, m_sms_phone_no, m_sms_carrier_url,
            m_email, m_ip_address, m_cache_ts, m_cache_addr
        FROM hr.v_emp_mobile_nos m, hr.v_employees_public e,
            hr.v_sms_carrier_host s, v_two_fact_cd_cache c
        WHERE m.user_id = os_user
        AND e.employee_id =  m.employee_id
        AND s.sms_carrier_cd (+)=  m.sms_carrier_cd
        AND c.employee_id  (+)= m.employee_id

        AND c.application_id (+)= m_application_id;

EXCEPTION
        -- User must exist in HR.V_EMP_MOBILE_NOS to send 2Factor, even to email
        WHEN OTHERS THEN
            m_err_no := SQLCODE;
            m_err_txt := SQLERRM;
            appsec.app_sec_pkg.p_log_error( m_err_no, m_err_txt,
                'app_sec_pkg.p_get_emp_2fact_nos' );
END p_get_emp_2fact_nos;
```

The query in Listing 10-8's procedure is almost identical to the select query that we had in the previous version of the distribute2Factor() method. The only difference is the addition of the last line: AND c.application_id (+)= m_application_id. With that addition, we are selecting from the two-factor cache for this user, and only for the specific application ID. Again, the (+) symbol indicates an outer join, so we will return the primary data (e.g., pager number), even if no two-factor code already exists in the cache for this user and this application.

Stored Procedure to Update Two-Factor Code Cache

The second Oracle statement that we are moving out of Java as dynamic SQL into an Oracle stored procedure was what we used in distribute2factor() for updating the two-factor cache. Our parameters for this procedure are primarily IN parameters. We pass in the user ID and the application ID for which the two-factor code was generated. We also pass in the two-factor code and the distribution code—a numeric value indicating which routes were used for distribution of the two-factor code. Listing 10-9 shows this procedure. We will place p_update_2fact_cache in the appsec_only_pkg package.

Listing 10-9. Procedure to Update Two-Factor Code Cache

```
PROCEDURE p_update_2fact_cache(
    m_employee_id       v_two_fact_cd_cache.employee_id%TYPE,
    m_application_id    v_two_fact_cd_cache.application_id%TYPE,
    m_two_factor_cd     v_two_fact_cd_cache.two_factor_cd%TYPE,
    m_distrib_cd        v_two_fact_cd_cache.distrib_cd%TYPE,
    m_err_no        OUT NUMBER,
    m_err_txt       OUT VARCHAR2 )
IS
    v_count         INTEGER;
BEGIN
    m_err_no := 0;
    SELECT COUNT(*) INTO v_count
        FROM v_two_fact_cd_cache
        WHERE employee_id = m_employee_id
        AND application_id = m_application_id;
    IF v_count = 0 THEN
        INSERT INTO v_two_fact_cd_cache( employee_id, application_id,
            two_factor_cd, distrib_cd ) VALUES
        ( m_employee_id, m_application_id, m_two_factor_cd, m_distrib_cd );
    ELSE
        UPDATE v_two_fact_cd_cache SET two_factor_cd = m_two_factor_cd,
            ip_address = SYS_CONTEXT( 'USERENV', 'IP_ADDRESS' ),
            distrib_cd = m_distrib_cd, cache_ts=SYSDATE
        WHERE employee_id = m_employee_id
        AND application_id = m_application_id;
    END IF;
EXCEPTION
    WHEN OTHERS THEN
        m_err_no := SQLCODE;
        m_err_txt := SQLERRM;
        appsec.app_sec_pkg.p_log_error( m_err_no, m_err_txt,
            'app_sec_pkg.p_update_2fact_cache' );
END p_update_2fact_cache;
```

You can see that we have three Oracle statements in the body of this procedure: a SELECT, an INSERT, and an UPDATE. If you recall, in the distribute2factor() method in the last chapter, we only required two statements. There we attempted an update and read the value of a returned integer. If the return value was 0, then no records were affected by the update, and we did an insert. Here, however, we must do the SELECT COUNT manually to see if there are any records to update. If the count is 0, we do the INSERT, or else we do the UPDATE.

In each of these statements, you can see that we are dealing with records associated with both the user (employee) id and the application ID. A user may have multiple two-factor codes in the cache for multiple applications.

Changes to the Method to Distribute Two-Factor Codes

The changes in the OracleJavaSecure.distribute2Factor() method have mostly to do with calling and receiving output parameters from p_get_emp_2fact_nos and p_update_2fact_cache. One other addition is the receipt and use of the applicationID argument as shown in Listing 10-10. We are not going to go into the details of our call to our new procedures—you have seen similar calls before.

Listing 10-10. Header for Method to distribute Two-Factor Code

```
private static String applicationID = null;

public static final String distribute2Factor( String osUser, String applicationID )
    throws Exception
{
    // Set class static member equal to what passed here from Oracle
    OracleJavaSecure.applicationID = applicationID;
```

■ **Note** You can find the code just described, which you can see in Listing 10-10, in the file named *Chapter10/orajavsec/OracleJavaSecure.java.*

One change that might go unnoticed is suggested by our setting of the static class member, applicationID, from what we receive in this procedure. In the last chapter, we had a small issue with the twoFactorAuth member: we generated it in the distribute2Factor() method, used it there and handed it to the distribToSMS(), distribToPagerURL(), and distribToEMail() methods. Additionally, we entered it on the command line in the client, handed it to our secure application role procedure, and eventually handed it to the f_is_cur_cached_cd function. Thus, we had two different points of entry—this will continue. The problem is that we had two different references for the same thing in OracleJavaSecure; that is unneeded, because we can call it the same thing whether generated on Oracle database for distribution or entered on the client for return to Oracle database for testing. It is in our benefit to move that member to a static class member and have a standard location to refer to. Then we can stop passing it from method to method and just refer to it locally in each method.

We have a couple more static class members that we will similarly put to use in this chapter, the first of which is coming into play here in the distribute2Factor() method. You can see that we pass the applicationID to this method and use it to set a static class member. We will refer to this in many places, and be thankful we don't have to list it in method arguments and pass it around from method to method.

We pass applicationID into the distribute2Factor() method because this is the first Java method called on the Oracle database. On the client side, the applicationID is entered by the user and passed to OracleJavaSecure from the specific application that is using our services. We will discuss that process later in this chapter.

Update to Two-Factor Distribution Formats

Now, because we will be sending two-factor authentication codes to the user for multiple applications, we will have to identify them in the messages we send. We will use the application ID to identify what app the code is used for. We will place the words "for APPID" on the Subject line and in the message body, where "APPID" is the specific application ID we are referencing. Here is an example.

```
From: response@org.com
To: 8005551212@txt.att.net
```

Subject: Response **for HRVIEW**
1234-5678-9012 **for HRVIEW**

Application Authorization Overview

We are going to implement this entirely with Oracle database as the backend, of course running with the Oracle JVM. That means we have to deal with one important security aspect. To talk to Oracle database at all, we need to connect with a user and password. We will spend significant time addressing that issue.

In a nutshell, here is how we will do Application Authorization, which we will also refer to as Application Verification:

1. We will first connect to Oracle, proxying through a new user, `appver.`

2. As in the past, we will need to pass the SSO and two-factor authentication requirements.

3. Once we have attained two-factor authentication, we exchange encryption keys.

4. We also retrieve an encrypted list of connection strings that we can use in our current application.

5. When we use one of those application connection strings, we again assure our SSO and we exchange additional encryption keys to query encrypted data, as before; however, we do not re-do our two-factor authentication.

All of this looks well and good, but the question arises: how do we know what application is being used? Well, we certainly don't want to merely take the application's word for it. A standard assumption in secure computing is that given an opportunity, a hacker's code will lie—a sort of application identity theft. We are distributing a list of connection strings, including user names and passwords, to known applications. They are encrypted, but we don't want to hand them to just anyone.

In order to assure an application is who it says it is, we are going to ask the application to give us a piece of itself, one which we have already received and registered. We will compare what the application provides with what we have registered, and if they are "equal," then we recognize the application.

The piece of an application that we demand be presented is an inner class. This class must have the same name as the one we registered. We may register multiple versions of the same inner class, to handle application upgrades, but connection strings need to be recreated or duplicated to the new version.

When I say that we assure that the inner classes are "equal," that is the litmus test. The default equality test, which we do not override, is that the classes are equivalent; they reside at the same memory address and are the same class. We can also say `class1 == class2`.

In a JVM, classes are modeled in memory, but only a single place in memory is required to model a specific class. There can be multiple instances, but they all use the same model. When we say `class1.equals( class2 )`, the class has to be the same model. I'll give you more insight: if these classes (the one the application provides and the one we have registered) claim to be the same—same package and same class name—but are not, then even before we get to the `.equals()` method, we will see an exception. When we attempt to deserialize a `Class` based on the serialized object in hand, if it is not the same as one we've already instantiated, then it looks like a square peg trying to fit in a round hole. Specifically, an `InvalidClassException` is thrown. A JVM only has room for one name to class instance image relationship. Try to introduce another, different class as the same name and the JVM will reject it.

Let me be subtle and say that you will probably find ways that this will need to be improved. One obvious way to improve it would be to run our applications on a server, perhaps as web applications, so we do not need to deal with client-side application authentication. However, even in that case, you may still want to have application authentication for server applications in order to restrict Oracle connection strings to specific applications.

User for Application Authorization

We need a doorkeeper. He will be our bouncer, rejecting the riff-raff and troublemakers. We will call him our application verification, **appver** user. In this analogy, the applications (not people) are our clients. Some applications are permitted because they have pre-registered and present their identities and submit to and pass identity checks.

In addition to guarding the entrance, **appver** provides every successful entrant with the keys needed to enter the inner doors where they are allowed to go. Again in our analogy, the keys are Oracle connection strings that have user ids and passwords to connect to Oracle database. These are not personal users and passwords, but application passwords, permitting secure application roles with access to application data.

Like a doorkeeper, **appver** is available to all and has sufficient information to grant passage and direction. He also has sufficient power to prevent passage, as needed.

A New Profile with Limits and Unlimited

Normally, we would limit user accounts for security, but in setting up our application authorization, we are going to need some flexibility. We will assign the limits and permissions for this account through a unique profile, **appver_prof**, shown in Listing 10-11.

Listing 10-11. Profile for Application Authorization

```
CREATE PROFILE appver_prof LIMIT
    CONNECT_TIME          1
    IDLE_TIME             1
    SESSIONS_PER_USER     UNLIMITED
    PASSWORD_LIFE_TIME    UNLIMITED
    FAILED_LOGIN_ATTEMPTS UNLIMITED;
```

⬚ **Note** You can find this script in the file named *Chapter10/SecAdm.sql*.

Contrary to our ordinary standards, our application verification, **appver** user, will have a password that will never expire. We will also allow this user to type in the wrong password an unlimited number of times without locking it out (keeping it from further login attempts, even with the correct password). And, we will allow this account an unlimited number of concurrent sessions.

I know that all sounds backwards from security, but we have the potential of hundreds of persons attempting to access applications, verified by this user. We need to tightly control when this password expires—we will periodically, manually reset the password—some file distribution will probably be required to the clients. However, we don't want it to expire automatically. Also, we do not know how many people will concurrently want to authorize for applications, hence the unlimited sessions. Perhaps down the road, once we have some history, we will know what the correct number of sessions is.

Sure we can say unlimited sessions, but in reality there is a limit. The hard limit is the number of processes that the Database was created to service. The default number of processes is 150. Looking ahead, when we create a dedicated database for application authentication in Chapter 11, we will bump the number of processes up to 500.

The unlimited failed login attempts are a bit harder to justify, because it gives a hacker a wide open door to use brute-force attack to guess the password. The alternative, however, is the potential for a slew of broken applications. If a hacker, or errant application, made several attempts to log in with the wrong password and locked out the user, all our applications that depend on this user for authorization would fail until the account was reset.

We are going to limit this account as much as possible. There will be only a few privileges we will give it. It will need to pass SSO, two-factor authentication, encryption, and application authorization—the reason for its existence. A couple of the limits we will set for this user will be set through parameters in the `appver_prof` profile. We will only allow this account a one minute connect time, and one minute of idle time (the minimums).

Application Verification User

It's time to create our application verification user, which we will name **appver**. Listing 10-12 shows the commands to create the appver user. We assign a password to this user, but for now, we are treating it more like a line of code or an address. It gets people to the workplace, but doesn't do any work, itself. For now, this password will be hard-coded into the `OracleJavaSecure` class, on the client. In Chapter 11, we will obfuscate and encrypt the password. In any case, please assign a complex password to **appver**.

Listing 10-12. Create Application Verification User

```
CREATE USER appver
    IDENTIFIED BY password
    QUOTA 0 ON SYSTEM
    PROFILE appver_prof;

GRANT create_session_role TO appver;
```

Notice that we assigned the `appver_prof` profile to **appver**. We also give **appver** no space, 0 QUOTA for storage. Finally, we grant the `create_session_role` to **appver** so that he can connect to Oracle database.

The Application Verification Logon Trigger

We are going to create a logon trigger for the **appver** account. We have already seen database triggers, but this one is different—it defines an action we will have Oracle database take whenever a user logs onto the **appver** schema. Listing 10-13 shows that our logon trigger simply calls a procedure, `p_appver_logon`.

Listing 10-13. Logon Trigger for Application Verification

```
CREATE OR REPLACE TRIGGER secadm.t_screen_appver_access AFTER LOGON ON appver.SCHEMA
BEGIN
    appsec.p_appver_logon;
END;
/
```

Application Verification Logon Procedure

The procedure for our **appver** logon trigger, **p_appver_logon** is shown in Listing 10-14. It would have been nice if we could have done a complete SSO check during the logon trigger, but alas, the proxy session and the CLIENT_IDENTIFIER setting in the USERENV are not available at logon time. However, we can still assure that the session user is **appver** (who else could it be?), and that our IP Address is acceptable. We also call a function, **f_is_user** to assure that the **os_user** is also a database user. That may be the most significant test since it is also what we will assure for our proxy login.

Listing 10-14. Application Verification Logon Procedure

```
CREATE OR REPLACE PROCEDURE appsec.p_appver_logon
AUTHID CURRENT_USER
AS
    just_os_user    VARCHAR2(40);
    backslash_place NUMBER;
BEGIN
    just_os_user := UPPER( SYS_CONTEXT( 'USERENV', 'OS_USER' ) );
    backslash_place := INSTR( just_os_user, '\', -1 );
    IF( backslash_place > 0 )
    THEN
        just_os_user := SUBSTR( just_os_user, backslash_place + 1 );
    END IF;
    -- For logon trigger - limited SSO, no PROXY_USER and no CLIENT_IDENTIFIER
    IF( SYS_CONTEXT( 'USERENV', 'SESSION_USER' ) = 'APPVER'
    AND( SYS_CONTEXT( 'USERENV', 'IP_ADDRESS' ) LIKE '192.168.%' OR
        SYS_CONTEXT( 'USERENV', 'IP_ADDRESS' ) = '127.0.0.1' )
    -- Requirements must be applicable to all applications - time may not be
    --AND TO_CHAR( SYSDATE, 'HH24' ) BETWEEN 7 AND 18
    -- Assure that OS_USER is a database user
    AND( appsec_only_pkg.f_is_user( just_os_user ) = 'Y' ) )
    THEN
        app_sec_pkg.p_log_error( 0, 'Success APPVER logon, ' || just_os_user );
    ELSE
        app_sec_pkg.p_log_error( 0, 'Problem getting APPVER logon, ' || just_os_user );
        --just_os_user := sys.f_get_off;
        -- This causes logon trigger to fail -- so not connected to Oracle
        RAISE_APPLICATION_ERROR(-20003,'You are not allowed to connect to the database');
    END IF;
END p_appver_logon;
/
```

We run this logon trigger procedure as AUTHID CURRENT_USER; that is with invoker's rights. That's the only way we can accurately gauge the user's identity—similar to the way it is for secure application role procedures. So, we need to grant execute on this procedure to PUBLIC:

```
GRANT EXECUTE ON appsec.p_appver_logon TO PUBLIC;
```

Get Off Function

There is always a longing to have complete control. It would be wonderful to be able to spot a problem in our logon trigger and immediately kill the session. Do you see the commented line saying just_os_user := sys.f_get_off in our logon trigger procedure, p_appver_logon, Listing 10-14? It is a nice idea that won't work. The f_get_off function shown in Listing 10-15 could accomplish the task for us; however, Oracle Database does not allow us to kill the current session.

Listing 10-15. Non-functional Kill Switch, f_get_off

```
CREATE OR REPLACE FUNCTION sys.f_get_off
RETURN VARCHAR2
AS
    PRAGMA AUTONOMOUS_TRANSACTION;
    p_sid v$session.SID%TYPE;
    p_serial v$session.serial#%TYPE;
BEGIN
    p_sid := SYS_CONTEXT( 'USERENV', 'SID' );
    SELECT serial# INTO p_serial
    FROM v$session
    WHERE sid = p_sid;
    EXECUTE IMMEDIATE 'ALTER SYSTEM KILL SESSION ''' ||
                p_sid || ',' || p_serial || '''';
    RETURN 'OFF';
END f_get_off;

GRANT EXECUTE ON sys.f_get_off TO appsec;
```

■ **Note** You can find Listing 10-15's function in the file named *Chapter10/Sys.sql*.

The heart of the function is in the EXECUTE IMMEDIATE command. An alternative along these lines that would work would be if we inserted the SID and SERIAL# to be killed into a table. Then using an independent, scheduled task, read the table and kill the sessions, then delete the records from the table.

Anyway, manhandling in the most direct way is not going to work. Just as well, because our call in p_appver_logon to RAISE_APPLICATION_ERROR does the same thing. Because we are in a logon trigger, when we raise an exception, the logon fails.

Function to Find Database User

There is a function that we have, for use in the **appver** logon trigger procedure, **f_is_user**, which tests whether the OS user is also a database user. This is an important test, because it enforces a portion of our SSO requirements—if we haven't created an Oracle user with the same name as this person's operating system user name, then he cannot use our applications. This function, Listing 10-16, will be added to the package, **appsec_only_pkg**.

Listing 10-16. Function to Find Database User

```
FUNCTION f_is_user( just_os_user VARCHAR2 )
RETURN VARCHAR2
AS
    return_char VARCHAR2(1) := 'N';
    v_count     INTEGER;
BEGIN
    SELECT COUNT(*) INTO v_count
    FROM sys.all_users
    WHERE username = just_os_user;
    IF v_count > 0 THEN
        return_char := 'Y';
    END IF;
    RETURN return_char;
END f_is_user;
```

▪ **Note** Return to file *Chapter10/SecAdm.sql* for reference in this discussion.

Notice from where we get the indicator that the user is an Oracle user. We read from the Oracle data dictionary view, SYS.ALL_USERS. That view is granted select to PUBLIC. I believe this is a bit of a security problem. If a hacker gets access to any Oracle user account, he can read the ALL_USERS view and *get a list of all the user names* he might try to access. There are other views of the data dictionary that are likewise granted for select by PUBLIC, which I believe oversteps security. Another particular view is SYS.ALL_SOURCE, which lists the entire body of every stored procedure in every schema, and other code to which a user is granted execute. Letting a hacker see our code (whether he's a legitimate but rogue user or an infiltrator) is inviting further compromise.

When we create a dedicated database for application authentication in Chapter 11, we will revoke select by PUBLIC for these particularly sensitive views. There are a few additional views that we will also remove from PUBLIC access.

Proxy Through Application Verification and Other Proxies

Finally, with regard to our application verification user, we need to permit every user to proxy through appver. Our logon trigger will not see the proxy, but when we execute the procedure to get the secure application role related to the current application, we will use our proxy test as part of SSO. For example:

```
ALTER USER osuser GRANT CONNECT THROUGH appver;
```

Do not forget to create an Oracle user for every OS user that you want to give access to your applications. And grant that each user may proxy through appver. Also for each OS user, grant that her account may proxy through the role associated with the specific application.

For example, to give an OS user named "coffin" access to the hrview application, you'd need to execute these commands:

```
CREATE USER coffin IDENTIFIED EXTERNALLY;
GRANT CREATE_SESSION_ROLE TO coffin;
```

```
ALTER USER coffin GRANT CONNECT THROUGH APPVER;
-- APPUSR is the account that gets access to HRVIEW_ROLE
ALTER USER coffin GRANT CONNECT THROUGH APPUSR;
```

Additionally, for user coffin to pass two-factor authentication, he will need entries in both HR.EMPLOYEES and HR.emp_mobile_nos.

Auditing Application Verification

It would be nice to know everything that the appver user does—there should only be a select number of statements he makes. However, we anticipate he will get called many, many times, and we do not want to audit all the legitimate calls he makes. The first clue that appver is doing something unofficial will probably be when he tries to select data. So we will use the audit log, by the uncommented commands in Listing 10-17 to watch for that.

Listing 10-1., Auditing Application Verification

```
--AUDIT ALL STATEMENTS BY appver BY ACCESS; -- WHENEVER SUCCESSFUL;
AUDIT SELECT TABLE BY appver BY ACCESS;

AUDIT EXECUTE PROCEDURE
    BY appver
    BY ACCESS
    WHENEVER NOT SUCCESSFUL;
```

Also, we might catch some application errors and attempted abuse by auditing when appver fails to execute procedures. So we audit when those calls are NOT SUCCESSFUL. We wouldn't want to audit successful procedure calls, because we know he will be calling procedures, and we hope he succeeds.

Structures for Application Authorization

We discussed one of the tasks that appver accomplishes—comparing an inner class object provided by the application with one that has been registered. Registration occurs when the inner class gets inserted on first sight (when there is no existing registry entry for the application). That's right: the first time you (a new application) show up, we write your name in the guest book and save the inner class you provided. Your application had to leap several obstacles to get this far, and we give you credit for that. However, at this point, it's not much more than a mug shot.

Your application has to come back with the same identity in order to register your connection strings. You also have to show up with the same identity from now on to get those connection strings returned to your application.

More Space for Application Security

Because we are committing to store a couple objects per application that use these services, we should give a bit more space to the appsec schema to use for storage. Execute this ALTER USER command to accomplish that:

```
-- Increase quota to hold app verification data
ALTER USER appsec DEFAULT TABLESPACE USERS QUOTA 10M ON USERS;
```

Application Connection Registry Table

We will create a table (see Listing 10-18) to hold the object each application provides, as a RAW data type. It needs to be less than 2K to be stored as a RAW, so developers shouldn't expand on the template class that we provide to them. Along with each object, we will store a binary large object (BLOB) data type that holds a list of the associated connection strings.

It is difficult to index and select on RAW or BLOB types, as you might imagine. So we are going to index on the class name and class version as VARCHAR2 data types. These identifiers can be garnered from the object, so we never pass them: passing the object is sufficient for us to find out who the application is claiming to be.

Setting the table of Oracle connection strings (the BLOB) is not a one-time occurrence; they can be updated. So we include an update_dt column in our table to keep track of that. We use the empty_blob() directive to allocate a BLOB locator address by default, pointing at no particular BLOB, but an address nonetheless—not a null.

Listing 10-18. Application Connection Registry Table

```
CREATE TABLE appsec.t_app_conn_registry
(
    class_name      VARCHAR2(2000) NOT NULL,
    class_version   VARCHAR2(200) NOT NULL,
    class_instance  RAW(2000),
    update_dt       DATE DEFAULT SYSDATE,
    connections     BLOB DEFAULT EMPTY_BLOB()
);
```

■ **Note** You can find this script in the file named *Chapter10/AppSec.sql*.

We create an index and primary key on class_name and class_version, not shown. We also create a view of this table for regular reference.

A Set of Connection Strings for an Application

On the client side, we are going to handle our table of connection strings as a HashMap, which we will call connsHash. You must assure that it is marked private so only the OracleJavaSecure class can see it. Here is the declaration:

```
private static HashMap<String, RAW> connsHash = null;
```

We will have exchanged keys with the Oracle database, so we can receive this table of connection strings encrypted with the shared password key. We will only decrypt them as needed, creating a connection and then freeing the connection string for garbage collection (retaining no class member reference to it.) Note that until the garbage collector runs (automatically, self-scheduling), the clear-text connection string will be in the machine memory, but not easily retrieved, even with a debugger.

A HashMap is a Collection class that has a key and value relationship. It is like a two-column table with unique keys and associated values. Both the keys and values are Java objects, not primitives. In this case, our keys are Strings, and our values are RAWs. Specifically, our RAW values are the encrypted form of each connection string used by the application. This declaration of connsHash uses generics to require that the keys be Strings and the values be RAW, with the <String, RAW> syntax.

HashMaps can be created without generics; that is, without specifying the object type of the key and value, but each time you retrieve a key or value, you would need to cast it to the appropriate type. Additionally, by specifying the object types, we are assured that our application will only place objects of that type in our key and value fields. Otherwise, HashMaps can hold a variety of Object types all at once.

An Inner Class to Represent the Application

Our applications will identify themselves to this application authentication process by passing an object that implements a specific interface: the RevLvlClassIntfc interface. An interface is like a class, but it is hollow—it has no guts. An interface can specify a list of methods, and all classes that implement that interface will need to implement those methods; that is, they will need to have methods with the same signature (same name, arguments and return types). Hopefully, they will also provide the guts or functional code to accomplish whatever's required.

The RevLvlClassIntfc interface is in the *orajavsec* package, just like OracleJavaSecure. Also like OracleJavaSecure, the interface needs to exist in the Oracle database as well as on the client. RevLvlClassIntfc needs to be loaded into Oracle, as the first line of Listing 10-19 suggests, and needs to be distributed to developers along with *OracleJavaSecure.class*, most likely in the same *jar* file.

Listing 10-19. Revision Level Class Interface

```
//CREATE OR REPLACE AND RESOLVE JAVA SOURCE NAMED appsec."orajavsec/RevLvlClassIntfc" AS
package orajavsec;

public interface RevLvlClassIntfc {
    //private static final long serialVersionUID = 2011010100L;
    //private String innerClassRevLvl = " 20110101a";
    public String getRevLvl();
}
```

■ **Note** You can find this code in the file named *Chapter10/orajavsec/RevLvlClassIntfc.java*.

There is one method in the interface, getRevLvl(). This returns a revision level, innerClassRevLvl that we can use to support multiple versions of an application. For instance, if you are moving your application data to new Oracle tables or a new Oracle database, you could update innerClassRevLvl in your inner class and use our processes to register the updated application and generate a new set of connection strings associated with it. Both the old application/version and the new one would be able to get their respective connections simultaneously. Also, to force everyone to move to a new version of an application and to disable the old version, we can delete the old version of our inner class from the application registry, or just delete the associated connection strings list.

We will ask the implementers of this interface (the developers) to also provide a static long named serialVersionUID that is used in object serialization (packaging for storage in the database and for transmission across the network.) We will discuss this more shortly.

Implement an Inner Class in OracleJavaSecure

For testing purposes in this chapter, we will define an inner class, InnerRevLvlClass, in the OracleJavaSecure class that implements RevLvlClassIntfc. To generate an inner class, just include the class definition within an existing class definition. In our case, it looks like Listing 10-20. Inside the body of the definition for OracleJavaSecure, we declare the inner class, InnerRevLvlClass.

Listing 10-20. OracleJavaSecure Inner Class for Identity and Versioning, InnerRevLvlClass

```
public class OracleJavaSecure {
    ...

    public static class InnerRevLvlClass

        implements Serializable, RevLvlClassIntfc
    {
        private static final long serialVersionUID = 2011010100L;
        private String innerClassRevLvl = "20110101a";
        public String getRevLvl() {
            return innerClassRevLvl;
        }
    }
}
```

> **Note** For most of the rest of this chapter, we will be referring back and forth to Java code that you will find in the file named *Chapter10/orajavsec/OracleJavaSecure.java*, and to SQL and PL/SQL code that you will find in the file named *Chapter10/AppSec.sql*.

Notice that our inner class is designated as public static. The static is not necessary, but assures us that the class exists when the parent, OracleJavaSecure, is instantiated. On the other hand, the public designation is significant from a security standpoint. We would prefer to make this inner class private, and we could for OracleJavaSecure.InnerRevLvlClass. But for other independent applications, the inner classes will need to be public so that OracleJavaSecure on the Oracle Database can instantiate them.

Our inner class also must implement the Serializable interface (another required element of the template we provide to our developers.) By implementing Serializable (no methods are required), we are assuring that we can take our inner class, get the bytes of the object and pass them to Oracle database for storage. We can only handle objects in that way if they implement the Serializable interface.

The serialVersionUID for the class that the application hands to us must be identical to the serialVersionUID for the class definition in Oracle database (this discussion is continued in the next section). We set a static member variable for serialVersionUID, but if we didn't have that member, the JVM would calculate a value. If that value is not identical, then the class cannot be realized, and the object cannot be instantiated, and an exception will be thrown. Most often, unless we make structural changes to the class, the calculated serialVersionUID will be identical, but that statistic of "most often" poses a risk that we are unwilling to take.

Note that the values we provide for innerClassRevLvl and serialVersionUID are pretty much whatever we want; however, I think a form of the date with flexibility for multiple values for any one date will make a good value. If I release a new application on February 14, 2012, I might give these values:

```
private static final long serialVersionUID = 2012021400L;
private String innerClassRevLvl = "20120214a";
```

If I release a revision later that same day, it might have these changed values (for example only, these are usually modified independently and for different reasons):

```
private static final long serialVersionUID = 2012021401L;
private String innerClassRevLvl = "20120214b";
```

It may be obvious, but the L at the end of the value for serialVersionUID is part of the number and indicates that it is a long value. It is a way of casting what would by default be interpreted as an integer to another type of primitive value. Use an upper case L to keep from having the lower case l (ell) confused with a 1 (one). There are other *literal* value casts that consist of suffixes (for example f for float) and prefixes (for example 0x for hexadecimal). Take one, as needed.

Deserialization and Version UID

Bringing an object back to life after serialization requires deserialization. But there is one huge requirement for this to happen—a class definition for the object must exist in the JVM. This is a requirement that is often overlooked or assumed in the documentation on serialization. Usually, an application is responsible for serializing an object, and an equivalent application handles the deserialization. The application has a class definition, perhaps in a separate *.class* file, or as an inner class, and so it already knows how to build an object of the type being deserialized. The serialized object does not contain all the details of the class definition; rather, it should be considered to only retain the data or state of the object when serialized. To deserialize the object in a JVM, the existing class definition must provide a skeleton on which to build the body of the object.

That all makes sense to us now, but consider this twist: We are going to deserialize the object in the Oracle database, in a place where the application does not run. To do this, we do have to have the class definition; so for each application, we will be storing the inner class definition (we'll see how we do that later). In the case of the inner class, InnerRevLvlClass of OracleJavaSecure, the class definition is there on the Oracle database because we create OracleJavaSecure on the server. For other applications, we will have to create the inner class on the Oracle database.

In the interim between object serialization and deserialization, some non-structural changes may be made to the class definition, and the Java compiler and runtime versions may continue to advance; but we should be able, even ten years down the road, to deserialize our object. This is where the serialVersionUID member variable comes into play. At the outset of use of our serialized objects, we may have no problem depending on the runtime calculation of the *suid* (another name for this value when the serialVersionUID member does not exist.) However, as time progresses and things change, we may begin to experience mismatches between what we've serialized and what we are attempting to deserialize into.

We can avoid problems with serial version mismatches (caused by technological progress rather than by changes to our classes) by simply encoding a serialVersionUID member, rather than relying on the runtime calculation.

If we do make structural changes to our class definition, we will need to do the following two things:

1) Change the serialVersionUID value in our class definition.

2) Store a new version of the class definition in Oracle.

Note that this situation is different from the situation where we are only encoding a new innerClassRevLvl in our class definition. We will do that to handle application version changes (and provide an updated list of Oracle connection strings.)

Set Application Context

You will recall from our discussion in the previous section that we are gathering all our application-specific elements in one place. We will store the applicationID, appClass, and twoFactorAuth code in OracleJavaSecure as static class members, so we needn't pass them around to all the methods where they will be referenced.

When an application initially comes to OracleJavaSecure, the first thing it will likely do is identify itself by calling the setAppContext() method, Listing 10-21. setAppContext() takes the applicationID, inner class, and twoFactorAuth code as arguments. The first time we run a client application, the twoFactorAuth code is not provided. It will not be until the user has received the two-factor code on their cell phone or other device that they will be able to return and redo this identification and proceed.

In order to request connection strings, we will have to pass muster with the application verification, appver security guard. That means we will have to present our inner class to the application authorization procedures. In the setAppContext() method, we assure that the inner class we will be presenting implements both the RevLvlClassIntfc interface, and the Serializable interface by calling the instanceof operator.

Listing 10-21. Set Application Context, setAppContext()

```java
private static String applicationID = null;
private static Object appClass     = null;
private static String twoFactorAuth = null;

public static final void setAppContext( String applicationID,
    Object appClass, String twoFactorAuth )
{
    twoFactorAuth = checkFormat2Factor( twoFactorAuth );
    if( null == applicationID || null == appClass ) {
        System.out.println( "Must have an application ID and Class" );
        return;
    }
    // Assure the app class has implemented our interface
    if ( !( ( appClass instanceof RevLvlClassIntfc ) &&
        ( appClass instanceof Serializable ) ) )
    {
        System.out.println(
            "Application ID Class must implement RevLvlClassIntfc" );
        return;
    }
    // Set class static member equal to what passed here at outset
    OracleJavaSecure.applicationID = applicationID;
    OracleJavaSecure.appClass     = appClass;
    OracleJavaSecure.twoFactorAuth = twoFactorAuth;
}
```

As a side note, we have seen methods like this before where we pass in references that are the same as class member names. We typically have set the class members with a statement like this:

```java
this.varName = varName;
```

Notice the difference in this case. Because we are setting static class members, there is no this to refer to–this is a reference to the current instance, but static classes are not instantiated. So we use this syntax to set static class member variables from a method arguments:

```
Class.varName = varName;
```

Format the User-Input Two-Factor Code

We introduced the checkFormat2Factor() method in the last chapter, but we didn't discuss its implementation. We want to assure that users who make an effort to enter the two-factor code get some leniency with regard to format. This is especially important in this chapter, and from now on because we are delivering the application ID along with the two-factor code to the user's cell phone and other devices.

We want to assure that we always deliver the two-factor code as the first item in our message. If the user includes the application name after that, we should find it easy to truncate the two-factor code at the appropriate place. If extra data comes as separate arguments on the command line, we ignore the additional arguments.

Occasionally, an old-style pager may drop non-numeric characters from a message. As a general rule, dashes are always included. Perhaps the pager might also drop spaces and include underscore characters. In preparation for any of those exigencies, and without burdening the user with our format requirements, we pass the two-factor code that comes to us in the setAppContext() method on to the checkFormat2Factor() method in Listing 10-22.

Listing 10-22. Format User-Provided Two-Factor Authentication Code, checkFormat2Factor()

```java
public static String checkFormat2Factor( String twoFactor ) {
    String rtrnString = "";
    if( null == twoFactor ) return rtrnString;
    // Use only numeric values and insert dash after every 4 chars
    StringBuffer sB = new StringBuffer();
    int used = 0;
    char testChar;
    int twoFactLen = twoFactor.length();
    for( int i = 0; i < twoFactLen; i++ ) {
        testChar = twoFactor.charAt( i );
        if( Character.isDigit( testChar ) ) {
            sB.append( testChar );
            if( sB.length() == twoFactorLength ) {
                rtrnString = sB.toString();
                break;
            }
            // Insert dash if we have accepted a multiple of 4 chars
            used++;
            if( 0 == ( used % 4 ) ) sB.append( "-" );
        }
    }
    return rtrnString;
}
```

This method reads each character of the user-input two-factor code. If a character is not numeric, it is discarded. Numeric characters are appended to a StringBuffer, and after each four characters, a dash is appended. This continues until we run out of input or we reach the required two-factor code length, `twoFactorLength`. If we have sufficient numeric characters, we return the `StringBuffer` as a `String`, else we return an empty string.

There is a perception among programmers, especially those (like me) who have worked extensively with perl, that checking the format of a string is best accomplished by using regular expressions. Regular expressions are a succinct way to express patterns of characters, including optional formatting. For example, this regular expression represents a SSN pattern: `"^\\d{3}[- ]?\\d{2}[- ]?\\d{4}$"`. I believe pattern matching has limits that need to be recognized and respected. In `checkFormat2Factor()`, for instance, we are going to throw away extraneous data (words or spaces) that a user might have seen on their cell phone or pager screen and entered. Pattern matching does not work well for free-form user input like this. The second issue I have with complex regular expressions is that to read them often requires a decoder ring and a sheet of scrap paper. (The same can too often be said of perl code in general.)

Save Connection Strings from the Client Perspective

We are going to explore saving connection strings and associating them with an application from both the client side and the server side. In some cases, developers may choose to use all our security except the application authorization, so they will benefit from having an independent method for using connections strings on the client that have not been stored on Oracle database. These can even be combined with a set of connection strings that are maintained by our application authorization.

However, if a developer elects to not store his connection strings under `appver`'s supervision, he will need to find another way to secure the password. Also, he will lose two-factor authentication, which we have delegated to the application authorization process.

Method to Put Connection Strings in the List for an Application

On the client, we have a method, `putAppConnString()` that we can use to add connection strings to `connsHash`. It takes 5 arguments (see Listing 10-23): the instance name, user name, password, host name, and port (as a `String`). By taking these components separately, it leaves the assembly of a connection string to us. We can assure that the connection string format is acceptable. We do take a moment to trim off any whitespace from the head and tail of each argument, calling the `String.trim()` method.

As an optional parameter, by way of an overloaded method, we accept a `boolean` value, which can direct us to test the connection string before saving it in `connsHash`.

We assume the connection string, as we've formatted it, is okay to be added to `connsHash`; however, if we've been directed to test the connection string, we may change that evaluation. If we are testing the connection string, we simply instantiate a new `Connection` based on the connection string and use it to query the database. If that fails, we have determined that the connection string is not good.

*Listing 10-23. Put Connection Strings in List, **putAppConnString()***

```
public static void putAppConnString( String instance, String user,
    String password, String host, String port )
{
    putAppConnString( instance, user, password, host, port, false );
}
public static void putAppConnString( String instance, String user,
    String password, String host, String port, boolean testFirst )
{
    instance = instance.trim();
```

```
        user = user.trim();
        password = password.trim();
        host = host.trim();
        port = port.trim();
        String key = (instance + "/" + user).toUpperCase();
        String connS = "jdbc:oracle:thin:" + user + "/" + password + "@" +
            host + ":" + port + ":" + instance;
        boolean testSuccess = true;
        if( testFirst ) {
            Connection mConn = null;
            try {
                mConn = DriverManager.getConnection( connS );
                Statement stmt = mConn.createStatement();
                ResultSet rs = stmt.executeQuery(
                    "SELECT SYSDATE FROM DUAL" );
                System.out.println( "Connection string successful" );
            } catch( Exception x ) {
                System.out.println( "Connection string failed!" );
                testSuccess = false;
            } finally {
                try {
                    if( null != mConn ) mConn.close();
                } catch( Exception x ) {}
            }
        }
        if( testSuccess ) {
            try {
                appAuthCipherDES.init( Cipher.ENCRYPT_MODE,
                    appAuthSessionSecretDESKey, appAuthParamSpec );
                byte[] bA = appAuthCipherDES.doFinal( connS.getBytes() );
                connsHash.put(key, new RAW( bA ) );
            } catch( Exception x ) {}
        }
    }
```

Finally, if we've decided we like the connection string (testSuccess is true), we add it to connsHash. And, like the connection strings we (perhaps) received from Oracle, we store it here in encrypted form, based on the shared password key we got from Oracle database.

The HashMap, connsHash, is keyed on the string "INSTANCE/USER" that we assembled from the instance name and user name that were provided to us. If we are calling this method with the same instance and user as an existing entry in connsHash, the new connection string will overwrite the old (assuming it's acceptable).

Client Call to Store List of Connection Strings on Oracle

Once we've filled out the ranks of one or more connection strings that we want to use with our application, we can call the putAppConnections() method to submit the connsHash to Oracle Database. We see this method in Listing 10-24.

Note again that we need to have already exchanged keys with Oracle database. Assuredly we have, else we wouldn't have been able to get the previously existing connsHash from Oracle, nor would we have been able to add new connection strings to connsHash—we would have nothing to submit.

We will assure that we have a connection to **appver**, which we can use. We test whether **appVerConn** is null, a reference to the connection we are using to converse with **appver**. If it is null, one of two problems exist: either we haven't connected yet as **appver** (call getAppConnections()), or we have overwritten our connection to **appver**, so it is no longer available to execute the update, putAppConnections(). The solution is to always call putAppConnections(), if needed, before getting one of the connection strings from the list for use in the application.

It is a trivial matter to convert a Java object, as long as it implements Serializable, into a byte array. However, it does look at bit daunting at first. Drilling down into this code, we write our object into an ObjectOutputStream, oout. The ObjectOutputStream is tied directly to a ByteArrayOutputStream, baos. After we write our object, we flush oout and close it, assuring that our entire object is delivered to baos. At that point, we call the toByteArray() method of baos to get our object out as a byte array.

Listing 10-24. Store Connection Strings List in Oracle, putAppConnections()

```
public static void putAppConnections(){
    OracleCallableStatement stmt = null;
    try {
        if( null == appVerConn ) {
            if( null == conn ) {
                System.out.println( "Call getAppConnections to establish " +
                    "connection to AppVer first, " +
                    "else can not putAppConnections!" );
            } else {
                System.out.println( "Connection to AppVer overwritten - " +
                    "can not putAppConnections!" );
            }
            return;
        }

        ByteArrayOutputStream baos = new ByteArrayOutputStream();
        ObjectOutputStream oout = new ObjectOutputStream( baos );
        oout.writeObject( appClass );
        oout.flush();
        oout.close();
        byte[] appClassBytes = baos.toByteArray();
        baos.close();

        baos = new ByteArrayOutputStream();
        oout = new ObjectOutputStream( baos );
        oout.writeObject( connsHash );
        oout.flush();
        oout.close();
        byte[] connsHashBytes = baos.toByteArray();
        baos.close();

        stmt = ( OracleCallableStatement )conn.prepareCall(
            "{? = call appsec.appsec_public_pkg.f_set_decrypt_conns(?,?)}" );
        stmt.registerOutParameter( 1, OracleTypes.VARCHAR );
        stmt.setBytes( 2, appClassBytes );
        stmt.setBytes( 3, connsHashBytes );
        stmt.executeUpdate();
```

```
        String checkReturn = stmt.getString( 1 );
        if( ! checkReturn.equals( okReturnS ) )
            System.out.println( checkReturn );
    } catch ( Exception x ) {
        x.printStackTrace();
    } finally {
        try {
            if ( null != stmt )
                stmt.close();
        } catch ( Exception y ) {}
    }
}
```

We perform this same operation both on our application inner class, appClass, and the connsHash HashMap object, which also implements Serializable (as do the String keys and RAW values held by connsHash).

We submit our application class and connsHash to Oracle Database as byte arrays. We send them to the f_set_decrypt_conns Java stored procedure (function). That function merely calls Java on the Oracle database side, passing these objects to the setDecryptConns() method on the Oracle database, discussed in detail in the sections that follow.

Save Connection Strings from the Server Perspective

On the Oracle database side, we go through a rather elaborate process in order to get the connsHash table of connection strings into the shape we want before storing them. You see, when we submit them to Oracle, they are encrypted with the secret password key that is unique to this session. If we were to store them as is, we could never decrypt them after this session closes; so we will decrypt them before storage on Oracle database. We will explore and apply encryption to data on disk when we get to Chapter 11. The decryption process, however, is preceded by an equally elaborate process to assure that the application class being submitted is appropriate for either overwriting an existing entry in the registry, or inserting a new one.

Function to Call Java to Decrypt the List of Connection Strings

From the client, we call a Java stored procedure, f_set_decrypt_conns on Oracle Database to deliver the connections HashMap. f_set_decrypt_conns simply passes the objects to our Java code on the Oracle database for processing. Java stored procedures can be seen simply as a doorway to pass data through, and a call to methods in Java on the Oracle database. We add this function to a new package, appsec_public_pkg, see Listing 10-25.

Listing 10-25. Function Call to Decrypt List of Connection Strings, f_set_decrypt_conns

```
CREATE OR REPLACE PACKAGE BODY appsec.appsec_public_pkg IS

    FUNCTION f_set_decrypt_conns(
        class_instance RAW, connections RAW )
    RETURN VARCHAR2
    AS LANGUAGE JAVA
```

```
    NAME 'orajavsec.OracleJavaSecure.setDecryptConns( oracle.sql.RAW, oracle.sql.RAW ) return
java.lang.String';
```

...

```
GRANT EXECUTE ON appsec.appsec_public_pkg TO PUBLIC;
```

For now, we will be proxying from a variety of users through **appver** to submit the **connsHash** to **f_set_decrypt_conns**, so we will grant execute to **PUBLIC** on the package **appsec_public_pkg**.

Obviously, we do not want just anybody submitting objects to this function, so we need to protect it in one or more of the following ways:

1) Revoke the **GRANT EXECUTE** on **f_set_decrypt_conns** from **PUBLIC**, and add grants only to those users (OS user names) who need access.

2) Protect the code used to accomplish this function—separate it out into an administrative application.

3) Implement some additional test in this code, possibly checking for a user's existence (listing) in an Oracle table, built for this purpose.

We will do all of these things in Chapters 11 and 12.

Method to Store List of Connection Strings for Application

Certain actions that we might take are considered risky or uncertain in Java. Java is a strongly typed language, so it doesn't abide uncertainty in object type identity. However, in cases where we are in control of both the origination and the receipt of the object, we can ignore any warnings in this regard and proceed.

In the **setDecryptConns()** method given in Listings 10-26 through 10-35, we engage in such an endeavor. We will be reading an object from an **ObjectInputStream** and then treating it as if we know what kind of object it is. We do this twice. First, we read in the application inner class object and then call its **getRevLvl()** method, assuming it has the wherewithal to respond. The second case is when we read in the **connsHash** object and cast it as a **HashMap**.

When compiling, *javac* will report to us that there are "unchecked or unsafe operations". We can, by way of the **@SuppressWarnings("unchecked")** annotation, ask *javac* not to bother us. That annotation applies directly to the method that follows, and only to that method. Notice in Listing 10-26 that there is no punctuation between the annotation and the method declaration. Unfortunately, those annotations are not accepted in the Oracle JVM, so we need to comment them out and just live with the compile-time warnings.

Listing 10-26. SuppressWarnings() Annotation, setDecryptConns()

```
@SuppressWarnings( "unchecked" )

public static String setDecryptConns( RAW classInstance, RAW connections ) {
    String rtrnString = "function";
    OracleCallableStatement stmt = null;
    try {
```

Build a Class from a Byte Array

Getting a class back from the RAW data type that we received on the Oracle database is the flipside of what we saw earlier when we converted our class objects into byte arrays. The first step here in Listing 10-27, part of setDecryptConns() is to get a byte array from the RAW that we are calling classInstance. We feed that byte array to a ByteArrayInputStream, bAIS. Then we instantiate an ObjectInputStream, oins, coupled to bAIS. We call the readObject() method of oins to rebuild an Object named classObject. After closing the streams, we get an instance of Class, providedClass for the classObject.

Listing 10-27. Build a Class from a Byte Array

```
byte[] appClassBytes = classInstance.getBytes();
ByteArrayInputStream bAIS = new ByteArrayInputStream( appClassBytes );
ObjectInputStream oins =
    new ObjectInputStream( bAIS );
Object classObject = oins.readObject();
oins.close();
Class providedClass = classObject.getClass();
```

Use Java Reflection to Call Method

With the Class object, we can use *reflection* to get the name of the class and even to call its methods. This is also part of setDecryptConns() method. Getting the class name is a single call to the getName() method. To call the getRevLvl() method in the inner class, we get a Method object, classMethod from providedClass by calling the getMethod() method, as shown in Listing 10-28. Then we call the invoke() method of classMethod, passing the classObject we got in Listing 10-27, to retrieve the actual return value from getRevLvl(). Cast the return Object value as a String.

Listing 10-28. Call Methods Through Reflection

```
String className = providedClass.getName();
Method classMethod = providedClass.getMethod( "getRevLvl" );
String classVersion = ( String )classMethod.invoke( classObject );

// Do this once we get to Oracle
// Before we store any class, let's assure it has a package (.)
// noted before being an inner class ($) - our planned requirements
if( -1 == className.indexOf( "." ) ||
    className.indexOf( "$" ) < className.indexOf( "." ) )
    return "App class must be in a package and be an inner class!";
```

We are going to place some requirements on developers for their application inner classes. First, we are going to require that their inner classes are declared public. We would also prefer that they are declared static, but don't require that (however, it will be included in the template code we provide them). Next, we require that they are inner classes and that their containing classes are contained in a package. We can assure these requirements are met by assuring that the name of the inner class includes a period, "." character, indicating a package, and that it also includes a dollar sign, "$" character sometime after the period, indicating an inner class of a class in a package. The javac compiler concatenates the class and inner-class names, adding a dollar sign between them, to formulate the fully qualified inner-class name.

Find Out Whether This Class Has Been Registered

If we have never seen this class before, then we will assume this is the initiation, and we will register a new application by inserting the class in the v_app_conn_registry view. We find out if we have ever seen this class before by selecting from the view where classes are registered with that same name and version. The p_count_class_conns Oracle procedure accomplishes that for us. See Listing 10-29.

Listing 10-29. Determine if the Application Class Is Already Registered

```
stmt = ( OracleCallableStatement )conn.prepareCall(
    "CALL appsec.appsec_only_pkg.p_count_class_conns(?,?,?)" );
stmt.registerOutParameter( 3, OracleTypes.NUMBER );
stmt.setString( 1, className );
stmt.setString( 2, classVersion );
stmt.setInt(    3, 0 );
stmt.executeUpdate();
```

If it turns out that p_count_class_conns tells us there are no classes registered by that name / version, then we go on to insert; otherwise we need to check if the class we just received is equal to the class that we have registered by that name. If it's "equal," we will overwrite the existing, stored connsHash; but if not equal, we are dealing with an imposter.

SOME DEVELOPER GOTCHA'S AND RESOLUTIONS

Unfortunately, our application developers can be victims of their own actions. If the developers change the code of their inner class without changing the version number, this will cause our equality test to fail. In that case, the developer should change both serialVersionUID and the innerClassRevLvl in his inner class, register it through our processes, and create a new list of connection strings or copy the connection strings from the previous version.

Another way the application developer might shoot himself in the foot, so to speak, is by moving his inner class around in his code. For instance, if he moves his inner class outside the public class definition, it becomes an outer class, or if he moves it out of the main body of the class into a method (a perfectly acceptable move, technically), the package and hence the class name changes to reflect that move. In these cases, the inner class will be seen as a new entity and registered, but won't have any associated connection strings until the developer rebuilds the list for the new version. In this case, he cannot copy his connection strings list from the previous version, because this is considered to be a new class, being found in a new path (and it may even have the same version number as the previous class).

Get the Application ID Class and HashMap List of Connections

Back to the task at hand in setDecryptConns(), we call the p_get_class_conns stored procedure to get our registered class and the connsHash associated with this class name and version. In Listing 10-30 we handle the connsHash as a BLOB. You will recall that in the t_app_conn_registry table definition, we define it as a BLOB; that allows us to store a connsHash object that is larger than 2K bytes. When we defined the procedure p_get_class_conns, we also specified the fourth parameter as a BLOB by reference to its definition on the table, like this:

```
m_connections     OUT v_app_conn_registry.connections%TYPE
```

Elsewhere in our code, we handle the connsHash as a RAW. Interestingly, in PL/SQL, that is in code, a RAW can attain 32K in size, but in storage in an Oracle table, can only be 2K. It is easy to handle the BLOBs as RAWs in code, but why not just always call a BLOB a BLOB? BLOBs are tightly coupled to either a database table or to a connection. They do not fare well in transmission, so we rely on the RAW data type.

Listing 10-30. Get the List of Connections from Oracle Database As a BLOB

```
if( stmt.getInt( 3 ) == 0 ) {
    // Do insert!
} else {
    // Assure provided instance and cached, if same version, are equal
    // NOTE: handling BLOBs with getBytes and setBytes is new to 11g
    stmt = ( OracleCallableStatement )conn.prepareCall(
        "CALL appsec.appsec_only_pkg.p_get_class_conns(?,?,?,?)" );
    stmt.registerOutParameter( 3, OracleTypes.RAW );
    stmt.registerOutParameter( 4, OracleTypes.BLOB );
    stmt.setString( 1, className );
    stmt.setString( 2, classVersion );
    stmt.setNull(   3, OracleTypes.RAW );
    stmt.setNull(   4, OracleTypes.BLOB );
    stmt.executeUpdate();

...

    byte[] cachedBytes = stmt.getBytes(3);
    oins = new ObjectInputStream( new ByteArrayInputStream(
        cachedBytes ) );
    classObject = oins.readObject();
    oins.close();
```

Pulling the inner-class object and the connsHash out of Oracle database is a two-step process. We get the bytes of the RAW and BLOB, respectively. Then we move the bytes through streams, as we've seen before, to reconstitute our objects. That process is shown for the inner class in Listing 10-30.

Test for Class Equality

We arrive at a crossroads. We have already instantiated an object (from the byte array that the client provided) from which we got the name and version number. Now we are going to instantiate another class from the bytes stored as a RAW in our registration table. The Oracle JVM will complain in a big way if these two objects are not identical: it will throw an InvalidClassException.

We will go ahead and assure that the object handed to us by the client and the object stored in our registration table are equal by calling the equals() method, as shown in Listing 10-31. In Java, this means more than just that the objects have equivalent values for their variables—it means they are based on the same model in memory. They are, at the core, from one and the same class.

Listing 10-31. Test for Class Equality

```
Class testClass = classObject.getClass();

    if( testClass.equals( providedClass ) ) {
        // further tests are unnecessary
    } else return "Failed to setDecryptConns()";
}
```

Decrypt Connection Strings for Storage and Reuse

Once we have the identity questions settled (still in the `setDecryptConns()` method), whether we are poised to insert or overwrite a registration entry, we are left to deal with the `connsHash` we received from the client. Currently, the connection strings are encrypted with our shared session DES key—a key that will disappear when the current session closes. That would be an unusable state to store them in. The next user in our application would not be able to read them, nor would we in our own next session.

So, we will decrypt all the connection strings and store them unencrypted. When the next session comes to get the connection strings for this application, we will encrypt them with that session's key before delivery. Notice in Listing 10-32, when we set the `cryptConnsHash` member that we cast it as a `HashMap<String, RAW>`, no questions asked. This kind of blind trust, which is appropriate at this point, is what the Java compiler warns about with the "unchecked" warning. Notice also that we will transition from a `HashMap<String, RAW>` to a new `HashMap<String, String>`.

Listing 10-32. Cast Encrypted List of Connections and Prepare to Decrypt

```
oins = new ObjectInputStream( new ByteArrayInputStream(
    connections.getBytes() ) );
classObject = oins.readObject();
oins.close();
HashMap<String, RAW> cryptConnsHash =
    (HashMap<String, RAW>)classObject;

HashMap<String, String> clearConnsHash =
    new HashMap<String, String>();
oins.close();
```

We initialize our shared secret password cipher to do decryption (see Listing 10-33), then walk through the `cryptConnsHash HashMap` to decrypt each value. We store each decrypted value, using the same key in our new `clearConnsHash`. With classes like the `HashMap`, from the *Collections* classes, we can traverse their members using the for each syntax. You can read our `for` statement as "for each key in the `cryptConnsHash` set of keys."

Listing 10-33. Decrypt Each Connection String and Save to New List

```
cipherDES.init( Cipher.DECRYPT_MODE, sessionSecretDESKey, paramSpec );
for( String key : cryptConnsHash.keySet() ) {
    // Decrypt each one
    clearConnsHash.put( key,
        new String(
```

```
            cipherDES.doFinal(
                ( cryptConnsHash.get( key )).getBytes()
            )
        )
    );
}
```

That syntax for storing our decrypted connection keys looks a bit complex, but we are simply putting a new entry in the clearConnsHash using the key we got in this pass through the for each loop and a new String. The new String is derived from the bytes we got back from decrypting the value associated with this same key in the former cryptConnsHash.

Store the connsHash for this Application

We will use a now-familiar process to get a byte array from the clearConnsHash HashMap. This is shown in Listing 10-34.

Listing 10-34. Get Byte Array of List of Connection Strings

```
ByteArrayOutputStream baos = new ByteArrayOutputStream();
ObjectOutputStream oout = new ObjectOutputStream( baos );
oout.writeObject( clearConnsHash );
oout.flush();
oout.close();
byte[] connsHashBytes = baos.toByteArray();
baos.close();
```

The final step in setDecryptConns() is to store the new connsHash in the **v_app_conn_registry** view. We do that by passing the byte arrays for our application ID class and the clearConnsHash to the p_set_class_conns procedure in Listing 10-35. This is another of our procedures that handles the connsHash as a BLOB. In Oracle Database 11g, we are able to get and set BLOBs from Java using the Statement.getBytes() and .setBytes() methods.

Listing 10-35. Store List of Connection Strings in Oracle

```
// NOTE: handling BLOBs with getBytes and setBytes is new to Oracle Database 11g
stmt = ( OracleCallableStatement )conn.prepareCall(
    "CALL appsec.appsec_only_pkg.p_set_class_conns(?,?,?,?)" );
stmt.setString( 1, className );
stmt.setString( 2, classVersion );
stmt.setBytes(  3, appClassBytes );
stmt.setBytes(  4, connsHashBytes );
stmt.executeUpdate();
```

Oracle Procedure to Set Values in the Application Registry

The p_set_class_conns procedure has three sections. This is shown in Listing 10-36. The first gets a count of records that already exist with the specific class name and version number. If there are 0, we will insert a new record in the second section; and if 1, we will update the existing record in the third. In the same way as in p_get_class_conns, you can see that we handle m_connections as a BLOB by reference to v_app_conn_registry.connections%TYPE.

Listing 10-36. Procedure to Set Values in Application Registry, p_set_class_conns

```
PROCEDURE p_set_class_conns(
    m_class_name      v_app_conn_registry.class_name%TYPE,
    m_class_version   v_app_conn_registry.class_version%TYPE,
    m_class_instance  v_app_conn_registry.class_instance%TYPE,
    m_connections     v_app_conn_registry.connections%TYPE )
IS
    v_count INTEGER;
BEGIN

    SELECT COUNT(*) INTO v_count

        FROM v_app_conn_registry
        WHERE class_name = m_class_name
        AND class_version = m_class_version;

    IF v_count = 0 THEN

        INSERT INTO v_app_conn_registry ( class_name, class_version,
            class_instance, connections ) VALUES
            ( m_class_name, m_class_version, m_class_instance, m_connections );

    ELSE

        UPDATE v_app_conn_registry SET class_instance = m_class_instance,
            connections = m_connections, update_dt = SYSDATE
        WHERE class_name = m_class_name
        AND class_version = m_class_version;
    END IF;
END p_set_class_conns;
```

Oracle Procedures to Get Entries from the Application Registry

We will look briefly at the Oracle stored procedures we use for getting data from v_app_conn_registry. There are no surprises here. We have established these procedures so that we do not need to have any dynamic SQL queries in our Java code.

Find if a Registry Entry Exists for this Application

p_count_class_conns returns an integer number that indicates how many records exist in v_app_conn_registry with this specific class name and version number. Because records in that view are keyed on those two columns, we expected the count to only be 0 or 1. The code is in Listing 10-37.

In review, we use this to determine whether we need to check the identity of a class provided by the client against a registered class, or whether we can simply insert this as a new class. We don't have any prejudice against new applications being registered, if the application class meets our standards.

Listing 10-37. Find Existing Application Registry Entry

```
PROCEDURE p_count_class_conns(
    m_class_name        v_app_conn_registry.class_name%TYPE,
    m_class_version     v_app_conn_registry.class_version%TYPE,
    m_count         OUT NUMBER )
IS BEGIN
    SELECT COUNT(*)
    INTO m_count
    FROM v_app_conn_registry
    WHERE class_name = m_class_name
    AND class_version = m_class_version;
END p_count_class_conns;
```

In hindsight, this was a good candidate for an Oracle stored function. It returns a single value. As a procedure, we return a value through an OUT parameter.

Get the List of Connection Strings for a Registered Application

p_get_class_conns gets the application ID class and associated connsHash from v_app_conn_registry for a specific class name and version number. This is shown in Listing 10-38. Not obviously, but again by way of referring to m_connections as type v_app_conn_registry.connections% TYPE, we are handling this column as its native type, a BLOB.

Listing 10-38. Get List of Connection Strings from Registry

```
PROCEDURE p_get_class_conns(
    m_class_name         v_app_conn_registry.class_name%TYPE,
    m_class_version      v_app_conn_registry.class_version%TYPE,
    m_class_instance OUT v_app_conn_registry.class_instance%TYPE,
    m_connections    OUT v_app_conn_registry.connections%TYPE )
IS BEGIN

    SELECT class_instance, connections
    INTO m_class_instance, m_connections

    FROM v_app_conn_registry
    WHERE class_name = m_class_name
    AND class_version = m_class_version;
END p_get_class_conns;
```

Get an Application Connection String: The Java Client Side

There are so many administrative tasks to address with this code that the practical application can be too easily forgotten. We turn now to that practical application. A client application wants to do work using Oracle database. The app uses our code to accomplish security—SSO, two-factor authentication and encryption, along with good Oracle and Java secure programming practices.

To make this easy on the developer for that application, we give the developer just a bit of template to follow to make all this happen. We have him do the following four things:

1) Include the *OracleJavaSecure.class* and *RevLvlClassIntfc.class* files in his
   `CLASSPATH` (we provide a *jar* file).

2) Write an Application ID inner class that implements `RevLvlClassIntfc` and
   `Serializable`.

3) Call `OracleJavaSecure.setAppContext()` method, passing his application
   name, ID class, and two-factor authentication code (yes, he will have to handle
   the loop from the first request to make a second call with the two-factor code).

4) Ask `OracleJavaSecure` for the Oracle connections he needs by calling the
   `getAppAuthConn()` method.

In the end, we are able to provide some Oracle connections to the developer's application. Those connections are based on connection strings (including passwords) that are transmitted and maintained securely, in encrypted form.

Get an Oracle Connection from the List for an Application

Our `getAppAuthConn()` method provides connections based on the list of connection strings that already exists in memory. However, this is a great starting place, because if the connection strings do not already exist in memory, `getAppAuthConn()` calls the `getAppConnections()` method to retrieve them form Oracle database, based on the application ID class. This is shown in Listing 10-39.

We also test whether appAuthSessionSecretDESKey is null. This will be the case when we call this method for the first time—we will not have generated or received our two-factor authentication code. If it is null, we return a null, which lets the application know it, needs to loop and let the user come again with a two-factor code. When we have provided the two-factor code and we call this method again, then we will have exchanged keys and appAuthSessionSecretDESKey will not be null.

Listing 10-39. Get an Oracle Connection from the List, getAppAuthConn()

```
public static OracleConnection getAppAuthConn( String instance, String userName ) {
    OracleConnection mConn = null;
    try {
        if( null == connsHash ) getAppConnections();
        // If we entered without twoFactorAuth, apAuth...DESKey is null
        if( null == appAuthSessionSecretDESKey ) return mConn;
        instance = instance.trim();
        userName = userName.trim();
        String key = ( instance + "/" + userName ).toUpperCase();
        appAuthCipherDES.init( Cipher.DECRYPT_MODE, appAuthSessionSecretDESKey,
            appAuthParamSpec );
        mConn = setConnection( new String( appAuthCipherDES.doFinal(
            connsHash.get( key ).getBytes() ) ) );
```

We need to observe two facts about this method. First, it returns an `OracleConnection`, not a connection string. In fact, we discard the connection string in relatively short order to reduce the possibility of exposing the clear-text password. Second, the connections we return are configured to proxy through an application user in order to pass further SSO testing.

We get the specific connection string that was requested by concatenating the instance name and user name that were requested in the arguments to this method call. As with all data coming from

245

elsewhere, we need to get it in shape (validate and format it) before use. We trim the white space at the head and tail of each argument and uppercase the concatenated key.

With that key in hand, we are ready to get the required connection string from connsHash, but recall that the strings are encrypted. So we set appAuthCipherDES to decrypt mode using the shared secret password key.

We then stack several calls together. We get the encrypted connection string from connsHash based on our key. Then we get the byte array and pass it to the Cipher for decryption. We create a new String based on the decrypted bytes, and pass the clear-text connection string to the setConnection() method, which returns an OracleConnection.

By stacking our method calls in this way, we do not need to identify method member variables for each step along the way. In this case, we could have an additional RAW, two byte arrays, and a String member variable.

Get List of Connection Strings from Oracle Database to Client App

Although we may instruct the developers to call the getAppAuthConn() method, the getAppConnections() method gets called behind the scene. Behind the scenes, we get the list of connection strings from the Oracle database, then the application calls getAppAuthConn() to get individual Oracle connections based on those strings. OracleJavaSecure does all the heavy lifting, decrypting the string and making the connection to Oracle, before handing the connection to the application (Listings 10-40 through 10-44).

Start Our Method to Get Connection Strings from Oracle

Here again, we are in control of a procedure that the Java compiler warns us is unchecked and /or unsafe. We cast the object we get from Oracle database as the connsHash HashMap without checking that it fits the bill—if we were wrong, a ClassCastException would be thrown. Because we control both the source and the receipt of this object, we are justified in ignoring that warning. We could use the SuppressWarnings() annotation (see comment in Listing 10-40) to keep the compiler from complaining, but the Oracle JVM compiler does not accept that, so we will live with the compile-time warning.

Listing 10-40. Get Connection Strings from Oracle, getAppConnections()

```
//@SuppressWarnings( "unchecked" )
public static void getAppConnections() {
    OracleCallableStatement stmt = null;
    try {
        if( null == appVerConn ) setAppVerConnection();
```

Before we go any further, we check to see if we've got a connection to appver, calling setAppVerConnection() to create one if needed.

Call Stored Procedure to Get Application List of Connection Strings

Our call from getAppConnections() to p_get_app_conns is easily one of the most complex Oracle stored procedure calls we make, but only because of the variety and scope of data we are exchanging. There is really nothing new here in Listing 10-41. There are a dozen arguments to the procedure: five IN and seven OUT. But two of those OUT arguments are for error handling.

One of the IN parameters is a byte array representing the application ID class. We get this byte array through two Streams classes, as we have seen before in this chapter. The other IN parameters are the artifacts of our local RSA public key, the modulus and exponent, and the two-factor authentication code (if provided).

Our OUT parameters, besides the error message, are the four encrypted artifacts of our shared secret password key and the connsHash object associated with the application ID object that we are submitting.

Listing 10-41. Procedure Call to Get List of Application Connection Strings, p_get_app_conns

```
stmt = ( OracleCallableStatement )conn.prepareCall(
    "CALL appsec.appsec_public_pkg.p_get_app_conns(?,?,?,?,?,?,?,?,?,?,?,?)" );
stmt.registerOutParameter( 5, OracleTypes.RAW );
stmt.registerOutParameter( 6, OracleTypes.RAW );
stmt.registerOutParameter( 7, OracleTypes.RAW );
stmt.registerOutParameter( 8, OracleTypes.RAW );
stmt.registerOutParameter( 9, OracleTypes.RAW );
stmt.registerOutParameter(11, OracleTypes.NUMBER );
stmt.registerOutParameter(12, OracleTypes.VARCHAR );
stmt.setString( 1, locModulus );
stmt.setString( 2, locExponent );
stmt.setString( 3, twoFactorAuth );
stmt.setBytes(  4, appClassBytes );
stmt.setNull(   5, OracleTypes.RAW );
stmt.setNull(   6, OracleTypes.RAW );
stmt.setNull(   7, OracleTypes.RAW );
stmt.setNull(   8, OracleTypes.RAW );
stmt.setNull(   9, OracleTypes.RAW );
stmt.setString(10, applicationID );
stmt.setInt(   11, 0 );
stmt.setNull(   12, OracleTypes.VARCHAR );
stmt.executeUpdate();
...
    if( null == stmt.getRAW( 9 ) ) {
        System.out.println( "Please rerun with two-factor Auth Code!" );
        return;
    }
    if( null == sessionSecretDESKey ) {
        makeDESKey( stmt.getRAW( 9 ), stmt.getRAW( 8 ),
            stmt.getRAW( 6 ), stmt.getRAW( 7 ) );
```

We check to see whether any error is being reported. If not, we test one of the values returned as our shared password key artifacts, stmt.getRAW(9). If it is null, we assume that the Oracle database has just now sent a two-factor code and must wait until the client application returns with a two-factor code to proceed. We ask the client to rerun this method with a two-factor code and exit (return from) this method.

Based on the artifacts of our shared password key, we build the key by calling the makeDESKey() method. The test of whether the sessionSecretDESKey is currently null is unnecessary during normal operation, but feels more complete. I can't think of an instance where we would arrive here and the sessionSecretDESKey not be null.

Use Static Class Members to Retain APPVER Connection and Keys

We establish several static class members in Listing 10-42 to retain the **appver** connection and session-specific keys. These keys, generated for the session for **appver** use, will continue to be required when the application later attempts to decrypt connection strings in **connsHash** for application use. Those connection strings were encrypted with the shared password key associated with the **appver** session.

Listing 10-42. Static Class Members to Retain Application Verification Decryption Keys

```
private static OracleConnection appVerConn = null;
private static byte[] appAuthSalt;
private static int appAuthIterationCount;
private static char[] appAuthDESPassPhraseChars;
private static AlgorithmParameterSpec appAuthParamSpec;
private static String appAuthSessionSecretDESAlgorithm;
private static SecretKey appAuthSessionSecretDESKey;
private static Cipher appAuthCipherDES;
```

You may want to refer to Chapter 3 where we discuss objects, static members, pointers, and references. Because our primary encryption keys and all the artifacts and related members are static, we cannot just assign a new member name to refer to and retain them while we point the primary references at a new instance. We need to set our new static members, those retaining the **appver** session data, to a new value, referencing a different place in memory. Within the getAppConnections() method in Listing 10-43, we set those retainer members to copies or clones of the current key artifacts. We create new instances where that process is supported.

Listing 10-43. Set Static Class Members for Application Verification Keys

```
// Cant just set new pointers to existing members
// Since static, updates to one will update both
// Must instantiate, clone or copy values
appAuthSalt = salt.clone();
appAuthIterationCount =
    (new Integer( iterationCount )).intValue();
appAuthDESPassPhraseChars =
    sessionSecretDESPassPhraseChars.clone();
appAuthParamSpec = new PBEParameterSpec( appAuthSalt,
    appAuthIterationCount );
KeySpec keySpec = new PBEKeySpec( appAuthDESPassPhraseChars,
    appAuthSalt, appAuthIterationCount );
appAuthSessionSecretDESAlgorithm =
    new String( sessionSecretDESAlgorithm );
appAuthSessionSecretDESKey = SecretKeyFactory.getInstance(
    appAuthSessionSecretDESAlgorithm ).generateSecret( keySpec );
appAuthCipherDES = Cipher.getInstance(
    appAuthSessionSecretDESKey.getAlgorithm() );
resetKeys();
```

At the end of our effort to retain those members for further use by **appver** in updating the **connsHash** for this application, and for decrypting the connection strings in **connsHash**, we call the resetKeys() method, which points all our primary keys and artifacts at null. We first saw resetKeys() in Chapter 7, where we used it in testing. Here it is identical, with one exception. We do not set the existing sessionSecretDESKey to null because, by experimentation, we have determined that doing so invalidates the appAuthSessionSecretDESKey. For that reason, we are going to modify several methods to test sessionSecretDESPassPhraseChars for null, instead of testing sessionSecretDESKey for null: getCryptData(), getDecryptData() and the set of methods getCryptSessionSecretDESPassPhrase() / Algorithm / Salt / IterationCount. I know some would prefer I not elaborate on gotcha's and tests and alternate scenarios, but the goal here is not just to develop an application, but also to develop an understanding. If we don't explore these issues here, you will be left to find them out on your own, which is not bad, but can be time-consuming.

Get the List of Connection Strings

From the RAW bytes returned as the application connsHash object, we generate the object by passing the bytes through a ByteArrayInputStream and an ObjectInputStream. If the resultant object is not null, we cast the object as a HashMap<String, RAW>, as shown in Listing 10-44. This is where our compiler reports an "unchecked" warning. If, however, the object we got from Oracle database is null, we assume that no connsHash has been stored yet for this registered application, and we set connsHash to a new, empty HashMap<String, RAW>. After one of those scenarios, we are then free to put new connection strings into connsHash via the putAppConnString() method, and to store them in the v_app_conn_registry view via the putAppConnections() method.

Listing 10-44. Cast Connections List Object from Oracle Database as a HashMap

```
if( classObject != null ) {
    connsHash = (HashMap<String, RAW>)classObject;
} else {
    connsHash = new HashMap<String, RAW>();
}
```

Establish a Connection for Application Verification Processes

I have reservations about the form of the setAppVerConnection() method that we have in this chapter—see Listing 10-45. I have already intimated that it is our plan to have this connection available to all, like a bouncer in a night club, treating his user name and password as little more than data, but that is not how I want to leave it.

It's just that this chapter is already quite weighty in scope, and I have a number of rather lengthy considerations in this regard that I feel will be best delayed until the next chapter. Please continue on to the next chapter for that discussion.

Listing 10-45. Method to Set Application Verification Connection, setAppVerConnection()

```
private static void setAppVerConnection() {
    setConnection( "jdbc:oracle:thin:appver/password@localhost:1521:orcl" );
    appVerConn = conn;
}
```

For now, ignore the man behind the curtain. This is reminiscent of passwords embedded in our application code; something we hope to get away from.

Notice also the last line of Listing 10-45. We set a static class member (see also Listing 10-42) to retain the application verification connection.

Get a List of Application Connection Strings: The Server Side

Here we are at that foreboding Oracle stored procedure with a dozen IN and OUT parameters, p_get_app_conns. But that is not what is notable about this procedure. Rather, the internal workings are what we need to give attention to. However, even those are familiar.

If we pass SSO, then we deal with two-factor authentication. If the user did not submit a two-factor code, we call the f_send_2_factor function, passing our validated user name and the application_id in order to create, distribute and cache (store in a table) a two-factor code for this user in this application.

However, if the user did submit a two-factor authentication code, then we call the f_is_cur_cached_cd function, passing the validated user, the application_id and the two-factor code. If the two-factor code equals the one cached for this user and this application, then we proceed to set return values for the secret password key, and we call f_get_crypt_conns to return the encrypted list of connection strings.

We will add p_get_app_conns to the appsec_public_pkg package since it gets called by any user using our proxy connection. The core code from this procedure is displayed in Listing 10-46.

Listing 10-46. Get List of Connection Strings to Return from Oracle, p_get_app_conns

```
return_user := f_is_sso( m_app_user );
IF( return_user IS NOT NULL )
THEN

    IF( m_two_factor_cd IS NULL )

    THEN
        m_err_txt := appsec_only_pkg.f_send_2_factor( return_user, m_application_id );
    ELSIF( appsec_only_pkg.f_is_cur_cached_cd( return_user, m_application_id,
        m_two_factor_cd ) = 'Y' )
    THEN
        secret_pass_salt :=
            app_sec_pkg.f_get_crypt_secret_salt( ext_modulus, ext_exponent );
        secret_pass_count :=
            app_sec_pkg.f_get_crypt_secret_count( ext_modulus, ext_exponent );
        secret_pass :=
            app_sec_pkg.f_get_crypt_secret_pass( ext_modulus, ext_exponent );
        secret_pass_algorithm :=
            app_sec_pkg.f_get_crypt_secret_algorithm(ext_modulus, ext_exponent);
        m_crypt_connections := appsec_only_pkg.f_get_crypt_conns( m_class_instance );
    ELSE
        -- Wrong two-factor code entered
        RAISE NO_DATA_FOUND;
    END IF;
    app_sec_pkg.p_log_error( 0, 'Success getting App Conns, ' || return_user );
ELSE
    app_sec_pkg.p_log_error( 0, 'Problem getting App Conns, ' || return_user );
END IF;
```

There are a couple ways for this process to exit with a failure. If the user's connection/session fails to pass our SSO requirements, then we log the error "Problem getting App Conns" and return without sending a two-factor code. Something is seriously wrong with that user, and we don't want to deal with him at all. If however the user is good (passes SSO) but he submits a bad or old two-factor code, then we raise a `NO_DATA_FOUND` exception, which we log here and report back to the application. In both these error cases, we exit without returning a list of connection strings.

The `getCryptConns()` method is called from the `f_get_crypt_conns` Java stored procedure. `f_get_crypt_conns` passes the application ID object through from `p_get_app_conns` (Listing 10-46) to Java on Oracle database.

In `getCryptConns()` method, we will get the `connsHash` object that is associated with the application ID object from the `v_app_conn_registry` view. Then we will encrypt each clear-text connection string in the `connsHash` before delivering it to the client, via the `p_get_app_conns` procedure.

This is the third of three methods we discuss that evoke "unchecked" warnings from the Java compiler. Here we cast the alleged `connsHash` object coming out of `v_app_conn_registry`, sight unseen, as a `HashMap<String, String>`. We also presume the application ID object provided to us is an implementation of `RevLvlClassIntfc`, on which we call the `getRevLvl()` method. Both of those actions are questionable in the eyes of the compiler, but we know all the parties involved and are doing what we truly want.

This method, `getCryptConns()` mirrors the functionality we've already discussed in `setDecryptConns()`. We are going to skip the description of the inner workings, except that we will point out the code used to encrypt each connection string in Listing 10-47. Recall that the `connsHash` stored in Oracle Database is stored in clear-text form, as a `HashMap<String, String>`, `clearConnsHash`. We use the session secret password key to encrypt the connection strings and place them in a new `HashMap<String, RAW>`, `cryptConnsHash`. Oracle database returns the encrypted connection strings to the client application.

Our Cipher is set to encrypt mode. Then we walk through all the keys in `clearConnsHash` using the for each syntax.

Listing 10-47. Encrypt Each Connection String in the List

```
cipherDES.init( Cipher.ENCRYPT_MODE, sessionSecretDESKey, paramSpec );
for( String key : clearConnsHash.keySet() ) {
    // Encrypt each one
    cryptConnsHash.put( key,
        new RAW(
            cipherDES.doFinal(
                (clearConnsHash.get( key )).getBytes()
            )
        )
    );
}
```

The stacked method calls get the connection string from `clearConnsHash` that is associated with the key we got in the for each loop. We pass that `String` to `cipherDES` for encryption using the secret password key. We then create a new `RAW` from those encrypted bytes, and we put the `RAW` into `cryptConnsHash`, keyed with the same key value. At the end of this method, we will return `cryptConnsHash` from Oracle Database to the client application.

Test Application Authentication, Phase 1

As in the last chapter, here again we need to edit the code to provide our company-specific addresses for two-factor authentication.

■ **Note** Edit the code found in the file named *Chapter10/orajavsec/OracleJavaSecure.java*.

```
private static String expectedDomain = "ORGDOMAIN" ; // All Caps
private static String comDomain = "org.com";
private static String smtpHost = "smtp." + comDomain;
private static String baseURL =
    "http://www.org.com/servlet/textpage.PageServlet?ACTION=O&NEWPID=";
```

We also have an embedded password in the **setAppVerConnection()** method and several more in the **main()** method. Change each of those to the appropriate password for **appver** and other users. Also change other connection string components in **setAppVerConnection()** and each **putAppConnString()** method call: the server name, port number, and instance name.

Get New Structures into Oracle

Load the new *orajavsec/OracleJavaSecure.java* code into Oracle Database. Again, uncomment the top line that begins "CREATE OR REPLACE AND RESOLVE JAVA…" and execute it in your SQL client (SQL*Plus, SQL Developer, JDeveloper, or TOAD). Remember to set the role and set define off, if using a SQL client that tries to do variable substitution, as documented in the comments:

```
// First
//      SET ROLE APPSEC_ROLE;
// Also having ampersands in the code without substitution variables
//      SET DEFINE OFF;
// To run in Oracle, search for and comment @Suppress
```

Next, execute all the commands in *AppSec.sql* and *SecAdm.sql* files. Execute the commands in that order, because of dependencies in *SecAdm.sql*.

■ **Note** You can find these scripts in the files named *Chapter10/AppSec.sql* and *SecAdm.sql*.

Review Steps of Testing

In order to test our application authentication, we are going to take the following steps:

- Set our application context: application ID, inner class, and two-factor code.

- Call getAppConnections() to get our list of connection strings for this application—the first time will register our application.

- Call putAppConnections() to upload our list of connection strings to Oracle.

- Call getAppAuthConn() to get a specific connection for use in this application.

- Use the connection to get data from Oracle.

For this first phase of testing, we will accomplish all these steps in the `main()` method of `OracleJavaSecure`.

We are going to run through this test code at least twice. The first time, we will not have a valid two-factor authentication code, so we will exit the program at a certain point. In short, the point we will exit is just after we know a two-factor code has been sent to us, and before we try to use connection strings associated with this application.

Set the Application Context

If we have a two-factor authentication code, we should pass it to the application on the command line as an argument to the application. Alternatively, if you are running this test from an IDE, it may be easier to embed the two-factor code, once received, into this class. You can do that where shown, then recompile and execute it. See Listing 10-48. Remember that each two-factor code is only good for 10 minutes!

Listing 10-48. Application Authentication Testing, Phase 1, main()

```
public static void main( String[] args ) {
    OracleCallableStatement stmt = null;
    Statement mStmt = null;
    ResultSet rSet;

    try {
        // Submit two-factor auth code on command line, once received
        String twoFactorAuth = "";
        if( args.length != 0 && args[0] != null ) twoFactorAuth = args[0];
        // You may place two-factor auth code here for testing from IDE
        // Remember, it's only good for 10 minutes from creation
        //twoFactorAuth = "1234-5678-9012";
```

We call the `setAppContext()` method in Listing 10-49 to set our context for this application. In this case, our application ID is `HRVIEW`, the only application we have configured so far; the one that can get encrypted data from the `HR` schema. Recall that there is a user, `appusr` and a secure application role, `hrview_role` associated with this application ID.

Listing 10-49. Testing Call to setAppContext()

```
String applicationID = "HRVIEW";
Object appClass = new InnerRevLvlClass();
setAppContext( applicationID, appClass, twoFactorAuth );
```

Multiple Java applications can gain access through that application ID. They will all get the same application user and role. Each Java application will be identified by a specific, representative application inner class that it will hand to Oracle database for validation. If the currently authenticated user (for whom the two-factor code was distributed) has been granted to proxy connect through the application verification, `appver` user, and the application class that he hands Oracle database is valid, then he will receive the connection strings associated with the application class. If the current user has also been granted proxy connect through the Oracle application user embedded in the connection string, then he will be free to use the connection to work with Oracle data.

There is another layer of control that you might consider applying, but which seems superfluous. You might control which users have access to which applications. In my mind, you have already granted the user access to data through whatever application interface they care to use by granting them proxy connect through the application user associated with the secure application role. If they have access to the data, do we really want to be bothered with controlling how they get there? I don't think so.

If two applications see different data, then they should have different application IDs and different application users and roles.

Call to Get Application Connections

The first time we call getAppConnections() from a specific application there will be no list of connection strings stored in Oracle database for us to retrieve. That is almost an ancillary concern, because we will be turned back earlier in the process when a two-factor code is generated and sent to us.

So, even the second time we call getAppConnections(), we will get a null in return from Oracle, and we will set our list of connection strings to a new, empty HashMap. This will be the case until we have called putAppConnections() for this application. However, we can use the application in this state by pushing connection strings into the list for our own, local use as shown in Listing 10-50.

Listing 10-50. Test Call to getAppConnections() and Put Connections in Local List

```
getAppConnections();
// Go no further until we have a two-factor Auth Code
if( twoFactorAuth == null || twoFactorAuth.equals( "" ) ) return;
System.out.println( "connsHash.size = " + connsHash.size() );

putAppConnString( "Orcl", "hr",
    "password", "localhost", String.valueOf( 1521 ) );
putAppConnString( "Orcl", "appusr",
    "password", "localhost", String.valueOf( 1521 ) );
```

Send List of Connection Strings to Oracle Database for Storage

Storing our list of connection strings in Oracle database is a task we will only need to do periodically, as we change our application passwords. We will do it here in Listing 10-51 to save the initial set of connection strings (from Listing 10-50) with a call to putAppConnections().

Listing 10-51. Send Connection String List to Oracle

```
putAppConnections();
```

Get a Unique Connection for Use in This Application

If we did not call getAppConnections() previously, it will be called automatically when we call getAppAuthConn() (see Listing 10-52). This would be our instruction to application developers who want to use our security structures—just call getAppAuthConn(). Note that by getting this application-specific connection, we will no longer be able to use the original appver connection to do putAppConnections().

Listing 10-52. Get and Use a Specific Oracle Connection for This Application

```
getAppAuthConn( "orcl", "appusr" );
mStmt = conn.createStatement();
rSet = mStmt.executeQuery( "SELECT SYSDATE FROM DUAL" );
if ( rSet.next() )
```

```
        System.out.println( rSet.getString( 1 ) );
```

Notice that the key values we use to select a specific application connection are the instance name and the user name. These are two of the same values we provided when we called putAppConnString(). Once we get the connection, we can use it to query Oracle database.

Use or Lose Initial Application Verification Connection

Both getAppConnections() and putAppConnections() do their work using an appver user connection. This is an important point. In establishing the appver connection, we have exchanged encryption keys that are specific for that connection. We will retain sufficient vestiges of those keys in order to continue to decrypt the connection strings in connsHash; however, once we have connected to a different Oracle user for this specific application and exchanged keys for that connection, we will no longer be able to call putAppConnections() using the previous appver connection. In other words, we need to run putAppConnections() before using any of the connections returned by getAppConnections().

We make another call to putAppConnections() in our test code, and it will fail because we already built and used an application connection. The connection to Oracle database as appver user is no longer available—we only retained the decryption keys associated with that session.

Get an Application Connection and the Associated Secure Application Role

After we get an application connection from our call to getAppAuthConn(), we want to get the secure application role associated with this application. Instead of calling p_check_hrview_access to get that specific application role, we call our generic p_check_role_access procedure, which grants us the secure application role that is associated with our application ID. In Listing 10-53, notice that we pass the application ID as parameter number 1.

Listing 10-53. Get and Application Connection and Set the Application Role

```
int errNo;
String errMsg;
getAppAuthConn( "orcl", "appusr" );
stmt = ( OracleCallableStatement )conn.prepareCall(
    "CALL appsec.p_check_role_access(?,?,?)" );
    stmt.registerOutParameter( 2, OracleTypes.NUMBER );
    stmt.registerOutParameter( 3, OracleTypes.VARCHAR );
    stmt.setString( 1, OracleJavaSecure.applicationID );
    stmt.setInt(    2, 0 );
    stmt.setNull(   3, OracleTypes.VARCHAR );
stmt.executeUpdate();
errNo = stmt.getInt( 2 );
errMsg = stmt.getString( 3 );
System.out.println( "DistribCd = " + errMsg );
if( errNo != 0 ) {
    System.out.println( "Oracle error 1) " + errNo + ", " + errMsg );
} else if( twoFactorAuth.equals( "" ) ) {
    System.out.println( "Call again with two-factor code parameter" );
} else {
    if( null != stmt ) stmt.close();
```

```
        System.out.println( "Oracle success 1)" );
```

In our call to p_check_role_access, we do not have to test whether the two-factor authentication code exists, though we do it here out of habit. You will recall that we are only doing two-factor authentication in the initial application verification connection, not in each specific application connection. We removed two-factor authentication from p_check_role_access and added it to our application verification procedure to get the list of connection strings for an application, p_get_app_conns.

Rehashing the security chain to this point; the user must be granted proxy connect through the application user account, and by extension, was granted access through the secure application role associated with this application connection.

Get Encrypted Data with the Application Connection

The full demonstration of our application authentication is provided when we get encrypted data from our application connection as shown in Listing 10-54.

Listing 10-54. Test Getting Encrypted Data from Oracle

```
...
String locModulus = OracleJavaSecure.getLocRSAPubMod();
String locExponent = OracleJavaSecure.getLocRSAPubExp();

stmt = ( OracleCallableStatement )conn.prepareCall(
    "CALL hr.hr_sec_pkg.p_select_employees_sensitive(?,?,?,?,?,?,?,?,?)" );
...
OracleJavaSecure.closeConnection();
```

We have seen this procedure call before, multiple times. The only difference here is that we are using a connection that we got from our application verification list

Add More Application Connection Strings

A developer may have some call to use connections in her application that are not stored in the connsHash list that has been stored in Oracle Database. Those application strings can be added to the local application connections list by calling putAppConnString(). This call can even overwrite existing connection strings coming from the Oracle Database store (table), perhaps for testing against a new Oracle instance or a development or acceptance instance:

```
putAppConnString( "Orcl", "appusr",
    "password", "localhost", String.valueOf( 1521 ), true );
```

If a subsequent call to putAppConnections() is not made, then the modified connection strings list is not stored in Oracle, and they are only seen by and used by the local client application. The plan is to call putAppConnections() once, to store the strings in the Oracle database, and from then on, to remove the connection strings from the application and use only what is stored in the database. We will avoid putting our connection strings into the application at all, and will make that process easy with the administrative interface we build in Chapter 12.

Testing a Second Application

Reflect for a moment on what we have done so far in the previous tests. We have an inner class in the OracleJavaSecure class that implements RevLvlClassIntfc, and we pass that to Oracle database for application validation. How does the Oracle JVM handle that inner class? Is it on the CLASSPATH or otherwise known to the Oracle JVM?

In this specific case, we actually loaded the class to Oracle Database when we loaded the outer class, OracleJavaSecure. If you have a SQL client application that lets you browse structures in Oracle, you can see the *orajavsec.OracleJavaSecure.InnerRevLvlClass* listed in the database. You can also execute this query to see it:

```
SELECT * FROM SYS.ALL_OBJECTS
WHERE OBJECT_TYPE = 'JAVA CLASS'
AND OWNER = 'APPSEC';
```

Unfortunately, occasionally the object name will have been modified by Oracle, and you may see something like "/fddfb98e_OracleJavaSecureInne". In addition to the expected inner class, for OracleJavaSecure you may also see an inner class named *OracleJavaSecure$1*—a class that represents our use of reflection to generate a heretofore unknown class.

This is probably the only application inner class for verification whose outer class is loaded into Oracle, so we have to ask, "how will Oracle database instantiate classes from other applications?"

Objects We Have Never Seen

I have repeatedly said that the application will hand us its inner class, which we will validate in order to authorize an application. I have made it sound like the Oracle JVM is able to create the class and object out of thin air using only the class bytes that we are providing from the application, or those stored in Oracle Database for this application. However, that is not really the case.

I am not saying that it is not possible to generate classes and objects based just on a byte array—it certainly should be possible by defining a BytesClassLoader class, based on a URLClassLoader that takes a byte array rather than a URL directory or jar file. However we will be taking the easy way out.

There are two reasons for taking the easy way out: to avoid the security issues raised by an alternate ClassLoader, and because an easy solution exists.

Our approach bears some resemblance to remote method invocation (RMI). In RMI, a local stub class exists that represents the remote object. In RMI, the local stub class and the RMIClassLoader handle calls to the actual methods that are running remotely, on the RMI server. That is not what we will be doing.

I say that our approach bears resemblance to RMI because we will have a representation of the application inner class pre-loaded in the Oracle JVM. The class in the Oracle JVM needs to bear strong resemblance to the class that will be passed to us from the client application, but doesn't need to match exactly. In particular, we are going to instantiate client classes with, potentially, different revision labels.

Place Stub Class on Oracle

Here is where and why we can enforce at least a partial code review for every application that intends to use our security structures. This will be a good thing, since you are the expert now, having reviewed all the secure programming concepts discussed in Chapters 2 and 3.

We need to distill the inner class that will be used to validate each application down to its essential structure. This includes the outer, containing class structure. We are going to load just those essentials into Oracle database to serve as a stub on which to realize classes and objects of this type in Oracle database.

Take a moment to compare the original inner class, *in situ* with the stub for our second application, testojs/TestOracleJavaSecure.

▪ **Note** Compare the files named *Chapter10/ testojs/TestOracleJavaSecure.java* (the original) and *TestOracleJavaSecure.sql* (the stub).

Looking at certain aspects of our stub, I'd like to point out what's required. First in Listing 10-55, notice the package name, *testojs*. We are going to require that application inner classes exist in a package, in order to assure that applications may even name their inner classes the same, but have unique names based on the package prefix. Second notice the outer, containing class definition for TestOracleJavaSecure. This outer class definition needs to match exactly what we see in the original code. The inner class is named AnyNameWeWant.

Listing 10-55. Stub Class for Second Test Application

```
CREATE OR REPLACE AND RESOLVE JAVA SOURCE NAMED appsec."testojs/TestOracleJavaSecure" AS
package testojs;
import java.io.Serializable;
import orajavsec.RevLvlClassIntfc;

public class TestOracleJavaSecure {

    public static class AnyNameWeWant
        implements Serializable, RevLvlClassIntfc
    {
        private static final long serialVersionUID = 2011013100L;
        private String innerClassRevLvl = "20110131a";
        public String getRevLvl() {
            return innerClassRevLvl;
        }
    }
}
```

The definition of the inner class itself should be exactly the same as in the original code, with the exception of the innerClassRevLvl string (whether you've defined it in the class or in the getRevLvl() method). Note that in all cases, the public and private modifiers should be maintained. We want the inner class to be declared as static so that we are dealing with a single object rather than potentially multiple instances.

In addition to being in a package, the inner class needs to be declared public so that the OracleJavaSecure class can generate the object, even though it's in a different package. The containing, outer class should also be public for this reason.

There is a lot of flexibility in placement of the inner class within the containing class. First of all, the containing class need not be a top level class for the application—it can be an ancillary class. In this way, a diligent programmer may withhold sensitive code from perusal by the application security personnel who will be generating the stub.

There is another reason why we may want our application inner class in an ancillary outer class. There is some concern because inner classes have access to the private members of their outer, containing classes. So having the application inner class in an ancillary outer class would be potentially less sensitive than having the inner class in the core application class.

The inner class can also be placed inside a method, instead of in the main class body. Generally, inner classes that are defined within methods are given a "$1" style marker in the middle of their class name. You can see that when examining the compiled class names.

Get Application Authentication Connection and Role

We should always be on the lookout to make using security easier for developers. With that in mind, we are going to combine into a single step, what had previously been a couple steps that asked our developers to implement separately. Up to this point we have asked our developers to, at a minimum, set their application context, then get an application connection and finally call Oracle Database to set their secure application role. We are still going to have the developers set their application context, but we are going to combine the request for an application connection with the request to get the secure application role. We will do this with a new method, getAAConnRole() shown in Listing 10-56.

When we call getAAConnRole(), we will have an OracleConnection returned to us, and the connection will already have the secure application role set. This new method takes the same arguments that we were providing to the getAppAuthConn() method.

Listing 10-56. Get Application Authentication Connection and Role, getAAConnRole()

```
public static OracleConnection getAAConnRole( String instance, String userName ) {
    OracleConnection mConn = null;
    OracleCallableStatement stmt = null;
    try {
        mConn = getAppAuthConn( instance, userName );
        // If mConn is null, probably did not send twoFactorAuth
        if( null == mConn ) return mConn;
        int errNo;
        String errMsg;
        stmt = ( OracleCallableStatement )mConn.prepareCall(
            "CALL appsec.p_check_role_access(?,?,?)" );
            stmt.registerOutParameter( 2, OracleTypes.NUMBER );
            stmt.registerOutParameter( 3, OracleTypes.VARCHAR );
            stmt.setString( 1, applicationID );
            stmt.setInt(    2, 0 );
            stmt.setNull(   3, OracleTypes.VARCHAR );
        stmt.executeUpdate();
        errNo = stmt.getInt( 2 );
        errMsg = stmt.getString( 3 );
        //System.out.println( "DistribCd = " + errMsg );
        if( errNo != 0 ) {
            System.out.println( "Oracle error 1) " + errNo + ", " + errMsg );
        } else if( twoFactorAuth.equals( "" ) ) {
            System.out.println( "Call again with two-factor code parameter" );
        }
    } catch ( Exception x ) {
        x.printStackTrace();
```

```
    } finally {
        try {
            if( null != stmt ) stmt.close();
        } catch( Exception y ) {}
    }
    return mConn;
}
```

Note that the call to p_check_role_access is identical to what we had been asking our developers to do for themselves. The applicationID we use in that call is what we set our static member to when we called setAppContext().

Test Application Authentication, Phase 2

If you haven't already, execute the script to create the stub inner class for TestOracleJavaSecure in Oracle database.

■ **Note** Execute the script in *TestOracleJavaSecure.sql* on the Oracle database.

You can query Oracle database to see the Java structures that you have just created. There will be one Java structure for the TestOracleJavaSecure outer class, and one for the inner class, resembling this list. Here's the query to execute:

```
SELECT * FROM SYS.ALL_OBJECTS WHERE OBJECT_TYPE = 'JAVA CLASS' AND OWNER = 'APPSEC';
testojs/TestOracleJavaSecure
/545c0b44_TestOracleJavaSecure
```

Next, edit and compile the TestOracleJavaSecure class on the client. Modify the call to putAppConnString() with the password, server name, instance name and port number for your Oracle instance.

■ **Note** Edit the code found in the file named *Chapter10/testojs/TestOracleJavaSecure.java*.

The tests here will be relatively simple, but everything we have described so far in this book will have taken place by the time we display a line of encrypted data from the database. This can also serve as an example of what an application developer will have to do to use our security structures.

First you will note that this application implements an inner application class in Listing 10-57.

Listing 10-57. Second Test Application Inner Class

```
package testojs;

public class TestOracleJavaSecure {
    public static class AnyNameWeWant
```

```
        implements Serializable, RevLvlClassIntfc
    {
...
```

Set the Application Context

The body of test code resides in the main method. In this case, we are presuming that the client user will call the application from the command line. After the first call, he will need to call it again, including the two-factor authentication code on the command line.

See in Listing 10-58 how the application sets the application context in `OracleJavaSecure` by calling the `setAppContext()` method.

Listing 10-58. Set Second Test Application Context

```
public static void main( String[] args ) {
    OracleCallableStatement stmt = null;
    Statement mStmt = null;
    ResultSet rSet;
    try {
        // Submit two-factor auth code on command line, once received
        String twoFactorAuth = "";
        if( args.length != 0 && args[0] != null ) twoFactorAuth = args[0];
        String applicationID = "HRVIEW";
        Object appClass = new AnyNameWeWant();
        OracleJavaSecure.setAppContext( applicationID, appClass, twoFactorAuth );
```

Store the Connection Strings in Oracle

If this is the first time we have run the `TestOracleJavaSecure` class, both before and after we have a two-factor authentication code, then we can run a few lines to populate the `connsHash` list of connection strings and store them in Oracle, as shown in Listing 10-59.

Listing 10-59. Store Connections for Second Test Application

```
// Only do these lines once
// If we provided an old twoFactorAuth, will not have connHash -
// null pointer exception here
OracleJavaSecure.getAppConnections();
OracleJavaSecure.putAppConnString( "Orcl", "appusr",
    "password", "localhost", String.valueOf( 1521 ) );
OracleJavaSecure.putAppConnections();
```

After we have succeeded in submitting our application-specific connection strings to Oracle, we can comment those lines of code and simply use the connection strings that we've stored in and retrieved from Oracle Database.

Get an Application Connection with Role

For this test, we are going to call our new method, `getAAConnRole()`, which as you'll recall gets the application connection and sets the secure application role. This call is shown in Listing 10-60.

Listing 10-60. Call to Get Application Connection with Role

```
OracleConnection conn =
    OracleJavaSecure.getAAConnRole( "orcl", "appusr" );
```

See the Proxy Connection

Now that we have our connection, let's see how we have been identified by Oracle database. There are a number of Oracle SYS_CONTEXT settings that we can query. We will query and display those having to do with our identity in Listing 10-61.

Listing 10-61. View the Proxy Connection Settings

```
mStmt = conn.createStatement();

rSet = mStmt.executeQuery( "SELECT SYS_CONTEXT( 'USERENV', 'OS_USER' )," +
"SYS_CONTEXT( 'USERENV', 'PROXY_USER' ),SYS_CONTEXT( 'USERENV', 'IP_ADDRESS' ),"+
"SYS_CONTEXT( 'USERENV', 'SESSION_USER' ), "+
"SYS_CONTEXT( 'USERENV', 'CLIENT_IDENTIFIER' ) " +
"FROM DUAL" );
if ( rSet.next() ) {
    System.out.println( rSet.getString( 1 ) );
    System.out.println( rSet.getString( 2 ) );
    System.out.println( rSet.getString( 3 ) );
    System.out.println( rSet.getString( 4 ) );
    System.out.println( rSet.getString( 5 ) );
}
rSet = mStmt.executeQuery( "SELECT * FROM sys.session_roles" );
if ( rSet.next() ) {
    System.out.println( rSet.getString( 1 ) );
}
```

Get Encrypted Data from Oracle

Finally, we will call our standard demonstration stored procedure, **p_select_employees_sensitive**. This requires additional encryption key exchange with the connection listed in the **connsHash**. The call is shown in Listing 10-62. Our first encryption keys that we exchanged for the **appver** connection cannot be reused with a different Oracle connection, as **appusr** for instance.

Listing 10-62. Call to Get Sensitive Employees Data

```
String locModulus = OracleJavaSecure.getLocRSAPubMod();
String locExponent = OracleJavaSecure.getLocRSAPubExp();
stmt = ( OracleCallableStatement )conn.prepareCall(
    "CALL hr.hr_sec_pkg.p_select_employees_sensitive(?,?,?,?,?,?,?,?,?)" );
...
```

Chapter Review

So, what have we got working so far? This whirlwind description will attempt to cover the secure programming ground traversed by this test application, TestOracleJavaSecure.

We call the TestOracleJavaSecure class without a two-factor authentication code for starts. The test application sets its application context in OracleJavaSecure by passing its inner class and application ID. Then (in a standard run mode) the test app calls OracleJavaSecure.getAAConnRole().

Behind the scenes, in OracleJavaSecure, we proxy connect to Oracle Database as the OS user, proxying through the Oracle appver user. Initially, the login trigger for the appver schema checks to assure that the OS user is a valid Oracle user.

Once connected to Oracle database as appver, we test if the user passes our SSO tests. Then, because we didn't provide a two-factor authentication code, Oracle database generates a code and sends it to the devices and accounts registered for the OS user.

Once we receive the two-factor authentication code, we call TestOracleJavaSecure again, passing the two-factor code. The two-factor code gets passed to OracleJavaSecure when TestOracleJavaSecure sets the application context. Now when we call Oracle database as appver and pass SSO, we check the two-factor code; and if it passes, and the inner class from our app context matches something in Oracle, we return the list of encrypted connection strings that has been stored for this application.

Another behind-the-scenes process that occurred is our key exchange for application verification processes. The client sent his RSA public key to Oracle, and Oracle database generated a shared password key, encrypted it with the RSA key, and returned it to the client. The connection strings are encrypted with the shared password key.

Continuing the behind-the-scenes activity of the getAAConnRole() method, we decrypt the requested connection string and connect to Oracle database with it. We connect in order to request the secure application role needed by the application in order to read data from Oracle database. In an effort to acquire the secure application role, we once again assure that we pass SSO (perhaps on a different Oracle instance from appver), but we do not do two-factor authentication again for this connection.

OracleJavaSecure.getAAConnRole() will return an OracleConnection, which the developer can use to call one of his application procedures in order to get encrypted application data. When he makes that call, he will exchange encryption keys for the new connection, and will retrieve data encrypted with a new shared password key. We decrypt the aspects of the shared password key and build that key, and then we decrypt the data using that key.

Figures 10-1 and 10-2 illustrate this process. In Figure 10-1 we see the process of getting a list of application Oracle connection strings from Oracle database. This is a two-phase process, with phase one being the first connection when requesting a two-factor authentication code, and phase two being the user's return with a two-factor authentication code in hand. The two outlined boxes illustrate the activities of each of those phases.

At the outset (top) of Figure 10-1, we call the setAppContext() method, which simply stages data for the particular client application in the static class member variables of OracleJavaSecure. After that, the client application makes one additional call to getAppConnections(). Near the end of the second phase of that process, note that the list of connection strings is not returned to the client application, but rather is held in escrow within the client-side OracleJavaSecure class. The list is a private class member of OracleJavaSecure. You can also see within the second phase that before the connection strings are returned, they are encrypted with secret password key, and they are returned in encrypted form.

Along with the list of encrypted Oracle connection strings for the application, the encrypted artifacts of the DES shared password key are also returned from Oracle database. OracleJavaSecure on the client builds an equivalent shared password key for use in decrypting the application connection strings. After building the DES shared password key and storing the key for later use in clone or new static members, the resetKeys() method is called so that further Oracle connections as application users may be made.

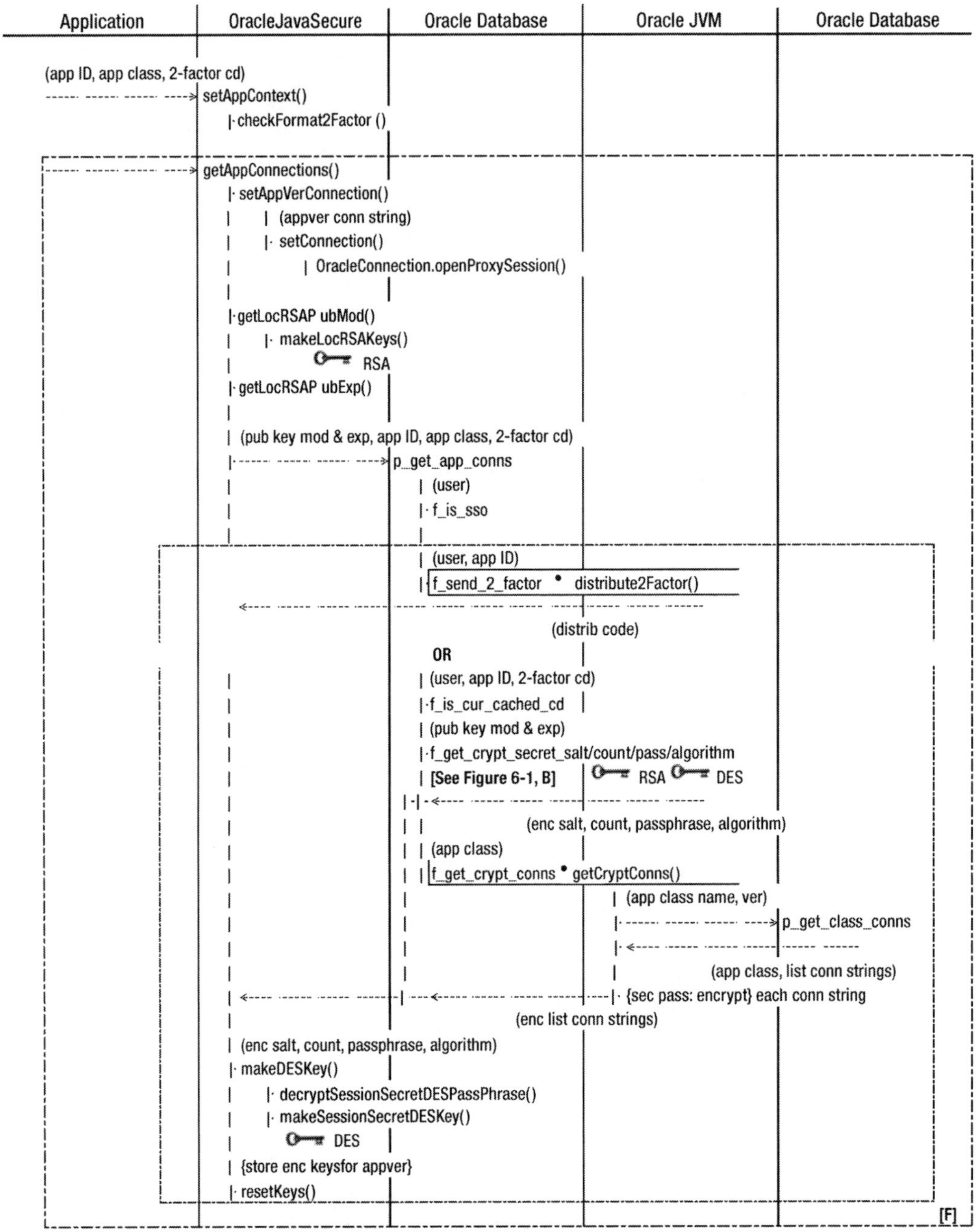

Figure 10-1. *Getting a list of application Oracle connection strings*

The top half of Figure 10-2 illustrates the process of storing Oracle connection strings in a list for the client application. All connection strings in the list on the client are maintained in encrypted form. The first call the client application may make, at the top of Figure 10-2 is a call to put a new connection string into the local list. This addition is only made locally on the client, and does not yet exist in the list stored on Oracle database. Notice that we call an encryption function using the secret password key to encrypt the connection string for storage.

The next call in Figure 10-2 that the client application may make is a call to putAppConnections(), which stores the entire list of connection strings in the Oracle database. This process illustrates best our use of different processing environments for different purposes. The individual columns of our illustration are informative. The client application (far left column) calls functions in OracleJavaSecur— this is Java calling Java. OracleJavaSecure calls Java stored procedures in the Oracle database, which passes the call through to the Oracle JVM—Java running on Oracle database. We also have the need from the Oracle JVM to call stored procedures and functions in Oracle (the far right column.) The two columns labeled "Oracle Database" are one and the same Oracle instance, just called from different directions.

In that process of storing the list of connection strings for the application in the Oracle database, you can see that we decrypt each connection string. We build a new HashMap of decrypted connection strings and we store them unencrypted in the Oracle database.

The bottom half of Figure 10-2 illustrates the acquisition of a specific Oracle connection for use by the application. The client application asks OracleJavaSecure.getAAConnRole() for a connection that uses a specific Oracle instance and user. Note that the connection string is only briefly decrypted for use in creating the new OracleConnection. The getAAConnRole() method not only creates the OracleConnection, but also sets the role to the secure application role needed for access to the sensitive application data. This OracleConnection with secure application role set is returned to the client application for use.

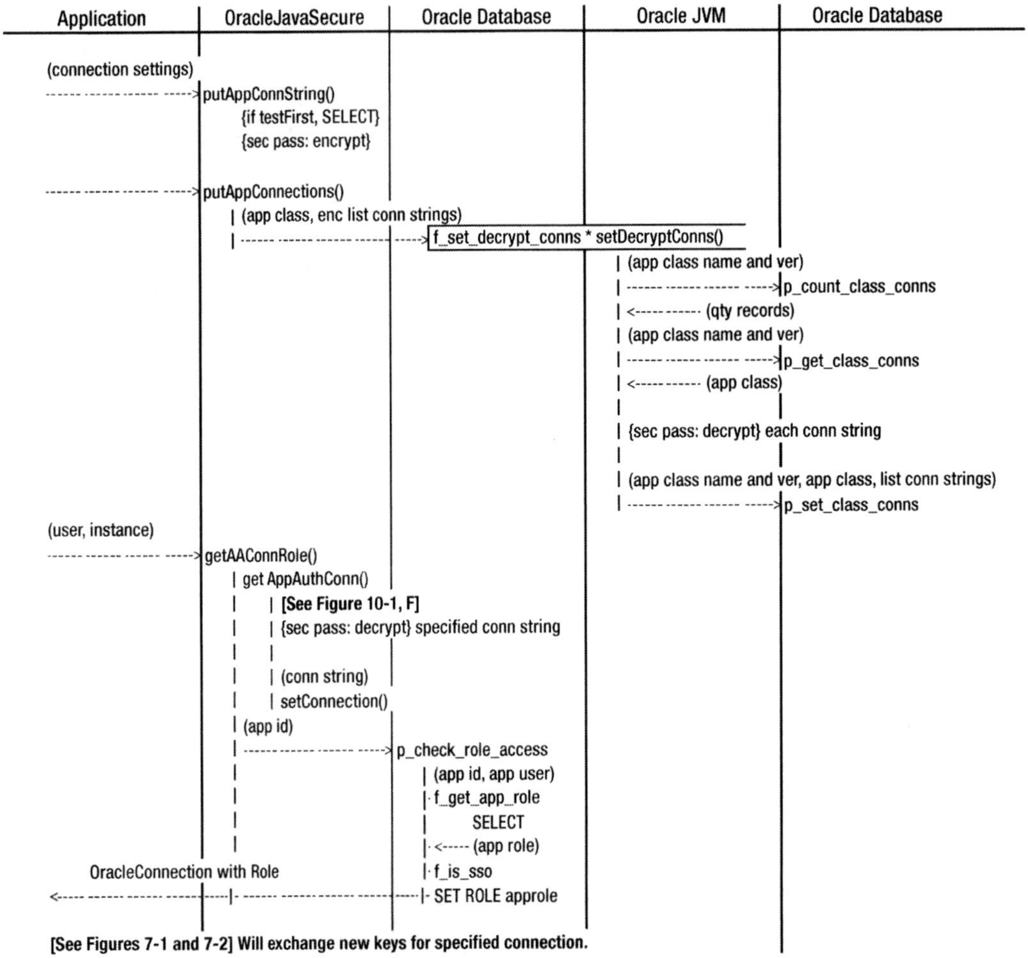

Figure 10-2. *Store the list of application connection strings in Oracle database, and get a specific application Oracle connection for use.*

Enhancing Security

Every year, the president of my company gives us a pep talk. Generally, he talks about the good things we've done throughout the year as a company, and shares an itemized list of our failures or less-than-stellar moments. At the end of the talk, the president recognizes the skills and commitment of the employees and encourages us not only to continue doing what we're doing, but to do even more, taking on every new challenge.

We need to have this is the same pep talk regarding computer security. We are doing well and succeeding, but there are always new challenges and areas where we can do even more.

We have one specific area to address, which I've mentioned in earlier chapters. It has been a weakness in all our Oracle applications: we have embedded passwords. And this problem is not going away. We have removed all passwords from the code except the one for the application verification user, appver. Now we need to take additional steps to protect that password.

An additional weakness we have is risk of privileged user attack. Currently, if a rogue DBA (or hacker with DBA privileges) wants, he can read all our passwords in the t_app_conn_registry table. Granted, he would have to know some Java to reconstitute the HashMap. Anyone with access to the backup tapes or archives might also be able to pull out the table and get access to all our application passwords. What we need is data encryption at rest; that is, data encryption in the Oracle table and on disk.

In the previous chapter, we produced code that will store application connection strings from any application running as any local user. This was convenient, but we need to formalize that process and delegate it to an application verification administrator. We will introduce the appver_admin role for that purpose and discuss the process of managing our application connection strings.

If an attacker succeeds in getting the appver password, we want to severely limit what he can do and see in the database. We already have our login trigger, and appver only has access to a few procedures and limited data for our application security process. But we will see that every user in Oracle database has access to PUBLIC data that we would prefer to not expose, so we will attempt to tighten our general Oracle application security.

Hide the APPVER Connection String

We are not going to solve the embedded password problem, and you might be wondering why. In a nutshell, this is a "chicken or egg" problem. Perhaps we could hide our passwords in Oracle database, but we would need an Oracle password to request them from the database.

You cannot talk to Oracle database without a user/password, so the question arises of where to store the password. We have solved that issue for all our application passwords except for the gatekeeper account, appver. So let's look at some of the prospective solutions for hiding that password.

Get It from a Second Source/Server

Well, if we don't want the password in our code, and we can't get it from Oracle database (without a password), perhaps we need to store it and retrieve it from a secondary server. At the end of the day, I'm going to promote the idea of just sticking with Oracle database as our server. Supporting and securing one server well beats distributing your security roles across many platforms, primarily because it's easier to account for and easier to keep an eye on.

From a Port Server

Where I work, we have a port server (a multithreaded application that opens a ServerSocket and listens on a network port) that performs some of the same activities as the appver structures we described in Chapter 10 and returns connection strings. That was a brilliant solution, and one I can't take credit for—my associate conceived it. That server does just what it is intended to do, and delivers the connection strings securely. It was homegrown before J2EE.

We could implement some additional security in our port server, like SSO and two-factor authentication, things that are not there at present. However, the primary faults of this server are twofold: first, there is less-than-Oracle-quality security of the storage of the connection strings. Now, instead of an Oracle account to get access, there is an operating system account or group that gives access. And second, managing another kind of server with its unique configuration and code means potentially greater support requirements and unique knowledge.

From RMI

Remote Method Invocation (RMI) is a system for separating Java functionality in half. Some Java code runs on the client, and some on the RMI Server. Using RMI, you could retrieve your connection strings from a Java RMI service.

This approach has very much the same strengths and weaknesses as the port server described previously. Its one advantage is that it is an industry-standard approach rather than a home-grown port server, so perhaps there is less concern with unique requirements for support.

From a URLClassLoader

If you have ever run an Applet in a browser, you have seen the URLClassLoader in action. With this approach, some of your application code, perhaps that which retrieves and delivers your connection strings, is not stored on the client computer. This is a separation of code, but not a separation of processing. When needed, the local application pulls down jar files or class files from an HTTP (web) server and runs the code in those files. Your application is running stand-alone on the client computer, and provides no server-side authentication. Additionally, if an application can read the files from a URL, so can any other web client on the local machine.

Briefly, if we were running in a browser, we might have server-side authentication. There can be realm authentication from a browser to certain document/application realms, which generally means another username/password prompt to access the URL. Or in a browser, there might also be SSO if the web page or server directs the browser to authenticate the logged-in user to active directory (or similar) before returning the jar file (still talking about the URLClassLoader). But in the present discussion, let's stick to client applications.

Perhaps we could modify the standard behavior of the URLClassLoader and read code from a secure repository, and hence get our connection strings securely. Well, we're talking about pretty much a combination of an RMI server (with the unique class loader) and a port server, again with the same weaknesses.

Weaknesses in All These Approaches

A computer hacker will do better to attack the client than the server. In Java, eventually all those connection strings are converted into a human-readable form in memory. No matter how fleeting and transitory, that is our biggest security weakness, and one that we have not solved. Our best efforts in the utility OracleJavaSecure class only succeed at keeping the connection strings out of the application code, and in keeping them encrypted until the moment they are needed, then discarding the unencrypted string.

It is beyond the scope of this book to look at an obvious protection from an attack on the client – that is connecting to Oracle database only from a server. Web applications are an example of this: the user sees the web page, but it is generated from data that is queried by the web server. We have mentioned RMI, and it could play a potential role in this. With RMI, the client may request data from the RMI server, and the RMI server would be responsible for querying Oracle database.

If you decide to run all your Oracle queries from a web services, HTTP, or RMI server, then you need to turn your attention to securing acquisition and use of the Oracle passwords on the server, which is an identical prospect, albeit more centralized, to what we have been discussing for client application security.

Get It from a Native Call: JNI

Perhaps we can protect our Oracle password by using a different programming language from Java for storing and reading our password, maybe even for querying Oracle database. We can write a procedure in C+ and call it from our Java application using Java native interface (JNI).

Granted, because Java is compiled into byte code that is interpreted by the JVM, the byte code is slightly more susceptible to decompiling back into source code than compiled C+ code. But code written in any language can be decompiled or disassembled. Dynamic link libraries (DLLs) and executable programs are just as open to attack.

I recommend just sticking with Java. For security, maintaining and applying one secure programming skill set well is better than being semi-fluent and semi-trustworthy in multiple languages.

Get It from an Encrypted Java Class

Okay, we're back to our client Java code, and we're trying to secure our embedded Oracle password. If we could encode our password so that only our program can read it, that would be good. But we'd have to hide how our program reads it to keep hackers from duplicating the process and reading the password.

The question has been asked, and we ask it here again, can we hide what we're doing in Java by encrypting our class files doing byte code encryption? The answer is yes, and an excellent description of the process and results was provided by Vladimir Roubtsov in his *JavaWorld* article, "Cracking Java byte-code encryption" from May 2003. He subtitles his article "Why Java obfuscation schemes based on byte-code encryption won't work."

The heart of Roubtsov's article describes his EncryptedClassLoader. If you recall, we discussed class loaders in the last chapter regarding realizing our application object and class in the Oracle database. We said that the ClassLoader cannot realize a class for which he has no prior knowledge, so we put a stub class on the Oracle database.

RMI has an RMIClassLoader that can load a class from a stub or skeleton class and match it with the implementation class on the RMI server. The URLClassLoader can load classes from a jar file or class files located remotely, for instance on a web server.

In the case of Roubtsov's EncryptedClassLoader, the byte code needs to be decrypted before the object or class is realized. That is all well and good, and we're all thinking green light!

However, Roubtsov points out the fallacy of trusting in this security. At some point in every class loader, the byte code is passed to the defineClass() method, which must present the class in a form readable by the JVM. It is at that point that the form and function of our classes are revealed to any Java hacker.

I'm not saying that encrypted byte code is a bad idea, just that we are not achieving meaningful encryption—just a complex obfuscation. Perhaps that can be said about all encryption: it is only encryption up to the point that it needs to be decrypted for use.

There are some concerns with implementing our own class loader: it is so close to the core of the JVM that we will need to take caution and may need to revisit it with every Java update. An error there in the ClassLoader could be devastating to our applications. That alone repels us from byte code encryption.

Get It from an Encrypted String

Why don't we just encrypt our password and only decrypt it as needed? That's a good idea, but what about the encryption key, how do we protect that? Is this another "chicken and egg" problem? I think so. Exposing the key is tantamount to exposing the password.

Get It from an Encoded String

What if we encode our string so that it is unrecognizable? This is perhaps as good as encrypting it, but it doesn't require an encryption key. We will look at some example Java code in a class we will call OJSCode to encode our password.

Using the Encode Method

In brief, our OJSCode.encode() method will take the connection string and encode it byte by byte by doing a binary Exclusive Or (XOR) with other bytes. An XOR conversion can be done twice to get back to the original byte. In XOR, the resultant bit is 1 only if the analogous bit in one or the other, but not both original bytes is 1. This is what the process looks like:

```
Original Byte    0 1 0 0 1 1 0 1
Other Byte       1 1 1 0 0 1 0 1
Result of XOR    1 0 1 0 1 0 0 0 (resultant bit is 1 where only one of bits is 1)
Other Byte       1 1 1 0 0 1 0 1
Result 2nd XOR   0 1 0 0 1 1 0 1 (notice this is the same as our original Byte)
```

For security reasons that we'll discuss later, we will reach outside the OJSCode class to get our "other" bytes. Our intent for OJSCode is only to use it from the OracleJavaSecure class, so how about we reach back to that expected class to get our other bytes? We will assemble our other bytes from a static string named "location" in OracleJavaSecure.

Because we know we are going to be doing an XOR on our original bytes, we will need to have the same number of other bytes as we have original bytes. Listing 11-1 shows how we get two byte arrays representing our connection string (encodeThis) and an array of other bytes of the same length.

Listing 11-1. Get Two Same-Length Byte Arrays for XOR Encoding

```
{ static String location = "in setAppVerConnection method."; }

    String location = OracleJavaSecure.location;
    byte[] eTBytes = encodeThis.getBytes();
    int eTLength = eTBytes.length;
    while( eTLength > location.length() ) location += location;
    String xString = location.substring( 0, eTLength );
    byte[] xBytes = xString.getBytes();
```

First, we get a local copy of the location string from OracleJavaSecure. It was defined with default (package) scope so code outside of the orajavsec package cannot see it. We concatenate that to itself sufficient times to get a string equal in length or longer than encodeThis. Then we get the substring of equal length to encodeThis.

To do byte XOR, we simply use the "^" operator. In Listing 11-2, we walk through both the original and other byte arrays and do an XOR on each byte pair, casting the bytes as ints for this process. We cast the result as a byte and store it in the code[] byte array.

Listing 11-2. Byte-by-Byte XOR encoding

```
    byte[] code = new byte[eTLength];
    for( int i = 0; i < eTLength ; i++ ) {
        code[i] = (byte)( (int)eTBytes[i] ^ (int)xBytes[i] );
    }
```

Our connection string resembles this:

"jdbc:oracle:thin:appver/password@localhost:1521:orcl"

We want to store an encoded replacement for that in the OracleJavaSecure class—something that will fit between quotation marks and be handled as a string. So the OJSCode.encode() method will return a String, but not just any string. Strings can contain unprintable characters such as carriage returns (character 13, decimal) and beeps (character 7). Those are difficult to represent as symbols between quotation marks.

When we do the XOR on our original bytes, we will end up with some unprintable characters, so we need a process to convert them all to readable characters without losing any fidelity, without losing information. We shouldn't need to solve this problem from scratch—we are not the first folks to have this concern.

An industry-standard approach for representing unprintable characters as strings is by Base64 encoding the characters. In Base64 encoding, the bits from a string of bytes is concatenated and broken up into 6-bit sequences that are translated into characters from a table of 64 printable characters. One or more "=" signs are often seen at the end of the Base64 encoded string as a padding character (for when the 6-bit values extend across an 8-bit boundary). When a string of those printable characters is seen with an equals signs at the end, it is a clear indication of Base64 encoding, and a give-away as to the process used to do encoding, if that's a concern. This is not necessarily a problem, because Base64 encoding is only intended to make extended characters palatable to web browsers and such where regular alphanumeric characters are about all that is expected. However, if we are additionally trying to disguise text, then Base64 encoding fails. Base64 encoding is surprisingly often used to convey passwords for basic authentication to proxy servers and web server realms, as if it were encryption. Listing 11-3 shows the Java call we make to do Base64 encoding.

Listing 11-3. Base64 Encoding

```
String decodeThis = (new BASE64Encoder()).encode( code );
```

Oracle has included Base64 encoding in the JVM; however, it is a bother to use. We can call upon **sun.misc**.BASE64Encoder to do our encoding, but look at the package it is in. This is a part of the JVM, but is proprietary. When we compile code that uses that class, we get this warning message:

```
sun.misc.BASE64Encoder is Sun proprietary API and may be removed in a future release
```

We can acquire the Base64 algorithm form many free sources, if we want. But fortunately, Base64 encoding is not the only game in town. We can create our own printable encoding. Look at Listing 11-4. Let's take every int resulting from the XOR and get the String representation in hex format by calling Integer.toHexString(). Our hex strings will be either one or two characters in length, ranging from 0 (0x00) to fe (0xfe) in hexadecimal (0 to 254 in decimal). When the number is less than 0x10, it will have only one character, but we want to know how to break up our encoded string, so we will prepend those hex strings with a "0" character. That way each byte is represented by two characters, and we know how to parse and decode each character. We might call this Padded Hex XOR Coding.

Listing 11-4. Padded Hex XOR Encoding

```
StringBuffer sBuf = new StringBuffer();
String oneByte;
for( int i = 0; i < eTLength ; i++ ) {
    oneByte = Integer.toHexString( (int)eTBytes[i] ^ (int)xBytes[i] );
    if( oneByte.length() == 1 ) sBuf.append( "0" + oneByte );
    else sBuf.append( oneByte );
}
String decodeThis = sBuf.toString();
```

Decoding this OJSCode'ed connection string is just the same process, in reverse. We call Integer.parseInt() on each pair of characters, using a *radix* of 16, so we convert from hex to decimal. Then we XOR the integer with the same other byte from our "location" string that we had used before. This gets us back to the original characters from which we rebuild our connection string.

Using Base64 encoding, the coded string is shorter. Here is an example (notice the telltale "=" sign padding at the end):

```
IE5DEgtTNVAUOUUGKw4aQkUnFR8KQA==
```

Our own encoding creates longer strings. This is the same string encoded with our algorithm.

```
204e43120b533550143945062b0e1a424527151f0a40
```

Obfuscating the Algorithm/Code

Our plan for OJSCode is to encode our appver password. In this case, our Java code is analogous to an encryption key. With a key, what we encrypt can be decrypted. With OJSCode, our encoded password can be decoded and read by anyone who has access to the OJSCode class.

If a hacker has this class but cannot see the OJSCode Java code, then she won't be able to reproduce the logic, and there is one hidden aspect that he won't be able to duplicate: we call out of the class to get the location string in the OracleJavaSecure class. That isn't much of a security feature, but if we hide it, it will be a major hindrance to the hacker.

What I am suggesting here is code obfuscation. The logic is hidden in plain sight. It is hard to know whether this produces much of an obstacle to reading our code, but it would require several conversion steps—the same steps we take to obfuscate our code, in reverse.

Obfuscate the Logic

One of my favorite aspects of Java code is its readability. I do compress my code with stacked method calls, and there is the object-oriented aspect to Java code that must be comprehended, but in all it is very readable. What if we make it our goal to make it less readable? The first step we can take is to use our hex encoding rather than the standard Base64. The rest of the ideas here are intended to give you an idea of what can be done to obfuscate code. Be aware that what makes your code harder for a hacker to understand will also make your code harder for you to understand and to maintain. For that reason, keep a copy of your original code in a secure location for your own reference.

We have a calculated field called eTLength, which is the length of our initial connection string, but we don't need a method member if we are willing to get the length of the string each time it's needed. We can add complexity by concatenating Strings rather than using a StringBuffer. It is not as efficient—in fact, it clutters memory with transient strings, but the logic is less obvious. Let's also convert the for loop to an eternal do while true loop. We will break the loop by breaking to a label, GT: we are creating the Java equivalent of a GOTO statement. We have a bit of inside knowledge about the expected input/output; the encoded string (using our padded hex encoding) will be twice as long as the connection string. Using that knowledge, we will break out of our loop when the encoded string is long enough; that is, twice the length of the connection string, modulus the length of the connection string equals 0. We know the next position in our original byte array that we need to deal with is the one at half the length of our encoded string as it is being concatenated together. There may be insufficient characters in our other byte array to XOR with the connection string bytes, so let's wrap around to the front of the "other" byte array by using modulus. We do that instead of concatenating location to itself until long enough. So far our obfuscated code is as shown in Listing 11-5.

Listing 11-5. Obfuscated Logic, Step 1

```
static String encode( String encodeThis ) {
    byte[] eTBytes = encodeThis.getBytes();
    byte[] xBytes = OracleJavaSecure.location.getBytes();
    String decodeThis = "";
    String oneByte;

    GT: do {

        oneByte = Integer.toHexString(
            (int)eTBytes[decodeThis.length()/2] ^
            (int)xBytes[( decodeThis.length()/2 ) % xBytes.length] );
        if( oneByte.length() == 1 ) decodeThis += "0";
        decodeThis += oneByte;
        if( ( ( decodeThis.length()/2 ) % eTBytes.length ) == 0 )
            break GT;
    } while( true );
    return decodeThis;
}
```

Looking at our code, we see a number of hard-coded integers, most of them equal to 2. Let's create a member integer that by complex calculation works out to be 2 and use it in pace of those integers. We will also capitalize on the fact that our integer divided by itself is 1 and subtracted from itself is 0. Once we get the bytes of the original connection string, we can reuse that original connection string as our return string. Several places in OJSCode we get a byte array from a String by calling the String.getBytes() method. Let's rewrite that as a method called traverse() to replace String.getBytes(). We will allow traverse() to take a null and to get the bytes of location string in that case. Further, we will create an additional member in OracleJavaSecure, named lower case 1 (ell) that we will set equal to location, and we will point at that instead. Now our code looks like Listing 11-6.

Listing 11-6. Obfuscated Logic, Step 2

```
static String encode( String encodeThis ) {
    byte[] eTBytes = traverse( encodeThis );
    byte[] xBytes = traverse();
    encodeThis = "";
    String oneByte = "*";
    int twoI = Integer.parseInt(
        String.valueOf( Integer.toHexString(
        (int)(oneByte.charAt(twoI - twoI)))).charAt(twoI - twoI)));
    GT: do {
        oneByte = Integer.toHexString(
            (int)eTBytes[encodeThis.length()/twoI] ^
            (int)xBytes[( encodeThis.length()/twoI ) %
            xBytes.length] );
        if( oneByte.length() == ( twoI/twoI ) )
            encodeThis += "0";
        encodeThis += oneByte;
        if( ( ( encodeThis.length()/twoI ) % eTBytes.length )
            == ( twoI - twoI ) )
        {
            System.arraycopy( xBytes, twoI - twoI,
                eTBytes, twoI * 0, twoI );
            break GT;
        }
    } while( true );
    return decodeThis;
}

static byte[] traverse( String encodeThis ) {
    int twoI = 0;
    if( encodeThis == null )
        encodeThis = OracleJavaSecure.l;
    byte[] eTBytes = new byte[encodeThis.length()];
    do eTBytes[twoI] = (byte)(encodeThis.charAt(twoI++));
    while( twoI < eTBytes.length );
    return eTBytes;
}
```

We have also added some misdirection. Now, in the final if statement of our do while loop, before we break to the GT label, we do an arraycopy(). We copy the first two bytes from our "other" byte array to the beginning of our connection string bytes. This is essentially meaningless, because we are through dealing with those arrays; however the tactic of misdirecting is often used in obfuscating code.

Obfuscate the Naming

Let's take just one more step—although, numerous other obfuscation processes could be accomplished. This step is merely replacing our member names with meaningless names that are difficult to read. Let's swap names according to Table 11-1. These sequences of the number 1 (one), capital I, and lowercase l (ell) are selected to be confusing. They all start with an alphabet character to comply with the compiler. The greatest loss in this step of obfuscation is the loss of meaningful names for these methods and members.

Table 11-1. Obfuscated Naming

Previous Name	Obfuscated Name
OJSCode	OJSC
encode()	x()
decode()	y()
traverse()	lI1ll()
encodeThis	I1ll1
eTBytes	lII11
xBytes	ll1I1
oneByte	ll11I
twoI	IlIl1
GT	I11lI

After these translations, our code is barely recognizable. Only the code structure looks like Java, and a few general method references. Listing 11-7 shows the encode() [x()] and traverse() [lI1ll()]methods.

Listing 11-7. Obfuscated Naming

```
public class OJSC {
    static String x( String I1ll1 ) {
        byte[] lII1l = lI1ll( I1ll1 );
        byte[] ll1I1 = lI1ll( null );
        I1ll1 = "";
        String ll11I = "*";
        int IlIl1 = Integer.parseInt(
            String.valueOf( Integer.toHexString(
            (int)(ll11I.charAt(0))).charAt(0)));
        I11lI: do {
            ll11I = Integer.toHexString(
```

```
                    (int)lII1l[I1ll1.length()/IlIl1] ^
                    (int)ll1I1[( I1ll1.length()/IlIl1 ) %
                    ll1I1.length] );
            if( ll11I.length() == ( IlIl1/IlIl1 ) )
                I1ll1 += "0";
            I1ll1 += ll11I;
            if( ( ( I1ll1.length()/IlIl1 ) % lII1l.length )
                == ( IlIl1 - IlIl1 ) )
            {
                System.arraycopy( ll1I1, IlIl1 - IlIl1,
                    lII1l, IlIl1 * 0, IlIl1/IlIl1 );
                break I11lI;
            }
        } while( true );
        return I1ll1;
    }

    static byte[] lI1ll( String I1ll1 ) {
        int IlIl1 = 0;
        if( I1ll1 == null )
            I1ll1 = OracleJavaSecure.l;
        byte[] lII1l = new byte[I1ll1.length()];
        do lII1l[IlIl1] = (byte)(I1ll1.charAt(IlIl1++));
        while( IlIl1 < lII1l.length );
        return lII1l;
    }
```

Generating an Encoded APPVER Connection String

We will add code to the main() method of OracleJavaSecure, as shown in Listing 11-8, to accept the password for appver as a command line argument and encrypt a connection string for appver. We check the format of the argument to see if it is possibly a two-factor authentication code. If it's not, then we call the obfuscated code in OJSC to do encryption and decryption for display. This uses the additional appver connection string attributes defined here.

Listing 11-8. Utility Encoding of appver Password and Connection String

```
if( args.length != 0 && args[0] != null ) {
    String encodeThis = args[0];
    if( ! encodeThis.equals(checkFormat2Factor(encodeThis)) ) {

        encodeThis = "jdbc:oracle:thin:appver/" + encodeThis +

            "@localhost:1521:orcl";

            //"@localhost:1521:apver"; // for use later in Chapter 11
        String encoded = OJSC.x( encodeThis );
        System.out.println( encoded );
        encodeThis = OJSC.y( encoded );
        System.out.println( encodeThis );
    }
} else System.out.println(
```

```
"You may enter APPVER password on command line." );
```

The intention at this point is that you would call OracleJavaSecure once with your intended appver password, then copy the encoded connection string into the code of *OracleJavaSecure.java* in the setAppVerConnection() method.

Hard Coding the Encoded APPVER Connection String

We will modify the setAppVerConnection() method by hard-coding our encoded appver connection string, and by calling the OJSC.y() method to decode it when calling setConnection(). (See Listing 11-9.) By decoding the connection string at the last moment when calling setConnection(), and not setting a member variable to the decoded value, we minimize the attack profile and duration when a hacker may view the clear-text password.

Listing 11-9. Hard-Coding the Encoded appver Connection String

```
String prime =
"030a42105f1b3311133a0048370707005f020419190b524215151b1c13411b0a601f0a17201c18391606795e5b5c5
4591b1b0c02"
    setConnection( OJSC.y( prime ) );
    appVerConn = conn;
```

Create an Oracle Client Wallet

There is a standard way for obfuscating/encrypting passwords stored on the client computer that is provided in the Oracle client. It is called the secure external password store, but it is better known as the wallet. Because wallets can be used on both the server and the client, we should call this the client wallet. I hope to give you a good overview of Oracle client wallets, but we will not end up using them in our security infrastructure.

The first thing about client wallets that you should know is that, by default, they must exist in each OS user's home directory. Client wallets are considered to be personal stores for Oracle credentials. This is quite the opposite of what I'd like to achieve, which is no Oracle user credentials on the desktop. And now, if we mix our appver user password in with potentially other additional user passwords, there is no practical way we can centrally manage it, e.g., update the password.

The second thing you should know about Oracle client wallets is that they can be copied and used by anyone who possesses them. I can create a client wallet and put the appver password in it, then copy it to every computer user' s home directory, and they can all use the wallet to log in as appver. This might appear to be a way to do centralized distribution of password updates. Perhaps, but it is also problematic. These wallet files can be given away like candy, e-mailed to buddies, stolen from backup tape—whatever. That is not protection. The assumption is that the OS is providing access control to user home directories and can protect the files.

The third thing to know is that client wallets are protected from modification and viewing by a wallet password, but there is no authentication required in order to use the client wallet if you have the files. If we place our appver password in a client wallet, then literally anyone who has the wallet files can connect to Oracle database as appver.

Install the Oracle Client

The Oracle client is included with the Oracle database installation, but you can also download and install the Oracle client separately. Having the Oracle client installed on a separate computer is the best way to test your client applications, rather than running them on the Oracle database, which you can also do. In the following discussions, we will assume that you have set your ORACLE_HOME environment variable to something that resembles one of these:

```
SET ORACLE_HOME=D:\app\oracle\product\11.2.0\dbhome_1
```

```
SET ORACLE_HOME=C:\app\oracle\product\11.2.0\client_1
```

Create the Wallet

The first thing you will do when you decide to place your connection passwords in a client wallet is pick a location for the wallet. While there is no restriction on where wallets can be created, when you go to use the wallet to connect to Oracle database, the presumed location is within the current OS user's home directory. You can create your client wallet in any secure location, but you might as well create it where it needs to be for your own use. Otherwise, you'll need to copy it to your home directory for your use and testing.

The expected wallet location is in a subdirectory with the same name as the OS user ID in the user's home directory. For example, if the user's OS user ID is FredF, then we will create a fredf directory in his home directory and create or copy the wallet files there. We will use FredF as the OS username in our examples. Create a directory for your client wallet.

```
mkdir C:\Users\FredF\fredf
```

Note In Windows XP, you will substitute *Documents and Settings* for *Users* in these commands.

To create your password store, you will issue commands to the *mkstore* utility. One command will create the store and one will create the password credential. In each of these commands, you will point to the directory location for your wallet files. The first *mkstore* command creates the wallet. It will prompt you to enter a wallet password that meets certain complexity rules.

```
%ORACLE_HOME%\bin\mkstore -wrl C:\Users\FredF\fredf –create
```

The second command creates the encrypted password/credential. The command will prompt you to enter the password for the appver user twice; then it will prompt you to enter the password for the wallet—that is the same password you entered for the first *mkstore* command. While we are here, let's also create an entry in the client wallet for the appusr user:

```
mkstore -wrl C:\Users\FredF\fredf –createCredential orcl_appver appver
mkstore -wrl C:\Users\FredF\fredf –createCredential orcl_appusr appusr
```

There are several commands you may use to view the contents of your client wallet. You will need to enter the wallet password to use these commands:

```
mkstore -wrl C:\Users\FredF\fredf -list
mkstore -wrl C:\Users\FredF\fredf -listCredential
```

```
mkstore -wrl C:\Users\FredF\fredf -viewEntry oracle.security.client.connect_string1
mkstore -wrl C:\Users\FredF\fredf -viewEntry oracle.security.client.username1
mkstore -wrl C:\Users\FredF\fredf -viewEntry oracle.security.client.password1
```

Notice that we give the name of the first credential as orcl_appver – that stands for the appver user on the *orcl* Oracle database instance. We need to make some additions to the *sqlnet.ora* and *tnsnames.ora* files that configure the *TNSNames* (transparent network substrate) search for database instances. TNS is to *SQLnet* (Oracle's database network communication protocol) as domain name services (DNS) is to TCP/IP. TNS allows us to have multiple names (aliases) for a single Oracle database instance and to write our applications with references to aliases that can at various times point at different Oracle instances. This flexibility is a primary reason for naming services; the other primary reason is to do remote lookup (not storing all names and addresses locally) and its corollary reason: centralized management of name/address associations. Of course we need to use LDAP or something similar for our TNSNames service to achieve that second goal.

There are many features of the TNSNames service that we are not covering in this book. Please refer to the Oracle Database Net Services Reference book for more information.

The *sqlnet.ora* and *tnsnames.ora* files exist or need to be created in a specific directory of the client. Both of them are in a directory like *%ORACLE_HOME%\network\admin*, depending on your installation. Add the line in Listing 11-10 to your *sqlnet.ora* file. For a basic client wallet installation, you only need to specify the WALLET_OVERRIDE directive. You could also specify the WALLET_LOCATION directive, but it would most likely be unused. I have found that the format for the WALLET_LOCATION directive is a bit sensitive; while (for specific Oracle client versions) drive letters are allowed, quotation marks and a trailing "\" character are not. Also note that wallets created by the Oracle 11g client cannot be used with Oracle 10g clients, but 10g wallets can be used in 11g clients.

***Listing 11-10.** Addition to Client sqlnet.ora File for Wallet*

```
SQLNET.WALLET_OVERRIDE=TRUE
```

▪ **Caution** Placing the WALLET_OVERRIDE directive in a **server** *sqlnet.ora* file (e.g., *%ORACLE_HOME%\NETWORK\ADMIN\sqlnet.ora*) can keep the Oracle database from responding to client connections. My suggestion, if you are testing the client wallet on the same computer as the Oracle database, is that you start the database without WALLET_OVERRIDE in the *sqlnet.ora* file, and then add that directive *temporarily* when testing the client wallet.

Add the lines in Listing 11-11 to your client *tnsnames.ora* file. The first section is a standard TNSNames entry for an Oracle instance. For each password we enter in the wallet, we will need an additional entry in *tnsnames.ora*. If you have made entries in *tnsnames.ora* before, but never used the wallet, this may seem a bit strange to you. But consider that you are giving the password for a specific user for each credential in the wallet, so you are coordinating that password with an entry in *tnsnames.ora*. For example, orcl_appver is an entry in *tnsnames.ora* that is specifically for use by the appver user.

Listing 11-11. Additions to Client tnsnames.ora File for Wallet

```
orcl =
        (DESCRIPTION=
                (SOURCE_ROUTE=YES)
                (ADDRESS=(PROTOCOL=tcp)(HOST=orcl.org.com)(PORT=1521))
                (CONNECT_DATA=(SERVICE_NAME=ORCL)))

orcl_appver =
        (DESCRIPTION=
                (ADDRESS=(PROTOCOL=tcp)(HOST= orcl.org.com)(PORT=1521))
                (CONNECT_DATA=
                        (SERVER=DEDICATED)
                        (SERVICE_NAME=ORCL)
                        (SID=ORCL)))

orcl_appusr =
        (DESCRIPTION=
                (ADDRESS=(PROTOCOL=tcp)(HOST= orcl.org.com)(PORT=1521))
                (CONNECT_DATA=
                        (SERVER=DEDICATED)
                        (SERVICE_NAME=ORCL)
                        (SID=ORCL)))
```

■ **Note** At least the HOST name will be different in your case, so modify those settings.

Use the Wallet from SQL*Plus

This is the slickest aspect of using the wallet. You can connect to Oracle database without entering the password, presuming the wallet is created and placed where needed and that your configuration files are correct. Just enter this SQL*Plus command to connect:

```
%ORACLE_HOME%\bin\sqlplus /@orcl_appusr
```

Keep in mind that the password is acquired somehow through the wallet; therefore, it still exists on the client. One might examine the computer memory during processing to capture the clear text password as it is acquired from the wallet. One might also examine the Java code, obfuscated Java code, DLLs, and obfuscated DLLS used by Oracle database to maintain and use the wallet, thereby revealing the process for independently deciphering the wallet password. I don't pretend to know how difficult that would be.

Use the Wallet from Java

Using the client wallet for authentication in a Java application requires an additional jar file in your CLASSPATH. The *oraclepki.jar* file is required for reading the wallet files. On the command line, you can run a test in the *Chapter11/wallet* folder.

```
java -cp %CLASSPATH%;%ORACLE_HOME%\jlib\oraclepki.jar TestWallet
```

In the *TestWallet.java* file, you'll find a main() method with the code shown in Listing 11-12. You may need to modify this code to run the test.

Listing 11-12. Configure Java to Use Client Wallet

```
System.setProperty("oracle.net.tns_admin",
    "C:/app/oracle/product/11.2.0/client_1/NETWORK/ADMIN");
Properties info = new Properties();
String username = System.getProperty( "user.name" );
info.put("oracle.net.wallet_location",
    "(SOURCE=(METHOD=file)(METHOD_DATA=(DIRECTORY=C:/Users/" +
    username + "/" + username + ")))");
```

We set the tns_admin system property so that we can find the *tnsnames.ora* file, and the connect identifier, orcl_appusr inside that file. We instantiate a Properties object that we will pass when we get the Connection. One of the properties we need to set is the wallet_location property. You'll recall that we created or copied the wallet files into the user's home directory in a directory by the same name as the user. In order to set that wallet property, we get the user.name System property, and concatenate a directory location from that value.

We use an OracleDataSource class to get our connection as shown in Listing 11-13. We saw OracleDataSource in Chapter 8 when we looked at single sign on with one of the varieties of pooled connections. In this case, we set the connection URL to use our wallet connect identifier, orcl_appusr. We also pass in the Properties class we instantiated earlier, and we call the getConnection() method.

Listing 11-13. Get a Connection in Java Using Client Wallet

```
OracleDataSource ds = new OracleDataSource();
ds.setURL("jdbc:oracle:thin:@orcl_appusr");
ds.setConnectionProperties(info);
Connection c = ds.getConnection();
```

In *TestWallet.java*, we also set up a proxy connection, identical to what we are using in OracleJavaSecure. For that reason, only OS users who can do SSO (who have matching Oracle users) can run TestWallet.

Administer Wallet Security

A client wallet might be the perfect solution for protecting our application verification appver user password. I would encourage you to use it in this one instance, except for my reservations.

True, the wallet protects the password from being read by hackers, probably better than anything we have developed so far in this book. It works as described—once you get it working. It is easy to copy around to each person's home directory for his or her use. Additionally, we have already portrayed the appver password as little more than data: a gatekeeper or bouncer for the real application accounts.

Yet some of the positives of the wallet have their dark side. Anyone who has the wallet files can connect to Oracle database as the user specified. That connection doesn't have to happen through your application; it can happen through a SQL*Plus session, as we saw. With the appver user, that is not much of a concern—but with most any other Oracle database user, it is a big problem. Don't only think of legitimate computer users, but also (for example) those users who get access to your offsite backup repositories and glean the wallet files from there. It is assumed that protection of the wallet files is incumbent on the OS permissions, but that is not reliable—what if a legitimate user e-mails the files to a hacker posing as a computer support technician?

Another concern is just a practical one that has to do with file distribution, management, and updates. Possibly you already have a system for that, but getting the files to each user's home directory and keeping them updated is not a trivial concern.

Finally, a concern that is not mentioned in regard to client wallets and security but follows logically from an examination of the files used to configure wallet authentication is the disconnect of the password from the host/Oracle database instance specification. A user might try substituting other Oracle instances for the one you have specified in the tnsnames.ora file; thereby testing a specific wallet user and password against every instance. For example, if a hacker changes the tnsnames.ora file on his machine so that the orcl_appusr entry points to (SID=TestOrcl), he can attempt to connect to that instance as appusr with this same command:

```
sqlplus /@orcl_appusr
```

Caution With the Oracle client wallet files, an attacker can connect as the specified user you configured on any instance where that user exists and has the same password.

Perhaps your users only exist on one instance, or have only the exact same privileges on each instance; however, it is more likely that a user may have extended privileges on lower priority (sandbox, development, or acceptance) regions than on production. Those extended privileges on any instance may provide additional attack vectors.

Trace Oracle Client Code

Often you will have the experience during development that things are not working, and your application can't tell you what's wrong. The error is happening in the underlying protocol somewhere, and is hidden or obscured. You may even see misleading error messages.

At that point, you may have to call in the reserves, asking your network administrators to put a network sniffer on your subnet and capture packets to analyze; hopefully, you'll spot the problem.

However, before it comes to that, you have some options yourself, when dealing with Oracle database. You can turn on trace in your client to see that underlying protocol dialog between the client and the Oracle database. Simply set the trace level in the client *sqlnet.ora* file. A value of 16 is the maximum detail trace; you can also choose less detail in levels 8, 4, 2, and 1.

```
TRACE_LEVEL_CLIENT=4
```

Caution When you are done troubleshooting your current problem, be sure to disable trace logging. It generates lots of files with potentially lots of data that can be both a hog of disk space and revealing in a security sense. At higher levels of trace logging, the data returned from a query is also presented in the trace file.

One of the default locations for trace files (there are several) is a folder named like this:

```
%ORACLE_HOME%\log\diag\clients\user_UserID\host_##########_##\trace
```

On the Oracle database, you may have to make the basic directory tree and grant all users the privilege to write to it.

```
mkdir %ORACLE_HOME%\log\diag\clients
```

Here is an example of what you would see with level 4 trace enabled (only the first few lines are shown):

```
Trace file D:\app\oracle\product\11.2.0\dbhome_1\log\diag\clients\
user_UserID\host_##########_##\trace\ora_2988_5952.trc
2011-07-09 07:22:35.826970 : --- TRACE CONFIGURATION INFORMATION FOLLOWS ---
2011-07-09 07:22:36.058905 : New trace stream is
D:\app\oracle\product\11.2.0\dbhome_1\log\diag\clients\
user_UserID\host_##########_##\trace\ora_2988_5952.trc
2011-07-09 07:22:36.058968 : New trace level is 4
2011-07-09 07:22:36.059012 : --- TRACE CONFIGURATION INFORMATION ENDS ---
2011-07-09 07:22:36.059057 : --- PARAMETER SOURCE INFORMATION FOLLOWS ---
2011-07-09 07:22:36.059105 : Attempted load of system pfile source
D:\app\oracle\product\11.2.0\dbhome_1\network\admin\sqlnet.ora
2011-07-09 07:22:36.059203 : Parameter source loaded successfully
2011-07-09 07:22:36.059241 :
2011-07-09 07:22:36.059275 : Attempted load of local pfile source
C:\OraJavSecure\Chapter11\wallet\sqlnet.ora
2011-07-09 07:22:36.059308 : Parameter source was not loaded
2011-07-09 07:22:36.059337 :
2011-07-09 07:22:36.059367 : -> PARAMETER TABLE LOAD RESULTS FOLLOW <-
2011-07-09 07:22:36.059402 : Successful parameter table load
2011-07-09 07:22:36.059435 : -> PARAMETER TABLE HAS THE FOLLOWING CONTENTS <-
2011-07-09 07:22:36.059472 :   TRACE_LEVEL_CLIENT = 4
2011-07-09 07:22:36.059504 :   SQLNET.WALLET_OVERRIDE = TRUE
...
```

Logging Oracle Thin Client Trace Data

When you are using Java thin ojdbc drivers, you cannot configure trace by the setting in sqlnet.ora. You will need to use the logging features of the ojdbc drivers. To accomplish this, you need to place a different ojdbc drivers jar, *ojdbc6_g.jar*, on your CLASSPATH (in front of or as a replacement for *ojdbc6.jar*). This alternate, logging jar file is available in the Oracle Client directory %ORACLE_HOME%\jdbc\lib, or on the Oracle downloads web site:

http://www.oracle.com/technetwork/indexes/downloads/index.html.

Change directories to wallet. To run the TestWallet class using this driver file (and the wallet), you can run a single Java command line. Trace logging and client wallet are unrelated; we are just using TestWallet as a convenient example to show trace logging.

```
cd Chapter11/wallet

java -Doracle.jdbc.Trace=true
    -cp .;%ORACLE_HOME%\jdbc\lib\ojdbc6_g.jar;%ORACLE_HOME%\jlib\oraclepki.jar
    -Djava.util.logging.config.file=OracleLog.properties TestWallet > temp.txt 2> temp2.txt
```

Several things about that command line are worth mentioning. The directive -Doracle.jdbc.Trace=true turns on trace logging. Notice the *ojdbc6_g.jar* in the CLASSPATH, -cp directive. Using that jar file enables logging. We also have the *oraclepki.jar* file on the CLASSPATH for enabling the wallet.

The -Djava.util.logging.config.file=OracleLog.properties directive tells the logging classes to find their properties settings in a file named *OracleLog.properties*. An example properties file for logging may have the entries shown in Listing 11-14.

Listing 11-14. Configure Java (ojdbc) Trace Logging, OracleLog.properties

```
handlers = java.util.logging.ConsoleHandler
java.util.logging.ConsoleHandler.level = ALL
java.util.logging.ConsoleHandler.formatter = java.util.logging.SimpleFormatter
.level=CONFIG
oracle.jdbc.level = FINE
oracle.jdbc.connector.level = FINE
oracle.jdbc.driver.level = FINE
oracle.jdbc.pool.level = FINE
oracle.net.ns.level = TRACE_20
```

■ **Note** You will find a complete configuration properties file at *Chapter11/wallet/OracleLog.properties.*

The first three property lines configure the console (command prompt window) as a logging handler. The ConsoleHandler.level = ALL directive indicates that we want everything that's generated to go to the console. That is my preference. Then, if there's too much logging data coming at me, I can redirect it to a file. The last portion of the command line shows a redirect of the two standard output streams of data, which normally come to the command prompt window, > temp.txt 2> temp2.txt. The first greater-than symbol redirects the "standard out" stream to a file named *temp.txt* in the current directory. The second greater-than symbol, with the "2" prefix redirects the "standard err" stream to a file named *temp2.txt*. You can send both these streams to the same file with this directive at the end of a command: > temp.txt 2> &1.

The last few lines of the properties file configure the level of detail of trace logging. The first property, .level=CONFIG, sets a default level of logging for all aspects of the ojdbc classes to use. CONFIG level is medium detail. The other levels are set at FINE and TRACE_20, which are more detailed levels. The example *OracleLog.properties* file lists of all the aspects to which logging applies, and all the levels that can be set.

With the setting provided in *OracleLog.properties*, a very large trace output is generated in temp2.txt. The following lines are just a snippet of the output produced:

```
Jul 9, 2011 8:32:37 AM oracle.jdbc.pool.OracleDataSource <init>
TRACE_1: Public Enter:
Jul 9, 2011 8:32:37 AM oracle.jdbc.pool.OracleDataSource <init>
TRACE_1: Exit
Jul 9, 2011 8:32:37 AM oracle.jdbc.pool.OracleDataSource setURL
TRACE_1: Public Enter: "jdbc:oracle:thin:@orcl_appusr"
Jul 9, 2011 8:32:37 AM oracle.jdbc.pool.OracleDataSource setURL
TRACE_1: Exit
```

```
Jul 9, 2011 8:32:37 AM oracle.jdbc.pool.OracleDataSource setConnectionProperties
TRACE_1: Public Enter: {oracle.net.wallet_location=(SOURCE=(METHOD=file)
(METHOD_DATA=(DIRECTORY=C:/Users/OSUSER/OSUSER))), oracle.net.encryption_types_client=AES192}
Jul 9, 2011 8:32:37 AM oracle.jdbc.pool.OracleDataSource setConnectionProperties
TRACE_1: Exit
...
 00 00 00 00 00 53 45 4C      |.....SEL|
 45 43 54 20 55 53 45 52      |ECT.USER|
 20 46 52 4F 4D 20 44 55      |.FROM.DU|
 41 4C 01 01 00 00 00 00      |AL......|
```

The last few lines are a portion of a packet sent to Oracle database, showing the query that was used. The entire contents of every packet in both directions are included in the trace log. Data encryption is not being used. Using trace logging is something to be done while troubleshooting, but it should not be done in production.

Encrypt Data Stored on Oracle Database

So far, we have encrypted data as it traversed the network between the client and the Oracle database. We have also encrypted data while in memory, but not in use on the client (the list of connection strings.) However, we have stored data on the Oracle database in clear text. In particular, we are concerned for the connection string lists that we have stored on Oracle in clear text. Well, we are going to address that concern here.

DBMS_CRYPTO Package

Oracle database provides a PL/SQL package that can assist us in doing data encryption at rest (while data is in storage in the database). By using the DBMS_CRYPTO package, we can selectively encrypt specific columns of data. Other alternatives exist, including full-table encryption. The Oracle Advanced Security product, which can be purchased separately from Oracle, can be used to accomplish that.

The DBMS_CRYPTO package is installed by default in the Oracle Database 11g, but it is not enabled by default. We will enable it for our application security, appsec user. We are going to accomplish encryption/decryption using a stored procedure that is owned by appsec, but is executed by appver. I'm telling you this to explain why we are granting execute on DBMS_CRYPTO to appsec instead of to the app_sec_role. The reason is that no roles exist unless you are in a session, and in the scenario I just described, no session exists for appsec. At an Oracle SQL command prompt as SYS, we will execute this command.

```
GRANT EXECUTE ON sys.dbms_crypto TO appsec;
```

Passwords and Keys

Now, as a matter of full disclosure, I hasten to add that DBMS_CRYPTO can be used for a variety of encryption/decryption tasks. Theoretically, we could do encryption on the client using Java and JCE, and do decryption on Oracle database using DBMS_CRPTO. There are two problems with that proposal. First, DBMS_CRYPTO is not nearly flexible enough for us to achieve the same level of security as we have with the OracleJavaSecure process. And second, DBMS_CRYPTO doesn't act like a single side of an encryption/decryption communication; rather, it assumes it is the party doing both encryption and decryption. It doesn't readily exchange encryption keys, nor expose its algorithms.

To meet the requirements of encrypting data at rest, we need to be able to decrypt data at a different time, in a different place by a different user. That said, it should be obvious that we cannot "negotiate" a key or set of keys at the time they are needed. Somewhere we need to store the encryption key, and retrieve it at some unspecified time in the future to decrypt the data.

The burden falls on the developer to decide where to store the encryption keys for use with DBMS_CRYPTO. There are benefits of having the password stored right in the Oracle database with the encrypted data. One benefit is that when we restore a backup of the encrypted data, we also restore the decryption key. The risk here is that, if someone gets access to the encrypted data, they might also get access to the decryption key.

One viable alternative would be to store the decryption key in the client application and to pass it to Oracle database when we want to decrypt the data; however, that hardly seems more secure. No, we will stick with storing the encryption key in the database, and we will take a couple steps to assure that it can't be used by anyone outside our application. Before I tell you how I do it, think about how you would do it.

Encryption at Rest Key Store

We will store our encryption/decryption keys, at least the genesis of the keys, in an ordinary Oracle table, t_application_key—see Listing 11-15. It is possible we may want to store these keys on a separate Oracle instance and acquire them across a DB link. In that way, the encrypted data and encryption keys will be backed up separately. We will provide a version number column, in case we want more than one key per database, possibly for a different application. You'll see why that's probably unnecessary. We also create an index and a view, v_application_key, of this table.

■ **Note** You will find this SQL script in a file named *Chapter11/AppSec.sql*.

Listing 11-15. Table of Encryption at Rest Keys

```
CREATE TABLE appsec.t_application_key
(
    key_version NUMBER(3) NOT NULL,
    -- Max Key size 1024 bits (128 Bytes)
    key_bytes   RAW(128) NOT NULL,
    create_ts   DATE DEFAULT SYSDATE
);
```

One assurance we want to make is that the key is never changed. We are going to do that with an on update/delete trigger. This trigger, shown in Listing 11-16, will basically turn the attempted update around and reject it.

Listing 11-16. Before Update/Insert Trigger on Table of Encryption at Rest Keys

```
CREATE OR REPLACE TRIGGER appsec.t_application_key_budr BEFORE UPDATE OR DELETE
    ON appsec.t_application_key FOR EACH ROW
BEGIN
    RAISE_APPLICATION_ERROR(-20001,'Cannot UPDATE or DELETE Records in V_APPLICATION_KEY.');
END;
```

```
/
```

```
ALTER TRIGGER appsec.t_application_key_budr ENABLE;
```

Let's go ahead and insert several records into v_application_key, one of which we will use. See Listing 11-17. We will use the RANDOMBYTES function in the DBMS_CRYPTO package to generate a string of 128 random bytes to use as our key genesis. I'm saying *key genesis* because, as you'll see, the real encryption/decryption key is assembled from these key bytes later on.

Listing 11-17. Insert Several Random Encryption at Rest Keys

```
INSERT INTO appsec.v_application_key
( key_version, key_bytes )
VALUES
( 1, SYS.DBMS_CRYPTO.RANDOMBYTES(1024/8) );
```

Also insert values for key_version numbers 2 through 5 using the same INSERT command.

Functions to Encrypt/Decrypt Data at Rest

We are going to build two Oracle stored functions to do server-side encryption of data to be stored in the database, and to decrypt it for use, as required. They are keyed to a specific version of the key genesis bytes in t_application_key, and they use DBMS_CRYPT package to do encryption. We will make this difficult to duplicate by not taking our data and our key bytes and going straight to encryption; rather, we will perform several operations on the key bytes first. Anyone reading these functions will be able to tell what we are doing, and will be able to duplicate it, so we are going to hide the function code by passing these functions through the Oracle Wrap utility to obfuscate the code.

I encourage you to take these functions as a starting place, and modify them sufficiently to change the encryption process, then save a copy somewhere safe but hidden. You will convert them to wrapped functions, which will not be legible.

Our original f_mask function, shown in Listings 11-18 through 11-21, takes the clear text connection strings list in the form of a RAW. It also takes the class name and version of the application inner class. It returns an encrypted RAW holding the list of connection strings.

Listing 11-18. Signature of Function to Encrypt Data for Storage

```
CREATE OR REPLACE FUNCTION appsec.f_mask(
    clear_raw        RAW,
    m_class_name     v_app_conn_registry.class_name%TYPE,
    m_class_version  v_app_conn_registry.class_version%TYPE )
RETURN RAW
```

We hard-code a specific key_version number of the genesis key bytes—version 4 in this instance (see Listing 11-19). This is a rather random decision on our part. We select the key_bytes for that version from v_application_key. We get the key_bytes into a variable named app_key.

Listing 11-19. Hard-Code Key Version

```
AS
    crypt_raw RAW(32767) := NULL;
    app_ver    v_application_key.key_version%TYPE := 4;
    app_key    v_application_key.key_bytes%TYPE;
    iv         RAW(16);
BEGIN
    SELECT key_bytes INTO app_key FROM v_application_key WHERE key_version = app_ver;
```

app_key is like the cup with the marble under it in that three-cups concentration betting game. The code is quicker than the eye. We are going to process the bytes of the app_key. The first process we perform is to take the class_version and concatenate with the string "SufficientLength". Then, as shown in Listing 11-20, we XOR the app_key with that concatenated string. Perhaps only the first 20 or so bytes of app_key are modified by XOR.

Note We have just made this process unique to the specific version of the specific application (the one presenting the inner class).

Listing 11-20. XOR the Key with the Class Version and Get MD5 Hash of Key

```
app_key := SYS.UTL_RAW.BIT_XOR( app_key,
    SYS.UTL_RAW.CAST_TO_RAW(m_class_version||'SufficientLength') );
app_key := SYS.DBMS_CRYPTO.HASH( app_key, SYS.DBMS_CRYPTO.HASH_MD5 );
app_key := SYS.UTL_RAW.CONCAT( app_key, app_key );
```

Our next process sets app_key equal to the Message Digest (MD5) hash of app_key. Listing 11-20 shows this. MD5 is a one-way hash algorithm that creates a 16-byte (128-bit) hash representing the initial value. Any modification to the initial value will cause the hash to change, and if the initial value doesn't change, MD5 will always calculate the same hash. Then, to get 32-byte key, we set app_key equal to the concatenation of two of the MD5 hashes.

For the encryption algorithm we will be using, we will also need a 16-byte RAW initialization vector (IV). We are going again to make this function *specific to the application* by using the application inner class name as part of the IV. See Listing 11-21. Actually, we concatenate the class_name with the string "SufficientLength," cast that to a RAW, and get the first 16 bytes as the IV.

Listing 11-21. Get Initialization Vector with Class Name and Call DBMS_CRYPTO.ENCRYPT

```
iv := SYS.UTL_RAW.SUBSTR(
    SYS.UTL_RAW.CAST_TO_RAW(m_class_name||'SufficientLength'), 0, 16 );
crypt_raw := SYS.DBMS_CRYPTO.ENCRYPT( clear_raw,
    SYS.DBMS_CRYPTO.ENCRYPT_AES256 + SYS.DBMS_CRYPTO.CHAIN_CBC +
    SYS.DBMS_CRYPTO.PAD_PKCS5, app_key, iv );
RETURN crypt_raw;
END f_mask;
```

Then it's just a matter of calling the DBMS_CRYPTO.ENCRYPT function as in Listing 11-21. We pass our clear text connection string list clear_raw, the app_key and the iv. We also tell the function to use 256-bit Advanced Encryption Standard (AES256) with Block Chaining and PKCS padding.

Ta-da! We have an encrypted list of connection strings that we can trust for storage on disk and in backup. Our f_unmask function that decrypts the data is almost identical to f_mask. We build the app_key and iv in the very same way, then pass the encrypted connection string list to the DBMS_CRYPTO.DECRYPT function, using the same encryption algorithm series. Voila, we have our clear text connection strings back from cold storage.

Wrap Utility

Oracle Corporation has been in the business of protecting its intellectual property for decades. The company has developed a process whereby it can publish business-sensitive PL/SQL code, much like our Oracle procedures, functions, and packages, and distribute it to customers without exposing the inner workings of the code. Oracle devised the wrap utility, which will obfuscate PL/SQL code so that it can't be read. I should only say that wrapped procedures cannot be read without some effort, because there are purported to be tools that will unwrap procedures.

We will use the wrap utility to obfuscate the f_mask and f_unmask functions. As a reminder, you should first modify f_mask and f_unmask so that they are unique to your company, then wrap them. That is to avoid the obvious loose lips of this book from sinking your ship.

Save a copy of your *F_MASK.sql* and *F_UNMASK.sql* files in a secure location, then pass the files to the wrap utility. The wrapped files will have a ".plb" extension, and are viewable in any text editor— they are not binary code. The resulting Oracle 11g wrapped procedure will always resemble Listing 11-22.

```
%ORACLE_HOME%\BIN\wrap INAME=F_MASK.sql
%ORACLE_HOME%\BIN\wrap INAME=F_UNMASK.sql
```

Listing 11-22. *Wrapped Version of Mask Function*

```
CREATE OR REPLACE FUNCTION appsec.f_mask wrapped
a000000
b2
abcd
abcd
abcd
abcd
abcd
abcd
abcd
abcd
abcd
abcd
abcd
abcd
abcd
abcd
abcd
abcd
8
3d9 237
GehnTGWDxAhWnsVg2jYOTJ2/sF4wg/BeTCCsfI5VgpOGvFbmFJFF9PpfKGM8NUbmI21KsMmT
9YLZz1gSTsZkw/skypO3G2z+bhL/AGJObl6IY3bf/PjNwdlhZ5argmaJytVXORDALqjMIRvj
```

GLdGjZoM6cJZs4nHbLQMRgmOh9ZTnOnUOfQMGOvDHhtBLOCZSmx1ROSWpFQ2OIui96EL3CD4
...
1atpfb/f+oVZAZkY78TOYBdSmyOSgifZtmOIiEdc5rh/Lbn5pmTzHV8=

/

Notice the first line of the wrapped procedure is a CREATE OR REPLACE statement. We can copy and paste this code to any SQL editor, like SQL*Plus, and create the Oracle structure in the database.

I know there is a lot going on, so let me reiterate our goal. In wrapping these functions, our intent is to keep folks, whether hackers or just snoopers, from knowing how we encrypted the list of connection strings, and from being able to independently decrypt the strings and read them.

Changes to setDecryptConns()/getCryptConns()

In the middle of the setDecryptConns() method that runs as a Java stored procedure, we take the list of connection strings that we are about to store in Oracle database, and we pass them to the f_mask function. Listing 11-23 shows this. The encrypted bytes that are returned from f_mask are then stored in the database.

Listing 11-23. Call to Encrypt Connection Strings for Storage

```
stmt = ( OracleCallableStatement )conn.prepareCall(
    "{? = call appsec.f_mask(?,?,?)}" );
stmt.registerOutParameter( 1, OracleTypes.RAW );
stmt.setBytes(  2, connsHashBytes );
stmt.setString( 3, className );
stmt.setString( 4, classVersion );
stmt.executeUpdate();
connsHashBytes = stmt.getBytes(1);
```

▪ **Note** This code can be found in *Chapter11/orajavsec/OracleJavaSecure.java.*

We also modify the getCryptConns() method to decrypt the list of connection strings before we return them to the client application. This is shown in Listing 11-24.

Listing 11-24. Call to Decrypt Connection Strings from Storage

```
bA = stmt.getBytes(4);
stmt = ( OracleCallableStatement )conn.prepareCall(
    "{? = call appsec.f_unmask(?,?,?)}" );
stmt.registerOutParameter( 1, OracleTypes.RAW );
stmt.setBytes(  2, bA );
stmt.setString( 3, className );
stmt.setString( 4, classVersion );
stmt.executeUpdate();

oins = new ObjectInputStream( new ByteArrayInputStream(
```

```
        stmt.getBytes(1) ) );
    Object currentConns = oins.readObject();
```

Manage Connection Strings for Applications

We have already seen, and have been using the functionality to add and update connection strings in our list, and to save them in Oracle database. Recall that those are two separate steps. The first step, adding or updating connection strings in our list, happens on the client and only affects the list currently being used by the client application. It is only when we save the list to Oracle database that we make the new or replacement connection string available to all future application users.

In the same way, we will need to remove connection strings from the list. Again, we will make the removal permanent by saving the list to Oracle database in a separate step.

Finally, we will want to be able to replicate the list of connection strings for use by a new version of our application. This replication process must be application-specific, so a poser application can't grab our list of connection strings for her illicit use.

Be forewarned that anyone who gains access to the application security, appsec user has access to copy connection strings from one application to another. Fortunately, we have taken care of that issue by making the f_mask and f_unmask functions both application and version specific. Another application may lay hold of our list of connection strings, but they won't be able to decrypt them. That means, though, that when we replicate our list of connection strings to a new version of the application, we will have to f_unmask them with the old version and f_mask them with the new version.

Create an Application Administrative User

Up to this point, we have described an application user named OSUSER whom I suggested was probably you (your OS user ID). This is an ordinary application user who was granted access to see sensitive data in the HR schema by way of having been granted CONNECT THROUGH appusr.

Now it has come time for us to differentiate between regular application users and administrative application users. We need a second user, whom I am going to call OSADMIN. The difference between these users will come in the next section through a single role grant. The reason for that additional role will be to manage the update of connection string lists for applications on the Oracle database.

For now, let's create a second application user. First of all, you will need to have an additional OS user account named osadmin in our example. As a Windows administrative user, you can create that account through the Control Panel/User Accounts utility. Once that exists, run the commands in Listing 11-25 to create the OSADMIN user (substitute the OS user ID of the OS user you just created) and grant him the same access to sensitive data in the HR schema that we have given to OSUSER. We do this so we can test just the difference that is made by the new administrative role.

Listing 11-25. Create the OSADMIN Oracle User

```
CREATE USER osadmin IDENTIFIED EXTERNALLY;
GRANT create_session_role TO osadmin;
ALTER USER osadmin GRANT CONNECT THROUGH appusr;


INSERT INTO hr.employees
    (EMPLOYEE_ID, FIRST_NAME, LAST_NAME, EMAIL, PHONE_NUMBER, HIRE_DATE,
    JOB_ID, SALARY, COMMISSION_PCT, MANAGER_ID, DEPARTMENT_ID)
VALUES
    (EMPLOYEES_SEQ.NEXTVAL, 'First', 'Last', 'OSADMIN.MAIL',
```

```
    '800.555.1212', SYSDATE, 'SA_REP', 5000, 0.20, 147, 80);

COMMIT;

SELECT EMPLOYEE_ID FROM EMPLOYEES WHERE EMAIL='OSADMIN.MAIL';

INSERT INTO hr.v_emp_mobile_nos
    ( employee_id, user_id, com_pager_no, sms_phone_no, sms_carrier_cd )
    VALUES ( (SELECT EMPLOYEE_ID FROM EMPLOYEES WHERE EMAIL='OSADMIN.MAIL'),
      'OSADMIN', '12345', '8005551212', 'Verizon' );

COMMIT;

SELECT * FROM hr.v_emp_mobile_nos WHERE user_id = 'OSADMIN';
```

The significant aspects of this code are as follows:

1. We create an Oracle user by the same name as our new OS user ID.

2. We grant the new user permission to CONNECT THROUGH appusr so that he can select encrypted sensitive data from the HR schema.

3. We insert a record for this user in the HR.EMPLOYEES table and get the next sequential value from EMPLOYEES_SEQ as the new EMPLOYEE_ID.

4. We can select the new user based on EMAIL address, which is a unique field.

5. Using that selection (for simplicity here), we can insert a matching record into hr.v_emp_mobile_nos with the user_id field set to the new OS user ID.

6. We finish by selecting the record we just created from hr.v_emp_mobile_nos.

We require the records for this user in the EMPLOYEES table and the hr.v_emp_mobile_nos view so that we can accomplish two-factor authentication for this user. Our administrative users will have to accomplish both SSO and two-factor authentication, just like every other user.

Create an Administrative Role for Application Verification

So far, we have allowed any successful application user to both insert and update the list of connection strings and store them in Oracle database for the application. Let's tighten up that process by creating an Oracle role that is required in order to administer the lists of connection strings for applications. We will use the application verification administrator, appver_admin role for this duty. As SYS, execute these commands.

```
CREATE ROLE appver_admin NOT IDENTIFIED;
```

Still, any user can manage her own copy of the connection strings in the local instance of the client application (we give users that freedom), but inserting, updating, or replicating the connection strings in Oracle database will require preapproval. We will preapprove certain persons, via the user IDs they have in the operating system that is SSO'd to Oracle database. To those user IDs, we will grant our new administrative role. It is a default role for that person.

```
GRANT appver_admin TO osadmin;
```

In order to put that role to work, we will categorize a certain set of the appver functions and procedures as being for use only by appver_admin. We place those functions and procedures in a package, appsec_admin_pkg, and grant execute on the package only to appver_admin. This command can be run as either SYS or appsec user.

```
GRANT EXECUTE ON appsec.appsec_admin_pkg TO appver_admin;
```

We have one existing function, f_set_decrypt_conns that we will move from appsec_public_pkg to this new package. No longer will just any application user be able to insert or update lists of connection strings for an application. Only users with the appver_admin role will.

Delete Connection Strings

Deleting a connection string from the list is a task we accomplish in the local client application. We simply formulate the key of the connection string value that we plan to remove, and then remove the entry from connsHash. Use the removeAppConnString() method, shown in Listing 11-26.

Listing 11-26. Remove Connection String from List, removeAppConnString()

```java
private static void removeAppConnString()( String instance, String user ) {
    instance = instance.trim();
    user = user.trim();
    String key = (instance + "/" + user).toUpperCase();
    connsHash.remove( key );
}
```

In order to make the change permanent for all future users of the application, we need to save the list to the Oracle Database. This is done by calling putAppConnections(), which we studied in Chapter 10 (see Listing 10-24).

Copy Connection Strings from Previous Version of Application

When the developer releases a new version of her application, she will want to use most of the same connection strings as the old version. If she kept her inner class version number/name the same, then she wouldn't need to worry about replicating connection strings; she would just continue using the existing list. However, it may be that she will want a new version of her inner class, and hence a new list of connection strings, for one of the following reasons:

- To modify the list of connection strings for the new version.

- To eventually disable the old version of her application by deleting the list of connection strings associated with it.

If her application only used a single Oracle connection or possibly two, it would be no problem rebuilding the list from scratch for the new version. However, if the application has many potential connections from which it may draw data, then the ability to replicate connection strings from one version of her application to the next will be a welcome feature.

Application Client Call to Copy List of Connection Strings

From the client application, we will call a new method in OracleJavaSecure, copyAppConnections(). It takes one parameter, the old inner class version name. When the current (new) inner class is evaluated on the Oracle database, we will be able to determine the new version right from the inner class.

We model copyAppConnections() on a method we have already examined, putAppConnections(). Our new method calls the Oracle procedure, appsec_admin_pkg.p_copy_app_conns, passing the application inner class and the old version name. In this case, we do not pass the connsHash list of connection strings—it is obviously not needed.

It will be a rare event when we call our procedure, p_copy_app_conns, to copy an application's connection strings list from one version of the inner class to the next version. We wouldn't create a new version of our inner class each time we update the application; only when we want to retire a previous version of the application, when our changes make a previous version of an application either dysfunctional or unacceptable.

We call p_copy_app_conns with an instance of our new version of the application inner class. We also designate the old version name so we know from where to get our connection strings. This procedure, in Listing 11-27, bears strong resemblance to various procedures we've examined before. We assure SSO and 2-factor authentication, before moving on.

If this connection is acceptable, then we call the function, f_copy_conns, which accomplishes the duplication of the list of connection, strings to the new version.

Listing 11-27. Copy List of Connection Strings to New Version, p_copy_app_conns

```
PROCEDURE p_copy_app_conns(
    m_two_factor_cd       v_two_fact_cd_cache.two_factor_cd%TYPE,
    m_class_instance      v_app_conn_registry.class_instance%TYPE,
    m_prev_version        v_app_conn_registry.class_version%TYPE,
    m_application_id      v_two_fact_cd_cache.application_id%TYPE,
    m_err_no        OUT NUMBER,
    m_err_txt       OUT VARCHAR2 )
IS
    return_user VARCHAR2(40);
    m_app_user  v_application_registry.app_user%TYPE := 'APPVER';
BEGIN
    m_err_no := 0;
    return_user := f_is_sso( m_app_user );
    IF( return_user IS NOT NULL )
    THEN
        IF( m_two_factor_cd IS NULL )
        THEN
            m_err_txt := appsec_only_pkg.f_send_2_factor(return_user, m_application_id);
        ELSIF( appsec_only_pkg.f_is_cur_cached_cd( return_user, m_application_id,
            m_two_factor_cd ) = 'Y' )
        THEN
            -- Reuse existing VARCHAR2, RETURN_USER
            return_user :=appsec_only_pkg.f_copy_conns(m_class_instance,m_prev_version);
        ELSE
            -- Wrong 2-Factor code entered
            RAISE NO_DATA_FOUND;
        END IF;
        app_sec_pkg.p_log_error( 0, 'Success copying App Conns, ' || return_user );
```

```
        ELSE
            app_sec_pkg.p_log_error( 0, 'Problem copying App Conns, ' || return_user );
        END IF;
-- Raise Exceptions
EXCEPTION
    WHEN OTHERS THEN
        m_err_no := SQLCODE;
        m_err_txt := SQLERRM;
        app_sec_pkg.p_log_error( m_err_no, m_err_txt,
            'p_copy_app_conns' );
END p_copy_app_conns;
```

Java Stored Procedure to Copy Connection Strings

Once again, we call an Oracle stored function, which is really just a wrapper for a method written in Java that will accomplish the task. This function, f_copy_conns in Listing 11-28 calls the copyPreviousConns() method.

Listing 11-28. Java Stored Procedure to Copy Connection Strings, f_copy_conns

```
FUNCTION f_copy_conns( class_instance RAW, class_version VARCHAR2 )
RETURN VARCHAR2
AS LANGUAGE JAVA
NAME 'orajavsec.OracleJavaSecure.copyPreviousConns( oracle.sql.RAW, java.lang.String )
return java.lang.String';
```

Database Java Method to Copy Connection Strings

copyPreviousConns() is perhaps the most complex method we will study; however, it is only complex in managing multiple versions of our application at once, not in the process. We are going to be performing steps that we have accomplished in other methods that we have examined. Here, though, we will go back and forth between the new and old versions of the inner class.

Our first step is to get the current inner class name and version number (shown in Listing 11-29) directly from the inner class, classInstance RAW parameter. We do this by getting the bytes of the RAW and pushing them through a ByteArrayInputStream, then through an ObjectInputStream, from which we read an Object as the providedClass member. From that Object, we can read the name into the className member. We can also get the getRevLvl() method and read the revision level into the classVersion member.

Listing 11-29. Get New Class Version and Name

```
byte[] appClassBytes = classInstance.getBytes();
ByteArrayInputStream bAIS = new ByteArrayInputStream( appClassBytes );
ObjectInputStream oins =
    new ObjectInputStream( bAIS );
Object classObject = oins.readObject();
oins.close();
Class providedClass = classObject.getClass();
```

```
String className = providedClass.getName();
Method classMethod = providedClass.getMethod( "getRevLvl" );
String classVersion = ( String )classMethod.invoke( classObject );
```

Next, we want to get an idea of how this is going to go. Do we really have anything to copy? We get the list of connection strings using the current inner class name, which we just got from the Object, and using the previous version name that was passed here in the prevVersion parameter. (See Listing 11-30.) By passing those arguments (1 and 2) to the stored procedure p_get_class_conns, we can get back the list of connection strings (OUT parameter 4) for the previous version of our inner class (OUT parameter 3). If we get a null back for our previous inner class, then there is nothing to copy, so we return.

Listing 11-30. Select Connection Strings for Previous Version

```
stmt = ( OracleCallableStatement )conn.prepareCall(
    "CALL appsec.appsec_only_pkg.p_get_class_conns(?,?,?,?)" );
stmt.registerOutParameter( 3, OracleTypes.RAW );
stmt.registerOutParameter( 4, OracleTypes.BLOB );
stmt.setString( 1, className );
stmt.setString( 2, prevVersion );
stmt.setNull(   3, OracleTypes.RAW );
stmt.setNull(   4, OracleTypes.BLOB );
stmt.executeUpdate();
if( null == stmt.getBytes( 3 ) ) return "Nothing to copy";
```

Listing 11-31 shows another application of our new f_unmask Oracle stored function. Now that we are encrypting the connection strings as we store them on disk, we need to also decrypt them as we read them from storage.

Listing 11-31. Decrypt Connection Strings from Previous Version

```
byte[] prevConnsBytes = stmt.getBytes(4);
stmt = ( OracleCallableStatement )conn.prepareCall(
    "{? = call appsec.f_unmask(?,?,?)}" );
stmt.registerOutParameter( 1, OracleTypes.RAW );
stmt.setBytes(   2, prevConnsBytes );
stmt.setString( 3, className );
stmt.setString( 4, prevVersion );
stmt.executeUpdate();
```

```
prevConnsBytes = stmt.getBytes(1);
```

We read the decrypted bytes for our list of application connection strings, but we do not need to assemble a HashMap object to represent the list; rather, we will be storing the byte array as-is for the new version.

However, before we proceed to copy our list of connection strings to the new version, we will assure we are not overwriting an existing list. We will call the p_count_class_conns procedure for the current inner class name and version to see if an entry exists in the database (see Listing 11-32). If none exists, then we are okay to insert; otherwise, we need to examine the list of connection strings that exists for the new version of the application.

Listing 11-32. Count Connection Strings Stored for Current Version

```
stmt = ( OracleCallableStatement )conn.prepareCall(
    "CALL appsec.appsec_only_pkg.p_count_class_conns(?,?,?)" );
stmt.registerOutParameter( 3, OracleTypes.NUMBER );
stmt.setString( 1, className );
stmt.setString( 2, classVersion );
stmt.setInt(    3, 0 );
stmt.executeUpdate();
boolean okToOverwrite = false;
if( stmt.getInt( 3 ) == 0 ) {
    // Do insert!
    okToOverwrite = true;
} else {
```

If an entry exists in the database, we will assure that the inner class instance that we provided as an argument to this method is the same as what is stored. We do this by simply getting an object from the stored bytes based on the current class name and version (see Listing 11-33). Recall that the Java class loader cannot load two substantially different classes by the same name; a runtime exception would be thrown.

Listing 11-33. Get Connection Strings and Class Stored for Current Version

```
stmt = ( OracleCallableStatement )conn.prepareCall(
    "CALL appsec.appsec_only_pkg.p_get_class_conns(?,?,?,?)" );
stmt.registerOutParameter( 3, OracleTypes.RAW );
stmt.registerOutParameter( 4, OracleTypes.BLOB );
stmt.setString( 1, className );
stmt.setString( 2, classVersion );
stmt.setNull(   3, OracleTypes.RAW );
stmt.setNull(   4, OracleTypes.BLOB );
stmt.executeUpdate();

byte[] cachedBytes = stmt.getBytes(3);
oins = new ObjectInputStream( new ByteArrayInputStream(
    cachedBytes ) );
classObject = oins.readObject();
oins.close();
```

When we read the object from the ObjectInputStream, it had better be identical to the object we passed as the classInstance argument to this method; otherwise an InvalidClassException will be thrown. For good measure, we get a class instance from the object and test to see if it is equal to the class we got earlier in Listing 11-34. If it's not, we would have already failed (unless the inner class name is different, in which case it shouldn't be stored in the database with this name).

Listing 11-34. Test Stored Class and Connection Strings

```
Class testClass = classObject.getClass();

if( testClass != providedClass )

    return "Failed to setDecryptConns";
```

```
if( null == stmt.getBytes(4) ) okToOverwrite = true;
else {
```

It could be that we stored an entry for this inner class, but stored a null for the associated list of connection strings. Listing 11-34 tests this. If the connection strings are null, we can overwrite this entry.

It is more likely that an empty HashMap was stored for this new inner class version as a placeholder. We can test this by getting the list of connection strings and reading it to see if there are any entries in the list. But first, we revisit our new f_unmask function to decrypt the connection strings list that we read from storage for the current class name and version, as shown in Listing 11-35.

Listing 11-35. Decrypt Stored Connection Strings List for Current Version

```
byte[] connsBytes = stmt.getBytes(4);
stmt = ( OracleCallableStatement )conn.prepareCall(
    "{? = call appsec.f_unmask(?,?,?)}" );
stmt.registerOutParameter( 1, OracleTypes.RAW );
stmt.setBytes(  2, connsBytes );
stmt.setString( 3, className );
stmt.setString( 4, classVersion );
stmt.executeUpdate();
```

Create an object from the decrypted list of connection strings and cast it as a HashMap. Next, test the size of the HashMap. If the size is zero, we can overwrite this entry; however, if it is not empty, we return without copying the old version connection strings to the new version. See Listing 11-36.

Listing 11-36. Test if Stored Connection Strings List is Empty

```
        oins = new ObjectInputStream( new ByteArrayInputStream(
            stmt.getBytes(1) ) );
        Object currentConns = oins.readObject();
        oins.close();
        HashMap<String, String> currConnsHash =
            (HashMap<String, String>)currentConns;
        if( 0 == currConnsHash.size() ) okToOverwrite = true;
    }
}
if( ! okToOverwrite ) return "Current connsHash is not empty!";
```

If we have gotten this far, then either there was no entry in v_app_conn_registry for the current (new) version of the application inner class, or the associated list of connection strings was null or empty. So we are free to copy the old connection strings to the new version. But first, we will encrypt them as in Listing 11-37, specifically for the new version, by calling our new f_mask function.

Listing 11-37. Encrypt Old Connection Strings List for New Version Before Storing

```
stmt = ( OracleCallableStatement )conn.prepareCall(
    "{? = call appsec.f_mask(?,?,?)}" );
stmt.registerOutParameter( 1, OracleTypes.RAW );
stmt.setBytes(  2, prevConnsBytes );
stmt.setString( 3, className );
stmt.setString( 4, classVersion );
stmt.executeUpdate();
```

```
prevConnsBytes = stmt.getBytes(1);
```

Now we store the encrypted list of connection strings for the new inner class version by calling the p_set_class_conns procedure. Listing 11-38 shows that call.

Listing 11-38. Store Encrypted Connection Strings List for New Version

```
stmt = ( OracleCallableStatement )conn.prepareCall(
    "CALL appsec.appsec_only_pkg.p_set_class_conns(?,?,?,?)" );
stmt.setString( 1, className );
stmt.setString( 2, classVersion );
stmt.setBytes(  3, appClassBytes );
stmt.setBytes(  4, prevConnsBytes );
stmt.executeUpdate();
```

Figure 11-1 illustrates the process of copying connection strings from a previous version of an application to the new, current version. The only item in the diagram that I want to mention is the first call to Oracle database, the p_copy_app_conns procedure. That procedure is in the appsec_admin_pkg package and can only be execute by users who have been granted the appver_admin role.

Application	OracleJavaSecure	Oracle Database	Oracle JVM	Oracle Database

(app ID, app class, 2-factor cd)
------ ------ ------> setAppContext()
       | checkFormat2Factor()

(prev version)
------ ------ ------> copyAppConnections()
    | (prev version, app ID, app class, 2-factor cd)
    | ------ ------ ------> p_copy_app_conns
       | ("appver")
       | f_is_sso

       | (user, app ID)
       | f_send_2_factor • distribute2Factor()
    <------ ------ ------ ------ ------ ------ -------- (distrib code)

           OR

       | (user, app ID, 2-factor cd)
       | f_is_cur_cached_cd
       | (pub key mod & exp)
       | (prev version, app class)
       | f_copy_conns • copyPreviousConns()
                    | (new app class)
                    | {get class name and version}
                    | (app class name, ver)
                    | ------ ------ ------ ------> p_get_class_conns
                    | <----- ------ ------ ------
                          (prev list conn strings - encoded)
                    | (prev conn strings)
                    | ------ ------ ------ ------> f_unmask
                    | <----- ------ ------ ------
                          (decoded prev conn strings)
                    | (app class name, ver)
                    | ------ ------ ------ ------> p_count_class_conns
                    | <----- ------ ------ ------ (count)
                    | 0 OK overwrite
                    | else (app class name, ver)
                    | ------ ------ ------ ------> p_get_class_conns
                    | <----- ------ ------ ------
                          (app class, list conn strings)
                    | ?new app class = app class
                    | list conn strings null, OK overwrite
                    | else
                    | (conns bytes, name version)
                    | ------ ------ ------ ------> f_unmask
                    | <----- ------ ------ ------
                          (decoded prev conn strings)
                    | ?conns list size = 0, OK overwrite
                    | if not OK overwrite, return error message
                    | else OK overwrite
                    | (prev conn strings, name, version)
                    | ------ ------ ------ ------> f_unmask
                    | <----- ------ ------ ------ (conns bytes)
                    | (app class name, ver, app class, bytes)
                    | ------ ------ ------ ------> p_set_class_conns
                      {select count}
                      {insert or update}

Figure 11-1. Copying application connection strings to a new version

300

Add Other Authentication Credentials

We are not limited to storing only Oracle connection strings in v_app_conn_registry. Recall that the HashMap is simply a list of string keys and associated string values. Once you get the HashMap back to your application, you can request a specific value based on any key you please.

Of course you could store connection strings or at least passwords for connections to non-Oracle databases. You might also store such things as passwords for secure FTP connections. Our current methods in OracleJavaSecure are tailored for storing Oracle connection strings, but you could add a method for storing, for example, secure FTP passwords. Listing 11-39 shows a sample method you might employ.

Listing 11-39. Example Method for Storing Other (FTP) Credentials

```
public static void putAppFTPString( String key, String password ) {
    appAuthCipherDES.init( Cipher.ENCRYPT_MODE,
        appAuthSessionSecretDESKey, appAuthParamSpec );
    byte[] bA = appAuthCipherDES.doFinal(password.getBytes() );
    connsHash.put( "FTP" + key, new RAW( bA ) );
}
```

For security purposes, you would want to devise your method (as shown) to prepend the key with the string "FTP" or something. We would use this as a filter to keep this method from decrypting non-FTP entries in the connsHash list. Listing 11-40 provides an example method for getting FTP passwords from connsHash.

Listing 11-40. Example Method for Retrieving Other (FTP) Credentials

```
private static String getAppFTPString( String key ) {
    return new String(
        appAuthCipherDES.doFinal( connsHash.get( "FTP" + key ).getBytes() ) );
}
```

Notice that this method is designated as private—you would want another method in OracleJavaSecure that establishes the FTP connection and returns the connection to the client application, rather than returning the clear text FTP password to the application. We do not want to give our passwords to applications.

Update Application Security Structures

Before moving on to new topics, please run all the commands and scripts that we have described thus far. At a SQL*Plus prompt or other SQL client, as SYS user, run the commands in *Chapter11/Sys.sql*. Substitute the name of an OS user who will be doing administrative tasks (you?) in the GRANT appver_admin command.

Then, as the application security, appsec user, run the commands in *Chapter11/AppSec.sql*. That should be easy. Additionally, execute the code from *Chapter11/F_MASK.plb* and *Chapter11/F_UNMASK.plb* (the masked versions).

Still as appsec user, remove the comment from the first line, CREATE OR REPLACE AND RESOLVE JAVA in *Chapter11/orajavsec/OJSC.java* (the obfuscated version) and execute that as SQL code. And finally, uncomment the first line of *Chapter11/orajavsec/OracleJavaSecure.java* and edit the expectedDomain and URL strings at the top of the code. Remove the passwords from the main() method, at the bottom. Then execute that as SQL code. Recall, you may have to SET DEFINE OFF to keep from being prompted for variable substitution at each & symbol in the code.

Authenticate on a Separate Oracle Instance

I'm going to describe something now that reveals the extent to which we might want to pursue security. What if we segregated the application verification tasks from the actual application data? What security would that buy us? The primary benefits we will achieve are the following:

- Fewer accounts with passwords, so fewer accounts to attack

- Reduced ancillary functions (fewer optional database programs), so reduced vulnerabilities

- Ability to revoke some PUBLIC access to particularly revealing data dictionary views without hampering database development

- A first database hurdle for hackers to overcome before sensitive data in the second database can be pursued by attack

In this section, we will create a new database instance, perhaps on the same server. This instance will have sufficient privileges to accomplish application verification, but no more. In order to ensure that, we will not create the privileged roles that we have discussed, secadm_role and app_sec_role; rather, we will do all our configuration steps as the SYS user.

▪ **Caution** If you do not intend to create an additional database instance for application verification, then do not issue any of the commands in this section. You can skip down to *Test Enhanced Security*; however, to learn about creating and hardening an Oracle database instance and about database links, read through this section in any case.

What about our application verification, appver user password? Is it still susceptible to snooping? Well, it isn't encrypted, and it could be recovered by anyone diligent enough to reconstruct our obfuscated OJSCode class. So the question we need to ask is what is our security exposure from having that password revealed.

We might pat ourselves on the back and say that we've got it covered with our login trigger, t_screen_appver_access, on the appver schema that calls the p_appver_logon stored procedure. And we might smirk and scoff at those who think they can get by the SSO proxy requirements, and down the road our two-factor authentication, encryption key exchange, and application verification process.

However, in the back of our minds, we realize that a hacker having a password to an account on a production Oracle database must be a bad thing. And the back of our minds would be correct. Even if there is nothing else that the account has access to, there is still PUBLIC data, and that data can be revealing. From standard PUBLIC access, a hacker can learn all the users of the database, setting him up to conduct a social engineering attack. The hacker can also see all the code of any procedures and Java that is granted to PUBLIC, and he can see the logic that is contained in triggers and views. PUBLIC grants provide an entrée into the database for every user account.

I believe that the Oracle Corporation could make a sweeping change to the database that would improve security. The sweeping change would be to make PUBLIC a regular role. Perhaps the PUBLIC role would be granted by default and additionally not lost when a user does a SET ROLE. However, PUBLIC would not be whatever it is now. Currently, when access is granted to PUBLIC, it is like saying that no grants are required. We cannot revoke PUBLIC from users. Every Oracle user always has PUBLIC access.

I can see how the use of PUBLIC is like making certain things a part of an Oracle user's identity. Maybe what I'm really shooting for is an almost-PUBLIC role that Oracle database could grant as a default and that would not get removed when a user does SET ROLE. At database install, some or most of the things that are normally granted to PUBLIC (anything that is not strictly required for logon and select) could be granted to almost-PUBLIC. Then for restricted users, we could revoke the almost-PUBLIC role.

Have I gone off the deep end? Well let's take a look. First, select from a public view to see all the users in the database:

```
SELECT * FROM ALL_USERS;
```

By listing all the database users, an attacker has multiple opportunities to try password guessing, or perhaps finds multiple individuals to contact in an attempt to do a social engineering attack. I'd like to turn off access to that PUBLIC view.

What if we'd like to know the names of all the Oracle procedures that are used by the application security, appsec user? We could query the ALL_PROCEDURES PUBLIC view:

```
SELECT * FROM ALL_PROCEDURES WHERE OWNER = 'APPSEC';
```

Now let's view the code for one of those procedures, p_check_role_access by querying the ALL_SOURCE PUBLIC view:

```
SELECT * FROM ALL_SOURCE WHERE OWNER = 'APPSEC' AND NAME = 'P_CHECK_ROLE_ACCESS';
```

Granted, the user can only see the source of procedures that have been granted to PUBLIC, but is that source really something the user needs to see? We shall see that it is not.

Create a New Oracle Database Instance

We need about 2 GB of space on the hard drive to create a sufficiently large database to hold just what we need to do application verification. "Why that much?" you might ask. Remember that to do application verification we need a basic Oracle database, and we need the data dictionary views, and we need to run PL/SQL, and we need to run Java. On top of that, for two-factor authentication, we need to send e-mail, and we need configure system privileges to read data across the network (URLs). All of these functions require space.

We will call our new database instance apver (notice it is like the appver user name, except with only one "P"). We need an initialization/parameter configuration file in order to build our new database instance. If you are creating the apver instance on a server that already has an installed instance, e.g., ORCL, then you can copy some files that will be helpful. One of those files is called *init.ora*. Change directory to where these files reside, outside your server Oracle home directory:

```
D:
cd \app\oracle\admin
```

Copy the entire *orcl* directory to a new directory named *apver*. This command will copy the directory and all the contents.

```
xcopy orcl apver /ei
```

Now change directory to the new parameters file, *pfile* directory and rename the existing *init.ora* file template to *init.ora*. Then edit the *init.ora* file.

```
cd \app\oracle\admin\apver\pfile
ren init.ora.* init.ora
edit init.ora
```

Search and replace the following strings:

```
Replace         With
=======         ====
=orcl           =apver
\orcl           \apver
```

Your final file should have parameters like those in Listing 11-41. Your db_domain and directory names may be different. The local_listener will the same for apver as for the primary database.

Listing 11-41. Initialization File for the apver Instance

```
db_block_size=8192
open_cursors=300
db_domain=org.com
db_name=apver
control_files=("D:\app\oracle\oradata\apver\control01.ctl",
"D:\app\oracle\flash_recovery_area\apver\control02.ctl")
db_recovery_file_dest=D:\app\oracle\flash_recovery_area
db_recovery_file_dest_size=4039114752
compatible=11.2.0.0.0
diagnostic_dest=D:\app\oracle
memory_target=1288699904
local_listener=LISTENER_Orcl
processes=150
audit_file_dest=D:\app\oracle\admin\apver\adump
audit_trail=db
remote_login_passwordfile=EXCLUSIVE
dispatchers="(PROTOCOL=TCP) (SERVICE=apverXDB)"
undo_tablespace=UNDOTBS1
```

We want to copy this *init.ora* file into its default location. This will come in handy later when we import the parameter settings into a system parameter file. Execute the copy command:

```
copy D:\app\oracle\admin\apver\pfile\init.ora %ORACLE_HOME%\DATABASE\INITAPVER.ORA
```

Create a directory for the secondary control file:

```
mkdir D:\app\oracle\flash_recovery_area\apver
```

Also, let's create a directory for our new instance database files:

```
mkdir D:\app\oracle\oradata\apver
```

Create a New Oracle Service

Each Oracle Database instance is started, usually on system reboot, by a Service. You can see these services in Windows by going to your **Start** menu and running the Computer Management application.

You will need to use system administrator privileges. Go to Services and Applications, then to Services and scroll down to the Oracle services. They are all normally named with the prefix "Oracle," and are sorted alphabetically. We are not going to explore creating, starting or stopping processes on Unix or Linux; the steps are the same, but the commands (Run Command level files) are different.

Because we are not using any Oracle web administrative services for the work covered in this book, all the Oracle services can be set to manual; however, do not do that on a production Oracle database server. Then we can manually start the standard `OracleServiceORCL` service to start the ORCL instance. We also start the standard `OracleOraDb11g_homeTNSListener` service to start the listener. Those 2 Oracle services are all we need. Typically, clients connect over the network to a listener service that then connects them to the database instance.

For the following discussions, we will assume you have set your `ORACLE_HOME` to something like:

```
SET ORACLE_HOME=D:\app\oracle\product\11.2.0\dbhome_1
```

Our new Oracle instance will be named apver, so we can use a command like the following to add a service to start the instance. You need to be working in a Windows command prompt window with administrative privileges, so right click on Command Prompt in your Start menu and select Run as administrator.

```
%ORACLE_HOME%\BIN\oradim -NEW -SID apver -STARTMODE manual
    -PFILE "D:\app\oracle\admin\apver\pfile\init.ora"
```

We also want to set the new service to automatically start the Oracle database process. This is in addition to starting the Service automatically. It is telling the service to issue a `STARTUP` command to the database. We can set the service to `MANUAL` startup later, and when we manually start the service it will automatically start the database.

```
oradim -EDIT -SID apver -STARTMODE AUTO -SRVCSTART SYSTEM
    –PFILE "D:\app\oracle\admin\apver\pfile\init.ora"
```

▨ **Note** We will get an error here about not being able to start the service. That is okay, because we haven't really created the database yet, but now the service to get it started is configured.

Write the Create Database Command

We are going to put our database creation command in a script file named `ApVerDBCreate.sql`. CREATE DATABASE is a single command, but there are many aspects to it, and we don't want to depend on our typing skills to enter everything correctly at the SQL*Plus prompt. Also, we want a script file so we can refer to it if we have any questions about the command we issued.

The first thing I'd like you to notice about our database creation script is that we have not hard-coded passwords for `SYS` and `SYSTEM` (we have commented lines in Listing 11-42, meant to remain commented and unchanged). Those users will be created with the default passwords, "change_on_install" and "manager," respectively. Placing the passwords in this command script is typical, but less secure. It is essential that you change these passwords from the default, but ask yourself this question: will you be more likely to issue an `ALTER USER` command once you log in and continue the installation steps, of which that is step one, or will you remember to go back and edit the database creation script, `ApVerDBCreate.sql`, removing the real passwords from that file? We are going to immediately change the passwords once the database is created, and we will not have to expunge passwords from the script file later on.

Listing 11-42. Create Database Command

```
CREATE DATABASE apver
--USER SYS IDENTIFIED BY password
--USER SYSTEM IDENTIFIED BY password
```

■ **Note** This command is contained in a file named *Chapter11/apver/ApVerDBCreate.sql*.

The next few aspects of the database creation command in Listing 11-43 simply define the redo log files we will be maintaining, and their sizes. These log files will be used in case we need to restore the database from backup, and reapply the transactions that have taken place since the backup, also those that were not applied before a database failure. Ideally, these transaction log files would be on a different hard drive from the database files.

Listing 11-43. Create Database Log Files

```
LOGFILE GROUP 1 ('D:\app\oracle\oradata\apver\REDO01a.log',
    'D:\app\oracle\oradata\apver\REDO01b.log') SIZE 16M,
GROUP 2 ('D:\app\oracle\oradata\apver\REDO02a.log',
    'D:\app\oracle\oradata\apver\REDO02b.log') SIZE 16M,
GROUP 3 ('D:\app\oracle\oradata\apver\REDO03a.log',
    'D:\app\oracle\oradata\apver\REDO03b.log') SIZE 16M
```

After that, our command includes some basic parameters that may suffice, or can be adjusted later. See Listing 11-44.

Listing 11-44. Create Database Configuration

```
MAXINSTANCES 3
MAXLOGFILES 6
MAXLOGMEMBERS 2
MAXLOGHISTORY 1
MAXDATAFILES 10
CHARACTER SET AL32UTF8
NATIONAL CHARACTER SET AL16UTF16
EXTENT MANAGEMENT LOCAL
```

Next, in Listing 11-45, we will define the database files we will use for the apver instance. We define our primary System database file, *SYSTEM01.DBF*, and an Auxiliary System file, *SYSAUX01.DBF*, which is used by some database components that had historically been placed in separate *tablespaces*. Additionally, we create the default tablespace files for USERS, TEMPORARY and UNDO tablespaces. Be sure to give the UNDO tablespace the same name that you gave it in your *init.ora* file, described previously. And with this, we come to the end of our CREATE DATABASE command (note the semicolon).

Listing 11-45. Create Database Files and Tablespaces

```
DATAFILE 'D:\app\oracle\oradata\apver\SYSTEM01.DBF' SIZE 512M REUSE
SYSAUX DATAFILE 'D:\app\oracle\oradata\apver\SYSAUX01.DBF' SIZE 512M REUSE
DEFAULT TABLESPACE users DATAFILE 'D:\app\oracle\oradata\apver\USERS01.DBF'
    SIZE 256M REUSE AUTOEXTEND ON MAXSIZE UNLIMITED
DEFAULT TEMPORARY TABLESPACE tempts1 TEMPFILE 'D:\app\oracle\oradata\apver\TEMP01.DBF'
    SIZE 16M REUSE
UNDO TABLESPACE undotbs1 DATAFILE 'D:\app\oracle\oradata\apver\UNDOTBS01.DBF'
    SIZE 64M REUSE AUTOEXTEND ON MAXSIZE UNLIMITED;
```

Create and Configure the Database

With your configuration and initialization files in place and edited for your unique installation, and with the required directories created, you are ready to create the new database instance, apver. First, let's set our environment to specify the instance we want to deal with to apver. This keeps us from tramping on the parameters and identity of the default database, orcl.

In an administrator command prompt window, set the ORACLE_SID environment variable. This setting will be in effect as long as the command prompt window is open. After it is closed, the setting will go away, so redo this if you need to come back to these procedures in a new command prompt window.

```
SET ORACLE_SID=apver
```

You already created a new Oracle service for the apver instance (it will have a name like OracleServiceapver), and that service should be running. You can check what Oracle services are running from the Services area of the Computer Management Windows program—scroll down to the services that start with "Oracle." All other Oracle services can be stopped and, in fact, it is safer while manually installing a new Oracle instance if you stop all the others.

We are going to run SQL*Plus and basically connect to NO instance (No Login or NOLOG) AS SYSDBA. This is the equivalent to what CONNECT INTERNAL had been in earlier versions of Oracle database. You must be an administrator on the server, or the account that installed Oracle Database, in order to run this CONNECT command.

```
%ORACLE_HOME%\BIN\sqlplus /NOLOG

CONNECT/AS SYSDBA
```

▪ **Note** These commands can be found in the file *Chapter11/apver/ApverSys.sql*

We want to be sure we are working on the apver instance. The CONNECT command should display the message "Connected to an idle instance." If you see the error message "ORA-12560: TNS:protocol adapter error," then your apver instance service is not running. Start it as described previously, using the Services area of the Computer Management program.

If an Oracle database instance is running, the message will simply be "Connected." If you see that message, check what instance you are using with this command:

```
SELECT VALUE FROM V$PARAMETER WHERE NAME = 'db_name';
```

If this shows the instance to be apver, review your progress so far to recall if you've already created the database. If not, just shut down the template apver instance with the shutdown command. (Note that if you stop the service and restart it (or reboot your computer), a template Oracle instance will be started as apver.)

```
SHUTDOWN
```

However, if that SELECT query shows that you are connected to a different instance, you need to stop the Oracle service that runs that instance and assure that your ORACLE_SID environment variable is set to apver.

Continuing on, we will request that messages from our SQL*Plus session be spooled to a log file. We will have to remember to close the spool file before we exit this session of SQL*Plus.

```
SPOOL apver.log
```

Now, we start a database instance defined by the *init.ora* parameters file. There are no database files to mount, in fact we haven't even defined the database files yet, so we say NOMOUNT.

```
STARTUP NOMOUNT PFILE=D:\app\oracle\admin\apver\pfile\init.ora
```

This will show you the System Global Area memory allocation, which is available to Oracle database. It is out of this memory pool that Java resources will be allocated (discussed later).

```
Total System Global Area 2522038272 bytes
```

Now call the script to create our database (modify this command with the path to your command file). This will take a few minutes as the large database files are created. (This is an example of how you call a file with SQL commands from within SQL*Plus; prefix the file name with an at (@) sign.)

```
@Chapter11\apver\ApVerDBCreate.sql;
```

You can examine the existence and sizes of the database files by browsing the directories we created previously: *D:\app\oracle\oradata\apver* and *D:\app\oracle\flash_recovery_area\apver*. If you don't get the "Database created" success message, you may have to delete files in those directories and start over—it is probably a typo in the initialization or command files that you will need to fix.

Change the Passwords for SYS and SYSTEM Users

Even without logging in as a SYS user, we can and must set the passwords for both the SYS and SYSTEM users. Substitute a complex password in each of the following commands:

```
ALTER USER SYS IDENTIFIED BY sys_password;
ALTER USER SYSTEM IDENTIFIED BY system_password;
```

■ **Caution** This is security step one. Do not proceed until you have accomplished this step.

Store Database Parameters in the Database

It is in our best interest to import our parameters settings from init.ora into a server parameter file. This is done through a command on the database.

```
CREATE SPFILE FROM PFILE;
```

This pulls the settings from the *init.ora*, PFILE file in the default location, *%ORACLE_HOME%\DATABASE\INITAPVER.ORA* and places them in a server-formatted (not hand-editable) file that corresponds to this database instance, *SPFILEAPVER.ORA* in the same directory. The main benefit of having our parameter settings in the server parameter file is that they can be dynamically modified by database commands, and the effects occur (often) both in the SPFILE and in the running Oracle instance. Because the SPFILE is modified by those commands, they are retained across Oracle instance restarts and server reboots.

Restart the database to use the new parameter settings. Notice that you don't have to specify the *init.ora* file. This time when we call STARTUP, we will use our newly created server parameter file (SPFILE) and will mount the database files:

```
SPOOL OFF;
SHUTDOWN;
STARTUP;
SPOOL apver2.log;
```

■ **Note** These spool log files will be created in the current directory of your command prompt.

Increase the Quantity of Processes

You may recall seeing in the *init.ora* file a standard setting of 150 processes. That sets a limit on concurrent Oracle connections. We would like to handle a large number of concurrent connections to do application verification. Imagine everyone getting to work on Monday morning and logging into one or more of our secure Oracle applications. We could easily exceed 150 concurrent connections.

Also recall that we configured a special profile for the Application Verification, appver user, appver_prof. For that profile, we set the SESSIONS_PER_USER to be unlimited. However, we made note that the actual limit was controlled by the number of processes. Let's bump up the number of processes.

First connect as SYS, and enter the new SYS password that we just set. You can connect using the TNSlistener service through the first syntax shown in the following, or connect directly to the database as in the second syntax, as long as your ORACLE_SID environment variable is set to apver. In either case, you might want to start the listener service from the Windows Computer Management application.

```
CONNECT SYS@apver AS SYSDBA;
CONNECT SYS AS SYSDBA;
```

We will increase the number of processes for this special-purpose instance, apver to a quantity of 500. Issue the command to set the number of process to 500.

```
ALTER SYSTEM SET PROCESSES=500
    COMMENT='Allow more concurrent Application Verification sessions.'
    SCOPE=SPFILE;
```

We give the scope of the change to be SPFILE, which means that we only change the stored parameter. This is a specific case where we can issue an ALTER SYSTEM database command to modify the SPFILE settings, but we cannot immediately update this parameter (the number of processes) in the running database instance. To realize the increased number of processes, we need to shut down and restart the Oracle database instance.

```
SHUTDOWN IMMEDIATE
STARTUP
```

Now log back in and check the parameter setting for the number of processes:

```
CONNECT SYS@apver AS SYSDBA;
SELECT VALUE FROM V$PARAMETER WHERE NAME = 'processes';
```

Run Oracle Scripts to Add Basic Database Capabilities

When we run the following scripts to add basic database capabilities, we will enter the path to each script at the SQL*Plus command line. For best practices, enter the complete path so that no other/older/alternate script is run by accident.

The first script we will run is one that will build the data dictionary views. We need the ALL_USERS view to do our proxy authentication and SSO. Beyond that, other aspects of running an Oracle database are heavily dependent on the Data dictionary, so we need this.:

```
@D:\app\oracle\product\11.2.0\dbhome_1\RDBMS\ADMIN\catalog.sql
```

Next, we will run the scripts to build the PL/SQL Procedural Option and the SQL*Plus Product User Profile. We need these capabilities in order to configure and run stored procedures and functions. These scripts also create some views in the data dictionary. Note that *catproc.sql* takes a good long while to run. I suggest you get a cup of coffee—that's what I do.

```
@D:\app\oracle\product\11.2.0\dbhome_1\RDBMS\ADMIN\catproc.sql
-- catproc also calls catpexec.sql calls execsec.sql calls
--   secconf.sql, which configures default profile and auditing settings
@D:\app\oracle\product\11.2.0\dbhome_1\sqlplus\ADMIN\pupbld.sql
```

The next script we need to run will build the Extensible Markup Language (XML) Database (XDB). XML is a syntax that permits us to present relational data in a structured text format, and XDB specifically allows Oracle data to be presented and delivered by XML. You might wonder why we need this capability—we don't seem to use XML anywhere in this book. However, we do URL lookups (browse to a web page) to accomplish our two-factor authentication, and granting access to use network ports (DBMS_NETWORK_ACL_ADMIN) is a feature provided when we build XDB. So we need this.

The script to build XDB requires that we pass a number of arguments. The first argument is the SYS user password. After that, we list the user and temporary tablespaces where this script will be applied. And lastly we indicate that we will not (NO) use SECUREFILE Large Objects (lobs) – they are not supported in non-ASSM (Automatic Segment Space Management) tablespaces. We don't need it, but if you want to include ASSM (automatically handles pctused and free lists), then specify SEGMENT SPACE MANAGEMENT AUTO when you create your tablespace, not included here:

```
@D:\app\oracle\product\11.2.0\dbhome_1\RDBMS\ADMIN\catqm.sql sys_password users tempts1 NO
```

Configure Database to Use UTL_MAIL Package

The ability to send mail is not an automatically included feature of an Oracle database. As you recall, we added that feature to the original orcl instance when we implemented two-factor authentication. We will add it to the apver instance as well. In fact, we will be doing two-factor authentication now as a function within application verification, not in relation to each Oracle connection we make.

```
@D:\app\oracle\product\11.2.0\dbhome_1\RDBMS\ADMIN\utlmail.sql
```

```
@D:\app\oracle\product\11.2.0\dbhome_1\RDBMS\ADMIN\prvtmail.plb
```

The extension on that second script file (*plb*) should look familiar to us now. It is a wrapped procedure.

Install DBMS_JAVA package

If you have installed Java in Oracle database before, or if you've looked at the instructions for doing so, you may have seen a precursor step listed. It used to be that you needed to specify memory pool sizes for java, setting java_pool_size and shared_pool_size to 150M each. This is no longer required, as of Oracle Database 11g. These allocations are handled automatically as a part of 11g Automatic Memory Management.

You can see the current settings for these parameters by selecting them from the database.

```
SELECT NAME,VALUE FROM V$PARAMETER WHERE NAME IN ('SHARED_POOL_SIZE','JAVA_POOL_SIZE');
```

You'll see that in 11g, these parameters are both set to 0. The required memory will be automatically provided from the global MEMORY_TARGET and TARGET_SGA settings. Recall that when we mounted the database we saw a report of the Total System Global Area. That is the memory that is partially available to Java in the database.

A number of scripts are used to configure and enable the Oracle JVM. We will only be running two of them—the ones we need for our application verification security processes. Of the five scripts generally listed to build Java into the Oracle database, we will only execute *initjvm.sql* and *catjava.sql*. Again, our reasoning for being selective is that we will only enable the capabilities we need, thus avoiding some potential security weaknesses.

```
@D:\app\oracle\product\11.2.0\dbhome_1\javavm\install\initjvm.sql;
--@D:\app\oracle\product\11.2.0\dbhome_1\xdk\admin\initxml.sql;
--@D:\app\oracle\product\11.2.0\dbhome_1\xdk\admin\xmlja.sql;
@D:\app\oracle\product\11.2.0\dbhome_1\RDBMS\ADMIN\catjava.sql;
--@D:\app\oracle\product\11.2.0\dbhome_1\RDBMS\ADMIN\catexf.sql;
```

Running *initjvm.sql* will take a while, so take a break. After all that, it is time to close our spool log file, so execute the SPOOL OFF command. Then you can browse the spool file for errors—it is in the current directory from which you started SQL*Plus.

```
SPOOL OFF
```

See What's Installed

Shut down the database and restart the TNSListener and database services from the Computer Management application (type Computer Management at the Start menu/Run command):

```
SHUTDOWN IMMEDIATE;
EXIT

Computer Management
        Restart TNSlistener service
        Start orcl instance service
        Restart apver instance service
```

Then run SQL*Plus and connect to each of our Oracle instances, one at a time. Sometimes, the TNSListener service takes a minute or two to register the database services after being restarted. If your SQL*Plus connect doesn't work, try again in a minute. Execute the SELECT command from ALL_REGISTRY_BANNERS to see what services have been built.

```
SQLPLUS SYS@ORCL AS SYSDBA
SELECT * FROM ALL_REGISTRY_BANNERS;

CONNECT SYS@apver AS SYSDBA
-- compare to what's installed in initial database
SELECT * FROM ALL_REGISTRY_BANNERS;

Oracle Database Catalog Views Release 11.2.0.1.0 - 64bit Production
Oracle Database Packages and Types Release 11.2.0.1.0 - Development
Oracle XML Database Version 11.2.0.1.0 - Development
JServer JAVA Virtual Machine Release 11.2.0.1.0 - Development
Oracle Database Java Packages Release 11.2.0.1.0 - Development
```

Connect from Remote AS SYSDBA

You may want to be able to connect to the apver instance as SYS from a remote GUI administrative application, like TOAD, or from any remote application (including SQL*Plus); however, there is a constraint on the ability to connect to a database instance remotely with the AS SYSDBA privilege. In order for that connection to succeed, a remote login password file must exist for the database instance. In order to remotely login as SYS AS SYSDBA to the apver instance, we will need to create the remote login password file for apver.

First of all, check that we do not have a remote login password file for the apver instance. This can be accomplished by executing an innocuous command that touches that file, GRANT SYSDBA. As SYS user, execute this:

```
GRANT SYSDBA TO SYS;
```

If the remote SYSDBA login password file already exists, you will not get an error, but on the apver instance you will probably see this error:

```
ERROR at line 1:
-ORA-01994: GRANT failed: password file missing or disabled
```

You can create a remote login password file by executing the orapwd command (found in the ORACLE_HOME bin directory). You will need to provide the default file name for the apver instance, *PWDapver.ora* and the password for the SYS user.

```
orapwd file=%ORACLE_HOME%\database\PWDapver.ora password=sys_password
```

Configure CREATE_SESSION_ROLE and APPSEC User

We should now be able to connect to the apver instance as SYS from either a local command prompt or from a remote session. Go ahead and connect as SYS AS SYSDBA so that we can create the structures needed for application verification.

■ **Note** These commands can be found in the file *Chapter11/apver/NewSys.sql.*

Create a `create_session_role` role identical to what we created on the `orcl` instance, and then create the appsec user. See Listing 11-46. Be sure to give a complex password for appsec. Also give a sufficiently large QUOTA on a default tablespace for appsec in order to hold structures and data for application verification.

Listing 11-46. Create Initial Role and User

```
CREATE ROLE create_session_role NOT IDENTIFIED;
GRANT CREATE SESSION TO create_session_role;

GRANT create_session_role TO appsec IDENTIFIED BY password;

ALTER USER appsec DEFAULT TABLESPACE USERS QUOTA 10M ON USERS;
```

Create a Database Link to the ORCL Instance

As I mentioned at the onset of this section, we will be configuring the bare minimum configuration in order to do application verification in this new, apver instance. For that reason, we will rely on the SYS user to configure all our structures, even those in the appsec schema. Well, that is except for one item that we might as well get out of the way right now.

We want to create a database link to be used by the appsec structures in particular to do two-factor authentication. Recall that we have stored an e-mail address in the HR.EMPLOYEES table, and we created another table with addresses to use for two-factor authentication in the HR schema, emp_mobile_nos. However, those tables are on a different Oracle instance, orcl. As a part of our application verification process, occurring on the apver instance, we need to read those tables across a database link.

Update TNSNAMES.ora for our Database Link

The way we read data from a different instance is by using a database link. To use the database link, the database that wants to read data, apver needs to know how to find the other database instance. This location and direction information is normally retained in a *TNSNAMES.ora* file on the Oracle database, as in Listing 11-47. Assure you have an entry for the orcl instance. While we are here, add another entry for the new apver instance.

Listing 11-47. Edit TNSNAMES.ora File

```
edit %ORACLE_HOME%\NETWORK\ADMIN\tnsnames.ora

ORCL =
  (DESCRIPTION =
    (ADDRESS = (PROTOCOL = TCP)(HOST = localhost)(PORT = 1521))
    (CONNECT_DATA =
      (SERVER = DEDICATED)
      (SERVICE_NAME = orcl)
    )
  )

APVER =
  (DESCRIPTION =
    (ADDRESS = (PROTOCOL = TCP)(HOST = localhost)(PORT = 1521))
    (CONNECT_DATA =
      (SERVER = DEDICATED)
      (SERVICE_NAME = apver)
    )
  )
```

Permit appsec to Create a Database Link

As SYS user grant the privilege for appsec user to create a personal database link in the appsec schema. Unlike most other create statements, this is one that cannot be done in a different schema; we need to be appsec user to create a personal database link in the appsec schema. As SYS, execute the commands in Listing 11-48 to create a limited appsec_role for this grant.

Listing 11-48. Grant Create Link Privilege to appsec

```
-- Must grant to user, not role since roles not exist without session
-- This is used in MASK/UNMASK - not needed on apver instance
GRANT EXECUTE ON sys.dbms_crypto TO appsec;

CREATE ROLE appsec_role NOT IDENTIFIED;
-- Give Application Security privilege to create Database Link
GRANT CREATE DATABASE LINK TO appsec_role;
GRANT appsec_role TO appsec;
-- Make the APPSEC_ROLE a non-default role for the APPSEC user
ALTER USER appsec DEFAULT ROLE ALL EXCEPT appsec_role;
```

Create the Personal Database Link as APPSEC

We made the appsec_role a non-default role, so now we need to log in as appsec and set our role to appsec_role.

```
SET ROLE appsec_role;
```

※ **Note** These commands can be found in the file *Chapter11/apver/NewAppSec.sql*.

Execute the command in Listing 11-49 to create the database link we need to attach to the `orcl` instance (substitute the password for `appsec` user on `orcl` instance into this command).

Listing 11-49. Create Database Link as appsec User

```
CREATE DATABASE LINK orcl_link
CONNECT TO appsec
IDENTIFIED BY password
USING 'orcl';
```

Test the new database link by selecting from a table that is available to `appsec` on the `orcl` instance:

```
SELECT * FROM hr.v_emp_mobile_nos@orcl_link;
```

We are returning to the SYS user now in order to accomplish much of the rest of this installation of our Application Security structures on the new apver instance.

Now that we have created the database link as `appsec`, we will no longer need to log in as our `appsec` user, so we will want to disable logins. The quickest way to do that is to expire the password for `appsec`. To do that, execute the following command as SYS user:

```
ALTER USER appsec PASSWORD EXPIRE;
```

You will want to remember that you did this so you don't worry when you cannot connect to apver as appsec. In effect, you can only connect to apver instance as SYS. You could connect as appver user, but the logon trigger and other security will prevent or limit what you can do.

Grant Access for APPSEC User to Reach out of the JVM Security Sandbox

In order to accomplish two-factor authentication, our `appsec` user will need to send e-mail and open connections to web servers. These abilities require that `appsec` be able to reach out from the Oracle JVM, outside the standard security sandbox. We will grant the privilege to do that here in Listing 11-50, as we did for the `orcl` instance in Chapter 9.

Listing 11-50. Grant Oracle JVM Security Sandbox Permissions

```
BEGIN
  DBMS_NETWORK_ACL_ADMIN.CREATE_ACL (
    acl         => 'smtp_acl_file.xml',
    description => 'Using SMTP server',
    principal   => 'APPSEC',
    is_grant    => TRUE,
    privilege   => 'connect',
    start_date  => SYSTIMESTAMP,
    end_date    => NULL);

  COMMIT;
END;
```

```
/

BEGIN
  DBMS_NETWORK_ACL_ADMIN.ASSIGN_ACL (
    acl        => 'smtp_acl_file.xml',
    host       => 'smtp.org.com',
    lower_port => 25,
    upper_port => NULL);
  COMMIT;
END;
/

CALL DBMS_JAVA.GRANT_PERMISSION(
    'APPSEC',
    'java.net.SocketPermission',
    'www.org.com:80',
    'connect, resolve'
);
```

Revoke PUBLIC Grant on Sensitive Data Dictionary Views

One of our primary reasons for establishing a separate Oracle instance in order to do application verification/authorization is that we want to be even more restrictive on what a hacker would be able to see and do if he gained access to the appver password. Remember, we have only obfuscated the password; we have not encrypted it.

Besides limiting the number of users with passwords on the new apver instance, we also want to remove the ability to SELECT on certain by-default PUBLIC views from the Oracle Database Data Dictionary. In particular, we are going to remove PUBLIC access from the ALL_USERS, ALL_SOURCE, ALL_TRIGGERS and ALL_VIEWS views. These particular data dictionary views expose accounts and code that can be leveraged in a computer security attack. Even though for most of these views, the exposure is only to code that has been granted to the user, we prefer to allow the user to run code without being able to see the code.

The ALL_USERS view will still need to be accessible by appsec in order to successfully execute procedures for 2-factor authentication. In Listing 11-51, we will GRANT SELECT on ALL_USERS directly to the appsec user, not to a role. The appsec user password is expired, so the ALL_USERS view will remain inaccessible to hackers.

Listing 11-51. Secure Public Data Dictionary Views

```
GRANT SELECT ON sys.all_users TO appsec;

REVOKE SELECT ON sys.all_users FROM PUBLIC;
REVOKE SELECT ON sys.all_source FROM PUBLIC;
REVOKE SELECT ON sys.all_source_ae FROM PUBLIC;
REVOKE SELECT ON sys.all_triggers FROM PUBLIC;
REVOKE SELECT ON sys.all_views FROM PUBLIC;
REVOKE SELECT ON sys.all_views_ae FROM PUBLIC;
```

■ **Note** If this were being used in production at the moment, you would grant the appropriate narrow privilege (as shown) before revoking the inappropriate broader privilege in order to keep appropriate functions working during the update.

Create the Remaining Structures for Application Authorization

The remainder of the *NewSys.sql* script for the apver instance configures all the structures we need to do application authorization. Most of the structures are created in the appsec schema. To do this as SYS user, we simply prefix the name of the structure we are creating with the schema name appsec.

We are doing this as SYS user to keep from granting administrative privileges to any other user, even appsec. This is the most secure, but control of the SYS password is mandatory.

Before running the script, copy and paste over the wrapped functions, f_mask and f_unmask, with the versions that you created and wrapped. Table 11-2 provides a list of the structures we will be creating, in creation order.

Table 11-2. Structures Created in apver Instance

TABLE	APPSEC.T_APPSEC_ERRORS
TABLE	APPSEC.T_APPSEC_ERRORS_MAINT
PACKAGE	APPSEC.APP_SEC_PKG
PROCEDURE	APPSEC.P_APPSEC_ERRORS_JANITOR
TRIGGER	APPSEC.T_APPSEC_ERRORS_IAR
TABLE	APPSEC.T_TWO_FACT_CD_CACHE
PROFILE	APPVER_PROF
USER	APPVER
USER	OSUSER
USER	OSADMIN
TABLE	APPSEC.T_APPLICATION_REGISTRY
TABLE	APPSEC.T_APP_CONN_REGISTRY
TABLE	APPSEC.T_APPLICATION_KEY

TRIGGER	APPSEC.T_APPLICATION_KEY_BUDR
FUNCTION	APPSEC.F_IS_SSO
PACKAGE	APPSEC.APPSEC_ONLY_PKG
PROCEDURE	APPSEC.P_CHECK_ROLE_ACCESS
PROCEDURE	APPSEC.P_APPVER_LOGON
TRIGGER	APPSEC.T_SCREEN_APPVER_ACCESS
PACKAGE	APPSEC.APPSEC_ADMIN_PKG
ROLE	APPVER_ADMIN
PACKAGE	APPSEC.APPSEC_PUBLIC_PKG
FUNCTION	APPSEC.F_MASK (wrapped)
FUNCTION	APPSEC.F_UNMASK (wrapped

Note Because we are not creating the secadm user on the apver instance, we cannot create the
t_screen_appver_access trigger in the secadm schema. We will create it in appsec schema instead.

There are a couple places in the script where you will need to substitute a real OS User ID (i.e.,
Windows login name) for a placeholder. Search and replace both OSUSER and OSADMIN. OSUSER is a person
(or multiple persons) who wants to run our secure applications. OSADMIN is a person, like you, who will
need to connect in order to register application connection strings in the database.

On apver, a couple stored procedures go across *database links*, f_is_cur_cached_cd and
p_get_emp_2fact_nos. In those structures, we see the reference types (like that for os_user in Listing
11-52) were converted to standard type declarations; we can't reference across a database link. Look at
the FROM clause in the SELECT statement in Listing 11-52. We are getting data from three views across the
database link: v_emp_mobile_nos@orcl_link, v_employees_public@orcl_link, and
v_sms_carrier_host@orcl_link.

Listing 11-52. Get Data Across Database Link into Procedure

```
PROCEDURE p_get_emp_2fact_nos(
    --os_user             hr.v_emp_mobile_nos.user_id%TYPE,
    os_user               VARCHAR2,
    fmt_string            VARCHAR2,
    m_employee_id     OUT NUMBER,
```

```
        m_com_pager_no     OUT VARCHAR2,
        m_sms_phone_no     OUT VARCHAR2,
        m_sms_carrier_url  OUT VARCHAR2,
        m_email            OUT VARCHAR2,
        m_ip_address       OUT v_two_fact_cd_cache.ip_address%TYPE,
        m_cache_ts         OUT VARCHAR2,
        m_cache_addr       OUT v_two_fact_cd_cache.ip_address%TYPE,
        m_application_id       v_two_fact_cd_cache.application_id%TYPE,
        m_err_no           OUT NUMBER,
        m_err_txt          OUT VARCHAR2 )
    IS BEGIN
        m_err_no := 0;
        SELECT e.employee_id, m.com_pager_no, m.sms_phone_no, s.sms_carrier_url,
            e.email, SYS_CONTEXT( 'USERENV', 'IP_ADDRESS' ),
            TO_CHAR( c.cache_ts, fmt_string ), c.ip_address
        INTO m_employee_id, m_com_pager_no, m_sms_phone_no, m_sms_carrier_url,
            m_email, m_ip_address, m_cache_ts, m_cache_addr
        --FROM hr.v_emp_mobile_nos m, hr.v_employees_public e,
        --    hr.v_sms_carrier_host s, v_two_fact_cd_cache c

        FROM hr.v_emp_mobile_nos@orcl_link m, hr.v_employees_public@orcl_link e,

            hr.v_sms_carrier_host@orcl_link s, v_two_fact_cd_cache c
```

Create Java Structures

Open each of these files and execute them on the apver instance from a SQL client. For each of the *.java* files, uncomment the top line with the SQL CREATE OR REPLACE AND RESOLVE JAVA SOURCE statement, and for *OracleJavaSecure.java*, edit the domain, SMTP host and base URL members, as before. Execute each of these to create the Java structures in the apver instance. Be sure to substitute values for domains and hostnames appropriate to your corporate environment into the *OracleJavaSecure.java* before creating the Java structures in Oracle.

> *Chapter11/orajavsec/OracleJavaSecure.java*
> *Chapter11/orajavsec/RevLvlClassIntfc.java*
> *Chapter11/orajavsec/OJSC.java*
> *Chapter11/testojs/TestOracleJavaSecure.sql*

Remove Application Verification from the ORCL Instance

At this point, we no longer need application verification in the ORCL instance. We will disable connections by the application verification, appver user to ORCL. Do that from a SQL client connection to ORCL instance as appsec or SYS user with the following command.

▓ **Note** This is to be done on the ORCL instance only, and only if you are installing a second database instance, apver, to do application verification.

```
ALTER USER appver PASSWORD EXPIRE;
```

Test Enhanced Security

We are at the point now where we can test everything we have established, including the segregation of Application Authentication on a separate Oracle instance, apver. We will do our testing in two parts: first using the main() method in OracleJavaSecure, then using the separate application, testojs.TestOracleJavaSecure.

Once again, assure that you have set the domain and other addresses at the top of *OracleJavaSecure.java* to be appropriate for your organization. Also assure that the SQL command at the top of the file has been commented. (The SQL commands at the top of the other *.java* files in this chapter should also remain commented in order to be compiled.)

Note The assumption in the following text is that you are running application verification on a separate database instance, apver. If you are not, then the only difference is that you will be able to connect as appsec user to the orcl instance—you will not have to connect as SYS.

Encode the APPVER User Password for APVER Instance

The first time we run OracleJavaSecure, we will have just one goal: to create a new encoded Oracle connection string for the appver user on the apver instance. Scroll down to the main() method in *OracleJavaSecure.java* and edit the encodeThis String components, shown in Listing 11-53, to point at the apver instance instead of orcl.

Listing 11-53. Switch appver Connection String from ORCL to apver

```
encodeThis = "jdbc:oracle:thin:appver/" + encodeThis +
    //"@localhost:1521:orcl";
    "@localhost:1521:apver";
```

Caution If you did not create an additional Oracle database instance dedicated to application verification, then do not make this change to the code. You do not need to update the encoded connection string, prime.

Then compile the class and run it. From the Chapter11 directory, execute:

```
javac orajavsec/OracleJavaSecure.java
java orajavsec.OracleJavaSecure appverPassword
```

You will see something like the following as a result:

```
Main encodes a new APPVER password if given.
After encoding, paste encoded string
in setAppVerConnection() method.
```

030a42105f1b3311133a0048370707005f020419190b524204041819015c390f5300121b3314303a

0a112203060116174e585a5c115704041e0a16

jdbc:oracle:thin:appver/appverPassword@localhost:1521:apver

We need to place that encoded string (see the bold data) into the setAppVerConnection() method in *OracleJavaSecure.java*. That method will look like Listing 11-54 when done (the prime String is all one line, though shown here with word-wrap onto a second line).

Listing 11-54. Embed Newly Encoded appver Connection String into OracleJavaSecure Code

```
private static void setAppVerConnection() {
    try {
        // Set this String from encoded String at command prompt (main)
        String prime =
"030a42105f1b3311133a0048370707005f020419190b524204041819015c390f5300121b3314303a0a112203060
116174e585a5c115704041e0a16";
        setConnection( OJSC.y( prime ) );
        appVerConn = conn;
    } catch( Exception x ) {
        x.printStackTrace();
    }
}
```

■ **Note** It is this one value, prime that directs our applications to use an alternate database instance for application verification.

Edit the Application Passwords to Be Used

We are going to upload a list of connection strings to Oracle database for the HRVIEW application. Update the main() method of OracleJavaSecure to have the correct passwords (substitute for the "password" string) for HR and appusr users, shown in Listing 11-55. Correct the other aspects of your Oracle application connection strings as well.

■ **Note** These connection strings are intended to connect to the orcl instance, not the new apver instance.

Listing 11-55. Connection Strings for Application, OracleJavaSecure.main()

```
putAppConnString()( "Orcl", "hr",
    "password", "localhost", String.valueOf( 1521 ) );
putAppConnString()( "Orcl", "appusr",
    "password", "localhost", String.valueOf( 1521 ) );
```

Then compile the class again. From the Chapter11 directory, execute:

```
javac orajavsec/OracleJavaSecure.java
```

Run Main to Test

Now we will run OracleJavaSecure at least five more times. You must run this as an OS (Windows) user whose matching Oracle user has been granted the appver_admin role: your equivalent of OSADMIN. The first time, we will generate a two-factor authentication code. The results will look like this:

```
Chapter11>java orajavsec.OracleJavaSecure
Main encodes a new APPVER password if given.
After encoding, paste encoded string
in setAppVerConnection method.
You may enter APPVER password on command line.
Domain: ORGDOMAIN, Name: OSADMIN
Please rerun with 2-Factor Auth Code!
```

We should either receive that code by two-factor authentication code distribution, or find it by querying the appsec.v_two_fact_cd_cache view on the apver instance. You will not be able to connect as appsec user to see that view, because we expired the appsec password; but you can select from the view as SYS user.

Then we execute the same command with the two-factor authentication code as a parameter on the command line:

```
Chapter11>java orajavsec.OracleJavaSecure 1234-5678-9012
Main encodes a new APPVER password if given.
After encoding, paste encoded string
in setAppVerConnection method.
Domain: ORGDOMAIN, Name: OSADMIN
connsHash.size = 0
connsHash.size = 0
Domain: ORGDOMAIN, Name: OSADMIN
2011-06-05 21:00:06
```

You can see that when we get the Oracle connections list for this application from the apver instance, the list is empty, connsHash.size = 0. We are able to insert connection strings into the list and use them. Using one of the connection strings, we query the database to get the SYSDATE.

When we run this command again, we see that for a minute our connsHash.size = 2, and later = 1. The first value is the number of connection strings in the list we get for this application from Oracle. The second value is the number we have after calling removeAppConnString(). We immediately call putAppConnString() twice to add and overwrite the connection strings, and then we call putAppConnections() to store the list of two connection strings in Oracle for this application. We again use one of them to get SYSDATE from Oracle.

```
Chapter11>java orajavsec.OracleJavaSecure 1234-5678-9012
Main encodes a new APPVER password if given.
After encoding, paste encoded string
in setAppVerConnection method.
Domain: ORGDOMAIN, Name: OSADMIN
connsHash.size = 2
connsHash.size = 1
Domain: ORGDOMAIN, Name: OSADMIN
```

2011-06-05 21:00:23

Run Main to Copy Connection Strings to New Version

We will edit *OracleJavaSecure.java* one more time in order to test our ability to copy a list of connection strings from an older version of an application to the new version. Open the file and edit the inner class InnerRevLvlClass (near the top), incrementing the version number, for example from 20110101a to 20110101b. See Listing 11-56.

Listing 11-56. *Change Version/Revision of Application Inner Class*

```
private static class InnerRevLvlClass
    implements Serializable, RevLvlClassIntfc
{
    private static final long serialVersionUID = 2011010100L;
    private String innerClassRevLvl = "20110101b";
    public String getRevLvl() {
        return innerClassRevLvl;
    }
}
```

> **Note** We do not have to CREATE a new version of this java code on the Oracle Database, because the serialVersionUID has not changed.

In the main() method, find the commented call to copyAppConnections() and uncomment that call. Assure that the old version number String in that call, Listing 11-57, matches the innerClassRevLvl you changed from previously.

Listing 11-57. *Copy List of Connection Strings from Previous Version*

```
copyAppConnections( "20110101a" );
```

Compile OracleJavaSecure and run it. Use the same two-factor authorization code if it has been less than ten minutes, else request and use a new one. This will exit after copying the list of connection strings from the old version to the new one.

```
Chapter11>javac orajavsec/OracleJavaSecure.java
Chapter11>java orajavsec.OracleJavaSecure
Chapter11>java orajavsec.OracleJavaSecure 1234-5678-9012
Main encodes a new APPVER password if given.
After encoding, paste encoded string
in setAppVerConnection method.
Domain: ORGDOMAIN, Name: OSADMIN
```

As SYS user on apver, you can see that there is a new version of the application class file and associated list of connection strings by querying the appsec.v_app_conn_registry view.

"CLASS_NAME"	"CLASS_VERSION"	"CLASS_INSTANCE"	"UPDATE_DT"

```
"orajavsec.OracleJavaSecure$InnerRevLvlClass" "20110101b"        "ACED00057372... "11-JUN-11"
"orajavsec.OracleJavaSecure$InnerRevLvlClass" "20110101a"        "ACED00057372... "11-JUN-11"
```

Once more we edit OracleJavaSecure.java and comment two areas of the main() method. First comment the line that copies the list of connection strings from an old version to the new version.

```
//copyAppConnections( "20110101a" );
```

Then comment the lines that would overwrite and insert new connection strings into the list.

```
//putAppConnString( "Orcl", "hr",
//    "password", "localhost", String.valueOf( 1521 ) );
//putAppConnString( "Orcl", "appusr",
//    "password", "localhost", String.valueOf( 1521 ) );
```

For the final times, compile OracleJavaSecure and run it. The first time it runs, you will see that there were already two connection strings (connsHash.size = 2) in the list that was copied from the previous version of the application. In the middle of the run, we call removeAppConnString() and then we run putAppConnections() to update Oracle with a list of only one connection string for this application. The second time it is run, you will see that, because we didn't update and add connection strings, there is only one to start with (connsHash.size = 1).

```
Chapter11>javac orajavsec/OracleJavaSecure.java
Chapter11>java orajavsec.OracleJavaSecure
Chapter11>java orajavsec.OracleJavaSecure 1234-5678-9012
Main encodes a new APPVER password if given.
After encoding, paste encoded string
in setAppVerConnection method.
Domain: ORGDOMAIN, Name: OSADMIN
connsHash.size = 2
connsHash.size = 1
Domain: ORGDOMAIN, Name: OSADMIN
2011-06-11 18:04:15
Chapter11>java orajavsec.OracleJavaSecure 1234-5678-9012
Main encodes a new APPVER password if given.
After encoding, paste encoded string
in setAppVerConnection method.
Domain: ORGDOMAIN, Name: OSADMIN
connsHash.size = 1
connsHash.size = 1
Domain: ORGDOMAIN, Name: OSADMIN
2011-06-11 18:04:26
```

We conclude that our copyAppConnections() process works to replicate an existing list of connection strings from one version of the application to the next (with an updated innerClassRevLvl in the inner class.) This will be a timesaver when we upgrade our application and don't need to change connection strings.

Test from a Different Application, TestOracleJavaSecure

TestOracleJavaSecure is independent from whatever instance is running application verification. It will act as a client application, calling methods in the OracleJavaSecure class in order to use those security features. Using OracleJavaSecure, the test application will do the following things:

- Accomplish SSO and 2-factor authentication.

- Register itself (its name and application inner class).

- Store a list of connection strings for the application.

- Retrieve the list of connection strings from Oracle.

- Transfer and store the connection strings in encrypted form.

- Decrypt and use the connection strings to query application data.

- Query sensitive data in encrypted form and decrypt it for use

Edit the file *Chapter11/testojs/TestOracleJavaSecure.java*. Correct the password for appusr shown in Listing 11-58. We will add this user to a list of connection strings for the TestOracleJavaSecure application. We are still using HRVIEW as our application ID, which means we will be connecting as appusr and using the role hrview_role (as registered in appsec.v_application_registry).

Listing 11-58. *Edit TestOracleJavaSecure to Test*

```
String applicationID = "HRVIEW";
Object appClass = new AnyNameWeWant();
OracleJavaSecure.setAppContext( applicationID, appClass, twoFactorAuth );

OracleJavaSecure.getAppConnections();
if( twoFactorAuth.equals( "" ) ) {
    return;
}

// Demonstrate copy connsHash from previous version
// Only do this once, make sure it worked (see appsec.V_APP_CONN_REGISTRY),
// then comment this line
//OracleJavaSecure.copyAppConnections( "20110131a" );
// Get copied list of connection strings for new version number
OracleJavaSecure.getAppConnections();

OracleJavaSecure.putAppConnString( "Orcl", "appusr",
    "password", "localhost", String.valueOf( 1521 ) );
//Only do this line once -- must be admin account
OracleJavaSecure.putAppConnections();
```

The last line in Listing 11-58 is a call to putAppConnections(). That method calls the Oracle function f_set_decrypt_conns, which we moved to the appsec_admin_pkg package. Only users with the appver_admin role can execute structures in the appsec_admin_pkg. In our example, we granted appver_admin to osadmin user. So, to test this facet of security, we will run TestOracleJavaSecure as both osadmin (an administrative account) and osuser (a non-administrative account). You can test copyAppConnections() for TestOracleJavaSecure by modifying the version number of the inner class and uncommenting copyAppConnections(), passing the previous version number.

Compile and Run as Administrative User, OSADMIN

In the code of TestOracleJavaSecure.main(), we have three attempts to connect to Oracle database before we try to get encrypted data. We attempt to do these things

- Call getAppConnections() to do key exchange and get the list of connection strings for this application.

- Call putAppConnections() to update the list of connection strings in Oracle.

- Call getAAConnRole() to decode and use a connection string to get a Connection.

We are going to compile and run TestOracleJavaSecure as an administrative user (a user with the appver_admin role, OSADMIN in our example—probably your OS user ID.) We start out running this application without a 2-factor authentication code. Here are the commands and results:

```
Chapter11>javac testojs/TestOracleJavaSecure.java
Chapter11>java testojs/TestOracleJavaSecure
Domain: ORGDOMAIN, Name: OSADMIN
Please rerun with 2-Factor Auth Code!
java.lang.NullPointerException
Please rerun with 2-Factor Auth Code!
```

The call to putAppConnections() reports a NullPointerException – we don't trap exceptions from that administrative command as closely as we trap exceptions from methods being called by regular client applications. The other attempts to connect to Oracle point out the need to return with a 2-factor authentication code.

Let's run the code again with a bogus two-factor authentication code:

```
Chapter11>java testojs.TestOracleJavaSecure 123
Domain: ORGDOMAIN, Name: OSADMIN
Oracle error 21) 100, ORA-01403: no data found
java.lang.NullPointerException
Oracle error 21) 100, ORA-01403: no data found
Wrong or old 2-Factor code parameter
```

The same NullPointerException was reported by putAppConnections(), and the other two attempts to connect to Oracle reported "no data found" error, which is what we get from a bad user or two-factor authentication code. We also trap a NullPointerException in Listing 11-59 when we attempt to use the Connection coming from getAAConnRole() to get an Oracle Statement. If we got this far, it is our understanding that we have provided a dubious two-factor authentication code, so we report the problem and exit.

Listing 11-59. Catch Incorrect Two-Factor Authentication Code

```
try {
    mStmt = conn.createStatement();
} catch( NullPointerException n ) {
    System.out.println( "Wrong or old 2-Factor code parameter" );
    return;
}
```

For this new user, there will be a new entry in the appsec.v_two_fact_cd_cache view. This new entry will be designated for the new employee_id, 304 in this example. Here is an example selection from appsec.v_two_fact_cd_cache.

```
SQL> select * from appsec.v_two_fact_cd_cache;

EMPLOYEE_ID APPLICATION_ID TWO_FACTOR_CD  IP_ADDRESS DISTRIB_CD CACHE_TS
----------- -------------- -------------- ---------- ---------- ---------
        304 HRVIEW         2747-4367-3056 127.0.0.1           1 12-JUN-11
        300 HRVIEW         3471-8557-5210 127.0.0.1           3 12-JUN-11
```

When we finally return to execute TestOracleJavaSecure with the correct two-factor authentication code, we are able to print out many aspects regarding our proxy connection to Oracle for data queries, connected through the appusr user, using the hrview_role. We also select and decrypt data from our familiar p_select_employees_sensitive procedure.

```
Chapter11>java testojs.TestOracleJavaSecure 1234-5678-9012
Domain: ORGDOMAIN, Name: OSADMIN
Domain: ORGDOMAIN, Name: OSADMIN
osadmin

APPUSR

127.0.0.1
OSADMIN
OSADMIN
HRVIEW_ROLE
Oracle success 2)
100, Steven, King, SKING, 515.123.4567, 2003-06-17 00:00:00, AD_PRES, 24000, null, null, 90
```

Run as Non-Administrative User, OSUSER

We are going to test our limitation of application connection string updates to just users who have been granted the appver_admin role. To do this, you need to log in as an OS user who corresponds to an Oracle user without the appver_admin role, your equivalent of OSUSER in our examples. Run TestOracleJavaSecure again. You will see that when the application calls the method putAppConnections() an exception is thrown with regard to the appsec_admin_pkg package. This user does not have privileges to execute the Oracle function, f_set_decrypt_conns that is called from that method.

```
Chapter11>java testojs/TestOracleJavaSecure
Domain: ORGDOMAIN, Name: OSUSER
Please rerun with 2-Factor Auth Code!
java.sql.SQLException: ORA-06550: line 1, column 13:
PLS-00201: identifier 'APPSEC.APPSEC_ADMIN_PKG' must be declared
ORA-06550: line 1, column 7:
PL/SQL: Statement ignored
```

We want to demonstrate other, non-administrative functions using the non-administrative user. To do that, edit *TestOracleJavaSecure.java* and comment the line calling the putAppConnections() method. Then recompile and rerun the application. You will see the following successful results:

```
Chapter11>javac testojs/TestOracleJavaSecure.java
Chapter11>java testojs.TestOracleJavaSecure
```

```
Chapter11>java testojs.TestOracleJavaSecure 1234-5678-9012
Domain: ORGDOMAIN, Name: OSUSER
Domain: ORGDOMAIN, Name: OSUSER
osuser
APPUSR
127.0.0.1
OSUSER
OSUSER
HRVIEW_ROLE
Oracle success 2)
100, Steven, King, SKING, 515.123.4567, 2003-06-17 00:00:00, AD_PRES, 24000, null, null, 90
```

Chapter Review

Our goal in this chapter has been to enhance the security of everything we had built so far. We accomplished that goal on the following fronts:

- We programmed Java to encode the appver user password (connection string).

- We obfuscated the Java program that does encoding/decoding.

- We accomplished secured data encryption for data being stored in the database—specifically our lists of connection strings.

- We established an administrative role that limits who can update connection strings for applications.

- We moved the application verification processes to a new, hardened Oracle database instance, apver.

In addition to working toward enhancing the security, we also delved into the following timely topics:

- Securing an Oracle user password by various means

- Using the Oracle client wallet

- Using Oracle client trace logging

- Using Oracle thin client (JDBC) trace logging

- Using the Oracle wrap utility to obfuscate Oracle functions

- Copying application connection strings from a previous version to the current application version

- Adding other authentication credentials, such as FTP passwords, to our application connection strings list

- Reviewing weaknesses in PUBLIC access to the data dictionary views

- Using database links to read data from another database instance

Administration of Security

Now that we have built Oracle structures and Oracle and Java code, we will need to maintain the data that keeps it running. Primarily, this data consists of users, proxy grants, application registrations, and application connection strings. It has not been too difficult to execute SQL scripts to insert records for one or two users, and one or two applications—especially while we are studying the issues and requirements. But in a year or so, the steps to accomplish these tasks will be long forgotten, along with the reasons for doing them.

However, if we can encapsulate the business rules, logic, and procedure steps in a user-friendly application, we will have a much easier time adding new users and applications. In fact, once we have done that, we will have developed a pretty handy interface, part of which we will provide as a template to the application developers in our organizations, so that they can implement our security code.

A Security Administration Interface

When I talk about user-friendly applications, what I mean is actually well designed, simple GUIs.

The security administration interface we will be exploring in this chapter consists simply of a Login screen, a Menu screen, and seven functional screens. The Login screen is where we expect the user to enter a two-factor authentication code that we send him. It is this screen that we will provide as a GUI template to other application developers so they can implement our security structures.

Note Files for the security administration interface application can be found in the directory *Chapter12/orajavsec*.

The functional screens will walk the administrator through tasks such as editing employee and user data (especially those elements that we use for single sign-on and two-factor authentication). There are also functional screens for granting both administrative and application proxy privileges. We need to be able to register a new application, and most of that process is done through the GUI. Then we want to edit existing connection strings for an application, and occasionally copy connection strings from a previous version of an application. All those functions are represented on screens in our GUI.

Application Login Screen

What do we mean by application login? Because we are using single sign-on, we don't actually have the users enter a user name and password, but we do have them enter the two-factor authentication code. Our plan will be to remain on the Login screen until they have entered the correct two-factor code or they have exited the program. We need to handle several cases:

- When their account cannot do SSO, we need to tell them

- When they enter the wrong or an old two-factor authentication code, we need to tell them

- When they enter the correct code we need to continue

Behind the scenes, a lot is happening. Before the user has an opportunity to enter the two-factor authentication code, the Login screen will get the user identity from the OS and attempt to do SSO and then proxy using that OS user ID to the apver instance as the appver user. Remember the lengths we went to in order to obfuscate the appver password and the Java code that decodes it—all that is part of the process here.

Once a proxy session is established, the Oracle database determines if the user has entered a two-factor authentication code; if not, it generates and sends one to the user's mobile devices. To find out where to send the authentication code, Oracle database looks across a database link from the apver instance to the orcl instance, to the HR schema EMPLOYEE, and emp_mobile_nos tables to find out what devices are available for this specific user. Sending the authentication code to each device and returning to the Login screen are the next steps.

Note We are going to build this administrative interface for two Oracle database instances, orcl and apver. If you have not created the apver instance, you will need to use the code that is modified to run on a single instance, in the *Chapter12/single* directory.

Then, when the user receives the two-factor authentication code on their devices, and enters the code on the Login screen, a slew of additional steps are taken. The first step that the Login screen takes is to pass certain data and objects to the Oracle database. It passes the two-factor code, an inner class instance specific to this application, and an application identification string. Additionally, an RSA public/private key pair is generated on the client, and the modulus and exponent artifacts are also passed to the database.

Oracle database first assures that the two-factor authentication code the user entered matches what was sent to the user within the last ten minutes for this particular application, from this particular client network address. Then, if it is the correct code, the database assures the inner class instance matches what is stored for the application in question, and then retrieves the list of connection strings that is associated with it. Recall that the list of connection strings is stored in encrypted form on the database, and the code to encrypt and decrypt has been "wrapped" using the Oracle database *wrap* utility.

The Oracle database builds a RSA public key using the artifacts provided by the client, and generates a DES secret password key. Artifacts of the DES key are encrypted using the RSA public key to return to the client.

The list of connection strings for this specific application is encrypted with the secret password key, and that encrypted list is also returned to the client. At this point, the Login screen is about finished.

However, before it is closed and we continue on with the application, we use the artifacts of the DES secret password key to build a matching key on the client. We will use this key as long as we are in this particular application to decode connection strings for the application; so we clone or duplicate all the associated key components for continued use. Thereafter, the basic RSA and DES encryption key members are available for reuse by new keys associated with each Oracle connection we will be making for application transactions.

Everything I just described amounts to quite a list of functions, but it all occurs from the relatively simple interface presented in Figure 12-1. A single input field for the two-factor authentication code, and a Continue button are all we need to get the job done.

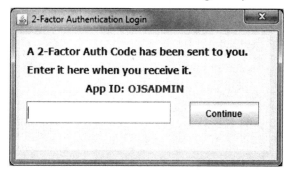

Figure 12-1. *Login screen*

The Application Inner Class

We are providing an application inner class structure in our Login class for use by any application. The code for the inner class is shown in Listing 12-1. By changing the package for the Login class, we can use this inner class for multiple applications, taking the burden off individual developers to include an inner class in their code. In the case of our security administrative interface application, the package is orajavsec. The complete inner class name will orajavsec.Login$InnerRevLvlClass. If there were another application that defined the Login class in a package named mynewpkg, then the inner class would be named mynewpkg.Login$InnerRevLvlClass. This difference is sufficient to distinguish different and separate applications and their associated application connection strings. This is true even if the definition of the inner class is identical except for that package name.

Listing 12-1. *The Login Class, Inner Class*

```
package orajavsec;

public class Login extends JDialog {

    public static class InnerRevLvlClass
                implements Serializable, RevLvlClassIntfc
        {
        private static final long serialVersionUID = 2011010100L;
        private String innerClassRevLvl = "20110101a";

        public String getRevLvl() {
            return innerClassRevLvl;
```

```
        }
    }
...
```

The code for Login is something we can give to other application programmers for inclusion in their applications. It is a template and a reusable piece of code—they just need to include it in their package. Then they don't need to worry about any of the setup details. After login is completed, they can just get their connection strings from OracleJavaSecure by calling the getAAConString() method.

In order to use the Login$InnerRevLvlClass in the Oracle database, we need to have a representative class to instantiate in the database. We need to execute the script shown in Listing 12-2 to create that Java structure in the database. We will be creating a similar Java structure in the database for each application. The only difference between classes for different applications will be the package name.

You may execute this script as the sys user on the apver instance, but you do not need to. When we get to the end of this chapter, we are going to use this security administration interface to register itself through a bootstrap process. That process will include creating the representative inner class in the Oracle Database and generating the connection strings that will be used by this application.

Listing 12-2. Script to Build Login Inner Class

```
CREATE OR REPLACE AND RESOLVE JAVA SOURCE NAMED APPSEC."orajavsec/Login" AS

package orajavsec;

import java.io.Serializable;

import orajavsec.RevLvlClassIntfc;

// Drop the "extends JDialog" from class definition
// It is unneeded and will be invalid on Oracle server
public class Login {
    public static class InnerRevLvlClass implements Serializable,
                                                    RevLvlClassIntfc {
        private static final long serialVersionUID = 2011010100L;
        private String innerClassRevLvl = "20110101a";

        public String getRevLvl() {
            return innerClassRevLvl;
        }
    }
}
/
```

■ **Note** This script can be found in the file *Chapter12/Login.sql*.

Center Method

We need to have the Login screen centered on the user's monitor, or else it may appear but be unnoticed in the top left corner of the monitor. Centering GUI interfaces is standard practice, and is something we will use for all our user interface screens. Because we want to center all our GUI screens, we will place the method in Login , as shown in Listing 12-3, and make the method both public and static—anyone can call it without referring to an instance of Login. It is part of the template and is code we do not need to duplicate for each screen. We hand whatever item we want to have centered to this method, and the method adjusts the item's location.

Listing 12-3. GUI Center() Method

```
public static void center(Component item) {
    Dimension screenSize = Toolkit.getDefaultToolkit().getScreenSize();
    Dimension frameSize = item.getSize();
    if (frameSize.height > screenSize.height) {
        frameSize.height = screenSize.height;
    }
    if (frameSize.width > screenSize.width) {
        frameSize.width = screenSize.width;
    }
    item.setLocation((screenSize.width - frameSize.width)/2,
                    (screenSize.height - frameSize.height)/2);
}
```

The code for the center() method is often generated automatically by the IDE for GUI applications (this version is from JDeveloper). I've just moved the code from a standard GUI main() method into this static method. Listing 12-3 shows the code.

```
┌─────────────────────────────────────────────────────────────────────┐
│                            JAVABEANS                                  │
└─────────────────────────────────────────────────────────────────────┘
```

I have mentioned JavaBeans, but this is our first introduction to them. JavaBeans are Java classes that have a required set of methods and interface. In particular, a JavaBean is a GUI object that has getter and setter methods for each property of the user interface. In this way, a JavaBean can be provided to an IDE, and the IDE automatically knows how to present it on screen and how to provide access to its properties. Each piece of text, input box and button that we have in our GUI application is a JavaBean.

Each IDE handles JavaBeans a little differently, placing the property settings code in a bit different location. Often the IDE will flag this code with a comment like, "This code is automatically generated, do not modify it." On the contrary, you generated the code when you drug or painted the component on the GUI application screen in the IDE, and you can edit the code. However, if you modify the code in unexpected ways, the IDE may no longer be able to present it to you on the screen. Perhaps a better wording for the flag comment would be, "This code lets the IDE display your components, please don't modify or add code that the IDE can't understand."

In JDeveloper, one of the free Java IDEs from Oracle (the other being NetBeans), when you develop GUI applications, most of the code for managing the user interface is placed in a method named jbInit(). Because we find all the parameter settings there initially, it is tempting to add our modifications to the UI in that method also. However, I have found that it is better to generate another method (what I will call ojsInit()) and to code our modifications to the UI in that method instead. We change the standard constructor to call our method right after the call to jbInit(). No matter what IDE you are using, you will want to have a similar segregation of code.

Login Screen Constructors

In Listing 12-4, you can see how we call ojsInit() right after the call to jbInit() in the constructor. Additionally, we have provided a third constructor that takes a Frame class. We will call that constructor, rather than the default constructor, and provide a reference to our main application class, parent. Then when the login process is complete, we will use this reference to return to our application.

Listing 12-4. Login Screen Constructors

```
public class Login extends JDialog {

    public Login() {
        this(null, "", false);
    }

    public Login(Frame parent, String title, boolean modal) {
        super(parent, title, modal);
        try {
            jbInit();
            ojsInit();
        } catch (Exception e) {
            e.printStackTrace();
        }
    }

    public Login(Frame parent) {
        // For Oracle Java Secure, call this constructor
        this(parent, "two-factor Authentication Login", true);
    }

    public Login(Frame parent, String applicationID, String appClassName) {
        // This replacement constructor is used when managing a selected application
        super(parent, "two-factor Authentication Login", true);
        try {
            this.applicationID = applicationID;
            Class applicationClass = Class.forName(appClassName);
            appClass = applicationClass.newInstance();
            jbInit();
            ojsInit();
        } catch (Exception e) {
            System.out.println("Specified application class is not available");
            System.exit(0);
        }
    }
...
```

There is also a fourth constructor that bypasses (repeats code from) the other constructors. That fourth constructor takes an alternate application name and inner class name. When called, this constructor uses reflection to instantiate a class of the type named, and will use that class in place of the inner class of Login. This will rarely be used, but is needed in our security administration interface. We have to become different applications in order to modify the associated connection strings. We will talk about that in detail later in this chapter.

The JDialog class, which Login is extending, has a constructor that takes three arguments. You can see our call to the JDialog constructor, super(). The last of those three arguments is a boolean that designates whether the JDialog is modal. We set the modal boolean to true for the Login screen. We want it to appear on top of whatever other screens are visible for the current application.

■ **Note** When calling other constructors, even super class constructors, those calls need to be the first line in the calling constructor. That is why we needed an independent fourth constructor. We needed to instantiate a new alternate inner class before we call the initialization methods. That could not have happened if we wanted to call our original constructors to do initialization. That call to the original constructors would have to be done first.

The "Wait While Processing" Modal Dialog

In a GUI application, bad things can happen if a user is impatient and your application code is off doing some complex calculation or data retrieval. The user may press a button repeatedly, possibly causing your application's code to do a function multiple times; or the user may quit the application in frustration. When your application is going to do something complex or possibly taking a long time, it is best to put up a little notification in front of the application, letting the user know you are busy working for them and asking them to be patient. Having described the complex list of tasks that take place in the Login screen, you can understand why it might take a few moments to process, during which time we will want the user to wait patiently.

I have defined a very simple JDialog class, sayWaitDialog, which I placed in the Login class. sayWaitDialog is a static member of Login, and it is configured by a static initializer block. This dialog screen is defined as a *modal* dialog—see the bold code in Listing 12-5. Modal dialogs appear on top of other windows on the user's monitor, and they can't easily be hidden behind other windows, at least those associated with the current application, even if the user clicks on other windows. I'm sure you have seen and noticed that kind of behavior in other dialogs before.

Listing 12-5. Modal Dialog Asking User to Wait Patiently

```java
public static JDialog sayWaitDialog = new JDialog();

static {

    sayWaitDialog.setDefaultCloseOperation(WindowConstants.DO_NOTHING_ON_CLOSE);
    sayWaitDialog.setModal(true);
    sayWaitDialog.setTitle("Please Wait");
    JPanel jPanel1 = new JPanel();
    sayWaitDialog.setSize(new Dimension(255, 93));
    sayWaitDialog.getContentPane().setLayout(null);
    jPanel1.setBounds(new Rectangle(5, 5, 230, 45));
```

```
        jPanel1.setLayout(null);
        jPanel1.setBackground(new Color(255, 222, 214));
        JLabel jLabel1 = new JLabel();
        jLabel1.setText("Working. Please wait!");
        jLabel1.setBounds(new Rectangle(5, 5, 220, 35));
        jLabel1.setHorizontalAlignment(SwingConstants.CENTER);
        jLabel1.setFont(new Font("Tahoma", 0, 16));
        jPanel1.add(jLabel1, null);
        sayWaitDialog.getContentPane().add(jPanel1, null);
        Login.center(sayWaitDialog);
    }
```

Notice that the last line in the definition of sayWaitDialog is a call to our center() method to place the dialog in the center of the monitor. The last thing to mention about this dialog is in the first line. We set the dialog to do nothing on close. We disable the ability of the user to click on the X in the top right corner of the window to close the dialog. We actually never open or close the dialog; we simply make it visible when we want it and invisible when we don't.

Background Processing Thread

Now let's look at the ojsInit() method that we use to set additional properties of the Login screen GUI and to jump-start to login process. Listing 12-6 shows the code. In the bottom half of the method code, we see the call to set the static Login.sayWaitDialog to be visible and our call to center the Login screen and then make it visible. We also slightly modify the Login Screen by setting the reEnterLabel to be invisible. If the user enters an incorrect two-factor authentication code, we will set that help message to be visible.

Listing 12-6. Self-Managed GUI Initialization and Background Processing Thread

```
    private static String applicationID = "OJSADMIN";
    private static Object appClass = new InnerRevLvlClass();

    private void ojsInit() {

        SwingUtilities.invokeLater(new Runnable() {

                public void run() {
                    OracleJavaSecure.setAppContext(applicationID, appClass, "");
                    // Under some circumstances, this will throw an exception
                    // if OS User not allowed, also test isAppverOK
                    OracleJavaSecure.getAppConnections();
                    // on success, original error message will be blanked out
                    if (OracleJavaSecure.isAppverOK())
                        twoFactCodeTextField.setText("");
                    Login.sayWaitDialog.setVisible(false);
                }
            });
        Login.sayWaitDialog.setVisible(true);
        Login.center(this);
        reEnterLabel.setVisible(false);
        appIDLabel.setText(applicationID);
        this.setVisible(true);
```

```
        return;
    }
```

So what's that complex bit of code at the top of our `ojsInit()` method? There is a block of code that we want to run in the background while our modal `sayWaitDialog` is being displayed. That sounds easier than it is. You see, a Java GUI application like this is generally *single-threaded*—that is, only one track of code is processed at a time. This single focus is made even more stubborn by the fact that we are using a modal dialog. The modal dialog completely dominates the single-threaded processing until the dialog is removed (made invisible, in our case).

In older versions of Java, I have had to write separate `Thread` pools to handle out-of-band processing, but in current Java versions, the `SwingUtilities` class provides a standard approach to this problem. We hand a new `Runnable` instance (`Thread`) to the `SwingUtilities.invokeLater()` method (you can see this in Listing 12-6), and it delays running the `Thread` until your current code has processed a bit further. The delay seems to work well enough for our purposes.

You can see the new `Thread` that's created in the `new Runnable()` syntax. This is an anonymous class definition. In the class definition, we define a single method named `run()` that does our work. You can see that the `run()` method does the significant initial work of the `Login` class—everything up to waiting for the user to enter a two-factor authentication code. Most of that work is accomplished in the two calls to methods in `OracleJavaSecure`, `setAppContext()` and `getAppConnections()`.

The call to `getAppConnections()` is prone to failure under one specific condition that we need to address—whenever the OS user is not authorized to proxy connect through the Oracle application user. This can occur under some circumstances with an exception being thrown, and in other circumstances with the Oracle connection as appver user being null. We have added a method in `Oracle Java Secure` to test whether the appver connection is null: `isAppverOK()`. In both sets of circumstances, we need to inform the user. However, in the delayed `Thread`, it is difficult to catch the exception and do anything helpful with it. The situation here is one where we only need to notify the user of the fact. They need to log out and back in as a different user to use the application. Here's how we will tell them: the initial value we set in `jbInit()` for the `twoFactCodeTextField` is "Your OS User account cannot log in." If we succeed at making our proxy connection, then no `Exception` will be thrown, and we will continue on through our delayed `Thread`. This will set the `twoFactCodeTextField` equal to a blank string. However, if there is an exception we will not change that value, and the text field will remain as the original error message. Instead of calling this approach "error reporting," I would call this "lack of success reporting". Keep "lack of success reporting" in mind as a viable approach in cases like this.

At the end of our delayed `Thread`, `run()` method, we make the `sayWaitDialog` invisible. The code order in `ojsInit()` is opposite of the chronological order of execution. So we end up making the `sayWaitDialog` visible before we make it invisible.

The Continue Button

The last set of activities we want to address are those that occur after the user has entered a two-factor authentication code and either pressed the enter key or clicked on the Continue button. Both of those events call the `continueButton_actionPerformed()` method. This method is shown in Listing 12-7. Notice that we call the same two methods of `OracleJavaSecure` that we called earlier; however, this time we provide the two-factor authentication code from `twoFactCodeTextField` that the user presumably received and entered.

Listing 12-7. Continue with Provided two-factor Authentication

```
private void continueButton_actionPerformed(ActionEvent e) {
    if (twoFactCodeTextField.getText().equals("Bad two-factor code"))
        twoFactCodeTextField.setText("");
```

```
    if (twoFactCodeTextField.getText().equals("") ||
        twoFactCodeTextField.getText().equals("Your OS User account cannot log in"))
        return;
    OracleJavaSecure.setAppContext(applicationID, appClass,
        twoFactCodeTextField.getText());
    OracleJavaSecure.getAppConnections();
    if (!OracleJavaSecure.test2Factor()) {
        twoFactCodeTextField.setText("Bad two-factor code");
        reEnterLabel.setVisible(true);
        return;
    }
    this.setVisible(false);
    return;
}
```

This time, after we return from the getAppConnections() method, we can test whether the two-factor code that was entered was successful by calling OracleJavaSecure.test2Factor(). This is a new method added in this chapter, the code for which is shown in Listing 12-8. We simply test the size of our list of connection strings that was returned as a result of providing our two-factor authentication code to the getAppConnections() method. A size of 0 is okay, and any other value is okay—it means the two-factor code was successful and test2Factor() returns a true. However, if the call to consHash.size() results in an Exception being thrown, then the list of connection strings is null, and we determine that the two-factor code was not acceptable, so we return a false.

Listing 12-8. Test Success of two-factor Code from OracleJavaSecure

```
public static boolean test2Factor() {
    try {
        connsHash.size();
    } catch( Exception x ) {
        return false;
    }
    return true;
}
```

Back in our Login class, in Listing 12-7, if the two-factor code is not good, we set our message in twoFactCodeTextField to "Bad two-factor code" and we make the reEnterLabel text visible. We are presenting user-feedback in the same text field used for user entry. Look back at the top of that method, continueButton_actionPerformed(). You can see how we handle messages in the field where we want the user to enter the two-factor authentication code. If they have a blank or one of our error message strings in that field, we do not try to submit it as a two-factor authentication code, but simply return.

A successful login event, where the two-factor code is acceptable and a list of connection strings has been returned causes the last lines of continueButton_actionPerformed() to be run. In that case, we basically set the Login screen to be invisible.

The Login Screen Closes

One final trick you might be interested in here: if the user exits the Login screen without completing the intended activities, then we exit the entire JVM that is running the application. This is handled through the this_WindowClosing() method with a call to System.exit(), which is shown in Listing 12-9. The method, this_WindowClosing() gets called automatically whenever the user clicks the X in the upper right-hand corner of the window to close it. In the normal process of entering an application, we will not close the Login screen, but will simply make it invisible.

Now you might be asking how the Login screen became visible in the first place, and what happens when it is no longer visible. The Login screen is called from an application, and control is returned to the application after the Login screen process, but I'm getting ahead of myself, and we will see this in the next section.

Listing 12-9. Closing the Login and Exiting the Application

```
private void this_windowClosing(WindowEvent e) {
    System.exit(0);
}
```

Security Administration Menu

We will build an application that uses all the security features we've described in this book, and we will use the application to manage the security features—we will "eat our own dog food," so to speak. We can call this application OracleJavaSecure (OJS) administration and it will consist of a Menu, shown in Figure 12-2, and several Functional screens.

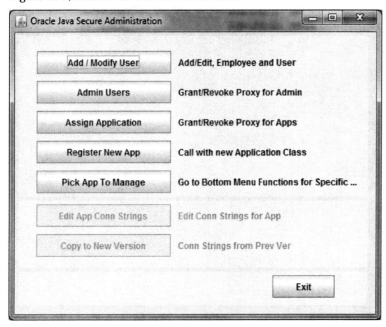

Figure 12-2. Security administration menu

The menu will reside in a class named OJSAdmin, and that class has a main() method that simply instantiates a new OJSAdmin class. See Listing 12-10. On instantiation, the OJSAdmin class runs through its JavaBeans initialization method, jbInit() and our additional initialization in the ojsInit() method.

Listing 12-10. Security Admin Menu main() method and Constructor

```java
public static void main(String[] args) {
    // Put main() method right in this JFrame
    new OJSAdmin(args);
}

public OJSAdmin(String[] args) {
    try {
        jbInit();
        // Add extra init in separate method
        ojsInit(args);
    } catch (Exception e) {
        e.printStackTrace();
    }
}
```

The OJSAdmin.ojsInit() method is shown in Listing 12-11. Its primary functions are to instantiate a new Login class, which we discussed previously, and then center itself and make itself visible. Instantiating the Login class is all that is needed to use the security features of this book. Note in Listing 12-11 that we call one of the Login constructors if there are two (or more) arguments to ojsInit(), and another Login constructor if there are not. There will be arguments if we are calling the menu in order to act on behalf of a different application (discussed later).

Listing 12-11. Additional OJSAdmin Menu Initialization

```java
private void ojsInit(String[] args) throws Exception {
    // Method for initializing OJS functionality
    JPanel disablePanel = bottomMenuPanel;
    // Login does SSO, two-factor Auth and Application Authorization

    if (args.length < 2)

        new Login(this);
    else {
        // Call Login with alternate Application ID and Class name
        new Login(this, args[0], args[1]);
        disablePanel = topMenuPanel;
    }
    // By default, we only use the top menu, so disable bottom components
    // When managing alternate application, we only use bottom menu
    Component[] comps = disablePanel.getComponents();
    for (int i = 0; i < comps.length; i++) {
        comps[i].setEnabled(false);
    }
    // This static utility method centers any component on the screen
    Login.center(this);
    // Finally, to see this frame, it must be made visible
    this.setVisible(true);
}
```

In the menu, we are going to differentiate two sets of menu buttons that we are going to display. These sets of buttons are located on two Java Swing JPanel components, topMenuPanel and bottomMenuPanel. Collecting the buttons in this way allows us to disable one of the sets of buttons by walking through all the components on a JPanel in a for loop and calling the setEnabled() method for each component.

We split the buttons into two sets because for functions represented by the topMenuPanel we will be acting with the privileges of the security administration interface (this application) and using Oracle connections associated with that application. However, for the functions represented by the bottomMenuPanel we will connect as a different, designated application and will be managing the connection strings associated with that application.

When the Login screen closes, after a successful two-factor authentication, the OJSAdmin screen becomes visible, because thread processing for the instantiation of Login has completed, and returns to the OJSAdmin.ojsInit() method, Listing 12-11. At that point, the application user can select from the menu options. If, for example, the user selects the **Add/Modify User** button, the event will call the addUserButton_actionPerformed() method (Listing 12-12), which instantiates a JavaBean for that activity, new AddUser(). Each of those activity screens that are available from the OJSAdmin menu will both hide the OJSAdmin menu screen and make it visible once again. They can do this because we pass the menu by reference to the constructor for the activity screen—note the reference to this in the call to instantiate a new AddUser class in Listing 12-12.

Listing 12-12. Action Method for the Add /Modify User Button

```
private void addUserButton_actionPerformed(ActionEvent e) {
    new AddUser(this);
}
```

Add/Modify User Functional Screen

Before we delve into the code and operation of our Add/Modify User functional screen, let's review the reasons we have this screen in the first place. Recall that we added a table in the HR schema named t_emp_mobile_nos. We are using that table to store cell phone and pager numbers, and we also store (for convenience) the operating-system user ID of the employee. We need to maintain that data to accomplish both single sign-on and two-factor authentication. Additionally, we use the e-mail address in the HR.EMPLOYEES table for two-factor authentication, so we want to be able to edit that.

In order to maintain the HR data, we want a functional screen like our Add/Modify User screen, shown in Figure 12-3. This security administration interface is not the right place to maintain employee data, but we will permit it here in order to demonstrate our secure query and update procedures that we developed in Chapter 7. We will enable viewing and updating the sensitive SALARY and COMMISSION_PCT columns.

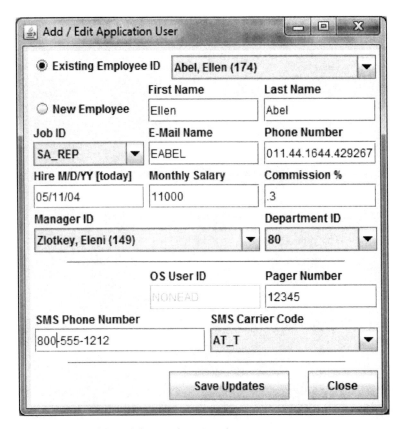

Figure 12-3. Add/Modify User functional screen

Instantiate the AddUser Screen

The Add/Modify User code is found in the file *Chapter12/orajavsec/AddUser.java*. We will begin exploring this functional screen by examining the constructors. Both constructors are shown in Listing 12-13. The first constructor is the one we call from the OJSAdmin menu. We pass a reference to OJSAdmin, so that we can hide it by calling the parent.setVisible() method. At about the same time, we set the Add/Modify User screen visible. Note that the first line in any constructor may be a call to a super-class constructor or another constructor in the same class. Here we call this(), which is a call to the default constructor (with no arguments); that is, the second constructor shown in Listing 12-13.

The last thing I'd like to point out about the first constructor shown in Listing 12-13 is that we end it by testing for the database connection being null. The connection would be null for at least a couple possible reasons, but the most important are that the operating system user account does not have access to the database. Specifically, the OS user may not have the right to proxy through the Oracle application user account that needs to be used for this function. When that occurs, we do not proceed; rather, we throw up a Dialog screen to notify the user. In this GUI single-threaded world, we will wait until the user clicks on the button to acknowledge our message before we hide the Add/Modify User screen and make the OJSAdmin menu visible once again.

Listing 12-13. Add/Modify User Screen Constructors

```java
public AddUser(JFrame parent) {
    this();
    this.parent = parent;
    // Post jbInit visual setup
    userMessageLabel.setVisible(false);
    userMessageLabel1.setVisible(false);
    ButtonGroup empGroup = new ButtonGroup();
    empGroup.add(existingEmpRadioButton);
    empGroup.add(newEmpRadioButton);
    existingEmpRadioButton.setSelected(true);
    Login.center(this);
    parent.setVisible(false);
    this.setVisible(true);
    if (null == conn) {
        JOptionPane.showMessageDialog(thisComponent,
            "Your account is not permitted to use this functional screen!");
        parent.setVisible(true);
        this.setVisible(false);
    }
}

public AddUser() {
    try {
        jbInit();
        conn = OracleJavaSecure.getAAConnRole("orcl", "appusr");
        // Possibly reentering - need new keys for new Oracle session
        OracleJavaSecure.resetKeys();
        locModulus = OracleJavaSecure.getLocRSAPubMod();
        locExponent = OracleJavaSecure.getLocRSAPubExp();
        sessionSecretDESPassPhrase = null;
        dataInit();
    } catch (Exception e) {
        e.printStackTrace();
    }
}
```

In our second constructor shown in Listing 12-13 we do the following four things:

- Call jbInit() to initialize the GUI components.

- Call getAAConnRole() to get a connection, specific for this function. Because we are performing tasks related to the employee data in the HR schema, we are going to need the hrview_role that we get through the appusr user on the orcl instance.

- Reset the encryption keys for this new connection.

- Call dataInit() to populate the drop-down combo boxes with existing values.

Probably the most important thing to know here is that we need to establish new encryption keys whenever we get a new connection, even if we are re-entering this same screen multiple times from the OJSAdmin menu. In order to assure we are cleaning up after ourselves, we call closeConnection()

whenever we close this window. That happens in the this_WindowClosing() method shown in Listing 12-14. We also see in Listing 12-14 what we described about the AddUser class making itself invisible and making the OJSAdmin menu screen visible again when done. Please use this approach as a template for opening and closing connections and resetting encryption keys.

Listing 12-14. Window Closing Method

```
private void this_windowClosing(WindowEvent e) {
    OracleJavaSecure.closeConnection();
    parent.setVisible(true);
    this.setVisible(false);
}
```

In addition to calling resetKeys() in the default constructor for AddUser, we get a new RSA key pair, storing the exponent and modulus in static members. We also have static members in AddUser for the artifacts of the DES secret password key. We set one artifact, sessionSecretDESPassPhrase to be null in Listing 12-13. We test this static member later to see whether we need to re-acquire the secret password key. If we are doing an update or insert before we do a select, then we may need to call an additional stored procedure to exchange keys, p_get_shared_passphrase.

Each of the functional screens in our application requires that we connect to a specific Oracle instance (orcl or apver) and that we connect as a specific user. The screens, instances, users, and roles are listed in Table 12-1. Different users are required because each screen requires different security privileges that we will acquire through different Oracle roles that are set based on the specific application and proxy user. The role is set through our getAAConnRole() method and the p_check_role_access procedure. That procedure finds the relation between the application/proxy user and the required role by querying the appsec.v_application_registry view. We need to insert the relationship data shown in Listing 12-15 as the appsec user on the orcl instance.

Table 12-1. OJSAdmin Functional Screen Users

Screen Class	Instance	User	Role
AddUser	orcl	appusr	hrview_role
AdminUsers	orcl	ojsaadm	ojs_adm_admin
AssignApp	orcl	ojsaadm	ojs_adm_admin
RegNewApp	apver	avadmin	appver_admin
PickAppManage	apver	avadmin	appver_admin
EditAppConns	apver	appver	{none}
Copy2NewVer	apver	appver	{none}

Listing 12-15. Script to Associate Application Users to Roles

```
INSERT INTO appsec.v_application_registry
(application_id, app_user, app_role) VALUES
('OJSADMIN','APPUSR','HRVIEW_ROLE');

INSERT INTO appsec.v_application_registry
(application_id, app_user, app_role) VALUES
('OJSADMIN','OJSAADM','OJS_ADM_ADMIN');

INSERT INTO appsec.v_application_registry
(application_id, app_user, app_role) VALUES
('OJSADMIN','AVADMIN','APPVER_ADMIN');
```

■ **Note** This script can be found in the file Chapter12/OrclAppSec.sql

During the call to the Login class associated with the OJSAdmin application in Listing 12-6, we designated OJSADMIN as the application ID. For that application ID and the specific application inner class, ojsadmin.Login$InnerRevLvlClass, there is (or will be) a list of connection strings stored in the v_app_conn_registry view. It is this list that we got from the processing in Login. Using connection strings from the list, we can connect as the different users required for the various security administration functions. The current function, Add/Modify User, requires that we have a connection to orcl as appusr with the hrview_role.

There is a lot of code in AddUser to make the GUI operate like it should, depending on user selections and entries. I will leave most of those details for you to explore and discover in the code, but I will mention a few important aspects. For instance, if the user is creating a new employee, they cannot enter data for the OS user identity until they have saved the employee and selected her from the drop-down combo box list. In the first constructor in Listing 12-13, we added a ButtonGroup and added our two radio buttons, existingEmpRadioButton and newEmpRadioButton as members. The button group assures that only one of the radio buttons is selected at a time. We also assure that personal data that was previously shown in the screen is blanked out when creating a new employee and/or user. Keeping track of what all is available and what becomes invalid as users click around on a GUI interface makes the programmer into a "bean counter" accountant.

Initialize the Data Selection Components

From the default constructor, shown second in Listing 12-13, after getting a new Oracle connection and resetting our encryption keys, we call a method to populate the drop-down combo box lists, dataInit(). The dataInit() method in Listing 12-16 has several static Oracle queries to non-sensitive views in the HR schema. Although the data is non-sensitive, we have not granted PUBLIC access to the data; rather, we granted access to the hrview_role, which we acquire and use in this Add/Modify User functional screen. The applicationID is OJSADMIN and the application user is appusr, so the corresponding role that we acquire from v_application_registry is the hrview_role according to Table 12-1 and Listing 12-15.

Using that Oracle role, we can select the list of employees from the public view, hr.v_employees_public. We created that view in Chapter 2, in the *Chapter2/HR.sql* script file. We order the list by last name of the employee, and we concatenate the last name, a comma, the first name, and the employee_id in parentheses. We do similar queries in dataInit() to populate the job ID, department ID, and manager drop-down combo lists. Notice in Listing 12-16 that, before we process the results through the while(rs.next()) loop, we first remove all existing items in the list and we add a blank string as the first item. We may call dataInit() repeatedly, after every update, because the lists of values may have changed as a result of our update. So, we clear the old listings and add new listings during initialization. We add the blank string as our first item in each list, as the default selection.

Listing 12-16. AddUser Data Initialization Method

```
private void dataInit() throws Exception {
    Statement stmt = null;
    ResultSet rs = null;
    try {
        stmt = conn.createStatement();
        rs = stmt.executeQuery("SELECT last_name || ', ' || first_name || " +
            "' (' || employee_id || ')' " +
            "FROM hr.v_employees_public ORDER BY last_name");
        // This throws event to run existingEmpComboBox_actionPerformed() method
        // Calls blankAll()
        existingEmpComboBox.removeAllItems();
        existingEmpComboBox.addItem("");
        while (rs.next()) {
            existingEmpComboBox.addItem(rs.getString(1));
        }
        if (rs != null)
            rs.close();
...
```

The list in existingEmpComboBox becomes our source for determining which employee the application user wants to view or edit. When the application user selects an employee, we need to find the corresponding data in the HR schema, and we want to find that data by employee_id. The plan will be to pull the employee ID out from between the parentheses of the selected item in existingEmpComboBox, so we will create a static utility method named pullIDFromParens(), Listing 12-17, that we will place in a class named Utility. We will use this in several places in this application, so we want it to be centrally located and not repeated as a member method of several functional screens.

Listing 12-17. Get Data Index from Data Value

```
static String pullIDFromParens(String inValue) {
    String rtrnValue = "";
    try {
        int openPlace = inValue.indexOf("(");
        int closePlace = inValue.indexOf(")", openPlace);
        if (openPlace > -1 && closePlace > -1)
            rtrnValue = inValue.substring(openPlace + 1, closePlace);
    } catch (Exception x) {
    }
    return rtrnValue;
}
```

We feel confident in using a static Oracle query instead of a stored procedure to get the list of employees and other lists in our dataInit() method (see Listing 12-16) because there are no application-user-provided parameters, so no chance of SQL injection and the data is non-sensitive, though still protected by a role grant (it's not PUBLIC). This doesn't go against what we've said about using stored procedures for queries; it is in addition to that approach. Again, querying the data directly from a view is safe as long as the query is static with no application-user-provided parameters.

In order for the hrview_role to query data from the HR.v_employees_public view, we need to grant the SELECT privilege to hrview_role. We make that grant as the HR user, along with a grant to select from HR.v_sms_carrier_host in Listing 12-18. In dataInit(), we also populate the contents of the job ID, department ID, manager, and SMS carrier drop-down boxes, so we need to select from both these views.

Listing 12-18. Grant Further Select on HR Views

```
GRANT SELECT ON hr.v_employees_public TO hrview_role;
GRANT SELECT ON hr.v_sms_carrier_host TO hrview_role;
```

■ **Note** The script for these grants is located in the file named *Chapter12/OrclHR.sql*.

Select an Existing Employee

After the AddUser screen is initialized, the application user may elect to enter data and add a new employee, or they may select an existing employee from the combo-box list. When an existing employee is selected, the existingEmpComboBox_actionPerformed() method is called. We again want to request that the application user be patient, so we make the sayWaitDialog visible—see the bottom of Listing 12-19. We show the structure of the existingEmpComboBox_actionPerformed() method in Listing 12-19, but the bulk of the run() method of our delayed Thread will be shown in later listings.

Listing 12-19. Method for Selecting Existing Employee

```
private void existingEmpComboBox_actionPerformed(ActionEvent e) {
    // When action from dataInit() at removeAllItems(), getItemCount() = 0
    if (0 == existingEmpComboBox.getItemCount() ||
        0 == existingEmpComboBox.getSelectedIndex()) {
        osUserIDTextField.setEnabled(false);
        blankAll();
        return;
    }

    employeeID = Integer.parseInt(Utility.pullIDFromParens(
        (String)existingEmpComboBox.getSelectedItem()));

    blankAll();
    SwingUtilities.invokeLater(new Runnable() {
            public void run() {

    // The bulk of the run() method has been removed from this Listing

                Login.sayWaitDialog.setVisible(false);
```

```
            }
        });
        // It may take a while to get the user data, esp while we set up encryption
        // So ask the user to be patient while working
        Login.sayWaitDialog.setVisible(true);
    }
```

That method, existingEmpComboBox_actionPerformed() gets the employee ID from the selected item by using the Utility.pullIdFromParens() method. Before we display the modal sayWaitDialog that will dominate the current GUI Thread process until dismissed or made invisible, we create a new Runnable Thread and pass it to the SwingUtilities.invokeLater() method. This delayed Thread will populate the AddUser screen with data for the selected employee.

In our delayed thread run() method, we call two Oracle stored procedures, shown in abbreviated form in Listings 12-20 and 12-22. The first procedure is one of our standard encrypted data queries from Chapter 7, p_select_employee_by_id_sens. That procedure accomplishes key exchange, if not already done, and selects data from the HR.EMPLOYEES table for the selected employee id. The salary and commission_pct values are returned in encrypted form. We call OracleJavaSecure.getDecryptData() to decrypt the values and then populate each field on AddUsers with the value we retrieved.

If there is an error with our call to p_select_employee_by_id_sens, we display an error message dialog, which is a modal dialog. If there is no error, then we get the components of the shared password (DES) key from the Oracle database. Our first call to OracleJavaSecure.getDecryptData() will have the side effect of building an equivalent DES key for use in the client.

Listing 12-20. Abbreviated run() Method when Selecting Existing Employee, Part 1

```
public void run() {
    int errNo;
    String errMsg;
    OracleCallableStatement stmt = null;
    OracleResultSet rs = null;
    try {
        stmt =
            (OracleCallableStatement)conn.prepareCall(
            "CALL hr.hr_sec_pkg.p_select_employee_by_id_sens(?,?,?,?,?,?,?,?,?,?)");
...
        stmt.setInt(10, employeeID);
        stmt.executeUpdate();

        errNo = stmt.getInt(8);
        if (errNo != 0) {
            errMsg = stmt.getString(9);
            JOptionPane.showMessageDialog(thisComponent,
                "Oracle error p_select_employee_by_id_sens) " + errNo + ", " + errMsg);
        } else {
            sessionSecretDESSalt = stmt.getRAW(3);
...
            rs = (OracleResultSet)stmt.getCursor(7);
            // Should be only one record for this Employee ID
            if (rs.next()) {
                firstNameTextField.setText(rs.getString(2));
...
                // Our stored procedure passes Hire Date back as sql.Date
```

```
    // So process here to format
    java.sql.Date sDate = rs.getDate(6);
    Date hDate = new Date(sDate.getTime());
    hireDateTextField.setText(hDateFormat.format(hDate));
    jobIDComboBox.setSelectedItem(rs.getString(7));
    deptIDComboBox.setSelectedItem(rs.getString(11));
    // Find this user's manager id in parentheses of combo box
    for (int i = 0; i < managerIDComboBox.getItemCount(); i++) {
        if (rs.getString(10).equals(Utility.pullIDFromParens(
            (String)managerIDComboBox.getItemAt(i))))
        {
            managerIDComboBox.setSelectedIndex(i);
            break;
        }
    }
    // Decrypt salary and commission pct using shared password key
    salaryTextField.setText(OracleJavaSecure.getDecryptData(rs.getRAW(8),
        sessionSecretDESPassPhrase, sessionSecretDESAlgorithm,
        sessionSecretDESSalt, sessionSecretDESIterationCount));

    commissionPctTextField.setText(

        OracleJavaSecure.getDecryptData(rs.getRAW(9),

        sessionSecretDESPassPhrase, sessionSecretDESAlgorithm,
        sessionSecretDESSalt, sessionSecretDESIterationCount));
    }
    if (rs != null) rs.close();
    if (stmt != null) stmt.close();
}
```

You can see in Listing 12-20 how we populate the AddUser form with certain data elements. We simply set the text of text fields on the form. For the date field, we take pains to convert the java.sql.Date into a java.util.Date, and we format the date using our static hDateFormat member, which was defined like this:

```
static SimpleDateFormat hDateFormat = new SimpleDateFormat("MM/dd/yy");
```

For our drop-down combo boxes, e.g., jobIDComboBox, we select the item in the existing list that corresponds with the value from our query. In the particular case of the managerIDComboBox, we walk through all the items in the existing list and call the pullIDFromParens() method to get the manager's employee ID. If that matches the manager ID we got from our query, we set that manager as our selected item. Also, you can see, we set the value for the salaryTextField and commissionPctTextField to the value we get from decrypting the data we received from our query.

We also populate the user data on the bottom half of the AddUser screen with data from the user mobile numbers view, hr.v_emp_mobile_nos. To do that, we call a new procedure in a package that we are defining in the HR schema, hr_pub_pkg.p_select_emp_mobile_nos_by_id. The script for creating this package is shown in Listing 12-21. This script should look very familiar to you at this point. Notice there are two procedures defined, the select procedure we already mentioned, and a procedure that we will use to update the data in v_emp_mobile_nos, named p_update_emp_mobile_nos. We grant execute on this package to hrview_role.

Listing 12-21. Script to Create the HR Public Package

```
CREATE OR REPLACE PACKAGE BODY hr.hr_pub_pkg IS

    PROCEDURE p_select_emp_mobile_nos_by_id(
        m_employee_id              emp_mobile_nos.employee_id%TYPE,
        resultset_out       OUT RESULTSET_TYPE,
        m_err_no            OUT NUMBER,
        m_err_txt           OUT VARCHAR2)
    IS BEGIN
        m_err_no := 0;
        OPEN resultset_out FOR SELECT
            user_id, com_pager_no, sms_phone_no, sms_carrier_cd
        FROM v_emp_mobile_nos
        WHERE employee_id = m_employee_id;
    EXCEPTION
        WHEN OTHERS THEN
            m_err_no := SQLCODE;
            m_err_txt := SQLERRM;
            appsec.app_sec_pkg.p_log_error( m_err_no, m_err_txt,
                'HR p_select_emp_mobile_nos_by_id' );
    END p_select_emp_mobile_nos_by_id;

    PROCEDURE p_update_emp_mobile_nos(
        m_employee_id       emp_mobile_nos.employee_id%TYPE,
        m_user_id           emp_mobile_nos.user_id%TYPE,
        m_com_pager_no      emp_mobile_nos.com_pager_no%TYPE,
        m_sms_phone_no      emp_mobile_nos.sms_phone_no%TYPE,
        m_sms_carrier_cd    emp_mobile_nos.sms_carrier_cd%TYPE,
        m_err_no        OUT NUMBER,
        m_err_txt       OUT VARCHAR2 )
    IS
        test_emp_ct     NUMBER(6);
    BEGIN
        -- Note: Use of this procedure assumes you have already done a select
        -- and that you are using the same Session Secret PassPhrase
        m_err_no := 0;
        SELECT COUNT(*) INTO test_emp_ct FROM v_emp_mobile_nos WHERE
            employee_id = m_employee_id;
        IF test_emp_ct = 0
        THEN
            INSERT INTO v_emp_mobile_nos
                (employee_id, user_id, com_pager_no, sms_phone_no, sms_carrier_cd)
            VALUES
                (m_employee_id, m_user_id, m_com_pager_no, m_sms_phone_no,
                m_sms_carrier_cd);
        ELSE
            UPDATE v_emp_mobile_nos
            SET user_id = m_user_id, com_pager_no = m_com_pager_no,
                sms_phone_no = m_sms_phone_no,
                sms_carrier_cd = m_sms_carrier_cd
```

```
                WHERE employee_id = m_employee_id;
        END IF;
    EXCEPTION
        WHEN OTHERS THEN
            m_err_no := SQLCODE;
            m_err_txt := SQLERRM;
            appsec.app_sec_pkg.p_log_error( m_err_no, m_err_txt,
                'HR p_update_emp_mobile_nos' );
    END p_update_emp_mobile_nos;

END hr_pub_pkg;
/
```

```
GRANT EXECUTE ON hr.hr_pub_pkg TO hrview_role;
```

The process of selecting data from the new hr_pub_pkg.p_select_emp_mobile_nos_by_id procedure is very similar to the procedure we reviewed earlier for selecting data from the v_employees_public view. However, in the case of the data from v_emp_mobile_nos, there is no sensitive data, so none of the columns is returned in encrypted form. This procedure also gets called from the delayed Thread run() method of the existingEmpComboBox_actionPerformed() method of AddUser. That call is shown in Listing 12-22. The only unique thing here is that we disable the osUserIDTextField when we populate it from this query. We do that because we do not allow the user ID to change once set for an employee. Disabling this field allows the value to be presented, albeit in grayed-out form, but doesn't allow the data value to be edited. If this query does not find values in v_emp_mobile_nos for the employee ID, then we enable the osUserIDTextField.

Listing 12-22. Abbreviated run() Method when Selecting Existing Employee, Part 2

```
    // Select from mobile_nos where emp id
    stmt = (OracleCallableStatement)conn.prepareCall(
        "CALL hr.hr_pub_pkg.p_select_emp_mobile_nos_by_id(?,?,?,?)");
...
    stmt.setInt(1, employeeID);
...
        if (rs.next()) {
            // Will not let you change a user ID for an employee
            osUserIDTextField.setEnabled(false);
            osUserIDTextField.setText(rs.getString(1));
            pagerNumberTextField.setText(rs.getString(2));
            smsPhoneNumberTextField.setText(rs.getString(3));
            smsCarrierCodeComboBox.setSelectedItem(rs.getString(4));
        } else {
            osUserIDTextField.setEnabled(true);
        }
```

These two Oracle stored procedures (shown in Listings 12-20 and 12-22) represent dynamic queries where the query includes the requirement that employee_id = user_selected_employee_id. Dynamic queries like this are susceptible to SQL injection, unless they are encapsulated in Oracle stored procedures like these. This is a design for security concern that should be considered in every security code review.

Create a New Employee

We can create new employees from the Add/Modify User functional screen. In that case, a new employee ID will be assigned. Until the employee has been created, we do not permit the application user to enter a user ID. In this way it is a two-step process. Once the employee is created, we can then select him from existingEmpComboBox and enter user and mobile number data for him.

Save Data for the Employee

Once the application user has entered data that she would like to save for the selected or new employee, she will select the Save button. That action calls the saveButton_actionPerformed() method. We show the structure of that method in Listing 12-23. In that listing, we have left out the bulk of the delayed thread run() method, which will be presented later. We test the values entered on the AddUser form to assure that values have been entered for all required fields. After we test them, we once again make the modal sayWaitDialog visible. In the meantime, we define another delayed Thread to do our work. At the end of the delayed thread run() method, we set the sayWaitDialog invisible. As I have described the use of the delayed Thread and the sayWaitDialog several times now, I will stop mentioning them; although, we will continue to use those features throughout this application.

Listing 12-23. Save Employee and User Data

```
private void saveButton_actionPerformed(ActionEvent e) {
    if (lastNameTextField.getText().equals("") ||
        jobIDComboBox.getSelectedIndex() == 0 ||
        eMailNameTextField.getText().equals("") ||
        managerIDComboBox.getSelectedIndex() == 0 ||
        deptIDComboBox.getSelectedIndex() == 0) {
        JOptionPane.showMessageDialog(thisComponent,
            "Must have values for Last Name, Job ID, E-Mail, Dept ID and Mgr ID!");
        return;
    }
    if (existingEmpComboBox.getSelectedIndex() > 0 &&
        osUserIDTextField.getText().equals("") &&
        (!(pagerNumberTextField.getText().equals("") &&
            smsPhoneNumberTextField.getText().equals("")))) {
        JOptionPane.showMessageDialog(thisComponent,
            "Must have value for User ID, else blank mobile nos!");
        return;
    }
    SwingUtilities.invokeLater(new Runnable() {
        public void run() {

...

            Login.sayWaitDialog.setVisible(false);
        }
    });
    // Ask the user to be patient while working
    Login.sayWaitDialog.setVisible(true);
}
```

The delayed Thread that is defined in the saveButton_actionPerformed() method does our Oracle update processing. In this case, the real processing occurs in two update Oracle stored procedures. The first is our encrypted sensitive data update procedure, p_update_employees_sensitive, from Chapter 7. The second is a new update procedure in the hr_public_pkg package for data in the hr.v_emp_mobile_nos view, p_update_emp_mobile_nos shown in Listing 12-21.

In Listing 12-24, we see the code used to call the p_update_employees_sensitive procedure. We pass the current employee ID to indicate which employee we are updating. Notice that we set parameters eight and nine to the encrypted values of the salary and commission percent fields. We also take the formatted date entered for hire date and parse it using the hDateFormat.parse() method into a java.util.Date, then convert it into a java.sql.Date to pass to the Oracle stored procedure for update. If no entry exists in the Hire Date field, we submit the current date to the procedure. One of the user-interface protections we enforce in AddUser is that the application user may not edit the hire date of an existing employee.

■ **Note** This process removes time significance from the hire date. We are doing that just for simplicity here.

Listing 12-24. Update Employee Data

```
stmt = (OracleCallableStatement)conn.prepareCall(
"CALL hr.hr_sec_pkg.p_update_employees_sensitive(?,?,?,?,?,?,?,?,?,?,?,?,?)");
stmt.registerOutParameter(12, OracleTypes.NUMBER);
stmt.registerOutParameter(13, OracleTypes.VARCHAR);
stmt.setInt(1, employeeID);
...
if (hireDateTextField.getText().equals("")) {
    stmt.setDate(6, new java.sql.Date((new Date()).getTime()));
} else {
    Date hDate = hDateFormat.parse(hireDateTextField.getText());
    stmt.setDate(6, new java.sql.Date(hDate.getTime()));
}
stmt.setString(7, (String)jobIDComboBox.getSelectedItem());
stmt.setRAW(8, OracleJavaSecure.getCryptData(salaryTextField.getText()));
stmt.setRAW(9, OracleJavaSecure.getCryptData(commissionPctTextField.getText()));
...
stmt.executeUpdate();
```

We only call the p_update_emp_mobile_nos procedure in Listing 12-25 if we have selected an existing employee and if the osUserIDTextField is not blank. We do not do any further data validation here, but you may want to.

■ **Note** Adding an entry in the hr.v_emp_mobile_nos view does not equate to creating an Oracle user with the user ID we entered in the view. However, we will need to create the Oracle user in order for that user to have access to our applications. As a corollary situation, we may drop (delete) an Oracle user, but the entry in hr.v_amp_mobile_nos will not be automatically deleted.

Listing 12-25. Update User and Mobile Numbers

```
if (existingEmpComboBox.getSelectedIndex() > 0 &&
    (!osUserIDTextField.getText().equals(""))) {
    stmt = (OracleCallableStatement)conn.prepareCall(
    "CALL hr.hr_pub_pkg.p_update_emp_mobile_nos(?,?,?,?,?,?,?)");
...
```

If we are creating a new employee without having selected an existing employee previously, then we would not have exchanged encryption keys yet. If that's the case, then the sessionSecretDESPassPhrase member (among others) will be null. We test sessionSecretDESPassPhrase for null, and if it is we call an additional Oracle stored procedure, p_get_shared_passphrase, from Chapter 7, to exchange keys before calling the data update procedures.

WHEN DOES THE ORACLE USER GET CREATED?

As of yet, we have not created the Oracle user corresponding to user ID we entered on the Add/Modify User functional screen. For each employee in the HR.EMPLOYEES table, we can create a record in hr.v_emp_mobile_nos that contains a user ID. The user ID is the same as the name of a Windows (operating system) account. We will create an Oracle user with that same name, and we will use the fact of having identical names to do single sign-on. The Oracle user will be granted access because the person has already logged in as an identical operating system user.

You may now wonder why we never ran a procedure to create the Oracle user from our Add/Modify User functional screen. It wasn't an oversight, but merely a delay until the last minute. We have no reason to create an Oracle user if he does not have access to any applications, so we will only create the user when we first grant him access to an application. That will happen in either the Admin Users or Assign Application functional screens, described next.

User Administration Screen

In the security administration interface application, each of our functional screens has many similarities to one another. We discussed many of those features already in looking at the Add/Modify User functional screen, and we won't repeat those details. However, there are plenty of new ideas introduced in each screen that will give us food for thought. The Admin Users functional screen is our current topic of discussion.

In the Admin Users screen shown in Figure 12-4, we have a drop-down combo box where we will find a list of all the users, userComboBox. This is not a list of all employees, but rather a list of all those employees with records in the hr.v_emp_mobile_nos view. For each user, we get the user ID from hr.v_emp_mobile_nos and the first and last name from hr.v_employees_public. We accomplish this in the dataInit() method of the AdminUsers class, and the process is identical to what we did in the dataInit() method of AddUser, as described previously.

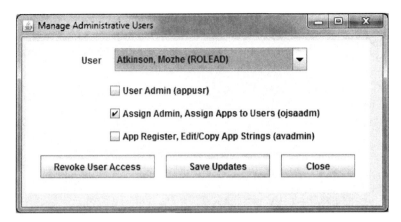

Figure 12-4. *Admin Users functional screen*

Also on the Admin Users screen, you will see three check boxes: one for each administrative proxy user: appusr, ojsaadm, and avadmin. When a user is selected from the drop-down list, these checkboxes will be populated with checkmarks or blanks corresponding to the current proxy grants for the user. By selecting or deselecting these check boxes and clicking on the Save Updates button, the application user can grant and revoke those privileges from the selected user.

There is one more button on the Admin Users screen, the Revoke User Access button. The function of this button stops short of deleting the Oracle user account; however, it revokes all the application grants that the user has, including the grant to proxy through appver—so the user in effect can no longer use our applications.

Create the OJSAAdm User

In the Admin Users functional screen, we are connecting to the orcl instance as the ojsaadm user. This is one of the proxy users we listed in Table 12-1. We need to create that Oracle user, and we need to grant him access to the HR views needed to populate the userComboBox. We will do this on the orcl instance as the Security Administrator, secadm user. The commands we are going to use are shown in Listing 12-26. When you execute those commands, substitute the OS username of the person you want to have manage the lists of administrators for the placeholder osadmin, and give the new ojsaadm user a strong password.

Listing 12-26. *Create the OJSAAdm User*

```
GRANT create_session_role TO ojsaadm IDENTIFIED BY password;
CREATE ROLE ojs_adm_admin IDENTIFIED USING appsec.p_check_role_access;
ALTER USER osadmin GRANT CONNECT THROUGH ojsaadm;

GRANT SELECT ON hr.v_employees_public TO ojs_adm_admin;
GRANT SELECT ON hr.v_emp_mobile_nos TO ojs_adm_admin;

GRANT CREATE DATABASE LINK TO ojsaadm;
GRANT CREATE VIEW TO ojsaadm;
GRANT CREATE PROCEDURE TO ojsaadm;
```

■ **Note** These commands are listed in the file *Chapter12/OrclSecAdm.sql*.

In addition to granting our new user the privilege to select from the HR views to populate the users list, you can see in listing 12-26 that we are giving this user some additional privileges. We are granting ojsaadm the system privileges to create database links, views, and procedures. We are going to put this Oracle user account to work. In fact, we are enlisting this Oracle user to talk across a database link from the orcl to the apver instance to accomplish user administration on both sides. That being said, we need to create an identical user on the apver instance. Listing 12-27 shows the script we will use to accomplish that. As usual, we are connecting as the SYS user to accomplish most of our work on the apver instance.

Listing 12-27. Create the OJSAAdm User on the apver Instance

```
GRANT create_session_role TO ojsaadm IDENTIFIED BY password;
GRANT SELECT ON sys.proxy_users TO ojsaadm;
```

■ **Note** The script that is partly shown in Listing 12-27 is included in the file `Chapter12/ApverSys.sql`.

From what we have described for the functions of the Admin Users screen, you might imagine that this user needs to read some unusual data from the Oracle database in order to accomplish his tasks. One thing ojsaadm needs to do is to read from the data dictionary view, sys.proxy_users. It is from that view that we will observe the avenue of access from the Oracle user through whom our OS user is matched by SSO, to the application role which is aligned with the Oracle user acting as the proxy. By adding or removing the ability to proxy through one of our application users, the individual person user is able or not to access the application.

Not just any Oracle user can modify data in the sys.proxy_users view. In Listing 12-27, you see that we granted SELECT on that view to the ojsaadm user on the apver instance. We are going to make the same grant to ojsaadm on the orcl instance. It is not sufficient to accomplish our plan to just have SELECT privilege on that view. To grant and revoke proxy privileges, we need the ALTER USER privilege. Additionally, as I described at the end of our discussion of the Add/Modify User screen, we need the ability to CREATE USER at the time we grant them their first application proxy. To do this, we will create a package in the SYS schema called usr_role_adm_pkg with procedures that will create users and grant and revoke proxy privileges. On the orcl instance, the script to create this package is shown in Listing 12-28. An identical package will be created on the apver instance.

In the usr_role_adm_pkg package definition in Listing 12-28, you can see five procedures are defined. There are two procedures required to create a user, p_create_user_once and p_create_user_many. We have split that process up into two procedures because the first, where we actually create the Oracle user, will experience an exception if the user already exists. The second procedure, p_create_user_many, is also part of the process to create an Oracle user account for application access. In that procedure, we grant the create_session_role to the user and grant him the permission to proxy through the appver user. That proxy is required in order to do SSO and two-factor authentication. Even if an Oracle user already exists and was created with a password, he will not be able to use our applications unless he is able to proxy through appver. Notice that when we create new users strictly for application access, we do not give them a password; rather, we direct that they are IDENTIFIED EXTERNALLY. Usually, that would mean that we use the OS or a naming service to authenticate the user, but in our case, we authenticate our one, big application user (appver) and allow this IDENTIFIED EXTERNALLY user to proxy through. No authentication for the individual person Oracle user ever occurs.

There is also a procedure for revoking user access to our applications, p_drop_user. This name is a bit of an overstatement, because we do not actually drop the Oracle user account. That account may exist for some reason other than to access our applications. It may even have an associated password and allow the user to use the Oracle database in her own schema. All we really want to accomplish is to keep the user from accessing our applications, and we can do that by simply revoking the privilege to proxy through the appver user. That is all the p_drop_user procedure does.

Listing 12-28. Create the sys.usr_role_adm_pkg Package

```
CREATE OR REPLACE PACKAGE BODY sys.usr_role_adm_pkg IS

    PROCEDURE p_create_user_once( username sys.proxy_users.client%TYPE )
    AS
        PRAGMA AUTONOMOUS_TRANSACTION;
    BEGIN
        EXECUTE IMMEDIATE 'CREATE USER ' || username || ' IDENTIFIED EXTERNALLY';
        COMMIT;
    EXCEPTION
        WHEN OTHERS
        THEN
            appsec.app_sec_pkg.p_log_error( SQLCODE, SQLERRM,
                'sys.usr_role_adm_pkg.p_create_user_once for ' || username );
    END p_create_user_once;

    PROCEDURE p_create_user_many( username sys.proxy_users.client%TYPE )
    AS
        PRAGMA AUTONOMOUS_TRANSACTION;
    BEGIN
        EXECUTE IMMEDIATE 'GRANT create_session_role TO ' || username;
        EXECUTE IMMEDIATE 'ALTER USER ' || username || ' GRANT CONNECT THROUGH appver';
        COMMIT;
    EXCEPTION
        WHEN OTHERS
        THEN
            appsec.app_sec_pkg.p_log_error( SQLCODE, SQLERRM,
                'sys.usr_role_adm_pkg.p_create_user_many for ' || username );
    END p_create_user_many;

    PROCEDURE p_drop_user( username sys.proxy_users.client%TYPE )
    AS
        PRAGMA AUTONOMOUS_TRANSACTION;
    BEGIN
        EXECUTE IMMEDIATE 'ALTER USER ' || username || ' REVOKE CONNECT THROUGH appver';
        COMMIT;
    EXCEPTION
        WHEN OTHERS
        THEN
            appsec.app_sec_pkg.p_log_error( SQLCODE, SQLERRM,
```

```
                    'sys.usr_role_adm_pkg.p_drop_user for ' || username );
    END p_drop_user;

    PROCEDURE p_set_proxy_through(
        username sys.proxy_users.client%TYPE,
        proxyname sys.proxy_users.proxy%TYPE )
    AS
        PRAGMA AUTONOMOUS_TRANSACTION;
    BEGIN
        EXECUTE IMMEDIATE 'ALTER USER ' || username ||
            ' GRANT CONNECT THROUGH ' || proxyname;
        COMMIT;
    EXCEPTION
        WHEN OTHERS
        THEN
            appsec.app_sec_pkg.p_log_error( SQLCODE, SQLERRM,
                'sys.usr_role_adm_pkg.p_set_proxy_through for ' ||
                username || '/' || proxyname );
    END p_set_proxy_through;

    PROCEDURE p_drop_proxy_through(
        username sys.proxy_users.client%TYPE,
        proxyname sys.proxy_users.proxy%TYPE )
    AS
        PRAGMA AUTONOMOUS_TRANSACTION;
    BEGIN
        EXECUTE IMMEDIATE 'ALTER USER ' || username ||
            ' REVOKE CONNECT THROUGH ' || proxyname;
        COMMIT;
    EXCEPTION
        WHEN OTHERS
        THEN
            appsec.app_sec_pkg.p_log_error( SQLCODE, SQLERRM,
                'sys.usr_role_adm_pkg.p_drop_proxy_through for ' ||
                username || '/' || proxyname );
    END p_drop_proxy_through;

END usr_role_adm_pkg;
/

GRANT EXECUTE ON sys.usr_role_adm_pkg TO ojs_adm_admin;
```

In order to grant and revoke privilege to access specific applications, we need to execute commands to ALTER USER and either GRANT or REVOKE CONNECT THROUGH the specific application proxy user that is used for the application. Those steps are accomplished by the p_set_proxy_through and p_drop_proxy_through procedures.

In each of these procedures, we concatenate a SQL command that represents what we want to accomplish and call EXECUTE IMMEDIATE, which is extremely handy for executing dynamic data definition language (DDL) statements like CREATE USER and ALTER USER. All of these procedures are defined with the modifier PRAGMA AUTONOMOUS_TRANSACTION. That allows each procedure to commit its own transaction.

The question arises, "why didn't we just grant the system privileges to CREATE USER and ALTER USER to ojsaadm?" First, we would still want to wrap these commands in procedures to control the parameters and avoid SQL injection attacks. And second, we want to limit what `ojsaadm` can actually do. Notice that in these procedures, `ojsaadm` can only create users that are `IDENTIFIED EXTERNALLY`. Beyond that, he can only grant and revoke the privilege to proxy through other users—that is much more limited ability than the grant of `ALTER USER` provides.

I mentioned that an identical package is to be created on the apver instance. The script for that is in the file *Chapter12/ApverSys.sql*. There is one difference between the instances in this regard. On the `orcl` instance, we grant execute on `usr_role_adm_pkg` to the `ojs_adm_admin` role; while on the apver instance, we grant it directly to the `ojsaadm` user. Now the challenge for us is in how we will execute the commands on both database instances at one time. We will do this across a database link.

Enable the OJSAAdm User Across a Database Link

Connect as the `ojsaadm` user to the `orcl` instance. While there, you can test your access to the `sys.proxy_users` data dictionary view. That command is shown first in Listing 12-29. The second command in Listing 12-29 is the command to create the database link. Change the password placeholder to the password you used to create `ojsaadm` on the apver instance.

■ **Caution** Take a moment to assure that the password for `ojsaadm` on the apver instance in particular is very complex. We have opened another avenue of attack on our perimeter by creating another user on the apver instance. With a very strong password (for example 15 random characters, mixed case with numeric and special characters) we can shore up our defenses. This is a password that will be used in the database link, but rarely typed in. We would prefer to disable the password for `ojsaadm` or to create a login trigger that denies him access, but in order to use our database link, `ojsaadm` needs to be able to log in on the apver instance.

Listing 12-29. Create Link as OJSAAdm User

```
SELECT * FROM sys.proxy_users;

-- Private database link to apver as ojsaadm
CREATE DATABASE LINK apver_link
CONNECT TO ojsaadm
IDENTIFIED BY password
USING 'apver';

CREATE OR REPLACE VIEW ojsaadm.instance_proxy_users AS
SELECT 'APVER' INSTANCE, proxy, client FROM sys.proxy_users@apver_link
UNION SELECT 'ORCL' INSTANCE, proxy, client FROM sys.proxy_users;

-- Test the link and view
SELECT * FROM ojsaadm.instance_proxy_users;

GRANT SELECT ON ojsaadm.instance_proxy_users TO ojs_adm_admin;
```

```
-- To let appsec read view across database link
GRANT SELECT ON ojsaadm.instance_proxy_users TO appsec;
```

The third command in Listing 12-29 creates a view that will bring together the results of a select on
sys.proxy_users from both the orcl and apver instances. This view is a UNION of the results of two
queries, one from each instance, and includes a prefix column indicating the instance on which the
proxy was observed. Test the new view by selecting from it—this will also be a test of the grant on apver
for ojsaadm to select from sys.proxy_users. We will grant select on this view to all users who proxy
through ojsaadm and acquire the ojs_adm_admin role.

The last command in Listing 12-29 provides one more avenue of access. You see, sometimes we
need to be able to see all the proxy users on the orcl instance from procedures running on the apver
instance. On apver, the appsec user already has a link to the orcl instance. That link was set up initially
so that application security, appsec user could do two-factor authentication by selecting from
hr.v_emp_mobile_nos on orcl. Here we are extending the functionality of the appsec private database
link from apver to orcl by allowing it to select all the proxy users from our new view. This also saves us
from having to grant SELECT on sys.proxy_users to appsec on the apver instance; she will be selecting
from proxy_users on apver by selecting the view on orcl which selects from proxy_users across a link to
apver. If this sounds circular, that's because it is.

Well, as we have observed, selecting from sys.proxy_users does not meet the goals of our plan to
manage proxy grants. From the Admin Users screen, we want to be able to grant and revoke the privilege
to proxy through application users on both the orcl and apver instances. We also want to do that from a
single Oracle connection, if possible. Is it possible to do this across a database link? It certainly is. In
Listing 12-30 we see the definition of a package for just this purpose, ojsaadm.apver_usr_adm_pkg. We
will create the package in the ojsaadm schema, and the package will have access through the private
database link, apver_link to execute procedures on the apver instance.

Please notice in Listing 12-30 that we are calling the procedures across the link with a
parameterized, EXECUTE IMMEDIATE statement. Our PL/SQL style call is defined in the m_stmt string. For
the variable (e.g., user name) we don't concatenate it with the statement string; rather, we have a
placeholder for it, :1. We call that statement string from an EXECUTE IMMEDIATE command, and pass the
username in to fill the placeholder by specifying USING username. This is another form of parameterized
statement that is also impervious to SQL Injection like stored procedures and prepared statements in
Java, which we discussed in the section called "Avoid SQL Injection" in Chapter 7.

Listing 12-30. Package Definition for Executing Procedures Across a Link

```
CREATE OR REPLACE PACKAGE BODY ojsaadm.apver_usr_adm_pkg IS

    PROCEDURE p_create_apver_user( username VARCHAR2 )
    AS
        m_stmt VARCHAR2(100);
    BEGIN
        m_stmt := 'BEGIN sys.usr_role_adm_pkg.p_create_user_once@apver_link( :1 ); END;';
        EXECUTE IMMEDIATE m_stmt USING username;
        m_stmt := 'BEGIN sys.usr_role_adm_pkg.p_create_user_many@apver_link( :1 ); END;';
        EXECUTE IMMEDIATE m_stmt USING username;
    END p_create_apver_user;

    PROCEDURE p_drop_apver_user( username VARCHAR2 )
    AS
        m_stmt VARCHAR2(100);
    BEGIN
```

```
        m_stmt := 'BEGIN sys.usr_role_adm_pkg.p_drop_user@apver_link( :1 ); END;';
        EXECUTE IMMEDIATE m_stmt USING username;
    END p_drop_apver_user;

    PROCEDURE p_set_apver_proxy_through( username VARCHAR2, proxyname VARCHAR2 )
    AS
        m_stmt VARCHAR2(100);
    BEGIN
        m_stmt :=
        'BEGIN sys.usr_role_adm_pkg.p_set_proxy_through@apver_link( :1, :2 ); END;';
        EXECUTE IMMEDIATE m_stmt USING username, proxyname;
    END p_set_apver_proxy_through;

    PROCEDURE p_drop_apver_proxy_through( username VARCHAR2, proxyname VARCHAR2 )
    AS
        m_stmt VARCHAR2(100);
    BEGIN
        m_stmt :=
        'BEGIN sys.usr_role_adm_pkg.p_drop_proxy_through@apver_link( :1, :2 ); END;';
        EXECUTE IMMEDIATE m_stmt USING username, proxyname;
    END p_drop_apver_proxy_through;

END apver_usr_adm_pkg;
/

-- Grant to role
GRANT EXECUTE ON ojsaadm.apver_usr_adm_pkg TO ojs_adm_admin;
```

The procedures in the ojsaadm.apver_usr_adm_pkg correspond to procedures in the
sys.usr_role_adm_pkg, with one exception. The procedure in this package, p_create_apver_user, calls
both the p_create_user_once and p_create_user_many procedures in sys.usr_role_adm_pkg. No
exception is thrown by the sys.usr_role_adm_pkg procedures, so we will succeed in calling
p_create_user_many even if the user already exists and p_create_user_once fails. Finally, we grant
EXECUTE on this package to the ojs_adm_admin role.

Select an Existing User

We return now from examining the Oracle structures and grants needed to accomplish our plan to the
Admin Users functional screen. We will look first at the actions that occur when the application user
selects an existing user from the drop-down userComboBox. The userComboBox_actionPerformed()
method gets called. We first get the user ID from within the parentheses in the selected item by calling
the pullIDFromParens() method like this:

```
userID = Utility.pullIDFromParens((String)userComboBox.getSelectedItem());
```

Next, we create a delayed thread whose run() method contains the query shown in Listing 12-31.
Notice that we select all the rows of the instance_proxy_users view – this is a static query, not vulnerable
to SQL injection. We walk through the ResultSet testing each row for a value of client that matches our
selected user. Then we check if the value of proxy matches any of our administrative users, and we select
the corresponding check box on the Admin Users screen. Before we got to this point, in the
userComboBox_actionPerformed() method, we called the blankAll() method, which had deselected all of

the check boxes. So at the end of this procedure, the only check boxes that are selected are those representing proxy privileges that are granted to the selected user.

Listing 12-31. Query to get Administrative Proxy Grants for the Selected User

```
rs = stmt.executeQuery("SELECT INSTANCE, proxy, client " +
    "FROM ojsaadm.instance_proxy_users ");
while (rs.next()) {
    if (rs.getString(3).equalsIgnoreCase(userID)) {
        if (rs.getString(2).equalsIgnoreCase("OJSAADM"))
            ojsaadmCheckBox.setSelected(true);
        if (rs.getString(2).equalsIgnoreCase("APPUSR"))
            appusrCheckBox.setSelected(true);
        if (rs.getString(2).equalsIgnoreCase("AVADMIN"))
            avadminCheckBox.setSelected(true);
    }
}
```

Save Updates to the Administrative Privileges

When the application user has selected a user and made changes to the administrative privilege check boxes that are selected, he will need to save the changes. He does this by selecting the Save Updates button. When that button is selected, the saveButton_actionPerformed() method is called. Once again, the selected userID is pulled from the selected item in the userComboBox. A delayed thread is created with the code in Listing 12-32 in its run() method.

This method is extensive because we are independently calling procedures to grant or revoke each privilege represented by the check boxes on the Admin Users screen. We could have combined several of these calls into a dynamic loop, but we wouldn't have saved much code, and the clarity would have been diminished. The first step we take is to try to create the user on both the orcl and apver instances. The user may already exist, but this is an easy enough step and assures the user both exists and has the privileges needed to run our applications. We call three Oracle procedures to create the user—two operate on the orcl instance (sys.usr_role_adm_pkg.p_create_user_once and p_create_user_many), and one operates across a database link to the apver instance (ojsaadm.apver_usr_adm_pkg.p_create_apver_user). Each of these procedure calls has the identical syntax, so I'll only show the full syntax once. Some of the procedure calls take one parameter, the user ID; some take two parameters, the user ID and the proxy user.

Listing 12-32. Saving Updates to Administrative Privileges, Abbreviated

```
stmt = (OracleCallableStatement)conn.prepareCall(
    "CALL sys.usr_role_adm_pkg.p_create_user_once(?)");
stmt.setString(1, userID);
stmt.executeUpdate();
if (stmt != null) stmt.close();


stmt = (OracleCallableStatement)conn.prepareCall(
    "CALL sys.usr_role_adm_pkg.p_create_user_many(?)");
...
stmt = (OracleCallableStatement)conn.prepareCall(
    "CALL ojsaadm.apver_usr_adm_pkg.p_create_apver_user(?)");
```

```
...
    // Next, grant or revoke each proxy
    if (ojsaadmCheckBox.isSelected()) {
        stmt = (OracleCallableStatement)conn.prepareCall(
            "CALL sys.usr_role_adm_pkg.p_set_proxy_through(?,?)");
        stmt.setString(1, userID);
        stmt.setString(2, "OJSAADM");
...
    } else {
        stmt = (OracleCallableStatement)conn.prepareCall(
            "CALL sys.usr_role_adm_pkg.p_drop_proxy_through(?,?)");
...
    }
    if (appusrCheckBox.isSelected()) {
        stmt = (OracleCallableStatement)conn.prepareCall(
            "CALL sys.usr_role_adm_pkg.p_set_proxy_through(?,?)");
        stmt.setString(1, userID);
        stmt.setString(2, "APPUSR");
...
    } else {
        stmt = (OracleCallableStatement)conn.prepareCall(
            "CALL sys.usr_role_adm_pkg.p_drop_proxy_through(?,?)");
...
    }
    if (avadminCheckBox.isSelected()) {
        stmt = (OracleCallableStatement)conn.prepareCall(
            "CALL sys.usr_role_adm_pkg.p_set_proxy_through(?,?)");
        stmt.setString(1, userID);
        stmt.setString(2, "AVADMIN");
...
        stmt = (OracleCallableStatement)conn.prepareCall(
            "CALL ojsaadm.apver_usr_adm_pkg.p_set_apver_proxy_through(?,?)");
...
        stmt = (OracleCallableStatement)conn.prepareCall(
            "CALL ojsaadm.apver_usr_adm_pkg.p_grant_apver_appver_conns(?)");
        stmt.setString(1, userID);
...
    } else {
        stmt = (OracleCallableStatement)conn.prepareCall(
            "CALL sys.usr_role_adm_pkg.p_drop_proxy_through(?,?)");
...
        stmt = (OracleCallableStatement)conn.prepareCall(
            "CALL ojsaadm.apver_usr_adm_pkg.p_drop_apver_proxy_through(?,?)");
...
        stmt = (OracleCallableStatement)conn.prepareCall(
            "CALL ojsaadm.apver_usr_adm_pkg.p_revoke_apver_appver_conns(?)");
...
    }
    blankAll();
```

We call either p_set_proxy_through or p_drop_proxy_through for each of the administrative proxy users, depending on whether the check box is selected for that administrative proxy or not. In addition, for the proxy user avadmin, we also call the procedures that go across the link to grant or revoke proxy, ojsaadm.apver_usr_adm_pkg.p_set_apver_proxy_through or p_set_apver_proxy_through, because this proxy user is used on both instances.

If the avadminCheckBox is selected we run one more procedure, p_grant_apver_appver_conns, and if not selected, we run p_revoke_apver_appver_conns. We will discuss those procedures in detail when we get to the Register New Application screen. The procedures grant or revoke another role we will need at that point.

Revoke User Access to Run Applications

When the administrative user selects a user on the Admin Users screen and then selects the Revoke User Access button, the revokeUserButton_actionPerformed() method is called. The code that gets run in that method drops all the proxies for the selected user on both instances. This code is shown in Listing 12-33.

We instantiate an ordinary Statement class, stmt2, which will support a query that returns a ResultSet. This is in addition to the OracleCallableStatement that we instantiate to call our stored procedures. Similarly to the way we selected from ojsaadm.instance_proxy_users to set the administrative proxy grant check boxes when an existing user is selected from our userComboBox; here again, we select all the proxy users and only concern ourselves, as we walk through the ResultSet, with those proxy grants that were made to the selected user. Then if the instance where we saw the proxy grant is equal to "apver," we call the stored procedure to revoke the proxy grant across the database link. Otherwise, we call the stored procedure to revoke the proxy grant locally.

Listing 12-33. Dropping all Administrative and Application Proxy Privileges

```
stmt2 = conn.createStatement();
rs = stmt2.executeQuery("SELECT INSTANCE, proxy, client " +
    "FROM ojsaadm.instance_proxy_users ");
while (rs.next()) {
    if (rs.getString(3).equalsIgnoreCase(userID)) {
        if (rs.getString(1).equalsIgnoreCase("apver")) {
            stmt = (OracleCallableStatement)conn.prepareCall(
                "CALL ojsaadm.apver_usr_adm_pkg.p_drop_apver_proxy_through(?,?)");
        } else {
            stmt = (OracleCallableStatement)conn.prepareCall(
                "CALL sys.usr_role_adm_pkg.p_drop_proxy_through(?,?)");
        }
        stmt.setString(1, userID);
        stmt.setString(2, rs.getString(1));
        stmt.executeUpdate();
        if (stmt != null) stmt.close();
    }
}
if (rs != null) rs.close();
blankAll();
```

I considered writing this method a bit differently, only dropping those proxies that we know are related to our applications, and you may want to rewrite this (calling both p_drop_user and p_drop_apver_user procedures to revoke the proxy grant to appver) if that is your goal. This method as written will drop all application proxies, including the privilege to proxy through the appver user, which will keep the Oracle user from accomplishing SSO or two-factor authentication. We do not, however, drop the Oracle user account.

Application Assignment Screen

The Assign Application functional screen shares a lot of the concepts and code that we used in the Admin Users screen. Here, though, we are not dealing with the administrative proxy grants, but with grants to proxy for other applications. Figure 12-5 displays the Assign Application screen.

■ **Note** Users who are able to proxy through `ojsadmin` are able to assign any application to any users. Perhaps another level of filtering would be appropriate, but that has not been added in this book. On the positive side, these `ojsadmin` administrators can fill in for one another, assigning user access to each other's applications. The only application-specific administrative filtering we do here is in limiting which administrators can change connection strings (passwords) for which applications.

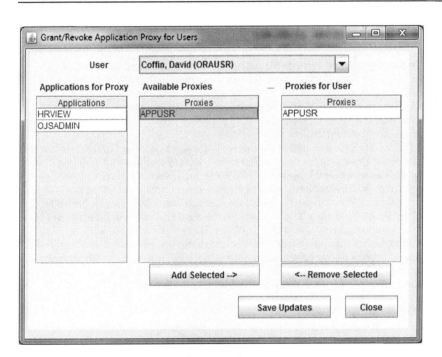

Figure 12-5. Assign Application functional screen

When there are many application proxies, having them all represented in a selectable table is easier than having a check box for each proxy. The one drawback in selecting from a list like this is the somewhat more likely possibility that an incorrect selection will be made and overlooked. For that reason, we don't show the administrative proxy users in this list.

The drop-down combo box at the top of the Assign Applications screen is where we select a user. We will be managing that user's access to applications. The far right table displays the list of proxy grants already given to the selected user, and the middle table lists all the available proxy grants. When an available proxy is selected, the far left table shows a list of applications in which that proxy is used. For example, the appusr proxy is assigned to users of the HRVIEW application as well as the OJSADMIN application.

These tables are a couple layers deep in nested GUI objects. Our tables reside in a scroll pane so that when the table grows beyond what can be seen in the little box we've provided, we will have vertical and/or horizontal scroll bars to give us access to the remaining data.

To add a proxy for the selected user, the Add Selected button will be pressed, and, likewise, to revoke a proxy from the selected user, the Remove Selected button will be pressed. To save these new settings, the application user will press the Save Updates button.

Initializing the Data Selection Components

When we instantiate a new AssignApp class, we will call the dataInit() method to populate three data-selection components. We will build the list of users for our userComboBox, as we have seen in other functional screens. We will also build a list of available application proxy accounts. And we will build a lookup table of lists of applications where a proxy user is used. Then, when a proxy user is selected from the available proxies list, we will display the associated list of applications in the far left column of the Assign Applications screen.

In our list of available proxy users for applications, we will not provide a true list of available proxies, because every Oracle user is in fact potentially a proxy-through user. We do not want to display all the Oracle users, or incorrect selections are bound to happen. Rather, the proxy users we will show in the available proxies list will be only those app_user entries from the appsec.v_application_registry view that are not also security administration proxies. Recall that we grant and revoke access to the administrative proxy users through the Admin Users screen. The available proxies will be the list of app_user entries for all registered, non-administrative applications.

For our available proxies list, we are going to populate a new GUI widget called a JTable. It is not so straightforward to populate the JTable as it was for our combo boxes. We cannot just call addItem(). In a JTable, there is an underlying table model that we populate. We are using instances of the DefaultTableModel that we declare as static members of AssignApps. This is shown in Listing 12-34.

Each table model has both data and column labels. The data and column labels can be provided to the table model in a variety of forms, and we elect to provide both the data and column labels as Vectors. We will only have a single column in our tables, which will be either a list of "Proxies" or a list of "Applications." Our column identifier vectors are defined as static members of AssignApp as shown in Listing 12-34. If we had multiple columns in our tables, we would add a label for each column to our column identifier Vectors. We do not have to tell the JTable how many columns of data we are going to have—it divines that from the number of entries in our column identifiers Vector.

Listing 12-34. Static Members of Assign Applications

```
static DefaultTableModel availableProxiesTM = new DefaultTableModel();
static DefaultTableModel userProxiesTM = new DefaultTableModel();
static DefaultTableModel appsTM = new DefaultTableModel();
static Vector columnIdentifiers = new Vector();
static {
    columnIdentifiers.add("Proxies");
}
static Vector appColumnIdentifiers = new Vector();
static {
    appColumnIdentifiers.add("Applications");
```

```
}
static Hashtable<String, Vector> appsHashtable =
    new Hashtable<String, Vector>();
```

The last static member we declare in Listing 12-34 is a Hashtable. The appsHashTable will have a key, the proxy user name, and a value, the Vector of applications where that proxy user is used.

A DefaultTableModel assumes that each row may have multiple columns, so it does not handle data as a simple list, even when there is only one column. Rather, in the case where Vectors are used, it expects each row to be a Vector of data elements, one for each column. So in the end, the data we provide to the table model in order to build our table will be a Vector of Vectors holding a list of potentially multi-column rows.

Now that you know where we are headed in building the data Vectors for our tables, let's look at the code from dataInit() that builds our available proxies list. This code is shown in Listing12-35. Look closely at the while loop where we handle the ResultSet from our query. We instantiate a new itemVector and populate it with one element, the first column of our ResultSet. The itemVector represents a row in our table. Then we add the itemVector to our dataVector. The dataVector represents a list of rows for the table. The last line in Listing 12-35 is a call to the available proxies table model setDataVector() method that will populate the table.

Listing 12-35. Build Data for Available Proxies Table

```
rs = stmt.executeQuery(
            "SELECT DISTINCT a.app_user FROM appsec.v_application_registry a " +
        "WHERE a.app_user NOT IN ('APPVER','AVADMIN','APPSEC','OJSAADM') " +
        "ORDER BY a.app_user");
// dataVector must be Vector of Vectors
Vector dataVector = new Vector();
Vector itemVector;
while (rs.next()) {
    itemVector = new Vector();
    itemVector.add(rs.getString(1));
    dataVector.add(itemVector);
}
if (rs != null)
    rs.close();
availableProxiesTM.setDataVector(dataVector, columnIdentifiers);
```

In the dataInit() method we also build the data for our applications for proxy table. The contents of this table will change to match whatever proxy user is currently selected. For each proxy user, we will have a Vector of Vectors to use to populate the table. Those Vectors of Vectors will be held as values in appsHashTable that we can select with the key of the proxy user name.

Listing 12-36 shows the code used to build appsHashTable. In building the data, we again skip administrative proxies that are handled by the Admin Users screen, and we skip proxies that are used on the apver instance. We are prepared to call dataInit() multiple times, whenever the data may have changed, i.e., after the Save Updates button is selected. Because we may be rebuilding the appsHashTable, we start out by removing any existing content by calling the clear() method. We also set the table model, appsTM to a null Vector—we don't want to show any applications until an available proxy is selected.

As we walk through the ResultSet, we check to see if we have already started a dataVector for the proxy user, rs.getString(2). We check if the appsHashTable contains a key by that name. If so, we get the value from appsHashTable which is our Vector of applications for the proxy, else we instantiate a new

Vector. Again, each application is an item in a new Vector that is added to the dataVector for this proxy. Then the dataVector is put into the appsHashTable with the proxy user name as the key.

Listing 12-36. Build Data for Applications for Proxy Table

```
rs = stmt.executeQuery("SELECT DISTINCT a.application_id, p.proxy " +
    "FROM ojsaadm.instance_proxy_users p, appsec.v_application_registry a " +
    "WHERE p.instance <> 'APVER' " +
    "AND p.proxy NOT IN ('APPVER','AVADMIN','APPSEC','OJSAADM') " +
    "AND a.app_user = p.proxy ORDER BY a.application_id");
// appsHashtable must be Hashtable of Vectors of Vectors
// empty static Hashtable each time you enter this screen
appsHashtable.clear();
appsTM.setDataVector(null, appColumnIdentifiers);
while (rs.next()) {
    if (appsHashtable.containsKey(rs.getString(2))) {
        dataVector = appsHashtable.get(rs.getString(2));
        itemVector = new Vector();
        itemVector.add(rs.getString(1));
        dataVector.add(itemVector);
    } else {
        dataVector = new Vector();
        itemVector = new Vector();
        itemVector.add(rs.getString(1));
        dataVector.add(itemVector);
    }
    appsHashtable.put(rs.getString(2), dataVector);
}
```

To build the table data for both the available proxies table and the applications for proxy table, we are selecting from the v.application_registry view, and in this functional screen, we are connected as the ojsaadm user with the ojs_adm_admin role. In order to select from the appsec schema view, the proxy user needs SELECT privilege. As the Security Administrator, secadm on the orcl instance, we execute this grant:

```
GRANT SELECT ON appsec.v_application_registry TO ojs_adm_admin;
```

Selecting an Available Proxy in the Table

When the application user selects an available proxy from the table, the availableProxiesTable_mouseClicked() method gets called. The significant code of that method is shown in Listing 12-37. To find the value of the data selected in a table, we need to get the value in a specified row, at a specified column. In a single-column table, all the data is in column index zero. So to get the value of the available proxy that was selected in the table, we get the value at the selected row and column zero. We use that selected proxy user name as the key to get the related dataVector from appsHashtable. Then we set the applications table model to use that dataVector.

Listing 12-37. Select Available Proxy from Table

```
String key = (String)availableProxiesTM.getValueAt(
    availableProxiesTable.getSelectedRow(), 0);
Vector dataVector = appsHashtable.get(key);
appsTM.setDataVector(dataVector, appColumnIdentifiers);
```

Having these pre-built lists of applications for each proxy saves us from having to make a call to Oracle to get the list whenever the application user clicks on a different available proxy user. Getting data from a local Hashtable is extremely fast, compared to opening an Oracle connection and querying the database and handling the ResultSet. However, we only want to build data structures like this in memory when we know the quantity of items to be stored is small.

Selecting a User from the List

Whenever a user is selected from the drop-down userComboBox, we will query Oracle to find what proxy grants the user has already been given. This is done by the userComboBox_actionPerformed() method. That method shows the sayWaitDialog message and executes a query in a delayed Thread, as we have seen before. The run() method of that thread is shown in part in Listing 12-38.

Listing 12-38 should look familiar. We build a dataVector of one-item itemVectors that represents our list of proxies granted to the selected user. In processing the ResultSet, we skip any returned rows that are not for the selected user. After we have gathered the list of proxies, we set that as the data Vector of the user proxies table model, userProxiesTM.

Listing 12-38. Selecting a User from the List

```
stmt = conn.createStatement();
rs = stmt.executeQuery(
    "SELECT DISTINCT p.proxy, p.client FROM ojsaadm.instance_proxy_users p " +
    "WHERE p.instance <> 'APVER' " +
    "AND p.proxy NOT IN ('APPVER','AVADMIN','APPSEC','OJSAADM') " +
    "ORDER BY p.proxy");
Vector dataVector = new Vector();
Vector itemVector;
while (rs.next()) {
    if (rs.getString(2).equals(userID)) {
        itemVector = new Vector();
        itemVector.add(rs.getString(1));
        dataVector.add(itemVector);
    }
}
if (rs != null)
    rs.close();
userProxiesTM.setDataVector(dataVector, columnIdentifiers);
```

Adding a Proxy to the User's List

When the Add Selected button is pressed, whatever proxy is selected in the available proxies list will be added to the list of user proxies. This is accomplished by the code shown in Listing 12-39, which comes from the addButton_actionPerformed() method.

We get the selected value from the available proxies table and add that as an item in a new Vector, itemVector. Then we test to see whether an identical itemVector (proxy) already exists in the users list. If not, we add the new itemVector to the list.

There are a couple things to observe here. We get a reference to the current dataVector from the userProxiesTM table model. We do not replace it with a new Vector at any point. Then at the end we set the data Vector for userProxiesTM back to the dataVector we got.

Was that necessary? Couldn't we have just added the new itemVector to the existing dataVector without getting a local reference? And couldn't we avoid calling userProxiesTM.setDataVector() with the local reference?

The answer to the first question is no, it is not necessary. The answer to the second question is yes, we could have referred to the existing dataVector in place in the table model without creating a local reference, but that would have made for longer references and more code after all. The answer to the third question is probably, but we are counting on a side effect of the setDataVector() method—it also updates the GUI display with the new data. There are other ways to update the displayed table data, but none is so concise.

Listing 12-39. Add Proxy to User's List

```
Vector dataVector = userProxiesTM.getDataVector();
String value = (String)availableProxiesTM.getValueAt(
    availableProxiesTable.getSelectedRow(), 0);
Vector itemVector = new Vector();
itemVector.add(value);
if (!dataVector.contains(itemVector)) {
    dataVector.add(itemVector);
    userProxiesTM.setDataVector(dataVector, columnIdentifiers);
}
```

Removing a Proxy from the User's List

When the Remove Selected button is pressed, the operation for removing an item from the user's proxies table is relatively simple. The code is shown in Listing 12-40. Just call the remove() method on dataVector. Once again, we call the table model setDataVector() method to assure the GUI display is updated.

Listing 12-40. Remove Proxy from User's List

```
Vector dataVector = userProxiesTM.getDataVector();
String value = (String)userProxiesTM.getValueAt(
    userProxiesTable.getSelectedRow(), 0);
Vector itemVector = new Vector();
itemVector.add(value);
dataVector.remove(itemVector);
userProxiesTM.setDataVector(dataVector, columnIdentifiers);
```

Saving Updates to the User's Proxies

When the **Save Updates** button is pressed, the saveButton_actionPerformed() method will be run. The significant code for this method is shown in Listing 12-41. This comes from the delayed thread run() method that is defined there.

In that thread, the first thing we do is attempt to create the user on both the orcl and apver instances. We did not need an Oracle user until we decided to grant the user access to the applications.

Then we assign applications. We get the dataVector from the user's proxies table model. That is our planned, resultant list of proxies for the user. Some of these may be added proxies. Some may be proxies the user had previously. There may also be proxy grants that the user had that have now been removed from this list. So we have to handle the following three cases:

- Retain existing proxies that are in the list.

- Add new proxies that are in the list.

- Remove existing proxies that are no longer in the list.

In Listing 12-41, we handle these three cases. We select the existing list of proxies from an Oracle query and walk through the ResultSet. We are only concerned with proxies for the selected user. For each existing proxy in the ResultSet, we create a new itemVector with that as an item. We can find if the dataVector has an itemVector like that by calling the contains() method. If it does, then this is a proxy we want to retain. We have dealt with that proxy, so we remove it from the dataVector. Later, we will see what proxies are still left in the dataVector—those will have to be newly granted to the user.

If the existing proxy we got from our query is not in the dataVector, then it was removed from the list, and we need to revoke the proxy grant. We do that by calling the p_drop_proxy_through procedure.

Finally, we are left with a dataVector with just those proxies that did not exist previously. For each of those, we call the p_set_proxy_through procedure to add a new proxy grant for the selected user.

***Listing 12-41.** Save Updates to User's Proxies*

```
OracleCallableStatement stmt2 = null;
Statement stmt = null;
ResultSet rs = null;
try {
    // First, try to create user on both instances
    stmt2 =
(OracleCallableStatement)conn.prepareCall(
"CALL sys.usr_role_adm_pkg.p_create_user_once(?)");
    stmt2.setString(1, userID);
    stmt2.executeUpdate();
    if (stmt2 != null)
        stmt2.close();
    stmt2 =
(OracleCallableStatement)conn.prepareCall(
"CALL sys.usr_role_adm_pkg.p_create_user_many(?)");
    stmt2.setString(1, userID);
    stmt2.executeUpdate();
    if (stmt2 != null)
        stmt2.close();
    stmt2 =
(OracleCallableStatement)conn.prepareCall(
"CALL ojsaadm.apver_usr_adm_pkg.p_create_apver_user(?)");
    stmt2.setString(1, userID);
    stmt2.executeUpdate();
    if (stmt2 != null)
        stmt2.close();
```

```
        stmt = conn.createStatement();
        rs = stmt.executeQuery(
            "SELECT DISTINCT p.proxy, p.client FROM ojsaadm.instance_proxy_users p " +
            "WHERE p.instance <> 'APVER' " +
            "AND p.proxy NOT IN ('APPVER','AVADMIN','APPSEC','OJSAADM') " +
            "ORDER BY p.proxy");
        Vector dataVector = userProxiesTM.getDataVector();
        Vector itemVector;
        String proxyID;
        while (rs.next()) {
            if (rs.getString(2).equals(userID)) {
                proxyID = rs.getString(1);
                itemVector = new Vector();
                itemVector.add(proxyID);
                if (dataVector.contains(itemVector)) {
                    //System.out.println("retaining proxy to: " + proxyID);
                    dataVector.remove(itemVector);
                } else {
                    //System.out.println("removing proxy to: " + proxyID);
                    stmt2 = (OracleCallableStatement)conn.prepareCall(
                        "CALL sys.usr_role_adm_pkg.p_drop_proxy_through(?,?)");
                    stmt2.setString(1, userID);
                    stmt2.setString(2, proxyID);
                    stmt2.executeUpdate();
                    if (stmt2 != null) stmt2.close();
                }
            }
        }
        if (rs != null)
            rs.close();
        for (Object element : dataVector) {
            itemVector = (Vector)element;
            proxyID = (String)itemVector.get(0);
            //System.out.println("adding proxy to: " + proxyID);
            stmt2 = (OracleCallableStatement)conn.prepareCall(
                "CALL sys.usr_role_adm_pkg.p_set_proxy_through(?,?)");
            stmt2.setString(1, userID);
            stmt2.setString(2, proxyID);
            stmt2.executeUpdate();
            if (stmt2 != null) stmt2.close();
        }
...
```

Application Registration Screen

Next on our Security Administration agenda, and the target of the next button on the OJSAdmin menu, is the Register New Application functional screen. We have a couple applications registered so far: HRVIEW and this application, OJSADMIN, if you have run some of the SQL in this chapter. You can see the list of fields required for registering a new application on Figure 12-6.

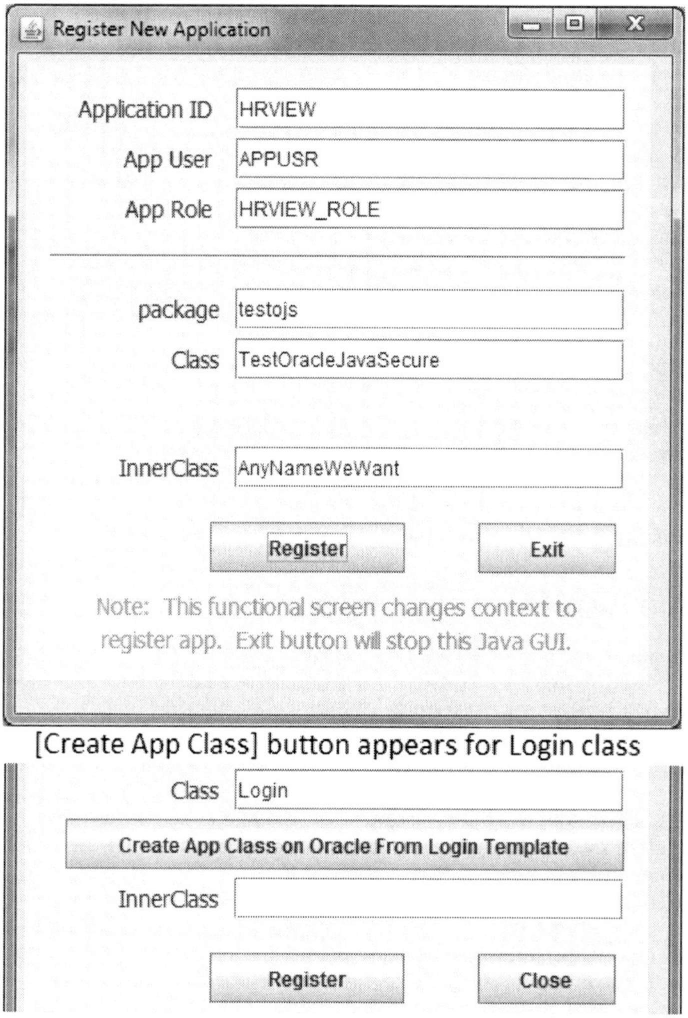

Figure 12-6. Register New Application functional screen

The Application ID is really just a name for the application—a way to refer to it in the database. The primary use for the application ID is as one of the keys to select the proper secure Application Role. The other key is the name of the Application User (proxy user). These three data elements are what we insert into the appsec.v_application_registry view.

At the bottom of the screen, there are three fields that make up the definition of an application inner class. The first field is the package, then the Class name, and finally the InnerClass name. We will create an instance of that class locally and submit it to Oracle in order to create a placeholder in the appsec.v_app_conn_registry view for a list of connection strings for this new application. In order for that entry to be made in appsec.v_app_conn_registry, a representative class needs to exist on the Oracle database.

373

There is an optional button on the Register New Application screen that appears if the user types "Login" into the Class field. In that case the Create App Class on Oracle From Login Template button appears. Be sure to document this feature for other application security administrators who will be using this screen to register applications. Might I suggest buying them a copy of this book?

If the application uses the Login class we developed in this chapter, then creating a representative class on Oracle is easy. The only change in this inner class from one application to another is the package in which the Login class is located. We take advantage of that fact in this button. When this button is selected, a new Java class is created on the Oracle database.

When the user selects the Register button, we do several things. For one thing, we insert the data from the top three fields on the form into the appsec.v_application_registry view. Also, we add the current Oracle user as an administrator for this specific application. That data goes into a new table named appsec.t_application_admins. And third, we enter a value in a new table that associates entries in the appsec.v_application_registry view with application inner class entries in the appsec.v_app_conn_registry view. This new table is named appsec.t_app_class_id. We will discuss these new tables later in this chapter.

There is only one concern when registering a new application. We actually change context from the OJSAdmin application to that of the new application in order to communicate with Oracle database as that application and enter the inner class in the appsec.v_app_conn_registry view. For that reason, the Close button turns into an Exit button after the Register button has been pressed, and instead of returning to OJSAdmin, the **Exit** button exits the JVM.

The Application Verification Administrator Role

In Chapter 11, we created a role named appver_admin. It is to that role that we delegated some administrative tasks, chief among those being the task of executing the procedures and functions in the appsec.appsec_admin_pkg package. Those procedures and functions include f_set_decrypt_conns, p_copy_app_conns, and the procedure we will introduce later in this chapter, p_create_template_class. These are procedures that handle our stored Oracle connection string lists for various applications, and they are due extra security measures.

In Chapter 11, we assigned the appver_admin role to a specific user that we have called osadmin in our example code (probably you.) In this chapter, we are going to change that role to operate more like one of our standard application roles, being set for persons who are allowed to proxy through an Oracle application account. You might have caught a hint of this from Table 12-1 and Listing 12-5 where we associated a new user, avadmin with the appver_admin role. We also saw how we can assign that proxy user to people in our discussion of the Admin Users functional screen.

Previously, we have defined the appver_admin role on both orcl and apver instances, and we had designated it to be NOT IDENTIFIED, and we granted the role to osadmin. Here we will revoke that grant and alter the role to be identified by our secure application role procedure, appsec.p_check_role_access. We do those tasks, shown in Listing 12-42, as SYS user on both the orcl and apver instances. At the same time we will create the new proxy user, avadmin, who will set this role. And we grant the right to connect through avadmin (proxy) to osadmin (you). Be sure to give a very strong password to the avadmin user. Also shown in Listing 12-42, on the apver instance we will repeat an insert into appsec.v_application_registry that we have already made on the orcl instance—setting up the association of the avadmin user and the appver_admin role.

Listing 12-42. Application Verification Administrator

```
REVOKE appver_admin FROM osadmin;
ALTER ROLE appver_admin IDENTIFIED USING appsec.p_check_role_access;
```

```
GRANT create_session_role TO avadmin IDENTIFIED BY password;
ALTER USER osadmin GRANT CONNECT THROUGH avadmin;

INSERT INTO appsec.v_application_registry
(application_id, app_user, app_role) VALUES
('OJSADMIN','AVADMIN','APPVER_ADMIN');
```

The Create App Class Button

When the application developer has included the Login class in his application, modifying the application ID and the package, he has made the registration of his application in Oracle database much easier. If he had not gone this route, then we would have to get his application inner class definition from him, and would have to execute the command CREATE OR REPLACE AND RESOLVE JAVA SOURCE NAMED. However, since he is following the preferred GUI development path, using Login, we know enough from his package alone to create a class on the Oracle database to represent his application.

So, when we get to the Register New Application screen, and we see the word "Login" typed in the Class field, we provide a button to allow easy creation of a representative application inner class on the database. The code in Listing 12-43 is used to display or hide that button. We use a keyReleased event to tell when the user has entered a character in the classTextField. If after entering the character, the text of the field equals "Login," then we make the button visible. Otherwise, we hide it.

Listing 12-43. Display or Hide the Create App Class Button

```
private void classTextField_keyReleased(KeyEvent e) {
    if (classTextField.getText().equals("Login"))
        createTemplateButton.setVisible(true);
    else
        createTemplateButton.setVisible(false);
}
```

When the button is visible, it can be selected and it then executes the code in the createTemplateButton_actionPerformed() method. In that method, we find the code shown in Listing 12-44. To create the template class in the database, we call the p_create_template_class procedure. That is a new procedure that we are defining in the appsec_admin_pkg package. We pass in the fully qualified class name; however, we don't read all the user-provided fields to get that. Rather we read the package name that the user provided and append the string ".Login$InnerRevLvlClass" to the package name.

Listing 12-44. Create a Template Class in Oracle

```
stmt = (OracleCallableStatement)conn.prepareCall(
            "call appsec.appsec_admin_pkg.p_create_template_class( ?,?,? )");
stmt.registerOutParameter(2, OracleTypes.NUMBER);
stmt.registerOutParameter(3, OracleTypes.VARCHAR);
stmt.setString(1, packageTextField.getText() + ".Login$InnerRevLvlClass");
stmt.setInt(2, 0);
stmt.setNull(3, OracleTypes.VARCHAR);
stmt.executeUpdate();
```

Listing 12-45 shows the code of the new p_create_template_class procedure. The procedure needs to live on the apver database instance, so the definition is included in the script file *Chapter12/ApverSys.sql*. The bulk of this procedure is given to the definition of the Java inner class. Notice that there are two places in that inner-class definition that we insert the package name: once in the name of the Java structure and once in the package statement. We do several tests before we decide to create the class. The first test is done to see whether the class has already been created in the database. We query all the Java classes (sys.all_java_classes) to see if one with the same name already exists. We don't create the class if that is the case. Because we are executing a CREATE command instead of a CREATE OR REPLACE command, we will get an exception if the class already exists. The second test we make will assure that the word "Login" is in the class name, and the third test assures that something is left, as a package, when we truncate the class name before the word "Login."

In the DDL command that we will EXECUTE IMMEDIATE, we are concatenating ASCII character codes 10, 13, and 34. These are used to give some format to our Java class. The pair of 13 and 10 are the carriage return/line feed characters that move to the beginning of the next line. The character 34 is a double quote that we want to have on both sides of our class name to set it off from the schema name, APPSEC.

Listing 12-45. Procedure to Create Template Class

```
PROCEDURE p_create_template_class(
    m_class_name      v_app_conn_registry.class_name%TYPE,
    m_err_no     OUT NUMBER,
    m_err_txt    OUT VARCHAR2 )
IS
    v_count    INTEGER;
    v_package v_app_conn_registry.class_name%TYPE;
BEGIN
    m_err_no := 0;
    SELECT COUNT(*) INTO v_count
    FROM sys.all_java_classes
    WHERE owner='APPSEC' AND name = m_class_name;
    IF v_count < 1 THEN
        v_count := INSTR( m_class_name, 'Login' );
        IF v_count > 0 THEN
            v_package := SUBSTR( m_class_name, 0, v_count - 2 );
            IF LENGTH( v_package ) > 0 THEN

                    EXECUTE IMMEDIATE

'CREATE AND RESOLVE JAVA SOURCE NAMED APPSEC.' || CHR(34) ||
v_package || '/Login' || CHR(34) || ' AS ' || CHR(13) || CHR(10) ||
'package ' || v_package || '; ' || CHR(13) || CHR(10) ||
'import java.io.Serializable; ' || CHR(13) || CHR(10) ||
'import orajavsec.RevLvlClassIntfc; ' || CHR(13) || CHR(10) ||
'public class Login { ' || CHR(13) || CHR(10) ||
'    public static class InnerRevLvlClass ' || CHR(13) || CHR(10) ||
'        implements Serializable, RevLvlClassIntfc{ ' || CHR(13) || CHR(10) ||
'        private static final long serialVersionUID = 2011010100L; ' || CHR(13) ||CHR(10)||
'        private String innerClassRevLvl = "20110101a"; ' || CHR(13) || CHR(10) ||
'        public String getRevLvl() { ' || CHR(13) || CHR(10) ||
'            return innerClassRevLvl; ' || CHR(13) || CHR(10) ||
'} } }';
                END IF;
            END IF;
        END IF;
    EXCEPTION
        WHEN OTHERS THEN
```

```
        m_err_no := SQLCODE;
        m_err_txt := SQLERRM;
        app_sec_pkg.p_log_error( m_err_no, m_err_txt,
            ' p_create_template_class' );
    END p_create_template_class;
```

To make this button work, there are requirements. The owner of the appsec_admin_pkg package, that is the appsec user, must be able to create Java classes. For that, we have to grant the CREATE PROCEDURE system privilege to appsec. Also she must also be able to select from the data dictionary view, sys.all_java_classes, to see what classes already exist. We do this as SYS user on the apver instance:

```
GRANT CREATE PROCEDURE TO appsec;
GRANT SELECT ON sys.all_java_classes TO APPSEC;
```

Tables of Specific Application Administrators and Application to Class Registry

At some point we are going to want to delegate administration of certain applications to one person, and other applications to another person—and we will not want them to have access to administer each other's applications. That eventual goal, which we will accomplish later in this chapter, is the reason that we are going to build the appsec.t_application_admins table. The definition of t_application_admins is given in Listing 12-46. It is simply a list of OS user names that are allowed to manage specific application inner class names. It is the lists of Oracle connection strings represented by those application inner classes that we are intending to protect.

■ **Note** These tables are only needed on the apver instance.

Listing 12-46. Application Administrators Table

```
CREATE TABLE appsec.t_application_admins
(
    -- match appsec.t_app_conn_registry.class_name
    class_name VARCHAR2(2000) NOT NULL,
    -- match hr.emp_mobile_nos.user_id
    user_id    VARCHAR2(20) NOT NULL
);
/

CREATE UNIQUE INDEX application_admins_pk ON appsec.t_application_admins
    ( class_name, user_id );

ALTER TABLE appsec.t_application_admins ADD (
    CONSTRAINT application_admins_pk
    PRIMARY KEY
    ( class_name, user_id )
    USING INDEX application_admins_pk
```

```
);
/

CREATE OR REPLACE VIEW appsec.v_application_admins
    AS SELECT * FROM appsec.t_application_admins;

INSERT INTO appsec.v_application_admins
    ( class_name, user_id )
    ( SELECT DISTINCT class_name, 'OSADMIN' FROM appsec.t_app_conn_registry );

COMMIT;
```

We are going to get a start on listing individual administrators for various applications by initially assigning administration of all the applications to the user we are calling osadmin. We do that with a single insert command shown in Listing 12-46, and we commit the insert.

There is a second table that we are going to create here, the appsec.t_app_class_id table. When each application was managed individually, as we have done up through Chapter 11, we automatically knew what application we were working on. However, in this security administration interface application, we are managing all applications. Now we need to symbolically associate an application with its application inner class and list of connection strings. This association is necessary in order to keep from having to type in both the application ID and the inner class name whenever we want to specify an application.

An example entry in the t_app_class_id table is for this application: the class name is orajavsec.Login$InnerRevLvlClass, and the application id is OJSADMIN. Listing 12-47 shows the script we will use to build and populate the table.

Listing 12-47. Application Class to ID Table

```
CREATE TABLE appsec.t_app_class_id
(
    class_name     VARCHAR2(2000 BYTE) NOT NULL ENABLE,
    application_id VARCHAR2(24 BYTE) NOT NULL ENABLE
);
/

CREATE UNIQUE INDEX app_class_id_pk ON appsec.t_app_class_id
    ( class_name, application_id );

ALTER TABLE appsec.t_app_class_id ADD (
    CONSTRAINT app_class_id_pk
    PRIMARY KEY
    ( class_name, application_id )
    USING INDEX app_class_id_pk
);
/

CREATE OR REPLACE VIEW appsec.v_app_class_id AS SELECT * FROM appsec.t_app_class_id;

INSERT INTO appsec.v_app_class_id
(CLASS_NAME, APPLICATION_ID) VALUES
('testojs.TestOracleJavaSecure$AnyNameWeWant','HRVIEW');
```

```
INSERT INTO appsec.v_app_class_id
(CLASS_NAME, APPLICATION_ID) VALUES
('orajavsec.Login$InnerRevLvlClass','OJSADMIN');

COMMIT;
```

I mentioned in the introduction to this section that we insert data into these tables when we register new applications. We enter the current Oracle user as an administrator for the new application, inserting a record in the appsec.v_application_admins view. Also we enter the application class to application ID relationship by an insert into the appsec.v_app_class_id view. The insert statements for our existing applications are shown in Listing 12-47.

Security Table Access Analysis

We are going to take a look at how we get to tables of data in the appsec schema and how we use the data. This will help us define who should get access and what access grants we need to make to each Oracle user.

First of all, we need to understand that most of the access to data in the appsec schema is accomplished by procedures, functions, and packages in the appsec schema, so no additional grants to the data are required. We have several packages that segregate procedures and functions into these groups:

- APP_SEC_PKG: Procedures and functions that applications need to access. We grant execute
  on this package to application schemas, like HR. Those application schemas have sensitive data access procedures that call on app_sec_pkg.

- APPSEC_ONLY_PKG: Procedures and functions that handle the inner workings of our Oracle and Java Security activities. No grants are made to this package.

- APPSEC_PUBLIC_PKG: Procedures that need to be accessible by all Oracle users. This package is granted execute to PUBLIC. Generally, this provides a jumping-off point, part of the application verification process, where users are proxying through appver, but have no roles except the create_session_role. One particular procedure in this package is the p_get_app_conns procedure, by which a user may acquire the list of connection strings for the application they are using after SSO, two-factor authentication and key exchange. Our plan is to secure SELECTs on this particular procedure so that users can only select applications that they have been granted.

- APPSEC_ADMIN_PKG: Procedures and functions that are only available to the application security administrators, those who can proxy through the avadmin user and acquire the appver_admin role. The execute privilege is granted to appver_admin for this package.

We also have a group of procedures and functions that do not reside in packages. All those structures have one of two aspects about them that keep them from working in a package: they either execute with the current user privileges, AUTHID CURRENT_USER, or they are obfuscated by the Oracle *wrap* utility.

We also support some direct access to the application security data from outside the structures of the appsec schema. In particular, we have queries in this security administration interface application that select data from three of the views: v_app_class_id, v_application_registry and v_app_conn_registry. These queries run in functional screens where the Oracle application user is proxying through avadmin. So, we grant SELECT on those views to the appver_admin role. Additionally, in the Register New Application screen, that we are examining now, we insert data into three views: v_app_class_id, application_registry and application_admin. We have currently set the appver_admin role, so we grant INSERT on those views to appver_admin.

There will come a time when we need to select, update and delete records in the v_application_admin view. We need to identify people, in addition to or in place of the person who initially registered the application, to manage connection strings for each application. We delegate that job of setting application administrators to specific users. We will grant SELECT, UPDATE, and DELETE on v_application_admin to the osadmin user (you, perhaps.)

On the Assign Applications functional screen, we need to select records from the v_application_registry view. That screen is operating with the ojs_adm_admin role by user proxying through ojsaadm. Recall that ojsaadm has a whole set of grants and package of procedures all of his own—look up at the description of the Admin Users screen for that discussion. We grant SELECT on v_application_registry to the ojs_adm_admin role.

Listing 12-48 shows the script used to make the remaining grants needed on the apver instance. Those grants take care of all the data requirements I mentioned earlier.

Listing 12-48. Grants to Appsec Data on Apver

```
GRANT SELECT ON appsec.v_app_class_id TO appver_admin ;
GRANT SELECT ON appsec.v_application_registry TO appver_admin;
GRANT SELECT ON appsec.v_app_conn_registry TO appver_admin;

GRANT INSERT ON appsec.v_app_class_id TO appver_admin ;
GRANT INSERT ON appsec.v_application_registry TO appver_admin ;
GRANT INSERT ON appsec.v_application_admins TO appver_admin;

GRANT UPDATE, SELECT, DELETE ON appsec.v_application_admins TO osadmin;
```

We still have one remaining security data access hurdle to deal with. Typically (that is up through Chapter 11), we have just embedded our passwords in the application and used the first pass through the application to set the connection strings. We don't want to have to do that! There was a reason for that which we have discussed. We need to be proxied through the appver user, as the application, in order to set the connection strings for the application. Once we call the getAAConnRole() method to get one of the application connections from the list, we can no longer update the connection strings associated with the application. I'm sure that OracleJavaSecure could be re-written to operate differently.

The issue arose when we moved some of our procedures into the appsec_admin_pkg package and required a secure role to get access. In effect, we have made the procedure to update our connection strings impossible for us to call. When we are connected by proxying through the appver user, we have not set a secure application role by executing the p_check_role_access procedure, or something similar. Individual Oracle users, proxied through appver, cannot execute appsec_admin_pkg, even if they are granted the privilege to proxy through avadmin to acquire the appver_admin role.

The solution we have is to create another role on apver instance that will be a default role for all users who need to update the connection strings for an application. Our application administrators will have both the grant to proxy through avadmin, and the grant to this new role, which we will call appver_conns. The code for creating the appver_conns role is shown in Listing 12-49.

Listing 12-49. Application Verification Connections Role

```
CREATE ROLE appver_conns NOT IDENTIFIED;
GRANT EXECUTE ON appsec.appsec_admin_pkg TO appver_conns ;
GRANT appver_conns TO osadmin;
```

Notice that we grant appver_conns to the osadmin user. We will make that same grant to all application administrators who will be maintaining the connection strings for their applications through this security administration interface. This gives them access to the appsec_admin_pkg, which they will need to update connection strings.

When we add administrators, we will need to grant both the privilege to connect through avadmin, and the grant to appver_conns role. For this reason, we have additional procedures in a package on apver instance named sys.appver_conns_role_pkg. The package code is given in Listing 12-50. There are two procedures, p_grant_appver_conns_role and p_revoke_appver_conns_role for both granting and revoking appver_conns.

Listing 12-50. Grant Appver Conns Role on Apver Instance

```
CREATE OR REPLACE PACKAGE BODY sys.appver_conns_role_pkg IS

    PROCEDURE p_grant_appver_conns_role (
        username sys.proxy_users.client%TYPE )
    AS
        PRAGMA AUTONOMOUS_TRANSACTION;
    BEGIN
        EXECUTE IMMEDIATE 'GRANT appver_conns TO ' || username;
        COMMIT;
    EXCEPTION
        WHEN OTHERS
        THEN
            appsec.app_sec_pkg.p_log_error( SQLCODE, SQLERRM,
                'sys.p_grant_appver_conns_role for ' ||
                username );
    END p_grant_appver_conns_role;

    PROCEDURE p_revoke_appver_conns_role (
        username sys.proxy_users.client%TYPE )
    AS
        PRAGMA AUTONOMOUS_TRANSACTION;
    BEGIN
        EXECUTE IMMEDIATE 'REVOKE appver_conns FROM ' || username;
        COMMIT;
    EXCEPTION
        WHEN OTHERS
        THEN
            appsec.app_sec_pkg.p_log_error( SQLCODE, SQLERRM,
                'sys.p_revoke_appver_conns_role for ' ||
                username );
    END p_revoke_appver_conns_role;
```

```
END appver_conns_role_pkg;
/

-- From New Application Registration
GRANT EXECUTE ON sys.appver_conns_role_pkg TO appver_admin ;

-- From Admin Users, grant to user, not to role
GRANT EXECUTE ON sys.appver_conns_role_pkg TO ojsaadm;
```

When we register a new application, we will call p_grant_appver_conns_role for the current session user, as we will see in the next subsection of this chapter. At that point, we are proxying through the avadmin user, with appver_admin role; so you see in Listing 12-50 that we grant execute on sys.appver_conns_role_pkg to appver_admin.

When we are adding administrators through the **Admin Users** screen, we want to call either p_grant_appver_conns_role or p_revoke_appver_conns_role, depending on whether the App Register check box is selected. However, at that point we are proxying through the ojsaadm user with ojs_adm_admin role, and we are on the wrong instance (orcl as opposed to apver.) We already have a package and a database link to solve this issue, so we will create two additional procedures in the ojsaadm.apver_usr_adm_pkg package and use them to call the sys.appver_conns_role_pkg package across a database link. The code for this is shown in Listing 12-51. Look back up to the end of Listing 12-50 and you will see that we grant execute on the sys.appver_conns_role_pkg to the ojsaadm user.

Listing 12-51. Grant Appver Conns Role Across Link

```
    PROCEDURE p_grant_apver_appver_conns( username VARCHAR2, proxyname VARCHAR2 )
    AS
        m_stmt VARCHAR2(100);
    BEGIN
        m_stmt :=
'BEGIN sys.appver_conns_role_pkg.p_grant_appver_conns_role@apver_link( :1 ); END;';
        EXECUTE IMMEDIATE m_stmt USING username, proxyname;
    END p_grant_apver_appver_conns;

    PROCEDURE p_revoke_apver_appver_conns( username VARCHAR2, proxyname VARCHAR2 )
    AS
        m_stmt VARCHAR2(100);
    BEGIN
        m_stmt :=
'BEGIN sys.appver_conns_role_pkg.p_revoke_appver_conns_role@apver_link( :1 ); END;';
        EXECUTE IMMEDIATE m_stmt USING username, proxyname;
    END p_revoke_apver_appver_conns;
```

The Register Application Button

With all the data entered on the Register New Application screen, and a representative application inner class created in the Oracle database, we are ready to register the application. That representative inner class may have been created in the database using the Create App Class button that I described previously, or you will need to execute a CREATE OR REPLACE AND RESOLVE JAVA command to create it.

When the Register button is selected, that event calls the registerButton_actionPerformed() method. Again we are using a delayed thread process, and we are displaying the sayWaitDialog while we are processing. In brief, this method does four things. It creates a local instance of the class described by the user entries; it executes three insert statements to register various aspects of the application; it grants the current session user an administrative role; and it sets the context to the new application and calls methods to create a placeholder in the v_app_conn_registry view for a future list of connection strings. There is no two-factor authentication, nor is there key exchange for the new application in this process.

Listing 12-52 shows the code used to create the local instance of the described application inner class. We discard any trailing dot (.) on the package name.

Listing 12-52. Create Local Instance of Defined Class

```
String innerClassName = packageTextField.getText();

if (innerClassName.endsWith("."))

    innerClassName.substring( 0, innerClassName.length() - 1 );
innerClassName = innerClassName + "." + classTextField.getText() +
    "$" + innerClassTextField.getText();

Class classToRegister = Class.forName(innerClassName);

Object appClass = classToRegister.newInstance();
```

■ **Note** This application inner class must exist in compiled form on the same client where the Register New Application screen is running in order to register the application. The application inner class must also be on the current CLASSPATH.

The first insert we execute will add the current user as an application administrator for this application. The insert command is shown in Listing 12-53. Notice we use the system context value of the client identifier that we have set equal to the SSO user. He is the designated initial administrator of the application associated with the fully qualified inner class name that we set as the first parameter.

Listing 12-53. Insert Application Administrator

```
String updateString =
    "insert into appsec.v_application_admins " +
    "( class_name, user_id ) values ( ?, " +
    "SYS_CONTEXT( 'USERENV', 'CLIENT_IDENTIFIER' ))";
PreparedStatement pstmt =
    conn.prepareStatement(updateString);
pstmt.setString(1, innerClassName);
pstmt.executeUpdate();
```

This is a dynamic update statement, but it is not susceptible to SQL Injection. It is a parameterized, prepared statement. We discussed and tested the security of this kind of statement in Chapter 8.

The second insert we make is into the appsec.v_app_class_id view. We will associate the fully qualified inner class name with a specific application ID. The code for this insert command is provided in Listing 12-54. This is also done using a prepared statement.

Listing 12-54. Insert Application Class to ID Relationship

```
String updateString =
    "insert into appsec.v_app_class_id " +
    "( class_name, application_id ) values ( ?, ? )";
PreparedStatement pstmt = conn.prepareStatement(updateString);
pstmt.setString(1, innerClassName);
pstmt.setString(2, applicationIDTextField.getText().toUpperCase());
pstmt.executeUpdate();
```

The last of the three insert statements is our application registration entry into the appsec.v_application_registry view. This data entry correlates the proxy user for this application with a secure application role. The code for the insert command is given in Listing 12-55.

Listing 12-55. Application Registration Entry

```
String updateString =
    "insert into appsec.v_application_registry " +
    "( application_id, app_user, app_role ) values ( ?, ?, ? )";
PreparedStatement pstmt = conn.prepareStatement(updateString);
pstmt.setString(1, applicationIDTextField.getText().toUpperCase());
pstmt.setString(2, applicationUserTextField.getText().toUpperCase());
pstmt.setString(3, applicationRoleTextField.getText().toUpperCase());
pstmt.executeUpdate();
```

When we make an entry into the v_application_registry view on the apver database instance, we need to have an identical entry in the v_application_registry view on the orcl instance. That is pretty easy to arrange with an insert trigger across a database link. (There are also more robust ways to do this with message queues or streams.) Because we already have a private database link from appsec on the apver instance to apsec on the orcl instance, all we need is the trigger. (Previously we had used the orcl_link to access data in the HR schema on the orcl instance from procedures running on the apver instance.) Listing 12-56 shows the trigger we will use to insert an identical record in the v_application_registry view on the orcl instance to the one we inserted on the apver instance.

Listing 12-56. Insert Trigger on Application Registry

```
CREATE OR REPLACE TRIGGER appsec.t_application_registry_iar
    AFTER INSERT ON appsec.t_application_registry FOR EACH ROW
BEGIN
    INSERT INTO appsec.v_application_registry@orcl_link
    ( application_id, app_user, app_role ) VALUES
    ( :new.application_id, :new.app_user, :new.app_role );
    -- OJDBC will auto-commit this insert on orcl instance
END;
/

ALTER TRIGGER appsec.t_application_registry_iar ENABLE;
```

We want to give the current user access to edit the connection strings for this application they just registered. To do that task, the user needs to be granted the appver_conns role on the apver instance. This is in addition to being able to proxy through the avadmin user. We create a prepared statement to call the stored procedure sys.appver_conns_role_pkg.p_grant_appver_conns_role. This is shown in Listing 12-57.

Listing 12-57. Grant Appver_Conns Role to the Current User

```
String updateString =
    "BEGIN sys.appver_conns_role_pkg.p_grant_appver_conns_role( " +
    "SYS_CONTEXT( 'USERENV', 'CLIENT_IDENTIFIER' ) ); END;";
PreparedStatement pstmt =
    conn.prepareStatement(updateString);
pstmt.executeUpdate();
```

Finally, we take one last step in the registerButton_actionPerformed() method. We create a placeholder in the v_app_conn_registry view for the connection strings to be used by this new application. To do that, we change contexts to the context of the new application by calling setAppContext(). Then we execute the getAppConnections() method, and follow that with a call to putAppConnections(). That series of commands, shown in Listing 12-58, will create the entry in v_app_conn_registry.

Listing 12-58. Insert Entry into Application Connections Registry

```
OracleJavaSecure.setAppContext(
    applicationIDTextField.getText().toUpperCase(), appClass, "");
OracleJavaSecure.getAppConnections();
OracleJavaSecure.putAppConnections();
```

When we set the new application context in Listing 12-58, we provide the application ID that the user entered along with the class we instantiated from the description on the screen and an empty string in place of a two-factor authentication code.

Note We have not accomplished two-factor authentication nor key exchange for this new application. When we call putAppConnections() with an empty list of connections, Oracle database does not balk at decryption and encryption, but rather inserts an empty conn string list for the new application.

When these steps are complete, the new application has been registered. It still remains that we need to enter some application connection strings into the list for this application. We can do that on another functional screen of the Security Administration Interface application.

Recall that after the Register button has been pressed, the **Close** button changes to an Exit button that will exit the JVM. Because we have changed application contexts, we cannot return to the OJSAdmin menu and continue working with the list of connection strings for the OJSAdmin application.

Application Selection Screen

In the functional screens we have discussed so far, we have done all the application security administration we can as the OJSAdmin application. We even set our context to be that of another application in order to act on behalf of the application and to register it. But in order to manage the connection strings associated with a different application, we will have to start out with the identity of that application.

In the Pick Application to Manage functional screen shown in Figure 12- 7, we will be selecting a specific application from the list of registered applications that we want to manage. The list is shown in the top drop-down box, and the Manage Selected Application button will start a new application in a new JVM. Because practically all our security structures, especially those in the OracleJavaSecure class, are static, we need to start each different application in a separate JVM in order to have application-specific settings of our static members.

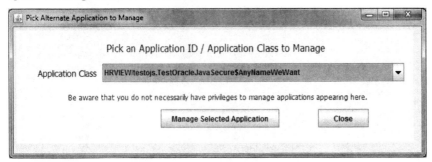

Figure 12-7. Pick an Application to Manage functional Screen

Initializing the List of Applications

We will run the Pick Application to Manage screen, PickAppManage class, with a connection that is proxied through the avadmin user. We will have the appver_admin role in order to read the list of applications that are registered. In our dataInit() method, we have a single query that we use to get the list of applications. This query is shown in Listing 12-59. Notice in the query that we are getting the application ID and the related application inner class name to represent the application. We display this list in the drop-down combo box at the top of the screen.

Listing 12-59. Query to get List of Registered Applications

```
stmt.executeQuery(
    "SELECT DISTINCT application_id || '/' || class_name o FROM appsec.v_app_class_id "
    + "where class_name in " +
    "( select distinct class_name from appsec. v_app_conn_registry_filtered ) " +
    "ORDER BY o");
```

We haven't configured it yet, but our intent is to limit the list of applications shown here to just those that the current user has been assigned to administer. This will be accomplished by restricting what entries in the v_app_conn_registry_filtered view are accessible to the current user. Once we have restricted that view, then the query in PickAppManage, Listing 12-59 will also be restricted by the where clause.

Selecting the Manage Selected Application Button

When you have selected an application to manage and you press the Manage Selected Application button, the event will run the manageAppButton_actionPerformed() method. We start that method by making sure an application has been selected from the list, and then by parsing out the application ID and the application inner class name from the selected item. The code for this is shown in Listing 12-60.

Listing 12-60. Parse Selected Application

```
if (0 == appClassComboBox.getSelectedIndex())
    return;
String appId = (String)appClassComboBox.getSelectedItem();
int place = appId.indexOf("/");
String appClass = appId.substring(place + 1);
appId = appId.substring(0, place);
```

With those two data elements, the application ID and the application inner class name, we can start a new JVM as that specific application. We plan to start a new instance of the OJSAdmin, security administration interface application with the identity of the application we selected here, instead of the default identity of OJSAdmin. The code we use to start the new JVM and new instance of OJSAdmin is shown in Listing 12-61.

Notice in the last line of Listing 12-61 that we are going to run the main() method of OJSAdmin, and we are providing the application ID and application inner class name as arguments. In our discussion of the Login constructors in Listing 12-4 and the OJSAdmin.ojsInit() method in Listing 12-11, I mentioned how we can take on the identity of a different application. There we saw code that uses reflection to create an instance of the application inner class that is named in argument two, and we set the application ID of Login to the value of argument one.

Listing 12-61. Start a New JVM and new Instance of OJSAdmin

```
Runtime rt = Runtime.getRuntime();
Process proc =
    rt.exec("C:/Java/jdk1.6.0_24/bin/javaw -classpath " +
            "C:/dev/mywork/OraJavSec/Project1/classes;C:/dev/ojdbc6.jar " +
            "orajavsec.OJSAdmin " + appId + " " + appClass);
BufferedReader stdError =
    new BufferedReader(new InputStreamReader(proc.getErrorStream()));
String inLine;
while ((inLine = stdError.readLine()) != null) {
    System.out.println(inLine);
}
```

We get a new instance of Runtime and call its exec() method. The exec() method returns an instance of Process, and we set a local member variable. Typically, you might get the output and error streams that are coming from the Process, and you might print them or handle them. In our case, we have intentionally requested not to have the output stream generated by our Process. We did that by running the version of the Java runtime that starts *windowless, javaw.exe*. Notice the "w" at the end of the executable name. In this way, we don't get an output stream and we don't have to deal with it. We do, however, choose to print the error stream to the current system out of the current JVM that called the new Runtime.exec(). We want to see any exception messages that are thrown, and if we don't deal with the error stream, our process may lock-up while waiting for us to deal with it.

If you can, I recommend that, in your corporate environment, you give full paths to your *javaw* executable and to the current application, OJSAdmin and Oracle drivers jar file in the CLASSPATH setting. If that doesn't work for all the computers that will be running this code in your environment, you will need to set environment variables for the Runtime. You might also consider using the ProcessBuilder class to get more fine-grained control of the environment settings. You might also consider placing these paths in a properties file that will accompany the code. You can read these specific values from the properties file; however, you will need a different properties file for each different client computer environment.

A different reason for why you might want to place these setting in a properties file and read them from there is to make handling an upgrade to the JVM easier. When the path to java.exe changes from the jdk1.6.0_24 directory to the jdk1.6.0_28 directory, you only need to edit the properties file. This presumes that it is easier to edit a text file on all your client computers than it is to recompile the code and distribute a new jar file to all. That might be a personal preference.

One argument against recompiling is the possibility of introducing errors in the process, but I have never seen that happen just from the compilation process, and perhaps we want to recompile our classes in order to gain from any efficiency provided by the updated compiler. Maybe this is a personal preference based on experience or standard practice.

▪ **Note** When the new Runtime Process starts, the Login Dialog will be instantiated again with the new application identity. That will result in a new prompt for entry of a two-factor authentication code—one specific to the selected application.

Connection String Editor

You can see in Figure 12- 8 that all the elements of an Oracle connection string are represented by text fields on the Edit Application Connections screen, EditAppConns. We provide two functional buttons there: one to add the newly described connection to the list, and one to save the list to the Oracle database.

When we select the button to add the connection to our list, the Update Connection String button, it only updates the local list; it does not store the new/updated connection string in the database. After editing or adding connections to the local list, select the **Save List** button to update the database.

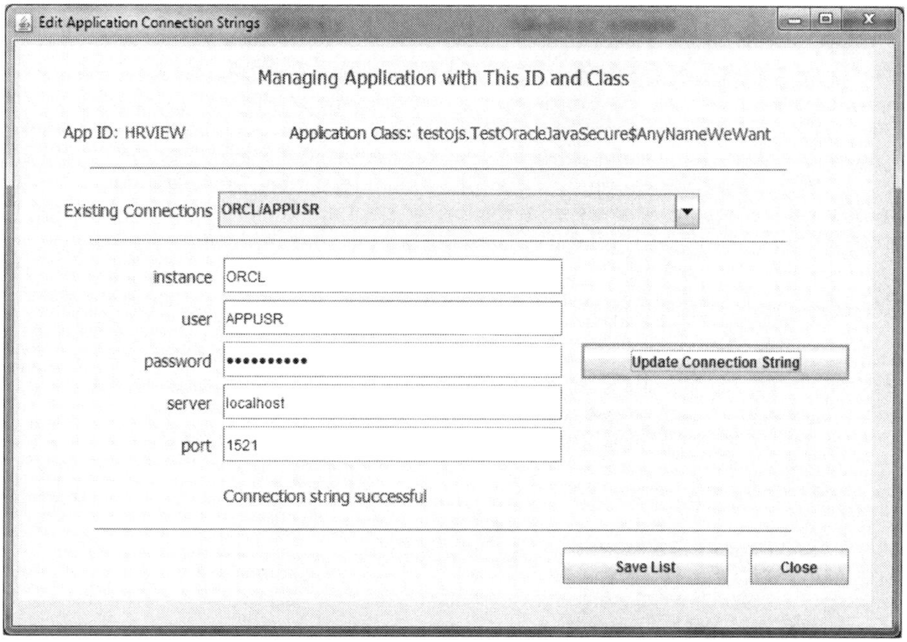

Figure 12-8. *Edit Application Connections functional screen*

Initializing the List of Connection Strings

In the dataInit() method of the Edit Application Connection Strings screen, we call a new method in the OracleJavaSecure class, listConnNames(). The list itself, connsHash is private, so we have to ask OracleJavaSecure to provide the names, keys of the Hashtable. The code for the listConnNames() method is given in Listing 12-62.

Listing 12-62. *Get List of Connection Names*

```
static Vector listConnNames() {
    Vector<String> rtrnV = new Vector<String>();
    try {
        for (String key : connsHash.keySet())
            rtrnV.add(key);
    } catch (Exception x) {}
    return rtrnV;
}
```

This method has the default access modifier, because we don't specify private or public. That default modifier is "package" accessibility. Only classes that are part of the same package, orajavsec can execute this method. Fortunately for us, OJSAdmin is in the orajavsec package.

The call to this new method from the EditAppConns.dataInit() method looks like the following. We use the returned Vector to populate the drop-down list of connection string names.

```
Vector<String> connList = OracleJavaSecure.listConnNames();
```

Selecting an Existing Connection String

There is little value in showing the list of existing connection strings for the application. We cannot edit individual parameters of the string, like the password, leaving other parameters as is. That is because we are not going to decrypt and expose the password here despite the convenience it would provide. What we gain by showing the list of connection strings is that we can see our progress as we enter multiple strings, and we can assure that at least the key names of an updated entry are spelled correctly.

When a user selects a connection string name from the list, we populate the first two text fields with the database instance name and user name from the selected item. The other fields remain blank.

Updating a Connection String in the List

When all the text fields on the **Edit Application Connection Strings** screen have been filled appropriately, the user may select the **Update Connection String** button. This action will call the updateButton_actionPerformed() method, whose primary duty is to call the OracleJavaSecure.putAppConnString() method. This call is shown in the code in Listing 12-63.

Listing 12-63. Update Connection String in the List

```
connSuccessLabel.setText(OracleJavaSecure.putAppConnString(
    instanceTextField.getText().toUpperCase(),
    userTextField.getText().toUpperCase(),
    new String(passwordField.getPassword()),
    serverTextField.getText(),
    portTextField.getText(),
    true));
```

We pass the text field values to putAppConnString(). For the password field, it is a JPasswordField type, which displays an asterisk for each character entered in the text field. We cannot get the text of the password field as a String; rather, we call the getPassword() method to get a character array, from which we instantiate a String to pass to putAppConnString().

When we call putAppConnString(), we pass a boolean set to true as the last argument. That tells putAppConnString() to test the resultant connection string to see whether we are able to make a connection to the database with the designated string.

We have modified the putAppConnString() method that takes this final boolean to return a String instead of a void. Previously, we had only sent a success or fail message to the System.out stream. Now we are additionally returning the success or failure message. We set the value of connSuccessLabel on this screen to the value of the message being returned. After we have updated the connection strings in the list, we want to refresh the list in existingConnComboBox, so we call OracleJavaSecure.listConnNames() like we did in dataInit() to repopulate the drop-down combo box.

Saving the List of Connection Strings to the Database

The final action to be taken on the Edit Application Connection Strings screen is a call to the saveButton_actionPerformed() method, which occurs when the Save List button is selected. In this method, we simply call OracleJavaSecure.putAppConnections(). That was easy!

Connection String Copy Screen

If you have modified the `innerClassRevLvl` member of the application inner class in order to designate a new version of the application, with a new/modified set of Oracle connection strings, then you can use the Copy to New Version screen shown in Figure 12-9 to duplicate the previous application version connection strings to the current version.

■ **Note** It only works to copy connection strings from a previous version to the current version if the list of connection strings for the current version is empty, that is the list in the database.

Figure 12-9. *Copy to New Version functional screen*

The Copy to New Version screen is very simple. It has a text field to enter the previous version number, from which the connection strings will be copied, and a button labeled Copy Existing Conn Strings. When that button is selected, the result is a call to the `OracleJavaSecure.copyAppConnections()` method, passing the user-entered previous version number.

Limiting Certain Administrators to Certain Applications

Before I end this chapter, let me elaborate on something I have alluded to several times: limiting which applications an administrator may manage. You will recall in our discussion of the Register New Application screen, we created a new table to designate an administrator for the new application, `appsec.t_application_admins`. We have not done anything with that table yet, except maintain the data in it.

You may recall from Listing 12-48 that we limited certain privileges on that table of administrators to just a single user, `osadmin`. This administrator of administrators job could be extended to more individuals, but we didn't create a role to handle this. That might be a good future improvement. We do not limit the insert privilege, because we are inserting the current session user as an initial administrator for the application from the Register New Application screen.

Virtual Private Database

How will we use this table of application administrators? One way is to use a feature of the Oracle database that goes by many names. The feature is implemented in a database package named DBMS_RLS, which stands for "Row Level Security." I suppose that might be the best name, but this feature is more often referred to as "Virtual Private Database" (VPD), as in the *Oracle Database Security Guide* document. You might also see it called "Dynamic Where Clause" or "Fine-Grained Access Control," depending on how it is being used.

It amounts to a dynamic where clause being applied to queries and execute commands on a table, and it is enforced by a database security policy. The main benefits of this feature are that it is transparently applied to all specified user interactions with the data table, and there is no way around the policy for the user.

As an example, let's say I define a policy that says every time a user deals with the HR.EMPLOYEES table, we will apply the dynamic where clause, "where employee_id = this_employee_id" assuming we have already calculated this_employee_id. Because this policy is applied to the table, even if the employee with ID 300 is selecting or updating the data through a view or procedure (as AUTHID CURRENT_USER), they still can only deal with their own record, for their employee_id, 300.

■ **Note** Procedures that operate with schema privileges, not AUTHID CURRENT_USER will be restricted to data available to the schema user, not the current user. However, if the VPD policy is restricting access by a different aspect of the user's identity, such as a session context parameter, then a user's access through these procedures is also restricted by the VPD policy.

■ **Note** If you are connected as SYS user or the schema user who owns the table, VPD policies do not apply to your access to the table. You see it all, unless the VPD function depends on a session context parameter.

For all our application connections, we are setting the SYS_CONTEXT parameter CLIENT_IDENTIFIER to the user ID from our SSO process. We would like to restrict access to the appsec.t_app_conn_registry table to just those users whose SSO user IDs are listed in appsec.v_application_admins as administrators for the specific application. That is the easy part—our dynamic where clause will be:

```
WHERE class_name IN ( SELECT class_name FROM appsec.t_application_admins
    WHERE user_id = SYS_CONTEXT( 'USERENV', 'CLIENT_IDENTIFIER' ) )
```

But we also want to allow any administrators of administrators to see all rows. We can find out who those individuals are by finding who has been granted extra privileges, like UPDATE on the appsec.v_application_admins view. We will add this to our dynamic where clause:

```
OR SYS_CONTEXT( 'USERENV', 'CLIENT_IDENTIFIER' ) =
    ( SELECT GRANTEE FROM SYS.DBA_TAB_PRIVS
        WHERE TABLE_NAME='V_APPLICATION_ADMINS'
        AND OWNER='APPSEC'
        AND PRIVILEGE='UPDATE'
        AND GRANTEE=SYS_CONTEXT( 'USERENV', 'CLIENT_IDENTIFIER' ) )
```

That addition will also allow the current user to select rows from appsec.v_app_conn_registry where it is true that the current user is found in the SYS.DBA_TAB_PRIVS data dictionary view with the privilege to UPDATE the appsec.v_application_admins view. If this is true, our dynamic where clause will return all rows. This requires that we grant select on the data dictionary view, SYS.DBA_TAB_PRIVS to the appsec user who will execute the VPD code:

```
GRANT SELECT ON SYS.DBA_TAB_PRIVS TO APPSEC WITH GRANT OPTION;
```

In a couple sections form here, we are going to use a similar dynamic where clause in a view, v_app_conn_registry_filtered. Then we will let other users select from that view. This reveals a potential limitation to the grant we issued earlier. In this case we specified WITH GRANT OPTION, as if appsec was interested in granting select on the sys.dba_tab_privs view to others. Appsec will not be doing that, but she wants to permit other users to view data that is selected from that data dictionary view. If we had not specified WITH GRANT OPTION, then appsec would not be able to let others see what she sees in the dba_tab_privs view. Grants cannot be transferred to others without specifying WITH GRANT OPTION.

The first step in using VPD is to create a function using a specific template form, that will return the dynamic where clause as a VARCHAR2. Listing 12-64 shows the function that encapsulates the dynamic where clause I just described, appsec.apps_for_admin.

Listing 12-64. *VPD Function for Administrators*

```
CREATE OR REPLACE FUNCTION appsec.apps_for_admin(
    m_schema_nm VARCHAR2,
    m_table_nm  VARCHAR2 )
RETURN VARCHAR2
IS
    rtrn_clause VARCHAR2(400);
BEGIN
    rtrn_clause :=
    'class_name IN ( SELECT class_name FROM appsec.t_application_admins '
    || 'WHERE user_id = SYS_CONTEXT( ''USERENV'', ''CLIENT_IDENTIFIER'' ) ) '
    || 'OR SYS_CONTEXT( ''USERENV'', ''CLIENT_IDENTIFIER'' ) = '
    || '( SELECT GRANTEE FROM SYS.DBA_TAB_PRIVS '
    || '  WHERE TABLE_NAME=''V_APPLICATION_ADMINS'' '
    || '  AND OWNER=''APPSEC'' '
    || '  AND PRIVILEGE=''UPDATE'' '
    || '  AND GRANTEE=SYS_CONTEXT( ''USERENV'', ''CLIENT_IDENTIFIER'' ) )';
    RETURN rtrn_clause;
END apps_for_admin;
/
```

We create this procedure on the apver instance, where it is applied to the t_app_class_registry table. Listing 12-65 shows the command that creates the policy to use this function. Notice that we only apply this policy to the statement types: INSERT, UPDATE, and DELETE. We consider this a restriction on administrators. Notice also that the policy is declared to be STATIC. That lends it great speed since it will reside in and execute from the system global area, SGA memory. See the Oracle Database Security Guide document for more information on VPD.

Listing 12-65. *VPD Policy for Administrators*

```
BEGIN
```

```
DBMS_RLS.ADD_POLICY (
    object_schema => 'appsec',
    object_name => 't_app_conn_registry',
    policy_name => 'apps_for_admin_policy',
    function_schema => 'appsec',
    policy_function => 'apps_for_admin',
    statement_types => 'INSERT,UPDATE,DELETE',
    policy_type => DBMS_RLS.STATIC );
END;
/
```

If we can do that, then surely we can restrict what application connection string lists our application users can SELECT. We want to apply the same where clause as before, with an additional allowance. If the user has been granted the privilege of proxying through the application user associated with an application, then the user should be able to select the list of connection strings. That addition to the where clause looks like this:

```
WHERE class_name IN ( SELECT class_name FROM appsec.t_app_class_id '
    WHERE application_id IN ( '
        SELECT application_id FROM appsec.t_application_registry '
        WHERE app_user IN ( '
            SELECT proxy FROM ojsaadm.instance_proxy_users@orcl_link '
            WHERE client = SYS_CONTEXT( ''USERENV'', ''CLIENT_IDENTIFIER'' ))) '
```

Reading from the inside out, that where clause looks at the cross-instance view of proxy users that we configured in Listing 12-29, getting all the proxy users that have been granted to the current user, then selects all applications from the t_application_registry table that are associated with that proxy user, then selects all application inner class names for those applications. The current user will be able to select application connection string lists from v_app_conn_registry that are associated with those application inner classes. Listing 12-66 shows both the function that returns the dynamic where clause and the policy that applies it to SELECT statements on the appsec.t_app_conn_registry table.

Listing 12-66. VPD for Users

```
CREATE OR REPLACE FUNCTION appsec.apps_for_user(
    m_schema_nm VARCHAR2,
    m_table_nm  VARCHAR2 )
RETURN VARCHAR2
IS
    rtrn_clause VARCHAR2(400);
BEGIN
--      appsec.app_sec_pkg.p_log_error( 122, 'dave',
--      'appsec.apps_for_user: ' || SYS_CONTEXT( 'USERENV', 'CLIENT_IDENTIFIER' ) );

    rtrn_clause :=
    'class_name IN ( SELECT class_name FROM appsec.t_app_class_id '
    || 'WHERE application_id IN ( '
    || 'SELECT application_id FROM appsec.t_application_registry '
    || 'WHERE app_user IN ( '
    || 'SELECT proxy FROM ojsaadm.instance_proxy_users@orcl_link '
    || 'WHERE client = SYS_CONTEXT( ''USERENV'', ''CLIENT_IDENTIFIER'' ))) '
    || 'UNION SELECT class_name FROM appsec.t_application_admins '
    || 'WHERE user_id = SYS_CONTEXT( ''USERENV'', ''CLIENT_IDENTIFIER'' ) '
```

```
    || 'OR SYS_CONTEXT( ''USERENV'', ''CLIENT_IDENTIFIER'' ) = ( '
    || 'SELECT GRANTEE FROM SYS.DBA_TAB_PRIVS '
    || 'WHERE TABLE_NAME=''V_APPLICATION_ADMINS'' '
    || 'AND OWNER=''APPSEC'' '
    || 'AND PRIVILEGE=''UPDATE'' '
    || 'AND GRANTEE=SYS_CONTEXT( ''USERENV'', ''CLIENT_IDENTIFIER'' )))';
    RETURN rtrn_clause;
END apps_for_user;
/

BEGIN
DBMS_RLS.ADD_POLICY (
    object_schema => 'appsec',
    object_name => 't_app_conn_registry',
    policy_name => 'apps_for_user_policy',
    function_schema => 'appsec',
    policy_function => 'apps_for_user',
    statement_types => 'SELECT',
    policy_type => DBMS_RLS.STATIC );
END;
/
```

One of the biggest benefits of VPD is also one of its biggest problems. The problem is that it can be hard to deal with. It is a hidden restriction, not listed in the grants or in the application code. The dynamic where clause gets applied behind the scenes, transparent to the user. That difficulty is a feature, a feature worth paying for in some secure computing environments. If you need VPD on steroids, you can acquire Oracle Label Security.

To disable the VPD policies we configured, you would execute the statements in Listing 12-67. I am going to do that, because for our efforts we can take a different, more manageable approach to achieve the same effect. Also disable VPD because certain procedures in appsec packages running as "definer's rights" could not select from v_app_conn_registry when appsec cannot.

Listing 12-67. Disable VPD Policies

```
BEGIN
DBMS_RLS.DROP_POLICY (
    object_schema => 'appsec',
    object_name => 't_app_conn_registry',
    policy_name => 'apps_for_admin_policy' );
END;
/
BEGIN
DBMS_RLS.DROP_POLICY (
    object_schema => 'appsec',
    object_name => 't_app_conn_registry',
    policy_name => 'apps_for_user_policy' );
END;
/
```

Adding a Dynamic Where Clause to Procedures

There are only two procedures that access the t_app_conn_registry table in a manner that concerns us. Both of these procedures are in the appsec.appsec_only_pkg package: p_get_class_conns and p_set_class_conns. Outside of those procedures, only SYS, the appsec schema user account and users who have been granted proxy through avadmin (with appver_admin role) have access to the table or a view of it.

I propose that instead of using VPD to restrict data access, we modify the specific procedures of concern with the same dynamic where clauses that we proposed for VPD. The resulting procedures are shown in Listing 12-68.

Listing 12-68. Procedures Protected by Dynamic Where Clause

```
PROCEDURE p_get_class_conns(
    m_class_name        v_app_conn_registry.class_name%TYPE,
    m_class_version     v_app_conn_registry.class_version%TYPE,
    m_class_instance OUT v_app_conn_registry.class_instance%TYPE,
    m_connections    OUT v_app_conn_registry.connections%TYPE )
IS BEGIN
    SELECT class_instance, connections
    INTO m_class_instance, m_connections
    FROM appsec.v_app_conn_registry
    WHERE class_name = m_class_name
    AND class_version = m_class_version

    AND class_name IN ( SELECT class_name FROM appsec.v_app_class_id
    WHERE application_id IN (
    SELECT application_id FROM appsec.v_application_registry
    WHERE app_user IN (
    SELECT proxy FROM ojsaadm.instance_proxy_users@orcl_link
    WHERE client = SYS_CONTEXT( 'USERENV', 'CLIENT_IDENTIFIER' )))
    UNION SELECT class_name FROM appsec.v_application_admins
    WHERE user_id = SYS_CONTEXT( 'USERENV', 'CLIENT_IDENTIFIER' )
    OR SYS_CONTEXT( 'USERENV', 'CLIENT_IDENTIFIER' ) = (
    SELECT GRANTEE FROM SYS.DBA_TAB_PRIVS
    WHERE TABLE_NAME='V_APPLICATION_ADMINS'
    AND OWNER='APPSEC'
    AND PRIVILEGE='UPDATE'
    AND GRANTEE=SYS_CONTEXT( 'USERENV', 'CLIENT_IDENTIFIER' )));

END p_get_class_conns;


PROCEDURE p_set_class_conns(
    m_class_name     v_app_conn_registry.class_name%TYPE,
    m_class_version  v_app_conn_registry.class_version%TYPE,
    m_class_instance v_app_conn_registry.class_instance%TYPE,
    m_connections    v_app_conn_registry.connections%TYPE )
IS
    v_count INTEGER;
    v_count_able INTEGER;
```

```
BEGIN
    SELECT COUNT(*) INTO v_count
        FROM appsec.v_app_conn_registry
        WHERE class_name = m_class_name
        AND class_version = m_class_version;

    SELECT COUNT(*) INTO v_count_able
        FROM appsec.v_app_conn_registry
        WHERE class_name = m_class_name
        AND class_version = m_class_version
        AND class_name IN (
        SELECT class_name FROM appsec.v_application_admins
        WHERE user_id = SYS_CONTEXT( 'USERENV', 'CLIENT_IDENTIFIER' )
        OR SYS_CONTEXT( 'USERENV', 'CLIENT_IDENTIFIER' ) = (
        SELECT GRANTEE FROM SYS.DBA_TAB_PRIVS
        WHERE TABLE_NAME='V_APPLICATION_ADMINS'
        AND OWNER='APPSEC'
        AND PRIVILEGE='UPDATE'
        AND GRANTEE=SYS_CONTEXT( 'USERENV', 'CLIENT_IDENTIFIER' )));

    IF v_count = 0 THEN
        INSERT INTO v_app_conn_registry ( class_name, class_version,
            class_instance, connections ) VALUES
            ( m_class_name, m_class_version, m_class_instance, m_connections );
    ELSE

        IF v_count_able > 0 THEN

            UPDATE v_app_conn_registry
                SET class_instance = m_class_instance,
                connections = m_connections, update_dt = SYSDATE
            WHERE class_name = m_class_name
            AND class_version = m_class_version;
        END IF;
    END IF;
END p_set_class_conns;
```

In p_set_class_conns we freely allow insert, which will happen during new application registration, but if an entry already exists for this application, we apply a test that uses our administrative dynamic where clause. If the record is found (v_count_able > 0) while using the dynamic where clause, then we allow update to the record.

Adding a Dynamic Where Clause to a View

To complete our emulation of VPD on the appsec.t_app_conn_registry table, we need to limit the rows returned by a select on a view of that table, appsec.v_app_conn_registry_filtered. Only SYS, the appsec schema user and users who have been granted proxy through avadmin will be able to select from the view, but we can limit what those folks see as well. Our plan is really only to limit what administrative users, proxying through avadmin will see, since SYS and the schema owner can see all the data in the table without using the view.

The dynamic where clause in this view selects from sys.dba_tab_privs, which was granted to appsec. Appsec grants this view to the appver_admin role. Fortunately, appsec was granted select on dba_tab_privs with WITH GRANT OPTION permission, so she can allow others to see what she sees in that data dictionary view; otherwise, other users couldn't select from v_app_conn_registry_filtered, even though they have the role appver_admin.

The definition of appsec.v_app_conn_registry_filtered includes a dynamic where clause that limits access like the administrative limitation we put on p_set_class_conns in Listing 12-68. We will not add the allowance to permit users of applications to select for applications they have access to by proxy grants. The code for v_app_conn_registry_filtered is shown in Listing 12-69. You may recall that we already used this view in one of our functional screens, the Pick App to Manage screen. Look back at Listing 12-59 to see how we limit the applications an appver_admin user may select from in order to manage connection strings. This view limits what the user sees, but the limit to what the user can do is enforced by the dynamic where clauses we added to p_get_class_conns and especially p_set_class_conns.

Listing 12-69. View Protected by Dynamic Where Clause

```
CREATE OR REPLACE VIEW appsec.v_app_conn_registry_filtered
AS
    SELECT * FROM appsec.t_app_conn_registry
    WHERE class_name IN (
        SELECT class_name FROM appsec.v_application_admins
        WHERE user_id = SYS_CONTEXT( 'USERENV', 'CLIENT_IDENTIFIER' )
    OR SYS_CONTEXT( 'USERENV', 'CLIENT_IDENTIFIER' ) = (
        SELECT GRANTEE FROM SYS.DBA_TAB_PRIVS
        WHERE TABLE_NAME='V_APPLICATION_ADMINS'
        AND OWNER='APPSEC'
        AND PRIVILEGE='UPDATE'
        AND GRANTEE=SYS_CONTEXT( 'USERENV', 'CLIENT_IDENTIFIER' )));

GRANT SELECT ON appsec.v_app_conn_registry_filtered TO appver_admin;
```

Scripts Execution and Code Compilation

If you have been running the code in the files in Chapter 12 as we've been discussing it, then you are mostly through this section. You can skip down to where we discuss editing the Java code. Otherwise, you need to execute the following scripts (note that there are some dependencies between them):

Execute *Chapter12/OrclSecAdm.sql* as the secadm user on the orcl instance (your primary database instance). Change the passwords for both the ojsaadm and avadmin users before executing the script.

Execute *Chapter12/OrclSys.sql* as SYS on the orcl instance. Change the placeholder OS user ID, osadmin to your OS user ID or whoever is the primary application security administrator.

Execute *Chapter12/OrclHR.sql* as the HR schema user on the orcl instance.

Execute *Chapter12/OrclAppSec.sql* as the appsec user on the orcl instance.

Execute *Chapter12/ApverSys.sql* as SYS on the apver instance. Change the passwords for both the ojsaadm and avadmin users before executing the script.

Execute *Chapter12/OrclOJSAAdm.sql* as the ojsaadm user on the orcl instance. Change the password for the ojsaadm user on the apver instance, in the database link before executing the script.

From the *Chapter12* directory, edit the code as listed here:

- At the top of *orajavsec/OracleJavaSecure.java*, edit the values for expectedDomain, comDomain, smtpHost and baseURL. Also, insert the correct value for prime (the encoded connection string for appver user on the apver instance) into place in the setAppVerConnection() method.

- In *orajavsec/PickAppManage.java*, edit the paths to *javaw.exe*, your classes, and *ojdbc.jar* file that are used in the Runtime.exec() command in the manageAppButton_actionPerformed() method.

- In *orajavsec/RegNewApp.java*, edit the password for the avadmin user in the default constructor. Also, temporarily uncomment the calls to putAppConnString() and putAppConnections().

■ **Note** Having the avadmin password, and the calls to putAppConString() and putAppConnections(), in *RegNewApp.java* is only temporary. After bootstrapping OJSAdmin, discussed shortly, be sure to remove the password and comment those method calls. Then recompile OJSAdmin.

Execute the following command to compile OJSAdmin and all related classes:
javac orajavsec/OJSAdmin.java
Finally, uncomment the command to CREATE OR REPLACE AND RESOLVE JAVA SOURCE at the top of *OracleJavaSecure.java*, and execute that code as a script on both the orcl instance (as appsec or SYS) and the apver instance (as SYS).

Final Updates to OracleJavaSecure

There are several legacy methods that we used differently in earlier chapters: getAppAuthConn() and three setConnection() methods. Initially we declared these methods to have public visibility, but now we are using the getAAConnRole() public method to handle those calls. So we will change the access modifiers for those legacy methods to be private.

There is also one method that we haven't yet put to use: removeAppConnString(). It is our intent to someday implement that from the OJSAdmin application. OJSAdmin resides in the orajavsec package, just like the OracleJavaSecure class. So to make removeAppConnString() visible to OJSAdmin, we will change the access modifier to default (package).

Single Oracle Instance Code

If you did not create a second Oracle instance to run the appver processes separately, then you need to run the code in *Chapter12single*. Execute all the scripts and commands listed in the last section, except there is no *ApverSys.sql* script. One example of the names for the scripts you will use is *Chapter12single/OrclSecAdm.sql*.

You will edit and compile the Java code similarly as well, except you will compile and run the code in the *Chapter12single* directory.

Bootstrap OJSAdmin

We need a way to get the security administration interface, OJSAdmin started. We will be able to get all future applications started by using OJSAdmin, but for OJSAdmin itself, we are going to take a couple steps to bootstrap the application. Did you realize we have been bootstrapping our applications this whole time, from Chapter 7 through Chapter 11? That's right, when we ran each application with a couple calls to putAppConnString() and another call to putConnections(), we were priming the pump and getting the application engine started with those password strings. The call to putConnections() entered a record in the appsec.v_app_conn_registry table that we could use from then on.

After our discussion of the register new application, RegNewApp functional screen, you can conclude that getting a new application registered has become more complex in just this chapter. Part of that complexity is for enhanced security – only allowing certain administrators to modify connection strings for certain applications. And part of it is for allowing this Security Administration Interface to manage multiple applications; and even more, to become those applications in order to edit associated connection strings.

It is no longer the case that just inserting a record into v_app_conn_registry is sufficient to register an application; however, that is the most significant step. Now we must designate an administrator for the application in v_application_admin and we must associate the application ID with the application inner class name in v_app_class_id. We have always needed an entry in the v_application_registry table that associates a secure application role to a specific application ID and application user.

For the OJSAdmin class, Security Administration Interface, we have entered a number of those data elements from the scripts. We have an entry in v_application_registry on both orcl and apver instances. We inserted those records independently into v_application_registry on orcl and apver, but in the future we will make inserts on apver, and they will be automatically inserted in orcl by means of the insert trigger. We have also made entries in both v_application_admins and v_app_class_id for the OJSAdmin application. Now all we need is an entry in v_app_conn_registry, which will include our application inner class and a list of connection strings (starting out empty).

We are going to call on the facility of our Register New Application functional screen to get the entry into v_app_conn_registry. This is where we experience the chicken or egg quandary (by the way, the chicken came first). In this case, we need to acquire a connection string from v_app_conn_registry before we can use Register New Application. At the same time, we want to use Register New Application to insert the initial (blank) list of connection strings into v_app_conn_registry.

As we have in the preceding chapters, we are going to bootstrap the application connection list. In Chapter 12, we need to do that in two steps. As before, to bootstrap the application, we place a connection string in memory on the client application by calling putAppConnString(). We do that in the ojsInit() method of RegNewApp as shown in Listing 12-70. We also call putAppConnections() but that has no effect when an there is no existing connection string list in the database—that call, at this point, does not save the list in the database.

Listing 12-70. Bootstrap Register New Application for OJSAdmin

```
public RegNewApp() {
    try {
        jbInit();
        // First times through way to build conn string list, or use this tool
        OracleJavaSecure.putAppConnString("apver", "avadmin", "password",
            "localhost", String.valueOf(1521));
        OracleJavaSecure.putAppConnections();

        conn = OracleJavaSecure.getAAConnRole("apver", "avadmin");
    } catch (Exception e) {
        e.printStackTrace();
    }
}
```

We are going to enter some representative data on the Register New Application screen shown in Figure 12-6. The top three entries for application ID, app user and app role will not be needed – we have already entered records with the necessary data values in our scripts, and we haven't acquired the appver_admin role needed to do the associated inserts. However, enter ojsadmin, avadmin, appver_admin in the top three text fields. Enter the correct package, orajavsec, and enter the class name, Login. At this point the **Create App Class** button will appear. Click the **Create App Class** button to create the Java structure. If you ever mistype a package name, and create an incorrect class, you can drop the class with a command like this (don't do this, for information only):

```
DROP JAVA SOURCE appsec."badPackageName/Login";
```

Notice when you click the **Create App Class** button that the last text field on the screen is automatically populated with the default inner class name of the Login class, InnerRevLvlClass. With all the fields populated, you are now ready to click on the **Register** button. When you do that, the **Register New Application** screen will instantiate the class described by your package name and the class name Login$InnerRevLvlClass. Some errors will be reported because this event normally inserts data into the v_application_registry, v_application_admins and v_app_conn_id views. Those inserts fail, but inserting the application inner class and an empty list of connection strings into v_app_conn_registry succeeds. This was the bootstrap process!

The **Close** button turned to **Exit** because we have changed the application context. You can select the **Exit** button at this time. Your application is registered, but you still need to insert connection strings into the list in order to use the functional screens of OJSAdmin. Start OJSAdmin again, and provide the two-factor authentication code that is sent to you. This may seem like an odd step, but you need to enter the Register New Application screen again. This time as you go in, the putAppConnString() method is called to again add the avadmin connection string to the list in memory, but this time when we call putAppConnections(), that connection string will be saved in the list that resides in the database. Since our connection strings list contains the avadmin connection string, we entered this screen with the appver_admin role, and we can UPDATE the v_app_conn_registry view.

▪ **Note** You must be the equivalent of osadmin, or have been granted proxy through avadmin and listed in v_application_admins for this application, OJSADMIN, to accomplish this final step.

At this point you can Close the screen and Exit the application, or you can just close the Register New Application screen and go on to our next step. In either case, when you finally do Exit the application, be sure to remove the bootstrap password from the code in *RegNewApp.java*.

There are several Oracle connections required to accomplish the various tasks of the security administration interface application. So far, we have only one connection string in the list, so we need to add the others. Run OJSAdmin and click on the Pick App to Manage button. In the drop-down selection box, select the OJSAdmin application OJSADMIN/orajavsec.Login$InnerRevLvlClass. You will receive another prompt for two-factor authentication; however, this is the same application. If it has been less than 10 minutes since the first two-factor code was sent to you, enter that code; otherwise wait for a new code.

You will see that the menu items at the bottom of the OJSAdmin menu screen are available. Select the Update Connection Strings menu item. Enter two additional connection strings as listed in Table 12-2.

Table 12-2. Additional Connection Strings for OJSAdmin

instance	user	password	server	port
orcl	appusr	password	localhost	1521
orcl	ojsaadm	password	localhost	1521

After each entry, click the Update Connection String button and assure the connection success message is displayed. After both entries are made, click on the Save List button to store the complete list of connection strings in the database. That completes the configuration of the OJSAdmin application, and all of its features are now ready for use. Exit OJSAdmin in both JVMs, then reenter to reload the connection strings.

Chapter Review

This chapter has perhaps been more fun to write and read because it provides a visual representation of the concepts we've been studying. The various menus and screens make managing the application security infrastructure much easier and more approachable. Also, by encoding the rules into a GUI application, we don't have to remember all the pieces and parts.

In addition to discussing the operation of the functional screens, we discussed GUI development in general, with specific attention to the single-threaded operation and the use of delayed threads and the SwingUtilities.invokeLater() method. We also explored modal dialog boxes and making dialogs and functional screens visible and invisible as required.

To make this security administration interface application work, we added a couple tables, several packages, a database link, a couple users and roles, and various other Oracle structures. We also added a couple utility methods to OracleJavaSecure, and modified a couple existing methods. A developer's job is never done, and those who implement the security infrastructure presented in this book will find reasons to modify it and expand it.

When you have finished reading and working your way through this book, you will want to continue on to read and work through the Supplemental material included in the source code download. In the supplement, we address several scenarios that you can use as templates and guides for accomplishing computer security. These are the scenarios we will cover:

- Testing with new applications, users and administrators

- Responding to an emergency – securing a new application and data

- Changing all the passwords

- Auditing and logging

- Performing an asset-centric risk assessment

- Tailoring installation and implementation

I encourage you to work on these issues, and I hope you have complete success in Application Security using Oracle and Java! Having finished this book, you are now the expert in Oracle and Java security.

List of Methods from OracleJavaSecure Class

Method	Listing	Access	Platform	Called By	How
Constructor	5-7	Private	Neither	none	none
byteArrayToCharArray	6-17	Package	Client	decryptSessionSecretDESPassPhrase	Internal
charArrayToByteArray	6-17	Package	Oracle	getCryptSessionSecretDESPassPhrase	Internal
checkFormat2Factor	10-22	Public	Client	setAppContext and main	Internal and Java
closeConnection	8-26	Public	Client	all applications	Java
copyAppConnections	ref 11-27	Public	Client	some applications	Java
copyPreviousConns	11-29ff	Public	Oracle	f_copy_conns	Stored Procedure
decryptSessionSecretDESPassPhrase	6-16	Private	Client	makeDESKey	Internal
distribToEMail	9-26ff	Private	Oracle	distribute2Factor	Internal
distribToPagerURL	9-27	Private	Oracle	distribute2Factor	Internal
distribToSMS	9-26	Private	Oracle	distribute2Factor	Internal

Method	Listing	Access	Platform	Called By	How
distribute2Factor	9-19	Public	Oracle	f_send_2_factor	Stored Procedure
getAAConnRole	10-56	Public	Client	all applications	Java
getAppAuthConn	10-39	Private	Client	getAAConnRole	Internal
getAppConnections	10-40ff	Public	Client	all applications	Java
getCryptConns	10-47 & 11-24	Public	Oracle	f_get_crypt_conns	Stored Procedure
getCryptData	6-9	Public	Both	f_get_crypt_data and sensitive apps	Stored and Java
getCryptSessionSecretDESAlgorithm	6-6	Public	Oracle	f_get_crypt_secret_algorithm	Stored Procedure
getCryptSessionSecretDESIterationCount	6-8	Public	Oracle	f_get_crypt_secret_count	Stored Procedure
getCryptSessionSecretDESPassPhrase	6-5	Public	Oracle	f_get_crypt_secret_pass	Stored Procedure
getCryptSessionSecretDESSalt	6-7	Public	Oracle	f_get_crypt_secret_salt	Stored Procedure
getDecryptData	6-14	Public	Client	sensitive applications	Java
getDecryptData RAW	6-15	Public	Both	f_get_decrypt_data and sensitive apps	Stored and Java
getLocRSAPubExp	5-6	Public	Client	getAppConnections and sens apps	Internal and Java
getLocRSAPubMod	5-6	Public	Client	getAppConnections and sens apps	Internal and Java
getOSUserID	8-4	Private	Client	setConnection	Internal
getOSUserName	Supplement	Public	Client	TestAppA class	Java

APPENDIX A ■ LIST OF METHODS FROM ORACLEJAVASECURE CLASS

Method	Listing	Access	Platform	Called By	How
getRSACryptData String	6-4	Private	Oracle	getCryptSessionSecretDESAlgorithm	Internal
getRSACryptData bytes	6-4	Private	Oracle	getCryptSessionSecretDESPassPhrase, IC, Salt	Internal
isAppverOK	ref 12-6	Public	Client	Login class	Java
listConnNames	12-62	Package	Client	OJSAdmin app	Java
main	11-8	Public	Client	none	Command Prompt
makeDESKey	7-7	Public	Client	getAppConnections, getDecryptData and sens apps	Internal and Java
makeExtRSAPubKey	5-3	Private	Oracle	getRSACryptData B	Internal
makeLocRSAKeys	5-1	Private	Client	getLocRSAPubMod and getLocRSAPubExp	Internal
makeSessionSecretDESKey	6-3	Private	Both	makeDESKey, getCryptSessionSecretDESPassPhrase…, getCryptData	Internal
makeSessionSecretDESPassPhrase	6-1	Private	Oracle	makeSessionSecretDESKey	Internal
putAppConnections	10-24	Public	Client	OJSAdmin and applications	Java
putAppConnString	10-23	Public	Client	applications	Java
putAppConnString test	10-23	Public	Client	putAppConnString A, OJSAdmin and applications	Internal and Java
removeAppConnString	11-26	Package	Client	[OJSAdmin app]	Java
resetKeys	7-9	Public	Client	OJSAdmin and getAppConnections	Internal and Java
setAppContext	10-21	Public	Client	Login class and applications	Java

Method	Listing	Access	Platform	Called By	How
setAppVerConnection	10-45 & 11-9	Private	Client	getAppConnections and copyAppConnections	Internal
setConnection URL	8-24	Private	Client	setAppVerConnection and getAppAuthConn	Internal
setConnection Connection	8-24	Private	Client	setConnection URL	Internal
setConnection OracleConnection	8-25	Private	Client	setConnection Connection	Internal
setDecryptConns	10-26ff	Public	Oracle	f_set_decrypt_conns	Stored Procedure
test2Factor	12-8	Public	Client	Login class	Java

APPENDIX B

Oracle Procedures, Functions and Triggers for Oracle and Java Security

Procedure/ Function/Trigger	Schema	Package	Listing	Special	Execute By	Called By
p_log_error	appsec	app_sec _pkg	7-6		App Users (HR)	all
f_get_crypt_secret _pass	appsec	app_sec _pkg	6-11	Java Stored Proc	App Users (HR)	p_get_app_conns
f_get_crypt_secret _algorithm	appsec	app_sec _pkg	6-11	Java Stored Proc	App Users (HR)	p_get_app_conns
f_get_crypt_secret _salt	appsec	app_sec _pkg	6-11	Java Stored Proc	App Users (HR)	p_get_app_conns
f_get_crypt_secret _count	appsec	app_sec _pkg	6-11	Java Stored Proc	App Users (HR)	p_get_app_conns
f_get_crypt_data	appsec	app_sec _pkg	6-11	Java Stored Proc	App Users (HR)	App Procedures
f_get_decrypt_dat a	appsec	app_sec _pkg	6-11	Java Stored Proc	App Users (HR)	App Procedures

Procedure/ Function/Trigger	Schema	Package	Listing	Special	Execute By	Called By
p_appsec_errors_janitor	appsec		7-4	Autonomous		t_appsec_errors_iar
t_appsec_errors_iar	appsec		7-5	Trigger		INSERT t_appsec_errors
t_application_key_budr	appsec		11-16	Trigger		UPDATE t_application_key
f_is_sso	appsec		10-3	CURRENT_USER		p_check_role_access, f_set_decrypt_conns, p_get_app_conns
f_copy_conns	appsec	appsec_only_pkg	11-27	Java Stored Proc		p_copy_app_conns
f_is_cur_cached_cd	appsec	appsec_only_pkg	9-13, 10-4			p_copy_app_conns, p_get_app_conns
f_send_2_factor	appsec	appsec_only_pkg	9-14, 10-4	Java Stored Proc		p_copy_app_conns, p_get_app_conns
f_get_app_role	appsec	appsec_only_pkg	10-5			p_check_role_access
p_get_emp_2fact_nos	appsec	appsec_only_pkg	10-8, 11-52			distribute2Factor
p_update_2fact_cache	appsec	appsec_only_pkg	10-9			distribute2Factor
f_is_user	appsec	appsec_only_pkg	10-16			p_appver_logon
p_count_class_conns	appsec	appsec_only_pkg	10-37			setDecryptConns, copyPreviousConns

Procedure/ Function/Trigger	Schema	Package	Listing	Special	Execute By	Called By
p_get_class_conns	appsec	appsec_only_pkg	12-68			setDecryptConns, copyPreviousConns, getCryptConns
p_set_class_conns	appsec	appsec_only_pkg	12-68			setDecryptConns, copyPreviousConns
f_get_crypt_conns	appsec	appsec_only_pkg	ref 10-46	Java Stored Proc		p_get_app_conns
p_check_role_access	appsec		10-6	CURRENT_USER	PUBLIC	getAAConnRole
p_appver_logon	appsec		10-14	CURRENT_USER	PUBLIC	t_screen_appver_access
t_screen_appver_access	appsec		10-13	Trigger		LOGON appver
p_create_template_class	appsec	appsec_admin_pkg	12-45		appver_admin, appver_conns	OJSAdmin
f_set_decrypt_conns	appsec	appsec_admin_pkg	10-25	Java Stored Proc	appver_admin, appver_conns	putAppConnections
p_copy_app_conns	appsec	appsec_admin_pkg	11-27		appver_admin, appver_conns	copyAppConnections
p_get_app_conns	appsec	appsec_public_pkg	10-46		PUBLIC	getAppConnections
f_mask	appsec		11-18ff	Wrapped		setDecryptConns, copyPreviousConns

Procedure/ Function/Trigger	Schema	Package	Listing	Special	Execute By	Called By
f_unmask	appsec		ref 11-18	Wrapped		getCryptConns, copyPreviousConns
p_create_user_once	sys	usr_role_adm_pkg	12-28	Autonomous	ojsaadm or ojs_adm_admin	OJSAdmin app, p_create_apver_user
p_create_user_many	sys	usr_role_adm_pkg	12-28	Autonomous	ojsaadm or ojs_adm_admin	OJSAdmin app, p_create_apver_user
p_drop_user	sys	usr_role_adm_pkg	12-28	Autonomous	ojsaadm or ojs_adm_admin	[OJSAdmin app], p_drop_apver_user
p_set_proxy_through	sys	usr_role_adm_pkg	12-28	Autonomous	ojsaadm or ojs_adm_admin	OJSAdmin app, p_set_apver_proxy_through
p_drop_proxy_through	sys	usr_role_adm_pkg	12-28	Autonomous	ojsaadm or ojs_adm_admin	OJSAdmin app, p_drop_apver_proxy_through
p_grant_appver_conns_role	sys	appver_conns_role_pkg	12-50	Autonomous	ojsaadm, appver_admin	OJSAdmin app, p_grant_apver_appver_conns
p_revoke_appver_conns_role	sys	appver_conns_role_pkg	12-50	Autonomous	ojsaadm, appver_admin	[OJSAdmin app], p_revoke_apver_appver_conns
t_application_registry_iar	appsec		12-56	Trigger		INSERT t_application_registry
apps_for_admin	appsec		12-64	For VPD		apps_for_admin_policy
apps_for_user	appsec		12-66	For VPD		apps_for_user_policy

Procedure/ Function/Trigger	Schema	Package	Listing	Special	Execute By	Called By
p_create_apver_user	ojsaadm	apver_usr_adm_pkg	12-30		ojs_adm_admin	OJSAdmin app
p_drop_apver_user	ojsaadm	apver_usr_adm_pkg	12-30		ojs_adm_admin	[OJSAdmin app]
p_set_apver_proxy_through	ojsaadm	apver_usr_adm_pkg	12-30		ojs_adm_admin	OJSAdmin app
p_drop_apver_proxy_through	ojsaadm	apver_usr_adm_pkg	12-30		ojs_adm_admin	OJSAdmin app
p_grant_apver_apver_conns	ojsaadm	apver_usr_adm_pkg	12-51		ojs_adm_admin	OJSAdmin app
p_revoke_apver_appver_conns	ojsaadm	apver_usr_adm_pkg	12-51		ojs_adm_admin	OJSAdmin app
p_check_secadm_access	sys		2-1	CURRENT_USER		Logon secadm

411

Index

413

▒ M

▒ N

■ T

■ W

■ X

■ Y, Z

CPSIA information can be obtained at www.ICGtesting.com
Printed in the USA
LVOW120206121111

254680LV00004B/1/P

9 781430 238317